SECOND EDITION

MOTIVATION

The Organization of Action

SECOND EDITION

MOTIVATION

The Organization of Action

DOUGLAS G. MOOK

University of Virginia

W · W · NORTON & COMPANY

New York · London

This one is for Nell

The text of this book is composed in Bembo
with the display set in Geometric Slabserif
Composition by ComCom
Manufacturing by Haddon Craftsmen
Book design by Jack Meserole
Cover Illustration: Credit Kevin O'Neell

Library of Congress Cataloging-in-Publication Data
Mook, Douglas G., 1934–
    Motivation: the organization of action / Douglas G. Mook. —2nd ed.
      p. cm.
    Includes bibliographical references and index.
    1. Motivation (Psychology)   I. Title.
BF503.M65   1996
153.8—dc20   95-32839

ISBN 0-393-96717-4

W. W. Norton & Company, Inc., 500 Fifth Avenue, New York, N.Y. 10110
W. W. Norton & Company, Ltd., 10 Coptic Street, London WC1A 1PU

1 2 3 4 5 6 7 8 9 0

Contents

v

PART 2   Basic Action Systems

4 Biological Motives: Sex and Aggression   111

7   Acquired Drives and Rewards   247

Purposive Behavior

PART 3

Human Motivation PART 4

11 Motivation and Cognitive Processes 405

14 Long-Term Goals 540

Preface

This Second Edition of *Motivation: The Organization of Action* has the same goal as the first: to present a coherent view of theory and research in motivation. It is intended not as an exhaustive (and exhausting) review of facts, nor as an anthology of theories. Rather, it seeks to bring out certain ideas that link together the great diversity of topics that are called "motivational"—or if not all of them, at least adjacent ones, so that readers can move from topic to topic without ever finding themselves on wholly unfamiliar ground. These include such concepts as hierarchical organization (a principle that applies from mating in the stickleback through human schema structure), negative feedback, interaction of external and internal influences on action, and the interplay of excitatory and inhibitory influences. All these were emphasized in the First Edition. To these is added the concept of a *schema,* which, it seems to me now, is as central to motivation as it is to cognition.

There are four major changes in the present edition as compared with the first one. First, there has been some reorganization in an attempt to carve the material at more natural joints. Decision theory now has a chapter of its own, where before it was divided awkwardly between two chapters. The section on altruism has been moved to the chapter on social motivation. The schema concept is introduced earlier and given the more elaborate treatment it deserves.

Second, topics have been added and expanded to reflect the interests of today's pragmatic students. Among the topics added are sexual orientation; drugs and behavior; similarity, contagion, and "magical thinking"; stress and coping; and mental self-control and the psychology of obsession. Expanded topics include phobias, attachment, love, and the motivational uses and implications of imagery (as in behavior therapy, goal-setting, and mental rehearsal). There is expanded treatment of Clark Hull (in response to instructors' requests) and of Sigmund Freud (in response to students', and some instructors', requests).

Third, the decisive role of *culture* in human motivation receives more detailed treatment. It was alluded to repeatedly in the First Edition, but in this one I have emphasized it even more, drawing on anthropological concepts and findings in an attempt to get across not only *the fact that* culture influences what we do, at every step in every domain, but also what we have learned about *how* it does it. The emerging discipline of cultural psychology (or "cognitive anthropology"; see D'Andrade and Strauss, 1992) provides yet another instance of how ideas from different starting points converge.

Fourth, there is increased emphasis on applications of the ideas discussed. Illustrations are drawn from everyday life, as well as from research in clinical, industrial, and (now) sports psychology.

Along with these changes, much remains the same. I have done some updating, but I continue to resist the idea that the newest findings and concepts are necessarily the most important. Hence the emphasis on "classic" investigations and ideas remains. The text continues to "build bridges rather than fences," noting points of similarity and convergence, as well as conflict, among points of view in motivational psychology: cognitive, behavioral, and psychodynamic. And it continues to emphasize the interplay and cross-fertilization of animal and human research. Above all, it tries to make sense of the diverse field of motivation, showing that there *are* some conceptual landmarks by which we can stay oriented as we explore the sprawling and sometimes rocky terrain.

The first two chapters are introductory. Chapter 1 presents the field of motivation as concerned with the causation of action, illustrates the methods by which we seek to determine the causes of action, and presents three points of view—psychodynamic, behavioral, and cognitive—as to what the explanations will look like when we find them. Chapter 2 places these ideas in historical context.

Chapter 3 introduces the related concepts of homeostasis and negative-feedback control, and illustrates them with research on hunger and thirst. It shows how both internal and external influences affect feeding and drinking, and how the two interact with each other. But it also shows how even these "simple" biological motives are responsive to cognition and culture. Chapter 4 extends these ideas and adds some new ones: stimulus-bound as contrasted with goal-directed action, the notion of instinctive or "untaught" repertoires of action (with a discussion of what this does and doesn't mean), and the great difficulty of separating the untaught from the taught in human sexuality and aggression. Chapter 5 considers how these multiple influences are organized and translated into action by the brain, showing how the principles we have learned—feedback, summation, inhibition, convergence, divergence, and hierarchical organization—correspond to principles of nervous-system organization. Chapter 6 takes up the question of non-specific "energy" models of motivation, and looks again at the brain in treating arousal and optimal-arousal theories. Chapter 7 considers drives and incentives—"goads and goals," as someone has put it—that result from specific learning experiences. This chapter ends with a review of the basic ideas we have covered, in the context of a topic that draws on many of them: the problem of addiction.

Armed with these basics, we turn to the problem of goal direction in behavior. Chapter 8 presents the cornerstone of behaviorism—reinforcement theory. It attempts to present this view both critically and accurately (most treatments do one or the other). In Chapter 9 we take up the cognitive view, dealing with anticipated or "imagined" outcomes of action, and with plans and schemas. Chapter 10 builds on those ideas in presenting decision theory—the theory that action is guided jointly by one's beliefs about outcomes, and one's desires among them. (Some variant of this, as Jerry Fodor has said, remains about "the only game in town" by way of a cognitive theory of goal-directed action.) Some ramifications of the theory are presented, as are some serious troubles with it.

In the final section we focus on more complex motivational systems—or, better, systems that include motivational influences. We look at some of the relations between motivation and cognition (Chapter 11) and between motivation and emotion (Chapter 12). Chapter 13 is a sample—not a survey—of motivational systems that are specifically social: attachment, liking and loving, and altruism. The emphasis is on the human case, though even here we find animal findings helpful, as in attachment in monkeys and the sociobiological approach to altruism. In Chapter 14, we look at a sample of longer-term motivational systems, the kind that may extend over much of a lifetime and guide career choices and other long-term "strategies" for meeting life's vicissitudes: achievement motivation; control and self-determination, and the obverse of these, helplessness; and finally, Maslow's hierarchy of needs and the concept of self-actualization. We end with a coda: The topic of motivation raises fundamental questions about human nature, questions that have been debated for millenia. But now we are learning how to direct empirical investigations toward such questions. They needn't be argued in a vacuum any more.

Certain Pesky-Pronoun Problems are dealt with in this edition as they were in the first. I refer to an animal as *he, she,* or *it* as seems to me most natural in each instance. Where people are concerned and a generic pronoun is needed, I use sometimes the masculine, sometimes the feminine, quite arbitrarily.

While this book was being written and revised, many colleagues and friends saved me from opacities and outright blunders. Richard Nisbett, Paul Rozin, Barry Schwartz, and Tim Wilson read the entire First Edition in at least one draft form or in final form or both; and Professors Rozin and Wilson read draft chapters for this edition as well. Their suggestions were extremely helpful. In addition, various colleagues and students helped me with specific chapters of one or both editions: Peter Brunjes, James Deese, Bella DePaulo, Bob Emery,

Linda Gonder-Frederick, Igor Kusyszyn, George Manderlink, John A. Nevin, Peter J. Urcuioli, Carolyn Ristau, Sandra Scarr, Marjorie Schacher, Sue Wagner, Dan Wegner, and Deborah White. My thanks to them all. I'm also very grateful to Kate Fiore and Sue Wagner for invaluable secretarial and bibliographic assistance.

At Norton, Donald Fusting made many helpful comments on repeated drafts, both times around. His criticisms improved the writing; his encouragement sustained the writer. Then Cathy Wick took over as editor, offering her own brand of sound advice and warm support. Also at Norton, Adam Dunn, Dan Saffer, Tim Holohan, and especially Kate Brewster worked with energy, savvy, and wonderful patience and good humor to turn my cuts, pastes, printouts, and penciled hieroglyphics into a coherent text. And Carol Loomis added the final touches as copy editor.

But the book's greatest debt is to my mother, Nell, to whom it is dedicated. She taught me to read; then she gave me *good* books to read (without, of course, calling them that) and thereby taught me how to write. Above all, she taught me that ideas are fun. How neat it is that I can make a living by sharing that fun!—as here.

PART 1

The Concept of Motivation

CHAPTER 1

Introduction

One day in July, an unemployed security guard stormed into a fast-food restaurant in California and opened fire on the people eating there. He shot down twenty-one people, total strangers, before he was killed by police. Why did he do it?

Tomorrow morning (as this is written), a group of about eighty young women and men will sit in uncomfortable chairs, moving little and talking less, while someone lectures at them. They will keep that up for an hour and a quarter, which is quite a long time. Why will they do it?

One day while looking for a friend's house in a strange city, I knocked on the door of a house. A woman answered. She gave me, a total stranger, a brilliant smile and said, "Good morning!" Why did she do that?

And a minute ago, in deciding which of these vignettes to put first, I sat back in my seat and began doodling an owl. Why an owl? Why doodle at all? Why did I do it?

For any action a person or animal performs, we may ask: "Why did she or he do that?" When we ask that question, we are asking about the person or animal's *motivation*.

As these examples show, we can ask the question "Why did he or she or it do that?" about any action at all, important, like the shootings, or trivial, like the owl (Fig. 1-1). Moreover, the answers may have important consequences. Suppose A shoots and kills B. Was it intentional? Was he *trying* to kill? If so, he is guilty of murder. If not, he may be guilty of manslaughter, and so will probably receive a lighter sentence if convicted. The difference is one of motivation.

Figure 1-1   Why are they doing that?

Questions about motivation, then, are questions about the *causes of specific actions*. Why does this organism, this person or rat or chimpanzee, do this particular thing we see it do? The study of motivation is the search for principles that will help us understand *why people and animals initiate, choose, or persist in, specific actions in specific circumstances*.

We seek to assign causes to actions for two reasons at least. First, the way we explain an action affects what we do about it. In the case of the shootings, one person might explain it as an inevitable result of the availability of guns and the glorification of violence in our society. Another might explain it as a result of lenient judges and clever attorneys who let people literally get away with murder. Another might attribute it to a deranged mind. And these three people might even press for social action on the basis of their explanations—the first advocating gun control; the second, harsher and swifter penalties; and the third, research into treatment and prevention of mental disorders.

But there is another reason, and that is the human urge to understand, to make sense of things. We are a curious species, in more ways than one. To consider the shootings again, a whole evening of serious discussion might center around the reasons why a person might do such a thing—even if the discussants didn't intend to do anything about it. Let us discuss that point a bit further.

The scientific study of motivation is a recent development in human history. But the attempt to understand the world has been characteristic of the human mind for as far back as we have any records. Our ancestors poured much intellectual effort, and a great deal of poetic genius, into the making of myths and legends about the origins and workings of the world, for no other reason than to satisfy the human itch to understand. If a bolt of lightning was the hammer of an angry god hurled through the sky, that was intelligible. We could understand it.

Notice something about such myths. They explain physical events in terms of the urges, feelings, and wishes—the *motives*—of the supernatural beings who make them happen. Lightning bolts are explained by the anger of the gods who hurl them; rain, by the good will of the gods who provide it.

Empathic Understanding

As theories, these myths fulfilled our urge to make sense of things. They gave us what we might call **empathic understanding**; that is, they allowed us to *empathize* with the beings who made the world work as it does. If an angry god hurls thunderbolts, well, we can empathize with that. We throw things when we are angry, too, though thunderbolts are a bit beyond us. If a benevolent spirit gives us rain, we can empathize with that too; we do favors for people when we feel benevolent toward them. In such cases, we understand the actions of the spirits, in this sense: We see that, given the same wishes and feelings, *we would do the same thing.* That is what empathic understanding means.

But as theories about how the world works, there were two difficulties with such myths. First, they were wrong; or at least, they gave way to other theories that worked better. Second, they explained events piecemeal, one at a time. Rain came from the benevolence of a rain spirit, lightning from the anger of a thunder god. There were no *general principles* by which to relate one event to another.

Understanding and Science

The scientific method, we might say, developed as a way of avoiding these problems. It differs from the method of the poet and the mythmaker in at least two important ways.

SYSTEMATIC OBSERVATION   In the first place, for the scientist, empathy is not enough. Rather than seek psychological explanations of physical events, scientists **systematically observe** the events themselves. They observe physical phenomena—lightning, or the movements of compass needles—under different conditions, noting what conditions are present when the phenomenon is present, and absent when it is absent. Sometimes they *create* special conditions—that is, they perform experiments—to isolate one possible influence on the phenomenon from others. In that way, scientists identify the *causes* of events—in other words, the conditions required to produce them.

Moreover, it is a continuous process. Having arrived at a tentative explanation, scientists check that explanation with further observations. That way, if an explanation is mistaken, we will know it sooner or later. If we know when we are wrong, we can correct our mistakes; if we don't, we can't.

As our understanding developed, careful observations and experiments showed that lightning bolts do not, in fact, occur at the whim of gods. They occur under specifiable conditions and have specific causes. They follow certain general principles, or laws, of physics. That was important to know; but perhaps more important is the underlying idea that made these discoveries possible: We need to check our explanations, by making observations.

THE SEARCH FOR PRINCIPLES   The second characteristic of scientific method is the search for *general principles* that underlie specific instances. Knowing these, we can relate different events to one another. And we can use the principles to create new instances—that is, to put our knowledge to use.

To see this, let us consider what kind of explanation a scientist would give for a familiar physical event. We flip a switch, and a light bulb lights up. We ask, "Why?"

An explanation might go like this: "Well, when the switch was flipped, two pieces of metal came into contact. This permitted electric current to flow through that connection, through the wires attached to the bulb, and through a little wire (the filament) inside the bulb itself. Now the flow of electricity generates heat. When the filament in the bulb gets hot enough, it glows, just as white-hot steel gives off a glow. That glow is what we see."

Of course our expert might have to backtrack a bit, if we didn't know enough about electricity or the anatomy of switches to understand him; but you see the idea. We have a chain of events laid out for us, each causing the next. Notice too that at each step, there is an appeal to a *general* fact or principle. It is true *in general* that electricity flows through metal wires, that heat is generated in the process, and that metals glow if sufficiently heated. The explanation *relates the specific event to general principles* and shows how it is an instance of them.

Why do we want general principles? For one thing, they permit us to relate one event to another. Knowing the principles of electricity helps us understand light bulbs *and* thunderbolts, and magnets and compasses and much besides. Second, these principles can be put to use. If we understand the principles of electric circuits, then we can build a circuit for some special purpose— a circuit perhaps different from any that has ever been built before—and be reasonably confident that it will work. That is what has given us electric lights, telephones, television, computers, and space travel—the use of general principles to *predict* whether a new method or invention will work, and implement it if we predict that it will.

Understanding Behavior

The explosive growth of science over the past few centuries has affected every aspect of our lives. And as it progressed, it has moved ever closer to home: Beginning with the stars and planets, it expanded its methods to include physical events here on earth, then the biology of earthly creatures, and finally the behavior of living organisms—humans included. It has turned its methods on the human mind itself.

The physical sciences have transformed the way we think about the world. Progress in psychology, however, has affected our thinking less. We have changed the way we explain physical events; we no longer appeal to the psychology of gods and demons. But in explaining behavior, we usually stick to the original form of explanation in terms of urges, wishes, or feelings. If a person greets us in a warm, smiling way, we say that she has a friendly personality. If students sit quietly in class, they must want to learn (or want good grades).

Are these explanations wrong? Not necessarily—there is some dispute about that, as we will see. But at best, they are incomplete explanations. Why? First, because we need to check them; second, because we need to know the *principles* that underlie them. The plain fact is: We do not understand how wishes, urges, and feelings work! *The psychological mechanisms that once served to explain the physical world, as ascribed to gods and demons, now are seen to require explanation themselves.*

CHECKING OUR EXPLANATIONS   Take our new acquaintance who greeted us with a smile. She has a friendly personality, we say. But we'd better check. She may not really have a friendly personality; she may, for all we know, be pretty cold most of the time. Maybe the students we see sitting in a classroom are not eager for knowledge *or* for good grades; they might be frozen in fear, or trying to win a bet about who can sit longest without moving. Without more information, we do not know.

SYSTEMATIC OBSERVATIONS   Our first task, then, is to acquire the further information we need—to make some systematic observations.

Consider our new friend again. Suppose we find, as we investigate further, that she always greets people warmly—not just us, and not just today. She goes out of her way to put people at ease, whistles while she works, and sings in the rain. If so, then we have gone *some* way toward explaining her behavior if we say, "She was friendly toward us because she's a friendly person in general." We are saying that her actions resulted from something about her that was stable, not something temporary—say, some joyful news she had just received.

We have gone *some* way, we say. But not all the way; and here we meet the second aspect of scientific understanding.

THE SEARCH FOR PSYCHOLOGICAL PRINCIPLES   Even if we are right about our new friend's personality, we have the most interesting questions still before us. How are personality traits formed? How do they guide specific actions? Why did her friendly personality express itself in that way rather than some other way? What *principles* govern the formation and expression of personality traits?

Or consider the students. They want good grades, let us say. But getting good grades hasn't happened yet; it lies in the future. How can events that haven't happened yet affect action now? If it is *expectations* that affect us now— well, how are expectations formed? How do expectations control muscles? What *principles* are involved?

The whole situation is similar to the case in physics. We want to be able to relate the specific events of sitting and listening, or greeting with a smile, to general principles. These principles, if we knew what they are, would be analogous to laws of thermodynamics, electric circuits, energy exchange, etc., in physics.

Needless to say, we are quite some way from achieving that ambitious goal. We understand electric circuits far, far better than we understand the causes of action. However, we have made some beginnings. This book will look at many examples, but here is just one to show the parallel: Many scientists believe that rewarded actions are likely to be repeated. If so, that is a principle of behavior. The principle was established largely in laboratory studies of animal behavior. But, by assuming that the *principle* applied to human behavior as well, scientists were able to make *predictions* that could be tested in the human case. They predicted that, for example, if one stopped rewarding the disruptive or self-destructive behavior of mentally ill patients, such behavior should become less frequent. As we will see later (Chap. 8), this prediction has been confirmed in at least some settings.

POINTS OF VIEW IN MOTIVATION THEORY

The field of motivation seeks to understand the causation of specific actions. What will such explanations look like? What kinds of ideas will be most helpful in giving us causal explanations of behavior?

Let us face one fact at the outset: Motivation theorists do not agree with each other even about that. There are strong differences of opinion, good for many an argument, about what causal principles apply to human and animal actions.

Let's look again at the shooting episode. Some theorists might explain that action as the bursting loose of furious anger, anger perhaps pent up for many years and directed originally at the parents. Others would look for a history of reinforcement for violent actions in this person, perhaps coupled with emotional reactions to the absence of reinforcers now. Still others would see it as the result of a reasoned, if not rational, *decision*. Perhaps the man had somehow convinced himself that people in general—just people, any people—were responsible for his misery. And so he took furious revenge on whatever people were around.

Since these are important points of view in motivation, let's look at them in more detail.

Causation by the Environment: Behaviorism

Most of our commonsense theories of motivation explain behavior by looking for internal causes, such as wishes, urges, and desires. To see the diversity of viewpoints, let us begin by looking at a quite different approach. **Behaviorist** theorists reject all explanations of action in terms of internal events such as thoughts or desires. They seek to explain action by *influences from outside*.

Behavior allows us to meet the demands of our environment. We are here because our ancestors were able to find food in the environment, find mates in the environment, avoid being eaten by predators* in the environment, and so on. So, we have evolved organs that register the external situation (the sense organs), and ones that allow us to do something about it (the muscles and joints). Psychology, to behaviorists, is the study of how we go about adjusting to the environment by behaving within it.

It follows that *the causes of behavior are outside the organism, in the environment.* Environmental events may *elicit* actions directly, as in reflexive flinching away from a painful stimulus. Or certain actions may have been strengthened and made more probable because they have been *reinforced* by environmental events in the past. Why does a trained rat press a lever? Because that response has been reinforced with food, and thus strengthened.

A person who encounters the behaviorist view for the first time may find it very strange. It seems to leave much too much out of account. A critic might raise this objection: "Suppose you have two people in the same situation, the same environment. Let's suppose they both flunked the same quiz. One says, 'I'd better study harder for the next one.' The other says, 'I can't do it; I'm a failure.' Doesn't it make a great difference? Doesn't that show that internal thoughts and feelings count for more than the external environment does?"

Now no behaviorist would be so foolish as to deny that such things happen. A behaviorist would reply to that objection this way: "Yes, of course two people might react in those different ways, and of course it's important. But speaking of thoughts and feelings doesn't explain anything. Thoughts and feelings are also behavior; thinking a thought is something we *do*. Now, *why* do the two people think different thoughts? Presumably because they have different learn-

---

*A *predator* is anything that eats you. To a mouse, a cat is a predator; to a blade of grass, a cow is; to a human, an occasional shark can be. Notice that a cobra does not qualify; he might do you in, but not for food.

ing histories; they have had different life experiences. And life experiences are provided by the environment! If two people react differently to the same environment now, in what they do *and* in what they think and feel, it's because their environments have been different in the past."

In other words, the behaviorist says: If we appeal to thoughts and feelings in explaining an action, we now have to explain the thoughts and feelings as well as the action. And if we try to do that, we will be led *outside* the actor to his environment—his learning history—which is the cause of his thinking what he thinks, feeling what he feels, *and* acting as he does.

This, then, is the behaviorist's view of explaining behavior. Thoughts, feelings, and other internal events are not part of the causes of action. They *are* actions, to be explained in turn. They are caused by the same environmental events that cause the external, overt behavior (Fig. 1-2A). That is why we speak of the environment as cause.

Inner Causes: The Mediationist Point of View

In contrast to behaviorists, other theorists believe that internal events such as wishes, urges, expectancies, and thoughts are important in the causation of behavior. These writers grant the importance of the situation. But they insist that to understand what a person does, we must know how she perceives the situation, what she thinks about it, what it means to her, what she wants to have happen within it, and the like. These internal events occur in the middle of the causal chain, or, as we say, they *mediate* between the situation and the action (Fig. 1-2B). Hence we refer to this as the **mediationist** point of view.

Mediationist theorists can in turn be divided into two classes, depending on what they emphasize. First, there are the **psychodynamic** theorists, who

Figure 1-2 Behaviorist (A) and mediationist (B) conceptions of the causes of action.

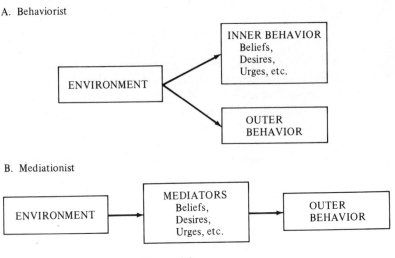

A. Behaviorist

ENVIRONMENT

INNER BEHAVIOR
Beliefs,
Desires,
Urges, etc.

OUTER
BEHAVIOR

B. Mediationist

ENVIRONMENT

MEDIATORS
Beliefs,
Desires,
Urges, etc.

OUTER
BEHAVIOR

Figure 1-2.
Behaviorist (A) and mediationist (B) conceptions of the causes of action.

emphasize urges or impulses, arising from within the actor,★ as sources of motivation. The most familiar of the psychodynamic writers is the founder of psychoanalysis, Sigmund Freud (1856–1939). Freud thought of our actions—including the internal actions of thinking, wishing, dreaming, and so on—as driven by *psychic energy,* produced in turn by tensions arising from within our bodies. Often we are unaware of these motivational forces; to Freud, *unconscious* motives are often the most important ones.

Second, there are the **cognitive** theorists, who emphasize the thinking, judging, rational processes that in turn lead to action. Such writers think of the actor as considering various possible actions, anticipating the outcome of each action, and choosing the action whose outcome is most desired. Considering, anticipating, and choosing—these are *cognitive* processes or operations that are assumed to determine what action takes place.

At first glance, the mediationist position sounds like such obvious common sense that one may wonder why there should be any dispute about it. There is dispute, however, for three reasons. First, it is challenged by behaviorists, who point out the incompleteness of appealing to mental events in explaining anything. A full explanation, they argue, must take us back to the environment to explain both actions *and* cognitions.

Second, mediationists are keenly aware that if we do not understand behavior very well, neither do we understand wishes, expectations, and the like. How do they work? What principles do they follow? We do not know. So, in insisting that wishes and expectations are important, the cognitivist is not so much offering explanations as telling us what she thinks an explanation will look like, what concepts it will use. We are a long way from complete explanations, and the mediationist knows that as well as anyone does.

Third, mediationist theories are not as close to common sense as they might seem. These theorists are convinced that complex mental operations—believing, desiring, deciding—take place in us. But that does not mean that we see them taking place. Much of our thinking and judging may go on without our awareness. If so—if there are internal causes of our actions that we do not know are there, and cannot describe—then our common sense will be a most unreliable guide to them.

The Biological Perspective

There is another point of view about motivation. This one is not really an alternative to the other two, for it cuts across them. Whether we see behavior as caused by internal mechanisms or by the environment, we can ask: How does the process work, within the *biological* system that is the behaving organism? There are two questions that can arise here in turn.

★The term *actor,* used this way, does not mean someone who performs on a stage. It is a shorthand term for "he, she, or it who acts"—that is, the organism whose behavior is under discussion.

First, there is the *physiological question:* How does the organism work? How do cells—in the brain, in the spinal cord, in the endocrine glands, in the muscles—cooperate to produce these effects? How are urges, or environmental impacts, or cognitions, translated into action by the physiological machinery of the body? This is the province of the neurophysiologist, the neuroendocrinologist, the neuroethologist, and the psychobiologist.

Second, there is the *evolutionary question:* How did this kind of organism get to be that way? How did this species evolve its repertoire of reflexes, its instinctive action patterns, and the mechanisms of perceiving, learning, and thinking that it now has? This question becomes: What advantages did these mechanisms provide, in the ecology within which the species evolved, so that ancestral forms that had them left more offspring than those that lacked them?—for this, as we will see in the next chapter, is how evolution works. This question is the province of the evolutionary biologist, the ecologist, the ethologist, and the sociobiologist.

The Prospects for Synthesis

This is not the place to get into the arguments that have arisen among these schools of thought. We will be doing that throughout this book. For now, the point is that there are fundamental differences of opinion about what motivational influences there are, and what they are like.

This is hardly surprising. The diversity in viewpoint is matched by the diversity of human behavior itself. After all, we are the species whose members invent computers, send people to the moon, crack genetic codes—and shoot one another. Approach this complex subject from different starting places, and you reach very different conclusions about it.

Then again, perhaps these viewpoints are not as different as they seem. Perhaps their differences arise because they are studying different aspects, or different parts, of a single complex system. Or they may sometimes be saying similar things in different words.

Two things at least are perfectly clear. First, each of these groups of investigators, using its own methods and concepts, has provided us with ideas, findings, and phenomena that the others, using their methods and concepts, would never have discovered. Second, some of our most productive and insightful scientists have been able to pull useful ideas from all of them.

By way of preview, here is just an example of how different approaches may be integrated.

Severe *depression* can be a paralyzing disorder. A severely depressed person may be unable to initiate any action, to think or reason clearly, or to find any pleasure in life. Freud thought of this as resulting from aggressive *urges,* turned inward. The depressed person, he concluded, is unconsciously angry at himself.

Martin Seligman had a different interpretation, based on his *behavioral* studies of learning in dogs.[1] The exposure to *uncontrollable events*—unpleasant events

1. Seligman, 1975.

from which the dogs could not escape—could produce symptoms in the dogs that paralleled many of the symptoms of human depression (see pp. 558–60). Going on to study humans directly, Seligman found evidence for his hunch: Uncontrollable unpleasant events could produce depressive symptoms in humans too. Here we see the behaviorist approach: It is events *in the environment* that trigger the symptoms. But Seligman added a *cognitive* interpretation of what was going on. He thought that dogs (and humans), when subjected to uncontrollable events, developed a *belief* in their own helplessness, and that this belief interfered with effective action. As his work continued to develop, he found that a great deal of cognitive theory was relevant—how people interpret events, what they think the causes are, what they believe about themselves—and, in particular, how depressed people *blame themselves,* whether consciously or not, for uncontrollable events.

The important thing to see is how the pieces from different viewpoints fit together here. Self-blame sounds similar to Freud's inner-directed anger, resulting from aggressive urges. But Seligman sees it as the result, not of urges, but of beliefs—a cognitive state. And yet it can also be an *unconscious* cognitive state—another contribution from Freud. Then again, those beliefs are beliefs about the causes of *environmental* events—uncontrollable events, whose effects on *behavior* started Seligman thinking about these issues in the first place.

Finally, one of the results of this work has been a new series of questions at the biological level, questions that we would not have thought to ask without this work. The role of *uncontrollability* in stress, and its effects on neurochemical function, on the body's defenses against infection, and much besides, is a rapidly growing field of research in psychobiology and behavioral medicine. Here we see a further convergence of ideas—behavioral and physiological.

METHODS IN THE STUDY OF MOTIVATION

We have seen that the questions asked by motivation theorists, and the kinds of answers they seek, are very diverse. So are the methods used to get these answers. We will discuss three such methods.

Case Studies

Case studies are in-depth observations of single individuals, groups, or events. The attempt is, by detailed examination of single cases, to see clearly the complex network of influences that affect that individual or event.

EXAMPLE 1: THE CASE OF ANNA O   One of the most influential case studies ever published dealt with a clinical case—the case of a woman called Anna O. The woman, when she came to her physician Josef Breuer (1842–1925), suffered from a distressing number and variety of physical symptoms, which had no identifiable organic basis. One of her arms was paralyzed, for example; and that was only one symptom out of many.

Breuer and his associate, Sigmund Freud, treated Anna by hypnosis. They found that under hypnosis, Anna was able to remember episodes that she had quite forgotten in the waking state. And these episodes often related to the symptoms in surprising ways. The paralysis of the arm, for instance, had first occurred at the time Anna's father died. Anna had dozed off at her father's deathbed, with her arm in an uncomfortable position.

After Anna had remembered that episode, the paralysis went away. Breuer and Freud concluded that it had been a reaction to the trauma of her father's death and her guilt at her neglectfulness in dozing off—as if it were a punishment imposed by one part of the mind on the rest of it. This case and the ones that followed led Sigmund Freud to the idea of *unconscious motivation*—the idea that the things we do, including the dreams we dream and the symptoms we suffer, have causes that come from within our minds, but of which we are unaware. This was surely one of the most influential ideas in the history of thought.

EXAMPLE 2: WHEN PROPHECY FAILS   In that example, the case study was of a particular person. However, the "case" might be a whole group of people, or an event. One team of researchers described a group of people who believed that the world was coming to an end, and that they knew the date on which this would happen.[2] These scientists followed the group through the period of waiting, the predicted day of doom, and the period following.

Doomsday came and went, and nothing happened. One would think that the group would accept this clear evidence that their prophecy had been wrong. They ought to change their minds and acknowledge their mistake. What happened was quite the opposite: The group members' beliefs actually intensified. They began publicizing their views and seeking new members— things they had never done before. Clearly, people *can* hang on to a strongly held opinion despite the clearest possible evidence that it is wrong.

This episode, by the way, is another example of how different theoretical perspectives converge. The group decided that the destruction of the world must have been averted by the "light of their faith." We could see that as an example of what psychoanalysts call *rationalization*—the invention of rational-sounding reasons for irrational actions. But we will also discuss it as an instance of *cognitive dissonance*—a concept from cognitive psychology (see Chap. 11). Finally, a behaviorist writer would point to the importance of the social *environment*—the influence of the group members on one another—as important in providing support, or reinforcement, for steadfastness of faith. As it happens, the cognitive psychologists who did the study were also struck by the importance of this social support; this again makes us wonder whether these perspectives are as different from one another as they look.

2. Festinger, Reicken, and Schachter, 1956.

LIMITATIONS OF CASE STUDIES   Case studies, then, can be extremely useful in showing us what *can* happen. They have, however, two severe limitations.

First, it is easy to overgeneralize them, to conclude, because something *can* happen, that it typically *does* happen. One of the major criticisms of Freud's theory is just this: From his conclusion that neurotic symptoms can express unconscious urges, he went on to propose that *all* neurotic behavior, and most normal behavior too, is of that kind. Many think that Freud simply went too far beyond his data, basing a whole theory of mind on a few neurotic people.

The second limitation is even more serious. Case studies look at individuals, or groups, in the natural setting where a great deal is going on. An interviewer cannot inquire about *everything* that happens, nor can the interviewee report everything—there is just too much of it. Both must be selective. And it is very easy to let one's selections be guided by one's theories or preconceptions.

Thus a Freudian therapist, listening to a patient, already believes that events in the patient's early childhood are important. So the therapist is likely to listen carefully when the patient describes such events; she is likely to remember such events and forget other things the patient says; she may even *elicit* reports of such events, by the questions she asks and the interest she expresses. Thus, she is likely to find and remember events that confirm the theory she began with. In a word, she is likely to find what she is looking for; and what she looks for will be determined by the theory.

This is a persistent and real danger in case studies. Because of it, the experimental scientist is likely to be skeptical of case-study research. He accepts it as a source of ideas and possibilities to be explored; but as a source of conclusions, he does not trust it.

Correlational Studies

Whereas case studies focus on single cases, correlational studies typically gather data from a large number of subjects. Typically, each subject will be measured on two attributes, X and Y. Then one asks: Are the sample members who are high in X also likely to be high in Y, and those who are low in X, low in Y? If so, we say that X and Y are positively correlated in the sample of cases. Or there may be an inverse relation: Those high in X tend to be low in Y, and conversely. Then we say that X and Y are negatively correlated. Think of it this way: A positive correlation says, "The more of this (X), the more of that (Y)." A negative correlation says, "The more of this (X), the less of that (Y)."

EXAMPLE 1: DEPRESSION AND EXPLANATIONS OF EVENTS   Each of the two variables X and Y can be anything that is measurable at all. Either or both could be taken from direct observation of behavior, or they could be paper-and-pencil measures. We will see, for instance, that score on a questionnaire test of depression (X) is positively correlated with a tendency, also measured by questionnaire, to blame oneself when bad things happen (*Y*). That is exactly the correlation that is predicted by Martin Seligman's theory of depression (pp. 564–65).

EXAMPLE 2: INFANTS AND MOTHERS   Correlations, we have said, hold across samples of subjects. As with case studies, however, a "subject" may be a group rather than an individual. (In that case we often speak of "sampling units" rather than "subjects," to avoid confusion.) For example, in one study, each sampling unit was a *pair* of people: a mother and her infant. Over a sample of such pairs, the researchers found a negative correlation between the frequency of infants' cries (*X*) and the promptness of the mothers' reactions to the cries (*Y*). Mothers who reacted promptly, in other words, tended to have babies who seldom cried; those who responded slowly tended to have babies who cried often.[3] This finding, and others like it, have implications for theories of infant-parent relations (see pp. 499–500).

LIMITATIONS OF CORRELATIONAL RESEARCH   Thus we see that correlational data can be used to test predictions based on theory. And, of course, the relations they establish may be worth knowing just for themselves; it is certainly important that, for instance, the severity of stress in one's life is correlated with the risk of illness.

Correlational studies do have a drawback, however: They cannot, by themselves, establish the *causes* of actions or events.

Take, for instance, the fact that smoking (*X*) is correlated with risk of lung cancer (*Y*). The more a person smokes, the more likely he or she is to develop lung cancer. But that fact by itself does not show that smoking *causes* an increased risk of cancer—as the tobacco industry was not slow to point out.

If smoking and cancer are correlated, maybe it is because smoking causes cancer. But, one could argue, maybe not. Instead, something else may cause both. Maybe people who are under stress are more likely to smoke *and* to develop cancer. It makes a big difference, because if that is so, then cancer-prevention programs should concentrate on reducing stress, and not on reducing smoking!

Now in this particular case, the causal relationship has been pretty well established. It turns out that smoking does cause increased risk of cancer. But that was established by experiment, not by correlational data. When experimental evidence is not available, we need to keep this caution in mind whenever we look at correlational data. A correlation shows that *X* and *Y* are related; but it does *not* show what causes what.

Experiments

Case studies and correlational research both look at what happens in nature as we find it. An **experiment** intervenes in nature, by *making* something happen so as to observe the effects. Ideally, some one influence is made to vary, in a sit-

3. Bell and Ainsworth, 1972.

uation where everything else is held constant. Some aspect of the subject's behavior is observed, and we can see how that one influence affects it.

The experimental method has two great strengths. First, it can tease apart a complex network of possible influences. It can show us which, of the many things that go on in nature, are the important things.

EXAMPLE 1: HORMONES AND HUNGER REDUCTION   A team of experimenters measured the amount of food eaten by a group of hungry young men. Before some of these meals, the subjects received an injection of a hormone (see p. 78). Before other meals, they received injections of a saline solution; this was a control for injection stress, expectancy effects, and the like. It turned out that the subjects ate less after hormone injections than after control injections. In other words, they became satiated sooner when the hormone was administered.[4] Now, the release of that hormone into the blood is one of the complex series of events that occurs when food is eaten. Many other things occur along with it; the stomach fills, the intestine fills, the nutrients are absorbed into the bloodstream, and so on. With all these things going on at once, it is hard to know how important any one of them is.

In this experiment, however, all these events took place under *both* experimental conditions; only the level of the hormone in the blood was different. And so, since everything else was constant too—the food that was offered, how long the subjects had gone without food, the stress of injection, the external setting—we know that it was the hormone, *and nothing else,* that led the subjects to eat less.

EXAMPLE 2: UNCONTROLLABILITY AND HELPLESSNESS   The second strength of experiments is that they can establish the direction of causal relations. Here again is an example.

Two groups of dogs were presented with a learning problem, in which they had to learn to make the correct response to avoid painful shock. One group was introduced to the problem without any previous experience in such situations. But the other group, before the training began, had received a series of shocks that they could not control; they could do nothing about those shocks. When faced with the learning task, the dogs in the first group quickly learned to avoid the shocks. The dogs in the second group never did. Even though they could easily turn off the shocks now, they did not learn to do so. The experimenters concluded that the earlier, uncontrollable shocks produced *learned helplessness,* so that the dogs simply gave up and did not even try to solve this new, solvable problem. This was the starting point of Seligman's work on depression, mentioned earlier.

Since the experimenters themselves subjected some dogs, but not others, to the early uncontrollable shocks, we are in no doubt here that the earlier experience *caused* the later failure to learn. Instead, we could do a correlational study, asking: Do dogs (or people) who experience uncontrollable events also

---

4. Pi-Sunyer, Kissileff, Thornton, and Smith, 1982.

show learning deficits? But even if the answer was yes, we would not know what caused what. Do some subjects have learning deficits because they have experienced uncontrollable situations? Or do they put themselves in uncontrollable situations because they have learning deficits?

In an experiment, these ambiguities disappear. We know what caused some dogs, but not others, to experience uncontrollable events. The experimenters did! And since the task was the same, and the dogs were comparable except for this prior experience, we know that it was the uncontrollable shocks *and nothing else* that caused the failure to learn a learnable task later on.

LIMITATIONS OF EXPERIMENTS   The experimental method has great strengths. But it does have limitations, too, and three in particular are worth noting here.

First, an experiment simply isn't always possible, for ethical or practical reasons. We might think it would be interesting to know whether uncontrollable shocks would lead to learning deficits in human babies. But we are not about to do that experiment, first because we don't shock babies, and second because we don't do things to them that might cause learning deficits! Questions about the origins and effects of learned helplessness in humans must be addressed in other ways.

Second, the experimental method is sure, but slow—very slow. In the feeding experiment, we know that the hormone suppresses feeding under given conditions, in men. What about women? What if a different food had been offered? What if the room had been warmer? Each of these questions requires its own experiment to answer. That is why it is very rare that a general conclusion can rest on a single experimental finding.

The third limitation is this: If we vary some influence on behavior, with all else constant, we see the effect of that influence—but we see nothing else. Take the hormone experiment, for instance. We know that the level of that hormone, by itself, *can* reduce the amount eaten. But it may well be that other events, such as stomach fullness, also can do so. In short, we have shown that the hormone is *an* influence on feeding. We have not shown that it is *the* influence on feeding—much less *the* mechanism of hunger or satiation. To know how important other mechanisms are, we must study other mechanisms.

This may seem an obvious point, but it is often overlooked. In fact, many of psychology's sillier arguments have arisen because we have forgotten this simple fact: To show that something is *an* important influence is one thing. To show that it is *the* important influence is another.

A Note on Animal Research

The case of the helpless dogs was chosen for a reason. Throughout this book, we are going to be hearing quite a bit about rats, dogs, and even stickleback fish, as well as about ourselves. But what do animal studies tell us about human behavior? I am often asked, "How can you generalize from animals to humans?"

I usually give a two-part reply, if my listener's patience permits. First, I point out that psychologists do a lot less "generalizing" from animals to humans than is popularly supposed. If one says, "Rats do it, therefore people do it"— that's generalizing, and you will rarely hear any such remark. What you will hear, often, is "Rats do it; *let's see* if people do it." Knowing about the rat case may give us ideas about humans that would not otherwise occur to us. Then we can test these ideas, and *see* if they help us understand the human case. That's not generalizing, for it does not state a conclusion; it asks a question instead.

The helplessness and depression story is one example of this. We will see many others.

My second answer is this: It's important to realize that not all animal research is *intended* to apply directly to humans. Animals are interesting and important in their own right. Moreover, if we know how this or that process works in an animal species, at the very least we have learned *one* way in which it *can* work. This may give us valuable insights about the characteristics that any set of mechanisms must have if it is to solve such a problem effectively. In this way, such knowledge can indirectly but importantly affect how we investigate the human case.

MEASURING MOTIVATION

If we wish to study how motivation works, we will be asking what sorts of things affect it. What influences make the desire to eat strong or weak? What about the desire to achieve, or to have control over our lives—what influences make those motives strong or weak? To find out, we must have ways of *measuring* the strengths of these motives.

The thing to remember is that *motivation,* or even this or that particular *motive,* is not something we ever observe directly. No one has ever seen *hunger.* We can observe how long a person has gone without food, or how rapidly he eats now, or how hard he will work or how much he will pay to get some food—but see hunger itself? Never. Even were we to look inside his head, what we would see there are brain cells—not motives.

The notion of motivation or of motives, then, is an invented concept; it is an idea, not something we observe. We use the concept to make sense out of the things we do observe. But that means that when we speak of "measuring motivation," we really mean that we are *inferring* strength of motivation from something else, something that we *can* observe and measure.

Motives as Intervening Variables

One might wonder, then: Why speak of motivation (or even hunger) at all? Why not just talk about what we observe and measure directly? Because it simplifies our thinking—or so it seems at first. Let us see how this could work.★

★This discussion is based on Miller, 1959.

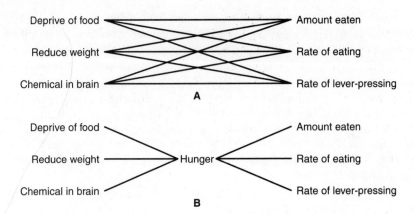

Figure 1-3 Hunger as an intervening variable.

Suppose we have three ways of making a rat hungry. We can deprive him of food for a time. Or, without taking his food away for any great length of time, we can reduce his body weight by giving only limited rations of food. Or we can inject a bit of chemical into the right place in the brain (as discussed in Chapter 5).

These things, we say, make the rat hungry; but how do we measure how hungry a rat is? Consider the following psychological yardsticks: We can measure how much he eats, or how fast he eats, or how hard he works, say, at pressing a lever to get food.

If we must deal only in what we can directly observe, then we have nine sets of relationships to specify (Fig. 1.3A). We must determine the relationship between each of the three procedures and each of the three measures of the rat's responsiveness to food.

However, let's suppose that there is a single variable—call it "hunger"— that *intervenes* between the procedures and the response measures. Such a theoretical variable is often called an *intervening variable*. We assume that it is affected by all three procedures, and affects in turn all three response measures. If we could specify *those* relationships, there would be only six of them, not nine (Fig. 1-3B). We have a simpler picture, with fewer relationships to worry about.

Some Complications

Now in fact it is not that simple, and we should recognize that at the very outset. Take just one example of the complications that arise. We measure, let us say, how much a rat eats—but of what food? Our results will depend on our choice of food. With some foods, as we reduce the rat's weight (making him skinnier and skinnier), he eats more and more of the food when it is offered. But with other foods, the rat will eat the same amount whether he is quite skinny, slightly skinny, or not skinny at all.[5] If we use the former kind of food in our experiment, we would conclude that weight loss markedly affects hunger; if the latter, we would conclude that it doesn't affect it at all.★

Well, what do we conclude? When measures disagree, what do we say? We can say either or both of two things.

First, we remember once again that motivation is inferred, not observed. *If there is something in the rat that we can call "hunger," it may affect our various measures, such as amount eaten or lever-press rate—but other things too will affect those response measures, perhaps in very different ways. As a result, the data we get will depend on the measures we use.* This principle, which is virtually a truism in psychology, means that we need to be very careful about drawing any sweeping conclusions from any one study. We must remember to wonder, "What if a different measure had been used?" That is why the strongest conclusions are those that reflect a convergence of different investigations, using different methods.

The second thing we can say is this: If different measures of a concept do not agree with each other, perhaps it's the concept that is wrong.

Perhaps what we call "hunger" is not a single state at all. Maybe it is a collection of states, reflecting different "kinds" of hunger with different mechanisms. For all we know, different kinds of hunger may be associated with different foods. This is not so strange as it sounds. Surely we have all had the experience of being, not just "hungry" in general, but "hungry for" this or that.[†]

This possibility is worth keeping in mind. Just because we have a single word—"hunger"—in our language, that does not mean that any single state, or set of mechanisms in the brain, corresponds to it. As we learn more, we may find that many of our commonsense concepts will need to be reconsidered. They may simply not do justice to what is really going on.

And all of this, just to consider relatively simple motives like hunger and thirst, in a relatively simple creature like the rat! How much more uncertainty will we face when we try to measure, say, the desire to achieve, in human beings! Later on, we will see much ingenuity devoted to the question: What measures can we take, from which the strength of complex human motives can be inferred?

TWO QUESTIONS ABOUT METHOD

When we discuss research methods in motivation, people often feel that we are missing some obvious bets. Two methods, in particular, often seem obvious ones to use, and students often are surprised that we do not use them more

5. Mook, 1990.
★Or "not hungry for. . . ." A personal example: "I'm starving!" said my Significant Other recently. "Okay," I said. "Want a ham sandwich?" "No; I don't want a ham sandwich." Starving?
†See Hinde, 1970, for some further complications.

than we do. There are reasons for this apparent neglect, however, and we should take a minute to discuss them.

Why Not Just Ask?

For the rat, we might suppose, part of our problem is a simple language barrier. For a person, it seems there is a straightforward way of finding out why he did this or that. Ask!

Sometimes we do that; and the answer can be useful for certain purposes. That is the good news.

At the very least, the person's reply can rule out some possibilities. Suppose a visitor asks, "Why are all you young people sitting in these hard seats?" and one of my students replies, "We're waiting to hear a lecture." That at least tells the visitor that the students are *not* being punished for sleeping on sentry duty, or trying to win a bet, or catatonic. Why did I doodle an owl? Because I felt like it—and *not* because I was entering an owl-sketch contest.

But now the bad news. When we are asked, "Why did you do that?" we find that, in a discouraging number of cases, we can give no reply. Why an owl? I felt like it—but what does that say? Yet, beyond that, I really have no idea.

Implied in "just asking" is that a person can look inside himself and see, with an inner eye, what his motives and feelings are. That sounds plausible; but is it? If we are asked "How hungry are you?" it seems that we can give an accurate reply; but can we? Think how we say, "Look how much I ate! I must have been hungrier than I thought," or, conversely, "My eyes were bigger than my stomach." It seems that we can be mistaken even about so simple a matter as how hungry we are.

That takes us to the worst news of all. We may be mistaken even if we think we do know how we feel or what our motives are. It is interesting that of the points of view we considered earlier—the psychoanalytic, the behaviorist, and the cognitive—*all agree* that we may simply be wrong about the causes even of our own actions.

THE PSYCHOANALYST'S OBJECTION Fundamental to psychoanalytic theory is the notion of *unconscious motivation*. Freud emphasized that we often are not, and cannot be, aware of the causes of our own actions. We do not permit ourselves to recognize them. So, if we ask a person "Why did you do that?" his answer may lead us far from the true causes—because the person may be doing a great deal of unconscious work to conceal the true causes from himself, as well as from us.

THE BEHAVIORIST'S OBJECTION The behaviorist takes a different tack. She points out that the original action, the one we want to explain, was produced by certain causes in the environment. If a subject tells us why he did the action, that is an action in itself. It is a new bit of behavior—verbal behavior—produced by its own causes. And the variables causing the verbal behavior might be quite different from the ones that caused the original action.

So, the behaviorist argues, if we ask a person "Why did you do that?" and get a reply, we have two bits of behavior to explain rather than one. We must explain why he did what he did, and we must explain why he said what he said. There is no reason to think that the causes of the two actions will always be related to each other in any simple way. Indeed, behaviorists have shown, by direct experiment, that environmental conditions can affect what a subject does, when the subject *cannot describe* either the conditions or the effect.

THE COGNITIVIST'S OBJECTION   For their part, some cognitive theorists have reached a remarkably similar conclusion. Some even make the same distinction behaviorists do. Certain cognitive processes affect action. Certain cognitive processes affect the explanations we give, to others and to ourselves, for our actions. And these may or may not be the same processes.

These writers too have supported their point with experimental data. Even when it can be shown by direct experiment that some factor affected the subject's behavior, the subject may deny that the factor was there, or that the behavior took place, or that the one had any influence on the other.*

There you have it. All three points of view, for different reasons, arrive at the same conclusion: "Just asking" can give us misleading answers, because we simply are not always able to identify the causes of our own actions. On the other hand, we also know that the answers we get *can* be accurate and useful. The real problem is to know when they are likely to be accurate and when not, and why. Until we do know that, "just asking" is suspect.

Why Not Wait till the Physiologist Comes?

A few paragraphs back, we noted that even if we look inside a subject's brain, we would not see "hunger" there. That may have been bothering some readers. What if we did "look inside," say by recording the activity of nerve cells in a "hunger center?" Wouldn't amount of nervous activity there be a measure of hunger? Wouldn't that solve our problem?

No, it wouldn't. After all, how would we know that this or that bit of brain tissue is in fact a "hunger center"? We would know it only if its activity were closely related to hunger as measured in some other way—and there we are, back in our original dilemma. Which "other way"?

More generally, the physiologist, who seeks an explanation of behavior in terms of the action of cells, must *first* know the properties of the behavior she is trying to explain—what the behavior is affected by, and what laws it follows. Otherwise she cannot know what properties a system of cells would have to have in order to explain that behavior.

*For examples from cognitivist theorists see Nisbett and Wilson, 1977; Wilson, 1985. For examples from behaviorist writers see Catania et al., 1982; Schwartz, 1982. This, by the way, is one of the many cases where different theories end up saying much the same thing, as noted earlier.

Therefore, there is a certain logical independence of the laws of behavior from the physiological laws of cellular activity. If we know the laws that some action follows, then those laws will hold even if we do not understand the physiology of the matter at all. In a similar way, many of the suggested laws of motivation are stated without any reference to physiology. These include statements like "The effect of a reinforcer decreases with the availability of other reinforcers," or "Other things equal, a person who is high in achievement motivation is more likely to go to business school than one who is low." We will see later what these statements mean, and discuss whether or not there is good reason to believe them. For now, the important point is: We can ask whether or not they are true, even though the physiology of the matter would, at present, be a total mystery either way.

None of this means that we should not make use of physiological knowledge when we can. Of course we should. What it does mean is that (1) we can also study behavior in its own right, apart from physiology, and (2) the properties of the behavior in question must be determined first, before we can know what sorts of physiological mechanisms to look for. We must discover *what* the system does, before we can investigate *how* it does it.

A LOOK AHEAD

Let us summarize the problem we have set ourselves. We want to know what sorts of ideas will help us answer the question, "Why did she or he or it do that, just then?" We will try to identify what causes operate to produce an action, and how. It will not be enough just to empathize with the actor, and see that we would have done the same thing; rather, we seek to understand the processes that cause the action, whether in someone else or in ourselves.

Often we will be contrasting the kinds of explanations offered by behaviorist writers on the one hand, and mediationists on the other. Just as often, though, we will be pulling ideas from both, seeing how they complement each other in seeking the *general principles* that apply to human or animal action.

We will seek these principles. We may or may not find them. Our ideas about motivation are in a state of rapid change, and definitive answers are few and far between. We will see what people think about the problem of motivation at this point in history, and why they think it. And we will want to consider carefully at each point, not whether we have reached our goal of understanding—we have not—but whether we are on the right path.

SUMMARY

Motivation deals with the causation of specific actions. When we ask, "Why did he or she or it do that?" we are asking about the actor's motivation.

We seek to understand the world, first because we use that understanding in dealing with its problems and second because we are a curious species; we want understanding for its own sake. Once we explained the physical universe in terms of the thoughts, wishes, and emotions—the motives—of spirits, gods, and demons. By doing so, we were able to gain *empathic understanding;* that is, we were able to relate the motives and actions of supernatural beings to what our own motives and actions would be. However, as scientific methods gained force, they changed the way we look at the world. We now check our conclusions to see if they are right; and we seek to go beyond empathy, to establish general principles that allow us to relate phenomena to each other and to create new phenomena—that is, to put the principles to use.

Now we are applying the methods of science to human behavior, seeking general principles and checking our theories against the facts. We realize that wishes, thoughts, and emotions need to be understood in their turn. There is dispute, however, about what role they play. The *mediationist* theorists believe that internal events such as wishes and thoughts are among the causes of action. These include psychodynamic writers, who emphasize the role of urges and desires, and cognitive writers, who emphasize thoughts, beliefs, and judgments. *Behaviorist* writers deny that these internal events cause behavior. Rather, they see both the inner events and the behavior as caused by the environment. Cutting across this dispute is the biological perspective, which asks how the mechanisms of behavior work at the level of cells or organ systems, or how the characteristics of the behaving organism evolved.

Three methods of investigating motivation were discussed, each having strengths and limitations. Case studies can give us important information about things that *can* happen, though it is easy to overgeneralize their results or to find in them what a theory leads us to expect. Correlational studies show what variables are related to each other. These relationships may be important in their own right, and they sometimes provide tests of theories, but they do not establish causality. Experimental research does establish causal relationships, but for one or a few variables at a time; so it is sure but slow. And we must remember not to mistake *a* causal variable for *the* causal variable.

Motivation, or even this or that motive (hunger, for instance) is never observed directly. It is a concept, or what is sometimes called an *intervening variable,* that we use to simplify our thinking. It is inferred from something that we do observe or measure. That means that our conclusions will depend on what we choose to observe or measure. Different measures can lead to different conclusions. When this happens, it could mean that one or another measure is faulty; or it could mean that the concept itself is too simple. Our strongest conclusions are those that are supported by a variety of different methods.

When we want to know a person's motives, we might simply ask: "Why did you do that?" This can rule out possibilities and may give accurate information, but all agree that it may also give very inaccurate information—and we are not sure when to expect accuracy and when not. Finally, physiological investigation can show how behavioral laws are mediated by the mechanisms of the body. But we must know what the laws are before we search for those mechanisms. At this stage of our knowledge, many theories and principles are stated without reference to physiology, so we test and evaluate them by other means.

CHAPTER 2

If you want new ideas, read old books.

—IVAN PAVLOV

A Brief History of Motivational Concepts

There is no way to know, but it seems likely that questions about motivation were asked before humankind appeared on earth. Surely there were occasions when a *Homo habilis* or some such proto-human looked at a neighbor and wondered, "Why would he do a dumb thing like that?"

What is certain is that by historical times, not only was the question "What makes people act as they do?" thoroughly familiar, but also some answers were taken for granted. The God of the Old Testament, having given the Hebrews a law to live by, did not depend solely on reverence to ensure their obedience. He promised:

> And it shall come to pass, because ye hearken unto these ordinances, and keep, and do them, that the Lord thy God . . . will love thee, and bless thee, and multiply thee; He will also bless the fruit of thy body and the fruit of thy land, thy corn and thy wine and thine oil, the increase of thy kine and the young of thy flock, in the land which He swore unto thy fathers to give thee. [Deuteronomy, 7:12–13]

But:

> . . . if thou shalt forget the Lord thy God, and walk after other gods, and serve them, I forewarn you this day that ye shall surely perish. As the nations that the Lord maketh to perish before ye, so shall ye perish; because ye would not hearken unto the voice of the Lord your God. [Deuteronomy, 8:19–20]

These promises and threats make it clear that an important behavioral principle was already well known: *What we do is affected by its consequences,* or its anticipated consequences. Our actions are initiated, selected, and maintained by what we expect their outcomes to be.

So, if we want a person to perform an act, we should arrange positive outcomes for him if he does it, and/or negative ones if he doesn't. Thus our principle has immediate application in politics, education, and criminal and civil law—anywhere the notion of *rewards and punishments* can apply.

PHILOSOPHICAL BEGINNINGS: ETHICS AND ACTION

Also early in history, people began wondering as they still do today: Is the notion of control by consequences an adequate theory of motivation in itself? If we assume that positive consequences are pleasant and negative ones unpleasant, the principle becomes: People (and animals) are motivated by the search for pleasure and the avoidance of displeasure. This is the point of view known as **hedonism.**

If that is true, then we know where to look for an explanation if we ask "Why did he or she do that?" We must identify the positive consequences of the action, and/or the negative consequences of other actions, for the behaving person.

Thrasymachus: Motivation as Self-Interest

About the fourth century B.C., the Greek philosopher Thrasymachus put forward a consistent defense of the self-interest theory and its social and political consequences. People are motivated by self-interest, he wrote; that is why rewards and punishments are set up by rulers and codified by law. The intent is just this: to make it in the self-interest of citizens to do the things the rulers want done. Of course society's rulers act in their own self-interest too. Their power is limited only by the fact that the subjects may rebel, if it is in their self-interest to do so. Any appearance of sympathy or altruism in the law is based solely on that kind of calculated, long-term self-interest. This view of **motivation as self-interest** is one that will recur over and over again as we survey this historical context—and the current scene.

Socrates: Motivation as Judgment

A very different point of view was held by Socrates, a contemporary of Thrasymachus. Socrates was unconvinced by the self-interest argument. In the first place, if *right* acts are those that benefit the actor and nothing else matters, then you and I could never agree on what acts are *right* or *good* and what ones are not. My self-interest is not always your self-interest. And we can sometimes agree that what X did was a good thing to do even if it harms both of us—for example, X did not show up when we needed him because he had to care for a sick child instead. This implies that there is some real standard of goodness, apart from our self-interests, that you and I are both in touch with.

Some actions, in short, are "really" good or "really" bad, and we know which is which, quite apart from our own self-interest. To Socrates, it appeared self-evident that people will do the right thing if only they know what it is. He found it impossible to imagine that a person could ever say, "Now I can do A or B; A is the right thing to do; so I'll do B." Even if a person does a very wicked thing, we might say, he must have *thought* he was doing the right thing or he wouldn't have done it.

Here is another view of motivation that will echo down through the centuries. Motivation is based, for Socrates, not on the self-interested search for pleasure but on a judgment of what is right. If we know what is right, we will do it. Intellect is not the servant of our desires, as in Thrasymachus' calculating hedonist; rather what we desire to do is based on our intellectual grasp of what is right.

Some Points of Controversy

There are several things we should notice about this ancient argument. First, we already see taking shape the issue of *external versus internal* determinants of action (see pp. 9–11). The hedonist's pleasures and pains come from outside, in the environment; we seek to gain the one and avoid the other. This view is ancestral to the modern behaviorist's theory of motivation, *reinforcement theory* (Chap. 8). But Socrates' judgments are internal events, based on our internal store of information and wisdom. In this view, we see the faint outlines of a *cognitive* theory of motivation. Since the time of Socrates, questions of knowledge and questions of motivation have been closely intertwined.

Second, we see different conceptions of the relation of motivation to other influences on behavior. Socrates, we have noted, linked motives to *knowledge* and *cognition*. A Thrasymachan view, emphasizing pleasure and pain, links the psychology of motivation with the psychology of *feeling* and *emotion*. The relations between motivation and emotion on the one hand, and between motivation and cognition on the other, were controversial then and remain so today.

Third, these two views began with opposite assumptions, so they faced opposite problems of explanation. To Socrates, right action comes automatically from knowledge of the good; if we know what is right, we will do it. He then must explain why people sometimes do act foolishly or destructively. His answer is that they lack the knowledge they need to do better. Is that an adequate answer?

To Thrasymachus, we are selfish creatures, moved by our own pleasures and pains. He then must explain why we ever behave kindly or in the long-term best interests of others rather than of ourselves. He might reply that these actions too arise from self-interest, for we must consider the pleasures of society's approval and the pains of its condemnation. Is that an adequate answer?

Fourth: Implied in Thrasymachus' argument is that what we do depends heavily on what we have learned. We must be taught what actions a society rewards (or at least tolerates), and what actions it punishes. For Socrates, we are not taught to do the right thing. We may need a great deal of learning to know what the right thing *is;* but once we decide that, the tendency to do it is not taught to us. It is simply human nature. Socrates might have said that we are naturally, or *innately,* inclined to do what is good.

And so we see an early form of the persisting argument, variously described as nature versus nurture, or the innate versus the learned, or, we might now say, heredity versus environment. How much of our mental apparatus, and how much of our behavior, is built in? How much is acquired through learning? Thrasymachus *might* have said (for we are putting words in both speakers' mouths here) that all we have by nature is the tendency to seek pleasure and avoid pain; the rest is a matter of learning how to do these things. Not so, Socrates might reply. What we have by nature is much more complicated: We have standards of goodness or rightness, and a motive to do what is right.

THE BEGINNINGS OF CAUSAL ANALYSIS

After our focus on these early conceptions of what motivates human beings, we must jump ahead quite some time to the next major developments. That is unfortunate, because much careful thought and much heated debate is to be found in the intervening period. But a chapter is only a chapter long.

The developments we will focus on next took place around the middle 1600s A.D. What was going on then in the Western world? First, printing had been invented—and not only printing but also inexpensive ways of making paper. Access to knowledge and ideas by way of books was far more widespread than ever before. Second, a new world was under exploration—and not only a new world but also a new conception of the universe and the world's place in it. Scientists such as Kepler and Galileo were showing that the orbits of planets, like the trajectories of cannonballs, could be understood as the result of a few simple physical laws.

Finally, these observers had also shown—and people were hearing about it—that our own planet has no special status in this vast but intelligible system of nature. We are part of it, that's all. The physical laws that the planets obey must apply to all parts of the universe, the earth and its cannonballs along with the rest. And if the laws apply to its cannonballs, why not to its inhabitants? Living things as parts of nature could be studied and understood as products of natural laws. Finally, if this is true of living things in general, how about living human beings? Must not human behavior also be subject to the universal laws of nature?

Descartes and the Reflex

One of the leaders of this scientific revolution was a remarkable man: a philosopher, mathematician, scientist, and professional soldier. His name was René Descartes (1596–1650).

Figure 2-1   Rene Descartes (1596–1650).

Besides inventing analytic geometry, setting the problems of modern philosophy, writing a textbook on scientific method to which later ones are footnotes, and performing fundamental experiments in physiological optics—among other things—Descartes left an idea that is still important to students of behavior. That was the concept of the **reflex.**

Descartes knew of the astronomers' work, showing that it is all one universe we live in, and of Galileo's work, which was increasingly leading toward the conception of the universe as a *machine.* The "laws of nature" were the laws of mechanics. If movement occurs, it is either inertial movement or the result of applied force. Now animals and their parts are material objects, and they move. What moves them? Forces applied to them must do so.

Sometimes, at least, an input from the environment, or what we call a **stimulus,** may cause movement quite directly. For example, if a child's foot comes too near a fire, the child's leg will flex so that the foot is drawn back, away from the painful stimulus. There are many other such cases. Tap the patellar tendon and the knee jerks; shine a light in a person's eyes and the pupils constrict. Such reflex actions seem machinelike in their reliability, and they are caused by forces applied from outside the organism. But caused how?

Descartes knew that inputs from outside the body are transmitted to the brain and spinal cord by nerves, and that commands from the brain and cord are transmitted to muscles, also by nerves. He thought that nerves were tiny tubes filled with fluid—which they are, though not in the way he supposed—and so were part of a hydraulic system along with the fluid-filled cavities of the brain and spinal cord. Perhaps when the child's foot is stimulated by too much heat, fluid is forced up through the nerves into those cavities. Then that fluid pressure is *reflected* back out through the nerves leading to the muscle (hence the term *reflex*), causing the muscle to swell. That, Descartes said, is muscle contraction, and that is what moves the foot (Fig. 2-2).

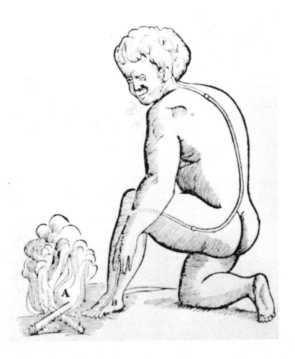

Figure 2-2 Descartes' illustration of reflex action. Stimulation of the foot by the fire is transmitted by fluid pressure to the brain. The fluid pressure is reflected back to the muscles that move the foot.

The mechanics of the theory were wrong, but the idea was ingenious, and scientists learned a great deal in showing it to be wrong (see Chap. 5). It also provided a specific theory about the workings of some behaviors that, in modified form, has dominated our thinking right down to the present. Most important, it added force to the idea that the behavior of animals, like a cannonball trajectory, could be analyzed as the workings of a machine.

Here we have the beginnings of a *causal* analysis of behavior. Descartes was trying for an account of the causes of some behaviors, in some animals; and his hope was to relate them to the principles of mechanics that underlay the world-machine as a whole.

"Some behaviors," we have said, and "some animals." Descartes was quite willing to suppose that animal behavior, and some human behavior, could ultimately be explained as a collection of reflexes and nothing more. However, he believed that most human behavior is not reflexive. Rather it is willed by the mind. Moreover, he held that the human mind is not a part of the vast world-machine of matter and force. Since it is not, it is not bound by the laws of mechanics; it stands outside the chain of mechanical causality. That is why a person has free will; and that, to Descartes, is the fundamental difference between an animal, which is a machine, and a person, who is not.

Thus we have from Descartes a fundamental distinction between two kinds of actions. There is *reflexive* behavior on the one hand, and willed or *voluntary* behavior on the other. The first, Descartes said, is caused by physical events; all animal behavior is like that. The second is caused by mental events; these have no causes in the physical sense, but only the choices made by the will. Only voluntary human behavior is of that kind.

Not everyone, however, was content with that distinction.

Hobbes: Empiricism and Hedonism

Thomas Hobbes (1588–1679) disagreed with his contemporary and correspondent, Descartes. Bodies are matter, and that includes human bodies. Matter moves or is moved in accordance with the principles of mechanics; if the mind moves the body, then the mind, too, must be part of a mechanical system. What we call mental events must reduce to matter in motion. Thus we have the doctrine known as **materialism.** Matter is all there is; even mind is material.

This, said Hobbes, is not all that hard to accept. After all, sensations are mental events, but they are physically produced. We see because light hits the eye; we feel because objects touch the skin. Sensations may be simply movements of particles or fluids in the brain, responsive to the energy impacting from outside. True, the mind also has ideas, dreams, and the like. But these are simply the residues or aftereffects of sensory input, persisting like ripples in a pond after a stone hits the water.

This implies in turn that all events in the mind begin with an impact from outside it. In the final analysis, said Hobbes, there is nothing in the mind— nothing at all—that did not first get into the mind by way of the senses. Let us try to imagine something we have never perceived. We can't. We can, it is true, create novel combinations, like a man's head on a horse's body. But we know what a horse's body and a man's head look like only because we have seen them before.

This important point of view is known as **empiricism.** An empiricist, in this sense of the word, is one who believes that all knowledge—indeed, all the furniture of the mind—begins with sensory experience. And if one believes that, then it is easy to accept the further belief that what we call mental events are really just part of a physical system. That is because mind is made up of sense impressions or their residues. And sense impressions are caused by physical stimuli.

How does all this bear on motivation? Very directly. The outside world, by its impacts, "furnishes" the mind with its ideas, memories, and so on. Stimuli cause the mind to be as it is. In turn, the mind causes behavior; the motion imparted by stimuli is transmitted, however faintly, to the muscles. If the motion is strong enough, the body itself is moved, toward or away from the stimulus. If toward, then we speak of *desire;* if away, we speak of *aversion.*

Thus, said Hobbes, movements in organisms, as in anything else, are caused by motion. Behavior is caused by stimuli; desired ones move us toward them, aversive ones move us away from them. Free will is an illusion. If we seem to deliberate and then make a choice, it really means only that we experience a mix of desire and aversion. The choice is simply the desire or aversion that first becomes strong enough to spill over into movement.

If all this begins to sound familiar, it should. A person, for Hobbes, is moved—literally—solely by his desires and aversions. This is the hedonism of Thrasymachus, linked to the mechanical view of the world and its creatures.

And of course the old problem arises again: If people are selfish to the core, how is a society possible at all? How can we restrain our urges and postpone our pleasures for the more general good, as obviously we do? Moreover, there is a new problem too—and it is a problem for any conception of behavior as part of a mechanical system. If stimuli move us this way or that, how can behavior have the foresightful, forward-looking character it has? How can we take account of future events, and not just respond to present ones?

Hobbes's answer was enormously influential. Ideas, for him, are the movement of particles in the brain; and as these move, they affect each other. In particular, if two sensory inputs enter the brain together, there will be a bond, or *association,* formed between their corresponding images or memories. Then, as one of the ideas occurs, the other is likely to occur as well. When we think of a person, our image of her is likely to include the image of other things that we associate with her—the sound of her name, for instance. In short, ideas tend to be thought together if their corresponding sensations occur together; that is the **principle of association.**

Suppose then that some action would bring pleasure, but that we also have been punished for doing it. Then if we think of the action, we may be moved to perform it; but by the principle of association, we will also think of the punishment that has followed the act before. That gives rise to aversion, which moves us away from the action.

That is how the *anticipation* of punishment suppresses the punished behavior. Anticipation of reward acts in the converse way, of course, to encourage the behavior that is rewarded. And that is what makes societies possible. We become socially acceptable beings, simply because society arranges that acceptable behavior will be rewarded and/or that unacceptable behavior will be punished. And when we think about performing an action, we think also of its consequences; thus our acts are encouraged or suppressed by the consequences society has set up.

None of this was really new. As we have seen, the use of reward and punishment is very ancient indeed. What Hobbes added was, first, an attempt to explain *how* rewards and punishments work. His achievement was to relate these concepts to a systematic causal theory of the mind. Second, he made explicit the role of association, as a psychological principle, in the motivation of human behavior.

Kant and the Organization of Mind

Hobbes's empiricism, the theory that all knowledge derives from the senses, did not have things all its own way by any means. Of the various objections and alternatives, the most influential were those of the German philosopher Immanuel Kant (1724–1804).

Kant pointed out that there are in fact concepts in our minds that sensory input does not account for. An important example is the notion of *causality*. We see causal sequences, Kant admitted, but the sequences are all we actually perceive. We see, let us say, one billiard ball moving and striking another billiard ball, and then the second one moving. In such cases, all that comes in through the senses is the succession of events. The idea that one *causes* the other is simply not part of the sensory input.

Where then does the idea of causality come from? It must be supplied by the observer. As we experience sensory inputs, we must bring with us certain concepts—and causality is only one—by which we interpret and organize the inputs from the sensory world. These concepts are like theories about the world, or about what events have to be like. Kant called them *categories of the understanding*. They are not derived from experience, but are necessary to permit us to make sense out of what we experience. If the "furnishings" of our minds were wholly the result of sensory input, Kant argued, then the concept of cause-and-effect could never have occurred to us.

At first glance, this argument is directed only at Hobbes's theory of knowledge, not at his theory of motivation. But consider this: If we have certain theories about the world that are not derived from experience, might these not include the theory that certain actions are right and others wrong—and that we ought to do the right thing? Kant thought so. Thus, just as Hobbes revived the Thrasymachan "selfish philosophy," so Kant argued for a variant of the Socratic view: We know, without being taught, that there are right and wrong actions, and we know that we ought to do the one and avoid the other.

Empiricists were not silent in the face of this challenge. Much effort was expended then, as it continues to be, in attempts to demonstrate that the seemingly inherent aspects of mind really are derived from experience after all. Once again we see the heredity-environment, or nature-nurture, controversy. What aspects of the human mind are unlearned or innate? What aspects are acquired by experience? "All are acquired," would be Hobbes's reply. "No, some are innate," would be Kant's; and he would add, as would Socrates: "Those that are innate are by far the most important."*

THE THEORY OF EVOLUTION

The 1800s saw an explosion of findings and ideas in the field of biology. Isaac Newton, in the seventeenth century, had shown that Galileo's laws of mechan-

---

*Actually, Kant himself never said that his categories were "innate." Indeed, he said specifically that he was not concerned with that issue at all; his concern was with what categories there were and what they implied about human thought, not with where they came from. However, many commentators have written as if Kant had held the categories to be innate, and certainly he could have done so without changing his argument in any important way.

ics and Kepler's laws of planetary motion were the same laws. The universe *really* was all one system. It was time for the scientific analysis of living creatures, their structure and their behavior, to move past the talking stage. In the nineteenth century, it did so.

By the middle of the century, physiology was advancing with giant strides. Scientists were working toward a clear understanding of the mechanisms of reflex action, and were beginning to assign different behavioral functions to different parts of the brain. Then came one of the most powerful ideas in all the history of science—one that showed *how* the vast world-machine could produce living, behaving creatures.

Darwin and Evolution

The developing conception of animals as machines posed a problem for nineteenth-century biologists. The machines worked! Most species of animals, it appeared, were remarkably well suited to the habitats in which they lived. If behaving animals are bundles of reflexes as Descartes supposed, how is it that they have just the reflexes necessary to perform their full-time jobs of finding food, avoiding becoming food, finding mates, and caring for the young?

The machines we build, of course, work because they are designed to do so. It was therefore natural to look to a Designer to explain the workings of the animal-machines as well. Another and quite different answer exploded on the world in 1859, with the publication of *The Origin of Species* by Charles Darwin (1809–1882).

Fearfully oversimplified, Darwin's idea was this: Animals "work" because, if they did not, they would not be here. And species that did not "work" are not here anymore. Animals had to have the structural and behavioral characteristics required to survive and to breed within their habitats. Those that lacked these requirements left no descendants. And living animals today *are* the descendants of those that possessed these requirements.

This theory explained not only why modern animals "work," but also where modern species come from, and how different species may evolve from a single common ancestor. There are three key ideas here. First is *variability:* Within a species, animals vary one from another. Second is *heritability:* Animals pass on their inherited characteristics to their offspring. Third is *selection:* Variation means that some members of the species are better adapted than others to the ecology in which they live. Those that are well adapted are more likely to have offspring, to which they will pass on their characteristics. Those that are poorly adapted will have fewer offspring, and so their characteristics will diminish over successive generations. This is known as *selection pressure* by the environment in which the species lives.

To take a somewhat threadbare example: Some members of a species will have longer necks than others. Now, suppose climatic changes or migration by the animals places them in an ecology where food is scarce on the ground and plentiful high in the trees. Here, the longer-neck animals will be more

Figure 2-3   Charles Darwin (1809–1882).

likely to go on eating long enough to have babies. If this goes on long enough, and if length of neck is a heritable trait such that long-necked parents tend to have long-necked offspring, the average neck length in the species will gradually increase.

There we have Darwin's **theory of evolution.** It is often presented as a struggle for survival among the animals of the world, but in fact that is not quite what Darwin said. It is not so much a struggle for *survival* as a race for *reproductive success*—that is, number of descendants. Animals that were well adapted to their environments left more descendants than those that were not. Therefore, modern animals are well adapted to their environments, because they *are* those descendants.

The long-neck example concerns the anatomical structure of a species. But the theory has fundamental implications for behavior as well.

First, it implies, as Darwin saw clearly, that the mechanisms controlling behavior in a species must evolve hand in hand with the anatomical structure of that species. Chickens peck at grain with their beaks. Tigers catch their food in their claws and bite it with their teeth. But the anatomical structures—teeth, claws, beak—would be useless if the controlling systems in the respective brains did not program the appropriate movements, and couple them to appropriate stimuli. Imagine a tiger trying to peck at grain, and the point will be clear.

Second, the theory implies continuity between humankind and other animals. Darwin drew back from this conclusion in *The Origin of Species*. But it was clearly implied there, and in his *Descent of Man* he spelled it out explicitly. Up to then one could argue, as Descartes did, that humankind's ability to reason made our species fundamentally different from others. Animals had built-in reflexes and instincts, but not minds. Mind was reserved for human beings.

But if the human species is a product of evolution like any other, this separation can no longer be maintained. If humans and other animals have a common ancestry, then our minds, like our bodies, should be related to those of animals. Our minds may be better than a badger's, as a badger's paws are better for digging than ours. But they ought to differ only in degree, not in kind.

If we abandon the dichotomy—animals have instincts, humans have minds—then two ways of bridging the human-animal gap are at once apparent. We may ask, first: Do humans have instincts? Second: Do animals have minds? Let us take the second first.

Do Animals Have Minds?

If humans have minds, and if there is continuity between human and animal, then animals ought to have minds. And if we could discover how animals' minds worked, then we should better understand the human mind as well.

ANIMAL LEARNING   And so, scientists began setting problems for animals to solve, and the study of learning in animals began. Prominent among the early investigations was the work of Edward Thorndike (1874–1949) in America.

Thorndike's experiments showed that in animals, as in humans, behavior is affected by its *consequences.* Animals are not fixed bundles of instincts; rather, their behavior could be modified by rewards or punishments. In that sense they do have minds of a sort; they could do things that would be called intelligent if humans did them. And so Thorndike titled his monograph *Animal Intelligence.*

THE LAW OF EFFECT   Thorndike summarized his conclusions in what he called the **law of effect.** He spoke of "effect," because the effect of an animal's actions determines what the animal will learn to do. If a response is followed by a reward, or what Thorndike called a "satisfying state of affairs," then that response is strengthened and likely to be repeated. If followed by punishment (an "annoying state of affairs"), the response is weakened and less likely to be repeated. Those are the two parts of the law of effect.

This strengthening or weakening is, of course, a learning process. But it is a motivational process too, inasmuch as satisfaction or annoyance is involved, and inasmuch as an animal's history of reward helps us understand its actions now. This line of work held forth the promise that these important processes could be studied in simpler creatures, under controlled conditions, and thus be understood.

The law of effect had one other important implication. It implied that the animal mind is not all that complicated. Thorndike saw the effects of rewards and punishments not as something his subjects thought about, but as an automatic strengthening or weakening of responses by their consequences—that is, *by the environment*. Clearly this idea takes us to the threshold of behaviorism.

Thorndike's law of effect is very much with us today. We call it the **reinforcement principle.** If a rat presses a lever and gets a bit of food, the rat will continue pressing; and we speak of pressing the lever as *reinforced* by the food. To some modern behaviorists, reinforcement is so important that they say: "Human behavior obeys the law of effect, *and nothing else.*"[1] Other writers take sharp exception, as we will see.

Do Humans Have Instincts?

While some writers were exploring the question of animal intelligence and reason, others were bridging the human-animal gap from the other side. Since we have space to consider only one of these, let it be the American philosopher and psychologist William James (1842–1910).

When James published his *Principles of Psychology* in 1890, many were saying, as many say now, that humans have no instincts. We don't need them; our intelligence and our capacity for learning make instinct superfluous. Not so, said James. We probably have more instincts than any other species, not fewer. Certainly we often act without, or even in the face of, rational considerations.

THE NATURE OF INSTINCTS   Instincts, to James, shade into simple reflexes. Like them, they are called forth by "determinate sensory stimuli." And "every instinct is an impulse." Unless inhibited by something else, it eventuates in action of a determinate kind. Thus distinguishing reflexes and instincts is "a somewhat arbitrary matter . . . it is best . . . to call an activity instinctive [if it is] *naturally* provoked by the presence of specific sorts of outward fact."[2]

By an "outward fact" James means something very similar to what we now call a *releasing stimulus* (see Chap. 4). And the "naturally" seems meant to imply that the act must *not* have come about as a result of learning. By an instinct, then, James means a complex unlearned response (more complex than a simple reflex) to a characteristic stimulus, which also may be complex.

HUMAN INSTINCTS   Moreover, James argued, instincts are by no means confined to animals. Humans have powerful instincts. Take *sympathy,* for example. James says:

> [Some psychologists argue] that it is no primitive endowment, but . . . the result of a rapid calculation of the good consequences to ourselves of the sympathetic act [Thrasymachus again!]. . . . It is hardly needful to argue against the falsity of this view. Some forms of sympathy, that of mother with child, for example, are surely primitive, and not intelligent forecasts of board and lodging and other support to be

1. Brown and Herrnstein, 1975, p. 169; italics in original.
2. James, 1890, p. 403; italics in original.

reaped in old age. Danger to the child blindly and instantaneously stimulates the mother to actions of alarm or defence. . . . In man, then, we may lay it down that the sight of suffering or danger to others is a direct exciter of interest, and an immediate stimulus, if no complication hinders, to acts of relief.[3]

James discussed a number of other human instincts ranging from crying and sucking in newborns, through such things as aggressiveness and the hunting instinct, to such things as secretiveness, cleanliness, and modesty. He concluded the chapter: "These are the most prominent of the tendencies which are worthy of being called instinctive in the human species. It will be observed that *no other mammal, not even the monkey, shows so large an array.*"[4]

Thus, just as Thorndike and others were showing that animal behavior could be modified by learning, so James was arguing that a great deal of human behavior does not require learning. We notice that what James was saying bears a distinct resemblance to what Kant had argued a century before. Kant said it about perception and knowledge; James said it about actions and the feelings that go with them. But what both were saying is this: There are complexities in our mental apparatus, and *the environment did not put them there.* They are innate. For Kant, we have knowledge of the principle of causality (for example), even though we never perceive causes as such, only events. For James, we react to an infant's distress with feelings of sympathy and actions of help or rescue, without regard for our own gain and, he argues, without having been taught to do so. Here again we meet the nature-nurture issue. Are our minds furnished wholly by experience, or is some of the furniture already there?

James's criteria for instinct seem perfectly reasonable. In practice, however, they proved difficult to apply. Can we really rule out the possible role of learning in the development of sympathy? Are aggressiveness, modesty, and the like really instinctive, or can we show that they are acquired after all? That problem also makes it hard to know how many instincts there are. Other writers drew up other lists of human instincts, some much shorter than James's list, some much longer. Whose lists were too long? Whose lists were too short? Whose were the most accurate? There was no good way to decide.

Worst of all, the vagueness and arbitrariness of the instinct label was an invitation to circular reasoning. Some later writers accepted the invitation, with the result that the label *instinctive* was used to "explain" any and all behaviors that seemed puzzling. This way of doing science has been summarized neatly: "If a man seeks his fellows, it is the instinct of gregariousness; if he walks alone, it is the solitary instinct; if he twiddles his thumbs, it is the thumb-twiddling instinct; if he does not twiddle his thumbs, it is the thumb-not-twiddling instinct. Thus everything is explained with the facility of magic—word magic."[5]

3. Ibid., pp. 410–411.
4. Ibid., pp. 440–441; italics in original.
5. Holt, 1931.

For these reasons, and others, the concept of instinct became an unpopular one for quite some time. It has made a strong comeback in recent years—but that story is for a later chapter.

In the meantime, the concept of human instincts, though suspect, at least had been proposed. It was a part of the intellectual atmosphere of the late nineteenth and early twentieth centuries. It alerted us to the possibility that, despite the reasoning power we humans are so proud of, our actions may have causes that are rooted in deeper and more primitive levels. We may be impelled to actions that are not based on reason and may even fly in reason's face.

This possibility received further support from an unexpected quarter. Five years after James published his *Principles,* a Viennese physician published, with a colleague, a book called *Studies on Hysteria.* The physician's name was Sigmund Freud.

FREUD AND PSYCHOANALYSIS

Now we come to the man who probably had more influence on subsequent thought than any other single person. Sigmund Freud's ideas are so very influential that we will be meeting them many times again in this book. Here we can give only the barest sketch.

Figure 2-4　Sigmund Freud (1856–1939).

Unconscious Motivation

Sigmund Freud (1856–1939) was trained as a physician, at a time when research on brain mechanisms and reflex physiology was in the air. Behavior, as a part of nature, was becoming intelligible! But as a clinical neurologist, Freud found himself confronted with patients whose problems did not fit what was known or believed about the functioning of the brain. Prominent among these were *hysterical* disorders. These are physical symptoms, such as blindness or paralysis, for which no organic basis can be found. Anna O's paralysis (see p. 13) was a hysterical disorder.

Such symptoms seemed quite irrational and senseless. Certainly they made no sense to the patients themselves. Yet Freud was convinced that they happened for a reason, that they must have intelligible causes.

Well, if hysterical disorders really are not disorders of the body, are they disorders of the mind? Some early investigators of hysteria had begun treating these disorders by hypnotizing the patient, and, in effect, "commanding" the symptoms to go away. Sometimes it worked. This showed Freud that a body ailment could indeed have a mental cure, suggesting that it was really a mental ailment all along.

To Freud, however, it was not enough to send the symptoms away; this was treating the symptoms, but it did not get at what had caused them in the first place. Anna O's case was a turning point, showing that the symptoms were actually related to, or *associated with,* life events and the emotions that went with these events—even though the patient could not remember the events. Moreover, the symptoms were relieved when the events were remembered and the emotions expressed. This suggested to Freud that the symptoms were caused by the energies of pent-up unconscious emotions, and would go away when the emotions were released, made conscious, and expressed. Here we have one of the fundamental principles of psychoanalysis: **unconscious motivation.** We are powerfully affected by thoughts, wishes, and memories of which we have no conscious awareness.

Urges from the Past

Freud eventually ceased to use hypnosis in treatment, partly because it was unreliable but also because it was unnecessary. In its place, Freud developed his method of **free association.** In this procedure, still in use by psychoanalysts, the patient is required to talk freely, without censorship or attempt to direct the flow of thought. He simply lets thought follow thought, describing his thoughts to the analyst as they come. Freud saw the mind, much as Hobbes had seen it, as a network of ideas and memories linked together by associations. By letting thoughts follow one another freely, a patient could show the therapist what associative bonds there were, and just what was linked with what in the patient's mind.

A patient might begin an analytic session by talking about a dream he had had the previous night. Then, as his continued talking revealed what ideas were linked to the content of the dream, and what ideas were linked to those in turn, the seemingly irrational dream would begin to make sense. The same could be said of irrational obsessions and fears. Freud found these to be connected, through a chain of ideas that might be long and indirect, to unconscious wishes or urges that could not be expressed directly. And thus came another fundamental idea that runs through all of Freud's work: Neurotic symptoms, dreams, slips of the tongue, and the like are *disguised or symbolic expressions of wishes.*

Why were the wishes disguised? Because they were highly threatening to the patient—too threatening even to be allowed into consciousness. As described above, free association sounds like an easy matter—the patient just talks along—but it is far from easy. Here is how Freud described it:

> The patient attempts to escape . . . by every possible means. First he says nothing comes into his head. . . . At last he admits that he really cannot say something, he is ashamed to. . . . Or else, what he has just thought of is really too unimportant, too stupid and too absurd. . . . So it goes on, with untold variations, to which one continually replies that telling everything really means telling everything.[6]

It was as if the unconscious wishes were pushing to be expressed, but, at the same time, another part of the patient's mind was fiercely resisting any such expression. The patient was at war with himself. We have another cornerstone of psychoanalytic theory: **unconscious conflict.**

Freud would persist, until the shameful, absurd, childish thoughts were expressed. And very often, they were indeed literally childish, for the chain of thoughts would work its way back into early childhood—to things that had happened, or that the patients unconsciously *wished* had happened, when they were children. Well then, there must be a reason for the importance of these early memories or fantasies. They must be expressions, Freud concluded, of persisting childhood desires.

This is another cornerstone of Freud's theory: the **persistence of infantile urges** into adult thought and action. Freud emphasized what Hobbes had only hinted at: If urges are inhibited, they do not just go away. If denied direct expression, they will seek expression in some other way. Like steam under pressure, the urge will flow along the pipes provided by the network of associations, until a pathway is found that permits the pressure to be released. Hence the roundabout expression of the urge in symbolic form, in dreams and in neurotic symptoms. The symbolism might be complex and sophisticated, but the urge was as primitive and infantile as it had ever been.

The Irrationality of Mind

Here, then, is the picture of the human mind that emerges. We humans are very proud of our ability to learn and to reason. But deep in our minds is an

6. Freud, 1917, p. 289.

important part of ourselves—the **id,** Freud called it—that does not reason, and has learned nothing. It does not think; it only wants. It is the bundle of urges we met in Chapter 1 (p. 11). And these urges seek gratification with the kicking, screaming, irrational, and uncompromising intensity of the small child. So, if our dreams or our neurotic symptoms are senseless and childish, it is because a senseless child is still part of us.

Freud's Impact

So wrote Sigmund Freud. The physicians of his day, and many laypersons as well, at first greeted his ideas with ridicule or revulsion or both. Partly this was because Freud saw many of our unexpressed urges as sexual, even in young children; this was an idea many found hard to accept. It was partly too because scientists found it hard to evaluate Freud's ideas with solid evidence. Precisely because the theory was so complex and rich in its possibilities, many felt that it could explain any conceivable action, and so could not be tested. Many people raised these objections then, and many still raise them today.

And yet, many other readers have found that Freud's ideas hit home; they ring true. Freudian concepts—id, ego, superego, repression—have become part of the educated person's everyday vocabulary (Fig. 2-5). Perhaps above all, we

Figure 2-5   "When Jud accuses Zack, here, of hostility toward his daughter, like he seems to every session, why, it's plain to me he's only rationalizing his own lack of gumption in standing up to a stepson who's usurping the loyalty of his second wife. The way he lit into him just now shows he's got this here guilt identification with Zack's present family constellation. Calling Zack egotistical ain't nothing but a disguise mechanism for concealing his secret envy of Zack's grit and all-around starch, and shows mighty poor ego boundaries of his own, it appears to me." (Drawing by Whitney Darrow, Jr., © 1976, *New Yorker Magazine.*)

respect Freud's intellectual courage. He faced squarely the manifest fact that we do act without knowing why, and in ways that our vaunted rational powers cannot account for. At the same time, he insisted that the irrational side of the human mind is a part of nature along with the rest; it must be respected, but need not remain mysterious. He held out the promise that even the irrational can be understood.

We may agree or disagree with what Freud says, but we cannot ignore him.

THE EMERGENCE OF BEHAVIORISM

By the early decades of the twentieth century, the science called *psychology* was a going concern. It was an academic department separate from philosophy, and psychological laboratories had sprung up over Europe and America. And it was generally agreed that the subject matter of psychology was the mind.

Any consensus about that, however, ended abruptly in 1913, with the publication of a paper titled "Psychology as the Behaviorist Views It."[7] The author's name was John B. Watson (1878–1958).

Watson's Challenge

Watson began his psychological career as a student of animal behavior. In his investigations, he naturally fell in with the tradition of trying to infer, from what animals did and how they went about solving problems, what their mental apparatus was like. Thorndike had pioneered that enterprise; after all, he had titled his monograph *Animal Intelligence.*

The problem was that conclusions about the animal mind were necessarily inferential. One could never observe directly what, if anything, was going on in an animal's mind. As a result, disagreements were hard to resolve, and solid conclusions about the animal mind were few. Impatient with this state of affairs, Watson said, in effect: Why make inferences? One cannot see what an animal *thinks, knows, or perceives,* but anyone can see what an animal *does.* Why not talk about that?

> The psychology which I would attempt to build up would take as a starting point, first, the observable fact that organisms, *man and animal alike,* do adjust themselves to their environment . . . secondly, that certain stimuli lead the organism to make the responses. In a system of psychology completely worked out, given the response the stimuli can be predicted; given the stimuli the response can be predicted. . . . The time seems to have come when psychology must discard all reference to consciousness; when it need no longer delude itself into thinking that it is making mental states the object of observation.[8]

7. Watson, 1913.
8. Ibid.; my italics

Figure 2-6 John B. Watson (1878–1958).

Therefore, said Watson, let us begin again; and his new beginning was nothing less than a redefinition of psychology. Psychology is to be the study of *behavior,* and of nothing else. It will relate what organisms do to the circumstances under which they do it. It will determine by direct experiment the laws relating stimulus to response.★

Moreover, this is to be so not only in animal psychology but in the psychology of human beings as well. The objections to making inferences about the animal mind apply, with equal force, to making inferences about the human mind. True, a human can speak to us, and thus describe his or her mental state. Even then, however, we do not observe the mental state itself. What we observe is what the person *says*—and verbal behavior is still behavior.

The Case against Consciousness

Watson's aim, then, was to get rid of the concept of consciousness altogether, as something unknown and unknowable. This includes *all* mental events—instincts, wishes, pleasures, and other motivating forces along with the rest. Our first reaction may be that this is much too radical; we do know something about other people's consciousnesses, their wishes, their feelings. But do we?

★A modern behaviorist would not express the matter this way, as we will see later. Behaviorism, like the rest of us, has changed quite a bit since it was born. Historically, though, this was its original program.

CONSCIOUSNESS AS UNOBSERVABLE   Think about this for a minute. Is your red the same as my red?

If we see a patch of a certain color, we will both *call* it red, because we both have been taught to do so. But how do you know that the color I see, looking at that patch, is not the color you would call "green," and vice versa?

If you worry seriously about that possibility for a while, I think you will conclude that the question is unanswerable. Even if we could somehow hook up your eyes to my brain, still it would be *my* brain that would "have" whatever color experience the patch gave rise to. You still would know only what I call it, not what it really is like for me.

On the other hand, you probably will not worry about the issue for very long. Not only is the question unanswerable; the answer simply *does not matter*. You and I both *call* the patch red; we both behave the same way when that color appears at a traffic intersection; we agree that it is not stylish for a man to wear a tie we call "purple" against a shirt we call "dark green." And so on. The knowledge that you and I make corresponding *responses* to color *stimuli* is all the knowledge we need. And that is fortunate, for it also is all we're going to get.

If the example strikes home, you have gone a long way toward sympathizing with Watson's argument. Questions about what another human's experience is really like cannot be answered and need not be asked. And Watson did not invent that circumstance; he only pointed it out. It has always been so.

CONSCIOUSNESS AS SUPERFLUOUS: PAVLOV AND CONDITIONED REFLEXES   There are other arguments on Watson's side. For one thing, his version of psychology is excellent Darwinism. In the last analysis, it is what an animal *does* about a situation, and not what it thinks about before doing it, that determines whether the animal survives that situation to leave descendants. Its thoughts and feelings, if any, are simply superfluous.

Finally, Watson thought that the clinching argument against consciousness was simply this: Psychology can do the job without it. The complexity and richness that we assign to "mental life" can be explained in a better way: by assigning it to the relation between behavior and its environment. To see why Watson was so optimistic about this, we must digress for a minute to pick up another major historical figure: the Russian physiologist Ivan Pavlov (1849–1936).

What Pavlov showed was this. Suppose we evoke a reflex action in a dog; say, we put a bit of food in its mouth, to elicit salivation as a reflex. While doing so, we present some stimulus that is wholly unrelated to food and does not evoke salivation in any sensible dog—a bell, let us say. If we do that a number of times, we will see a new reflex forming: The dog will begin to salivate at the sound of the bell alone. Now, in addition to the **unconditioned reflex,** salivation in response to food, the dog has a **conditioned reflex,** a learned reflex—salivation in response to the bell (Fig. 2-7).

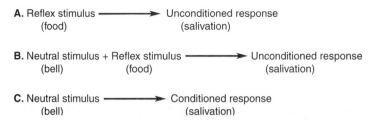

Figure 2-7   The conditioned reflex. (A) Food evokes the unconditioned response of salivation. (B) A neutral stimulus is paired with the food. (C) After several such pairings, the neutral stimulus comes to elicit the response by itself. That is a conditioned reflex. In all cases the *response* is salivation; the term *reflex* applies to the whole stimulus-response relation.

This discovery raised the hope that the psychological phenomenon of *learning* might be brought into articulation with the physiology of reflex action. It seemed indeed to be a physiological embodiment of Hobbes's *association*. For Hobbes, sensations (the units of mind) are associated with each other because they occur together. For Pavlov, reflexes (the units of behavior) are associated with stimuli because *they* occur together. Thus in Pavlov's experiment, the bell caused the dog to salivate because the bell, and a stimulus for salivation (food), occurred together. So important is this experimental demonstration that the procedure has come to be called **classical conditioning,** or **Pavlovian conditioning.**

Like Hobbes's association, it seemed that the classical-conditioning mechanism could, in principle, provide for almost unlimited complexity and richness. For Hobbes, *any* two ideas could become associated if their corresponding sensations occurred together. So for Pavlov. One could condition salivation as a response to a bell, or a light going on, or a light going off, or the sound of bubbling water—the response could, it appeared, be attached to any stimulus whatever. Conversely, we could condition any of a number of responses to a bell; we could condition salivation if we pair the bell with food, or a change in heart rate if we pair the bell with shock. What response we make, to any stimulus, depends on what has been paired with that stimulus before. It becomes clear how Pavlov's ideas clicked into the behavioristic view like a key into a lock.

Where is the limit? How much of the causation of human action, including its diversity and richness, might be understood in conditioning terms? This object you are holding could be called *a book,* or *ein Buch,* or *un libro*—vastly different responses to the same stimulus, depending on one's learning history. Or the same response could be attached to different stimuli in different individuals. One person fears heights, one fears exams, one fears members of the opposite sex, one fears failure. If we think of fear as a response, then we are saying: Different stimuli evoke the same response. Are different conditioning histories at the bottom of it?

No wonder so many behaviorists thought that the key to the causation of complex human behavior had come from Pavlov's research! If our various behaviors are complex and diverse, perhaps that's because our various learning histories are complex and diverse. Thus the behaviorist's emphasis on the *environment,* past and present, as the cause of action. The stimulus situation—the environment—accounts for what we do. And if different people react differently in the same present environment, says Watson, it is because of differences in the *past* environment—that is, in the conditioning they have had. And on the old nature-nurture issue, the behaviorists come down squarely on the nurture side. Simple reflexes are innate; but *all the complexity of behavior is learned.* Learned how? Through conditioning.

THE "GHOST IN THE MACHINE"   There is one more argument we must consider if we are to understand the impact of behaviorism on psychology. Watson's rejection of mental explanations for behavior was given added force by what he took the term "mental" to imply.

Descartes had argued that the human mind stands outside the physical chain of cause and effect. It was not part of the physical world at all. In modern everyday speech, the word "mind" often does carry the connotation of something non-physical. It can even sound like something mystical, something extra-natural or even supernatural. Certainly it sounded that way to Watson, and he was having none of it:

> The behaviorist . . . holds . . . that belief in the existence of consciousness goes back to the ancient days of superstition and magic[9] . . . the behaviorist began his own formulation of the problem of psychology by sweeping aside all mediaeval conceptions.[10]

The modern behaviorist B. F. Skinner implies something similar when he says that in turning from the mental events to the environment for our explanations, we turn "from the miraculous to the natural."[11]

It comes down to this. According to behaviorists, those who speak of the *mind* are flirting with downright superstition; they must believe that there is a mysterious spirit inhabiting the body, a "ghost in the machine." Psychodynamic and cognitivist theorists are most emphatically included in this accusation.

I have mentioned this argument because its historical importance requires that something be said about it. It is still sometimes used to argue against some concepts we will need in later chapters, for example, cognitive maps and search images (Chap. 9), beliefs (Chap. 11), and other such mental or cognitive terms.

But to me, it simply is not a serious argument and never was. Hobbes wrote about the mind, as did James and Freud; all three would have been surprised to

9. Watson, 1924, p. 2.
10. Ibid., p. 5.
11. Skinner, 1971, p. 201.

hear that they were talking about something supernatural! Mind, to them, was part of nature, to be studied as such. Today, most cognitivists take it for granted that the events we call "mental" have something to do with events in the physical nervous system. Many modern scientists are busy investigating how images or feelings reflect the actions of the material brain.

We simply do not need to regard mental events as non-physical—much less as supernatural or mystical. Once we recognize that, the issue disappears, and we have spent time on it here only to make that clear.

The Impact of Behaviorism

What are we to think of the behaviorist challenge?

On the positive side, the behaviorists' emphasis on *observable data* was distinctly beneficial. Behaviorists gathered, and continue to gather, solid facts about behavior. Even those who disagreed with them—scientists who were convinced that such things as purposes, goals, and likes and dislikes existed and were important—had to demonstrate that they were important by offering the kind of objective evidence a behaviorist could accept.

In one sense, therefore, we are all behaviorists now. For we all—or almost all—accept the propositions that our conclusions must be based on evidence, and that the evidence must be observable, so that any observer can see it and verify it for himself. That is what *objective evidence* means.

And yet it must also be said that as it became the dominant force in academic psychology—and it did—behaviorism imposed severe limitations on its subject matter. The study of cognition, of imagery, of wishes, preferences, likes and dislikes, goals and purposiveness in behavior—all these were ruled out of scientific court by behaviorists, simply because they had once been called "mental" phenomena. As a result, their investigation by scientists was long delayed.

But, though delayed, it was not abandoned. It has come back strong in recent years. Let us look briefly at what happened.

CHALLENGES TO BEHAVIORISM

For the twenty or thirty years following Watson, the behaviorist view was the dominant force in the study of motivation and learning. Its assumptions were very clear: (1) Most behavior is learned. Aside from a few simple reflexes, organisms begin as "blank slates" on which the environment "writes," by providing learning experiences. Therefore, if behavior is complicated, it is not so much because organisms are complicated as because the environment is. (2) Learning itself follows a few basic principles, revealed by experiments such as those of Thorndike and Pavlov; and *motivation* could similarly be reduced to a short list of "drives," as we'll discuss in Chapter 3. (3) Inner states and operations, such as thoughts, desires, and instincts, can be ignored if they exist at all.

To talk about them is to drag in some mystical mind stuff—a "ghost in the machine"—into a psychology that was well rid of such superstition.

It did not long remain that way. Around the 1950s, behaviorism received a series of hammer blows that left it, and the study of motivation, permanently altered.*

The Resurgence of Cognitive Psychology

THE DISSENTERS   There were dissenters, even within animal psychology. Wolfgang Köhler argued with vigor (and with data) that to understand even an animal's behavior, one had to know how the animal *perceived* the world, not just what the stimuli were.[12] On the response side, Edward Tolman showed, with good behavioral data, that rats did not just make the responses they were trained to make. They might make a brand-new response, never made before, to get to where the food was—implying that they *knew* where it was.[13] And Donald Hebb tried to show how thoughts, concepts, and even expectancies could be formed by the interaction of messages within the brain.[14]

In human research, we must mention the great social psychologist Kurt Lewin.[15] Lewin insisted that to understand actions, we must consider the situation *as the person perceives* it. Lewin also pioneered the experimental study of practical human problems. He showed how such complex processes as people's reactions to thwarting, or democratic versus authoritarian organizations of social groups, could be modeled in the laboratory and studied there. It was he who said, "Nothing is so practical as a good theory."

PURPOSIVE MACHINES   In the years following World War II, computers became sophisticated—small, fast, and very versatile. And in performing their tasks, these useful tools do things which, if done by humans, would be described as "cognitive" or "mental" operations.

A computer can accept input from the environment and, rather than acting on it now, store it for use later. A computer can build an internal representation, or "image," of some aspects of the outside world, and use the information that image provides (as a self-guided missile might do). A computer can decide among alternatives: It can calculate what would happen *if* this or that were done (without actually doing it), and then take the action whose calculated consequences are best for the purpose at hand. That's what a computer does when it plays chess, for example. (And computers can play chess very well indeed. In our own time, there are chess-playing programs that can give world champions a run for their money!)

The effect of these developments was twofold. First, they meant that the behaviorist "ghost in the machine" argument had lost whatever validity it ever

12. Köhler, 1925.
13. Tolman, 1932.
14. Hebb, 1949.
15. Lewin, 1935.

had had. Here were machines—literal, physical machines with no ghosts in them—performing cognitive operations or their equivalents. If machines made of silicon could do these things, there was nothing mystical in supposing that machines made of flesh and blood could do them too.

The second effect was that scientists interested in cognitive processes now had new ways of thinking about them. By itself, the fact that machines can do these things tells us nothing whatever about how humans do them. But it does lead to a wealth of ideas about how humans *might* do them. One hears of the "computer metaphor," which refers to this handy rule of thumb: If you want ideas about how this or that cognitive activity might work, think about how you might program a computer to do it.

In sum, the computer metaphor made mental operations at once less mysterious and more easily studied. Such operations are not the province of ghosts; and by seeing how they are accomplished by a machine, we get ideas about how the machinery of the brain might do analogous things.

The Impact of Ethology

Behaviorism received another challenge at roughly the same time. This time the challenge came from zoologists and naturalists who studied behavior in its natural setting. Watching what animals did in the world in which they made their living, rather than in the laboratory, these scientists, called *ethologists,* identified the patterns of action that characterized the members of a species, and the patterns of stimulation that triggered these actions.★

Early on, behaviorists had thrown the concept of instinct out the window. This was partly because it had been abused (see the thumb-not-twiddling instinct, p. 39), partly because instinct seemed to suggest a mystical force for which science had no place, and partly because it was believed that learning could account for all the complexity of behavior. Not so, said the ethologists. Like it or not, behavior has complexities that are not put there by the environment—that are not learned. William James had said the same thing, but he had only argued for that conclusion. The ethologists were *showing* it, by direct observation and experiment.

Consider the mayfly. This unfortunate creature mates exactly once—just once—in its whole short life. It has no opportunity to learn anything about the process. It must identify a mate, court the mate, and mate with the mate— and it must do these things the right way, the first time, or it will not reproduce. And since there are a substantial number of mayflies around, it is clear that many of them do get it right the very first time. That's a simple example, of course, in a (relatively!) simple species; but it makes the point: complex patterns of behavior can be "built into" the members of a species, with no opportunity, and no need, for learning them.

★See especially Tinbergen, 1951.

Both the concepts and the methods of ethology have had substantial impact on the study of motivation. As to the concepts, there can no longer be any doubt that a great deal of complex behavior is organized in a way that a creature's learning history does not account for. To understand what the creature does, to know its present environment and its past history is not enough; we must also know the internal organization of its repertoire of actions.

As to method: As long as it was assumed that behavior is shaped by the environment, it made sense to study it in simple environments where one can specify what is going on—environments such as Pavlov's conditioning laboratory, or Thorndike's puzzle box or its modern descendant, the operant chamber (Chap. 8). The study of behavior in natural settings may be more difficult, but it also reveals complexities that would never have been discovered in simplified laboratory settings.

In recent years, as we will see, ethologists and laboratory experimenters have stopped arguing and begun collaborating, each bringing to the union something of value: control over conditions in the one case, and in the other, an appreciation of the range of behaviors a species exhibits, and how its behavior is adapted to problems its natural environment poses. It has been a productive union!

This historical sketch takes us up to around 1960—not exactly "today," but a time by which the issues have taken recognizably modern forms. We have sketched out the antecedents of the modern points of view summarized in Chapter 1: behaviorism, psychoanalysis, and cognitive psychology. We see where the diversity comes from, and what some of the persisting issues are: internal versus environmental determinants of action; nature versus nurture, or the role of innate factors in behavior; and emotion versus cognition, feeling versus knowledge, in human conduct. With this background in mind, we should find the modern scene much easier to understand.

SUMMARY

The principle that behavior is affected by consequences was taken for granted even at the beginning of history. A popular form of this theory is the doctrine of *hedonism*—people and animals seek to obtain pleasure and to avoid pain. Such a theory points to the environmental determinants of action, because pleasurable and painful consequences of action come from the environment; and it links this study of motivation with the study of emotions and feelings.

Among the Greeks, Thrasymachus believed that that principle was in itself an adequate theory of human action: Humans are motivated solely by self-interest. Socrates disagreed: Human are basically virtuous, and will do the right thing if only they know what it is. Socrates' theory points to inner as opposed to outer determinants of action—there is an inherent tendency to seek the good. And it links motivation with cognition rather than with emotion—

action is guided not by what pleases or displeases us, but by what we think is right. The controversy still echoes today.

The scientific analysis of behavior began with Descartes's concept of the *reflex*. Some environmental stimuli drive movements mechanically, by way of the nervous system. Descartes restricted this idea to animals and involuntary movements in humans. But Hobbes showed how something like it could account for voluntary human behavior as well: We move toward pleasurable stimuli and away from painful ones. In addition, Hobbes's concept of *association* showed how these movements could be guided by anticipated consequences as well as present ones. We move toward stimuli *associated with* pleasure. Hobbes thus was led to a theory of motivation somewhat like that of Thrasymachus. In response, Immanuel Kant took up a position somewhat like Socrates'. We know more than what incoming stimuli there are or have been; and among the things we know is that certain actions are right, and that we ought to do them.

In the nineteenth century, Darwin's theory of evolution showed how natural processes could produce the good fit between animals' structures and the environment in which they live, through *natural selection* of well-adapted life forms. Animals poorly fitted to their environments left fewer descendants than those well adapted; and so modern animals, which *are* the descendants, are the well-adapted surviving forms. His theory recognized that mechanisms of behavior must evolve along with the structure of the body, so that an animal can use its body structures appropriately.

Darwin's theory also broke down the rigid distinction between animal behavior, guided by instinct, and human behavior, guided by the mind. Perhaps animals have minds, too. Scientists began to study learning and problem solving in animals under controlled conditions. This work led, among many other things, to Thorndike's *law of effect,* an early statement of the *reinforcement principle*. On the other side, William James argued that humans, like animals, have instincts. Instincts were thought of as complex reactions to complex stimuli, reactions produced by evolution and not by learning or by reason.

Soon thereafter, Sigmund Freud began the work which convinced him that much of the causation of behavior had little to do with reason. He saw much of neurotic behavior, and much of normal behavior too, as symbolic expressions of unfulfilled urges and wishes, dating back to early childhood. These urges, with attendant fear and guilt, operated as powerful *unconscious motives*.

The program of psychology took an abrupt turn under John B. Watson and *behaviorism*. Watson objected to talk of conscious *or* unconscious mental events. He doubted that such events could be studied scientifically, for they could not be observed; and they seemed to him to represent mystical, supernatural "ghosts in the machine." He argued instead that psychology should concern itself with relations between observable responses and observable events in the environment—stimuli—that evoke them. Then Pavlov demonstrated that learning could be studied by observing such stimuli and responses, that is, by the *conditioned-reflex* method. In light of the importance of learning in behavior, Pavlov's work added to the early behaviorists' conviction that behavior could be understood in stimulus-response terms. Modern behaviorism has moved away from the stimulus-response framework, but it continues to insist that the causes of behavior are *in the environment*.

Behaviorism dominated our thinking about motivation for a while, though there were dissenters from the outset. Later developments have substantially weakened its hold. Developments in guidance and computer technology gave us new ways of thinking about how internal, cognitive operations might affect action (the "computer metaphor"). Modern cognitive psychology, though it accepts the behaviorist insistence on objective data, now uses such data to test theories about *internal* mental operations as part of the causation of behavior. At about the same time, *ethologists*—students of behavior in its natural environment—reminded us that evolution of the species, as well as the complexity of the environment, contributes to the complexity of behavior.

Today, we shall see that behaviorists, ethologists, and cognitive psychologists are collaborating, sharing their methods and ideas with each other. These convergences of ideas are throwing new light on some very old issues: internal versus external determinants of action, nature versus nurture, and the relation of motivation to emotion on the one hand and to cognition on the other.

PART 2

Basic Action Systems

CHAPTER 3

Biological Motives: Hunger and Thirst

Water was the only thing on my mind. One of the men led me into a cabin where I downed four China mugs of water in quick succession. The skipper, who was barely my age, became alarmed. "Aren't you overdoing it?" he asked. I said yes, maybe too much water would be bad. So I had a couple of mugs of pineapple juice and a mug of hot beef broth, one after the other.

—EDWARD V. RICKENBACKER*

Let us begin with two motives that are essential to life. The motivational systems that keep the body supplied with fuel and, in land-dwelling animals, with water *must* be intact and functioning. Otherwise, we simply wouldn't be here. And if the demands of these motives were not met with some regularity, we would not stay around for very long.

In examining feeding and drinking, we will look for *principles*—what kinds of systems are we dealing with, and what do they do?—and we will see some investigations that illustrate these principles. These simple biological motives may seem a long way removed from attacks with guns, career choices, and other complex human actions. In fact, however, these motives are not so simple as they seem. As we go, we will find ourselves confronting the whole range of influences—biological, cognitive, cultural—that come to bear in accounting for why we do what we do.

DRIVES AND MOTIVATIONAL STATES

At the end of Chapter 1, we saw that behaviorism had become the dominant school of thought at least in American psychology. Its program, as John B. Watson declared it, was to determine the relations between objectively specifiable *stimuli* and objectively measurable *responses*.

Even to behaviorists, however, it became apparent that that program would not work. Something more was needed, for two reasons.

*Quoted by Wolf, 1958. Captain Edward Rickenbacker had just spent 21 days on a life raft floating in the Pacific, with seven companions (six survived).

Figure 3-1 Activity wheel for the rat. The rat turns the wheel as it runs, and each revolution of the wheel advances a counter, providing a record of the amount of running that occurs.

Behavioral Variation in a Constant Environment

First, responses may vary even when the stimulus is constant. Thus Curt P. Richter, one of the founders of modern motivational psychology, saw great differences from one day to another in the amount of activity displayed by rats in a *constant stimulus situation*.[1] When he measured this activity (Fig. 3-1), he found it to be affected by the internal state of the animal. Female rats showed peaks of activity every fourth or fifth day, and these peaks corresponded roughly to the times of sexual receptivity, or *estrus*. Male rats showed no such cycles of activity. But if food was withheld, both males and females became progressively more active as time without food elapsed—again, even in an unchanging external environment.

Clearly, in addition to the stimulus situation outside the animal, one has to consider its *internal state*. Behavior changes when the environment does not. If the causes of that change are not in the situation, then they must be in the rat.

1. Richter, 1922.

Multiple Outputs: Goal-Directed Action

Second, an effect of internal state can be expressed by any of a number of specific responses. Offer solid food to a hungry rat, and it will chew; offer it liquid food, and it will lap. But it may do *none of these things* if it is not hungry.

ARBITRARY RESPONSES AND PURPOSIVE BEHAVIOR   Appropriate training can add more members to the class of actions. If food is available, a food-deprived rat will approach it directly. If food is not available and if the rat has been trained to run a maze for food, it will run that maze. If trained to press a lever for food, it will press the lever.

This is an important fact. It is the reason we speak of *motivation,* and not just of *feeding or drinking behavior.* The behavior itself is not fixed; rather, the rat will make any of a variety of specific responses to get its food. More important, the connection between, say, lever-pressing and food is a totally arbitrary one, set up by the experimenter. There is nothing in the nature of food, or of rats, that connects lever-pressing with food.

To many writers, it is this *arbitrariness* of the response that is diagnostic of purposive, goal-directed behavior.[2] It is how we distinguish goal-directed behavior from reflexive or instinctive behavior that is not arbitrary, but a natural part of an animal's feeding repertoire. Some writers would say that it shows *desire* or *wanting.* If we see that the rat will make an arbitrary response—that it will *do whatever it has to do, make whatever response is available* to obtain food—then we may say that it *wants* food.

HIERARCHICAL ORGANIZATION   All this suggests some mechanism, or state, that is different from any specific response. For convenience, we will call such a state a **motivational state.** Here, such a state is activated by food deprivation, and it can activate in turn any of a number of specific actions. We might as well call it *hunger.* Figure 3-2 shows the idea and also introduces another important concept: the *hierarchical organization* of behavior.

A **hierarchy** is any system that is organized from top to bottom, so that its units are composed of sub-units which in turn are composed of sub-sub-units, and so on down. Think of a military chain of command, in which the general can order any or all of his field officers to get something done, the officers order their sergeants to get it done, and the sergeants order their foot soldiers to do it.

Well, feeding and food-getting behavior are organized in that way. A state of hunger, the general, can tell the officer in charge of running, "Run in that direction." (Or it could tell the lever-pressing officer, "Press the lever.") The

2. For example Tolman, 1932; Teitelbaum, 1966.

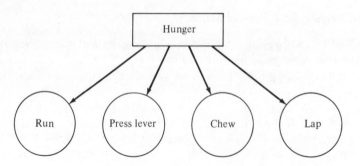

Figure 3-2   Hunger as a motivational state that can be expressed by any of a number of responses.

running officer gives orders to the leg-moving sergeants, which control patterns of muscle contractions: "Advance the left foot, then the right foot . . ." The muscles themselves are the foot soldiers that perform the actual movements.

Further examples abound. Later we will see that a male stickleback fish in reproductive condition will fight a rival male, court a female, or build a nest if he has no nest. But he will do *none of these* unless his hormonal state puts him in reproductive condition.[3] The hormones must act at the level of *reproductive motive(s)* to activate the whole system, with all its components.

Before moving on, it is worth noting that such a motivational state is not observed directly. It is *inferred* from behavior. Or, better: It is a way of *talking about* the behavior. If we see that an actor may achieve the same end in a variety of ways, or that a number of specific movements are affected together by some condition, then *we say* that a motivational state exists.

A Look Backward: The Drive Concept

Now let us put these pieces together. A **drive,** we will say, is a hierarchically organized **motivational state,** evoked by some change or condition inside the animal. We need such a concept for two reasons: (1) Behavior can vary in an unchanging environment, and (2) any of a number of specific responses, including arbitrary learned ones, can be activated. That is why we distinguish motivational states from the specific behaviors that express them.

MOTIVATION, NEGATIVE FEEDBACK, AND HOMEOSTASIS

The concept of drive was attractive to scientists who sought to understand the physiological causes of action. It provides a direct link between motivated behavior and physiological regulatory processes. These relationships introduce two concepts that are fundamental to motivational thinking: homeostasis and negative feedback.

3. Tinbergen, 1951.

Homeostasis

The body has mechanisms for regulating a number of physiological variables within the narrow limits that the body requires. This regulation is called **homeostasis.**★ It is achieved both by physiological means and by behavioral means.

For example, if temperature rises too high, our bodies can drive it down again by perspiring: if it falls too low, our bodies drive it up again by shivering. But behavior extends our range of options. If temperature rises too high, we can move into the shade; if it falls too low, we can build a fire or put on a sweater. In other words, behavior can be a part of the homeostatic system that maintains temperature at or near an optimum value.

Other basic biological drives play a similar role. Because thirst leads us to find and drink water, our bodies receive water when they need it. Because hunger drives us to eat, our bodies' fuel is replenished as it begins to run low. Thus a relative constancy of body water and of available fuel is maintained by behavioral as well as physiological means.

Negative Feedback

Homeostatic regulation depends on **negative feedback,** another fundamental concept of motivation. A *negative-feedback loop* is any case in which the output of a system is fed back to reduce the input. An air conditioner controlled by a thermostat is such a system. The temperature in the room rises (input). That calls the air conditioner into play (output), and its action reduces room temperature. That is, it reduces the input; that is what makes it a negative-feedback system.

A separate loop could keep temperature from falling too low. If the temperature drops (input), the furnace is switched on (output), and the temperature rises again to take the input away (negative feedback). With these two back-to-back systems, one can *regulate* the temperature of the room as precisely as the sensitivity of the thermostat and the speed of action of the output mechanisms permit (Fig. 3-3).

Finally, in either case, the output of the system could be behavior rather than the action of a machine. If external temperature rises too high, we may move to a cooler place or turn on the air conditioner manually. If it drops too low, we put more clothes on, light a fire, or turn on the furnace.

The same sort of thing happens in the body. Take blood sugar level, for example. Sugar is supplied by the blood to the cells of the body, which burn it as fuel. If the cells are to work properly or even go on living, a steady supply of fuel must be maintained. The level of sugar in the blood must be regulated within quite narrow limits. And it is—an instance of homeostasis.

How does such regulation take place? Briefly, the body has a kind of sugar

---

★The term was coined by the physiologist Walter B. Cannon (1871–1945). It has come to mean either the optimal range of values necessary for life, or the processes by which they are kept within that range.

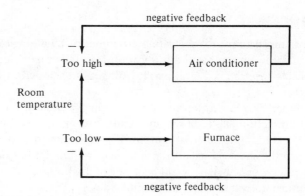

Figure 3-3 Control of room temperature by back-to-back negative-feedback loops.

bank, in which sugar is stored outside the bloodstream in the form of complex molecules known as *glycogen*. If the blood sugar level drops too low (input), there are reflex reactions that write a check on the account; glycogen is broken down into sugar molecules which are released into the blood (output), and blood sugar level rises again (negative feedback). Conversely, if blood sugar level rises too high (input), the body writes a deposit slip: Glucose molecules are withdrawn from the blood and stacked into glycogen molecules (output), and blood sugar level decreases (negative feedback). The result is regulation of blood sugar level within a narrow range, because these back-to-back feedback loops—these *homeostatic* mechanisms—prevent it from drifting either too high or too low.

Where then does behavior come in? It can be seen as another output of the homeostatic mechanism. If the body's stores of glycogen are used up, it can draw on its fat or even its protein to keep blood sugar level from dropping. But at some point, the body's fuel reserves must be replenished. How? By finding and eating food.

Thus at first glance, hunger and thirst look like elegantly simple *negative-feedback* systems. The body gets low on fuel (for example), and somehow senses this (input). This triggers behavioral systems that lead to the seeking and ingestion of food (output); and that removes the deficiency that started the process in the first place (negative feedback). Now one thing we will learn, before we are much older, is that this conception of hunger and feeding is far too simple to fit the facts—even the facts about laboratory rats. But it is a starting point, so we will begin by following it as far as it can take us. Then we will look at just a few of the factors we must consider besides.

THE LOCAL SIGN THEORIES

But how do these systems work? To present them as negative-feedback loops shows what they do; but how do they do it? In particular, what are the all-important *inputs* that call the systems into action? What tells an organism that it's time to eat or drink?

Cannon's Experiments

The most influential early experiments were the work of the physiologist Walter B. Cannon. He regarded hunger as a sensation arising from the gastrointestinal tract, the stomach in particular.

In his most famous experiment, Cannon had a human subject swallow a balloon that in turn was coupled to a pneumatic system (one worked by air pressure) that permitted Cannon to record muscle contractions in the subject's stomach. When the empty stomach showed a series of rhythmic contractions, that was when the subject reported feeling hungry. The discovery was verified and extended by many others, who also discovered that the stomach contractions (already known as "hunger contractions") could be caused in turn by a decrease in blood sugar level. Since sugar carried by the blood is the fuel used by the cells, a drop in blood sugar level would indicate the need for food. That need is made conscious, so the argument went, by way of stomach activity, which the person senses.★

Thus Cannon concluded that hunger was a sensation evoked by a stimulus, or "sign," coming from a particular location in the body; hence the term *local sign*. *Thirst* received a similar analysis. Cannon concluded that the sensation of thirst was elicited by the local stimulus, dryness of the mouth.

There was a subsidiary assumption in these theories—that the sensations of hunger and thirst are unpleasant. That accounts for the negative-feedback characteristics of these motives, and also for the fact that they can be expressed by multiple responses. When we experience these unpleasant sensations, we try to get rid of them (negative feedback), and we do it by whatever means is available (multiple outputs).

The Shift to Behavior

More recent investigations have made Cannon's theories unpopular. In the first place, his data were correlational. A person may feel hungry when his stomach contracts, but that doesn't mean he feels hungry *because* his stomach contracts. Moreover, it is clear that hunger does not *require* the experience of stomach contractions. Human patients, for example, have undergone cutting of the *vagus nerve,* the nerve that carries sensations from the stomach up to the brain, and have still reported feelings of hunger. Similarly, numbing the interior of the mouth, which ought to block sensations of dryness, does not prevent thirst from arising.

This does not mean that local signs play no role in hunger and thirst. It does mean that if they do, they are not the *only* sources of these motives; there must be others as well. Therefore, scientists began looking at how the *internal state of the body* influences feeding and drinking, and food- and water-getting behaviors. Often these experiments used animals as subjects. Animals can't tell

---

★For a detailed presentation of this theory see Carlson, 1916.

Animal studies

us whether they feel hunger or thirst sensations, but they can eat and drink, and we can ask how conditions inside the body affect their doing so. Let us turn to these investigations.

THIRST

Land-dwelling animals lose water continuously, humans along with the rest. The loss occurs through many channels. You and I are losing water all the time through the lungs as we exhale moisture, and through the skin as we perspire. Still more water is lost in urine and feces.

We lose water in all these ways, but we have only one way of replenishing it. We must drink. But how do we, and other animals, know when it is time to drink?

The Arousal of Thirst

As it became clear that the dry-mouth theory could not be the whole story of thirst, investigators began looking for the internal changes that trigger drinking.

To understand this work, we must consider that the water in our bodies can be divided into two parts, or compartments. Some of our body's water is inside the cells. That is the intracellular fluid. The rest of it is outside the cells—in the blood plasma and in the fluid that surrounds and bathes the cells (Fig. 3-4). This is the extracellular fluid. The thirst system, it turns out, is responsive to both fluid compartments.

INTRACELLULAR THIRST   A classic experiment was performed by Alfred Gilman in 1937, to show that *cellular dehydration* is a stimulus for thirst.[4] Gilman injected a solution of sodium chloride into the bloodstreams of his subjects (dogs). Sodium and chloride, so injected, do not penetrate the cells of the body; they stay outside the cells. If the solution injected has a higher concentration of dissolved particles than do the body fluids (as Gilman's solution did), then the fluid outside the cells, the **extracellular fluid,** will have a higher concentration than the fluid inside the cells, the **intracellular fluid.** To dilute the concentrated fluid outside, water rushes out of the cells (this action is known as **osmosis**). That expands the extracellular fluid but leaves the cells dehydrated and shrunken (Fig. 3-5). Gilman injected control solutions of urea at other times; these do not have this effect, because urea does move into the cells, so that the concentration of dissolved particles remains the same inside and outside the cells.

Thus, injections of concentrated sodium chloride solutions draw water out

4. Gilman, 1937.

A

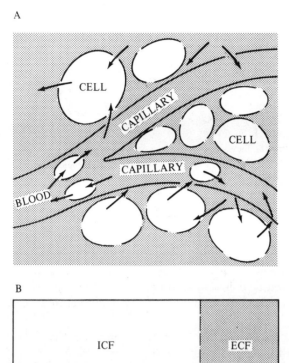

Figure 3-4 (A) Distribution of body fluids outside the cells (shaded areas) and inside the cells (unshaded areas). Arrows show movement of water into and out of the bloodstream and into and out of the cells. (B) For simplicity, we often speak of the body fluids as if they were divided into two compartments, one containing all the fluid inside all the cells (intracellular fluid, ICF) and the other containing all the fluid outside the cells (extracellular fluid, ECF).

B

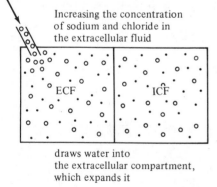

Increasing the concentration of sodium and chloride in the extracellular fluid

draws water into the extracellular compartment, which expands it

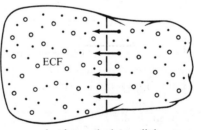

but leaves the intracellular compartment shrunken.

Figure 3-5 Gilman's experiment. Sodium and chloride particles in the body fluids are shown as open circles, water molecules as dots.

of the cells and leave them dehydrated. Injections of concentrated urea solutions do not do that. Sure enough, Gilman's sodium chloride injections caused copious drinking, but urea injections did not.

This demonstration in the dog has since been repeated in various species, humans included. The results are the same: Strong sodium chloride solutions lead to copious drinking and, in humans, reports of intense thirst. Moreover,

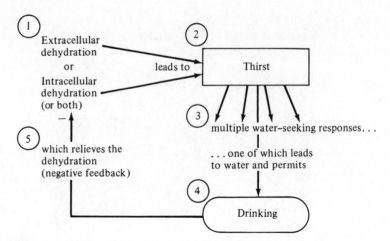

Figure 3-6 Thirst as a motivational state with multiple response outputs, and two inputs. It is a negative-feedback loop inasmuch as the result of its action—drinking—takes away the dehydration(s) that acted as input.

rats will run a maze, or press a lever, to obtain water after such injections. Therefore, cell dehydration arouses not just drinking per se, but a drive or motivational state with its multiple specific responses (see Fig. 3-6 above).

EXTRACELLULAR THIRST   It later became clear that cell dehydration, like a dry mouth, could be only one stimulus for thirst, not *the* stimulus. For example, extensive bleeding from wounds can provoke very severe thirst. Yet in these cases, the fluid is lost not from the cells but from the extracellular fluid. This is the fluid outside the cells, which includes the blood plasma and the fluid that surrounds the cells themselves. Might a decrease in extracellular fluid volume also be a stimulus for thirst?

Apparently it is. James Fitzsimons[5] in England and Edward Stricker[6] in America showed that a reduction in extracellular fluid volume could provoke drinking. This happened even though direct measurement of the body fluids showed that no cell dehydration was present. Reduction of extracellular fluid also evoked a motivational state, not just drinking; a rat would press a lever for water in response to such reduction.

These findings and later ones led to the *double-depletion hypothesis,* which is now generally accepted. There is not one state of the body that evokes thirst, but at least two. Reduction of fluid inside the cells is one; reduction of fluid outside the cells is another; and either of these can say to a rat or a human, "Time to drink." The two sources of thirst seem to have additive effects. If one reduces the fluid both inside and outside the cells, the drinking that results is about equal to the sum of the drinking that each alone would produce.

Not one thirst, but two. Let us pause for a minute and look at the system that is taking shape (Fig. 3-6). Remember that a motivational state has *multiple*

5. Fitzsimons, 1961.
6. Stricker, 1966.

outputs—the various responses it controls, like lapping, running, or bar-pressing. Now we see that it also may have *multiple inputs*. Shrinkage of the extracellular fluid can produce thirst; shrinkage of the intracellular fluid can also do so. Either one can act alone, or both can act together and sum their effects. This kind of multiple-input, multiple-output organization is characteristic of motivational states.

Satiation of Thirst

Now let us turn to another question. If either or both of these two inputs can turn thirst on, what turns it off?

VOLUNTARY DEHYDRATION   Matters would be simple if drinking continued until the body's fluid loss was made good. Satiation of thirst, in that case, would be just the absence of the conditions that initiate it. But this is not so. A water-deprived rat, when offered water, stops drinking well before its water deficit is made good. The extracellular compartment, in particular, may remain shrunken. This phenomenon is called *voluntary dehydration.*[7]

There is an excellent reason for it. When a rat drinks water, most of the water gets back to the body fluids eventually; but this takes time, and during that time the rat would load too much water into its stomach if it continued to drink. If the rat did not stop drinking until it was fully hydrated, then the water still remaining in its stomach would move on from there to *overhydrate* the body later. That could seriously disrupt the body's functions. Indeed, the state known as *water intoxication*—disruption of cellular functioning by drinking too much water—can actually cause death in rats or humans.★

The animal, then, must drink the right amount of water and then stop, even though its body is still dehydrated, especially the extracellular compartment. There are two solutions to that problem. First, the rat (or human) might *learn* to calibrate its intake, so that it drinks appropriate amounts and no more. There is evidence that this can in fact happen, but we will defer it till later (p. 99).

Second, the controlling system may have an *inhibitory* component. Some short-term consequence of drinking water might shut down, or *inhibit,* the seeking and drinking of water even though a fluid deficit remains. That also happens, and we turn to it now.

INHIBITION OF THIRST IN THE RAT   Consider what happens when a rat drinks. Water passes through the mouth; it is swallowed and enters the stomach; then it passes to the intestine, from which it is absorbed into the extracellular fluid; and finally, most of it (about two-thirds of the water ingested) passes into the cells. Somewhere in that chain of events must lie

7. Adolph, 1943.

★It is true that the kidney can get rid of excess water by producing urine, but that too takes time, and a serious excess could occur before it happened.

the inhibitory conditions that switch off thirst. A series of experiments by Elliott Blass and Warren Hall explored the possibilities one by one (see Fig. 3-7).[8]

What contribution do mouth factors alone make to satiety*? To determine this, the experimenters equipped their rats with gastric fistulas, permanently implanted tubes that drain the stomach contents to the outside. When these fistulas were closed, the rats were in effect drinking normally (Fig. 3-7A); but when the fistulas were open, water drained out of the stomach as fast as it entered it (Fig. 3-7B). The water drunk, therefore, passed through the mouth but did not fill the stomach or, of course, reach the body fluids. This is known as *sham drinking*.

When the rats drank normally (with fistulas closed), the amounts drunk varied with how severely deprived of water they were, as one might expect. When the rats sham-drank (with fistulas open), the amount passed through the mouth still varied directly with deprivation. These amounts were much higher throughout, however, than those drunk under normal conditions.

This tells us two things. (1) Just passing water through the mouth makes *some* contribution to satiety. Sham drinking stops eventually, even though the water hasn't gone anywhere in the body. And the amount sham-drunk varies with deprivation, as if a thirsty rat needs more of that oral stimulation to satiate thirst than a less thirsty rat does. (2) However, passing a normal amount of water through the mouth is *not* enough to satiate thirst. Sham intake was much higher than normal intake.

If mouth factors alone are insufficient, what if we add stomach filling? Now the rats were permitted to drink with fistulas closed, so that the stomach filled; but the passage from the stomach to the intestine was pinched off with an ingenious "noose" arrangement, so that the water did not pass into the intestine and from there to the cells. As Figure 3-7C shows, intake was still higher than normal. Also, under these conditions, the amount drunk did *not* vary with severity of deprivation. Perhaps stomach filling sets an upper limit on intake, so that the rat could drink only so much and no more. Clearly, though, a *normal* amount of stomach filling is not enough to satiate the rat.

Well, let us add still more. Suppose the water empties from the stomach and is absorbed from the intestine, but does not enter the cells? That too can be arranged. Suppose a rat drinks a salt solution rather than water. Then the water, the sodium, and the chloride will all be absorbed into the extracellular fluid. But sodium and chloride do not enter the cells; and since they are confined to the extracellular fluid compartment, osmotic action holds the water in which they are dissolved in that compartment. By using an appropriate salt concentration, one can produce expansion of the extracellular fluid with no effect on the intracellular fluid—neither expansion nor shrinkage.

8. Blass and Hall, 1976.
*Satiety simply means the state of being satiated, or not inclined to drink any more.

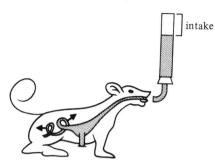

intake

A. Normal drinking with gastric fistula closed. Water enters the stomach and passes from there to the intestine (represented by loops), from which it is absorbed into the body fluids. A moderate amount of water is drunk.

B. Sham drinking. When the ingested water drains from the stomach through the open gastric fistula, the amount drunk is very much greater than normal.

C. Drinking without stomach emptying. The entrance to the intestine is clamped off, so that water is held in the stomach. Intake is lower than with sham drinking, but still higher than normal.

D. Drinking without cellular hydration. An appropriate salt solution, after it is absorbed from the intestine, expands the extracellular fluid (ECF) without supplying water to the cells. Intake is still higher than normal. It is only when water enters the cells, as happens in (A) above, that the rat's intake is limited to the normal amount.

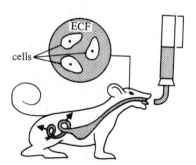

ECF

cells

Figure 3-7 Inhibition of thirst by the consequences of drinking.

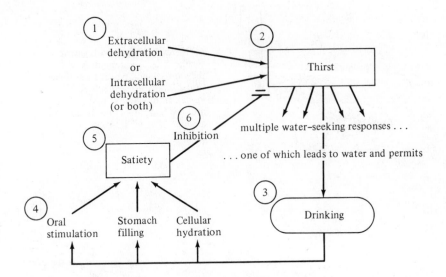

Figure 3-8 The role of satiety in thirst. Oral, gastric, and cellular consequences of drinking activate an inhibitory mechanism—satiety—that shuts off thirst and drinking *before* the body's dehydration is alleviated.

Drinking such a solution, then, sets up the conditions shown in Figure 3-7D. All the other consequences of normal water drinking take place, but the cells are not hydrated. The result? Intake remains abnormally high.*

In short, nothing that water does in the body reduces intake to normal levels *unless the water enters the cells and hydrates them.* It appears that cellular hydration provides an inhibitory stimulus for thirst, shutting off water intake even though the rat is not yet fully rehydrated by its drinking.

A Look Backward

Let us summarize what we have learned.

THE ORGANIZATION OF THIRST   Figure 3-8 shows the system as we have developed it thus far. It has already come quite a way from the simple negative-feedback loop we began with. In has its two inputs (and there may be more). It has its multiple outputs, so that the rat can take whatever means its environment makes available to get the water it seeks. The water it drinks activates a system that inhibits thirst, and the inhibitory sub-system too has multiple inputs—three at least, from the mouth, from the stomach, and from the cells.

PHYSIOLOGY AND BEHAVIOR REVISITED   Earlier, we noted that behavioral mechanisms combine with physiological ones to combat such threats to homeostasis as excess heat, excess cold—or dehydration. Now that we know

*Of course a salt solution also tastes different from plain water, but it has been shown that taste makes no contribution to this high intake (see Mook, 1963; Mook and Kozub, 1968).

more about thirst, let's look more closely at how it works hand in hand with physiological regulation.

We saw that shrinkage of intracellular fluid triggers thirst. It does so because certain detector, or as we say, *receptor,* cells in the brain detect the shrinkage and mobilize thirst. At the same time, other receptor cells detect the same change, but they do something different about it. They cause the brain to release a hormone into the blood, and the hormone tells the kidney, "Don't waste water in urine! Hang on to the water that remains in the body!" This the kidney does, by manufacturing a more concentrated urine with less water in it.

Similarly for *extracellular* fluid shrinkage. By a complex chain of events, this input causes an increase in the level of a chemical messenger, or *hormone,* in the blood. This hormone, called *angiotensin,* can act on the brain to mobilize thirst. But it also acts on the walls of the blood vessels, causing them to constrict; this reduces the volume of the whole system of vessels through which the blood must flow. And the effect of that is to oppose the drop in blood pressure that would otherwise occur: If a volume of fluid shrinks, but the container it has to fill shrinks too, then its pressure against the walls of the container can remain high.

In both these ways (and others), physiological and behavioral adjustments to dehydration are coordinated. The body responds physiologically by minimizing water loss or its effects, and also by behavioral means: finding water and drinking it. But we should note that of the two, it is the behavioral adjustment that ultimately is much the more important. The kidney can slow down the loss of water in the urine, but it cannot stop it altogether. The blood vessels can constrict just so much and no more. Sooner or later, the animal *must* replace the water it is losing, and it can do this only behaviorally—by finding and drinking water.

DIVERGENCE: MOBILIZATION OF MULTIPLE SYSTEMS   At several points, we have noted that multiple inputs can come together, or converge, to trigger a common output. Thus both intra- and extracellular dehydration converge to activate the thirst system.

There is also the converse possibility: A single input can *diverge* to affect multiple systems. Extracellular dehydration provides an example. Faced with that condition, a rat will seek and drink water, as we have seen. But it may be even more avid in seeking and drinking a salt solution—even a solution so concentrated that normally it would be avoided. The chain of events is complex, but the output is clear: another motivational state, "salt appetite," that seeks salt rather than water, is engaged (Fig. 3-9).[9]

This makes eminent homeostatic sense. As we saw earlier, salt in the water exerts osmotic action on the water it's dissolved in, holding that water outside the cells and thus *expanding the extracellular fluid.* So, if a shrinkage in that fluid compartment is the problem in the first place, water with salt in it will solve the problem much more quickly than will water alone. On the other hand, for the

9. DeCaro, Epstein, and Massi, 1986.

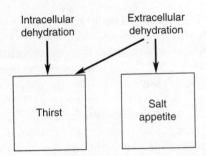

Figure 3-9 Intracellular dehydration evokes thirst only. Extracellular dehydration evokes two motivational states: thirst and salt appetite.

same reason, salt water will be less effective than plain water in repairing an *intracellular* shortage, as we saw in Figure 3-7. Sure enough, intracellular thirst is not accompanied by a "salt appetite," as the figure shows.

Thus, just as a motivational system can have multiple inputs, so inputs can have multiple effects. They can evoke more than one motivational state at the same time.

FEEDING: SIGNALS FOR STARTING

According to the homeostatic view, hunger is aroused, and food search and feeding begin, when some internal change signals the actual or impending depletion of fuel. What such signals might there be?

Decreased Glucose Availability

Cannon's gastric-pangs theory was coupled to the homeostatic control of food intake by the suggestion that a drop in blood sugar level was what started the whole process going. When blood sugar level drops, the stomach begins to contract, and that is what we feel as hunger. As Cannon's theory faded, the possibility gained ground that a low blood sugar level could stimulate hunger directly.

In this simple form, the idea runs into a major difficulty. The disease known as *diabetes* is characterized by insufficiency of insulin, a hormone that is required for the passage of glucose from the blood into the cells. As a result, diabetic people may have very high blood sugar levels. If the theory were correct, they should seldom get hungry. In fact, however, many of them report feeling hungry nearly all the time. Obesity is frequently a complication of diabetes.

There is a way out of the difficulty.[10] Perhaps what is important is not how much glucose is in the blood, but how much is available to the cells. If so, the diabetic's hunger would make sense; the sugar is in the blood all right, but it doesn't go from there into the cells. As a result the cells are literally starved for glucose, and hunger results.

10. Mayer, 1955.

If this is so, then preventing the cells from obtaining and using glucose should elicit hunger. One way of doing that is to inject a chemical known as 2-deoxy-D-glucose or 2-DG. This compound interferes with the uptake of glucose by the cells. That causes glucose to accumulate in the blood; but the cells are not receiving that fuel. The body is like a car with a full tank but a block in the fuel line. If the glucose-availability idea is correct, then this elevated blood sugar level should be accompanied by hunger and ravenous feeding. And that is exactly what happens, in rats and monkeys[11] and in humans.[12]

Problems for this *glucostatic theory* still remain, however. First, some investigators believe that whereas decreased glucose use by the cells may be *a* stimulus for hunger, it cannot be *the* stimulus. Selective damage to certain brain areas may produce rats that no longer respond by feeding to decreased glucose availability.[13] Yet such rats may eat voluntarily in a perfectly normal way, and maintain themselves in good health. If they eat, but no longer respond to 2-DG or related manipulations, then they must get hungry for other reasons than the unavailability of glucose to the cells. Other stimuli for hunger must exist.

Second, there is the question whether decreased glucose use is a stimulus that comes into play under normal conditions. Some think it is,[14] but others believe that the drop in glucose availability necessary to produce hunger is so extreme that it would occur in nature only as an emergency, not as a stimulus for normal hunger.[15]

Decreased Fatty-Acid Availability

Another possible signal for feeding has been identified. All cells, including brain cells, can burn the simple sugar *glucose* for fuel. Some cells (though not brain cells) can burn something else as well: free fatty acids, molecules that are building blocks for fats or lipids. And, just as we can block the cells' use of glucose with such drugs as 2-DG, so we can block fatty-acid usage by drugs such as 2-mercaptoacetate (abbreviated MA). Sue Ritter and her colleagues have found that treatment with MA can also induce feeding in laboratory rats.[16]

Moreover, the effect of MA seems to depend on a different mechanism from that of 2-DG. As we saw, damage to certain brain areas can abolish the effects of 2-DG; but these may leave the effects of MA unchanged. Conversely, we can interrupt the nerve pathways by which signals are sent to the brain from the abdominal organs, such as the stomach and liver (more on the liver in a minute). If we do that, we find the converse case: we can still elicit feeding with 2-DG, but now the feeding response to MA is abolished.

11. Smith and Epstein, 1969.
12. Thompson and Campbell, 1977.
13. Epstein and Teitelbaum, 1967; Blass and Kraly, 1974).
14. See LeMagnen, 1981.
15. See Geiselman and Novin, 1982; Smith 1982.
16. Ritter and Tayla, 1990.

MA, then, must block the use of free fatty acids by structures in the abdomen. These structures in turn complain to the brain about this state of affairs—"We have no fatty acids to burn! Find some food and eat it so that we will!"—so that the brain mobilizes food search and feeding. If the complaint cannot be heard (because the nerves are cut), then feeding does not occur—though it still occurs if we interfere with glucose use, to which the brain is directly sensitive.

One problem remains, however, and it is the same problem we saw earlier with the glucostatic theory. A severe reduction of fatty-acid availability would, in nature, represent a real physiological emergency. Does this mechanism operate in normal circumstances or in emergencies only? We are not sure.

A Look Backward

Let's again see what we have learned so far. Curiously enough, we can see already that there is more than one possible way of putting the facts together (Fig. 3-10).

It appears that decreased glucose use *or* decreased fatty-acid use can evoke feeding, by different pathways. We could still imagine these signals as con-

Figure 3-10 Two signals may contribute to a single hunger state (A), or each may contribute to a different hunger state with different goals (B), or both (C).

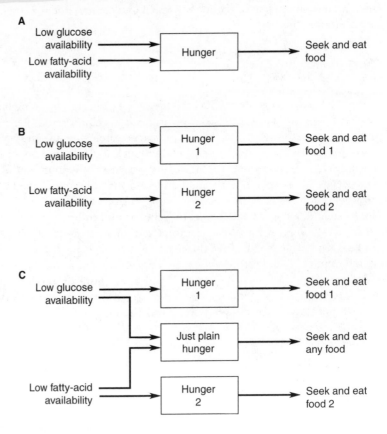

verging, perhaps adding their effects, to promote a single hunger state (Fig. 3-10A). Some writers adopt this view, arguing that feeding is responsive to the total amount of fuel available for burning (or to the rate of change in this quantity; for simplicity, the figure omits this possibility).[17] Such a view is supported by the finding that if both glucose and fatty-acid usage are blocked concurrently, food intake is greater than if either one alone is blocked.[18]

Alternatively, there could be more than one kind of hunger, so that the two signals remain separate and have different consequences for behavior. Maybe we should think of the animal not just as "hungry," but as "hungry for" this or that. There is evidence for this view as well. It has been found that food-seeking behaviors differ in response to the two inputs; that is, the rats select different foods in the two cases.[19] So we probably should distinguish among different hunger systems for the two cases.

Then again, both alternatives might be correct! Perhaps the two signals converge on a "general hunger" system that increases the rat's disposition to eat any food (hence the additive effects of the signals when both are activated and only one kind of food is available). In addition, each could activate its own "specific hunger" system that leads the rat to seek and ingest a particular kind of food if it is available.

But are there such "specific hungers"? How many hunger states are there? Let us turn to that question.

How Many Hungers Are There?

It is clear that even a rat may be "hungry for" a specific commodity. As one example, rats that are severely deficient in sodium are usually sluggish eaters of standard rat food; they reduce their intake of such food and lose weight. But they eat or drink vigorously when offered salt.[20] It is not that rats learn to do this, in order to feel better, for they do it even under sham-drinking conditions, where the salt they taste never does the body any good.[21] So there is a separate salt hunger, which can be high at a time when hunger for other commodities is low.

How many other such specific hungers might there be? We do know that at least in the rat, protein intake is regulated separately from the ingestion of other nutrients. One experimenter's rats lived in a "cafeteria," with separate sources of protein, carbohydrate, fat, vitamins, and minerals.[22] When the protein solution was diluted with water, the rats promptly increased their intake of the protein solution—but of nothing else—in compensation. And this was not just because they liked the dilute solution better; the increase occurred even if

17. Friedman, 1990; Friedman and Stricker, 1976.
18. Friedman and Tordoff, 1986.
19. Ritter, personal communication.
20. Richter, 1942–43.
21. Mook, 1969.
22. Rozin, 1968.

the solution was less preferred when diluted.★ Rather, protein and carbohydrate intake may be responsive to separate "hungers."

Finally, we recall the evidence that blocking glucose utilization on the one hand, and fatty-acid utilization on the other, leads the rat to seek different kinds of food. That sounds as if each such signal is activating a system that leads to the search for certain specific foodstuffs.

In short, rather than a hunger system per se, we may have separate systems controlling hunger for *this* and hunger for *that*. It makes eminent sense that both humans and rats should have evolved that way. We need not only energy, but fats, proteins, vitamins, and minerals; and we could easily eat enough of a particular food to satisfy one need while others persist. So we have developed a system in which hunger for *this* can be satiated, while hunger for *that* persists. Of course, this also means that the organism must have ways of identifying and responding to *this* rather than *that*—a problem that looks forward to the topic of stimulus factors in ingestion.

FEEDING: SIGNALS FOR STOPPING

Whereas we know only a little about the conditions that start feeding, we know much more about the conditions that stop it, producing satiation or satiety.

As with drinking, a whole chain of events happens when a rat or a person eats. By removing or retaining these selectively, we can see what contribution to satiety each one makes. The logic of these experiments is very similar to those we looked at in the case of thirst (pp. 66–70). The conclusion too is the same: We are dealing with yet another multiple-input system. Let's look briefly at some of these experiments.

Mouth factors. As with thirst, these may make some contribution to satiety, especially if a rat is not very hungry. But if it is, sham-feeding may persist literally for hours (Fig. 3-11A). Clearly, normal amounts of oral stimulation do not suffice to shut ingestion down.

The stomach. If the mouth alone does not account for satiety, what if we add the stomach? Researchers have permitted ingested food to reach the stomach, but prevented it from going further by a "clamp" that prevents the stomach from emptying into the intestine, and hence from being absorbed (very little absorption of foodstuffs takes place from the stomach itself).† When this

---

★One might say, "Well, if a rat takes a meal from a more dilute protein solution, he will get fewer calories for his efforts and get hungry again sooner. And so he will eat more." True; but if that were all, then the rat should increase his intake of all dietary components when the protein is diluted. Nothing of the sort happened; it was only protein intake that increased.

†The clamp consists of an inflatable cuff, similar to the one a physician wraps around your arm to measure blood pressure. The cuff is wrapped around the entrance to the intestine (while the rat is anesthetized, of course), and the tube that leads into it is led to the outside. Later during feeding tests, the cuff can be inflated to clamp off that entrance. This causes no signs of distress; and when testing is finished, things can be returned to normal simply by deflating the cuff.

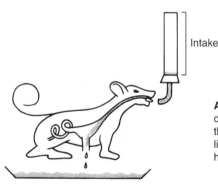

Intake

A. Sham feeding. If the liquid diet drains from the stomach as the rat feeds, then food intake, like water intake, is very much higher than normal.

B. Satiation of feeding by the stomach. If the food ingested enters the stomach, even though it goes no further, intake is limited to normal amounts.

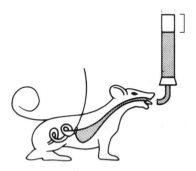

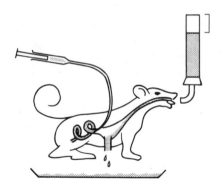

C. Satiation of feeding by the duodenum. When food is injected into the duodenum through flexible tubing while the rat sham drinks, the amount drunk is limited to normal amounts. Therefore, food in the stomach or in the duodenum can inhibit feeding after a meal of normal size has been ingested.

Figure 3-11   Inhibition of feeding by the consequences of eating a liquid diet.

was done, rats 3 hours without food (a period within the rat's normal meal interval) ate meals of normal size.[23] Therefore, filling of the stomach with food, even if the food does not move on from there, can produce satiety.

The intestine. Food in the stomach can produce satiety even if it never reaches the intestine. On the other hand, presentation of food to the duodenum, bypassing the stomach, can also produce satiety. (The duodenum is the portion of the small intestine that is nearest the stomach.) One team of experimenters infused liquid diet into the duodenum while the rats were sham-feeding a liquid diet through an open gastric fistula.[24] (That way, intestinal contents were prevented from mixing with the food the animal was eating.) The infusions depressed sham-feeding, to produce a meal of normal size. Moreover,

23. Kraly and Smith, 1978; Deutsch, Young, and Kalogeris, 1978.
24. Liebling, Eisner, Gibbs, and Smith, 1975.

the volumes required to do it were about the same as the volumes that were found in the intestines of rats that were satiated after feeding normaly.

The blood and the liver. The glucostatic theory implies that an increase in blood sugar, if the sugar enters and is used by the cells, ought to inhibit hunger. In fact, though, injection of glucose directly into the blood has surprisingly little effect on intake.

However, there is a part of the circulatory system that may be special. When nutrients leave the intestine for the bloodstream, they pass first into the *portal vein* that conveys them to the liver. When glucose was injected directly into the portal vein, it inhibited the rat's response to a liquid food. Injecting glucose into the jugular vein, bypassing the liver, had no such effect.[25] In other words, artificial elevation of blood sugar depressed feeding only if the elevation was in the blood going to the liver. Perhaps there are receptor cells in the liver that detect elevated glucose levels in the blood that bathes them, and respond by saying to the rat, "Eat less!"

CCK. There are other factors carried by the blood that can influence intake. These are not nutrients themselves, but they could signal the arrival of nutrients into the body. Of these, the one that has received the most attention is a hormone named *cholecystokinin,* mercifully abbreviated CCK.

When the intestine detects the arrival of food, CCK is released into the blood from the intestine. And it has been found that CCK by itself, when injected into the body and picked up in the bloodstream, can inhibit both normal feeding and sham-feeding.[26]

How does it do it? The CCK story is instructive, for it shows just how complicated these mechanisms (and the study of them) can be. There are at least three things CCK could be doing:

1. It could simply be making the animals sick, so that they feel less like eating. This is a problem for many studies of satiety. If we do something to a rat and it eats less, how do we know we haven't just made the rat feel a bit queasy? The possibility is usually checked by observing another behavior. Thus, if a treatment reduces food intake in hungry rats, but not water intake in thirsty rats, we assume that sickness is not responsible for the former effect. CCK passes this test. Some writers, however, are not convinced that this test is sensitive enough.[27] But CCK also depresses hunger in humans, who report little or no feelings of illness.*

    We now have very clear evidence, too, that CCK *can* depress intake without producing illness even in rats. We'll discuss that experiment later (pp. 100–101).

2. It could modulate the rate of some other inhibitory process. For example, CCK slows down the emptying of the stomach into the intestine.

25. Campbell and Davis, 1974; see also Friedman, 1990.
26. Smith and Gibbs, 1994.
27. See Deutsch, 1990.
*Pi-Sunyer et al., 1982. This is the study referred to in Chap. 1, p. 17.

Now if, as the rat eats, the stomach is filling at a normal rate but emptying more slowly, it follows that it will get full sooner; and that could lead to a smaller meal. Suggestive of some such possibility is that the suppressant effect of CCK can be reduced or abolished by cutting the *vagus nerve,* which carries messages from the abdominal organs to the brain. But this would not tell us why sham-feeding, in which the stomach does not fill, is suppressed by CCK.

3. It could be a signal in its own right to the controlling system. Assessing this possibility presents ferocious technical difficulties. The problem is that CCK does not readily pass from the blood to the brain; so how would the brain know how much CCK is in the blood? CCK is also manufactured in the brain itself (though no one is sure what it is doing there); and some researchers (but not others) find that feeding can be suppressed by injection of CCK directly into the brain. Possibly some other, peripheral event triggers release of CCK by the brain, and this in turn suppresses feeding.[28]

At present, that is where the mystery stands. CCK clearly promotes satiety, but where and how does it do it? We do not know.

A Look Backward

As we see, there are a large number of internal factors that can inhibit food intake, each by itself if need be. Again note the parallel with thirst: If what we call "hunger" is a multiple-input system, so is inhibition of feeding (Fig. 3-12). Which input is first to operate under normal conditions, or whether they all work together, we are not sure. Moreover, there is no particular reason to think that the same mechanism is most important under all conditions. Maybe the circumstances, or the kind of food one seeks and eats, determines which of the various signals is most influential.[29]

FEEDING IN HUMANS: INTERNAL CONTROL

The experimental analysis of human feeding has been guided by our developing understanding of animal mechanisms. Once specific questions are defined by animal research, one can often find a way to ask those questions of humans. Moreover, humans do have this advantage: They can tell you how their bodies feel. Rats cannot.

28. For further discussion see Smith and Gibbs, 1994.
29. Mook, 1990.

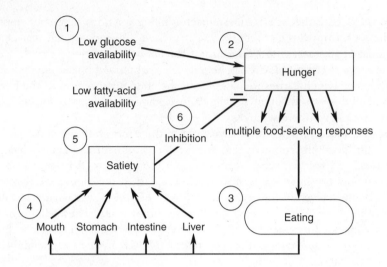

Figure 3–12 Hunger as a multiple-output, multiple-input negative-feedback loop. Like thirst, it has a satiety component that shuts off ingestion even before the inputs are removed.

Inhibition in Human Feeding

One experimenter, for instance, invited human volunteers to have breakfast with him in his laboratory over a number of sessions.[30] He fed them a standard liquid diet for breakfast, under controlled conditions where the distractions of the everyday could not interfere with their eating. Moreover, the better to examine biological controls over feeding, he took steps to minimize cognitive controls, such as the subjects' knowledge of how much they were eating. Subjects sipped the liquid diet through an opaque straw, from a hidden reservoir, so that they could not see how much they were taking in. And, in fact, they proved very poor at judging the amount they had eaten when asked to do so.

What does feeding look like under these conditions? It is rapid at first, then slows down gradually until it stops. If the subjects drink a large "preload" glass of liquid diet from a cup before the sipping session starts, then the meal is depressed—but usually not quite enough to compensate for the calories in the preload.

But why is feeding depressed at all? What inhibits it? Is it the volume of the preload in the stomach or the nutrients it contains that depress feeding? Here, you will be happy to know, is a distinct difference between humans and rats. Rats respond to the nutrients in a preload, but humans do not; they respond to its volume. When the preload is diluted with water, reducing the amount of nutrients it contains, this makes no difference to human subjects. A given preload volume causes about the same depression of feeding, whether it is very concentrated and supplies many calories, or very dilute and supplies few.

Let us look further. In humans as in rats, food passes from the mouth to the stomach to the intestine, and from there to the blood. Let us ask the ques-

30. Jordan, 1969, 1975.

tion we asked earlier of animals: Which of these events can play a role in controlling how much is eaten?

First of all, these subjects could not see the food they were eating, but of course they tasted it and felt themselves swallowing it. Can intake be controlled without oral cues at all? Yes, it can. In another experiment the subject swallowed a tube, which led directly from a pump into the stomach. By pressing a button whenever he wanted some food, the subject activated the pump which gave him a direct intragastric infusion. Result? The meals the subjects "ate" by such intragastric injections were of normal size. And again, it was the volume of the meal and not its nutrient density that was controlled. When the diet was diluted with water, intake was no greater than when it was full strength.

The important role of *volume* in human feeding makes us wonder whether simple mechanical distension of the stomach, thereby mimicking a full stomach, can alleviate or suppress human hunger. It can. In one study, human volunteers were given no nutrients, rather they swallowed balloons, connected through thin tubing to the outside world so that they could be inflated. When the balloons were inflated, and the stomach distended—sure enough, the subjects ate less.[31]

Well, then, what if the whole digestive tract is bypassed? The experimenters turned to a sample of hospitalized volunteers who were being fed intravenously, receiving a mixture of glucose and amino acids—the building blocks of proteins—directly into the bloodstream.[32] All these patients had lost considerable weight before intravenous feeding began, and they were receiving very substantial amounts of nourishment now. Yet most of the patients reported that they still felt hungry. Apparently carbohydrates and protein circulating in the blood fail to suppress human hunger, just as carbohydrates in the blood fail to suppress rat hunger.

However, an intriguing finding was obtained in four patients, for whom fats were added to the intravenous infusions. When this was done, hunger *was* suppressed. We noted earlier the evidence that there may be separate hungers for protein and carbohydrate. Is fat intake also regulated separately, by a system sensitive to fat constituents in the blood? Perhaps so.

Weight Regulation and Its Failures

So far we have focused on the short-term, meal-by-meal control of hunger and feeding. There is another regulatory system, however, that operates more slowly over much longer time periods.

Suppose you are an average woman, twenty years old. You can expect to gain about 11 kilograms—roughly 24 pounds—over the next forty years. That means that you are eating more than your energy needs require. How much more? If we do the arithmetic—so many calories in an average meal, so many calories expended in living and working, so many days—we find that you are

31. Geliebter, 1988.
32. Jordan et al., 1974.

eating more food than you need by an average of about 300 *milligrams* of food a day![33] (A milligram is very, very small.)

Obviously you don't adjust your meal-by-meal intake to your energy needs with anything like that kind of precision. Something must operate over a longer time, so that deficits or surfeits in intake are slowly and gently corrected to make long-term energy intake about equal to long-term energy expenditure.

That assumes that you are average. Not everyone is so fortunate. You surely know people who, despite continued efforts, weigh more than they should and more than they want. If obesity is severe, then its costs are also severe—to health, to social acceptance, and to one's acceptance of oneself.

Are obese people simply weak-willed or self-indulgent? Neither seems likely, for two reasons. First, many people avoid becoming obese without having to give the matter any thought. They don't need willpower or self-control. They avoid getting fat without even trying.

Second, the simple fact is that obese people do not overeat that much. Many studies, in both laboratory and natural settings, have found them not to overeat at all. They may even eat *less* than people of average weight, in attempts to lose the excess poundage. Because the body has multiple means of resisting weight loss, it may take surprisingly few calories to keep a fat person fat. As a result, even Spartan restriction of food intake may have effects on weight that are discouragingly small.

To see how all this could be, we must consider what a weight-regulating system might look like.

IS BODY FAT REGULATED?   Let us see how a long-term weight-regulating system might operate (Fig. 3-13A). We need a mechanism that keeps a kind of running total of the difference between energy intake and energy output. And we have tissue that keeps just such a running total. It is the *adipose tissue,* or fat stored in the body.

We mentioned earlier that as fuel in the blood gets low, glycogen is drawn on to keep the cells supplied with fuel. This "checking account," however, is quickly depleted. Then overdrafts are covered by the breakdown of fat, which in turn is converted to usable fuel. Thus, the fat stores are our long-term savings account. If output exceeds intake for any length of time, fat will be lost. Conversely, if intake exceeds output for any length of time, the excess fuel will be saved in the fat stores.

But how does this help us to regulate weight? In 1950, Gordon Kennedy suggested that it is not weight per se, but body fat, that is regulated.[34] There may be a *feedback loop* such that as fat accumulates in the body, appetite is depressed so that meals become smaller, fewer, or both; and excess fat is lost as a result (Fig. 3-13B).

In normal rats, this does happen. Rats can be made artificially fat by force-

33. Hervey, 1969.
34. Kennedy, 1950.

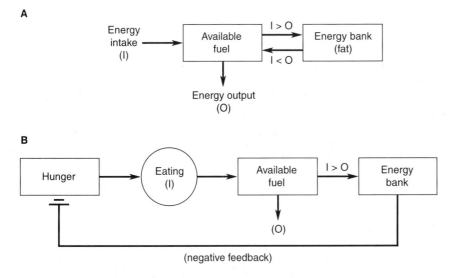

Figure 3-13 (A) The relations between energy intake, energy output, and energy storage as fat. (B) Accumulation of fat in the energy bank may provide a signal, not yet identified, that inhibits hunger (or augments satiety; not shown). If so, it is part of a negative-feedback loop by which amount of fat in the body is regulated.

feeding. Then, after force-feeding is stopped, the rat (a creature not noted for willpower, by the way) goes on a diet. It reduces its meal size and frequency until the excess weight is lost over the next few days or weeks.[35]

Such a rat does continue to eat meals, even while dieting. The short-term cycle of hunger and satiety continues to cycle along. Therefore, the effect of excess fatness must be to modulate these short-term controls, resetting them so that meals are slower to begin, quicker to end, or both, as Figure 3-13B shows.

Such a feedback loop would keep the body's fat stores from getting too high (barring force-feeding or other interferences with the system). Another feedback loop could keep them from getting too low; as fat is lost, meals may be biased in the direction of greater size and/or frequency. Over the long term, then, gains or losses in weight (i.e., fat) would be corrected and weight would be held nearly constant, just as a furnace and an air conditioner, controlled by a thermostat, would hold room temperature constant in summer and winter.

Obesity

Figure 3-13A makes an attractively simple picture, and it is one that dominated our thinking about weight control for a very long time. The major emphasis was on the intake variable *I*. If we eat more than our energy needs require, we will gain weight; if less, we will lose weight. Therefore, the overweight person is one who eats more than he needs to eat. Period.

ENERGY OUTPUT: MULTIPLE CONTROLS REVISITED   But it is just not that simple. We are coming to realize that the body can make choices as to what it does with excess calories. At one extreme, it can literally waste the

35. Cohn and Joseph, 1962; Hoebel and Teitelbaum, 1966: Mook, Talley, and Wagner, 1992.

excess calories: it can turn them into heat, which then dissipates into the environment.[36] At the other extreme, the body can hang grimly onto every calorie it receives, wasting none of them but storing them as fat under the skin in the adipose tissue.

What that means is this. Suppose John and Jim eat the same amount of food. But suppose that John's system wastes excess calories as heat, whereas Jim's system stores fat instead. Then Jim may gain weight whereas John may not—even if they eat the same amount and, just to make the point clear, even if they exercise the same amount as well!

Animal studies show that this can and does happen. There is a strain of rat that will spontaneously overeat and get fat. More interesting, though, is that such rats deposit excess fat even if their food intake is restricted to what a normal, lean rat would eat. Clearly, something is happening to promote the manufacture of fat in these rats, and it need have nothing to do with excessive intake of food. It probably has to do with hoarding, rather than wasting, the calories that food provides.

Finally, and what may be the worst news of all for would-be weight losers: it appears that the body's ability to hoard calories improves with practice. In one experiment, rats were allowed to get fat on a specially attractive diet.[37] Then their intake was restricted so that they lost the excess weight; then they were allowed to get fat again; then they were restricted again. The rats gained weight much faster the second time than the first and lost weight much more slowly on the second restriction than the first—even though, in both cases, food intake was the same on the first and second experiences. It seems that the body "learns" to hang onto calories, rather than waste them, with repeated dieting experiences. So it builds fat more rapidly, and gives it up more slowly, the second time around.

In any case, it appears that when one restricts one's food intake, the body resists loss of weight by every means available, just as it resists a drop in blood sugar in multiple ways. Metabolic rate goes down in dieters, so that less energy is wasted and so less fat is broken down. In addition, the chemical machinery that pulls fat constituents out of the blood, and makes them into stored fat molecules, goes into high gear—and it stays that way in persistent dieters. To lose weight, one must persist in the face of these multiple mechanisms by which the body resists one's attempts to do so.[38]

OBESITY OR OVEREATING: WHICH COMES FIRST? Excessive weight, then, may be very hard to take off and keep off once it is gained; and it may take surprisingly little food to maintain that excess weight. But why was it gained in the first place? At some point, energy intake had to exceed energy output to produce the excess weight or excess fat.

36. See van Itallie and Kissileff, 1990.
37. Brownell et al., 1986.
38. Garrow, 1978; Schwartz and Brunzell, 1981.

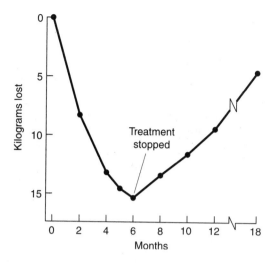

Figure 3-14   Patients receiving multiple treatments for obesity lost weight during treatment, but, on average, regained most of it within 12 months. (From Brownell, 1982.)

Even so, it is not clear whether the excess intake is cause or consequence of the excess fat. Metabolic abnormalities could lead directly to fat deposition, with overeating a result of this. How? Here is one way: they could drive fuels out of the blood and into the fat cells, which turn them into more fat. That would leave the other cells starved for fuel—the fat cells gobble up all the fuel before the other cells can get their share. A state of chronic hunger could result. If this is true, we just might have to turn our thinking right around. Such people may not get fat because they overeat. They may overeat because they are getting fat!

AN ELEVATED SET POINT?   Earlier, we compared a weight-regulating system to the thermostatic control of room temperature. Now, if the room temperature is too high, this could mean that the controlling system has broken down. Or it might be that the system is working just fine, but someone has set the thermostat too high!

Might the obese person be one whose fat thermostat, or body-weight "set point" is set too high? The idea has its critics,[39] but it has much to recommend it.

People who have lost weight have a distressing tendency to gain it back again, and to return to about the weights they were at before the loss occurred. This tendency is shown dramatically in Figure 3-14. Here the therapeutic book was thrown at a series of patients: behavior modification aimed at eating habits, an exercise program, and appetite suppressant drugs besides. The patients lost weight all right; but after treatment ended, their weights rose again until, on average, they were close to their starting points. This return toward the starting point suggests a negative-feedback system; and if the starting point is too high, then such a system may be "set" to keep it there.

39. See for example, van Itallie and Kissileff, 1990.

Further evidence for a body-weight set point comes from the converse case. If people find it hard to take weight off and keep it off, they also find it hard to put on weight and keep it on! Volunteer subjects have forced themselves to overeat, day after day. By doing so, they gain weight; but they gain less and less weight as time goes on, even though the high caloric intake is maintained. One reason is that in this case, energy output rises. More heat is generated, so that many of the excess calories are wasted rather than being stored as fat. The body resists gaining weight, just as fiercely as it resists losing it.[40]

A LOOK BACKWARD—AND A QUESTION   Why do some people become obese? There are many theories about that; and they could all be correct, for there is no reason to think that all these cases have the same cause.[41] Obesity could reflect a failure of a weight-regulating system, or a miss-setting of the system (an elevated set point), or, for that matter, it could reflect a swamping of the system by other factors.★

Thus some commentators have divided obesities into two kinds. In one, overeating comes first, in response to non-regulatory influences of the kind we'll consider later. For example, some obese patients may be overly responsive to good-tasting foods (pp. 87–89); others may eat in response to arousal or stress (pp. 87–89). In the other, the tendency to obesity may actually precede the overeating, as we have just seen. If such a person overeats at all, it may be because the greedy fat cells keep the rest of the body starved for fuel.

Now, none of this means that obese people are doomed to obesity forever. People take off weight and keep it off—perhaps more people than we think, because the ones who do it by themselves may not come to clinicians' attention.[42] It may mean, however, that for some people the struggle against obesity will be a lifelong battle—whereas others stay lean without even trying. And increasingly, researchers are beginning to wonder whether the battle is worth fighting.

Consider: Is there any such thing as an ideal height? People who are extremely tall, or extremely short, do have practical problems. But short of those extremes, we might speak of an *average* height, but not of an *ideal* height.

Well, we all have seen the charts that tell us what we ought to weigh for our height. When these are not pure guesswork, they represent averages—that is, what is statistically most usual. But if it makes no sense to speak of an ideal height, does it make any more sense to speak of an ideal weight per unit of height?

40. Keesey, 1980.
41. van Itallie and Kissileff, 1990.
★Perhaps this is the place to note that there is strong evidence for a hereditary factor in the tendency to obesity (for example, Stunkard et al., 1987). This leaves open the question of what it is that is inherited: metabolic characteristics, susceptibility to stimulus factors (pp. 223–25), or perhaps even certain personality characteristics.
42. Schachter, 1982.

The idea of a body-weight set point is helpful here. If each of us has a natural weight that the body "tries" to maintain, then that weight will vary among individuals as any other biological measure does. It might be better to accept that fact than to try for an abstract ideal. This is especially true inasmuch as our society encourages an unrealistic ideal of leanness, especially for women. Pictures of fashion models smile from magazine pages to show us that leanness is beautiful, and leanness is possible. We may forget that "pressure on aspiring models to maintain a skeletal physique is legendary; fashion models are notorious for the nutritional abuse to which they subject their bodies"[43]—and they are highly paid for submitting to this abuse! You and I are not.

The cure for overweight, in our culture, is the endless misery of guilt or dieting—or both—and since we are misled about what we "should" weigh by that same culture, the misery is widespread, especially among women. In 1984 a survey by *Glamour* magazine found that a full *75 percent* of the respondents between ages 18 and 35 thought they were fat, though only 25 percent were overweight by objective standards.[44] Is the cure worse than the disease? How often is there a disease at all?

It is true that extreme overweight carries risks to health. However, it is not clear that *mildly* overweight people are sick any more often or die any sooner than people of average build. Two things are clear, however. First, the "yo-yo" cycle of dieting and weight loss, discouragement and weight gain, dieting and weight loss again, . . . does put a severe stress on the body. Second, severe weight loss is dangerous, accompanied by low blood pressure and fainting, elevated serum cholesterol and gallstones, diarrhea, aching muscles, weakness and fatigue, heart-rate disturbances, anemia, and even death. In particular, fad diets, some nationally advertised and "recommended by doctors," are *extremely dangerous,* and they can and do cause deaths.

One wonders: What if the determination and willpower that are now directed toward saying "no" to food were directed instead toward saying "no" to this society's foolish insistence that lean is good, and leaner is better, and that any one body shape is "best"?

EXTERNAL FACTORS IN INGESTIVE BEHAVIOR

Thus far, we have considered the role of influences from *inside* the body on hunger and thirst. However, these motives are powerfully affected by *external* factors as well.

Think about the last beverage you drank. A cup of coffee, maybe, or a Coke, or a mug of beer. Were you really thirsty? Or was it that you wanted the *taste* of what you drank? How much of our eating and drinking is really *pulled* to the commodity by its sensory properties, rather than *pushed* by a state of need or drive? Quite a bit.

I don't usually get hungry until someone puts a menu in front of me.

—A COLLEAGUE

43. Polivy and Heiman, 1983, p. 101.
44. Brumberg, 1988.

Taste-Evoked Drinking

Consider a rat sitting placidly in his cage, with food and water freely available. We clip a bottle of sweet fluid to the cage—it may be sugar, which is nutritive, or saccharin, which is not—and the rat will rush to the bottle and drink phenomenal amounts, as much as two or three times his total blood volume.[45]

These rats are *not* hungry or thirsty in the physiological sense. They have access to food and water all the time. Yet at a time when feeding and drinking would otherwise be minimal, the presence of a sweet solution evokes a huge bout of ingestion that *would not occur if the tasty solution were not there*. The effect occurs with a variety of sweet solutions.

Now a special treat of this kind does not trigger just lapping behavior. It evokes a *motivational state*. We know that because the behavior itself is not fixed. Non-deprived rats will run down a runway to get a few drops of sweetened water.[46] Or they will work vigorously at lever-pressing for a few laps of glucose solution. In short, the rat will take *whatever action is available* to obtain the sweet fluid. And that gives us our familiar multiple-output system, or motivational state, expressed by any of several responses—running, bar-pressing, or lapping.

Clearly, *not all motivational states are evoked by drives*. The word *drive* connotes a physiological condition, a push from within. But here, we have a clear case of a motivational state *evoked by a stimulus from outside the body*—not a push from within, but a pull from without.*

Dietary Obesity

The prevalence of obesity in modern societies may very well depend in part on the availability of rich, high-calorie, *tasty* foods. Of course there are many factors that promote and maintain obesity in humans, and it is hard to prove that what foods are available is really an important influence. So, once again, we turn to the rat, where at least we can see what effects the properties of food *can* have, in the absence of all these complications.

Normal rats, fed normal rat food, regulate their weights very well, gaining weight through their adult lives only very slowly. But offer them special treats, and a perfectly normal rat will overeat and get fat. High-fat diets are especially good stimuli for this dietary obesity, but a sweet, high-carbohydrate eggnog will also do. We could look at this result as a kind of long-term analogue of the taste-evoked drinking phenomenon. As the sweet taste triggers a single meal that would not occur without it, so a special diet can trigger a persisting elevation in daily caloric intake that would not occur without it.[47]

45. See Ernits and Corbit, 1973.
46. Young and Shuford, 1954.
*Some writers refer to such a pull from without as *incentive motivation,* to distinguish these cases from *drives.*
47. Corbit and Stellar, 1964.

An especially worrisome case of this phenomenon has been reported in rats.[48] The animals were maintained cafeteria style on a variety of common, commercially available supermarket foods: chocolate chip cookies, cheese, bananas, salami, milk chocolate, peanut butter. . . . These rats gained nearly three times as much weight in 2 months as their rat-food-fed controls!

Inasmuch as these are not rat foods but people foods, no farther away than the grocery store, one must wonder what pressure their ready availability exerts on the weight-regulating systems of human beings in this society. Going further, one might wonder whether overweight people are especially responsive to the good taste of food. Some writers, notably Stanley Schachter, have suggested this.[49] The evidence is mixed; but there does seem to be a tendency for overweight people to be more responsive to good tastes than the non-overweight.[50] Of course, whether they are overweight *because* they are more responsive is a different question (pp. 84–85); but it may be that *some* cases of excess weight result from this. And the prevalence of obesity in some modern societies may depend in part on the availability of rich, calorific, and *tasty* foods.

The Effect of Variety

The supermarket diet that made rats fat offered not just one special treat, but a *variety* of special treats. That may be important in its own right.

To see this, consider the converse case. Few things are worse than having to eat the same food meal after meal, day after day—however nourishing and tasty it may be. We come to feel that we never want to *look* at another X—where X is whatever we have eaten again and again. This can have important clinical implications, too. It is not hard to get hospitalized obese patients to lose weight on a bland liquid diet offered as their only food. The problem is that patients refuse to stick with such a regimen, simply because it is killingly monotonous.[51]

The powerful influence of variety has been demonstrated by direct experiment in both rats and humans. In one study, hungry rats were offered either a series of four different foods, each for 30 minutes; or a single one of the foods for the full 2 hours. They ate about 30 percent more when the varied menu was offered, even though the foods were about the same in caloric density. Humans (nursing students) also ate more when offered a variety of sandwiches than when offered only one.

Later explorations showed the effects of more restricted variations in the sensory properties of foods. Even varying the *shape* of the food had some effect: Subjects ate more cooked pasta if it was offered sometimes as spaghetti, some-

48. Sclafani and Springer, 1976.
49. Schachter, 1971.
50. Drewnowski, 1990; Pliner, Herman, and Polivy, 1990.
51. Hashim and van Itallie, 1965.

times shaped as half hoops, and sometimes shaped as bow ties. The three of course were nutritionally identical.[52]

In short, simply changing the stimulus properties of the food can keep ingestion going longer. This effect may have evolved for good reason. It may be one of the ways in which an animal, satiated for one kind of food, can still eat another kind and thus get the various nutrients it needs (pp. 75–76). But, like the effect of a good taste, it could work against the precise regulation of ingestion. Both good taste and variety can encourage intake in excess of need, during a single meal, or day after day.

A Look Backward

We have seen some of the ways in which ingestion can be initiated and maintained from the outside, not the inside. Tasty foods can trigger ingestion even without input from internal need states. Conversely, simple exposure, producing boredom or perhaps *habituation* (pp. 239–41), can reduce the effectiveness of stimuli. The variety effect may reflect such a process—a process which, once again, is quite independent of the state of the body.

In all this, we notice that we are moving away from the image of feeding behavior as the output of a homeostatic, negative-feedback regulatory system, responding to the need for fuel and acting to eliminate that need. Feeding may be initiated, or maintained, in the absence of any such need. So, while feeding may occur as the output of such a system, it can occur for other reasons as well.

In later sections, this shift in emphasis will continue.

INTERACTION OF INTERNAL AND EXTERNAL INFLUENCES

To this point, we have divided factors affecting hunger and thirst into external and internal ones, in an either/or way. But they are not just two independent influences; they affect each other. In this section, we look first at some of the influences of the stimulus on the internal mechanisms that in turn affect what we do. Then we will consider the converse case: Internal states of the body can affect how we respond to stimuli from outside.

Stimulus Effects on Internal State: Can Food Make the Body Hungry?

External stimuli can evoke motivated behavior directly, as we have seen. However, they can also affect it indirectly by modifying the state of the body, which then in turn calls motivational systems into play.

In both animals and humans, the sweet taste alone can trigger the release of insulin into the blood. Insulin drives blood sugar level down, so that it is

52. Rolls, Rowe, and Rolls, 1982.

unavailable to the cells; and a drop in available sugar, we recall, can in turn promote eating and food-seeking.

In humans, just the sight and smell of a crackling, charcoal-broiled steak are sufficient to elicit insulin release.[53] Whether these effects are sufficient to influence feeding behavior in their own right is not clear, but some writers are beginning to wonder seriously whether food may actually increase hunger in just such ways.[54] Perhaps that is why it is easier to avoid the cake altogether than to have "just a bit."

Internal Modulation of Responses to Stimuli

Input from the environment, then, can modify the body's internal states in ways that in turn affect what the person or animal does. Conversely, internal factors can affect how one responds to stimuli coming in from the outside world.

THE RANGE OF EFFECTIVE STIMULI   First of all, internal states modify the range of stimuli to which the organism is responsive. If we get thirsty enough—say, after a few days in a lifeboat under a broiling sun in the Pacific— we will be willing to drink almost anything, even urine, or the sea water that actually dehydrates us further and will kill us all the sooner if no help arrives. Similarly for food. When hunger is severe enough, people have eaten grass, or shoe leather, or each other! In short, as the body's state of need becomes more and more severe, there is an increase in the range of stimulus objects that are treated as edible or drinkable.

The same thing can be seen under less drastic laboratory conditions. Rats, we saw earlier, will drink sweet solutions even if they are not hungry. But as we lower the concentration of sweetener, we soon reach a point at which the sweetness is too weak to support drinking in the nondeprived rat. Make the rat hungry, though, and it will drink the same weak solution with avidity.[55]

This is what we would expect if states of hunger and thirst enhance, or, as we say, *potentiate,* the responses to relevant stimuli. The more potentiation from inside, the less effective the external stimulus has to be to trigger ingestion.

THE IDENTIFICATION OF COMMODITIES   Internal states modulate not only *how many,* but also *which,* external stimuli will trigger ingestion. A thirsty rat responds to water, by drinking it. A hungry but non-thirsty rat does not do that; but it does respond to food, by eating it. The rat must identify these commodities, and it identifies them by their stimulus properties.

53. Rodin, 1981.
54. For review see Geiselman and Novin, 1982.
55. Mook and Cseh, 1981; Teitelbaum and Epstein, 1962.

A rat deprived of food, but not of water, will drink very little water. But put a bit of sugar or saccharin in the water, and the rat will drink with gusto; and the hungrier it is, the more saccharin-water it will drink. The sweet taste labels the commodity as food. It is as if the stimulus properties of the water say to the rat: "I am water. If you're thirsty, drink me," whereas the sweet taste says: "If you're hungry, drink me; I'm a source of nourishment." (In the case of the non-nourishing saccharin, that is a lie, but that is not the rat's fault.)

Think again about our military analogy. It is as if the thirst general says to the lapping officer, "Be ready to lap if you encounter *these* stimuli"—ones that identify water. The hunger general says, "Be ready to lap if you encounter *those* stimuli"—a sweet taste, for example, which identifies the fluid as having calories (Fig. 3-15). The salt-hunger general says, "Be ready to lap if you encounter *the other* stimuli"—those that identify salt.

If we think about it, we realize that the internal states must guide behavior in just such a way: by modifying the animal's response to external cues. Feeding takes place in the environment. A hungry animal must locate food, and identify it as food by its stimulus properties (taste, smell, texture, etc.), and then ingest the commodity if it has the right set of such properties.

Indeed, in a number of the studies we have summarized, these internal effects on responsiveness have been shown directly. Recall that not only feeding, but also sham-feeding, is depressed by such treatments as CCK injection, injection of glucose into the blood, or placement of food in the intestine (pp. 76–79).

Now in sham-feeding experiments, the food that is eaten does not go anywhere; it leaves the body before it can be digested and absorbed. Physiologically, the animal is as hungry at the end of a sham-feeding bout as it was at the beginning. How much it sham-feeds, therefore, is a measure of how responsive it is to the *external* cues—taste, smell, texture, etc.—that the food provides. Hungry rat, high responsiveness, and sham-feeding is vigorous and persistent. Non-hungry rat, low responsiveness, and sham-feeding may end quickly.

So, in Figure 3-15, we have included this complication. The effect of hunger is not to drive the lapping response directly, but to make it responsive to the stimuli that indicate food.

A LOOK BACKWARD AND A NEW COMPLICATION: LATTICE HIERARCHIES   Notice something else about Figure 3-15. A hungry rat, in some of the experiments we've described, was offered a liquid diet such as eggnog or a glucose solution. Offered such a liquid food, a hungry rat will lap, much as it would lap water if it were thirsty.

Therefore, the lapping response can act as a component of a hunger system *or* a thirst system. So can chewing. A thirsty rat is reluctant to chew dry food. But it will chew wet lettuce and obtain water that way. Just as it can eat by lapping, so it can drink by chewing.

Think again of a chain of command, and imagine an officer with specialized skills that can be made available to whichever superior officer requires them.

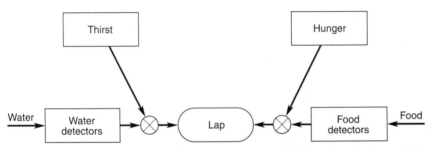

Figure 3-15   Hunger and thirst call the lapping response into play, not directly, but by making it responsive to the appropriate stimuli—water in the one case or liquid food in the other. The symbol ⊗ represents a point where converging inputs are combined.

Suppose it is the officer in charge of lapping—Lieutenant Lap. General Thirst can give orders to Lieutenant Lap when she needs his skills. So can General Hunger, when *he* needs Lieutenant Lap's skills.

   A hierarchical organization like this, in which lower components can be called into play by different higher-level systems at different times, is called a *lattice hierarchy*. Figure 3-16 shows why: the lines of influence from motives to action cross each other to form a lattice. Such organization provides for a great deal of the flexibility of behavior. It makes specific actions (like lapping) into general-purpose tools, which can be put to different uses at different times.

   We could say the same sort of thing about the arbitrary learned acts we require of an animal. A thirsty rat will press a lever if (1) there is a lever present, and (2) lever-pressing has led to water in the past. Similarly for a hungry rat, if lever-pressing has led to food. Thus lever-pressing (or maze-running, or approach) can be called into service by different motives at different times. We will have much more to say about this idea in the following pages.

Figure 3-16   Hunger and thirst, and the responses that express them, form a lattice hierarchy. Both are hierarchically organized, and they converge to control responses in common. Either system can call the lapping response into play—or the bar-press response or the running response if appropriate training has been given.

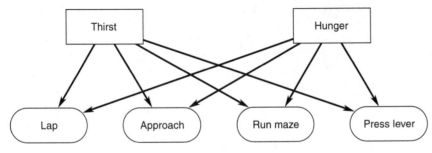

They surfeited with honey, and began
To loathe the taste of sweetness, whereof a little
More than a little
Is by much too much.
— SHAKESPEARE, *Henry IV,*
PART I: ACT III, SCENE 2

THE PLEASANTNESS OF STIMULI: ALLIESTHESIA Internal states, then, direct behavior by modulating responsiveness to external signals. But how do they do that? One influential idea goes as follows.

Michel Cabanac, in 1971, reported that the nutritional status of the body affected the *pleasantness* of sweet solutions. When first allowed to taste a series of sugar solutions, human subjects rated them more pleasant as the sugar concentration increased. The sweeter the solution, the better it tasted. But after the subjects had swallowed appreciable amounts of solution, the ratings were reversed: The sweeter the solution, the worse it tasted.

This effect, which Cabanac called **alliesthesia**[56] (literally, "changed sensation"), was not just an effect of too much taste input. If the subjects simply rinsed their mouths with the solutions and spat them out again, there was no such effect. It required that the solutions enter the stomach. It is therefore an internal effect on the pleasantness of taste inputs.

Cabanac and others have suggested that *satiety* may be mediated by such a change in the pleasantness of food. Perhaps, as the stomach (or duodenum, or portal vein, or whatever) is stimulated by food, that internal stimulation is reported back to the brain to make the food taste less good. It turns out too that alliesthesia, like intake itself, is responsive to variety (pp. 89–90). As a person continues to eat one food, its rating of pleasantness drops, but the pleasantness of other foods, not yet eaten, may change less or not at all.[57]

Later, Cabanac and his colleagues extended their work to the long-term regulation of body weight.[58] In some parts of Africa, there still survives an ancient custom: Young women deliberately overeat and make themselves fat prior to their weddings. Taking advantage of this natural experiment, the investigators asked the women to rate the pleasantness of sugar solutions, before and after the voluntary weight gain. Sure enough: After gaining weight, the women rated the solutions less pleasant. Perhaps excess fat, like a stomach full of glucose, makes a sweet taste no longer a good taste.

The idea is attractive, but the experimental evidence is mixed. Some people have had trouble replicating Cabanac's findings. Moreover, it is not clear that satiety is *necessarily* accompanied by diminished pleasantness of the food. Surely we can sometimes say, "It's delicious, but I really don't want any more," and mean it. Nor is it clear, if we think about it, that the good taste of food has much to do with keeping eating going in the usual course of events. C. S. Lewis reminds us: ". . . anyone who has watched gluttons shovelling down the most exquisite foods as if they did not know what they were eating, will admit that we can ignore even pleasure."[59]

On the other hand, there is another and quite different line of evidence that the sort of thing Cabanac described can occur. Experimenters have video-

56. Cabanac, 1971.
57. For example, Rolls, 1990.
58. Fantino, Baigts, Cabanac, and Apfelbaum, 1983.
59. Lewis, 1962, p. 93.

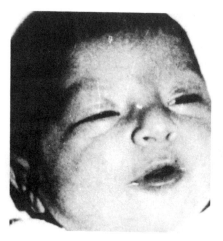 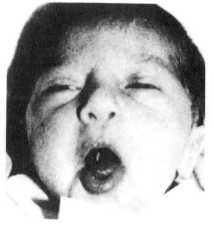

Figure 3-17   Facial expressions in a newborn, when a sugar solution (left) or a bitter quinine solution (right) is applied to the tongue. Note protrusion of the tongue in response to sugar and the wide gaping in response to quinine, with turning of the head and clenching of the eyes. (From Steiner, 1977.)

taped rats, close up, when the rats were drinking various solutions.[60] They find that rats make faces—and quite different faces depending on what they are offered to drink. Sweet solutions are accepted with protrusion and lateral movements of the tongue, as if seeking further contact. Bitter solutions, or intensely salty ones—the kind we rate "unpleasant"—are reacted to instead with a peculiar kind of yawn or gape. Human infants make faces similar to the ones rats make; and, like rats, they greet nice and nasty tastes with very different expressions (Fig. 3-17).

How does alliesthesia come in? It develops that the characteristic facial response to sweet solutions can be altered by manipulating internal state. If a rat's stomach has just been loaded with a large amount of glucose solution, then the taste of that solution evokes the facial expressions usually made to unpleasant tastes. It is as if glucose in the body changes the taste of sugar water from nice to nasty.

Of course this evidence is indirect. We do not really know what a rat finds nice or nasty (more on that in a minute). However, we can say this much: (1) Rats react in different ways to acceptable and unacceptable tastes, and (2) a fully fed rat treats a sweet taste as if it were unacceptable. Whether this mechanism plays an important role in normal satiety for a normally eaten meal, we are not yet sure.

A LOOK BACKWARD: INTERNAL AND EXTERNAL CONTROLS   We have seen how stimuli can evoke motivated behavior, how they can affect the body's internal state, and how that internal state can affect responses to them. Can we bring these ideas together, and link them to our discussion of internal factors, negative feedback, and homeostasis? We can try. But note well that the following attempt is *highly speculative;* it is not established truth by any means.

60. Grill and Norgren, 1978.

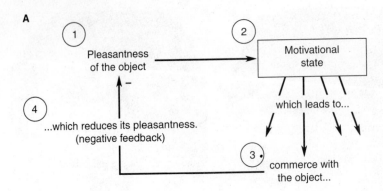

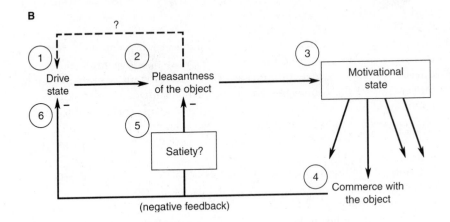

Figure 3-18   How pleasantness might affect motivated behavior. In A, the object—tasty food or a sugar solution—is pleasant in its own right, and evokes a motivational state directed toward obtaining commerce with it. In B, the system is the same, except that an internal drive state produces the pleasantness. Alleviation of that state, or its inhibition or satiety, reduces pleasantness, and the system shuts down.

In Figure 3-18, we see two kinds of systems that lead to *commerce with the object*—which simply means finding food and eating it, finding water and drinking it, or the like. In Figure 3-18A, the pleasantness of the stimulus leads the organism to seek such commerce, as in taste-evoked ingestion and perhaps dietary obesity. That commerce, or its consequences inside the body, reduces the pleasantness of the stimulus (alliesthesia), and the system shuts down.

In Figure 3-18B, the process begins not with the pleasantness of the object itself, but with a drive state that *makes* it pleasant. Such a state might extend the range of acceptable objects, or it might enhance responsiveness to all of them.★ If the state is one of need, such as dehydration or a low level of nutrients in the blood, then commerce with the object would reduce the need and restore homeostasis, and again the system would shut down. Or the effects of that commerce could reduce the pleasantness of the object (alliesthesia again),

---

★Or of course these two possibilities might amount to the same thing. If the responsiveness to *all* potential edibles were enhanced, then, all else equal, the number of them that meet our standards of good enough to eat would necessarily increase.

even *before* homeostasis was restored. The inhibitory mechanisms of satiety might work that way.

Even a system like B, however, could be activated by stimuli. For example, perhaps some foods can make our bodies "need" more food (p. 90). This is shown by the dashed line with question mark in the figure.

Notice that both these speculative systems are negative-feedback loops. But *only B is a homeostatic system*—and then only if the dashed line is not in the picture. System A is not triggered by the body's needs. Therefore, it could lead a person or animal to drink more delicious fluid than the body requires. Or it could lead the person or animal to overeat and (if this happens often) get fat. For that matter, there is no reason why individuals might not differ from one another as to which kind of system is operative.

Now all this speculation does tie some threads together, and it makes a good story. But it *is* speculative; and some of the links in the chain of evidence—for example, the alliesthesia experiments in humans—are weaker than we would like.

Then too, in giving *pleasantness* and *unpleasantness* a central role in our overview, we are taking on a difficult problem of method—a problem so difficult that it is worth our stepping back to look at it specifically.

A Note of Caution: The Problem of Self-Report

At several points in this chapter I have made use of data that purport to show us how subjects *feel* about stimuli. How pleasant is this taste? Are you hungry? Do you feel nauseous? And so on.

These are descriptions by the subject of his or her own consciousness. They are precisely the kind of data that John B. Watson would have thrown out of court (see Chap. 2). And yet they are the kind of data that only a human can provide, and they offer information we would like to have. The question is how to interpret them.

Consider: If a rat tastes a solution and makes a wide-mouthed gape, that is an objective *fact* for all to see. But when we call it a "nasty face," we are already going beyond the data. Nice faces and nasty faces may just be external indicators of an intention to accept or reject; we do not know what, if anything, the rat feels. Humans, we say, can tell us. But then, we don't really know what a fellow human feels, either—even if she tells us. If a person *says*, "This tastes pleasant," that too is a fact. But what does it mean? Do you and I mean the same thing by "pleasant," or even "sweet"? Is your red the same as my red?

The question is: Do we move on from the facts to make inferences about our subjects' *feelings* of pleasure or displeasure, hunger or satiety? A mediationist may be willing to do so. A behaviorist will remind us, with some justice, that we really don't know what we're talking about when we do.

To see the problem clearly, consider that our objective measures may go in one direction, subjective reports in another. Quite a few investigators have asked human subjects to rate how hungry they were, before eating a meal—and have found no correlation at all between how hungry the subjects said they were, and how much they ate.[61]

Now there are reasons why that might be so. Perhaps as eating progresses, satiety develops at a rate that is independent of how hungry we are when the meal begins. But there are other possibilities too:

1. We might not really *know* how hungry we are. Surely we have all said at some time, "Gosh, look how much I ate. I must have been hungrier than I thought."
2. Maybe our *feelings* of hunger arise from some internal signals that really have nothing to do with the signals that control the starting and stopping of feeding behavior.
3. Maybe "hunger" means different things to different people. Are my hunger sensations the same as yours?

This example brings the problem into focus, because objective and subjective measures do not agree. But the same problems arise even when they *do* agree. In the alliesthesia experiments, people refrained from eating any more of the food offered, and they said that it didn't taste good any more. That seems to make sense, but does it? Are the subjects confusing how good the food tastes with how much they want to eat it? Are they confusing a bad taste with the onset of nausea? Are they reporting what they think *ought to happen* to the pleasantness of tastes? And so on.[62]

It would be wonderful if it were clear that in *these* cases we can take subjects' self-reports at face value, and in *those* cases we cannot. But no such rules exist.

Perhaps the safest way to look at it is to realize that self-report data are just that—data, to be considered along with others. We take subjective data when we think they may tell us something; they are not to be dismissed automatically. *But they have no special privileged status either.* They are not automatically the last word. We should remember their ambiguities, and keep a bottle of salt tablets handy when we make inferences about our subjects' feelings on the basis of them.

That means in turn that all our knowledge about the role of sensations, feelings, and pleasure in behavior must have that salty flavor. For it rests squarely upon just such inferences, and upon nothing else.

LEARNING AND COGNITION IN FEEDING AND DRINKING

Early this afternoon (as this is written), a colleague stuck his head in the door and said, "Let's go eat." I looked at the clock and said, "Okay." And we did.

Now, until that time I had not been thinking about food at all. Did I suddenly become hungry? Did my glucose or fatty-acid availability take a sudden

61. Reviewed by Spitzer and Rodin, 1981.
62. Stellar, 1977.

nose dive, or did CCK cease to slosh within my body fluids? I doubt it. The simple fact is that in this society, simple *time of day* influences our meal-taking behavior at least as much as anything else. And that influence obviously is learned.

Rats, too, can be taught to feed in response to a signal that says "Meal time!" even if food is available *all* the time.[63] And if such "conditioned feeding" can be shown, so can "conditioned satiety." Rats eat less of a food if it bears the odor of a food which, *in the past,* supplied a heavy load of calories. It is as if the odor *predicted* the arrival of a large caloric load, and the rats ate less in anticipation of this.[64]

Anticipatory Drinking

An English and a French physiologist, James Fitzsimons and Jacques Le Magnen, collaborated in a study that was so simple, yet so informative, as to be a classic.[65] What they showed was that rats can anticipate how much water they are *going* to need, and drink it before the need arises.

Rats do most of their drinking along with meals, either at the beginning of a meal or just following it. Having established this, the researchers increased the protein content of their rats' diet. Now a high-protein diet eventually creates nitrogen-containing waste products that have to be eliminated in the urine. Thus, by increasing urinary water loss, such a diet increases the amounts of water rats must drink to replace what they lose.

Right after the dietary change was made, the rats began drinking water between meals. It is as if they waited until the urinary water loss occurred after each meal, and then drank to replace it. After a few days, however, water intake moved back into close association with meals. It now occurred, in other words, *before* the loss of water in the urine occurred. Yet it remained high. It is as if the rats were now drinking in *anticipation* of their heightened water need—not in *response* to that need, for it had not yet accrued.

Such drinking is not, strictly speaking, part of a negative-feedback system at all. A negative-feedback system operates to correct a disturbance once it has occurred. These rats were preventing the disturbance from occurring in the first place, thus providing a greater margin of safety. The ability to learn what one is *going* to need, before the need arises, permits just such an added safety margin.

Interaction of Internal and Anticipatory Effects

Earlier, we saw that internal and external influences on feeding are not independent, but affect each other. In a similar way, internal influences can interact with anticipatory ones.

63. Weingarten, 1983.
64. Booth, 1977.
65. Fitzsimons and Le Magnen, 1969.

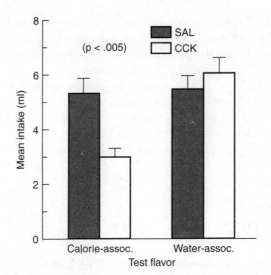

Figure 3-19 CCK, as compared to a control saline injection (SAL), reduces intake, but only for a flavor that has been associated with calories.

One example is an elegant experiment by Paul Fedorchak and Robert Bolles.[66] Rats were given experience at drinking either of two distinctively flavored solutions. Both flavors were non-nutritive in themselves; but for each rat, one solution had a source of calories mixed in with it. So for one solution, but not the other, the distinct taste became a signal that nutrients were about to arrive in the body.

After this training came the test phase. Rats were given an injection of the hormone CCK, or a placebo injection. (CCK we recall, promotes satiety [pp. 78–79]). They were then offered either the flavor that had been paired with calories, or the flavor that had not. However, *neither* fluid had any nutrients mixed with it now.

What happened? As Figure 3-19 shows, rats injected with CCK markedly reduced their intake for the fluid that had been paired with calories before. For the fluid that had not, the same dose of CCK had no effect at all.

What was the CCK doing, then? This beautiful experiment allows us to rule out a number of possibilities all at once. We cannot suppose that CCK was interacting in some way with nutrients, because there were no nutrients when the CCK was given. We can also say that CCK was *not* just making the rats sick; it was *not* acting as a direct inhibitory signal; and it was *not* augmenting the effect of some other inhibitory signal (pp. 78–79). If it had been doing any of these things, then it should have suppressed intake of both fluids equally. It didn't. It affected only the fluid whose taste "predicted" calories.

The authors conclude that the CCK was acting by way of learned "nutrient expectancies." It is as if the rat said, for the one fluid, "Hmm, this taste means I'm about to receive some nutrition [the result of conditioning]. Funny, though, I don't want much nutrition right now [the CCK effect]. I guess I

66. Fedorchak and Bolles, 1988.

won't drink much of this stuff." And for the other: "Well, I don't want much nutrition, but this fluid doesn't supply any nutrition anyway. I'll just drink the usual amount." If this is so, then CCK, a physiological factor, is exerting its effects by way of a cognitive factor—the "nutrient expectancy."

One wonders how general this is. Might other internal factors that promote satiety—food in the stomach, for example, or in the intestine (pp. 77–78)—exert their effects, not as direct physiological inhibitors, but by affecting a *decision* about how much to ingest, a decision that is also affected by learned expectancies?

Cognitive Control of Human Feeding

It is quite obvious that what, when, and how much we eat is affected by much more than the physiological signals our bodies provide. In the extreme case, people have starved themselves to make a political point. Short of that, we may refrain from eating this or that food, not because we are not hungry or because it doesn't taste good, but because we know it is not good for us. We may in fact expend quite a bit of cognitive effort—or even draw on the cognitive efforts of others!—in planning a healthful diet (Fig. 3-20).

Let us look at just one example of this active research area.

RESTRAINED EATING AND "COUNTER-REGULATION"   In our society, many people consciously limit their intake of food, not because their bodies dictate it but because they choose to do so, in the interest of losing

Figure 3-20 "That's right, Phil. A separation will mean—among other things—watching your own cholesterol." (Drawing by Maslin, © 1992, The New Yorker Magazine, Inc.)

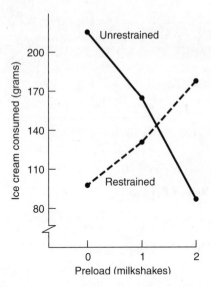

Figure 3-21 Counter-regulation in restrained eaters. Whereas unrestrained eaters ate less ice cream after drinking one or two milk shakes, restrained eaters actually ate *more* ice cream after doing so.

weight or preventing weight gain. An intriguing phenomenon was discovered by C. Peter Herman, Janet Polivy, and their collaborators, in investigating such "restrained eaters."[67]

The study was conducted as follows: On the basis of questionnaire data, the subjects (female college students, all of normal weight) were divided into "restrained eaters" who deliberately restricted their intake, and "unrestrained eaters" who did not do so. When the subjects came to the lab, some of them (but not others), within each group, were first asked to drink one or two big, rich milk shakes. Then all were offered dishes of ice cream, and were invited to eat as much ice cream as they wanted.

Consider what ought to happen. After having just drunk down a big milk shake or two, one will naturally be less hungry and so will eat less ice cream, right?

Right, for the non-dieters in the study. But for the "restrained eaters," quite wrong! The opposite occurred: These subjects ate much *more* if they had just had a milk shake than if they had not (Fig. 3-21).

This effect, which Herman and Polivy call **counter-regulation**, makes no physiological sense at all. The internal effects of the milkshake should have triggered or enhanced internal satiety signals, so a smaller meal of ice cream should have resulted.

However, it does make cognitive sense, in this way: If a person sticking to a rigid diet drinks down a whole milk shake, then the diet plan has already been violated. The subject may say, "Well, my diet is already ruined for the

67. Herman and Polivy, 1980.

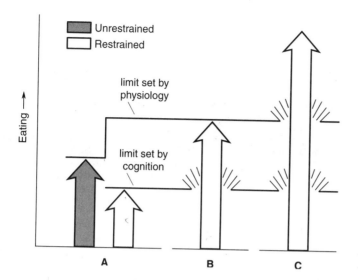

Figure 3-22 How counter-regulation occurs. (A) Unrestrained eaters eat until physiological inhibitory signals kick in. Restrained eaters eat until they reach the limit set by cognition ("all I'm allowed"). However (B), if the cognitive control collapses, eating proceeds until physiological inhibition ends it. (C) In some cases, even physiological inhibitory signals may be ignored, so that a very large binge occurs.

day. I might as well just go ahead and enjoy myself, and eat." Hence this phenomenon has also been called the "what-the-hell effect."★

There are limits to this effect. If subjects have swallowed a *very* large amount of food before being offered the ice cream, then counter-regulation does not occur: Both restrained and unrestrained eaters say, "I've had enough, thank you!" and eat little or nothing thereafter. A very large amount of food, in other words, does seem to trigger an inhibitory mechanism that affects both kinds of eater.

Perhaps, then, we need to consider two kinds of "stop-eating" mechanisms, one set by physiology, the other set by cognition (Fig. 3-22). Unrestrained eaters may be content to depend on physiological inhibitory controls; these, it seems, are sufficient to keep those subjects at acceptable weights without their having to worry about the matter. But in restrained eaters, the stop mechanism set by cognition is the more restrictive; it says, "You should stop now, even though physiological inhibition has not yet kicked in" (Fig. 3-22A).

However, that cognitive control seems to be very fragile. If the eater decides that the cognitive rule has failed—the diet is ruined for today anyway—then control seems to pop like a soap bubble. Then the meal may progress until the physiological limit is reached; and, if the physiological limit is set higher for dieters than for non-dieters, a large counter-regulatory meal will result (Fig. 3-22B).

★An alternative possibility is that the milk shake had internal effects that stimulated hunger or "whetted the appetite" (pp. 90–91). This was ruled out in an experiment in which counter-regulation was shown only by subjects who *thought* the milk shake was high in calories. Subjects who drank identical milk shakes, but thought they were low in calories, did not counter-regulate. Physiological appetite-whetting should have been the same for both; but here, as so often, it's the thought that counts.

BINGE EATING   In a provocative paper, Polivy and Herman relate their extensive research to a problem of human feeding.[68] This is the syndrome known as "binge eating", or *bulimia*. This condition is characterized by episodes of uncontrolled eating, in which a person may wolf down an enormous meal all at once. The quantities eaten in such a binge can stagger the mind. As much as 7 *pounds* of food have been eaten at one sitting!

Typically, the bulimic person feels remorseful after the binge, and if he is a dieter (as many binge-eaters are), he may diet all the more vigorously to make up for his "self-indulgence." Or he may go to the extreme of forcing himself to vomit up the food just eaten, converting the binge into a kind of sham binge. Laxatives and even enemas have also been used for this purpose.

It is natural to think of binge-eating as a cause of later dieting: one has overeaten, so one then diets to make up for it. But Polivy and Herman suggest that we try thinking of it another way—maybe dieting can cause binge-eating!

If a person persistently holds his weight below where the body "wants" it to be—the set point (pp. 85–86)—then he must suppress or ignore the signals to eat that his body is sending him. He must depend on conscious cognitive controls. But it is just these controls that have that soap-bubble quality: they may collapse under stress, or even after a minor "violation" of the diet (the what-the-hell effect). These are the conditions under which counter-regulation occurs; and the resulting bout of eating may escalate into a full-scale binge episode.

We can take the argument yet a step further. If one is accustomed to ignoring the body's hunger signals, one just might ignore its satiety signals as well! That could take the binge even past the point of physiological, as well as cognitive, inhibition (Fig. 3-22C). Binge-eaters not infrequently say things like this: "When I would binge, my stomach would get so full I would feel stuffed. I'd say, so what? And go on eating anyway!" In such cases it is not enough for the body to tell the brain, "Hey, I'm satiated!" The brain has to be listening.*

A Look Backward

Clearly, in both rats and humans, cognitive influences may have a decisive effect on feeding. A rat may say in effect, "I don't want much nourishment, and I've learned that *this* stuff delivers a lot of nourishment; so I'll go easy." A human may say, "I'm not allowed much of this stuff; it'll stick to my hips. So I'll go easy." Or, alternatively, "What the hell—I've blown my diet anyway. Why go easy now?"

As all these cases make clear, the size of a meal may not at all reflect a balance of physiological "go" and "stop" signals. It may reflect a *decision* about

68. Polivy and Herman, 1985.

*Implied in all this is that the bulimic's feeding behavior may become nearly independent of the internal signals that would otherwise promote feelings of hunger and satiety. There is experimental evidence for this (Halmi and Sunday, 1991).

when to stop, and that decision may or may not even take internal state into account. Even a "simple" biological motive like hunger and feeding may be affected by cognitive operations, as much as—or more than!—by the internal workings of the body.

CULTURE AND HUMAN FEEDING

Individual learning experiences, we have seen, can affect feeding profoundly. But many learning experiences are, in a sense, collective rather than individual. By growing up within a society, we all are taught the attitudes and values of the culture in which we live. Do these, too, affect feeding behavior? Definitely.

What Is Edible?

To see this clearly, let us do a thought experiment right now, you and I. Imagine this: You have come to visit my laboratory. It's lunchtime; you are hungry; and I offer you a heaping plate of delicious fried cockroaches. Would you eat them? Neither would I.

But why not? Cockroaches are a perfectly good source of nourishment. They are ugly, you might say. (And shrimp are pretty? We eat those.) Or, you might say, they are dirty and could carry diseases. But remember that this is a laboratory. Suppose I tell you, and you believe me, that these cockroaches are thoroughly washed and boiled—guaranteed to be absolutely, positively germ-free! Would you eat them then? No? Then it's not the threat of germs that is holding you back.

No, something is going on that is far beyond all these reasons and excuses. Indeed, I will hazard a guess, Reader, that you are uncomfortable even reading this passage! To you and me, there is something deep-down disgusting about the very idea of eating you-know-what. But that is because we live in a society in which those, well, commodities are defined as disgusting and as definitely not to be eaten.

Societies differ profoundly in their definitions of what is, or is not, to be eaten. For most Americans, beetles would rank not far above cockroaches. But natives of New Guinea eat beetles with gusto.

Food Associations and Symbolizations

Culture not only defines what does and does not count as food; it may embed food within a rich network of symbols and associations. In some societies, it is considered a very good thing if a respected or loved person spits on the food before the eater eats it. That way, some of that person's good spirit enters the diner's body along with the food.[69] In America, one suspects that for *anyone,* however respected, to spit on our food would at once make the food unacceptable.

Even as basic a human instinct as appetite is transformed by cultural and social systems and given new meaning in different historical epochs.
—HISTORIAN JOAN BRUMBERG (1988, p. 3)

69. Rozin, 1990.

Again in our own society, what we eat and how we eat it may say something about our ethnicity, our background, even our social status. Or consider this: In the United States, toward the end of November, it is the custom for family members to gather together for a large meal. And it is expected (though not strictly required) that the meal center around a roast turkey.

Why? We certainly will not understand this curious behavior by looking for specific turkey-hunger systems in the brain! We can better understand it if we realize that food has symbolic as well as nutritive properties. Americans eat turkey on Thanksgiving Day not to maintain homeostasis, but to commemorate certain historical events.

A "Lean Society"?

The culture in which we live does not only have direct effects on what we eat, and how we eat it. It also affects feeding indirectly, by affecting our conception of how much we should weigh or what our bodies should look like.

Consider our own society—which, we saw, is obsessed with thinness (pp. 86–87). Self-help books on dieting and weight control make the best-seller lists year after year. It certainly doesn't have to be that way. Compare all this with the East African societies in which women work hard (against the body's resistance) to make themselves fat (p. 94)!

Anorexia Nervosa

In fact, the standards of contemporary Western society have been held responsible, in part, for yet another disorder of feeding and weight regulation. This is the condition known as *anorexia nervosa*.

Imagine a young woman in her teens or early twenties (90 to 95 percent of anorexic patients fit that description). She is "dieting" to control her weight—and her idea of dieting is to restrict her food intake to, say, three Cheerios a day. She may have lost 25 to 30 percent of her original body weight, which may not have been excessive to begin with. Yet the anorexic typically will tell us that she is still too fat, and continue her drastic diet, often combining it with a vigorous exercise regimen, in an attempt to become *thinner still*. Thus the disorder has been well described as a "relentless pursuit of thinness."[70]

The disorder is indeed life-threatening; the anorexic may quite literally starve herself to death. In fact, the fatality rate among anorexics *who are receiving treatment* has been put as high 15 percent.[71] The popular singer Karen Carpenter died of complications resulting from anorexia.

Why does this happen? Various physiological abnormalities have been associated with this condition. However, as one writer put it, "Every observation [of such abnormality] has proven on follow-up after refeeding to be a symptom

70. Bruch, 1973.
71. Brumberg, 1988.

of the food-restricted and starved state and thus likely to be a result rather than a cause . . . of the behavior."[72]

On the other hand, demographic data suggest to many writers that our society's values have a lot to do with the problem: "Anorexia nervosa is a behavioral disorder that primarily affects (1) youthful females of the (2) upper classes in (3) developed nations in the (4) contemporary era."[73]

Why youthful females? Perhaps because of the cascade of chemical changes that accompany puberty; but also, perhaps, because puberty brings an increase in one's concern about sexuality, sexual acceptability, and personal attractiveness. Why the affluent in affluent nations, and why now more than in years past? Perhaps because it is young women living in such societies who—increasingly—are bombarded with two messages: (1) It's very important to be physically attractive, and (2) to be physically attractive, you must be lean. This idea is supported by another observation: In certain occupations in which leanness really is important—e.g., in ballet dancers or fashion models—the risk of anorexia nervosa is especially high. Thus some writers see anorexia as an exaggerated response to an already-unreasonable standard of leanness that our culture has imposed.[74]

Now there must be more to it than this. Even if the disorder is an exaggerated response to the ideal of thinness, still the exaggeration must be accounted for. In this regard, the evidence implicates a genetic "risk factor" for anorexia as for obesity (p. 86). That leaves open the question of what is inherited—certain personality characteristics, certain physiological vulnerabilities, or both—but either way, the "risk" is different for different people.

Even if physiological changes are results rather than causes of the initial starvation, still they could have effects of their own that could help keep the self-starvation going once it has begun. Many anorexics find that they are unable to resume eating even if they want to.[75] This of course makes the starvation still more severe, and so a vicious cycle is set in motion.

One possible way of putting these pieces together is this: Perhaps what we are seeing, over time and in certain social and occupational groups, is an *increase in the risk that the self-starvation cycle will begin.* The more people we have who are dieting, the more people there will be whose restrained eating will slip over an invisible line to fall into the vicious cycle of anorexia nervosa: One starves oneself until physiological changes preclude eating, and so one starves one self more. And more people *are* dieting, in response to the double message from the surrounding culture: (1) It's vital to be attractive, and (2) to be attractive, be thin.

One final point. If we identify an anorexic person, we think in terms of *treatment,* medical or behavioral or both. Well, that too is an outlook that char-

72. McHugh, 1990, p. 540.
73. Ibid., p. 541.
74. For example, Boskind-White and White, 1983.
75. Brumberg, 1988.

acterizes this society at this point in history. We see an incredibly emaciated young woman and we say, "This is a very sick person who should be treated." Not many centuries ago, we might have said something quite different: "This is a very holy person who should be venerated."[76] This is not to imply that the present view is wrong. It is only to say that it *is* the present view; it was not always that way, so it doesn't have to be; and it reflects the way our society has taught us to look at problematic behavior, feeding behavior or any other kind.

A Look Backward

In this last section, it is clear that we have moved even farther away from homeostatic considerations. A culture may define one commodity as edible, another, *equally nutritious,* as not. In some societies, the history of a portion of food—who prepared it and how—may be of great importance;[77] kosher food is an example in our own society. Then there are the food rituals that a culture recognizes, like Thanksgiving Day, and the indirect effects of culture on feeding via its definitions of desirable body weight or shape.

If anything is clear from this, it is that regulatory biology is not the whole story, even for biological drives such as hunger and thirst.

SUMMARY

The concept of drive arose from the observations (1) that behavior varies even in a constant situation and (2) that animals will make various responses, including arbitrary learned ones, to achieve a goal. That implies a hierarchical organization of behavior, so that a single motivation state can call into play any of a number of specific behaviors. When such a motivational state is evoked by a change or condition inside the body, we call it a *drive.*

Drives link behavior to *homeostasis,* or the regulation of physiological variables within the narrow limits the body requires. A drop in body temperature can be corrected by physiological means (increased metabolic rate) or by behavioral means (building a fire). A drop in blood sugar can be corrected by physiological means (release of stored sugar into the blood) or by behavioral means (eating). All these are examples of *negative feedback,* in which a system operates to reduce or remove the input—low temperature, low blood sugar— that produced the operation. Homeostasis is maintained by negative-feedback loops that correct deviations from optimal values.

The early local-sign theories thought of hunger as an unpleasant sensation from the stomach, and thirst as an unpleasant dryness of the mouth. However, these theories tell at most only part of the story; other inputs must exist as well.

76. Ibid.
77. Rozin, 1990.

There are two independent stimuli for thirst: reduction of fluid inside the cells, and reduction of fluid outside the cells. Either can occur without the other, or both can occur and add their effects. Thus thirst, a multiple-output motivation state, is also a multiple-input system called into play by different stimuli at different times. Inhibition of thirst, or *satiety,* is also a multiple-input system; it receives some input from the mouth and the stomach, though hydration of the cells is required to limit intake to normal levels. Thus thirst, a way of gaining water, cooperates with physiological mechanisms that slow down the rate of water loss. Both behavior and physiology act to prevent or correct dehydration, and thus promote homeostasis with respect to volume and concentration of body fluids. As yet a further complication, a single input can call forth multiple drive states. Thus extracellular (but not intracellular) dehydration calls forth not only a thirst for water, but also an appetite for salt.

A drop in the availability of glucose (blood sugar) to the cells can trigger hunger, but so can a drop in availability of fatty acids, and there may be yet other stimuli that can do so. Moreover, there may be several hungers rather than only one. Protein intake is regulated separately from carbohydrate intake, and sodium is regulated separately again. Perhaps what we call "hunger" is a collection of different states, not just one.

Satiety of hunger is another multiple-input system; stimuli from the mouth, the stomach, the liver, and the intestine can act to limit feeding. In humans, blood-borne fat constituents can also suppress hunger.

The short-term cycle of hunger and satiety is superimposed on a longer-term regulatory system that holds body weight remarkably constant over long periods. This may mean that the amount of fat in the body is regulated. Obesity might result from an elevated set point for body fat, so that the "normal" weight, which the body regulates, is set too high. The body does defend its normal weight vigorously; it is difficult to gain or to lose very much weight, for adjustments in body chemistry and metabolic rate oppose these attempts. As a result, overeating may have little to do with what we call "excess weight." People do lose excess weight and keep it off, but some scientists question whether the battle is worth it. We might do better to accept the fact that people vary in body weight and composition, just as they do in height.

Besides being *pushed from within* by physiological needs, ingestion may be *pulled from without* by stimulus factors. A sweet taste can evoke ingestion. Access to tasty and varied foods can make normal rats fat. Even simple variety can increase intake, in both rats and humans.

Internal and external influences interact with each other. Food-related stimuli may trigger internal changes that in turn promote feeding. Conversely, internal state affects how external stimuli are responded to. Thirst makes us responsive to water; salt deficiency makes us responsive to salt taste. Hunger may greatly extend the range of commodities we are willing to eat. Short-term satiety or long-term excess weight gain may make food taste less good, to humans and even to rats as judged by the faces they make. This effect is called *alliesthesia.* Moreover, feeding and drinking may use the same responses, as when a rat laps a liquid diet when hungry, or laps water when thirsty. The same lower-level movements may be called into play by different higher levels at different times. Such a *lattice hierarchy* suggests that the effect of internal states is to prime, or *potentiate,* ingestive responses to specific external stimuli.

Therefore, internal states direct behavior by modifying the actor's responsiveness to external stimuli. We might conceive of food-seeking behavior as responsive to the *attractiveness* of food. That attractiveness could arise either because the food is attractive in itself or because internal states of need enhance its attractiveness. In the former case we would have taste-evoked ingestion; in the latter, homeostatic control of ingestion. Such theorizing, however, depends on self-reports of pleasure or displeasure which are not always easy to interpret.

Cognitive and cultural factors also affect our feeding behavior. We eat when it is time to eat. We may also learn, for example, how much water we are *going* to need or how many calories a food is *going* to supply, and adjust our intake to these anticipated conditions, not just to conditions that are present now. Laboratory rats may do the same.

In human dieters, a load of calories may even increase the amount eaten subsequently if the dieter decides that the load has "blown" the diet, and abandons deliberate control over ingestion. This "counter-regulation" may play a role in binge eating.

The culture in which we live affects our feeding behavior in many ways. It defines what is or is not an acceptable food; in some societies beetles are a delicacy, in others they would be rejected with disgust. Culture embeds food and feeding in a dense network of symbols and associations, as with Thanksgiving dinners in the United States. It also affects feeding indirectly, by dictating the appearances or body shapes that it holds in high regard. The dangerous disorder *anorexia nervosa,* which can and does cause death by starvation, has been attributed in part to our society's obsession with physical attractiveness and with leanness as a component of this. Clearly even the "biological drives" like hunger and thirst are much more complex than simple negative-feedback, homeostatic systems.

CHAPTER 4

Biological Motives: Sex and Aggression

Drinking in land-dwelling animals, and feeding in all animals, are basic necessities if individuals are to survive. But reproduction is just as basic a necessity if the *species* is to stay around. And in some species, the same may be true of aggressive behavior, partly because it is closely linked with reproduction.

That is one reason we consider these two motives together in this chapter. Another is that they bear some resemblances to each other, and to hunger and thirst. But there also are some important differences.

First, the similarities: Like hunger and thirst, sex and aggression are affected by both internal and external factors. And internal and external factors interact: Internal state affects how the environment is reacted to, and environmental inputs affect the body's internal state.

Now, some differences: First, sex and aggression are *not* homeostatic motives. No internal commodity is *regulated* by sexual or aggressive behavior, and there is no threat to the animal's physical well-being if they do not occur. As a result, both are more variable and more sensitive to external circumstances than feeding and drinking are. Second, an animal may eat or drink all by itself, but sex or aggression takes two. Thus we must consider the interactions between *two* behaving organisms, and the factors influencing each.

Third, especially in humans, the role of *learning* adds formidable complexities to whatever biological mechanisms there may be. In fact, the culture in which one is raised has such profound effects on human sexuality, and human aggressiveness, that some scientists wonder whether they are still controlled by biological mechanisms at all. The old argument about inherited and learned mechanisms—the nature-nurture issue—has had these two motives as its principal battleground.

Therefore, let us begin by looking at the research that has given that ancient issue its modern form.

INSTINCT RE-EXAMINED: THE IMPACT OF ETHOLOGY

Back in Chapter 2, we saw how behaviorist researchers emphasized the study of behavior under controlled laboratory conditions. And the study of *learning* was a major part of their research program. In contrast, *ethologists* studied behavior in its natural setting; and these scientists were struck by how rich and complex an animal's *unlearned* repertoire of behavior could be. Sexual and aggressive actions were often particularly striking in this regard.

A Case Study: Sex, Aggression, and the Stickleback

An example that was worked out so early and so well as to be a classic of ethological analysis is the reproductive behavior of a river fish, the *three-spined stickleback,* as described by ethologist Niko Tinbergen and his co-workers.[1]

In the spring, the male three-spined stickleback is brought into reproductive condition by hormonal changes. These have physical effects: They give the male fish a characteristic red-colored underbelly, of which more in a minute. They also affect its behavior. The fish builds a tube-shaped nest, and then patrols the territory around the nest, as if waiting for the arrival of another fish.

What happens then depends on who comes around. If another fish with a red underbelly approaches, the male treats it as a rival male, and attacks. The attack begins with a characteristic *threat display,* an **action pattern** consisting of head-down posture and spread fins (Fig. 4-1A). This threat posture is elicited, or released, by the intruder's red underbelly. That is the **releasing stimulus.** Even very crude models, if introduced near the male, will be threatened if their undersides are red—and only then.

If it is a female fish that comes along, then courtship rather than attack is released. Here the action pattern is a peculiar back-and-forth swimming pattern, a zigzag dance. Its releasing stimulus is the swollen underbelly of the female fish heavy with eggs. Crude models with swollen undersides will be courted; good models without it will not be (Fig. 4-1B).

The affair is consummated by a meticulously choreographed series of releasing stimuli and action patterns. The male leads the female to his nest. If she follows, he points to the next entrance with his nose. If she swims into the nest, he nuzzles her posterior, causing her to release her clutch of eggs. He then swims in after her, depositing sperm to fertilize the eggs; fertilization takes place outside the body in this species. Then the male takes over the job of car-

1. Tinbergen, 1951.

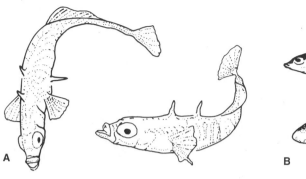

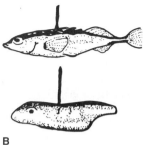

Figure 4-1 (A) A male stickleback fish (left) threatens his opponent. (B) Two model sticklebacks. The top one, a detailed female model without the swollen underside, does not release courtship in the male. The crude bottom one, with the swollen underside, does. (Both from Tinbergen, 1951.)

ing for the developing eggs. Experiments with models have shown that every stage of the sequence is an instinctive pattern of responses—an *action pattern*—evoked by certain stimuli provided by the partner's appearance and/or behavior—the *releasing stimuli*.

Organization of Instinctive Behavior

In Figure 4-2, we see the structure of a stickleback male's reproductive behavior as Tinbergen described it. Here we find many parallels to what we learned about hunger and thirst in the previous chapter.

First, there is the hierarchy, with components and sub-components like a military chain of command. A male fish in reproductive condition will fight a rival male, or court a female, or build a nest if he has no nest. But he will do *none of these* if his hormonal state is not appropriate. Therefore, hormones must act at the level of *reproductive motivation* to activate the whole system, with all its components. Hormones awaken the general, not the foot soldiers directly.

Second, the higher levels prime, or facilitate, *responsiveness to stimuli*. Once aroused, the reproduction general activates the officers in charge of fighting, courting, and so on. Each is made ready for action *if a specific releasing stimulus occurs*. The fighting officer is told, "Be ready to fight if you see a red underbelly." The courting officer is told, "Be ready to court if you see a swollen underbelly." When the releasing stimulus is encountered, the officer alerts the sergeants, who order coordinated patterns of movement by the body's parts. Finally, the foot-soldier muscle cells, which actually produce the movements, are ordered into action.

INSTINCTIVE BEHAVIOR AND MOTIVATIONAL STATES

We see that the stickleback's sex/aggression system has much in common with hunger and thirst. There is the hierarchical organization; the multiple-alternative, multiple-output system; and the priming of specific responses to specific stimuli.

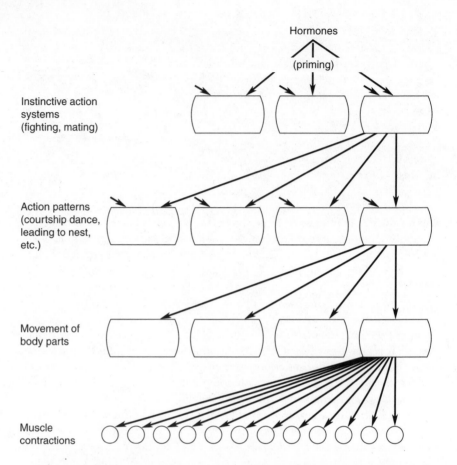

Figure 4-2 The hierarchical organization of reproductive behavior in sticklebacks. Each level, when activated, primes a collection of response patterns at the next level down. External stimuli, shown by the short arrows at the left, release one or more of those patterns.

But are these motivational states, like hunger in rats or humans? In the rat, we saw that the feeding hierarchy includes *multiple paths to a goal*—and some of these are arbitrary learned responses, like pressing a lever or running a maze. The rat will make *whatever response is available* to attain its goal—food. The stickleback does have alternative responses—to court, or to mate—but the response is not goal-directed. Rather, it is *stimulus-bound:* It depends on the releasing stimulus that precedes it, not on the goal that follows it. And it is not learned (see below).

To say that a motivational state exists, we must show that the animal will make an arbitrary learned response to attain a goal. This defining characteristic of motivational states—arbitrary goal-directed responses—is absent from the sexual behavior of many species, and for good reason. In many insects, for instance, mating occurs only once in a lifetime. The animal must identify a mate and make all the right movements the first and only time; it has no need and no opportunity to learn anything about it. In such species, mating is stimulus-bound and inflexible; there is no evidence for a motivational state.

The stickleback is an intermediate case. In this species, as in hungry rats, arbitrary responses may be learned, and these may be directed toward a goal rather than triggered by a releasing stimulus.[2] But this flexibility is there during the period *before* the releasing stimulus comes along. For example, a male fish will learn an arbitrary response to obtain access to a female, but then it courts the female in its unlearned, instinctive way. Or it will learn a response that gives it access to a rival male, but then it will threaten the rival in its unlearned, instinctive way.

In sticklebacks, therefore, there are two phases to sexual/aggressive behavior. During the first, arbitrary learned responses can expand the sexual or aggressive repertoire, and therefore we can speak of a state of sexual, or aggressive, motivation. But once the mate or the rival is at hand, behavior funnels down into inflexible, stimulus-bound instinctive reactions.

Actually, feeding and drinking in the rat are organized in a similar way; we just haven't discussed it until now. The various responses the animal can make—approaching, running a maze, pressing a lever—are alternative ways of *getting to* food or water. But once the commodity is there, it releases stimulus-bound, instinctive action patterns: Dry food triggers seizing and chewing, liquid triggers lapping.★ The rat does not have to learn these.[3]

Humans are different. In adults, feeding movements, as well as food-seeking ones, are variable and learned: Some of us eat with forks, others with chopsticks. That species difference has its parallel in sexual behavior, as we will see.

In summary, we can distinguish two classes of behavior. Some are flexible and goal-directed, leading us to speak of *motivational states*. Others are stimulus-bound, depending on the stimuli that precede them rather than on the goals that follow them, and when these are unlearned, we speak of them as *instinctive*. Various mixtures are possible, however. In some insects, mating appears to be all instinctive, as noted above. In sticklebacks, a motivational state can be shown early in the mating sequence, but the later behavior is instinctive. And in humans, the question is whether anything instinctive remains—a question to which we will return.

INSTINCT AND LEARNING: THE INNATE AND THE UNTAUGHT

Even in the stickleback, we have seen, learning can play a role in sex and aggression, at least early in the sequence. What impressed ethologists, however, was how much complexity there was in the fish's behavior even without specific learning experiences that might have put it there. Nest building, fighting, and mating happen in an essentially normal way on the fish's first breeding

2. Sevenster, 1972.
★One *can* teach rats to feed and drink with arbitrary responses; for example, by pressing a lever to inject fluid into their stomachs. The experiment is difficult, however, and there are questions about its interpretation (see Epstein, 1960; Teitelbaum, 1966; Holman, 1969).
3. Hall, 1975.

season, even in fish reared in isolation. They are unlearned; in the ethologists' language, they are **innate.**

The word *innate* is an unfortunate one. It seems to imply something forever fixed and unmodifiable, something that must inevitably occur. In fact, that is not at all what the ethologists showed. Let us look again at the data.

By the use of models, Tinbergen showed that a red underbelly, all by itself, is enough to release attack behavior in the male stickleback. That is what he meant by calling the red belly a releasing stimulus. That does *not* mean that nothing else affects attack behavior. Other conflicting motives, for instance, might suppress it altogether.

He also showed that the attack response occurred even with no opportunity for learning. That does *not* mean that learning cannot affect it.* It is entirely possible, for instance, that one might suppress courting in such a fish by punishing courting behavior, though I know of no data on this point.

In short, what terms like *innate* refer to is behavior, or some influence on behavior, that *is not acquired through specific learning experiences.* How modifiable it is, if specific learning experiences *are* brought to bear, is a different question altogether.

Because this confusion crops up so frequently, I offer a modest suggestion here. Let us drop the term *innate* altogether and substitute the term **untaught.** Then we can speak about action that was not taught to the animal by any specific learning experience. But *untaught* doesn't mean *unteachable,* and we are leaving open the possibility that learning might modify the behavior later. I will use the term *untaught,* for that purpose, throughout the rest of this book.

It is worth pausing to note explicitly that the term *untaught*—like the term *instinctive,* as used by writers like Tinbergen—is not an explanatory concept. It is a descriptive or classificatory one. It makes no sense to say, "The animal does such and such *because* the action is untaught (or instinctive)." Rather, the term says this to us: "Here is an action or set of actions that needs to be explained; and it does *not* look as if we can explain it by pointing to specific experiences that taught the animal to do it." In other words, such terms do not explain how the behavior develops, but only how it doesn't.

But that is no small thing. Considering that learning *can* account for a great deal of behavior in many species, it is worth identifying those cases for which it cannot account, and having a word—like *instinctive* or *untaught*—by which to refer to them.

A Look Backward: The Concept of Instinct

Ethologists have offered us concepts that are highly useful in describing animal behavior in the wild. Much of it is instinctive. That is, it consists of action pat-

---

*This takes us back to a point we saw in Chapter 1 (p. 18). It is one thing to show that something is *an* important influence on behavior. That doesn't mean that it is *the* important influence. The red underbelly is *an* important influence on the stickleback's attack, and learning did not make it so. But other influences, including learning, may be just as important or more.

terns, complex actions that (1) are characteristic of the species, (2) are triggered by certain stimulus inputs, or releasing stimuli, and (3) are untaught; that is, learning did not produce them, though it may modify them later.

The question then arises: How far will these concepts take us in explaining the behavior of more complex creatures? How much of the stickleback do we see in our mammalian cousins—or in ourselves?

SEX IN MAMMALS: INTERNAL FACTORS

The rat, like the stickleback, has a characteristic courtship routine. A male rat's initial reaction to a female is a thorough investigation, with particular attention to the female's genital region. If receptive, the female often responds with a swift, darting run for a short distance, then an abrupt halt with wiggling of the ears. If the male does not follow, the female then approaches and investigates the male's genital area, shifting back to the darting run if the male shows interest.

The dart-pursuit-dart sequence is repeated with mounting excitement. Mating itself begins when the male mounts the female from the rear, eliciting the *lordosis reflex*—the female's rump is elevated and the tail is moved to one side, exposing the vaginal opening. Copulation follows.

What produces this sequence of courtship and copulation? As in Chapter 3, we will look at internal and external influences, and then at how they interact.

Endocrine Glands and Hormones

We have referred to *hormones* several times in this discussion. These are the body's chemical messengers. They are manufactured by the *endocrine glands,* which release hormones into the blood. They are then carried by the blood to all the cells in the body.

The sex hormones produce their effects at a number of places in the body that react to their presence. At puberty, for instance, there is an outpouring of hormones from the male *testes*. These hormones are referred to collectively as *androgens;* among these, the hormone *testosterone* is the most important. The increased androgen level produces, in boys, the growth of facial and body hair, deepening of the voice, and growth of skeletal muscles. In girls, the development of breasts and the widening of hips is caused, and the growth of facial hair is inhibited, by the outpouring of hormones, especially *estrogen,* from the *ovaries*.

And in both sexes, these hormones may act on the brain to promote sexual interest and motivation. In animals at least, it is clear that they do.

Hormones and Sexual Motivation

We need to consider males and females separately, for the hormonal systems are quite different in the two. We will also need to be careful which species we consider, for there are very great species differences.

MALES   In the male rat, sexual behavior slowly declines and finally disappears altogether after castration. Injections of testosterone can restore it. Therefore, in the rat, the presence of the male hormone testosterone is an important condition for sexual motivation. Moreover, when the hormone is present, it produces a motivational state. A rat will learn an arbitrary response if rewarded with the opportunity to copulate.[4]

In higher species, too, hormones play some role. The following, however, is a safe rule of thumb: *As we move to higher animals, even within the mammals, hormones become less important; experience and stimulus factors become more so.*

In men, castration can produce a loss of sexual interest or failure of such interest to develop, especially if it occurs before puberty. On the other hand, sexual motivation—and potency as well—*can* persist for many years, especially in sexually experienced men. In short, absence of the male hormone does not *necessarily* lead to loss of sex drive or sexual behavior in human males, whereas in the rat, it does.

On the other hand, while male hormones are not *necessary* for male sexual motivation, they can enhance it if present. Sexual activity tends to be highest in late adolescence, when testosterone levels are highest. Men with low testosterone levels may have low frequencies of erection and of sexual activity, but testosterone injections increase the frequency of both.[5]

FEMALES   In female mammals, secretion of hormones is a cyclic process; the ovaries secrete a combination of hormones that changes over time, and repeats itself again and again. In female rats, this *estrous cycle* lasts four to five days; in women, the corresponding *menstrual cycle* lasts about a month.

In female rats and carnivores, sexual behavior is strictly limited to a brief period during the cycle, known as **estrus** or "heat." This is also the period during which impregnation can take place. It is characterized by high levels of certain ovarian hormones, especially the hormone **estrogen.**

If you have ever been owned by a female cat, you have seen the characteristic behaviors that signal the arrival of heat. There is the weird, contralto meow. Stroke the cat's back, and you see the reverse arching of the back that elevates the rump—the lordosis reflex—and the unmistakable treading with the paws. Let a male come around at that time, and we know just what to expect.

In female cats and rats, that state, and sexual behavior too, are totally dependent upon the sex hormones. Remove the ovaries, and sexual behavior and the other signs of heat are totally and permanently abolished. Injection of estrogen can restore them.

And, once again, what the hormones promote is a motivational state, not just responses to releasers. Female rates during estrus, or spayed rats treated with estrogen, will work at an arbitrary response to gain access to a male.[6]

4. Kagan, 1955.
5. Davidson, Camargo, and Smith, 1979.
6. See for example Meyerson and Lindstrom, 1973.

In adult human females, as with males, hormones play a less central role. Unlike female rats or carnivores, human females may mate at any time, not just during the fertile period. Moreover, neither removal of the ovaries, nor menopause when ovarian function ceases, has any dependable effect on sex drive in women. And attempts to correlate sexual activity with the menstrual cycle have led to inconsistent results.*

Interestingly, however, removal of the adrenal glands, which secrete appreciable amounts of the *male* sex hormones even in females, does depress sexual interest, both in female monkeys and in women.[7] And in both species, treatment with male hormones can restore it. Thus, the "male" sex hormone may play a greater role than "female" hormones in sexual arousal for women.

SEXUAL BEHAVIOR: STIMULUS FACTORS

We saw in Chapter 3 that external as well as internal influences can trigger ingestion and food-seeking. We also saw that internal factors can exert their effects by priming responses to external stimuli. These phenomena occur in sexual behavior, too. In sticklebacks, courtship reactions to releasing stimuli are primed by sex hormones. The sexual action patterns require appropriate hormonal condition *and* the releasing stimulus.

Pheromones and Other Sexual Signals

In some mammals, chemical messengers, or **pheromones**—odorous substances released by the animal—are powerful sexual attractants. Male rats or guinea pigs, for instance, are strongly attracted to the smell of the urine of a female in estrus. The urine of a non-estrous female evokes no such interest.[8] Pheromones are also the reason that all the male cats in the neighborhood seem to know when a female cat is in heat. They do know it, and it is pheromones released by the female that tell them.

Furthermore, these smelly signals do not just release action patterns; they can evoke motivational states of the kind we considered earlier. Male rats may press a lever to gain access to a hormone-treated female—but not if they are unable to smell.[9]

In some primates such as chimpanzees, the signal is visual. The tissue around the genitals becomes swollen, and sometimes brightly colored, during the female's fertilizable period (Fig. 4-3). This change in appearance, known as *sex skin,* brings a great deal of sexual attention from males in the vicinity.

*For discussion of the problems in this research see Matteo and Rissman (1984).

7. Everitt and Herbert, 1975.
8. Pfaff and Pfaffmann, 1969.
9. Michael and Keverne, 1968.

Figure 4-3 Estrus in the female chimpanzee is indicated by swelling of the vaginal lips, or sex skin.

Stimulus Arousal in Humans

In the human case, too, external stimuli can evoke signs of sexual arousal. The sight of an attractive person of the opposite sex, or pictures, can elicit penile erection in men, and vaginal lubrication and swelling of the vaginal walls in women. In homosexual men, pictures of same-sex individuals can have similar effects.[10]

It is tempting to think of these persons or pictures as releasing stimuli—or perhaps simply as stimuli that inherently evoke motivational states, as tasty foods do. It is true that physical attractiveness plays a powerful role in how sexually interesting we find a person.[11] On the other hand, conceptions of sexual attractiveness vary a great deal between one group of humans and another, so we must be careful here. In American society, slimness is considered attractive in women, but in many societies it is plump women who are considered attractive. Among the Hottentots of Africa, the condition known as *steatopygia*—enlargement of the buttocks—is considered a mark of great beauty, and the bigger the bottom the better. In certain groups in New Guinea, feathers in the nose are considered sexually provocative dress in males (Fig. 4-4).

10. See for example Barlow et al., 1972.
11. Walster and Walster, 1978.

Figure 4-4   Among the people of the New Guinea highlands, feathers in the nose enhance sexual attractiveness.

Thus these characteristics are not releasing stimuli. Our response to them is *not* untaught; we are taught by our society to consider them attractive or arousing.

Because of this diversity, many writers have argued that standards of sexual attractiveness are wholly learned; one is taught them by the culture one grows up in.[12] Other writers are not so sure. Maybe we have been so struck by the differences among cultures that we have neglected the similarities. It has been argued that certain standards of sexual attractiveness *are* universal among humans. One is the set of stimuli correlated with *health,* for example, a clear skin. Another, in women but not in men—and whether we like it or not—is the set of stimuli correlated with *youth*. To this we should add a fascinating finding: Pictures of people who are rated more attractive than others, by adults, are also preferred to those others even by tiny babies! (Preference was inferred from amount of time spent looking at the pictures.) Presumably, in those little subjects, culture has not had time to have much impact. So, underlying the cross-cultural diversity, there may be some universally attractive characteristics after all.[13]

Perhaps such stimulus patterns do evoke sexual motivation directly, apart from learning. If so, however, they still don't qualify as releasing stimuli, for it

12. For example, Mahoney, 1983.
13. For a review of these and other findings, see Symons, 1992.

is another question how such motivation is expressed. In humans, it certainly is not expressed by untaught action patterns (see below).

Touch and Sexual Arousal

Smells and sights are long-range signals. Especially as behavior progresses from courtship toward mating, close-up stimuli take over. The role of touching and caressing in sexual arousal may be almost too obvious to require comment. And it is tactile stimulation of the genitals during intercourse that builds up excitation in the spinal-cord centers that control the reflex patterns of orgasm and ejaculation.

Once again, however, the matter is not simple. The so-called **erogenous zones**—the genitals, breasts, and lips—are densely supplied with nerve endings, rendering them highly sensitive to touch. But the touch they are sensitive to is apparently just that—touch. There are no special sexual receptors in these places, and no special sexual touch (Fig. 4-5).

What makes touches sexual, then? As one writer points out, the lips are erogenous zones all right, but when was the last time you were turned on by eating a slice of pizza?[14] And anyone who has ever fended off an unwanted sexual advance knows that the touching of one's erogenous zones is not *automatically* arousing or even pleasant. The context of the touch has a great deal to do with our response to it: our relations with the toucher, the sexual attitudes and values our society and our upbringing have given us, the external situation, and what we expect will follow. In a word, culture and cognition can powerfully affect our response to sexual stimuli.

Internal Modulation of Responses to Stimuli

In the last chapter, we saw that internal and external influences on ingestion are not independent; rather, they interact with each other. Indeed, *internal* factors influence behavior by modifying how *external* signals are reacted to.

Well, exactly the same can be said of sexual behavior. Let us look again at sexual signals such as pheromones and sex skin in animals (pp. 119–120). In all such cases, one animal sends out signals to another, and these signals are produced by the sender's hormonal state. However, responsiveness to the signals depends on the *receiver's* hormonal state. A castrated male guinea pig, for example, will show no interest in the smell of a female's urine. Testosterone injections restore that interest. In short, the male's hormones make him responsive to the female's signals.

We notice a complication here that we did not see with feeding—for feeding, unlike sex, does not take two. The sequence of events goes from one partner's endocrine state—the fertile period—to the other partner's behavior. The one partner's endocrine state produces the signals, pheromones or sex skin, that arouse the other's sexual motivation.

14. Mahoney, 1983.

Figure 4-5   Even a tickle on the nose can be erotic, from the right person at the right time.

This link between one actor's hormones and the other's behavior may be an important way of synchronizing mating behavior with the fertile period, so that it occurs when offspring are most likely. When a female rat comes into estrus and is fertile, she produces urine with its characteristic odor, evoking the male's sexual interest. Thus, if copulation occurs, it will occur right about when it should, to maximize the likelihood of producing little rats with minimal risk and wasted energy.

Alliesthesia

In feeding, we saw some evidence that hunger can make food taste good, whereas satiety can make it taste less good. What about sexual behavior? Does sexual motivation affect the pleasantness or attractiveness of sexual stimuli? Perhaps.

In female rats, stroking of the flanks, even by a human experimenter, can evoke the lordosis reflex—the elevated rump that characterizes the female mating position—if the female is sexually receptive. Lacking the hormones that prime sexual readiness, the female reacts with escape or attack instead, as if touches on the flank were strongly unpleasant. And she may react much more violently to a second approach by a male than to the first one, as if the first one had left a painful memory. Donald Pfaff points out that many things which reduce the painfulness of stimulation also promote lordosis, and conversely.[15] He speculates that sex hormones may shift the effects of touch away from unpleasantness and toward pleasantness.

15. Pfaff, 1982.

In human sexual behavior, a kind of alliesthesia seems to affect the *visual* stimuli that people provide. Sexually aroused people, of both sexes, perceive attractive members of the opposite sex as even more attractive. Aroused males in this society see females as having better figures than non-aroused males do. Aroused females see males as having more attractive hips and genitals.[16]

Stimulus Effects on Internal Factors

The next topic extends the parallel between sex and feeding. Earlier, we saw that external stimuli can affect internal controlling systems; food can trigger insulin release which in turn leads to hunger. This kind of thing happens in sexual behavior, too, at least in some species. Stimulation can affect the release of hormones that in turn affect subsequent behavior.

LOVE IN THE DOVE   An especially clear case occurs in the female ring dove. The courtship process in ring doves normally takes several days. When a male and female have been properly introduced in the laboratory, the male begins to bow to the female repeatedly, making characteristic cooing sounds. After about two days of this, the female is ready for copulation. And it can be shown that this readiness occurs because of a gradual increase in estrogen level in the female.

But this buildup of estrogen occurs as a *response to the sight of the male's behavior*. To show this, a team of experimenters removed the gonads from the *male* dove—not the female.[17] This operation abolishes bowing and cooing in the male.

It also abolished estrogen buildup in the female. A perfectly normal female ring dove, placed with a castrated male, showed no trace of the hormonal changes that would otherwise have occurred in a male's presence. Appropriate controls ruled out sounds and smells as the missing signals; it was the *sight of the male's bow-and-coo display* that was necessary to start the female's estrogen flowing.

What this shows is that it is not enough, for the female, to be in the presence of a male bird. The bird may look like a normal male and feed like a normal male, but if it does not bow and coo like a normal male, the surge of estrogen that primes the female for mating does not occur. Thus this very complex input—the sight of the male's display—acts on the female's brain to effect the release of hormones that in turn control her sexual responsiveness.

STIMULUS EFFECTS ON HORMONE SECRETION IN HUMANS
There are similar effects in human women, but their behavioral effects, if any, are unclear. A classic study showed that women who lived together—as dormitory roommates, for example—tended to synchronize their menstrual

16. Stephan, Berscheid, and Walster, 1971.
17. Erickson and Lehrman, 1964.

cycles.[18] Some signal transmitted from woman to woman, probably a pheromone, must have produced this synchrony. More recently, it was found that over a 40-day period, women who simply slept in the same bed with a man were more likely to ovulate than ones who did not. This effect was independent of the frequency of intercourse; this suggests that the mere *presence* of the male was enough to produce the effect.[19] How this works we do not know, but some pheromonal signal is a likely possibility.

These phenomena may be important in preparing the body for fertilization and implantation of the egg. But, to my knowledge, no corresponding effects on sexual *behavior* have been reported. That makes good sense, for women's sexuality, we recall, is not much affected by ovarian hormones anyway.

On the male side, there is the fascinating experience, published anonymously, of a man who worked in isolation for considerable periods of time. On occasion he would return to civilization, with its opportunities for sexual contact; and as the times to do so grew nearer, he found that he had to shave more often! Actual measurement—weighing beard clippings to the nearest milligram—confirmed the fact: As sexual contact grew nearer, his beard grew faster.[20] The rate of beard growth is sensitive to androgen level, suggesting that the mere *prospect* of sex was enough to increase sex hormone secretion.

Variety: The Coolidge Effect

We saw earlier how simple *variety* in the diet can keep feeding going when otherwise it would end. Variety can also maintain sexual behavior, and the effect can be very large. In some species, sexual activity may persist much longer if the partner is varied than if the partner stays the same. This is known as the Coolidge Effect.★

EXPERIMENTAL DEMONSTRATIONS In male rats, one investigator found that sexual exhaustion and cessation of mating required an average of seven ejaculations if the rat was left with the same female throughout. But if the female was changed at every 15-minute mark, an average of thirteen ejaculations—almost twice as many—was required to produce exhaustion.[21] In

18. McClintock, 1971.
19. Veith et al., 1983.
20. Anonymous, 1970.
★The name comes from the following story (almost certainly untrue): One day, President Calvin Coolidge and his wife were visiting a chicken farm. The two went separate ways, the President with the farmer and Mrs. Coolidge with the farmer's wife. As Mrs. Coolidge walked past a particularly assertive-looking rooster, she wondered aloud how many times a day roosters copulated. "Dozens of times!" she was told. "Please tell the President that," she said. So the farmer's wife did so. Coolidge listened quietly and then asked, "Same hen every time?" "Oh no, Mr. President; different hen every time." The President nodded and said, "Tell Mrs. Coolidge that."
21. Fisher, 1962.

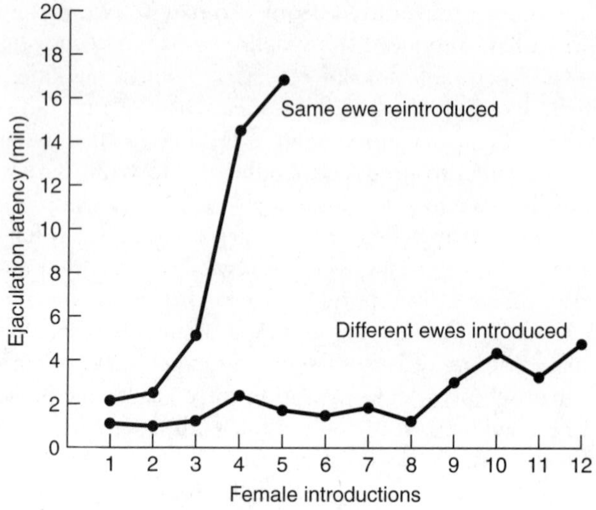

Figure 4-6 In rams, ejaculation latency gets longer and longer—that is, the rams take longer and longer to resume and finish mating—if the same ewe is offered every time. With different ewes, the rams mated promptly time after time. (From Bermant, 1976.)

rams, the effect is even more striking, as shown in Figure 4-6. When the same ewe was offered the male throughout, the ram was slower and slower to resume mating. With a different female every time, the ram mated promptly again and again, until the *experimenters* were exhausted.

There are few if any experiments dealing with the Coolidge Effect in *females*. Actually, it would make good biological sense if the Coolidge Effect were specifically a male phenomenon (see below). The matter needs direct study, however.

VARIETY AND HUMAN SEXUALITY   In humans, we have evidence that is mostly anecdotal, and one must remember how easily anecdotes or case studies can be selected to support a point. But consider the complaints of the men in a Pacific island society: When colonial authorities took their concubines away, they found it difficult to maintain sexual interest in their wives.[22] That variety may be arousing is also suggested by the frequency with which American adults—of both sexes, by the way—report the use of *fantasy* during intercourse to increase arousal. Very often, the fantasy centers around someone other than the partner—a former lover, or an imaginary one.[23]

But do males respond to variety more than females do? In our society, folk-lore certainly has it that they do; but is it true?

Across cultures, *polygynous* marriages, in which a man has many wives, are more common than monogamous marriages. And *polyandrous* systems, in which a woman may have many husbands, are very rare.[24]★ This by itself doesn't tell

22. Davenport, 1965.
23. Tavris and Sadd, 1977.
24. Ford and Beach, 1951.
★These terms are easy to keep straight. "Poly" means "many." Polygyny, in which a man has

us much, for in many societies men treat "their" women as property, and "having" multiple women may be a sign of status. Or it could reflect the (in)famous "double standard"—maybe women, more than men, are *taught* to be faithful to a single mate.

However, (1) among *gay* men and women in our society, where the issue of property rights should not be a factor, still the pattern holds. One study found that gay men had had, on average, sixteen different partners; gay women, on average, only two.[25] And (2) there are societies in which there is no sign of a double standard, at least prior to marriage. Among the Mangaians of Polynesia, sexual exploration is free and approved for both boys and girls. But even here, boys on the average had had about ten different partners prior to marriage; girls, three to four.

Now, none of this is definitive evidence that human males have an "untaught" urge to seek sexual variety more than females do (see below). The most we can say is that the data are *compatible with* that idea. However, we can also say that the idea makes a good deal of evolutionary sense.

SOCIOBIOLOGY AND THE COOLIDGE EFFECT   We noted a minute ago that the Coolidge Effect, or a search for variety in sexual partners, might make particularly good sense in males. Let us see why.

Once a female has mated and been impregnated, she cannot be impregnated again for some time—let us say, nine months. Then the total number of offspring she could possibly bear in her lifetime is strictly limited by the number of childbearing years, times 12/9. If her period of childbearing capability is, say, thirty years long, this means that she could have an absolute maximum of forty children.

Now look at it from the male view. If he remains faithful to one mate all her fertile lifetime, then his limit on offspring is the same as hers. He could leave forty children, at the very maximum. But a male, having fertilized one female, can soon be ready to fertilize another. A male *could* father literally thousands of children—*but not if he remains monogamous.*

Now, suppose that the tendency to seek sexual variety has some genetic basis. That is a big assumption, especially if we try to apply the theory to humans (see below). But there is nothing mysterious or absurd about the possibility. It sounds strange to speak of something like "genes for male philandering," but it really is not. It would mean something like: "An inherited characteristic of the masculine brain which makes novel sexual partners effective stimuli for courtship and mating, where familiar or just-mated-with sexual partners would not be effective." That takes a long time to say, so let us speak of a *Coolidge gene complex* or CGC, for short.

And, in at least some species—rams for instance—we know that there is a CGC. No one *taught* those rams to renew their sexual enthusiasm when offered

----

many wives, sounds like "many Ginnies." Polyandry, in which a woman has many husbands, sounds like "many Andys."
25. Schafer, 1977.

new partners. It must be a characteristic of a system within the ram brain, the development of which was programmed by the genes.

Now, if some species members have a CGC and others do not, then the males who have it will leave more offspring than those who lack it. That is because, by seeking variety, they will fertilize more females. Therefore, the CGC will spread through the population. In Darwinian language, the CGC will be *selected for* because of the advantage in reproductive success—number of descendants—it confers. For females, this is not true. A female, in our example, can have just forty children, no more—whether she mates with many men or only one. She cannot increase her number of offspring by seeking variety. So a tendency to seek variety should evolve—but only in males.

In theory, then, there might be a biologically based tendency for males to seek sexual variety. It could have evolved simply because ancestral forms that had that mechanism left more descendants than those that did not have it. And the life forms of today *are* the descendants.

So goes the argument. It is the kind of argument characteristic of the area of research and thought known as **sociobiology**—the application of evolutionary theory to social behavior.

Does this argument apply to humans? Human sexuality is subject to so many influences that it is hard to tell, as we noted earlier. However, Alfred Kinsey did conclude: "Among all people everywhere in the world, the male is more likely than the female to desire sex with a variety of partners."[26] For us, the important thing to see is how the responsiveness to subtle stimuli, such as those that signal novelty or variety, might have evolved, and how its evolution would depend on its effect on reproductive success.

WHAT SOCIOBIOLOGY DOESN'T SAY   Since we have touched on sociobiology here and will touch on it again, it is worth pausing a minute to get clear on what the theory says—and what it doesn't say. The approach has led to many misunderstandings (Fig. 4-7).

Even textbooks contribute to the confusion. Thus we read: "The male, sociobiologists argue, has one prime goal—to transmit as many personal genes as possible into the next generation."[27]

That's simply wrong. The theory says that animals have urges to *mate;* and perhaps, among males, a subsidiary urge to seek sexual variety. And the mechanisms that promote these variety-seeking urges might have evolved in males, because they *had the effect* of increasing reproductive success among ancestral forms. "Reproductive success" is not a cause or a goal, but an effect, of action—and an effect of our ancestors' actions, not our own.

A "goal to propagate our genes" need play no role in the behavior of any actor, modern or ancestral; and the theory assumes no such goal. No one says those rams are *trying* to pass on their genes. Rams know very little about genet-

26. Quoted by Barash, 1979, p. 49.
27. Weiner, 1989, p. 59.

Figure 4-7 "Because my genetic programming *prevents* me from stopping to ask directions—*that's* why!" How *not* to understand sociobiology. (Drawing by D. Reilly; © 1991, The New Yorker Magazine, Inc.)

ics, and one doubts that they grasp the connection between the pleasant activity they engage in now and the appearance of little lambs some time down the road. (Not all adult humans are aware of that connection!) They are trying to mate, that's all; and they are responsive to variety, presumably because their brains are "wired" that way. The question is why *that* is so, and sociobiology offers a possible answer.

Just as wide of the mark are questions like "How . . . could sociobiologists account for the fact that today so many males are undergoing voluntary sterilization?"[28] A sociobiologist would reply: "Not only is that not a problem, it is not even relevant. A vasectomized male can continue to enjoy sex; he might even display the Coolidge Effect, if he finds sexual variety arousing and/or rewarding. And if he does, this *might* be because the masculine brain has evolved that way; and ours is a theory as to how it might have evolved that way."

THE PRACTICAL NON-IMPLICATIONS   Another and even larger literature of needless controversy has swirled around the question: What are

28. Weiner, 1989, p. 60.

the practical implications of sociobiological theory? The answer, I think, is: There aren't any.

Here the misunderstanding is expressed by such remarks as this: "Sociobiologists also seem to suggest that aggressiveness is natural and desirable. Thus, efforts to control aggression can be seen as doomed to failure and even morally questionable, because they interfere with the natural order of things."[29] (Aggression is of course a different topic from sexual variety-seeking, but the issues that arise are similar.)

Wrong on all counts!

Let us be clear: *If* there is an untaught tendency for males to seek variety (or to aggress), this does *not* mean that they will necessarily do so, or that they must do so, or that they can't help doing so. This takes us back to the point I made earlier: Untaught means *untaught*. It doesn't mean *unteachable*.

We have evolved certain behavioral tendencies that are indeed very hard to modify. Prick the finger with a pin, and the reflex that jerks the finger away will be very difficult to suppress. At the other end, rats have evolved a preference for sweet fluids. That preference is untaught, and very strong. Yet it is not only possible, it is quite easy, to reverse that preference with a single learning experience (pp. 257–58). So the argument that "if a behavioral tendency is the product of zillions of years of evolution, it will be very hard to change" is simply false.

The human Coolidge Effect, *if* there is one, is certainly more like the sweet-fluid case than the finger-jerk case. Human males can learn to be monogamous. There is no possible argument here; the evidence is before us in every male who is in fact monogamous. And whether males today would be happier if they were *not* monogamous is a different question:

> Perhaps it is true that for many married couples, the quality and quantity of sexual experiences . . . would be enhanced by participation in sexual behavior outside the marriage. *But this does not mean, necessarily, that the marriage would be strengthened.*[30]

Human relationships, even sexual ones, involve much more than sex.

The point is this. *If* we have evolved untaught tendencies to seek variety (or to aggress in certain situations), they are just that—tendencies. Other influences—cultural and cognitive ones, for example—could be much more powerful influences in any given situation. And they could well override any untaught tendencies we might bring to that situation.

Thus, the importance of sociobiological theorizing is not in its social implications—it has none—but in that it invites us to look at human and animal behavior with some new ideas. It could help us understand how certain behavioral tendencies evolved over evolutionary time spans, and thus came to be the way they are in creatures living today.

29. Rathus, 1990, p. 25.
30. Bermant, 1976, p. 101; italics in original.

(I cannot resist one final point: The notion that interfering with the "natural order of things" is "morally questionable" is manifestly absurd, and no sociobiologist, to my knowledge, has suggested anything of the sort. Disease germs are part of the "natural order of things." Is it morally questionable to combat them?)

Sexual Motivation—A Look Backward

What sort of system is sexual motivation, as we have developed it so far? Figure 4-8 puts some of the pieces together.

INTERNAL AND EXTERNAL CONTROLS   In at least some species, internal hormonal factors are necessary for sexual arousal. Even in humans, if hormone levels are low, hormone treatments can enhance arousability. However, hormones exert their effects by promoting responsiveness to *external* stimuli—a partner or potential partner, or the signals the partner generates—just as internal factors may affect the response to food. In sex, as in feeding, this effect *may* be exerted by way of the attractiveness of the stimuli—alliesthesia.

But whereas hormones may provide a background priming or encouragement of sexual motivation, sexual arousal is produced over the short term by *external* means. In humans, even a picture of an attractive person can produce sexual arousal that was absent before. And sexual arousal is primarily a response to those stimuli, not to the hormones themselves. The Coolidge Effect shows dramatically the importance of external influences on mating. The effectiveness of a just-mated-with partner is reduced, while responsiveness to other partners remains strong.

We are reminded of taste-evoked feeding or dietary obesity (see pp. 87–89). In affluent societies, even eating is more often pulled from without than pushed from within. The same is true of sexual behavior, especially in complex creatures.

NEGATIVE FEEDBACK AND HOMEOSTASIS   Is sex a negative-feedback loop? Is it a homeostatic system? The answer to the first is yes; to the second, no.

As to the first question, we know that sexual activity is self-limited, producing a kind of satiety that brings arousal to an end. That qualifies the system as a negative-feedback loop: Sexual arousal leads to mating, and some consequence of mating decreases sexual arousal—at least as directed toward that partner. In that sense the behavior acts to reduce the motive that aroused it.

However, it is not a homeostatic system. In Figure 4-8, the negative feedback depresses *sexual arousal*. Or it *might* decrease the arousing properties of the specific partner, leaving arousability by other partners high. That is one way of interpreting the Coolidge Effect. Either way, it does *not* control internal hormone level.

Therefore, sex hormone level is not *regulated,* in a homeostatic sense, by sexual behavior. In thirst, the body loses water, the animal drinks, and water is

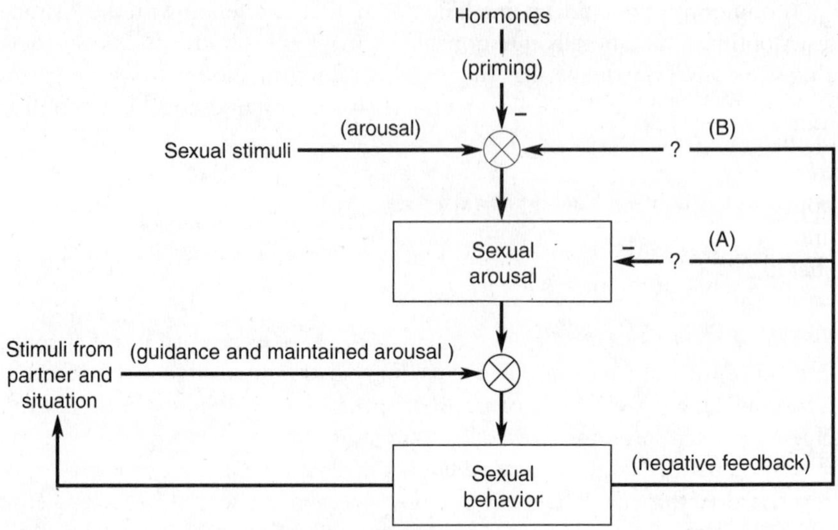

Figure 4-8 Sexual motivation as a negative-feedback loop. Mating depresses sexual arousal (A) or the arousing properties of the stimuli from that particular partner (B). It does not, however, feed back to affect hormone levels.

restored. But mating does *not* depress the male rat's androgen level from too high to normal. Indeed, androgen level may even *rise* after mating.

Rather than acting as regulated variables, then, the sex hormones act to *support,* or *permit,* sexual motivation when the appropriate stimuli arise. As one writer puts it:

> The individual deprived of sexual outlet does not perish, regardless of the length of time involved. No genuine tissue or biological needs are generated by sexual absti-nence. . . . To a much greater extent than is true of hunger or thirst, the sexual ten-dencies depend for their arousal upon external stimuli.[31]

Finally, before moving on we should remind ourselves just how oversim-plified this is. In Figure 4-8, the box innocently marked *sexual behavior* includes the whole complex hierarchy of Figure 4-2—and that figure just shows the stickleback's hierarchy. In more complex animals, we find learning and, in humans, culture modulate the system at every step and at every level. We turn to that topic now.

THE ROLE OF LEARNING AND CULTURE

The stickleback's mating pattern can be elaborated by learning. Its basics, how-ever, are untaught, and a quite uneducated stickleback can mate successfully the first time it sees another stickleback.

But we also recall our rule of thumb in sexual behavior. As we go to more complex animals, there is progressive emancipation from hormonal control,

31. Beach, 1956, pp. 4–5.

and other factors become more important. Among these other factors, learning is prominent and powerful.

Animal Investigations

Even in rats, experience plays a role. A male rat may mate normally on its first opportunity. In that sense, its sexual behavior, like the stickleback's, is untaught. However, castration in male rats has much more prompt and severe effects in sexually naive males than in experienced ones. And certain handicaps—inability to smell, for instance—are serious sexual stumbling blocks for an inexperienced male, but are readily overcome by experienced ones.[32] In short, sexual experience is not necessary for mating in male rats, but it helps.

In female rats, learning is even less important. Handicaps to mating seem to have about the same effect in experienced as in naive females. This sex difference, too, diminishes as we go to more complex creatures.

When we look at *primates,* learning may change from a luxury to a necessity, at least for some species. The psychologist Harry Harlow has observed sexual behavior—what there was of it—in male monkeys reared in isolation, and then given access to hormonally receptive females. He describes it thus:

> When these infant monkeys reached sexual maturity, we attempted to set up a breeding colony. . . . [But] of those lab-reared males who made any attempt at amorous advances, some created bizarre sexual scenes by mounting the head of the female, while others grasped the midbody of the female and thrust laterally, leaving them totally at cross purposes with reality. It was not surprising that the morale of our lab-reared monkeys was not very high . . .[33]

It appears at first glance that, deprived of learning opportunities, the monkeys were deprived of sexual behavior too. But when we look again, we see that some fragments survived. It is as if the monkeys knew that they wanted *something,* and that it involved the females, and even which organs of their own were crucial. What they lacked, it seems, was not sexual motivation but the skills necessary to express it. As Harlow comments mournfully, "Their hearts were in the right place even if nothing else was." They seemed to be confused about the means, and not, so to speak, the end.

If this is so, then we might suggest that the *top* levels of the Tinbergen hierarchy were functioning in these monkeys. Hormones, together with the stimuli from the female, promoted sexual arousal and directed it toward the female. But it was expressed ineffectively because the monkeys lacked specific skills at lower levels of the hierarchy. The motivational state was like a general with incompetent field officers: The aim was there, but not the tactics for achieving it.

We may see something like that in the human case, too. Let us look.

32. Beach, 1956.
33. Harlow, 1976.

Children without Cultures

In most human beings, sexuality is subject to intensive teaching by the society in which one lives, so much so that it is hard to tell what, if anything, is instinctive. However, there are a few rare cases in which such cultural conditioning is absent. What does sexuality look like then?

THE WILD BOY   On January 9, 1800, a boy about twelve years old wandered out of the woods into a village in France. His behavior was animal in almost every respect. He was naked except for the tatters of a shirt and showed no sign of relating himself to the people who captured him. He had no speech, and was, as a commentator delicately put it, "unhousebroken." No one knows where he came from or how he had lived to that time. No parents claimed him.

Most of what we know about the Wild Boy comes from the reports of Jean-Marc Itard, who worked with the boy, named him Victor, and tried to teach him to speak. These reports were concerned primarily with Victor's cognitive and linguistic development, but some notes on his sexual development are revealing.

When Victor was about seventeen, his training program hit a snag: puberty. Itard wrote:

> I saw this long-awaited puberty arrive, or rather explode. Our young Savage has been consumed by continuous and violent desires without the faintest idea of their object and without the slightest preference for any woman. . . . I have seen in him only a kind of groping and feeble instinct making him prefer the company of women to that of men. . . . Several times I have watched him in a group of women seek to calm his tenseness by sitting down next to one and squeezing her hand, her arms, her knees. Continuing these bizarre caresses, he would feel his unruly desires grow stronger instead of disappear. Then, seeing no way out of his uncomfortable emotions, he would change mood completely. He would push away the woman he had first sought out and go through the same process with another.[34]

As with all such case studies, it is always possible that Itard, or we ourselves, are reading too much into what happened. Yet the behavior does sound familiar. We mean no disrespect to Victor when we say that his behavior is reminiscent of Harlow's unsocialized monkeys. He seemed to want *something,* and to want it from women—but did not know how to seek it or even what it was. In any case, some fragments of apparently sexual urges were directed toward women, without, as far as we know, any explicit cultural conditioning that might have taught such actions to him.★

34. Quoted by Shattuck, 1980, p. 152.

★After Itard gave up his training, Victor lived on for 22 years with a Madame Guerin. He never did learn to speak, or to form any but the most rudimentary social attachments. A state pension kept him alive, and when he died, no one noticed.

GENIE   The case of Genie is one of the most dramatic episodes known of growing up without a society. It is also one of the most tragic.

Genie was discovered in 1970. Her father disliked children and wanted none; when his first child was born, he put the child in a garage so that he would not have to hear her cries. She died of pneumonia and exposure. Later, Genie was born into this family.

The details of Genie's first 20 months of life are unclear. We do know that after that, Genie was confined to her bedroom, harnessed, with a harness the father had sewn himself, to a baby's potty seat. She seldom heard speech, and, beaten for making noise, she made none. She was fed baby foods and cereals, hurriedly. She spent her days alone in that harness, her nights sewn into a sleeping bag, until she was *14 years old.*

Genie's mother, "too blind to even dial the phone and forbidden under threat of death to contact her own parents, felt helpless to do anything" over these years.[35] She finally did leave her husband, taking Genie with her. Genie was at once hospitalized for extreme malnutrition. The father committed suicide.

Susan Curtiss, a psychologist, worked with Genie as Itard had worked with Victor, trying, successfully this time, to teach her to speak. Like Itard, Curtiss focused on cognitive and linguistic development. But, as Itard had, Curtiss also saw puberty explode:

> Today Genie revealed an adolescent crush on Mr. B., her school bus driver. When I mentioned his name to her, she blushed and held her hands over her face. She also talks about him incessantly, mentioning him over and over. Today I asked her, *Who is Mr. B.?* Genie answered *Mr. B.* She was overcome—blushing, she was unable to verbalize.[36]

Elsewhere, Genie talked as specifically as she was able about her sexual feelings involving Mr. B. She said in her fragments of English:

> Mr. B. hand.
> Mr. B. have hand.
> Mr. B. tickle vulva.
> Finger tickle vulva.
> Genie vulva.

Now it seems clear that nothing like that had ever happened. These were fantasies, to which Genie clearly attached some desire. There are two dramatic implications here. One is that her adolescent body chemistry triggered her desire for that kind of touching. The other is that it targeted these desires on a

35. Curtiss, 1977, p. 7.
36. Ibid., p. 42.

specific person, from whom she wanted the touching. And the wish was not targeted on Susan Curtiss, whom Genie knew much better, but on a male.★

To summarize: In the actions of both Victor and Genie, there was evidence of vague sexual desires, but also evidence that they were *directed* in each case toward a member or members of the opposite sex. If so, then the stimuli that identify conspecifics as male (for Genie) or female (for Victor) must have become more powerful stimuli for approach, or simply for desire, than the converse set of stimuli. And it must have been hormonal state that made them so. We cannot see what else it could have been.

Quite possibly, then, certain hormonal conditions can produce *untaught* urges and orientations, in humans as in sticklebacks. But humans, unlike sticklebacks, must learn the means of implementing those urges. And, as we will see in the next section, such hints from the hormones can be modulated or even overruled by the learning experiences a culture provides.

Culture and Human Sexuality

Among the Mangaia of Polynesia, males and females become active in sexual relations at early adolescence. Sex is a highly and frequently enjoyed aspect of living. It is not unusual for couples to engage in intercourse three or four times a night, five or six nights a week, and to keep to that schedule for years on end.

In contrast, the Dani of New Guinea show little interest in sexual activity. Intercourse does not occur before marriage and, after marriage, may not occur for the first 2 years while the couple are establishing their residence. After childbirth, there is no sex within the marriage or, apparently, outside it, for 4 to 6 years.

One is led to wonder what rigid social controls, or what feats of self-control, permit the Dani to starve themselves sexually in this way. But the Dani reply: None. They do not report feeling any stress, tension, or deprivation. Sex just is not that big a part of life for the Dani.[37]

Multiple Levels of Cultural Influence

In human sexuality, cultural learning takes hold at every level of the already complex system.

★One might argue that if Genie was going to direct her urges toward anyone, the odds were about even that the target would be male. But Genie developed several other crushes, all on men, and Victor made repeated overtures to different women.

After Curtiss' book was published, the issue of who was to be responsible for Genie's care became a nightmare of conflicting claims and litigation. At the most recent report I have found (Rymer, 1993), Genie was living in a home for retarded adults.

37. Mahoney, 1983.

SEXUAL AROUSAL   First, consider the *stimuli* provided by the partner and the situation. We have already noted the wide cultural variation in standards of sexual attractiveness; beyond that, there is the matter of who is, or is not, even *considered* as a possible sexual partner. In our society, many people find the idea of homosexual relations disgusting, just as they are disgusted at the notion of eating toasted ants! But in one important cross-cultural survey, fully two-thirds of the societies studied regarded homosexuality as normal and permissible, at least for some age groups. Some societies even encourage it.[38]

Finally, the differences between three societies—the Dani, the Mangaia, and our own—suggest that the frequency of sexual arousal or interest, high in the hierarchy, varies greatly with culture and circumstances. If sexual arousal is a response to a set of sexual stimuli, then frequency of arousal will depend on what is *defined* by the actor as a sexual situation, and how many such situations there are. If there are few such situations, sexual interest will rarely be aroused. Perhaps that is the case with the Dani.

In short, hormones may provide a necessary underpinning for *potential* sexual arousal. But actual arousal depends on what situations we encounter, *and* how we have learned to interpret them. Our cultural training selects those stimuli that define permissible sexual partners and courtship situations. One culture filters out same-sex persons as sexual partners; another does not. One culture teaches its members to be aroused by large buttocks or feathers in the nose; another does not.

COURTSHIP   Once a sexual situation arises, culture selects those responses that are permissible, and that are effective—in that society—as ways of attaining the goal of sexual contact. The social skills that Victor lacked are taught to those who do grow up within a society.

Consider the preliminary courtship or approach phase. In some cultures, courtship may begin with a request for a date during a casual conversation. In others—for example, in traditional Japanese families—it begins with a conversation between the respective parents.

Conversely, we may be taught what *not* to do, and when not to do it. In an especially clear demonstration of this process, a group of young American men and women watched an erotic film, and then worked together for a while. After the film, there were *fragments* of sexual advance; the subjects stood somewhat closer to members of the opposite sex, and gave them more sidelong glances. But there were no overt sexual overtures, much less mating behavior. Of the many behaviors that the film may have primed or aroused, the ones expressed were strictly limited to those permitted in social situations in this society.[39]

38. Ford and Beach, 1951.
39. Griffitt, May, and Veitch, 1974.

MATING   After the male stickleback encounters a female—the releasing stimulus—its behavior becomes stimulus-bound and untaught. Human sexual behavior does not; it remains goal-directed and largely taught.

First, culture defines permissible mating situations. In this society, we seldom make love in public. Some other societies find nothing objectionable in doing so.[40]

Then there are the actual movements involved in mating. Sexual intercourse can be performed with a wide variety of movements in a wide variety of positions. But within a culture, only certain positions and movements may be permitted, whereas others are prohibited, labeled "not nice," or punished by law. In American society today, for example, oral-genital sex is a crime in some states, even between consenting adults.

Conversely, varied techniques of love-making can be *taught* by the culture one lives in. In this society, sources of such education range from peers, to more experienced people, to how-to books.

SEXUAL GOALS   Even the goal is not fixed. At first glance we might suppose that orgasm is the goal. But consider that, for many people in this society, the *partner's* sexual pleasure is an important goal, and ways of achieving that goal may have to be discovered (Fig. 4-9). In fact, in this society, some people of both sexes pretend to have orgasms, so that the partner may feel that he or she has pleased the other person!

A Look Backward: Of Sex and Sticklebacks

What can we say about all this? How much of the stickleback do we see in human sexuality? A bit, perhaps, but very little.

We might expect that the instinctive component of human sexuality, if any, would be seen at the low levels of the hierarchy—the level of movements.

Figure 4-9   "Look at the corner apartment on the 12th floor. That's what I want you to do to me."

40. Barash, 1979.

What evidence we have, however, suggests the opposite. There may be untaught influences that promote diffuse sexual arousal at the top of the hierarchy, as suggested by Genie, Victor, and Harlow's monkeys. These may include untaught stimulus influences, including, perhaps, novelty or variety itself. But the *expression* of that arousal, at every level, is a matter of goal-directed learned responses, not of stimulus-bound, untaught ones. The latter seem limited to unskilled, diffuse approach and touching, as in Victor's case.

Culture as Filter: From Possible to Actual

One way of representing the situation is as shown in Figure 4-10. In humans, there is a wide variety of inputs, from the partner and from the situation, that *could be* effective in promoting sexual arousal, depending on the culture in which one is raised. A particular culture then acts as a kind of filter, so that only some of these potential turn-ons become actual ones.

Similarly on the action side. There are a variety of ways in which sexual arousal *might* be expressed, including perhaps some clumsy "untaught" approaches. In a given culture, some of these ways will be permitted, but others will be filtered out as inappropriate, naughty, ineffective in that society, or even "unthinkable." This latter looks forward to the notion of *cognitive availability,* of which we will say more in later chapters.

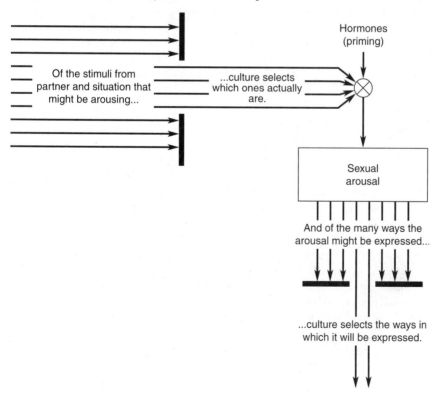

Figure 4-10 Culture as filter. A variety of stimuli are capable of arousing sexual interest—we know that because each one does so in some societies—but in any given society, only some of these will be arousing. By the same token, sexual arousal at each level can be expressed in a variety of ways, but in any given society, only some of them may occur.

We see this filtering at multiple levels of the hierarchy. Culture selects available actions from the range of possible ones at every step: how we approach a potential partner, how we form a sexual relationship with one, how we make love, and what the goals are when we do so.

Now this "filter" metaphor may be a useful way of visualizing the role of culture, but we need to remind ourselves that it is drastically oversimplified as shown. It omits the feedback features of goal-directed actions, for one thing. For another, it omits the role of skill acquisition: the ways in which our culture *teaches us how* to ask for a date, make a sexual advance, make love, and so on.

A Look Forward: The Problem of Internalization

One final point. As we have discussed it here, it is easy to think of culture as a set of commands, a set of dos and don'ts. The fact is, however, that the dos and don'ts of a society become *internalized* as our own values, preferences, and customs. We do not just *obey* them, we *share* them. We do not just do what society says, we also feel what it feels. Thus, for example, many heterosexual people in this society do not just refrain from homosexual activity, or oral-genital sex, because it is forbidden. Some find such ideas genuinely disgusting.

Why? How do we internalize a society's values so that they become our own? We do not know; indeed, that is one of the great mysteries of human motivation. What is clear is that it occurs, and with powerful effect.

SEXUAL ORIENTATION

The topic of sexual orientation looks backward over a number of topics we have considered to this point—internal and external influences, their interaction, and the role of learning and culture.

In the rat or the stickleback, mating is based on a stereotyped series of movements. Moreover, the male has his movements, the female has hers, and they are quite different from each other. Not so in humans. As you know, human beings have invented a great variety of postures and movements for love-making. And in face-to-face intercourse (which is almost uniquely human, by the way), the pelvic thrusts that create mounting excitement, perhaps leading to orgasm, can be performed by either partner or both.

In human, then, *sexual orientation* is not a matter of *what* one does, but with whom or toward whom. It is a matter of what *stimulus* complexes—what other persons—arouse sexual interest and can promote sexual approaches.[41]

In our own society, early survey data showed that about 40 percent of adult men had had some kind of homosexual experience at least once; and about 10 percent of adult women. Only about 10 percent of these, however, remained

41. For further discussion see Carlson, 1994.

exclusively homosexual. And a number of adults are bisexual, seeking and enjoying sex with both males and females. Thus human sexual orientation is not an either-or matter; there is a continuum from exclusive homosexuality, through bisexuality, to exclusive heterosexuality.

Again, these orientations have to do not so much with actions per se as with choice of partner. Thus we can compare sexual orientation to a kind of "window," through which, of all the cues from other people that *might* arouse sexual interest, only some actually do so for a given individual (compare Fig. 4-10). In bisexuals, the window is wide, so that cues from both males and females are effective.

What Determines Sexual Orientation?

There are a number of theories (including Freud's) that attempt to relate sexual orientation to early experiences or relations with the parents. We will deal with these very briefly, for a simple reason: There is no evidence for them. Study after study has failed to find any differences in home environment, early experiences, or relations with parents that distinguish people of different sexual orientations.

On the biological side, there also is no evidence that orientation is related to sex hormones in adulthood. As we saw earlier, very low levels of male hormones may be associated with low sexual interest in men, and treatment with hormones may raise it. Such treatment, however, only increases the level of sexual activity that ensues. It doesn't affect its orientation; if it was directed toward other males before, it continues to be.

If we don't see correlates of sexual orientation in blood chemistry, what about the brain? A great deal of interest has been generated by recent findings of differences in brain structure between hetero- and homosexual males. But as the investigators themselves point out, these findings—like all correlational ones—are ambiguous as to what causes what. Are the brain differences causes, or consequences, or just correlates, of sexual orientation?

We do know this much: What look like vague and awkward sexual advances can be directed consistently toward opposite-sex conspecifics, even without (as far as we know) any learning experiences that could have taught the subjects to direct them. We saw this in monkeys (p. 133), and something like it in Victor and Genie (pp. 134–36).

We also know this: Apart from their motivating role, sex hormones can have an *organizing* effect on the brain early in life. Let a genetically male rat be castrated shortly after birth, and then treated with estrogen at adulthood. He will display the female mating pattern. Converse effects occur in the genetically female rat treated with male hormones when newborn. Her brain is "defeminized" and "masculinized": She does not show the female mating pattern even if treated with estrogen, but she does show the male pattern if treated with testosterone.[42] In other words, the rat brain, in *both* sexes, is capable of

42. For review see Graham, 1990.

developing either as a masculine brain or a feminine brain, so far as sexual behavior is concerned—depending on the hormonal conditions to which it is exposed early in life.

Most of these studies have focused on the behavior patterns themselves. Surprisingly little is known about the key issue for the human case: Toward whom is sexual behavior directed? At least some studies do find, however, that "feminized" male rats show little interest in females, but attempt to attract males, and that "masculinized" female rats not only mount other rats in the male way, but specifically try to mount female rats. These findings suggest an inversion of the "target" of sexual interest, as well as of the movements that express it. If so, these data provide yet another example of the famous internal-external interaction. *Internal* hormonal events, early in life, affect how the brain handles *external* signals from fellow species members later on.

Now, that's rats; and we don't generalize from these to humans, for animals and humans may do analogous things for very different reasons. But the findings do tell us that it is *possible* for hormonal events early in development to affect sexual orientation in adulthood—to organize brains such that a creature responds sexually to opposite-sex cues on the one hand, or same-sex cues on the other—in some species at least.

Do early hormonal events affect sexual orientation in humans? Maybe they do, and many scientists expect a breakthrough along these lines in the next few years. But it hasn't happened yet.

It would obviously be impossible, and unethical, to conduct "masculinizing" or "feminizing" experiments in developing humans. Some researchers have taken advantage of natural "experiments" in which developmental abnormalities might have parallel effects on the organization of the human brain. We won't review these studies, for (1) they are complicated and would take much space to explain, which would be all right except that (2) their findings are inconclusive.[43]

A Look Backward

For now, we must leave the mystery at that. Putting all these pieces together, we still have only tantalizing fragments of the puzzle. Can sexual orientation be untaught? In some animals, clearly yes, and the cases of Genie and Victor suggest that it might be in humans as well. Do developmental events control the organization of the fine structure of the nervous system, so that the window of sexual interest comes to admit same-sex cues for some, opposite-sex cues for others? In some animals, it seems so. In humans the answer is: Maybe. It is not an inherently implausible idea, though it has yet to be demonstrated convincingly.

The fact that attitudes toward, and frequency of, homosexuality vary widely among cultures[44] does not weigh against this possibility. Cultural influences can

43. See Graham, 1990, for a review and critique.
44. Ford and Beach, 1951.

narrow or widen the window of potentially effective stimulus factors, or permitted actions, or both (pp. 136–40). And *if* the initial width and position of the window were set by biological events in the developing brain, cultural factors could still have this effect.

But "not inherently implausible" is the most we can say. Why do some people become homosexual? Well, why do some become heterosexual? The answer to both questions is: We don't know.

AGGRESSION: INTERNAL INFLUENCES

In some species, aggression is so closely linked with sex that the two might be considered a single motive. For example, let us return to the stickleback. In the male, both mating behavior and aggressive behavior are primed by male hormones. Whether the male fights or courts depends upon what releasing stimuli are presented, but the fish is prepared to do either one. And for good reason: The male must stake out its territory, defend it against intruders, and build a nest in it. No nest, no mate.[45]

Hormones and Aggression

This link between mating and aggression occurs in many species. Deer, for instance, are seasonal maters and seasonal aggressors. In the spring rutting season, the testes pour out androgens, and both sexual and aggressive motives appear: Males will court females, and fight each other vigorously.

All this suggests that fighting, like sexual behavior, might be responsive to male hormones, the androgens. It is. In many species, little or no serious fighting occurs before puberty, and after that it is mostly males who engage in it. A male rat castrated in adulthood is likely to show diminished aggression, which hormone treatment can reverse.[46]

In adult humans, the role of hormones is less clear. Throughout the world, men commit more violent crimes than women do, but this tells us little; is it a matter of sex roles, sex hormones, or what? Among males in this society, some studies do find that histories of violence and self-reports of irritability and hostility correlate with testosterone levels. Not everyone finds this, however.[47] And even if the finding were solid, what would it tell us? In some species, aggressive encounters may *cause* a rise in androgen level for the victors, and/or a drop in such levels for the losers. If some men have a history of violence— especially if violence has been effective in getting them what they want—then high testosterone levels could be a consequence of this, not a cause.

There are experimental studies in which effective testosterone levels have been reduced, as by castration or drug treatment; and reduction in aggression

45. Morris, 1958.
46. Brain, 1979.
47. Fausto-Sterling, 1992.

has followed. Many of these experiments, though, have been poorly done, failing to separate the effects of the hormones themselves from the effects of what we *expect* them to do. The matter remains controversial.

Lorenz's Hydraulic Theory

An influential theory of aggression also posits an internal factor that promotes aggressive action. This theory comes from the ethologist Konrad Lorenz.

VACUUM REACTIONS AND ACTION-SPECIFIC ENERGY   In birds and fish of several species, Lorenz noticed that if an action pattern has not been released for some time, it may be triggered at the slightest provocation. Most important, in animals who had not attacked or captured prey for a long time, the complete behavioral sequence of attack or prey capture might occur without *any* external releasing stimulus. Lorenz called such episodes **vacuum activities.**

To explain such actions, Lorenz proposed an internal pressure building up behind an action pattern, making it more and more likely to occur. Occurrence of the action releases the pressure, so that the response does not have much strength for a while. But then pressure builds up again, so that it takes a less and less powerful releaser to permit the response to occur. If the built-up excitation is very great, then the response can go off without any input from the environment. That, Lorenz thought, is why vacuum reactions occur.

The theory implies that if aggressive urges are denied expression, they will build up so that less and less provocation, or none at all, is required to evoke them. Earlier, Freud had taken a similar view: Unexpressed aggressive urges continue to press for expression, direct or symbolic (pp. 41–43).

All this is not so pessimistic as it sounds. Lorenz argued that in humans, aggressive energy can be drawn off in non-destructive symbolic ways (again compare Freud). Indeed, part of his argument in his influential book *On Aggression* is that we ought to seek more and better ways of accomplishing this, so that truly damaging human aggression, as in warfare, can be made less likely.[48] Aggression must have *some* outlet, though, and if it is denied one outlet, it will seek another. So the argument goes.

THE CATHARSIS HYPOTHESIS   We have presented Lorenz's theory because it introduced influential concepts and has received a great deal of attention. As a general theory of motivation and of aggression in particular, however, it has not fared very well. There are various reasons, but we will consider only one: the catharsis hypothesis.

A clear prediction from the theory is that an opportunity to fight should release the pent-up action-specific energy, and therefore reduce aggressiveness

48. Lorenz, 1966.

for a while. This is the **catharsis hypothesis**—that venting anger, or "letting off steam," allows aggressive urges to dissipate.

But this is not always true even in animals. In one experiment, a model male fish was presented repeatedly to a real male fish, who attacked it. Repeated presentations of the model led to an *increase* in the rate of attack reactions—not a decrease, as Lorenz would predict.[49]

Among humans *in this society,* something like the catharsis hypothesis has become part of the folklore. We speak of "ventilating" anger, or "getting it off our chests," or "letting off steam," as if these would drain off aggressive urges. The theory is often taken for granted. And yet there is a great deal of evidence that it is simply not true.

The fact is that expression of anger, either verbally or in action, is at least as likely to *increase* anger and further aggression as to dissipate it.[50] In one study, a group of boys was encouraged to play with violent toys, kick the furniture, and otherwise blow off aggressive steam. On later occasions, these boys were not *less* hostile and destructive, but *more* so.

What about verbal catharsis? In one study, a team of researchers interviewed 100 engineers who had been laid off by the local aerospace industry. Some of these subjects, but not others, were encouraged to express their anger at the company during the interview. Did this catharsis drain the anger out of their systems? Quite the contrary; the men who expressed anger at the company or their supervisors were *more* angry at the end of the interview than those who did not.[51]

Then there is the notion that watching violent games, or violent television shows, provides symbolic catharsis for our aggressive urges. This theory is argued vigorously by followers of Lorenz, followers of Freud, and television producers; but there is now a great deal of evidence on this point, and it says just the opposite. Watching violent television, for example, is much more likely to increase violent behavior than to reduce it.[52]

We sometimes do experience a feeling of relief and well-being after telling someone we are angry, and why. It seems, though, that this happens when our action is likely to have some useful effect on the cause of our anger.[53] In other words, it may be the positive feeling that comes with progress toward a solution of a problem. Perhaps it is the anger-arousing circumstances, not the anger itself, that we get off our chests in such cases.

In summary, the physical or verbal expression of anger is at least as likely to feed on itself, increasing anger further, as it is to drain anger off. As one commentator says, "Letting off steam can make the atmosphere very hot and humid."[54] And: "For most of the small indignities of life, the best remedy is a

49. Heiligenberg and Kramer, 1972.
50. See Hokanson, 1970; Baron, 1977; Tavris, 1982.
51. Ebbeson et al., 1975.
52. Liebert et al., 1973.
53. Hokanson, 1970.
54. Tavris, 1982, p. 129.

Charlie Chaplin movie. For the large indignities, fight back. And learn the difference."[55]

A Look Backward: Is Aggression Inevitable?

Lorenz's hydraulic theory of aggression, and Freud's closely related one, do not stand up to the evidence. Aggressive tendencies do not necessarily build up as opportunity to express aggression is denied; nor are they necessarily drained off when aggression is expressed.

Lorenz's observations still need explaining, especially the vacuum reactions. We know little about them. But Lorenz's explanation, that they represent the escape of pent-up energy, is unlikely to be correct. There probably is no buildup of aggressive energy over time, and certainly none that makes aggression inevitable.

The same could be said of other internal influences on aggressiveness: They do not make it inevitable. Male hormones may enhance aggressive tendencies perhaps; but "[i]t is perfectly possible for . . . 17-year-old men with very high levels of androgen to be perfectly peaceful."[56] They might be even *more* peaceful without all that androgen, but if so, it would make little difference.

Then again, if such a man is peaceful, it may be because he is not provoked. This takes us to the topic of *external* factors in aggression.

STIMULUS EVOCATION OF AGGRESSION

If aggressive action is not an escape of pent-up internal energy, our next thought is to look to the *external situation* for its causes. What sorts of situations or stimuli call forth aggressive actions?

Kenneth Moyer has listed a number of stimulus situations that frequently cause aggression. He distinguishes among different systems of aggressive behavior on the basis of their arousing stimuli.[57] Let's consider a few of them.

Predatory Aggression

Predatory aggression refers to an attack by an animal on its prey, which it kills and eats. Our first thought is that this behavior is part of a hunger system, and is not aggression per se; but satiated animals will sometimes kill prey without eating it. The attack reaction may be released by appropriate stimuli even in the absence of hunger.

In any event, this probably is a separate system from the others. In cats, for instance, the form of the action—quiet stalking and a pounce—is quite differ-

55. Ibid., p. 253.
56. Kalat, 1981, p. 345.
57. Moyer, 1976.

ent from the rage reaction to pain, which includes arching the back, loud hiss-ing, and striking out with unsheathed claws.

Irritable Aggression

This kind of aggression is aroused by a wide range of aversive conditions. *Pain* is one. Pairs of mice or rats can be induced to fight by painful electric shocks.[58] Moreover, pain-induced aggression can be a motivational state, expressed by arbitrary responses. A squirrel monkey that receives shock may learn to pull on a chain to produce an object that can then be attacked.

Frustration is another frequent cause of irritable aggression. For example, if a subject is accustomed to receiving reward for some response, then the failure of the reward to arrive when expected can lead to aggression in pigeons,[59] chim-panzees,[60] and humans.[61] This happened with Victor on at least one occasion.[62]

Irritability in Human Aggression

Something like irritable aggression has been intensively studied in the labora-tory, with humans in this society. A frequently used procedure is as follows: Someone insults the experimental subject, or otherwise treats him badly. A lit-tle later, the subject has a chance to deliver electric shocks to the nasty fellow. Sure enough, subjects angered in such a way will deliver more shock than sub-jects who have not been angered.*

We will not review this literature, for the results depend on a wide variety of factors.[63] What is important for us now is that it occurs at all. It means that the subject will make an arbitrary response—pushing a button, for instance—to cause pain to someone. And so we have a motivational state, induced by exter-nal means—the insult.

Moreover, subjects in such experiments, if they have been insulted and angered, often will give more shock even to a victim who was *not* the insulter. This is the kicking-the-cat phenomenon; one takes out one's aggressive urges against an innocent bystander. It implies that the motivational state *widens the range of effective stimuli*—that is, the range of target persons against whom aggres-sion will be directed. It suggests a kind of priming of responsiveness to a per-son-stimulus by the motivational state. And—a final blow to the catharsis

58. Azrin, Hutchinson, and McLaughlin, 1965.
59. Azrin, Hutchinson, and Hake, 1966.
60. van Lawick-Goodall, 1971.
61. Barker, Dembo, and Levin, 1941.
62. Shattuck, 1980.
*Such experiments are usually disguised as learning experiments, in which the subject punishes his victim—the one who angered him—for making errors. Typically the subject only *thinks* he is delivering shocks, whereas in fact no shocks occur. So the measure of aggressiveness here is the frequency, duration, or intensity of shock the subject *thinks* he is giving to another person.
63. See Berkowitz, 1982; Geen and Quanty, 1977.

hypothesis—this aggressive behavior typically becomes greater, not less, as it is repeated.

This effect can be far from trivial. For example, an early team of investigators found an inverse relationship between the price of cotton and the number of lynchings of black people in the South, over the period from 1882 to 1930. They suggest that the frustration of economic hard times was turned into aggressiveness, which in turn was murderously directed onto the black community.[64]

Maternal Aggression

Then there is *maternal aggression*. This is an interesting exception to the general principle of greater aggressiveness in males. Among rodents it is seen in pregnant or lactating females, which attack, and often defeat, males that approach their nests or their young.[65] This sex difference is less apparent in primates; adult male and female baboons, for instance, may defend a baby baboon with equal ferocity.

A Look Backward: Aggression and Regulation

What kind of system do we have here? Let us start by asking the same questions we asked about sex. Is it a negative-feedback loop? Is it homeostatic? The answer to the first is: sometimes, in a way. The answer to the second is no.

Aggressive action may remove the source of aggressive motivation. In that sense, negative feedback may describe what happens: A rival male comes along, the male stickleback attacks, and chances are that the rival goes away. The behavior removes the conditions that evoked it.

However, this is not homeostatic regulation in the original sense. Even if hormones enhance the reaction, the initiating condition is outside, not inside. There is no evidence for any buildup of energy, or any other physiological imbalance, which aggressive action corrects.

To what extent is it instinctive? Does Tinbergen's analysis of stickleback aggression shed light on more complex creatures? To address that question, we must ask how much of the system can be said to be untaught. We will turn to that topic in a minute.

A Look Forward: The Role of Interpretation

But before moving on, we should note that even in the examples discussed, two problems arise for human aggression that stickleback aggression never encounters. First, you can't apologize to a stickleback. Second, you can't insult one.

64. Hovland and Sears, 1940.
65. Svare, 1983.

To take the second one first: In laboratory studies, irritable aggression is often induced by insults. That means that at minimum, the subject must first draw upon all the cognitive apparatus required to *understand* the insult, before he becomes angry. This at once takes us out of the realm of releasing stimuli, and into the realm of **interpretation of the situation.**

Then again, consider how someone may anger us, perhaps quite severely, and then *apologize* or *explain*. He may say, "I tripped," or "I can't see without my glasses," and thus assure us that his blundering into us and almost knocking us down was not intended as an insult. And the effect may be to remove our anger as if by magic.

Clearly, the study of human aggression will have to consider our interpretation of the situations and the actions within it, the beliefs we hold about it, and the causal attributions we make within it. Later chapters will have more to say about these matters.

AGGRESSION, LEARNING, AND CULTURE

Like sexual behavior, aggressive behavior can be affected powerfully by experience. In humans, *culture* is of overwhelming importance in determining whether aggressive motives are aroused and, if they are, how they are expressed. Again the parallel with sexual behavior is a close one.

Studies of Children

As with sex, culture is such a powerful influence that we wonder whether the raw material includes anything untaught or instinctive. One way of finding out is to study aggressive action in children, asking: What is the system like *before* culture is brought to bear?★

John B. Watson, the founder of behaviorism, was also an experimental child psychologist. He studied the development of emotional expression in children, and concluded that anger, as an action pattern, is untaught. In newborns it is released by hampering of movement (frustration?). And the pattern is easily identified: "stiffening of the whole body, the free slashing movements of hands, arms, and legs, and the holding of the breath."[66] Thus, even this arch-critic of the instinct concept allowed that "rage," in babies, has the properties an ethologist would call instinctive.

Later writers also have noted the appearance of classic "temper tantrums" at about 3 months of age, with striking, kicking, and characteristic facial expres-

---

★Our "children without cultures" are of little help here. Genie was punished for any loud or violent behavior that might annoy her father, and no doubt that included any aggressive actions she might otherwise have displayed. As for Victor, he did display flashes of aggression, but he might have learned to fight for food or self-defense in the wild. It is much harder to imagine that he could have learned his apparent sexual urges there. (True, he might have seen animals mate; but how would he relate that to himself and to women?)

66. Watson, 1924, p. 154.

sions. These seem not to be directed toward any particular target. In this society at least, such displays become less frequent as a child matures, though they are better directed when they do occur. It seems that a child does not have to learn to throw tantrums, but can and does learn not to.

These undirected tantrums *might* constitute an instinctive core of untaught action patterns, which are then elaborated, directed, *and suppressed* as the child grows up within a society. The pattern is seen in very different cultures and may be universal in small children. One writer says of a highly peaceful society, "[T]heir children seem to exhibit typical behavior [presumably angry or aggressive] toward thwarting agents. But they are *taught to be different* when they reach adulthood . . ."[67]

Taught by what? By the culture in which they grow up. Let us turn to that topic.

Culture and Human Aggression

As with sexual behavior, by far the most potent determinant of a human's aggressive actions is the culture in which he or she was raised. The characteristics of whole societies determine the levels of aggressiveness and violence that their members display. As we did for sex, we will consider just two examples of this diversity.

> In Tahiti, children are not rewarded for aggressive behavior by parents or peers. They are punished for it, not by blows but by parents' assurance that ancestral spirits will cause them accidents and bad fortune if they strike out. Tahitians have been described as "affable people who are slow to anger, who quickly get over any ill feelings, and who lack vengefulness and hostile aggressiveness. They are disinclined to create anger-provoking situations, and when they show aggression, it is generally expressed in words rather than physical fights.[68]

Children can be raised in a society like that, and fit naturally into it as adults. Or they can grow up in a society like this:

> All accounts of the Yanomamo [a tribe that lives near the Orinoco River in South America] are in agreement: They are one of the most aggressive, unpeaceful groups of people anywhere in the world. Fighting and intimidating others is a constant feature of their existence. The men demand immediate obedience from their women and frequently beat them to ensure it. The men also constantly "test" each other's "fierceness" and often fight among themselves over issues ranging from real or imagined insults to charges of committing adultery with each other's wives. Moreover, villages frequently wage war against each other, when the men's continual challenges and provocations lead to the ultimate aggressive behavior, the killing of human beings.[69]

67. Mandler, 1984, p. 165; my italics.
68. Bandura, 1973, p. 109.
69. Hunter and Whitten, 1976, p. 397.

Clearly, levels of aggression and violence, like frequency of sexual activity, can be modified up or down by the course of instruction that characterizes a society. And—again as with sexual behavior—cultural training affects both the situational arousal of aggressive motivation, and its expression in action once it is aroused.

SITUATIONAL AROUSAL OF AGGRESSION

The young wife leaves her house one afternoon to draw water from the local well. . . . On her return from the well, a stranger stops her and asks her for a cup of water. She obliges, and in fact invites the man home for dinner. He accepts. The husband, wife, and guest spend a pleasant evening together, and eventually the husband puts the lamp out and retires to bed. The wife also retires to bed—with the guest. In the morning, the husband leaves early to bring back some breakfast for the household. Upon his return, he finds his wife again making love with the visitor.[70]

At what point in this scenario will the husband become angry or aggressive? It depends on the society in which the actors live. A century ago, a Pawnee Indian husband would hurl a furious magic spell at any man who dared request water from his wife. An Ammassalik Eskimo husband would be showing common courtesy in offering his wife to a visitor; he signals the offer by putting out the lamp. But he would be very angry if the episode were repeated the next morning, without a mutual agreement to exchange mates. Most American husbands would resent any man who made sexual advances to their wives; in some communities the husband might kill the guest, and local juries would acquit him—the famous "unwritten law." But a husband of the polyandrous Toda tribe of southern India, at the turn of the century, would have found no grounds for anger at any point in the scenario.

The point is clear. Whether a situation arouses aggression depends on how we *interpret* that situation, and the interpretations are taught to us by our culture. A peaceful people, then, may be a people in which few situations are *interpreted* as grounds for aggression.

THE EXPRESSION OF AGGRESSION   Suppose we do interpret a situation as grounds for anger. What do we do about it? In this society, most of us feel that only a very serious situation justifies physical violence, but we are likely to feel that the verbal expression of annoyance—scolding the offender, let us say—is usually permissible. But even this is by no means universal. "Try getting angry in front of an Utkuhikhalingmiut Eskimo, as anthropologist Jean Briggs did, and you will be ostracized for your childishness."[71]

Finally, just as the details of mating behavior itself are constrained by cultural influences, so are the fine-grained details of the aggressive actions we do emit. Observations of Tahitian children provide an instructive example:

70. Tavris, 1982, p. 46.
71. Ibid., p. 44.

[L]ack of fighting is particularly striking among children in public settings. . . . [But when anger does get] serious in children's conflicts (I saw only two such episodes), the fashion of expressing a threat is carefully ineffectual. An offended boy chases his tormentor but never catches him, while other children look on with serious expressions. Then, giving up, the boy throws a small piece of dry coconut husk at his antagonist but carefully misses. Children are excellent marksmen in other kinds of throwing.[72]

It is as if, in this case, culture took hold of the action at a low level in the hierarchy—the finger and arm movements that give a missile its aim. The throwing itself *might* have been an instinctive action pattern. It is most unlikely that Tahitian boys are taught by their elders to throw things at each other; and after all, if a throw is aimed to miss, why throw at all? Perhaps there was an instinctive core to the action; but, if so, its details, at the finger-movement level, were carefully modified so as to ensure its harmlessness.

THE "CODE OF THE STREETS"

The inclination to violence springs from the circumstances of life among the ghetto poor—the lack of jobs that pay a living wage, the stigma of race, the fallout from rampant drug use and drug trafficking, and the resulting alienation and lack of hope for the future.

ELIJAH ANDERSON
(1994, p. 81)

On May 7 it was James Todd, a 65-year-old retired plumber, who stopped at a store in a middle-class neighborhood. . . . He accidentally bumped into a teenager and apparently didn't say excuse me or didn't say it fast enough or with an appropriate degree of respect. According to a witness, the boy felt "dissed." An argument ensued; then Mr. Todd left. As he walked home, the teenager caught up to him on a bicycle, pulled out a gun, and shot him point-blank in the head. Mr. Todd died instantly.

—*New York Times*, May 26, 1994

We do not have to go so far afield to see such diversity. Within the United States, there are profound regional or sub-cultural variations in what is considered grounds for aggression and in what behaviors are appropriate expressions of it. Let us look at what sociologist Elijah Anderson calls the "code of the streets."[73]

As noted in the passage quoted above, poverty and discrimination are endemic among American urban poor, and no doubt they set the stage for irritable aggression (pp. 147–48). In addition, however, many inner-city people—especially young males—adopt a set of informal, but clearly understood, rules of conduct which actually *require* a constant readiness for violent action. These rules are the "code of the streets."

At the heart of the code is *status*—being treated respectfully by others. This depends, first, on demanding respectful treatment. If one is treated disrespectfully—"disrespected" or "dissed"—one's status is being challenged and one must defend against the challenge or avenge it, by violence if necessary. Second, one's status is determined by possessions—expensive jackets, sneakers, or gold jewelry. But these too are invitations to challenges: "A boy wearing a

72. Levy, 1973, p. 280.
73. Anderson, 1990, 1994.

fashionable, expensive jacket . . . is vulnerable to attack by another who covets the jacket and either cannot afford to buy one or wants the added satisfaction of depriving someone else of his."[74]

One retains status by being ready, and being *perceived* as ready, for violent defense of it—one must be seen as someone "not to mess with." And one gains in status by reducing someone else's, as by dissing him and getting away with it, or by taking a possession of his. Hence challenges are a constant of inner-city life; ". . . there are always people around looking for a fight to increase their share of respect . . ."[75]

Because of this, an act that seems incredibly trivial to a mainstreamer—maintaining eye contact, for example, or an accidental bumping—may be taken as a challenge, and reacted to. Here we see it again: The surrounding culture determines how we react to aggressive challenges, *and* what we perceive or define as being such a challenge.

The clash between the "code of the streets" and the code of mainstream America, Anderson says, has set up a vicious cycle. The code fuels violence. The violence fuels the negative feelings that many middle-class people, white and black, have toward ghetto dwellers; and this in turn helps perpetuate the limited options that make that code one's only available route to respect and self-respect, and thus tightens its grip on those who live by it. "Unless this cycle is broken, attitudes on both sides will become increasingly entrenched, and the violence, which claims victims black and white, poor and affluent, will only escalate."[76]

A Look Backward: Is Aggression Instinctive?

Is there an instinctive core to human aggression? Perhaps the most important thing to see is that this is a theoretical question. Its social implications, one way or the other, are minimal.

Confusion arises here because the question has often been confused with another question: Is aggression inevitable? The two questions are different.

If we ask the first question—is aggression instinctive?—we are asking: Do people have to be taught to be aggressive? We don't know the answer for sure. Little kids do express an apparently untaught "rage" pattern. In the description of Tahiti, we are told that children are punished for aggressive behavior—not that they don't express any.

It is possible that aggressive motives, like sexual ones, are evoked by certain situations, but that cultural influences determine whether they are expressed in action, and if so, how. This could then be an example of a motive that *may* be instinctive in origin, but still modifiable by training.

If we ask the second question, we are asking: Can people be taught *not* to be aggressive? We do know the answer to that, and the answer is yes. The evi-

74. Anderson, 1994, p. 88.
75. Ibid.
76. Ibid., p. 94.

dence is before us, in every peaceful person and every peaceful society. Perhaps we can stop arguing about that, and get on with the teaching.

A LOOK FORWARD: CONFLICT AND CONVERGENCE

Two final complications, and then we will move on.

Motives and the Lattice Hierarchy

First, we should remind ourselves once more that in complex creatures, even the simplest actions are subject to multiple controls. We can see this clearly in the case of aggression. Think about a bombardier who kills people he never sees, by pushing a button. He may be doing his duty, calmly and without anger. Is the action motivated by aggression at all?

We face a similar problem in sexual behavior. A prostitute's mating behavior may not reflect sexual motives at all, but economic ones. Or consider violent rape. The movements of forcible intercourse may be sexual, but the motive, most writers agree, is not sexual but aggressive. If so, then rape is not a sexually *motivated* act. It is the crime of assault.

The problem arises even in feeding behavior. Consider pie-eating contests, or, a less exotic case, consider how we may eat to be polite to a host, and not because we are hungry.

Such actions provide yet more examples of the *lattice hierarchy* in behavioral organization, in which a given action may be called into play by different motivational systems in different people or at different times (Fig. 4-11). Any action may reflect any of a variety of motives, and these in turn may have little or nothing to do with each other.

Figure 4-11 Drinking behavior can be called into play by a number of different motivational systems, including complex social ones that have little to do with the biological causes and effects of fluid intake.

Conflict: Priorities and Compromise

The other major complication is this. In most human societies, sexual behavior is embedded in a complex network of expectations, obligations, constraints, and beliefs. Therefore, sexual motives must be balanced against many other motives. Sexual behavior will occur—if it does—only after resolution of the conflicts.

As an obvious example: Is sexual action *safe* in this situation with this partner? Adultery is punishable by death in some societies.

A less obvious example: Men of the Mae Enga of New Guinea believe that sexual intercourse puts them at risk for illness and even death, unless appropriate magical steps are taken to ward off the dangers. This may require the recitation of protective spells during the act of intercourse itself. Where such a belief is sincerely held, it is hardly surprising that sexual relations may be infrequent. In short, *sexual motivation* must be weighed against *fear of consequences,* real or imagined.

These are examples from sexual behavior, but obviously they arise with respect to any motive. Can we afford to buy a meal? We must consider that question, however hungry we may be. Is it safe to eat now? Is it polite to do so? And so on.

All this only scratches the surface, but that scratch is enough to reveal the complexities we face. Any serious discussion of human motivation must look forward to discussions of decisions, costs, allocation of resources, and other considerations that later chapters will address. And it must consider the multiple reasons that may exist for feeding, fighting, or even mating actions. In humans, even the biological drives stubbornly refuse to stay within their biological context.

SUMMARY

Sex and aggression are closely linked in many species, and resemble each other in some respects. Like hunger and thirst, they are subject to both internal and external influences. Unlike hunger and thirst, they are not homeostatic and do not serve to regulate any internal commodity. As a result they can be more variable in their expression and more modifiable by learning.

Ethologists study behavior in its natural environment. Early ethological researchers identified instinctive *action patterns,* patterns of movement evoked by characteristic *releasing stimuli.* In male sticklebacks, for example, attack patterns are released by the red underbelly of another male; courtship patterns are released by the swollen underbelly of a female. Action patterns are hierarchically organized; higher levels of the system activate lower-level components by priming their responsiveness to appropriate external stimuli. Thus releasing stimuli trigger courtship or attack only if hormonal conditions are appropriate.

Such instinctive action systems are characteristic of a species. And they are *untaught.* This means that their appearance in the animal's behavioral repertoire is not produced by any specific learning experience. It does *not* mean that learning cannot modify the action—a frequent source of confusion.

In some species, instinctive systems can articulate with *goal-directed* motivational states. In sticklebacks, behavior is variable and goal-directed until the releasing stimulus is encountered. From that point it becomes *stimulus-bound*, elicited by stimuli rather than directed toward a goal.

Sex in mammals, as in sticklebacks, can be influenced by internal messengers, the *hormones*, borne by the blood. In men, for instance, sexual interest and potency may be low if hormone levels are very low, and can be restored by hormone treatment. In women, ovarian hormones have not been shown clearly to affect sexual interest, but hormones secreted by the adrenal gland may do so.

But these hormones operate, in mammals as in sticklebacks, by priming responsiveness to external stimuli. The animal's hormonal state affects responsiveness to chemical signals (pheromones) or to visual or tactile sexual excitants.

Conversely, external stimuli can affect the body's hormonal state. In some species that, in turn, can affect readiness to mate; this has not been demonstrated in humans.

In some species, varied partners can keep male sexual behavior going much longer than a single partner. This *Coolidge Effect* may have evolved because males, but not females, can increase their numbers of descendants by mating with many different partners. Whether such a tendency operates in humans is controversial, but it is clear that if it does, it is just that—a tendency, among many other influences.

Learning can affect sexual behavior even in animals, where it seems to affect not so much arousability as the skills mating requires. Studies of children without cultures suggest that the same might be true in humans. With normal development in a society, however, culture selects and defines both the stimulus conditions for sexual behavior and the responses by which it may be implemented. This happens at each stage of a courtship-mating sequence. Even the goals are defined by one's culture, as when the society teaches us to seek a partner's pleasure as well as our own.

Sexual orientation appears to consist not so much in what actions one performs, as toward whom they are directed. Some humans seek and enjoy sex with same-sex partners or with partners of either sex. Thus sexual orientation is primarily a matter of what external cues, from what potential partners, evoke sexual interest.

Sexual orientation is not related in any consistent way to early experience within the family or to sex hormone levels. Animal experiments do tell us (1) that the mammalian brain, in both sexes, is capable of developing so as to organize either masculine or feminine mating patterns and (2) that hormonal inputs early in life can bias the brain toward one or the other pattern. Whether such events affect sexual orientation in humans is unclear.

As with sex, hormones may prime aggressive behavior, but they do not cause it directly. There probably is no buildup of energy behind aggressive activity, as Lorenz proposed. The idea that aggression drains off such energy—the *catharsis hypothesis*—has not been supported by the data in humans or animals. As with sex (and hunger), aggressive reactions may be triggered by the environment—by prey, pain or frustration, perhaps threat to the young, and others.

Human aggression, like sexuality, is shaped at every level by cultural training. We are taught what to be angered by and what to do about it. There are substantial differences, even between sub-cultures in Western society, as to what are grounds for aggressive behavior and what kind of aggressive behavior is appropriate. In the United States, the "code of the streets" defines even seemingly minor expressions of disrespect as justifying violent retaliation.

Is human aggression instinctive? If this means, "Is it partly untaught?", we are not sure. If it means, "Is it an inevitable part of our behavior?", the answer is no. We may not have to learn to be aggressive. We clearly can learn not to be.

Finally, aggression, sex, and even feeding and drinking can be responsive to many motives beyond biological ones. A full understanding of them must look forward to more complex mechanisms of decision-making, choice, and allocation of resources.

Biological Motives: Integration by the Nervous System

In previous chapters, we have introduced some of the complexities of motivational systems. They are responsive to multiple inputs, and expressed by multiple outputs, at each level of a hierarchical control system. Internal states affect them. External stimuli affect them. Internal states affect how external stimuli are reacted to, and conversely. And beyond that, an individual's learning history—especially the course of instruction a culture provides for its members—modulates the effects of inputs, the expression of outputs, and the relations between the one and the other.

Even the simplest biological motives must put a formidable number of pieces together. All these influences must be taken into account and translated into action. In all but the simplest animals, that job of integration and translation is done by the *nervous system*.

THE NERVOUS SYSTEM

The cells of the nervous system are the message lines of the body. They permit rapid communication between one part of the body and another, so that the body as a whole can take effective action. They permit the left hand to know what the right hand is doing—both literally and figuratively.

Nerve Cells and Synapses

Nerve cells, or **neurons,** come in a wide variety of sizes and shapes. Figure 5-1 shows a selection. These are the nerve cells involved in a simple *spinal reflex,* as described below. The thick arrows show the direction in which messages, or nerve impulses, travel from the sensory neuron across the synapse to the motor neuron and from there to the muscle.

Nerve cells communicate with each other across a structure known as a **synapse,** which comes from a Greek word meaning "sitting together and holding hands." The sequence begins with the fingers or *endings* of the presynaptic cell—that is, the cell before the synapse in the path the nerve impulses take. In this case it is the sensory neuron. At the synapse, other fingers grasp the postsynaptic cell—that is, the cell after the synapse. Here it is the motor neuron carrying messages out to the muscle.

As nerve impulses reach the presynaptic endings, they cause opening of the **vescicles** in which packets of chemicals are stored. These chemicals are the **neurotransmitters,** and they carry the messages from one cell to the next. Once released from their vesicles, they diffuse over to the postsynaptic membrane, where they affect the activity of the postsynaptic cell.

Affect it how? There are two things these neurotransmitters may do. At some synapses, they *excite* the postsynaptic cell. They cause it to generate nerve

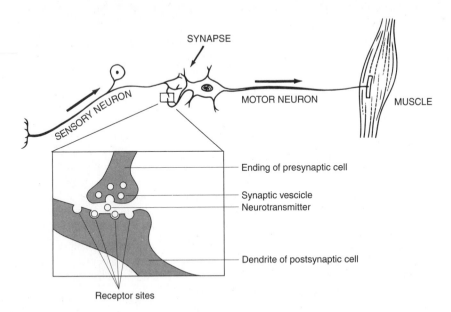

Figure 5-1 Two neurons and the synapse through which the sensory neuron affects the motor neuron.

impulses of its own, or make it more likely to do so. That is how a message is relayed from nerve cell to nerve cell. It is also how nerve cells can add their effects. If two cells converge on a postsynaptic cell, then input from the two of them together may produce more activity in that postsynaptic cell than either alone would do. This is known as summation, or **potentiation.**

At other synapses, the neurotransmitter *inhibits* the postsynaptic cell. It prevents it from generating nerve impulses, or makes it generate fewer. That is how one cell may shush another cell, silencing what it might otherwise say.

We notice that the list of a nerve cell's capabilities is not very long. A nerve cell's message can excite or inhibit the next cell in the chain. That's all it can do—and each synapse does either one or the other. And yet, these simple elements with their simple functions must somehow be able to generate all the subtlety and complexity of behavior. It is a dramatic study in how much can be done with how little.

PRINCIPLES OF NERVOUS SYSTEM FUNCTION

We have seen that what nerve cells do is excite, or inhibit, other cells. These provide the arithmetic of the nervous system—addition and subtraction, respectively. Further complexity and versatility arise from the geometry of the system. One input can trigger a *diverging* system of connections so as to have multiple effects. Or, different inputs can *converge* on a single output so that any or all of these inputs can affect it.

Let us see some examples of how these principles operate in producing behavior.

Inhibition and Excitation: Feeding in the Fly

The analysis of feeding behavior in the fly, strange as it seems, has set the standard for investigation of feeding mechanisms in other species. This is partly because of the elegance of the experimental analysis by Vincent Dethier and his colleagues,[1] but partly too because it shows just how engagingly simple a biological control system can be.

The next time you have a fly as a dinner guest, watch it carefully before chasing it away. Spill a few drops of something sugary on the table where the fly can find it. As it walks along, it probably will encounter your gift with one or the other of its forefeet. Then the feet on that side will stop moving, because movement is inhibited, while the legs on the other side keep walking. The result will be a tight pivoting movement that will bring both forefeet into contact with the fluid. The fly will then extend its *proboscis,* or mouthparts, into the fluid; and, like a little vacuum cleaner, the fly will suck the fluid in.

Proboscis extension is a reflex, whose stimulus is taste. We must get used to a wholly different world view at this point. The fly does not taste with its

1. See Dethier, 1969, 1976.

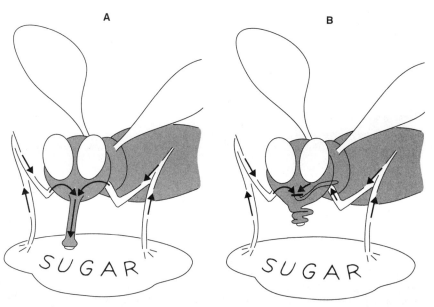

Figure 5-2 Feeding and satiety in the blowfly. (A) The fly, showing its taste receptors and mouth parts (proboscis). Taste receptors, triggered by a sugar solution, send messages to the brain that trigger the feeding reflex. (B) Satiety. Food in the digestive tract sends impulses upward to inhibit proboscis extension, even if the feet are still tasting food.

tongue, for the excellent reason that it doesn't have one. It tastes with its feet. The taste receptors are found in tiny hairs that extend out through the fly's external skeleton, on the soles of the feet (Fig. 5-2A).

If the sweet receptors of the foot are stimulated, nerve impulses are transmitted from the receptors up to the brain. If the fly is hungry, then several things happen. First, walking movements are inhibited, so that walking ceases. This keeps the fly from walking right on out of the nourishing fluid. If a foot on only one side is stimulated, then walking will be inhibited only on that side. The other side will keep walking, producing the tight turn into the fluid so that the sweet receptors on both sides are activated.

Second, proboscis extension and feeding will be elicited. In a hungry fly that tastes sugar, these occur as automatically as the withdrawal of our foot from a pinprick. This occurs because the nerve impulses, traveling from the feet up the sensory nerves, cause excitation of motor nerve cells that in turn drive the proboscis-extension muscles (Fig. 5-2A).

This reflex occurs if the fly is hungry. But when is the fly hungry? To make a long story short, the fly is hungry when this feeding reflex is not *inhibited*.[2] If the fly has recently eaten its fill, then the food inside its digestive tract stimulates internal receptors that trigger nerve impulses in another set of nerve cells. These impulses *cancel the excitation provided by the taste input* (Fig. 5-2B). Then, even if taste input is there, the fly stubbornly refuses to extend its proboscis and eat. Such a fly is satiated. Of course, once food has left the crucial place in the digestive tract, the inhibition is removed and the fly will be ready to feed again.

Here we have a system that can cause the fly to orient toward food and eat it, when—and only when—the fly has not recently fed. The cycle of hunger

2. Dethier, 1976.

and satiety, the process of food identification, the initiation and maintenance of the feeding response itself—all this could be provided for with only that much machinery.★ The body can do a great deal with very little, and the fly, a creature of reflex, gets around in the world very well indeed.

Divergence: Reflex Patterns

We now have some grasp of the basic functions of nerve cells—excitation and inhibition, the arithmetic of the nervous system. Now let us see how important the spatial layout of their interconnections is—the geometry of the nervous system.

When we discussed Descartes's theory of the reflex, we used as example a creature that flexes its leg in response to pain. Think again about such a creature. Suppose it has a four-point stance; it is a dog or a cat, let us say. We pinch its toe, and its leg flexes.

Obviously, if such a creature flexed its leg and did nothing else, it would topple over like a chair with a leg missing. Instead, the painful stimulus causes not only flexion but adjustment of the three other legs as well. The opposite foreleg tenses to take up the weight. So does the hind leg on the same side. The diagonally opposite hind leg flexes, to shift the center of gravity away from the limb that is no longer giving support. The result is a **reflex figure,** involving movements of *all four* legs even though only one foot was stimulated.

Each of these adjustments involves a pattern of contraction of one muscle, and relaxation of the opposing one. Each such pattern in turn reflects a pattern of excitation and inhibition of motor neurons, triggered through pathways in the spinal cord by the original painful stimulus.

Thus reflexes need not be isolated muscle twitches. They can be patterns of movement involving the whole body. These patterns are made possible by the *divergence* of nerve cells and their interconnections. A chain of events that begins with one foot, affects the actions of many.

Convergence and Multiple Control

We have seen that one input can have many outputs in the nervous system. Conversely, one output can be responsive to any or all of many inputs.

Think again about the response to pain in the foot. If we step on a tack, we are likely to flex that leg, and adjust the tension on the other leg so that it bears the added weight (a reflex figure).

That withdrawal reflex can occur without any involvement of the brain. It can be elicited in an animal without a brain, through the interconnections between nerve cells at the spinal cord. But we can make the same flexion movement *voluntarily,* and that does involve the brain. The motor nerve cells that drive the flexor muscles are the same. But this time, it is nerve impulses

★Though again there is in fact a great deal more; see Dethier, 1976.

coming down from the brain that excite those motor nerve cells. In short, we can flex a leg because of a painful stimulus—reflex flexion—*or* because we decide to do so—voluntary flexion. The two possibilities depend on two different communication lines that *converge* on the motor cells.

A Look Backward—and Forward

We have looked over the basic operations that nerve cells perform—excitation and inhibition. We have seen some implications of the spatial arrangements of nerve cells and their interconnections—divergence or multiple outputs, and convergence or multiple inputs.

As we move on to the brain, the thing to remember is that the *same principles continue to apply.* The concepts we have seen in action, in controlling movements, also operate in *whole organized systems* within the brain. Whole systems can be excited or inhibited; whole systems can respond to multiple inputs, with multiple outputs. The levels of complexity are vastly different; but the principles are the same.

Indeed, in looking back over this section, we recognize some familiar ideas. The nervous system provides communication lines by which multiple inputs can affect a single output. And we remember that motivational states, like hunger and thirst, also are affected by multiple inputs. The nervous system provides for divergence, or multiple outputs from a single input. Well, a motivational state can be expressed by different specific actions—it has multiple outputs! And we treated *satiety* as a mechanism that *inhibits* a hunger or a thirst system.

Let us look at how the brain performs these operations at the level of organized action systems.

THE CENTRAL NERVOUS SYSTEM

The **central nervous system** consists of the brain and the spinal cord (Fig. 5-3). These structures are densely packed collections of nerve cells and cells of other kinds. We do not show these cells individually, for there are about 100 billion of them in the human nervous system.

In Figure 5-3, the human brain is shown in side view, from the middle out. In other words, imagine that someone has sliced the brain down the middle, from front to back, and that we are looking at the cut. The shaded area shows a cavity in the middle, one of the **ventricles** of the brain. These cavities are filled with **cerebro-spinal fluid,** a kind of filtered blood plasma that can provide the brain with information about the composition of body fluids. The lower wall of that cavity, on each side, consists of clusters of nerve cells known collectively as the **hypothalamus.**

The entire system is a tube-shaped affair, closed at the top, with its fluid-filled central cavity. The figure shows the conventional divisions of the ner-

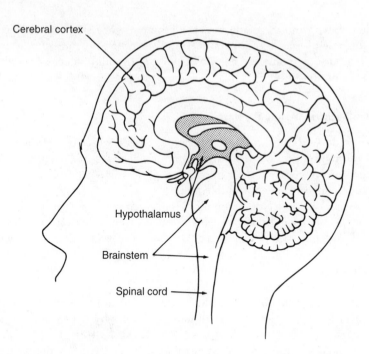

Figure 5-3   The human central nervous system, seen from the midline out.

vous system, which break it up into a series of *levels,* bottom to top. In the human brain especially, the structure appears to get more and more complex as we move upward. It does; and with that increase in anatomical complexity comes increasingly complex control over behavior.

LEVELS OF INTEGRATION IN THE NERVOUS SYSTEM

Now let's look at the *hierarchical organization* of control over movement. We will see how the brain directs action in the environment and integrates individual movements into *motivational states.*

Bard's Experiments: Hierarchical Organization

A classic series of experiments by the physiologist Philip Bard and his colleagues has shown the *hierarchical organization* of the mammalian nervous system.[3] The principle is: *Higher parts of the brain coordinate and direct the simpler components of action,* which themselves are controlled by levels farther down in the nervous system.

Figure 5-4 presents a highly schematized layout of the mammalian nervous system. It shows that the motor nerve cells, which drive skeletal muscles in mammals, emerge from the spinal cord.★ Above the spinal cord we find the

3. Bard and Rioch, 1937.
★There are exceptions to this that we will ignore.

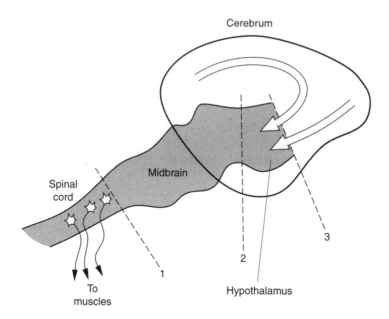

Figure 5-4 Schematic diagram of the cat central nervous system, showing levels of transection in Bard's experiments. The motor cells that drive the muscles emerge from the spinal cord. The cerebral hemispheres ("cerebrum") fold back over the brainstem on each side; their descending influences funnel down through the brainstem to affect the motor cells, as indicated by the open arrows. (From Gallistel, 1980.)

brain with its subdivisions. Its influence on movement is exerted by way of those motor cells that run out from the cord. In other words, the motor cells control the muscles directly, whereas the brain controls the muscles indirectly by controlling the motor cells.

It follows that if we *transect* the nervous system—simply cut it across—we will leave all structures *above the cut* out of communication with the motor cells, and hence unable to influence movement. Therefore, what we see in the behavior of the operated animal is the influence of structures *below the level of the transection.*

THE SPINAL CORD: REFLEX MOVEMENTS   Suppose then that the system is cut across at Level 1 in the figure. Now the brain is for practical purposes removed as an influence on behavior. The motor cells can only be affected by information coming from the sensory cells that enter the cord below the cut, and influence motor neurons there. Movements produced by that part of the system are called **spinal reflexes,** because they involve only the spinal cord, not the brain. The reflex withdrawal from a painful stimulus is such a reflex.

After transection at Level 1, then, the animal should be capable only of simple spinal-reflex responses to stimulation. That is exactly what Bard saw, using cats as experimental subjects. Once they had recovered from the operation, cats with Level 1 transactions were capable of local reflex movements. Prick the paw, and the limb would flex. Stretch the extensor muscle in one leg, and the leg would extend; this is the *extensor reflex*. That reflex is an important component of *standing,* and the Level 1 cat can make the movements involved in standing in each of its limbs individually. But it cannot put the individual movements together. It cannot stand up.

Some of the reflexes that remain, by the way, are specifically associated with higher-order systems. When its genitals are stimulated, a female cat in heat will respond by deflecting its tail to one side. That reflex is part of its mating pattern. A Level 1 cat retains this reflex. And, an interesting point to which we will return, it makes that response to genital stimulation whether it is in heat or not.

THE HIGHER BRAINSTEM: MOVEMENT PATTERNS   If one makes no cut at Level 1, but severs the nervous system at Level 2 instead, the picture is different. One now has a cat that can stand, and even walk. What remains lacking, however, is any adjustment of the movements to external or internal circumstances. The cat continues to deflect its tail upon genital stimulation, and it now may make the treading movements and arching of the back characteristic of the female in heat. But it does these things whether or not its hormonal state is one of heat. It does not approach males. It does not approach food. It can walk, but it walks without apparent purpose. It does not walk to or away from anything.

THE HYPOTHALAMUS: DIRECTED MOVEMENTS AND INTERNAL CONTROL   If the transection is still higher (Level 3), the result is different again. In this case, the cat does combine fragmentary acts into organized behavioral sequences. Thus, when its genitals are stimulated, such a cat displays the full-blown mating pattern, with loud growling, lowering the head and raising the rump, vigorous treading, and tail deflection. And—another distinct difference—the cat displays that pattern when its hormonal state is one of heat, and only then. Therefore, the pattern is controlled by hormonal state in a Level 3 cat, as in an intact one.

Strikingly similar findings were obtained with feeding behavior. A Level 2 cat could chew and swallow food placed in its mouth, but it never sought food, and it would chew and swallow the food whether it was starved or fully fed. A Level 3 cat would sniff, lick, and explore the floor with its mouth if food was placed in front of it—but only if it was hungry. And the longer it had been without food, the more vigorously it would explore. Clearly, with Level 3 transection, fragmentary movements are organized into effective locomotion and search, and the whole pattern is under the influence of nutritional status.

Also in Level 3 cats, emotional expression changed from isolated fragments to organized patterns. A pinprick on the paw would elicit reflex flexion in a Level 1 cat. A Level 2 cat might look angry or afraid, but would not withdraw or attack effectively. But a Level 3 cat would show the whole integrated pattern of rage, with crouching, hissing, erection of the hair, and striking movements of the forepaws with claws extended.

Before moving on, though, we should note that more recent findings have made the picture less clear. Harvey Grill and his co-workers have shown that

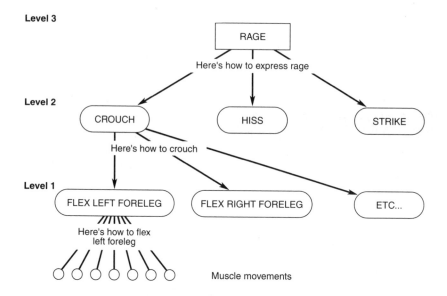

Figure 5-5 Hierarchical organization of control of movement by the nervous system. Each level combines elements or subsystems organized at lower levels.

laboratory rats, roughly equivalent to Bard's Level 2 cats, also do not approach food if hungry. However, they do seem to register hunger and satiety in their reflex responsiveness to liquid food placed in the mouth: If hungry, they will swallow the food; if not, they will let it dribble out. So some sensitivity to internal state does remain, even if the hypothalamus is disconnected from lower controlling systems.[4]

A Look Backward: Levels of Control

In short, when the hypothalamus and adjacent structures are in communication with the muscles, isolated movements are coordinated into organized behavior patterns and sequences—some writers call them *motivated* behavior sequences. It is tempting to see this as an example of *divergence* in the systems running down from the hypothalamus. Without it, fragments of behavior can be elicited *one by one*. But with it, descending systems diverge to excite *all the fragments at once* (Fig. 5-5).

We should note the definite parallels between levels of neural organization as discovered by Bard's work, the levels of organization of instinctive behavior suggested by Tinbergen (pp. 113–15), and the concept of hierarchical *motivational states* that we developed earlier. Lower-level movements—movements of individual legs in mammals or of fins in fishes—require only lower levels of nervous integration. Movement patterns—action systems at intermediate levels,

4. See Grill and Kaplan, 1990.

such as standing or walking—require that the midbrain be intact. Patterned sequences of behavior as in aggression or mating, adjusted to external *and* internal circumstances, are seen only if still higher levels of the brain remain in the controlling system.

Conversely, as we take more and more brain out of the system from the top down, the behavior falls apart. But what falls apart is the *organization* of components into patterns; the components themselves may remain. The organization must therefore be imposed by those higher levels.

DRIVES AND THE HYPOTHALAMUS

In looking over Bard's findings, we notice that the presence or absence of the *hypothalamus* makes a great difference in the organization of many forms of behavior. Since that time, much research in motivation has been concerned with that small bit of brain. It is a nexus within which multiple influences converge.

The next step was made possible by a technical advance. By the late 1930s, scientists had developed techniques that permitted manipulation of small clusters of cells deep in the brain. Small areas of damage, or *lesions,* could be made within the brain and their effects on behavior observed. Or one could place electrodes deep in the brain, fix them in place there, and later stimulate clusters of cells electrically in the conscious, awake animal. Finally, one could apply chemical stimuli—drugs, hormones, or neurotransmitters—to local sites within the brain.

The results of such studies led to an influential theory about how drives are mediated by the brain. Let us look first at the theory, and then at some of the findings.

Stellar's Dual-Center Theory

In 1954, Eliot Stellar presented a synthesis of the findings up to that time, and a theory of the role of the hypothalamus in motivation.[5] The basic idea (Fig. 5-6) is that motivated behavior reflects the output of **excitatory centers** located in the hypothalamus. These centers, or clusters of cells, are affected by sensory stimuli, whose messages are transmitted to the hypothalamus from elsewhere in the brain, and by stimuli arising from within the body and carried by the blood and cerebro-spinal fluid. The output of these excitatory cells is directed to other parts of the brain to produce motivated behavior. The consequences of that behavior influence the internal and external stimuli that began the process—the familiar *feedback loop.*

5. Stellar, 1954.

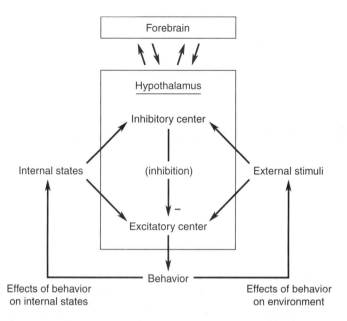

The activity of these excitatory centers is modulated by **inhibitory centers** that suppress them. These in turn receive multiple inputs from inside and outside the body. Thus the behavior that occurs is jointly influenced by inputs to the excitatory center that excites that behavior, and inputs to the inhibitory center that holds it in check. This already has a familiar ring, for we saw earlier that arousal of hunger and thirst (excitation) and their respective satieties (inhibition) both have multiple inputs (Chap. 3).

Notice one thing more before we go on. These excitatory centers are seen as exciting, or calling into play, whole organized motivational hierarchies *as units*. And when the inhibitory centers come into play, they exert their inhibition on entire hierarchies, again as units. This is the idea we looked at earlier: The principles of nerve-cell interaction, such as excitation and inhibition, also apply to *whole organized systems* of behavior.

Since Stellar wrote this paper, the picture has had to be modified in many ways, and many more details are known. Still, it remains a useful way of organizing our thoughts about motivation and the brain. Let us see how the data for specific motives fit into this framework.

Thirst

We saw earlier that there are two stimuli for thirst: dehydration inside the cells of the body, and dehydration outside them. It turns out that the two have different brain mechanisms, as well as different arousing conditions.

EXCITATION OF INTRACELLULAR THIRST   Gilman's original experiments dehydrated all the cells in the body by injection of strong salt solutions. In an elegant series of experiments, Elliott Blass and Alan Epstein showed that there are certain cells that signal their own dehydration, and thus serve as **receptors**—receiving stations—for the cell-dehydration signal.[6]

The receptors are in the **lateral preoptic area,** which lies just forward of the hypothalamus. Blass and Epstein first showed that localized lesions in this area could produce a rat that no longer drank in response to injections of salt solutions. The rat did drink in response to extracellular-fluid reduction—the other stimulus for thirst—showing that it was capable of drinking. It was only the intracellular stimulus for thirst that it no longer reacted to.

Then Blass and Epstein implanted cannulas in the brain, through which they could inject minute amounts of solution directly into the preoptic area. These injections were so small that they affected only the cells immediately surrounding the cannula tip. A fully hydrated rat, which ought not to have been thirsty at all, would drink vigorously when a tiny bit of concentrated salt solution was injected through the cannula. Conversely, if the rat's whole body was dehydrated by salt injection, but a bit of water was injected into the preoptic area, the rat would not drink.

It therefore appears that cells in the preoptic area are ones that register their own state of hydration or dehydration, and tell the rest of the brain about it. If we inject water into the vicinity of these cells, then even if the rest of the body is severely dehydrated, these cells say, "Don't bother to drink; there's plenty of water. We feel fine." And no drinking occurs. Conversely, the body as a whole may have plenty of water in its cells, but if *these* cells are dehydrated, they say, "Drink!"

These preoptic cells, then, may be ones that are excited by the dehydration of intracellular fluid and mobilize the drinking response.* Thus we have evidence for an *excitatory system* in the brain for intracellular thirst.

EXCITATION OF EXTRACELLULAR THIRST   The mechanism for this kind of thirst is much more complex, and will be summarized only briefly.**

One stimulus for extracellular thirst originates in, of all places, the kidney. James Fitzsimons showed that when there is a reduction in pressure of the blood flowing through the kidney, as a consequence of extracellular fluid depletion, a hormone called *renin* is released from the kidney into the blood.[7] Renin in turn reacts with a substance circulating in the blood to produce another hormone, called *angiotensin*.

Angiotensin in turn stimulates copious drinking. And it does so even if injected directly into the brain, suggesting that it activates cells there.[8] Here, then, is another excitatory system for thirst in the brain.

6. Blass and Epstein, 1971; see also Peck and Novin, 1971.
*There may be other such sensors as well; see Carlson, 1994.
**For discussion and other views see Stricker, et al., 1979; Epstein, 1982.
7. Fitzsimons, 1969.
8. Epstein, Fitzsimons, and Rolls, 1970.

It is likely that angiotensin affects the brain by way of certain specialized receiving areas, and these *circumventricular organs* are closely adjacent to—you guessed it—the hypothalamus. Injected into the right places, angiotensin (or the specific form of it, angiotensin II, that has this effect) is a phenomenally powerful stimulus for thirst, effective in picogram quantities. (A picogram is a *trillonth* of a gram, and a gram isn't much!)

INHIBITION OF THIRST   We have two excitatory systems, then, one for each thirst. What about inhibitory systems? One has been found.

Damage to the **septal area** of the brain, another structure just forward of the hypothalamus, produces a rat that drinks *too much* water.[9] The inhibition here is exerted specifically on the systems that respond to angiotensin, for the overdrinking is seen only when angiotensin injections, or manipulations that activate the renin-angiotensin system, are used to stimulate drinking. If cell dehydration is used to evoke drinking, the amounts taken in by rats with septal damage are quite normal. We have, then, not an *inhibitory center* for thirst as such, but something more specific—an inhibitory system, involving the septal area, that clamps down specifically on drinking stimulated by angiotensin.

Sexual Behavior

We saw in Chapter 4 how, in some species, adult sexual behavior is dependent on hormones. Castrated male rats gradually lose sexual interest, and spayed female rats do so abruptly and totally. Presumably the presence of these hormones in the blood is somehow conveyed to the brain, which in turn organizes and mobilizes the mating behavior itself.

In fact, the functioning of certain bits of brain tissue is quite critical for these hormone effects—and sure enough, the critical locations are in or near the hypothalamus. Mating in female guinea pigs, after it has been abolished by removal of the ovaries, can be restored by injection of estrogen—but only if the hypothalamus is intact. Lesions in the anterior part of the hypothalamus block mating even if estrogen is injected. In male rats, lesions in the preoptic area, forward of the hypothalamus, abolish mating behavior, and testosterone injections do not restore it.

Conversely, we can administer hormones to the brain through cannulas, to stimulate only the cells around the cannula tip. If these cells respond to hormones by promoting mating, then hormonal stimulation at just those sites should be enough to restore mating in spayed or castrated animals. And that is exactly what happens, in females and in males.[10] The whole story is very similar to the thirst one, summarized above. The animal's body may have no sex hormones in it; but if *these* brain cells see hormones, they say to the rest of the brain, "Sex hormones here!" And the brain knows just what to do about that.

9. Blass, Nussbaum, and Hanson, 1974.
10. Harris and Michael, 1964; Davidson, 1966.

It may well be that naturally occurring hormones act on these same brain sites to promote mating behavior. If so, then we have *excitatory* systems in the brain that couple mating behavior to the animal's hormonal state, just as other systems make drinking behavior sensitive to the state of hydration.

Hunger

Stellar's synthesis was strongly influenced by research on brain mechanisms in hunger. This research provides an especially clear picture of the strengths, and the limitations, of the theory.

THE VENTROMEDIAL HYPOTHALAMUS: HYPOTHALAMIC HYPERPHAGIA   The story began with the discovery of hypothalamic hyperphagia in the 1940s. Destruction of a bit of tissue near the midline in the hypothalamus, the **ventromedial nuclei,** caused rats to overeat and get fat.[11] A rat can easily double or triple its normal food intake after such damage to the brain. That is *hypothalamic hyperphagia*—"hyperphagia" coming from Greek words meaning "overeating."

Since destruction of a bit of brain tissue gives us an animal that eats too much, our first thought is that that bit of brain, when it is intact, must act to reduce the animal's hunger. And yet, paradoxically enough, such rats did not behave as if they were abnormally hungry. They might actually eat less than normal if their food was made slightly bitter. And if food was sweetened, they would overeat by even more than before, whereas intact rats might not change their intake at all.[12] It was as if, being less responsive than before to their internal state of fullness, the rats were that much more responsive to external influences such as taste. That idea, by the way, was one that influenced Schachter's *externality* theory of human obesity (p. 89).

All this fits well with the idea that the damaged tissue is normally responsible for signaling *satiety*. The hyperphagic rat may not be abnormally hungry, but may simply not know when to stop eating. Thus this part of the brain may be an *inhibitory center* of the kind Stellar described—an inhibitory center for hunger, a *satiety center*. This might be the place to which the different satiety signals from the periphery of the body—from the stomach, the intestine, the liver—send their messages that food has arrived. These messages could then activate the satiety center, and feeding would be inhibited.

THE LATERAL HYPOTHALAMUS   If one bit of brain inhibits feeding, does another bit of brain excite it? It certainly looked that way. Damage to the **lateral hypothalamic area,** just to the outside of the ventromedial nuclei, has effects opposite to ventromedial damage. It produces an animal that does not eat at all, and will starve to death unless rescued and force-fed.[13] Food may

11. Hetherington and Ranson, 1939; Brobeck, Tepperman, and Long, 1943.
12. Teitelbaum, 1955.
13. Anand and Brobeck, 1951.

be all around, but a rat with lateral hypothalamic damage ignores it, even while starving.

Added evidence came from studies using electrical stimulation of the brain to excite cells artificially. When such stimuli were applied to the lateral hypo-thalamus, fully satiated rats could be made to eat vigorously, and even to get fat if stimulated often enough.[14]

It all seemed to make a simple and coherent picture. The stimuli for hunger, whatever they are, may act directly or indirectly on cells in the lateral hypothalamus. Perhaps these cells are the generals, who send down a command that tells the body-moving field officers in the midbrain, "Eat!" or "Eat until further notice!" Then the meal ends when the satiety signals activate ventro-medial cells. These report, "Mission accomplished!" to the feeding cells; the command to eat ceases, and the animal can go on to other business. It seemed so straightforward that, for a while, researchers spoke of a lateral hypothalamic "feeding center" and a ventromedial "satiety center."

Unfortunately the situation is not so simple as all that; and while the basic idea may hold—an interplay of excitatory and inhibitory systems—few people talk about feeding centers and satiety centers any more. But before we look at the complications, let's explore the general theory further.

Brain and Environment: Modulation of Stimulus Effects

Stellar's dual-center theory, like Bard's work on hierarchical organization, sees the hypothalamus as combining fragmentary response systems, organized at lower levels, and calling them into play as units. How does the system do that? How does it produce movement patterns?

The most likely answer is the one we are familiar with. Systems higher in the brain may prime, or *potentiate,* systems that are in turn responsive to *external* stimuli. Let us see some examples.

ATTACK REFLEXES AND SUMMATION   Electrical stimulation of the lateral hypothalamus can induce cats to attack rats or other small animals. It does not just produce the attack movements; if stimulated in an empty cage, the cat will show circling movements and general arousal, but no attack. Present a rat, however, and the cat will attack it at once. The stimulation primes attack, but there must be an attackable stimulus.

J. P. Flynn and his colleagues have investigated the separate movements involved in the attack sequence.[15] For example, when the hypothalamus is stimulated, a touch on the lips will cause head turning and biting. Stimulation of the hypothalamus alone does not produce this; touch alone does not pro-duce it; but the two together do. There must be *potentiation* somewhere in the system.

14. Hoebel and Thompson, 1969.
15. MacDonnell and Flynn, 1966; Flynn et al., 1970.

More convincing still, there is a trade-off between intensity of hypothalamic stimulation and adequacy of the touch stimulation; if one is weak, increasing the other will compensate for the weakness. If the current is strong, then a touch anywhere on the cheek or snout, around the mouth, will provoke that response. If the stimulating current is weak, then it takes a touch right on the lip to provoke the biting response. A touch elsewhere will not do. Clearly, the effect of the stimulation is to widen the range of *external* stimuli that are effective in eliciting biting.

SEXUAL BEHAVIOR: THE LORDOSIS REFLEX AND DISINHIBITION
A more complex example is the *lordosis reflex*—part of the female mating pattern in rats, cats, and many other mammals. It consists of elevation of the rump, with deflection of the tail to one side.

Now this reflex is elicited by touch on the female's flanks, normally provided by the male. But there is more. The reflex will not occur without the touch; but in the intact cat or rat, even *with* the touch, it will not occur unless the hypothalamus is stimulated by estrogen. Donald Pfaff and his co-workers have traced the pathways through which cells in the hypothalamus, stimulated by estrogen, send messages that are relayed down into the spinal cord, to affect the lordosis-reflex mechanisms that are located there.[16]

Thus far, the picture looks much like Flynn's: External stimuli summing with descending influences from the hypothalamus, to evoke the response. There is a complication, however. We recall that in Bard's cats with transection at Level 1 or 2, the mating reflexes could be elicited by touch, whether or not estrogen was present. In Level 3 cats with the hypothalamus connected to the system, the reflexes could be elicited *only* if estrogen was present. At other times, the same touch would elicit violent rage instead.

The simplest explanation is to suppose that in the intact cat, descending messages from the hypothalamus are *inhibitory*. Their role is not to prime the lordosis reflex when estrogen is present, but to *suppress* that reflex when estrogen is *not* present. Then we can think of estrogen as producing *disinhibition*—literally, it inhibits the inhibitors, directly or indirectly—thus allowing the reflex to occur when its external stimulus, touch, occurs. If this is so, we see again the complex interplay of *excitation* and *inhibition* in behavioral organization.

THE LATERAL HYPOTHALAMIC SYNDROME   We noted earlier that damage to the lateral hypothalamus produces failure to eat or drink in rats. But if such a rat is kept alive by force-feeding and hydration, one will see a gradual recovery of ingestive behavior. Philip Teitelbaum and Alan Epstein traced the course of this recovery.[17]

Immediately after the operation, the rat simply refuses to eat or drink anything at all. After a while, however, it will begin to nibble at wet, highly palat-

16. Pfaff, 1982.
17. Teitelbaum and Epstein, 1962.

able foods: chocolate chip cookies, eggnog, and the like. It does not eat enough to maintain its weight at this stage, and still has to be force-fed. But later still, the rat will begin to eat larger quantities of food; it will now accept ordinary laboratory food, and it regulates its body weight. However, it still needs to be kept hydrated artificially; it will not drink water.

Eventually, most rats do come to accept water, though they seem to use it more as a means of swallowing dry food than as a response to dehydration.[18] But the rats eat and drink, no longer require special maintenance, and appear grossly normal.

Looking over these findings, we can see the effects of lateral hypothalamic damage as a sudden shrinking, followed by a gradual widening again, of the *range of effective stimuli* for ingestion. At first, even the most potent elicitors are ineffective. Later, powerful stimuli—special treats—will elicit ingestion in these rats. Later still, less powerful ones—laboratory chow and water—will do so. This is exactly what we would expect of a system that *potentiates responses to stimuli* for eating and drinking. If descending messages from the hypothalamus prime the feeding and drinking responses, then the less priming there is, the more powerful the external stimulus has to be. If lateral hypothalamic damage removes that priming, then only very potent stimuli—very attractive foods— will trigger ingestive behavior. If the gradual recovery of function gradually reinstates the priming, then we would expect that less and less powerful external stimuli will be needed to get ingestion going.* That is exactly what we see.

HYPOTHALAMIC STIMULATION AND FEEDING SEQUENCES   If we look at the effects of electrical stimulation in the hypothalamus, we see again the effect of brain activity on responsiveness to external stimuli. And this time, we will see how that mechanism provides for the organization of behavioral *sequences* over time.

When the lateral hypothalamus is stimulated, the rat walks over to where food is, seizes a bit of food with its forepaws, bites off a mouthful, and chews and swallows it. The behavior changes over time. But the brain stimulation does not—it is the same throughout the sequence. If the stimulation is constant, why does the behavior change?

A possible though speculative explanation is as follows.[19] We can think of all these responses—walking, seizing, biting, chewing—as components of the rat's food-getting hierarchy. Perhaps, therefore, *all* these responses are primed by hypothalamic stimulation. But in addition, each one requires a certain stimulus situation before it can occur (Fig. 5-7).

If no food is immediately at hand, that situation (plus the brain stimulation) leads the rat to walk to food. Then food is at hand, and that situation (plus the brain stimulation) triggers biting—and so on. Thus, whereas *all* responses in

18. Kissileff, 1969; Kissileff and Epstein, 1969.
*The mechanisms by which recovery occurs are not well understood; for discussion see Kolb and Whishaw, 1990.
19. See Gallistel, 1980.

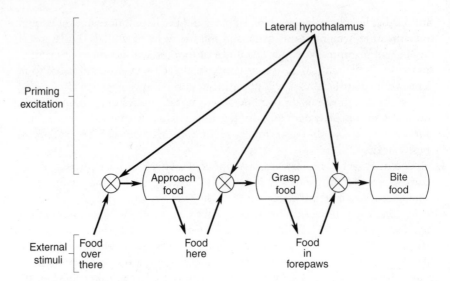

Figure 5-7 Hypothetical mechanism by which hypothalamic activity could combine with the changing external situation to produce a *sequence* of different feeding activities. See text for explanation.

the hierarchy are primed, their actual occurrence is organized as a chain, in which the occurrence of each response provides the stimulus conditions for occurrence of the next one. Each step in the chain involves *summation* of external stimulus effects with impulses descending from higher in the brain.

Second Thoughts about Centers: The Problem of Specificity

To this point, we have taken the experimental findings very much at face value, for we wished to get the ideas straight before critiquing them. As described, they fit well with Stellar's original idea: Excitatory centers prime certain responses to certain stimuli, and are held in check by inhibitory mechanisms. Now, however, we must shift ground and look more critically at these findings.

The logic of brain manipulations seems straightforward. We damage a bit of brain tissue, let us say; we find something that the operated animal does not do or refrain from doing; and we identify the bit of behavior that is missing with the bit of brain that is missing. The problem is that brain manipulations can have multiple effects, both direct and indirect, and we may easily mistake one for another.

Here are two examples, both of which have led us to think again about "feeding" and "satiety" centers. They have shown us that the idea is much too simple.

THE VENTROMEDIAL SYNDROME: DIRECT OR INDIRECT EFFECTS? Damage to the ventromedial hypothalamus, we have seen, can produce a rat that eats too much. Our first thought was that feeding has been released from inhibition, and so we spoke of a satiety center. But other, quite different mechanisms operate too, or instead.

Back in Chapter 3, we looked at some findings that just might revolutionize our views about human obesity. Some people, we realized, may not get fat because they overeat. They may overeat because they are getting fat!

Well, exactly the same suggestion has been made about the overeating rat. Within hours after damage to the ventromedial area, there is an outpouring of insulin from the pancreas. This and other internal changes drive fuel out of the blood, making it unavailable to the brain, and the formation of fat from fuel is enhanced.[20] Perhaps such a rat overeats, not because controls over feeding are damaged, but because the brain really *is* starved for fuel, and responds as it should to that state of affairs.

As it turns out, the insulin effect is probably only part of the picture, for rats overeat after such lesions even if insulin level is artificially held constant.[21] But they overeat less; and besides, there are other metabolic effects of the brain damage that also could act back on the feeding system. Any way we look at it, the important point remains: Brain damage, even to a specific area, can have multiple effects, indirect as well as direct; and it can be a challenging experimental task to separate one effect from another.

THE LATERAL SYNDROME: AKINESIA AND SENSORY NEGLECT
The effects of lateral hypothalamic lesions pose the problem even more dramatically. Such damage produces failure to eat and failure to drink, but it does a great deal more than that. It turns out that lateral hypothalamic damage causes depressed responsiveness to a wide variety of stimuli, not just to food and water.

A rat with lateral hypothalamic damage does not eat or drink; but it also does not attack mice as normal rats do, and it does not orient to sights, touches, and smells as normals do. Such rats may be reluctant to move at all, as if movements were no longer under the control of environmental events and, therefore, seldom occurred. These more global deficits are called **akinesia** (literally, absence of movement) and **sensory neglect.** These symptoms too, like failure to eat and drink, gradually recover over the days or weeks following the operation.[22]

Such damage has similar effects in other species. A cat with lateral hypothalamic damage, for instance, may fail to attack mice as it normally would. It may fail to turn its head toward a prominent visual object, or an odor, or a touch on the skin. It may show little or no spontaneous walking, and it may adopt strange postures, or stay in such a posture for a long time if placed there by the experimenter.

20. Han and Frohman, 1970; Powley, 1977; Friedman and Stricker, 1976.
21. Inoue and Bray, 1980.
22. Marshall, Turner, and Teitelbaum, 1971.

Finally, damage to the system has effects on other specific motivational states. Chemical depression of some of the nerve-cell bundles that run up through the lateral hypothalamus into the forebrain (see below) causes depression of mating behavior in male rats. However, the depression could be prevented and the male would mate if the female rat's behavior was sufficiently provocative. If she darted around, hopped, and wiggled her ears—all very sexy things for a female rat to do—then the male would pursue, mount, and mate normally. If she behaved in a less exciting way, the brain-treated male was less likely to pursue the matter than a normal rat would be. In other words, a powerful stimulus to mating will maintain mating, just as an especially palatable food will maintain feeding, even with damage to this system.

In any case, it is clear that damage to this system affects much more than just feeding. Rather than affecting a system concerned with feeding or mating as such, we may be affecting a system that governs the *arousability* of the animal, or promotes responsiveness to environmental stimuli generally.[23]

This line of thinking takes us far away from the original notion of a specific disorder in feeding. It is a whole new way of looking at the behavior. A rat with lateral hypothalamic damage may fail to eat, not because hunger has been removed, but because sensory input no longer produces reactions—to *any* object in the environment.[24]

CENTERS OR THROUGHWAYS? Thus far we have focused on problems in interpreting the *behavior* we observe. If a rat doesn't eat, is it absence of hunger or absence of arousability? We face similar problems in relating the behavioral changes to the brain systems we assume to underlie them. If we are not sure *what* is happening, we're also not sure *where* it is happening.

If we look at the anatomy of the lateral hypothalamus and the geometry of its connections, the problem becomes clear. There are indeed synapses in the lateral hypothalamus, where information exchange takes place, but there are also nerve fibers running up and down *through* it, connecting brainstem systems with systems in the forebrain (see Fig. 5-13, p. 192). It is quite possible that some of the effects of hypothalamic damage are the result of *disconnecting* lower and higher systems from each other. If so, the systems promoting response to food and other commodities may not be *in* the hypothalamus at all; rather, they may involve communications among far-removed systems, where the communication lines run *through* the hypothalamus.

There is evidence that this is so.[25] An important bundle of nerve fibers runs through this area from the midbrain up into the forebrain, where they release the neurotransmitter *dopamine*. Poisoning these cells, so that they no longer deliver their messages to the forebrain, can also produce failure to eat and drink.

23. Wolgin, Cytawa, and Teitelbaum, 1976.
24. Stricker, 1990.
25. Stricker and Zigmond, 1976.

But, like lateral hypothalamic damage, it does more than that. It also produces akinesia and sensory neglect.

The challenge to experimenters is to tease apart these multiple effects in multiple systems. What part of the system does what? Returning to feeding deficits: Do they result from damage to the synapses *in* the hypothalamus, or from damage to the fibers running *through* it? Probably both. In one study, a cell poison was injected into the lateral hypothalamus; this damaged the synapses *in* the area, but without destroying fibers running *through* the area.[26] This produced failure to eat and drink, suggesting that synapses specifically concerned with feeding and drinking do exist in that area. Perhaps hypothalamic lesions interfere with locally organized feeding and drinking systems, *and* with connections among more remote areas having to do with general arousability and responsiveness.

A Look Backward: The Status of the Dual-Center Theory

What are we to think of Stellar's dual-center framework for thinking about drives and the brain? The details have certainly undergone changes. It is clear that interference with a particular cluster of cells does not affect one and only one motivational system. Hypothalamic lesions that abolish feeding abolish much more besides. Perhaps what is really disrupted is responsiveness to *any* stimulus, not just to food. And the lesions themselves do not just destroy cells right *here* or right *there;* they interrupt communications among cells that may be far removed from the hypothalamus and from each other.

What does all this mean? It means that the systems controlling hunger, thirst, and sexual motivation may well *involve* the hypothalamus, but they are not *in* it. Stellar's notion of hypothalamic *centers,* with different centers for different motives, cannot be taken literally. A map of the brain will not look like a map of Europe: Spain for satiety, France for feeding, Denmark for drinking. It will look more like a map of the Los Angeles freeway system, with routes diverging, converging, and crossing over, and many different destinations even for those all traveling the same route at the moment.

The freeway analogy is a good one for another reason, too. Freeways permit cars to travel to and from distant places—and in the brain they permit messages to do just that. The organization of motivated behavior requires the cooperative action of forebrain, hindbrain, and spinal reflexes—and the hypothalamus—to get on with its business effectively. Organized feeding or mating behavior is not localized in any single collection of cells. The hypothalamus does not act alone.

But if some aspects of Stellar's theory have changed, others remain valid. In fact, the general principles that underlie his theory are the general principles of brain function we have learned.

26. Grossman et al., 1978; see also Dunnet, Björkland, and Stenevi, 1983.

First, the theory provides for *multiple inputs*. In linking the hypothalamus to the blood and to the rest of the brain, it shows how internal factors, but also stimulus factors, and other influences, converge on the final output—the behavior we observe.

Second, and related: *Internal and external factors jointly control motivated behavior.* Behavior must take account of both internal state and external situation, so that the demands of the one are met by appropriate action on the other. There must be communication channels so that the body's nutritive, hormonal, or hydrational state can converse with the brain systems that register the environment and direct action within it. Stellar's theory provides for points of convergence that would permit just such communication.

Third, *motivation reflects a balance of inhibitory and excitatory influences.* Living, like politics, is the art of compromise. A rat, or a human, must stop drinking when its cells are still thirsty, lest they become waterlogged a few minutes later (p. 66). An inhibitory system provides the needed stop mechanism. Then too, activation of one motive may require inhibition of another. A human who sees a tiger, with no cage around it, has more important things to do than eat—however hungry she may be. Stellar's model helps us to remember the ever-present role of stop mechanisms—inhibitory mechanisms—in motivated behavior.

THE PHYSIOLOGY OF REWARD

In the last section we saw how systems involving the hypothalamus can prime the response to stimuli such as food or touch, once those stimuli are encountered. But animals also *seek* appropriate stimuli, making arbitrary learned responses to obtain them; this, we recall, is how we identify *motivational states* as opposed to reflexes and action patterns. To a hungry rat, food is a *reward,* and the rat will learn what is required to produce it. If we knew how the brain handles learning and reward, we would know a great deal about how the brain produces motivated behavior.

We are a long way from understanding these matters, but we do have a starting point.

Brain Stimulation Reward

In the early 1950s, one of the most exciting discoveries in modern psychobiology was made. James Olds and Peter Milner found that electrical stimulation of certain areas of the rat brain, through implanted electrodes, had reinforcing properties.[27] A rat could be given access to a lever, and by pressing the lever could cause delivery of a brief series of electrical pulses to the brain. If the electrode was in the right place, the rat might press the lever over and over again, for hours at a time.

27. Olds and Milner, 1954.

REWARD AND AVERSION SYSTEMS   By varying the placement of electrodes in the brain, and seeing which placements would support this *self-stimulation,* Olds and other investigators were able to map out a *reward system* in the brain. Important sites include our old friend the lateral hypothalamus and the systems of nerve fibers that course into and through it, upward and downward. Additional rewarding sites were found in various structures of the brainstem and forebrain.

Over the same period, Olds and others identified electrode placements where stimulation appeared to be aversive. If pressing a lever delivered stimulation to these area, rats might actively avoid the lever, or they might press a lever to turn stimulation off, rather than to turn it on. The *aversion system* so identified runs closer to the midline than does the reward system, through the hypothalamus and down into the floor of the midbrain. It includes the ventromedial area—the old "satiety center." Stimulation there is highly aversive to rats.

In humans, too, stimulation of the brain in conscious patients can evoke feelings of pleasure. These tend to be described vaguely as warm, glowing, good feelings.[28] (Science-fiction writers to the contrary, no wallops of unendurably delicious ecstasy have been reported to date.)

RELATION TO NATURAL MOTIVES   We remember that the lateral hypothalamus is an area where electrical stimulation can produce feeding in otherwise satiated rats. It is also an important focus of the reward system. In fact, it is possible to obtain stimulus-bound feeding (with prolonged trains of electrical pulses) and self-stimulation (with briefer trains following a lever-press) through the same electrode in the same rat.[29]

Moreover, the rewarding value of lateral hypothalamic stimulation is affected by some of the same internal factors that affect feeding. If a rat's stomach is full of food, it will not eat spontaneously; it becomes harder to induce it to eat by brain stimulation; and the rate of self-stimulation goes down. Indeed, the previously rewarding stimulation may actually become aversive. A rat that would work to turn the current on when hungry, will work to turn it off when overfed.[30]

Other experiments have found similar parallels. In the posterior hypothalamus, a bit farther back than the lateral area, electrical stimulation can elicit mating behavior in the male rat, and rats will work to self-stimulate through electrodes implanted there. Sure enough, castration reduces self-stimulation just as it reduces readiness to mate, and treatment with male hormones restores both.[31]

Finally, the effects of deprivation and satiation can be specific to one or another brain site. Filling a rat full of food can depress self-stimulation of the lateral hypothalamus—the old "feeding center"—without affecting self-stimu-

28. Heath, 1964.
29. Hoebel, 1974.
30. Hoebel and Thompson, 1969.
31. Caggiula and Hoebel, 1966.

lation through another electrode farther forward in the brain.[32] This tells us at once that the system has multiple components. There is no one reward system; or if there is, it has multiple inputs—convergence again!—that can be affected separately from each other.

RELATION TO NATURAL REINFORCERS   But how does all this relate to natural motivational states? At first glance, there is a paradox about self-stimulation and stimulus-bound feeding. Stimulation in the lateral hypothalamus can produce feeding, as if it made the rat hungry. But the rat will also work to *produce* stimulation there. Isn't hunger unpleasant? Shouldn't the rat seek to avoid stimulation that mimics hunger?

The paradox disappears if we suppose that the effect of the stimulus is not to produce a drive state, but to set, or mimic, the *reinforcing properties of external stimuli*. To a hungry rat, food is a reinforcer. Perhaps the self-stimulation taps into a system that permits, or produces, that reinforcing effect.

Reward and External Stimuli: Modulation of Hedonic Response

There are other, quite different lines of evidence that point to the same conclusion: Brain reward and aversion systems modulate *hedonic* responses—responses of pleasure and displeasure, or approach and withdrawal—to external stimuli.

SENSORY NEGLECT AND SENSORY REJECTION   We saw earlier that rats or cats with lateral hypothalamic damage show a decreased responsiveness to stimuli in general. They do not orient to sounds or touches, do not attack mice, and may be reluctant to move at all. This *sensory neglect* can extend to both negative and positive stimuli. Animals with lateral hypothalamic damage may fail to withdraw from a painful stimulus or from an obnoxious odor. They are unresponsive to good *or* bad events.

But there is another common effect of lateral damage, and that is an *exaggerated negative response* to stimuli. Such a rat may gape and turn its head away if even a sweet solution is put in its mouth. It seems to treat *any* stimulation of its mouth as highly aversive. And even after recovery of feeding and drinking, the rat may refuse to drink if the slightest bitter taste is added to its drinking water.[33] In short, after lateral hypothalamic damage we may see not a passive *sensory neglect,* but an active *sensory rejection*. Even ordinary stimuli may be rejected as if they were bad, and bad ones, such as bitter tastes, are treated as if they were *really* bad.

In a careful exploration, Timothy Schallert and Ian Whishaw showed that these two different reactions to lateral hypothalamic damage depended upon

32. Hoebel, 1974.
33. Teitelbaum and Epstein, 1962.

just where the damage was done.[34] Lesions in one place produced a passive sensory neglect, in which the rats simply were not responsive to stimuli, good or bad. Lesions in a slightly different place produced active sensory rejection, in which the rats actively turned away from stimuli that should have been neutral or even positive. The first reaction, sensory neglect, presumably reflects a failure to react to incoming stimuli at all. The second, sensory rejection, reflects a failure of a *positive* reaction to incoming stimuli, and a swing toward negative reactions instead.

Let us try to put these findings together. Suppose there are *three* systems running close to each other, in or through the lateral hypothalamus. One system may have to do with arousal or alerting reactions to incoming stimuli. It says to the rest of the brain, "Isn't that interesting!" Another system permits positive or pleasurable reactions to stimuli. It says, "Isn't that nice!" Damage the first of these, and we get passive *sensory neglect;* nothing is very interesting. Damage the second, and we get active *sensory rejection;* everything is unpleasant. And that implies that there must be yet a third system that produces the negative reactions, a system that says, "That's awful!"

STIMULATION OF THE HYPOTHALAMUS   Some effects of hypothalamic stimulation also support this idea. Stimulation of the lateral hypothalamus can evoke feeding, as we have seen. But it also affects responses to a variety of other stimuli, and it seems to shift the responses in a positive direction.[35] During stimulation, rats ran to a sugar solution that was too weak to support running without the stimulation. They did not run to escape a mildly painful electric shock to their feet, as they did without the brain stimulation. They did not avoid, and sometimes they even approached, a strong ammonia smell that normally they would have avoided. In all these cases we see an increase in positive reactions to stimuli, and a decrease in negative ones.

Stimulation in the ventromedial hypothalamus had opposite effects. Now it took very strong sugar solutions to elicit running or drinking; the rats would not run to weaker solutions, though without the stimulation they would have done so. Shocks or ammonia smells were rejected with abnormal vigor. It appears that this is a brain area favoring negative reactions to stimuli. And we recall that stimulation in that area is aversive in its own right. It may be part of the "That's awful!" system suggested by the lesion studies.

The effects of these brain systems on feeding might be exerted in part by way of their effects on hedonic reactions to stimuli. Ventromedial hypothalamic tissue—the old "satiety center"—may be part of an inhibitory system that keeps our responses to pleasant stimuli, including foods, in check. We are reminded of the *alliesthesia* idea: Feeding ends when the hedonic response to food shifts

34. Schallert and Whishaw, 1978.
35. Stellar, Brooks, and Mills, 1979.

from "nice" toward "awful." Conversely, intact lateral hypothalamic tissue—the old "feeding center"—may support the pleasantness of stimulus inputs, including foods, so that in its absence the good is less good and the bad is worse. Remember, though, that these functions are not confined to food-related stimuli; they seem to apply to whatever stimuli the environment offers.[36]

In any case, all this is still too simple. As we have laid out the picture, damage to the ventromedial area should weaken the "awful" system, and a rat with ventromedial damage ought to respond to stimuli generally as if they were nicer than before. It does not. It shows exaggerated acceptance of nice foods, but it also shows an exaggerated rejection of nasty foods.[*][37] And it often shows vicious, rageful reactions to mild provocation—hardly the behavior of a rat for which everything is lovely. Clearly, a full-blown "awful" reaction can persist after damage to that portion of the brain.

A Look Backward: The Brain and Hedonic Reactions

It appears that among the bundles of fibers running through the hypothalamus, there are at least *three* systems that (1) have hedonic properties themselves and (2) control the hedonic effects of external stimuli. One system permits *attention* or *arousal* in response to stimuli; it says, "Isn't that interesting!" It may be closely related to other non-specific arousal systems, to be considered in the next chapter.

Another system permits *positive reactions* to stimuli; it says, "Isn't that nice!" Stimulation in that system exaggerates positive responses to stimuli, and is positively reinforcing in its own right. Conversely, damage to the system reduces the niceness of external stimuli in general.

Still a third system promotes *negative reactions;* it says, "That's awful!" Stimulation there exaggerates negative reactions to stimuli, and is punishing in its own right. And damage within the system, in the ventromedial hypothalamus, can release exaggerated positive reactions to *some* stimuli such as palatable foods. However, there can be exaggerated negative reactions as well, so there must be more to the "awful" system than this simple picture implies.

Even if oversimplified, however, these ideas offer a tantalizing glimpse of a Grand Design. We have seen in Chapters 3 and 4 how motivated behavior may be produced, and satiated, through the attractiveness or unattractiveness of the relevant commodity—its niceness or its awfulness. If that is so, then there must be systems in the brain that *make* commodities nice or awful to us. The brain's reward and aversion systems seem well suited to perform such functions.

---

36. Compare Kelley and Stinus, 1984; Neill et al., 1982.

*There is dispute about whether this happens because it is brain-damaged or because it is fat; see, for example, Weingarten, 1982; Graff and Stellar, 1962.

37. Teitelbaum, 1955.

In 1962, S. P. ("Pete") Grossman set the physiology of motivation off on a new tack. Briefly, here is what he did.[38]

We recall that a tiny wire, or electrode, can be implanted deep in an animal's brain while it is asleep, and that later it will wake up and walk around with the wire in place, so we can stimulate the brain cells that surround the electrode tip. In the same way, we can implant a tiny metal tube deep in the brain. Later, through flexible plastic tubing so that the rat is free to move, we can inject a tiny amount of fluid (a microliter or less) into the brain. If the fluid contains an appropriate chemical, we can look at the effects of *chemical stimulation* of the brain.

To see why we do this, look back at Figure 5-1. We recall that one nerve cell delivers its message to the next cell in the chain by releasing a bit of chemical messenger, or neurotransmitter. Now if, instead of waiting for a cell to deliver that chemical, we deliver it ourselves, we should be (approximately) mimicking the effect of the stimulation that the postsynaptic cell would naturally receive.

Grossman implanted his tiny tubes, or *cannulas,* into the lateral hypothalamus in a series of rats. Later, he looked at the effects of minute quantities of the chemical *norepinephrine* on some test sessions, and of the chemical *acetylcholine* on others. Both these are neurotransmitters that occur naturally in the brain.

A remarkable thing happened. When Grossman injected norepinephrine into the lateral hypothalamus, the rats ate. When he injected acetylcholine through the same cannulas in the same rats, they did not eat; instead, they sought and drank water! There seemed to be a "chemical coding" in that area of the brain: Cells responding to norepinephrine initiated feeding, cells responding to acetylcholine initiated drinking.★

Now let us not raise any hopes that will just have to be demolished again. We are not going to find a "hunger chemical" and a "thirst chemical," any more than we're going to find hunger and thirst centers. First, these chemicals occur at many junctions between cells, and have different effects at different locations. Acetylcholine is not a "thirst chemical." It also, for example, acts on skeletal muscle cells to excite them and cause them to contract; but it *inhibits* the muscle of the heart, slowing it down.

Second, the cells around the cannula tip, which Grossman stimulated with his injections, are parts of a whole functioning brain. When stimulated, those cells must have called into play whole systems of who-knows-what complexity,

---

38. Grossman, 1962.

★They probably were not the *same* cells, even though the injections were made through the same cannulas. Even very small injections reach a large number of cells, and different ones of these can have different functions and respond to different chemicals. A microliter is a millionth of a liter, which sounds pretty small; but it's also a cubic millimeter, which, when you're dealing with something as small and densely packed as nerve cells, is quite impressively large.

eventuating in feeding or drinking. What we do know is that cells in *just this area* (1) are responsive to *just these* chemical stimuli and (2) are able to call the whole systems into play. And we therefore know (3) that different cell systems that are too densely intertwined to be teased apart anatomically can be teased apart chemically. That is what "chemical coding" means.

Whole new chapters in neuroscience have been written because of this discovery and those that followed. We could not summarize it all without writing another, multivolume book. So, following our usual strategy, let's look at just a couple of samples of what is going on.

Case Study 1: Neurotransmitters, Drugs, and Reward

Take a look at Figure 5-8. Here we see again a schematic view of a synapse, and we see the packets of chemical messenger—the *neurotransmitter*—being released to affect the postsynaptic cell. The figure also shows that there are several steps in the process. Now it turns out that any or all of these steps can be affected by certain drugs, which *modify the rate* at which the step takes place. Which drugs? What steps? That depends on the neurotransmitter and the synapse we're talking about.

As a case study, let's look at the role of the neurotransmitter *dopamine* in mediating the rewarding effect of brain stimulation. We saw earlier that an

Figure 5-8 Another look at synaptic transmission, from presynaptic to postsynaptic cell. Appropriate drugs may affect any of the steps shown. For example, a drug could enhance the action of a neurotransmitter by increasing its rate of manufacture (1) or of release (2) or by decreasing its rate of metabolism (4) or reuptake (5), so that it stays around longer after being released. Drugs could antagonize the neurotransmitter if they had the opposite effects on any of the steps. In addition (not shown), a drug could show *competitive antagonism*—it could compete with the neurotransmitter for receptor sites (3), tying them up so that the transmitter could not deliver its message because the "line is busy."

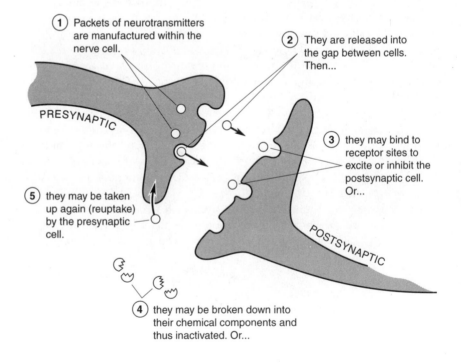

1. Packets of neurotransmitters are manufactured within the nerve cell.

2. They are released into the gap between cells. Then...

3. they may bind to receptor sites to excite or inhibit the postsynaptic cell. Or...

PRESYNAPTIC

5. they may be taken up again (reuptake) by the presynaptic cell.

POSTSYNAPTIC

4. they may be broken down into their chemical components and thus inactivated. Or...

ascending bundle of nerve cells runs up from the midbrain, through the lateral hypothalamic area, to end in the forebrain, and that electrical stimulation there is reinforcing. That reinforcing effect is dependent on the release of dopamine into the forebrain areas where these nerve cells end.

How do we know that? For one thing, dopamine *antagonists*—drugs that block the effects of dopamine—depress or abolish the reinforcing effects of the brain stimulation. For another, dopamine *agonists*—drugs that enhance the effects of dopamine—make the stimulation more rewarding.★ Rats treated with such drugs will work at a higher rate for stimulation in that pathway.

Again: We suggested earlier that what the brain stimulation does is to mimic the effect of natural rewards. An elegantly simple experiment supports this idea.[39] Rats were trained to press a lever for food. Then they were injected with a dopamine-blocking drug, and placed in the apparatus. A curious thing happened: Initially, the rats worked for food at their usual high rate, but they responded less and less as the session went on, as if the lever press were undergoing extinction through lack of reward.

The simplest interpretation is this. The rats were still hungry, as shown by their initial high rate of response. But the food, when it came, simply wasn't reinforcing any more. The rats discovered as the session went on that the food provided no reinforcement—no pleasure?—and so they quit, just as they would have done if the food itself had stopped coming.

Other experiments support the same conclusion. Treatment with a dopamine blocker, for instance, depressed sham-feeding of sugar solutions in rats. The rats, when drug-affected, treated a given concentration of sugar as if it were a lower concentration, hence less tasty.[40]

Conversely, measurement of dopamine release at these forebrain synapses also suggests its involvement in natural rewards.[41] Figure 5-9 shows the effects of sexual contact on forebrain dopamine release. When the male rat was placed in the experimental chamber (in which he had mated before), dopamine level increased. It increased again when a female was introduced behind a wire screen; and it increased *again* when the screen was removed so that the two could mate. When the female was removed, it declined.

Finally, dopamine release can be modulated by at least some of the factors that modulate the effectiveness of natural rewards. In a striking demonstration, it was found that a sweet taste in the mouth caused an increased dopamine release, *unless* the taste had been made aversive by pairing it with illness (as discussed in Chap. 7). In that case, the same sweet taste caused an actual *decrease* in dopamine release at the same terminals.[42]

★An *antagonist,* as its name implies, opposes something—here, dopamine. An *agonist* enhances that something, or helps it. Think of "antagonist" as short for "anti-agonist," and this terminology will make sense.

39. Wise et al., 1978.
40. Geary and Smith, 1985.
41. Pfaus et al., 1990.
42. Mark et al., 1991.

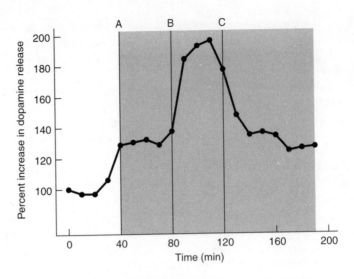

Figure 5-9 Dopamine release in the forebrain of the male rat. It increases when the rat is placed in a chamber where he is accustomed to mating (A). It rises again when a female is palced in the chamber (B) and falls when she is removed (C). (Adapted from Pfaus et al., 1990).

It may well be, then, that this *dopaminergic* system is one of the systems (there must be others as well) whose activity provides the "niceness" of nice things. If that is so, then anything that enhances activity in that system should itself be pleasurable. Well, at least two drugs, both of which have intensely pleasurable effects, turn out to be dopamine agonists. The drug *amphetamine* ("speed") enhances the effect of dopamine by speeding up its release at the axon terminal (Step 2 in Fig. 5-8), so that more transmitter is released per unit time. The drug *cocaine* enhances dopamine's effect by blocking its re-uptake by the presynaptic cell (Step 5 in Fig. 5-8), so that, once released, it stays around longer and thus has greater effect.

In other words, these drugs, which are so dangerous precisely because they are so pleasurable, probably produce that pleasure by activating the same systems that are activated by natural pleasures—only more so! When we understand the natural reward systems better, we should better understand the effects of certain "unnatural" rewards such as addictive drugs.

Case Study 2: Stress and Sweetness

Many writers have suggested that *eating,* as a response to stress, may have a calming effect. And it is widely believed that at least some people may eat, and perhaps overeat, because it does.

Much of the evidence here is very mixed and hard to interpret. People will tell us that they find eating stress-reducing; but is that because it *is,* or because they are aware of the popular theory that says it ought to be? Similar doubts attend the finding that, for example, eating during exam week—a stressful time, presumably—was correlated with self-reported anxiety in obese, but not non-obese, college women. And there is evidence of a correlation between obesity and depression, which might be considered a kind of chronic stress state. But which came first—the obesity, or the depression? Such ambiguity always attends correlational studies such as these (pp. 15–16).

There is, however, experimental evidence that feeding, or at least a fragment of it—the taste of food in the mouth—*can* have a calming, stress-reducing effect. Let us look closely at these experiments. They are an excellent example of how research in the human case can be informed and guided by animal experiments (pp. 18–19).

When a baby rat is removed from its mother, it protests long and loud—but inaudibly to human beings. What it does is to emit a series of shrill cries, at a pitch so high that humans cannot hear them. We have to tape-record the cries and play them back at a slower speed, to hear them ourselves.

Now Elliott Blass and his colleagues found that the cries would end, and the baby rats would calm down, if a tiny amount of sugar water were placed in their mouths.[43] Was this because a baby rat can't cry if its mouth is full of fluid? No, on two counts. First, the water had to be sweet; plain water would not do. Second, the effect could be blocked by certain drugs, and here we must digress for a bit more background.

The drug *morphine* is a potent painkiller in both animals and humans. It also turns out that the brain is capable of manufacturing its own morphine-like compounds in times of stress. These compounds, the *endorphins,* resemble morphine in their effects (reduction of pain), in their chemical structure, and in their susceptibility to certain drugs. The drug *naloxone,* for example, blocks the pain-relieving effects both of morphine and of the endorphins.

And, Blass's group found, naloxone also blocks the quieting effect of sugar solution in the mouth. That calming effect, therefore, seems to be produced by the release of endorphins, triggered in turn by the sweet taste in the mouth (Fig. 5-10).

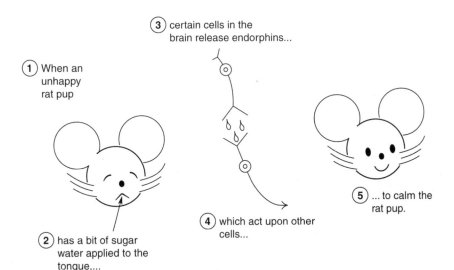

③ certain cells in the brain release endorphins...

① When an unhappy rat pup

② has a bit of sugar water applied to the tongue,...

④ which act upon other cells...

⑤ ... to calm the rat pup.

Figure 5-10 A sweet taste in the mouth calms distressed rat pups by triggering the release of endorphins, which in turn relieve the distress.

43. See for example Blass and Shite, 1994.

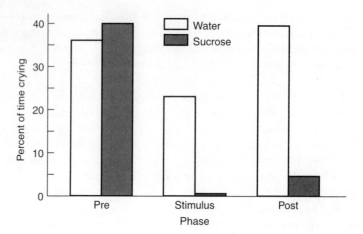

Figure 5-11   Crying in infant humans before, during, and after receiving sugar water (solid bars) or plain water (open bars). Sugar water, but not plain water, caused a profound and prolonged reduction in crying.

Does the same effect occur in humans? Blass's group turned their attention from baby rats to baby people. They found that in infants, newborn to 2 weeks of age, the same effect occurred. Placing a bit of sugar water in the mouth had a calming effect, leading to a prolonged cessation of the crying that had been in progress (Fig. 5-11). Other liquids containing palatable food components, such as suspensions of fat in water, had similar effects; but plain unflavored water did not.[44]

Finally, is this effect also mediated by endorphins? One could find out by treating the babies with drugs like naloxone, but here we face practical and ethical problems: One doesn't give powerful drugs to babies just to satisfy one's scientific curiosity! But Blass and his colleagues found another way. What if the baby were already, in the natural course of events, receiving drugs that had such effects?

Another drug, *methadone,* seems to block not the effect but the manufacture of these natural painkillers, the endorphins. This drug is sometimes administered to people recovering from heroin addiction, for it can reduce the craving for the drug during the initial period of abstinence. Finally, if such a patient is a pregnant mother, the methadone in her blood is transmitted to the blood of the fetus. And if treatment continues through childbirth, the baby will be born "methadone-treated," and its own manufacture of endorphins will be much reduced.

Blass's group repeated their experiments on four such "methadone babies." Sure enough, in these babies, the calming effect of sugar in the mouth was absent entirely. It appears that the effect in baby humans, as in baby rats, is endorphin-dependent.

Does all this mean that food is in fact an effective stress reducer in human adults? Not for certain; we cannot generalize from newborns to adults, any more than we can from rats to people (pp. 18–19). But these findings, which

44. Blass and Smith, 1992.

show that food in the mouth *can* reduce signs of stress in at least some creatures, certainly make the idea all the more plausible. They also suggest some specific, testable ideas about how the process might work.

A Look Backward

In this section, as in the previous one on reward, we find ourselves dealing with systems that cut across specific motives. The dopaminergic reward system may underlie the rewarding effects of feeding *and* of mating. Indeed, the same *behaviors* may cut across different motivational states, serving different goals on different occasions (the *lattice hierarchy,* pp. 92–93). The endorphins may be triggered by the sweet taste, normally a consequence of feeding behavior, to make that action effective for stress-reduction, not just for nutrition.

All this suggests that different motivational sequences reflect, not different parts or centers of the brain, but different *combinations* of components that serve more general purposes: reward or aversion, interest in and attention to the environment (compare sensory neglect), orientation and locomotion (compare akinesia), and so on. When we turn to the forebrain, we will meet this idea again.

THE ROLES OF THE FOREBRAIN

Above the hypothalamus, the tube-shaped brainstem opens out to form the great **cerebral hemispheres,** with the band of nerve cells, the **corpus callosum,** connecting them (Fig. 5-12). These hemispheres, the forebrain, have the layers of the **cerebral cortex** as their outer covering. There are also clusters of cells buried beneath the cortex, not visible in Figure 5-12. These assemblies of cells form complex interconnections with each other and with lower systems in the brainstem.

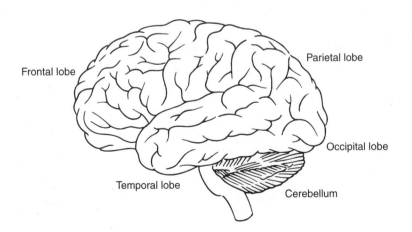

Figure 5-12 The external surface of the brain viewed from the left cerebral hemisphere, showing the lobes of the forebrain.

In looking over some forebrain influences on motivation, we can draw on an extensive body of human clinical literature. Because the cerebral cortex is at the surface of the brain, and because its very complexity makes it vulnerable, clinical neuroscientists frequently encounter patients with cortical damage. While trying to help these unfortunate people, we can also learn about the brain from what their symptoms tell us.

Relations of the Forebrain to Lower Levels

We have emphasized that the hypothalamus does not act alone. Motivated behavior may originate there—sometimes it surely does, as when we evoke motivated behavior with hypothalamic stimulation. But it does not end there. Excited hypothalamic cells reach up into the forebrain to interact with systems there (Fig. 5-13), as we will see in a minute. And they reach down into the midbrain and spinal cord to interact with these lower systems. Recall, for example, that food acceptance and rejection can be shown by rats with only the midbrain and lower structures operating (pp. 166–67). Perhaps (though we are speculating now) the role of higher systems, including the hypothalamus, is not to register or create states of hunger and satiety, but to translate them into goal-directed action.

Clearly we are dealing with systems that can be disrupted at many levels, and some of the symptoms produced by hypothalamic damage have their parallels after damage to the forebrain. For example, with damage in the *parietal lobe* of the cerebral cortex, a familiar symptom may appear: *sensory neglect*. Here is a case study.

> Mr. P., a 67-year-old man, had suffered a right parietal stroke. . . . Mr. P. neglected the left side of his body and of the world. When asked to draw a clock face, he crowded all the numbers onto the right side of the clock. . . . When he dressed, he

Figure 5-13 The forebrain includes the cerebral cortex (shaded) and various subcortical structures (not shown). The forebrain, the hypothalamus, and the midbrain are interconnected, so that mechanisms at any level can communicate with all levels. And all levels of the brain are connected, directly or indirectly, with the motor neurons in the spinal cord.

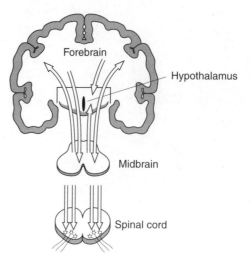

did not attempt to put on the left side of his clothing . . . and when he shaved, he shaved only the right side of his face. He ignored tactile sensations on the left side of his body. Finally, he appeared unaware that anything was wrong with him and was uncertain as to what all the fuss was about.[45]

We notice that the damage to the *right* side of the brain produced neglect of sensations on the *left* side of the body. This crossed control is characteristic of the brain, and it shows up at the level of the hypothalamus as well. Damage on one side of the hypothalamus can cause neglect for stimuli on the opposite side of the body and only for those.[46] It is likely that this neglect results from interference with communication between cortical cells and systems much lower in the brain.

Inhibitory Functions of the Forebrain

The role of the forebrain is largely one of *inhibition*. At least as often as its systems cause things to happen, they cause things *not* to happen. This is vitally important in organized, focused behavior, which involves doing things *only* at the right time and directing them *only* toward appropriate objects. Since this function of the forebrain is so important, it is worth looking at several examples.

SHAM RAGE   We recall that Bard's cats with Level 3 transection were capable of well-organized rage reactions. But there are differences between a Level 3 cat and a normal one. One is that in the operated cat, the rage reaction is on a hair trigger. Even a mild disturbance, which a normal cat would ignore or at most investigate, is enough to trigger violent attack from a cat with its forebrain disconnected.[47] This is *sham rage*.

It appears that in intact cats, forebrain mechanisms hold rage in check until there is something worth raging about. Lacking that inhibitory check, the cat flies off its handle at any little thing—hardly a recipe for effective action in the world.

Finally, notice that it is the whole pattern that is held in check, as a unit. Once again we see how the principles of nerve-cell interaction—inhibition, in this case—apply to the interactions among whole organized systems.

THE TEMPORAL-LOBE SYNDROME   Yet another kind of release from inhibition was discovered by Heinrich Klüver and Paul Bucy.[48] This occurred after damage, in monkeys, to the temporal lobes and the subcortical structures underlying them.

After the operation, the monkeys expressed simple motivated behaviors—eating, mating, exploring—in a perfectly normal way. What was missing was

45. From Kolb and Whishaw, 1990.
46. Marshall, Turner, and Teitelbaum, 1971.
47. Bard and Mountcastle, 1948.
48. Klüver and Buoy, 1939.

the *selectivity* in expressing them toward appropriate objects. The monkeys would eat monkey food, but they would also eat meat—which monkeys normally do not eat—or wooden blocks or paper bags or, it seemed, anything that could be put into the mouth. They masturbated frequently and mated, or tried to mate, with animals of different species or even with inanimate objects. They would carefully explore small objects such as nuts and bolts, find them useless, and throw them away in normal monkey fashion—but then, on encountering them again, they would carefully explore them again as if seeing them for the first time.

Since it is *removal* of brain tissue that produced these indiscriminate mating, eating, and exploring reactions, we must assume that systems involving that tissue had been keeping them discriminate before. In such cases, it is tempting to speculate that the failure is of inhibitory control on the *stimulus elicitation* of the action. The operation must have damaged systems that say to intact monkeys, "Eat, but don't eat *that;*" or "Mate, but not with *that;*" or "Explore new things, but not *that;* it isn't a new thing and is not worth exploring."

The syndrome also occurs in humans. One such patient

seemed unable to recognize a wide variety of common objects. He examined each object placed before him as though seeing it for the first time, explored it repetitively and seemed unaware of its significance. . . . , [When imitating another's actions, a common neurological test], he would perseverate, copying all movements made by another for extended periods of time. . . . All objects that he could lift were placed in his mouth and sucked and chewed. He was commonly observed to place his fingers in his mouth and suck them . . . he ingested virtually everything within reach, including the plastic wrapper from bread, cleaning pastes, ink, dog food, and feces.[49]

The Frontal-Lobe Syndrome

On September 13, 1848, Phineas P. Gage was the victim of a bizarre accident. A railroad construction foreman, Mr. Gage was tamping a charge of dynamite into rock when the charge exploded prematurely. The tamping iron, a 1-inch thick, 3-foot long pointed rod, was hurled like a rocket through Mr. Gage's face and skull and into the sky; it landed many yards away.

It seems miraculous that Mr. Gage survived the accident at all; but in fact, he was conscious and walking around within minutes, and he lived for about another 12 years. His speech, intelligence, and memory were intact. But he was a changed man. Once quiet, conventional, and dependable, he became profane and capricious, and so irresponsible that he could no longer hold a job. As his physician John Harlow put it, "the equilibrium . . . between his intellectual faculties and animal propensities" had been disrupted. And he was

49. Marlowe et al., 1975.

"capricious and vacilating, devising many plans of operation, which are no sooner arranged than they are abandoned in turn for others appearing more feasible."[50]

As with the temporal-lobe syndrome, the major problem would appear to be not in organizing and executing actions themselves, but in keeping them appropriate to the task and the situation. Thus we can *speculate* that we are again seeing failures of inhibition, applied to whole actions and action sequences. Mr. Gage's outbursts of profanity seem to reflect a failure of restraint. So do his irresponsibility and disorganization, abandoning plans for "others appearing more feasible." The effective execution of any plan may require the suppression, or inhibition, of others that come to mind.

Consider: After I finish writing this section, I think I'll walk around the corner for a coffee break. But to get any work done, I must refrain from acting on that idea—that is, I must *inhibit* that action—until I do finish this section. Similarly for the zillions of distracting stimuli, thoughts, etc., that would pull me off the track were I unable to refrain from acting on them. Quite possibly Mr. Gage's problem was an inability to refrain. He may, we might say, have become more *stimulus-bound* (pp. 113–116) at the expense of goal-direction in his behavior.

No autopsy was conducted when Mr. Gage died, but his skull was preserved. Recently, a team of neuroscientists, working from skull measurements and using modern imaging techniques, were able to make a good estimate as to where the brain must have been damaged (Fig. 5-14). They conclude that there must have been damage in the medial (toward the midline) portion of the *orbital cortex*. That is the cortex that lies at the bottom of the frontal lobes, and is so called because it lies right above the eyeball or "orbit." And the symptoms fit those of other patients with known frontal-lobe damage. In such patients, the

> ability to make rational decisions in personal and social matters is invariably compromised and so is their processing of emotion. On the contrary, their ability to tackle the logic of an abstract problem, to perform calculations, and to call up appropriate knowledge and attend to it remains intact. [These findings suggest] that emotion and its underlying neural machinery participate in decision making within the social domain and [that] participation depends on the ventromedial frontal region.[51]

Anatomical considerations make this idea attractive. Orbital cortex is connected to other cortical areas implicated in cognitive operations. But it also has two-way connections to systems implicated in motivational and emotional processes, including (you guessed it!) the hypothalamus. Possibly we are seeing

50. Quoted by Kolb and Whishaw, 1990, p. 483.
51. Damasio et al., 1994, p. 1104.

Figure 5-14 Three views of the brain and skull, showing what the trajectory of the tamping iron must have been in the case of Phineas Gage. Entering under the cheekbone, it must have penetrated the underside of the frontal lobe of the brain (the orbital cortex) on the left side, then passed through the frontal lobe to emerge at the midline.

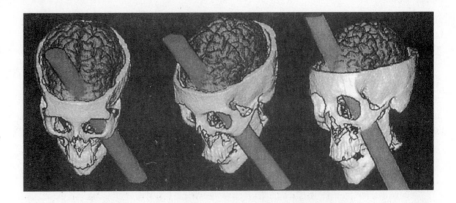

the disruption of a system in which how we appraise our alternatives (cognitive), and how we feel about them (emotional/motivational), come together.

Perhaps part of that system is concerned with the inhibition of emotional expression, suppressing such expression until and unless it is appropriate. If so, then it is easy to see how damage to that system could turn a quiet and serene man into a profane and cantankerous one, as in the case of Mr. Gage. As to his disorganization, being constantly pulled away from his ongoing plans by "others appearing more feasible," we can *speculate* that perhaps some inhibition must be applied to the emotional components of these "others" to prevent them from distracting us. Indeed, to go out for coffee would be very pleasant for me right now ("wouldn't that be nice!"). I might never finish this chapter if another part of my system, one that says, "Yes, but don't do it yet," were not in working order.

Skills, Tools, and the Forebrain

We could say a great deal more about the forebrain, but we could not do the topic justice without writing a whole book on neuropsychology (a thought whose implementation I shall inhibit). We can only allude to some functions of the forebrain here, to show their relations to our topic.

Suppose I do go out for coffee in a minute. Think what that action will entail. I must *remember* how to get to the coffee shop, *recognize* it when I get there, and remember why I'm there. (Surely we have all had the experience of ambling into the next room to look for something and, once there, forgetting what we were looking for!) I must *speak* to order my coffee and to specify sugar but no cream. Perhaps I will *read* the menu, and *comprehend speech* when I'm told what today's specials are (Fig. 5-15). I must know how to handle a cup full of coffee. And I'd better remember to pay for what I have.

All that for a cup of coffee? Yes, that's the point. Nay more—I might do any or all of the same things, with only minor modifications, if my goal were to see a movie instead. Clearly, if it would be naive to look for coffee-getting or movie-going *centers* in the brain, it would be almost as naive to look for coffee-

Figure 5-15   In humans, even feeding behavior may draw on speech production, speech comprehension, reading, and other specialized functions of the forebrain.

getting or movie-going *systems* in the brain, dedicated all and only to one action or the other.

Finally, any of these functions—spatial memory, recognition memory, speech production, speech comprehension, skilled movements, reading—may be disrupted, sometimes quite selectively, by damage to the forebrain. This points to the existence of complex systems, *involving* the forebrain (not necessarily *in* it), which can be called into play in the service of any motivational state. If we do not usually think of these functions as *motivational,* that is only because they are not linked to any specific motive, but are general purpose. Like tools in a toolbox, which could be used to build or repair almost anything, so these specialized functions can be called into play to express our motives and seek our goals, whatever these may be.

A Look Backward

All this means that we cannot expect to find a "box in the brain"—not even a system, much less a center—that "does" hunger, all of it and nothing else. Similarly for any other specific motive. We saw earlier how the brain's reward system may contribute "niceness" to any of a number of actions or objects. We can use our speech apparatus to ask for coffee, to ask for a date, or to yell for help; and we would be calling on our memories too, in doing any of these.

The *initiation* of different motivational states may be localized, it is true. Grossman was able to trigger the whole feeding sequence by activating one group of cells, and the whole drinking sequence by activating another, sensitive to norepinephrine and acetylcholine respectively. But once triggered, the affected systems surely call on processes that are shared by many, perhaps all, motivational states.

SUMMARY

The nervous system is composed of nerve cells, or *neurons*. A nerve cell communicates with another cell by liberating a chemical messenger, a *neurotransmitter*, which can either *excite* or *inhibit* the activity of the receiving cell. Even this much permits a surprising degree of organization in behavior. An example is the blowfly, whose reflex feeding movements are excited by taste stimuli, but inhibited by food in the digestive tract; thus food identification, feeding behavior, and satiety are all provided for. In addition to the arithmetic of excitation (addition) or inhibition (subtraction), the geometry of the nervous system adds possibilities for complexity. Connections in the nervous system can permit a signal to *diverge* so as to have multiple effects. Or different signals can *converge* on a common output, permitting multiple-control systems in which different inputs can have similar effects.

Bard's experiments in animals with transected nervous systems showed a hierarchical organization, in which fragments of behavior at lower levels are organized into units at higher levels. In particular, if the *hypothalamus* was left in the system, movement patterns were organized into sequences of goal-directed action.

Stellar suggested that the multiple controls over biological drives converged to affect *centers* in the hypothalamus. Excitatory centers were assumed to start motivated behavior sequences, inhibitory centers to stop them. There do appear to be sensitive cells in or near the hypothalamus, that detect internal states such as dehydration or the presence of sex hormones and mobilize drinking or mating, respectively, in response. And motivated behavior can be produced by artificial electrical stimulation in the hypothalamus. Conversely, damage to the lateral hypothalamus can produce failure to eat; this suggested to earlier writers that a "feeding center" had been damaged. Damage to the ventromedial hypothalamus produces an apparent lack of inhibition on eating, with resulting overeating and obesity, and this suggested that a "satiety center" has been damaged.

To the extent that these systems promote motivated behavior, they seem to do it by priming the responses to certain *external* stimuli. Hypothalamic stimulation can widen the range of stimuli that will elicit attack. If the hypothalamus is intact, estrogen can *disinhibit* the lordosis reflex in female cats and permit it to occur in response to touch. Feeding, elicited by hypothalamic stimulation, is a sequence of responses—approaching food, then grasping it, then biting and chewing. Since the stimulation remains the same, this may mean that each response sets up the *external stimulus* conditions for the next one.

The notion of localized *centers* for specific motives is no longer held. The systems controlling motivational states may well involve the hypothalamus, but they are not *in* it. The brain is like a freeway system, permitting rapid communication among distant places; it is not a collection of centers for this and that. Some effects of hypothalamic damage may be metabolic rather than directly behavioral. Others may be secondary to more general effects. Failures to eat after hypothalamic damage, for instance, are difficult to distinguish from a general reluctance to move—*akinesia*—and a generalized unresponsiveness to all stimuli—*sensory neglect*. Finally, a deficiency in some behavior after brain damage does not mean that the damaged structure controls that behavior. Such effects may occur, not because a *center* has been damaged, but because one part of the brain has been disconnected from another where the communication is essential for normal behavior. Despite all this, Stellar's theory helps us remember important principles of nervous-system functioning: converging multiple-input systems, joint internal and external control of motivated behavior, and the interplay of excitation and inhibition.

In some systems of the brain, running through the hypothalamus and related structures, electrical stimulation is rewarding. It also appears to bias the brain in the direction of positive responses to external stimuli, as if it said, "Isn't that nice!" Related systems promote arousal and exploration, as if they said, "Isn't that interesting!" Still others promote reactions of aversion and withdrawal, as if they said, "That's awful!" Parts of the reward system are affected by the same states of the body that affect motivational systems. In a well-fed rat, lateral hypothalamic stimulation becomes less rewarding. It is possible that stimulation in these systems mimics the rewarding properties of natural reinforcers. In nature, these systems may be essential for the rewarding effects of natural commodities such as food or opportunity to mate.

Localized areas of the brain can be stimulated not only electrically, but also by injecting minute amounts of certain chemicals to which the cells respond. A message goes from cell to cell by means of a chemical messenger, or neurotransmitter, released by one cell to affect the activity of the next. Certain drugs can modify this process at various stages. Thus the reward system of the brain seems to involve synapses at which the neurotransmitter *dopamine* is the messenger. Drugs that interfere with the effects of dopamine also depress the reward value of stimulation there, and ones that enhance the one enhance the other. Blocking the system with drugs can block the rewarding properties of food without, apparently, reducing hunger. As a second example, certain tastes in the mouth can reduce distress in baby rats or in baby people, and the effect seems to depend on certain morphine-like compounds, the *endorphins,* which are manufactured in the brain and act as neurotransmitters there. Thus unraveling the chemistry of the brain's reward system could teach us much about the physiology of drug use and abuse.

These reward systems that cut across specific motives again suggest that we must deal with systems rather than centers. The hypothalamus connects to both higher and lower parts of the brain. Damage to the parietal lobe of the cerebral cortex, like hypothalamic damage, can produce sensory neglect and thus impair the expression of many different motivational states. Vital too are the inhibitory functions of the forebrain, which keep motivated behaviors in check until the situation is appropriate for their expression. Failures of this system can lead to impulsiveness and disorganization, as in the frontal-lobe system. Finally, in any real-life situation, motivated action may draw on memory, recognition, and perhaps speech production and speech comprehension in humans. All these functions may be involved in translating *any* motive, not just this or that one, into action; and any of them can be compromised by damage to the forebrain.

CHAPTER 6

Energy, Arousal, and Action

I will do such things—
What they are, yet I know not;
but they shall be
The terrors of the earth.
—SHAKESPEARE, *King Lear,*
Act II, Scene IV

Nothing happens, nobody
comes, nobody goes, it's awful!
—SAMUEL BECKETT,
Waiting for Godot

Think of a car running along a road. Why does it do what it does? What makes it go at all, and what makes it go where it goes rather than somewhere else? What makes it go is the engine. And what makes it go in one direction rather than another is the steering apparatus.

Now some writers have suggested that we might break up the causation of behavior in a similar way. One set of influences, analogous to the steering mechanism, affects *what* a creature does if he does anything. It *selects* actions. The other, analogous to the engine, affects whether he does do anything and, if so, how vigorously and persistently he does it. It is a kind of behavioral gas pedal, making the difference between vigorous, persistent action and slow, sluggish, feeble action or no action at all. Finally, it seems natural to think of this latter set of influences as *motivational.*

Our everyday use of the term *motivation* often suggests an image like this one. There are days when we feel, well, *motivated*—just motivated in general. We are aroused, alert, ready to take action. Then there are those other days when we are unresponsive, sluggish, not inclined to do much of anything. Then we may say that we are *unmotivated,* and we often wish we could summon up the energy to do something about it!

In this chapter, we will look at how this conception—motivation as the energizer, the engine, of behavior—developed. One form of the idea arose primarily in the psychological laboratory. A second, Freud's theory of drives, emerged in the first instance from the clinic. A third, the *arousal* concept, originated in the physiological laboratory, but found psychologists eager to join forces with physiologists in exploring it. We will see that despite their very different origins, the three ideas have much in common.

HULL'S DRIVE THEORY

The experimental psychologist Clark L. Hull made an early and influential attempt to specify how drive, conceived as an "engine" of behavior, could fit into its causation. Hull envisioned nothing less than a mathematical theory of behavior, analogous to Newtonian physics as a model of the "behavior" of nonliving objects. He sought, in other words, to specify quantitative relations between behavior and its causes.[1]

Now in a natural environment, where many such causes operate all at once, the mathematics would be horrendously complicated. (They get pretty hairy in Newtonian mechanics too, once we get beyond simple two-body problems!) So Hull's strategy was to observe behavior under laboratory conditions in "simple" animals, where a few important causal influences could be systematically varied and their effects specified. That done, one could work up to more complex cases—and more complex species.

Drive, Habit, and Reaction Potential

Take a look at Figure 6-1. Each of the data points represents the average "score" of a separate group of rats, all trained to press a lever for food reward (or, as we say, food *reinforcement*). Some groups received only a few reinforcements during this training (the data points to the left); others received many (the points to the right). Finally, when tested, some groups of rats were only mildly hungry (lower curve), others were quite hungry (upper curve). The rats were tested under extinction conditions; lever-presses were no longer reinforced with food, and the measure, or "score," was how many times each rat would press the lever before quitting. This was assumed to be a measure of the "strength" of the lever-pressing tendency.

We see that the average score is higher, the more reinforcements the rats had received (the scores rise as we read from left to right). In addition, scores are higher under high hunger than low. Finally, the two curves diverge; the *difference between* the two sets of circles increases from left to right.

Now any theory of what is going on must account for this pattern of data. Hull's thinking went something like this:

Suppose that persistence of lever-pressing does reflect the "strength" of the rat's tendency to press the lever. It reflects, in other words, an underlying theoretical variable that *energizes* the response itself. Modifying Hull's notation, let's call it E (for *energy*).

Now E must increase with number of reinforcements, and also with level of drive. Suppose that successive reinforcements increase the value of another

1. Hull, 1943.

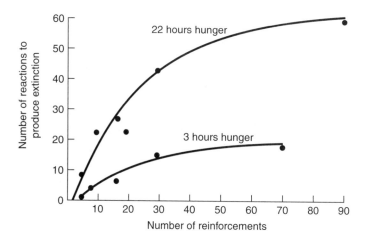

Figure 6-1 Resistance to extinction as affected jointly by number of prior reinforcements (contributing to habit strength, or *H*), and severity of food deprivation (contributing to drive, or *D*). (From Perin, 1942.)

theoretical variable, *H* (for *habit*). This represents the *strength of an association* between the situation and the response in question, for Hull, like Thorndike (pp. 37–38), saw the learning process as a matter of strengthening stimulus-response associations. The concave-downward shape of the curves then suggests that that association grows rapidly at first, then more slowly, with successive reinforcements.

Notice that the strength of the association, *H,* is not the same as the tendency to make the response here and now, *E.* In a well-trained rat, *H* (the association) may be very strong; but if the rat is not hungry, he will not bother to lever-press (see later). *H,* in other words, reflects what the rat has learned. But to show what he has learned, the rat must be—what else?—*motivated* to do so.

This takes us to a third theoretical variable, the motivational factor *D* (for *drive*), which increases as food deprivation does. Persistence of bar-pressing is higher in hungrier animals because *D* is higher.

Finally, the divergence between the two curves suggests a *multiplicative* relation between *H* and *D*. So we get Hull's basic equation:

$$E = H \times D.$$

Thus *E* will be higher as *H* increases (left to right), or as *D* increases (upper versus lower curves). As for the divergence, it follows directly from the algebra. If we multiply any two numbers, then increase one of them and multiply again, we will also increase the *difference between* the two products; that is, the products will diverge.

The whole idea was attractive to many psychological theorists, not only because one could account for a lot with just a little simple algebra, but because the theory made a great deal of sense, and made contact with other ideas as well.

Consider: It follows from Hull's equations that if either D or H is zero, then E should also be zero. That makes good sense. As noted earlier, an animal may be very well trained in lever-pressing (H is high); but if it is not hungry (D is zero), why should it bother to lever-press now? It won't; E will be zero. Conversely, an animal might be very hungry indeed (D is high), but if it has had no training at lever-pressing (H is zero), then E will be zero and the animal will do no lever-pressing (except occasionally by accident, which is what makes training possible). Here then are more data to fit the simple model! (But see later.)

Again: If Hull was right, then a very hungry animal would work hard for food, and so (under most conditions) obtain more food and get less hungry (*negative feedback,* though the term was not current in Hull's time). Thus behavior was used to regulate energy reserves—behavior in the service of *homeostasis.* Even Richter's observations on activity (p. 58) fit in: If drive multiplies all action tendencies, learned and unlearned, then a hungry animal should be an active animal—as it is. And an active animal is more likely to find food. Thus it makes sense that animals should have evolved that way; and we see the influence on Hull's thinking of the *theory of evolution* (pp. 35–37).

Anxiety as a Drive

Some writers influenced by Hull attempted to extend his theory to more complex behavior in humans.[2] Now, any attempt to do that—to account for complex human behavior by reference to a few biological drives—at once faces a problem. Most of what we do is not "driven" by any biological emergency at all.

Consider the author. Right now he is engaged both in the mental work of deciding what to say and how to say it, and the physical work of typing one word after another. He is not hungry or thirsty; he is in no identifiable state of deprivation at the moment. Nor will his efforts lead directly to food, drink, a mate, or anything of the sort. What then is "driving" all this activity?

One possibility is that the drive is *anxiety*. To put it baldly, maybe I do all this work because I'll feel anxious if I don't. I remind myself that if the book doesn't get written, then my ideas about motivation will have no audience, I'll earn no royalties, and my editor will scold me.

Fear, or anxiety, is an *acquired* motive (Chap. 7). It is something we learn; and so the complexity of our behavior reflects the complexity of our learning history (pp. 46–48). Nevertheless, anxiety could be a perfectly good drive if it has the properties of other drive states. Kenneth Spence, an associate of Hull, reasoned this way: If anxiety is a drive, it ought to multiply response tendencies. So, as we saw earlier, it should also multiply the *differences in strength* among different response tendencies.

2. See for example Dollard and Miller, 1950.

Now that could be a good thing or a bad thing. It all depends on whether it is the stronger or the weaker habit that best fits the occasion.

Let us look at the exam situation. Suppose an exam question for this course asks you, "Who was Watson?" Now, you of course will have mastered this book thoroughly. You will have a strong habit of responding to that question, "He was the scientist who . . . ," and you can fill in the rest. Other possible responses, that might intrude as wrong answers, have less strength. Therefore, you will do well in any case, but you will likely do even better if you are a bit anxious and eager and "up" for the quiz—that is, if drive is high. If your drive is high, the appropriate response will not only be the strongest one, but it will be strongest by a wider margin.

But think about the poor student who hasn't studied. Asked "Who was Watson?" his strongest habit is the reply, "He was Sherlock Holmes's biographer." Now the poor guy has to *suppress* that dominant habit before any other response, including the correct one, has any chance of being expressed in actual behavior. And *the more anxious he is, the harder that will be*—again, because anxiety will increase the difference between strong response tendencies and weaker ones.

Spence and his colleagues had their experimental subjects learn a list of word pairs—so-called paired-associate learning, in which, given the stimulus word, one learns to say the response word that goes with it. One such list was made up of easy items in which the stimulus-response connection was already strong, like the "Watson–Sherlock Holmes" connection (though that was not one of their items). Another list was made up of difficult items, like the "Watson–founder-of-behaviorism" connection (which would be weak for a student who has not studied the history of psychology, though of course it would not be weak for *you*).

For the easy list, high anxiety (high *D*) should make the correct response tendency all the stronger, so anxious subjects should do better than non-anxious ones. But for the difficult list, where existing habits interfered with good performance, high anxiety should make the incorrect habits all the stronger, hence harder to suppress; so anxious subjects should do more poorly than non-anxious ones at this task.

So Spence's group also varied anxiety. This was done by selecting subjects who were high (for one group) or low (for another) in chronic or "resting level" of anxiety as measured by a paper-and-pencil test.★

The results are shown in Figure 6-2. Sure enough: When the list was easy, the high-anxious subjects did better than the low-anxious ones. But when the list was hard, high-anxious subjects did slightly *less* well than their low-anxious counterparts.

★The test was the Manifest Anxiety Scale, developed by Janet Taylor (later Janet Taylor Spence) for this research project. A high score reflected "yes" answers to items like (1) "I cry easily," or (2) "I work under a great deal of tension."

Figure 6-2 How anxiety (*D*) interacts with *H* in human learning. With easy pairs of words, high-anxious subjects make fewer errors than low-anxious ones. With difficult pairs, the difference disappears or is even slightly reversed. (Data from Spence, Taylor, and Ketchel, 1956.)

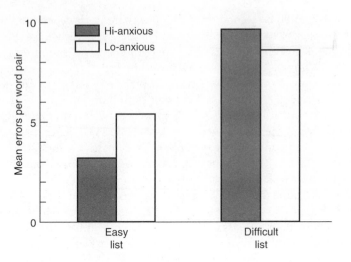

This example shows how the Hullian algebra can indeed be applied to complex human behavior, to lead to testable predictions. It also shows, by the way, how personality variables (here, high versus low chronic anxiety) can make contact with experimentally derived concepts (*D* and *E*) within a single theory. And it shows how a theory can lead to questions that would not occur to us, and findings that would be very puzzling, without it. Why should subjects' chronic anxiety level have *any* effect on their rate of learning a list of word pairs? The theory tells us why.

Some Problems with Hullian Theory

There was much more to Hull's theory than we have considered, but we have enough to see the guiding ideas and to have some feel for what such a theory can do. We also have enough to see why, as research continued, the theory has shown itself to be inadequate.

First, it is now clear that learning is not a matter of strenthening stimulus-response connections. As we will see in Chapter 8, animals learn not just *what to do,* but also *where things are* ("cognitive maps" and "search images," pp. 329–32). So an animal may make its way to a goal by means of a response that has never been reinforced in that setting.

Also too simple was the idea that reaction potential will be zero whenever drive is. It turned out that animals will learn quite complex tasks, such as taking a mechanical puzzle apart (Fig. 6-3) for no reward except, perhaps, satisfaction of curiosity (pp. 234–37); and they will do so when non-hungry, non-thirsty, and presumably non-lecherous.[3] Non-hungry, non-thirsty rats will drink copious quantities of a sweet solution, with no need to drive them to do so.[4] It

3. Harlow, 1953.
4. Sheffield and Roby, 1950; Ernits and Corbit, 1973.

Figure 6-3 Hasps, hooks, and hinges: Baby rhesus monkeys work busily to take apart a mechanical puzzle. If the experimenter then reassembles the puzzle, they will take it apart again. Persistent as it is, this activity is not motivated by any homeostatic drive.

simply is not true that a non-deprived animal (*D* zero) will just sit there doing nothing.

Finally, Hull's "generalized-drive" idea has not held up. Hull treated *D* as a non-specific multiplier, something to which *all* drive states contributed, and which activated *all* S-R connections (all *H*'s) indiscriminately.

Attempts to test this idea involved such things as, for example, adding an "irrelevant" thirst drive to hunger in experiments like the one in Figure 6-1 above. If Hull were right, then the added thirst should increase *D,* just as an increase in hunger would, and so increase the vigor or persistence of food-getting activity.

It did not. And later research discovered that there was good reason for this: Water deprivation, which enhances thirst, may actually suppress or *inhibit* hunger and feeding.★ These findings came later and Hull had no way of knowing about this. But the fact remains that different drives are not necessarily additive; they may inhibit each other instead.

A Look Backward: Hull's Legacy

You may well ask why, if the theory hasn't held up, have I spent so much time working through it with you? For four reasons. First, it is an instructive example of behavioristic theorizing. And its research logic—simplify the situation so that only a few key variables operate, rather than try to study everything at once—was then, and is now, a cornerstone of the experimental method in psychology.

★Some of the inhibition may simply reflect the mechanical difficulty of swallowing dry food with a dry mouth (for example, Kissileff, 1969). But there is also evidence that the activation of brain systems involved in thirst may have inhibitory effects on food-getting and feeding behavior (see for example Grossman, 1962).

Second, the idea that behavior is controlled jointly by a motivational factor (like *D*) and an associative, cognitive, or learning-based factor (like *H*) crops up again and again—as does the notion of a multiplicative relation between them. In modern decision theory (Chap. 10), for example, the tendency to choose a given alternative reflects the values of its possible outcomes (motivational), *times* what we judge the probabilities of those outcomes to be (cognitive). Variants of this idea have been proposed by many modern psychologists. So in working through a bit of Hull, we are previewing some important contemporary ideas.

Third, whereas the notion of "generalized drive" has been greatly modified since Hull's day, it has not disappeared entirely. Hull was surely wrong in this: It is not the case that *any* drive state will automatically enhance *all* behaviors in a generalized, non-specific way. But this much of it may be true: There are certain influences that affect, not just this or that action, but a variety of actions, raising or lowering the vigor or persistence of all of them at once. Such influences could make the difference between an active, alert, vigorous creature and a sluggish, unresponsive, or comatose one. That latter idea is still with us, as we will see later when we discuss *arousal*.

There is one further reason. In seeing how certain findings raise problems for Hull's theory, we see a good example of how we check our ideas by testing the predictions they make (pp. 5–6). That way, when we are wrong, we will know it. In science, the failure of a theory is not a step backward but a step forward. Every failed prediction says to us: Here is a place where our ideas do not square with the facts, and need to be revised.

We will see how important this process is when we contrast Hull's theory with another "engine model" of motivation—Sigmund Freud's.

FREUD'S THEORY OF DRIVES

A few weeks ago (as this is written), a certain Chuck Jones went to jail for theft. He had had dozens of stolen shoes, boots, slippers, and sandals, most of them belonging to Ms. Marla Trump (wife of the high-profile real estate developer Donald Trump), for whom he had worked as public-relations representative. Most of these had high heels; and this, according to a clinical psychologist who testified, is quite characteristic, because such shoes are more feminine and also because the heel is a phallic symbol. (He doesn't say how he knows this, and there is trouble ahead on that point, as we will see.) Mr. Jones himself had told a friend: "I don't know why I like shoes." He could not explain his own actions.

As a clinical neurologist of the late nineteenth century, Sigmund Freud faced, from very early on, the problem of symptoms that made no sense. These included physical symptoms with no reasonable organic basis, but also actions, fears, and preoccupations (as with shoes, for instance) that could not be explained—least of all by the patient himself.

Yet Freud insisted that these symptoms occurred for a reason. They were, in a word, *motivated.* Their study led him to a theory that was, right or wrong, the most influential theory of human motivation our society has yet produced.

Freud's Theory of Motivation

Freud regarded mental events as ultimately biological ones, reflecting operations of the brain. Like any other biological events, they take energy—biological energy, that comes from the food we eat. Therefore, some biological events motivate action, whether mental action or physical.

Freud's word for these, the German word *trieb,* is usually translated as "instinct;" but as many writers have pointed out, the word *drive* is a more accurate translation, and probably closer to Freud's intention. A drive is a source of tension and discomfort, which the actor will seek to remove. That is what gives it its motivating, energizing force.

DRIVES   Every drive has a *source,* an *object,* and an *aim.* The *aim* of all the drives is ultimately the same—the reduction of discomfort. It is the sources from which various drives arise, and the objects by which they are satisfied, that distinguish them.

Thus the source of hunger might be the discomfort of stomach pangs (pp. 63–64). Its object is food.

The source of elimination drives is pressure in bowel or bladder. As to their object—well, in this society (unless one can tolerate a lot of anxiety-arousing disapproval), their expression usually requires that one find a suitable enclosure. (The elimination drives have been neglected by psychologists, but if these drives are present in strength and no suitable object is around, we see—do we not?—why Freud thought of drives as sources of unpleasurable tension!)

The sexual drive also is experienced as tension. Its object is sexual contact broadly conceived—sexual intercourse perhaps, but also the pleasure of intimate touching, of and by another, or of and by oneself. Its aim, as always, is pleasurable reduction of tension.

As Freud saw it, all actions (physical and mental) are motivated by this small handful of biological drives. Of them, the sexual drive is much the most important. Freud was roundly criticized for this assertion, even by his associates. Yet, if one tries to reduce human motivation to biological drives at all, it makes good sense. Hunger, thirst, and elimination drives *must* be regularly satisfied if we are to survive; but sexual gratification can be postponed indefinitely. And in Western society, said Freud, that drive is in fact systematically frustrated. This, plus the great flexibility of our ways of expressing drives (see below), makes the sex drive a plausible candidate for a source of "general-purpose" motivational energy.

THE PLEASURE PRINCIPLE   Since the aim of all drives is the same—the reduction of tension—we could say for Freud, as for Hull, that ultimately there is only one motivator. For Hull it is the sum *D* of all drive states. For Freud, it

Every man has reminiscences which he would not tell to everyone . . . He has other matters in his mind which he would not reveal even to his friends . . . But there are other things which a man is afraid to tell even to himself, and every decent man has a number of such things stored away in his mind.

—FYODOR DOSTOYEVSKI,
Notes from the Underground

It's sexual energy, this energy that you control and channel into your performance. Without it, you can have the best technique in the world and sing beautifully, but you'll just be singing notes, and your audience will go to sleep.

—OPERATIC BARITONE
GEORGE MALDONADO

is discomfort, which is unpleasant; and the aim of behavior is the pleasure of reducing that discomfort. Hence, at bottom, the organism seeks pleasure, and *nothing else*. That is the *pleasure principle*.

A Look Backward   Even this brief preview shows that Freud's ideas mesh closely with those of other writers. His pleasure principle recalls the *hedonism* of Thomas Hobbes (pp. 32–33). His theory is a *homeostatic* one: a state of quiescence, or non-tension, is maintained as much as possible; and it is regulated, in the sense that deviations from it will be corrected if they can. Thus we could say that Freud, like Hull, saw behavior as an adjunct to homeostasis. And, here once again, homeostasis is defended by *negative-feedback* loops. Tension or disturbance (input) calls forth action (output) to make the tension go away (negative feedback).

Dynamics of Mind: Conflict, Redirection, and Disguise

The instincts or drives are biologically based and primitive. If we are to think of them as the wellsprings of motivation, then we face the same problem Hullian theory faces: How, from these few and simple building blocks, can we generate the richness and complexity of human behavior?

Freud's answer is as follows: Complex mental phenomena result from the complexities of the *interactions among* drives and urges and their respective strivings. They are perceived as "brought about by the play of forces in the mind, as expressions of tendencies striving toward a goal, which work together or against one another. We are endeavoring to attain a dynamic conception of mental phenomena."[4]

Thus we saw earlier (pp. 41–42) that Freud saw patients as at war with themselves: a tendency to express a thought or wish could be blocked by a countervailing tendency *not* to express it (Fig. 6-4A). We should remember, however, that both these mental forces had the same origin—the pool of mental energy, coming from the food we eat. We can elaborate Figure 6-4A so as to represent this (Fig. 6-4B).

The relation among forces in the mind can be more complex than this. Rather than simply blocking each other, conflicting forces can result in a *redirection* of energy in some third direction (Fig. 6-4C). Thus the outcome in thought or action can be a redirected, distorted, or *disguised* expression of the original forces. Or the forces may be directed toward a substitute *object*—like shoes!—if the more direct object is blocked, unavailable, or dangerous. The outcome may make no sense on the face of it; but penetrate the disguise, said Freud, and we will see that it does make sense after all.

---

4. Freud, 1977.

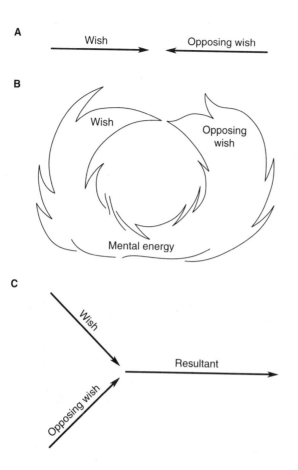

Figure 6-4 In Freud's theory, opposing wishes may block each other (A), though they both draw on the same pool of psychic energy (B). The resultant thought or action may represent a compromise between two wishes or impulses (C).

Freud's Theory of Dreams

This is a fundamental principle in Freud's thinking. Neurotic symptoms, fears, fetishes—but also quite normal actions, and even acts of creative genius—can be seen as disguised expressions of primitive impulses. If we want examples close to home, said Freud, we can look within ourselves. We all do irrational, apparently senseless things—at night, when we dream. In perhaps his most influential book, *The Interpretation of Dreams,* Freud applied his developing theory to the act of dreaming.

Think about the *act* of dreaming. We *do* irrational things in our sleep. Thinking and dreaming are actions. If you have a senseless, irrational, childish dream—well, you *did* it. You made it happen; it is, after all, your dream. So we can ask our motivational question: When you dreamed that dream, why did you do it?

Freud saw dreams as coming about in either of two ways. First, a strong unconscious impulse may by itself break through into consciousness while one sleeps, because the defenses that otherwise keep it from consciousness are weakened during sleep (Fig. 6-5A).★ Second, an event of the day might be *associated with* a deeper, more long-lasting, and unconscious idea (Fig. 6-5B). It may then "borrow" energy from that idea by fusing with it, so that what comes into the sleeper's consciousness is a fusion of the two (Fig. 6-5C).

An analogy may help. The event of the day may be compared to a human

Figure 6-5 Two ways in which unconscious wishes may appear in consciousness as dreams. (A) The wish may be strong enough to break through directly. Or (B) a recent event may be *associated with* an unconscious wish, represented by the joining hands. Then a fusion or "condensation" of the two may have enough total energy to break through.

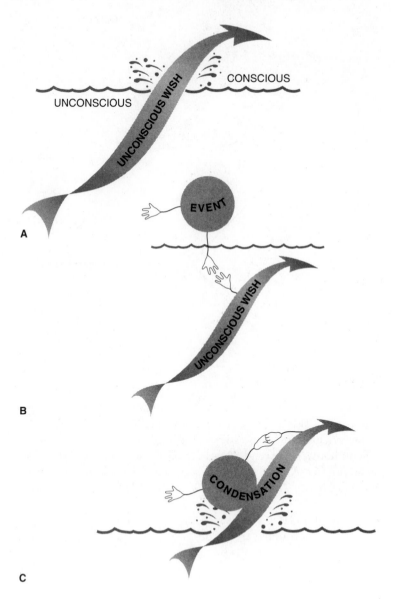

rider, a smallish jockey perhaps. It makes contact, through association, with a strong unconscious drive—the jockey mounts a big, powerful horse. Then he can use its great strength and speed to get somewhere—into the land of consciousness perhaps, as a dream.

As long as we're about it, let's take another step. Maybe the dream work will fuse together the horse and the jockey, so that we get a centaur—a human head and torso emerging from the shoulders of a horse. There are no such creatures, but so what? Our minds can combine these parts to create a new whole, which can symbolize in one image both the intelligence and skill of the jockey and the enormous power of the horse. Dream work, Freud believed, involved a great deal of such *condensation*—combining ideas or their fragments into an imaginary synthesis that expressed all of them at once.

And we can do one more thing with this metaphor (of which the author is becoming quite fond, as you see). Suppose the idea of riding a horse were threatening—a powerful and potentially uncontrollable animal between one's legs. What if the thought gave rise to troublesome anxiety? We might suppress the thought—generating a counterforce, borrowing some energy to oppose the horse image and thrust it out of mind.

Then the centaur, an image that *modifies and thus disguises* the horse, could be thought about (and dreamed about) with less discomfort. Thus the energy of the original thought could find indirect release, and no additional energy need be tied up in its suppression. As Freud saw it, very many dream images—and daydream images, and neurotic symptoms, and everyday activities too—are just such disguises. They mask the uncomfortable instinctive drives, the objects of these, or both, and thus they reduce the displeasure of anxiety.

How then do we interpret a dream? In essence, we follow the dream work in reverse. By the technique of *free association* to each element of the dream (pp. 41–42), we work backward—perhaps against great resistance—to discover what urges those elements represent in the patient's mind. We can sooner or later uncover an intelligible pattern, and see what interplay of tensions has expressed, distorted, condensed, or otherwise shaped those urges into the content of the dream itself.

To see this idea in action, let's take one of Freud's examples:[5]

"You're always saying to me," began a clever woman patient of mine, "that a dream is a fulfilled wish, Well, I'll tell you a dream whose subject is the exact opposite—a dream in which one of my wishes was *not* fulfilled. How do you fit that in with your theory? This was the dream:
I wanted to give a supper-party, but I had nothing in the house but a little smoked salmon. I thought I would go out and buy something, but remembered then that it was Sunday afternoon and all the shops would be shut. Next I tried to ring up some caterers, but the telephone was out of order. So I had to abandon my wish to give a supper-party."
Analysis.—My patient's husband . . . had remarked to her the day before that he was getting too stout and therefore intended to start on a course of weight-reduction . . . [He would] above all accept no more invitations to supper. —She laughingly added that her husband, at the place where he regularly lunched, had made

5. From Freud, 1980, pp. 180–182.

the acquaintance of a painter who had pressed him to be allowed to paint his por-
trait . . . [The husband replied that] he was sure the painter would prefer a piece of
a pretty young girl's behind to the whole of his face . . .

Notice how it is the woman, not Freud, whose thoughts flow from topic to
topic: from the dream to her husband's diet to the place where he eats lunch,
and then by way of the painter to a woman's figure. The relevance of that last
will be apparent shortly.

After a short pause, such as would correspond to the overcoming of a resistance,
she went on to tell me that the day before, she had visited a woman friend of
whom . . . she felt jealous because her (my patient's) husband was constantly
singing her praises.
Fortunately this friend of hers is very skinny and thin and her husband admires a
plumper figure. I asked her what she had talked about to her thin friend. Naturally, she replied, of that lady's wish to grow a little stouter. Her friend had
enquired, too: "When are you going to ask us to another meal? You always feed
one so well."
The meaning of the dream was now clear, and I was able to say to my patient: "It
is just as though when she made this suggestion you said to yourself: 'A likely thing!
I'm to ask you to come and eat in my house so that you may get stout and attract
my husband still more! I'd rather never give another supper-party.' [The dream]
was thus fulfilling your wish not to help your friend to grow plumper. The fact
that what people eat at parties makes them stout had been brought home to you by
your husband's decision not to accept any more invitations to supper." . . . [But
why did smoked salmon appear in the dream?] "Oh," [the patient] replied,
"smoked salmon is my friend's favourite dish."

Thus, by letting the patient tell us what ideas are connected with each other
in her own mind (by seeing how her mind flows by *association* from one to
another), we see the underlying pattern that the dream expresses. In a similar
way, we can trace neurotic symptoms—or the foibles of our daily mental
lives—back to their sources in unconscious motives.

The Structure of the Mind

It is worth emphasizing once again that the dream work, and the primitive
urges on which the work is done, are largely unconscious. This takes us to
Freud's conception of how the mind is organized. Figure 6-6 shows his famous
sketch. Most of what goes on in the mind, Freud believed, is unconscious; we
may be aware of its results, but not of its operations. These unconscious
processes include the collection of instinctive drives (the *id,* the source of motivation) and some, though not all, of the information-gathering and decision-
making parts of our minds (the *ego,* the source of cognition).

It also includes some, though not all, of the internalized sets of approvals
and disapprovals that we pick up from our culture by way of our parents and
other caretakers. These *superego* processes lead to our feelings of anxiety ("moral

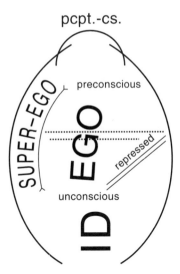

Figure 6-6   Freud's sketch of the organization of the mind. The "percept-conscious" includes material that one is conscious of at the moment; the much larger "preconscious" contains material that is not conscious but could be, such as your memory of what you had for breakfast or your knowledge that Rome is in Italy. Much of the mind, however, is unconscious, and much material is unconscious because it is *repressed*—forced out of consciousness and kept out by forces opposing its entry into consciousness. Both the *superego* and the *ego* are represented as in part unconscious; the *id,* as totally so. (From S. Freud, 1977.)

anxiety" or guilt) when we violate society's standards or contemplate doing so, and our feelings of pride or satisfaction at "doing the right thing" in society's eyes, at being the kind of person society says we ought to be. (Freud spoke of the latter as the "ego ideal.") However, since superego processes *are* in part unconscious, the sources of our anxiety or guilt may not be apparent to us. Many of our problems in living result from this.

PSYCHOANALYSIS IN ANOTHER CULTURE

Freud developed his ideas over the years into a detailed theory of human development: the oral, anal, and phallic stages, and the famous *Oedipus complex*—the growing boy's wish for sexual comfort from his mother and his terror of his powerful rival, the father. We will not review these ideas here, first because any good text in personality theory will do that, and second because one may reject these specific ideas—as many psychoanalysts do—while still holding onto the more general Freudian concepts of symbolism, association, the persistence of primitive urges, and, above all, unconscious motivation.

A Case Fragment

So let us look at a case in which both analyst and patient are from a different culture from ours. This example shows both similarities with, and differences from, a strictly Freudian interpretation of clinical material.

The therapist is a psychoanalyst in India, Dr. Sudhir Kakar. And the patient is a 26-year-old Indian man, M., who had been in analysis for 3 years.

Most of M.'s early memories about his female relatives were images of their sleeping together, in

> the crowded, public living arrangements of the Indian family . . . Sleeping in the heat with little or no clothes next to one of his caretakers, an arm or a leg thrown across the maternal body, there is one disturbing memory that stands out clearly. This is of M.'s penis erect against the buttocks of his sleeping mother and his reluctance to move away, struggling against the feelings of shame and embarrassment that she may wake up and notice the forbidden touch. . . . Embedded in this blissful abundance of maternal flesh . . . however, is a nightmare. Ever since childhood . . . M. would often scream in his sleep while a vague, dark shape threatened to envelop him. At these times only his father's awakening him with the reassurance that everything was all right helped M. compose himself for renewed slumber.[6]

That was then. Compare now:

> In the very first sessions of the analysis, M. talked about a sexual compulsion that he found embarrassing to acknowledge. The compulsion consisted of traveling in a crowded bus and seeking to press close to the hips of any plump, middle-aged woman standing in the aisle. It was vital for his ensuing excitement that the woman gave her back to him. If she ever turned to face M. with the knowledge of his desire in her eyes, his erection immediately subsided and he would hurriedly move away with intense feelings of shame. After marriage, too, the edge of his desire was often at its sharpest when his wife slept on her side with her back to him. In mounting excitement, M. would rub against her and want to make love when she was still not quite awake. If, however, the wife gave intimations of becoming an enthusiastic partner in the exercise, M sometimes . . . found his erection precipitately shrivel.[7]

A Freudian would immediately suspect that M. was reliving, as an adult, the childhood closeness to his mother. One would also suspect that the desire for such closeness triggered intense fear of the jealous father—hence the "discovery" of his actions by the woman would lead at once to impotence, as if to prevent any possible justification for that jealousy.

Kakar, while agreeing that there is unconscious conflict here, sees the terms of the conflict differently. It seems that the boundaries between genders are more fluid in India than in the West, and that in India it is not uncommon for a man to feel, and express, the wish to be a woman:

6. Kakar, 1991, pp. 437–438.
7. Ibid.

[W]hen Gandhi publicly proclaims that he has mentally become a woman or . . . talks of man's envy for the woman's procreative capacities, saying "There is as much reason for a man to wish he was born a woman as for woman to do otherwise," he is sure of a sympathetic and receptive audience."[8]

M., too, had fantasies—undisturbing ones—of being a woman.

The conflict faced by a growing boy in India, Kakar suggests, is not between desire for the mother and fear of the father (a conflict that Freud held to be universal), but between, on the one hand, the desire to be an independent, autonomous man and, on the other, the wish to merge again with the mother, to become one with the mother symbolically. If he did that, he would gain closeness to the mother, her nurturance and protection; but he would would also cease to be an independent, autonomous male. Hence the dark, threatening figure in the dream was not the father but the potentially devouring, all-consuming mother. It "has as its roots the fear of the mother's sexuality."[9] So, we might guess, did his impotence when his sexuality was acknowledged by a woman.

Symbolism in Myth and Folklore

Freud insisted that our literature and folklore, as well as our symptoms, expressed unconscious urges and conflict. His "Oedipus complex" is named after the Greek legend of Oedipus, who, unknowingly, murdered his father and married his mother. The story moves us, said Freud, because it expresses a conflict every boy feels. He wishes his father were out of the way (or expressing it childishly, as the unconscious often does, that his father were dead), so that his mother would be all his. But this wish in turn triggers fear of his father's jealousy, and so the wish must be punished, as was the act in the tragic myth.

In a similar way, Kakar sees the ubiquitous conflict of the Indian boy symbolized in folklore. Consider a folk story, which concerns two young gods. One is Ganesha, "god of all beginnings" represented as a pot-bellied toddler having the head of an elephant with one tusk missing. His brother Skanda is a handsome child, a youth of slender body and heroic exploits.

> Ganesha, in many myths, is solely his mother Parvati's creation. Desirous of a child . . . she created him out of the dirt and sweat of her body mixed with unguents . . . Skanda . . . is the son of more than one mother; his father Shiva's seed, being too powerful, could not be borne by one woman and wandered from womb to womb before Skanda took birth.[10]

It should come as no surprise that Skanda's sexual appetites were literally legendary.

8. Ibid., p. 439.
9. Ibid., p. 438.
10. Ibid., p. 440.

Now, the folk tale:

> A mango was floating down the stream and Parvati, the mother, said that whoever rides around the universe first will get the mango . . . Skanda impulsively got on his golden peacock and went around the universe. But Ganesha, who rode the rat, had more wisdom. He . . . [rode around] his mother, worshipped her and said, "I have gone around my universe." Since Ganesha was right his mother gave him the mango. Skanda was furious when he arrived and demanded the mango. But before he could get it Ganesha bit the mango and broke one of his tusks.[11]

Kakar sees this myth as expressing the conflict that the growing Indian boy confronts. He can be an autonomous, sexual male, and ride around the universe. But then he cannot rejoin, or become, the nurturing mother figure. Or he can rejoin the mother; he can nurse at her breast (the mango, we are told, is often compared to the breast) and be protected and comforted. But then he loses some of his masculinity (one tusk breaks off) and he does not get to explore the universe.

A Look Backward

Kakar's interpretation of M.'s case material obviously keeps the basics of Freudian theory: the persistence into adulthood of unconscious childhood conflicts which are expressed symbolically. It also suggests, however, that the exact nature of the conflict may vary, depending on the culture in which one lives. Fear of a father's jealousy need not be universal, as Freud had held it to be.

In a similar way, Kakar, like Freud, sees legend and folklore as expressive of deep-lying, persisting concerns (analogous to the horse in our earlier image). Just what these concerns are, however, may vary considerably in different societies.

WHAT SHOULD WE SAY ABOUT FREUD?

For just about a century now, the debate has continued: Is Freudian psychology a set of fundamental insights into the mind, or is it a century-long wild-goose chase? Do his ideas give us deep understanding of the human mind, both normal and pathological—or do they only allow us to spin ingenious stories that give us the *illusion* of understanding? The question is still before us.

Freud as Cognitive Psychologist

Many of the things Freud said about the mind are not, from a modern perspective, really controversial at all.[12] The ideas he dealt with include ones with

11. Ibid.
12. Erdelyi, 1985.

which modern cognitive psychologists are quite comfortable. That material can be distorted in memory to fit long-standing ideas, or that two episodes can fuse together in memory is well known. And clearly there can be associative links between ideas; this is only to say that one idea can remind us of another.

Can we be "reminded" of sexual material in this way? Of course; why not? Matthew Erdelyi gives a marvelous example. This took place on a television quiz show, hosted by comedian Groucho Marx. Groucho, a virtuoso of the unrehearsed "one-liner," would interview his contestants before playing the quiz game with them. On one such interview, the following exchange took place:

Groucho: How are you?
Man: Fine.
G. Well, tell me, are you married?
M. Yes, I've been married for nine years.
G: Gee, that's swell. Do you have any kids?
M. Yes, nine already and the tenth is on the way.
G. Wait a minute! Ten kids in nine years?
M. Well, I happen to love my wife very much.
G. Well, I love my cigar too, but I take it out of my mouth once in a while![13]

Can we be in any doubt as to the sexual reference here? Television audiences were not. Audience members who were offended by sexual innuendos (and there were more of these in the 1950s than there are now) called their stations in large numbers to complain.

Two questions arise, however. One is how far we can push such interpretations and still be on firm ground. What about Figure 6-7? Here we see a man and a woman at a tender moment. The ring is shown edge-on, but there is also a faint reflection that could remind us of the roundness and the *openness* of

Figure 6-7 Is this a sexy picture? (From Gleitman, 1995.)

13. Ibid.

the ring. And directly between the two people there is a silhouette of a very erect flower arrangement. We could easily see sexual symbolism in all this (the details are left as an exercise for the reader). But the question is: would we react to these symbols unconsciously in any case, with increased interest in the figure as a result? Or are we *reading them in* now, because we have psychoanalytic theory specifically in mind? And if the latter, might not a psychoanalyst, who also has the theory in mind, read symbolism into what she hears her patient say? Keep that question in mind; we'll return to it.

The "Dynamic Unconscious"

The second question is this: If we do accept such interpretations, do we need an energy metaphor to explain them?

Freud, as we have seen, regarded mental (and behavioral) events as reflecting the resolution of dynamic forces. Ideas and wishes are active, striving processes. If many of these are unconscious, it is because they are *made* unconscious; they are forced out of consciousness, or *repressed,* by other dynamic processes.

It has been pointed out that most people will tell us, if asked, that they do actively thrust ideas out of mind if these are unpleasant or anxiety-arousing. Yes, but in these cases, the ideas are preconscious; they remain accessible to consciousness and may still come to mind, all too easily it often seems. Freud is talking about ideas that are thrust so violently out of consciousness that the person *cannot* get to them, at least not without the patient help of a psychoanalyst.★

The idea of repression has become so commonplace that many of us are inclined to take it for granted. It is worth emphasizing, therefore, that such a process has *never been demonstrated* under controlled conditions—that is, under conditions where we know what is going on.

In other cases too, modern writers wonder whether unconscious mechanisms need reflect the clash of "hot" instinctual energies. Maybe they reflect instead some ways in which our minds process information, "coolly" as it were. Are we, as one team of writers happily put it, dealing with "psychodynamics" or with "psychologic"?★★

Freud's Interpretations

All this takes us to what many writers regard as the key question about Freudian psychology: In whose head(s) are these associations, symbols, and disguises? Are they in all our heads, or only in the heads of psychoanalysts? To

---

★For this reason, the Groucho Marx joke, delicious as it is, is only superficially Freudian. The sexual reference was fully apparent to the radio listeners and, surely, to Groucho himself.

★★Nisbett and Ross, 1980. Their book includes a very readable discussion of this issue, which we also will touch on again in later chapters.

what extent do psychoanalysts (Freud included) "read into" a patient's material what they expect to find there?

Take the case of M.'s problems on buses. The symptoms cry out, we might say, for interpretation as a reliving of childhood experiences. Perhaps so (since we have the theory specifically in mind), but that still doesn't mean the interpretation is right. For all we know, M. might have the same problems even if he had slept alone from earliest childhood. That is what an experimenter means when he points out that "real life doesn't run the control condition."*

Looking over this example, we begin to see the problem more clearly. *Freud's theory cannot be tested.* It is so flexible that it could be made to "explain" anything whatever—after the fact. But that means that if it is wrong, it gives us no way of discovering that it is wrong (see pp. 207–8). We must take it on faith or not at all.

There is obviously a problem of bias here—of reading into material what one expects to find there. This is frequently a problem with case studies, as we saw in Chapter 1. And in Freud's case, letters and documents recently made public have suggested that Freud's biases intruded blatantly into his work. He may have been, quite simply, a poor scientist, by the standards of our day and of his own.**

Freud was nothing if not confident of his own theories. And it now seems that he was capable of jumping to a conclusion based on his theories and forcing it on his patients. He might continue to insist that such and such must have happened in the patient's childhood, even if the patient never could recall any such event. And if the patient did recall it, what then? We now know that it is possible for a person to *create* false memories, of things that we *know* did not happen, in response to the insistence of an experimenter (or a well-meaning therapist). We'll discuss this "false-memory syndrome" in Chapter 11.

One other thing should be made very clear in all this: *A patient's assent to a Freudian interpretation is no guarantee of its correctness.* The patient, too, is puzzled by his own thoughts and actions. He would like to understand them. A story

*It does not help matters that many of Freud's followers—and, on occasion, Freud himself—have been ready to give quick and confident pronouncements about this or that action, based on no evidence at all. Here is an example of the sort of thing that makes scientists cringe:

In a letter, Freud speaks of Shakespeare's Hamlet, "who is positively hasty in murdering Laertes." A commentator writes of this: "[Freud's] slip about Laertes is an interesting commentary on the conflict he had stumbled upon in himself . . . Hamlet, of course, murders the father, Polonius, rather than Laertes, the son. It is as though, caught up in his self-analysis, Freud could not quite face the enormity of the son's homicidal oedipal hostility directed against his father." (Gay, 1990, p. 8.)

This bald assertion is true to the spirit of Freud's thinking. But we have no way of knowing whether or not it is correct. Was Freud's slip really an indication of "homicidal hostility" toward his own father? Suppose Freud had got it right, and written correctly of Polonius as the murderee—would that count against the theory? No, for then the commentator could as easily have said this: Since the fictional victim was someone else's father, not his own, Freud could express his hostility symbolically, hence safely, by writing of Hamlet's murder of a father. The theory wins, either way!

**For discussion and references, see Crews, 1993.

that gives him the *feeling* that he understands them may, right or wrong, be avidly accepted.

One may well wonder: If Freud's methods were so bad, why did his theory have such impact on the popular culture? There are a number of possible answers. Freud's case studies do spin intriguing stories. He wrote about sex, always a topic of interest. And there is a certain *fittingness* to the theories: If we do dark, mysterious, sometimes violent things, it seems natural to look for dark, mysterious, sometimes violent mechanisms to account for them.* None of this, however, argues for the rightness of the theory. It may instead only help to explain its seductiveness, in offering us the illusion of understanding in place of the real thing.

A Look Backward

Looking back over the chapter thus far, we can see several points of similarity between Freud's theory and Hull's. (1) Both writers saw motivation as springing ultimately from a handful of biological, homeostatic, energizing drives that reduce ultimately to one: Hull's *D,* and Freud's *pleasure principle.* (2) Both failed to make their case convincingly. In Hull's case, the theory was tested and found wanting; in Freud's, it could not be tested at all, and the invitation to bias in Freud's methods increases our suspicions of it. As a result, although (3) some recognizably Hullian and Freudian ideas are still with us, (4) neither theory in its original form is widely held by students of motivation today.

That said, we should note on the other hand, first, that some recognizably Freudian ideas *are* still with us: that one idea can symbolize another and that memories can fuse and condense with each other. And that our minds can process information *unconsciously* is about as well established anything in psychology could be. (Did you even notice, Reader, the mi   1g word in the last sentence? Or did you fill it in—unconsciously?)

Above all, it is clear that any theory of motivation must ace up to a simple but vital fact: *We do things without knowing why.* Mr. Jones doesn't know why he has his thing about shoes. I don't know why I doodled that owl. We are, as a modern writer put it, "strangers to ourselves" in very many ways.[15] We need to understand why this is so. Did Freud solve that problem? Probably not. Is the problem real and important? Definitely.

AROUSAL

At about the time when interest in Hull's theory was waning among psychologists, another non-specific, engine-like concept was gaining ground. This was the concept of *arousal.*

*Remember this when we discuss the *representativeness heuristic,* pp. 408–9.
15. Wilson, 1985.

We can look at the underlying idea in several ways. One is to consider that an organism may act in various ways—it may do this, that, or the other—depending on the situation. That action, however, occurs with more or less vigor or persistence depending on the state of arousal. High arousal, vigorous action; low arousal, feeble action (Fig. 6-8A).

Another way of looking at it is to consider not just how vigorous the action is, but how effective it is likely to be. If arousal level is too low, little or no effective action will occur, as before. If it is too high, action may be very intense, but it may also be frenzied and frantic and disorganized, so that nothing useful gets accomplished (Fig. 6-8B). This looks forward to the idea that there is an optimal, or best, level of arousal for behaving effectively (pp. 234–39).

Non-Specific Effects on Behavior

The first line of evidence for such ideas came from the study of reflex action (p. 165). It turns out that stimuli can have not only specific effects, calling forth just this or that reaction, but also *non-specific* effects, enhancing or priming a variety of reactions.

THE "CENTRAL EXCITATORY STATE"   At around the turn of the century, the English physiologist Sir Charles Sherrington noticed that the elicitation of a simple reflex in dogs would elicit not only a specific reaction (e.g., leg flexion in response to a pin-prick on the foot), but also a momentary

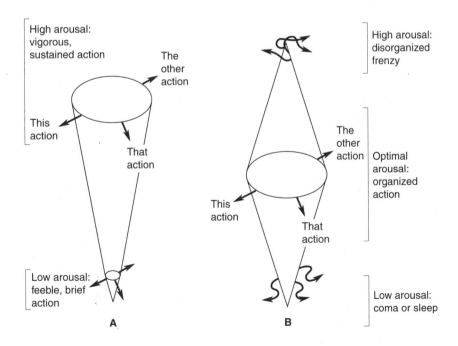

Figure 6-8   Two conceptions of the effects of non-specific arousal on behavior. In A, arousal enhances the vigor or energy level of whatever action occurs; the higher the arousal, the more vigorous the action. In B, there is an optimal, intermediate level of arousal for well-organized action. Action becomes less effective as arousal level moves away from the optimum, up or down.

state in which other reflexes, even unrelated ones, became more sensitive and vigorous. Besides eliciting leg flexion, then, the pinprick evoked what Sherrington called a *central excitatory state,* in which the whole family of reflex actions was made more excitable.

Something of the sort could easily be demonstrated in humans, too. In one classic study, subjects used one hand to squeeze a hand dynamometer—the gadget that measures the strength of one's squeeze. It was found that squeezing this instrument with one hand actually increased the speed with which one could react to a signal, where that reaction used the other hand—an entirely different set of muscles.

PAIN- AND STRESS-INDUCED BEHAVIORS   More recently, researchers have identified yet more examples of non-specific effects. Suppose a male rat is subjected to mild pain, produced by electric shock or a clamp attached to the tail. This of course will produce attempts to escape and expressions of annoyance; but if a receptive female is present, then the male rat may court and mate. Or if food is present in the situation, the rat may eat.[16]

Stressors of these kinds can also counteract the effects of interference with the brain. Certain forms of brain damage can reduce responsiveness in experimental animals, producing, for example, rats or cats that are unwilling to mate or eat or explore (pp. 177–78). David Wolgin and Philip Teitelbaum found that many of these deficits could be reversed, as if by magic, if the animal were stressed or aroused. After being picked up, pinched, or dipped in cold water, an otherwise sluggish and unresponsive cat would walk briskly around for a while, or lunge at a mouse, or eat a bit of food. Arousal by quite another means, injection of the stimulant drug *amphetamine,* had similar effects.[17]

Wolgin and Teitelbaum suggest that the directing and eliciting properties of stimuli are superimposed on a general arousal that makes the actor responsive to them. Conversely, arousal can be enhanced by stimuli, such as a pinch or a cold bath. In other words, stimuli coming in from outside can have two effects. They can trigger specific responses such as feeding or mating, and they can also arouse the animal, making it responsive to other, perhaps quite unrelated, stimuli. Drugs or handling can also produce that arousal.

In humans as well as animals, non-specific effects have been observed. For example, many people in our society report that they eat in response to stress (pp. 188–89). Again, both women and men have been found to be more sexually aroused by an erotic film if, prior to that film, they have watched a vivid and gory movie dealing with automobile accidents.[18] Perhaps relevant too is that in many cultures, bites and scratches that draw blood are a routine part of sexual foreplay.

16. Antelman and Szechtman, 1975.
17. Wolgin and Teitelbaum, 1978.
18. Hoon et al., 1977; Wolchik et al., 1980.

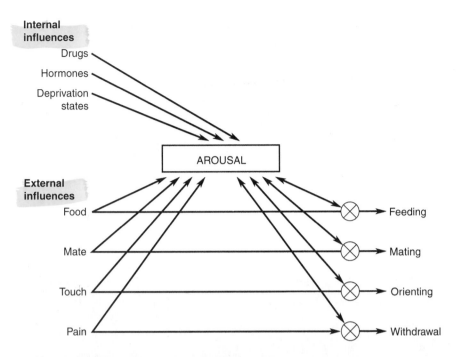

Figure 6-9 A possible role of arousal in behavior. Various stimulus situations elicit specific responses, but they also contribute to a generalized arousal state that enhances the effects of *all* stimuli. Internal influences also can contribute to that arousal state.

A Look Backward: Specific and Non-Specific Influences

What is underscored by these findings is this: A variety of manipulations can affect a variety of behaviors. Thus tail pinch, stimulant drugs, or prominent environmental stimuli can affect feeding, or mating, or attacking—among other things. We can represent these relations as in Figure 6-9, which shows some of the relations between non-specific arousal and some of its determinants and consequences.

The figure emphasizes several important ideas. First, specific stimulus factors, besides promoting and directing specific actions, can contribute to the generalized arousal state. So, presumably, can the occurrences of the responses themselves. Finally, there can be trade-offs among different influences. If food by itself is not an adequate stimulus for feeding just now, it might become so if pain-induced arousal is added to prime the feeding response. That is one way in which a pinch to the tail could elicit feeding.

THE PHYSIOLOGY OF AROUSAL

Yet another line of support for the arousal concept came from the study of organisms' reactions, physiological and behavioral, to emergencies. The physiologist Walter Cannon, who coined the term *homeostasis* (pp. 60–61), also pointed out that the body has a certain "emergency mode," in which it is prepared for vigorous action—"fight or flight," in Cannon's phrase—to deal with the emergency. Let us look more closely at this emergency state, and bring its investigation to modern times.

As with specific drive states, what happens inside and outside the body must be registered and translated into action by the nervous system. In complex creatures, this means integration in the spinal cord and the brain.

The Autonomic Nervous System

The **autonomic nervous system** is a part of the nervous system that has a specific role to play. Rather than producing behavior on the part of the creature—limb movements, for instance—it regulates the rate of the physiological processes that keep the body going. These include the processes of respiration, digestion, circulation of the blood, and the like.

The autonomic nervous system breaks down into two divisions, the **sympathetic** and the **parasympathetic** (Fig. 6-10). These systems place the body in different modes, depending on circumstances. We can think of this as a balance between a business-as-usual mode, controlled by the parasympathetic nervous system, and an emergency mode, mobilized by the sympathetic nervous system. In the latter function, the sympathetic system is reinforced by the **adrenal medulla,** an endocrine gland so closely related to sympathetic functioning that we might as well consider it as part of the package.

THE SYMPATHETIC-ADRENAL SYSTEM   When emergencies arise and we must take vigorous action, our whole bodies go into emergency mode. Rate of breathing increases, to supply more oxygen; blood glucose increases, to supply more fuel. Heart rate increases, to keep the glucose and the oxygen coming to the cells; blood pressure therefore rises sharply. Not only that, but the blood vessels in the muscles expand, while vessels supplying the digestive organs constrict; the effect is to divert more blood to the muscles, to fuel the effort that may be required of them.

This global preparation for **fight or flight** is mobilized as a unit by a system well designed to change a number of things at once. Figure 6-10 shows a schematic diagram of the sympathetic nervous system. Motor nerve cells run from the spinal cord into a chain of nodes running up and down the cord, the **sympathetic chain ganglia**. There they synapse with other nerve cells that in turn run out to the organs—the blood vessels, heart, and others.

The synapses in the chain ganglia use the neurotransmitter **acetylcholine**. But at the target organs, the transmitter is **norepinephrine**, or noradrenalin, as it is also called. It is this chemical that affects the organs, exciting some and inhibiting others, so that the emergency state is brought into being.

Chemically, the adrenal medulla, a part of the adrenal gland, is very much like the nerve fibers running out from the chain ganglia. It too is stimulated by nerve cells that release acetylcholine, and it too releases a chemical transmitter, in this case **epinephrine**, or adrenalin. The difference is that the epinephrine is released into the bloodstream, which then carries it throughout the

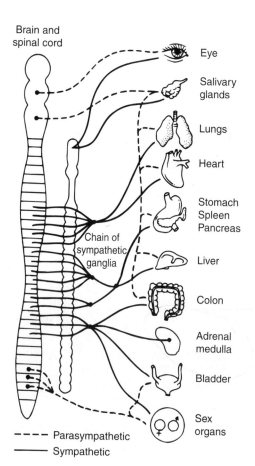

Figure 6-10 The autonomic nervous system, with its sympathetic division (solid lines) and parasympathetic division (dashed lines). The parasympathetic division has the following effects on its target organs: constriction of the pupils, stimulation of tears, stimulation of salivation, slowing of the heart, constriction of respiratory passages, promotion of movements in the stomach and intestine and the secretion of digestive fluids, contraction of the bladder, and flow of blood into the genital organs, producing erection in males and swelling of the vaginal walls in females. The sympathetic system has the opposite effects: dilation of the pupils, inhibition of tears, inhibition of salivation, acceleration of the heart, opening of the respiratory passages, inhibition of stomach and intestinal movements and digestive secretions, relaxation of the bladder, and inhibition of blood flow to the genitals. (After Cannon, 1929.)

body. It too inhibits some organs while exciting others, so that its effects closely resemble those of norepinephrine. It also has the important function of elevating blood-sugar level, supplying the cells with extra fuel.

The important thing to see is that this system is designed to function *as a unit*. The chain ganglia are closely connected with each other, so that an excitatory input anywhere in the system is likely to spread all up and down the chain, activating the whole system and thus mobilizing the entire body. The secretions of the adrenal medulla will have similar diffuse effects, for they are carried to all organs by the blood. In a word: *Input to the system from anywhere has effects everywhere.* Here we see again the important role of *divergence* in nervous system function.

Although the executive part of the system is organized at the level of the spinal cord, its effective inputs may of course come from elsewhere. Electrical stimulation of our old friend the hypothalamus may provoke a storm of sympathetic activity in an animal's body; if the animal is awake, signs of violent rage or fear may be evoked as well.[19]

THE PARASYMPATHETIC SYSTEM   The housekeeping, business-as-usual system, the parasympathetic, is quite different. Here, nerve cells run from the spinal cord and from certain areas of the brain, to synapse with clusters of cell bodies close to the individual target organs. Other nerve cells go to those organs. These cells, like the sympathetic cells, are stimulated by acetylcholine, but unlike those cells they also release acetylcholine at the target organs. By and large, the effects of acetylcholine on the organs are opposite to those of epinephrine and norepinephrine. Acetylcholine slows down the heart, and it promotes activity of the digestive system, emptying of the bladder and rectum, and other housekeeping chores.

There is no interconnected chain of ganglia here, and there is no parasympathetic hormone corresponding to the sympathetic hormone, epinephrine, released by the adrenal medulla into the blood. As a result, the parasympathetic system is much less a unit than the sympathetic; its various parts can act more or less independently of one another. This makes good sense. The body's business-as-usual mode involves independent action of different systems, each in response to local conditions. If too much light enters the eye, the pupil must constrict; if the bladder is full, it must empty. There is no particular reason why these reactions should be coupled together so that if one occurs the other does. On the other hand, an increase in heart rate, constriction of blood vessels in the interior of the body, and a rise in blood sugar all act to make emergency fuel available to the muscles. These responses *should* be coupled with each other, so that if any one occurs they all do. And they are so coupled, through the sympathetic system.

Arousal and the Brain

The brain is a communication network. It is made up in large part of billions of nerve cells, or *neurons,* whose job it is to transmit messages from source to destination. Once called into action by an event or *stimulus,* arising from inside or outside the brain, such a cell, we recall, will send a series of electrochemical blips—nerve impulses—along its thread-like *axon* to affect the next cell in the chain.

19. For example, Hess, 1957.

In much of the brain, these axons are gathered together in bundles, reminding us of telephone cables. These cell bundles, again like a cable that connects, say, Pittsburg with New York City, transmit information from just one location in the brain to another—from right *here* to right *there*.

But not all of the brain is organized that way. Gathered around the central core of the brain stem are networks of cells that connect to multiple output locations (Fig. 6-11). Networks of cells like these remind us of military warning systems: an emergency signal that originates at one base will be sent, not just to some one other base, but to all other bases in the network.

This system, then, has effects that are widespread and diffuse, rather than localized and specific. The parallel with the sympathetic nervous system is apparent: input from any of a number of sources will have effects that spread throughout the system. And because the system does seem to be involved in a generalized arousal or alerting reaction within the brain, we will refer to it as the *brainstem arousal system,* or BAS.

There are several lines of evidence that this system does have an arousing, alerting effect when it is called into play. One kind of evidence is obtained by "listening in" on the brain's internal conversations by the recording of brain waves. Such a recording is an *electroencephalogram,* or EEG.

THE EEG   To record an EEG, we simply paste electrodes to the scalp with conducting paste and attach the electrodes to a voltage-measuring device. We can then record the electrical fields that the activity of nerve cells generates.

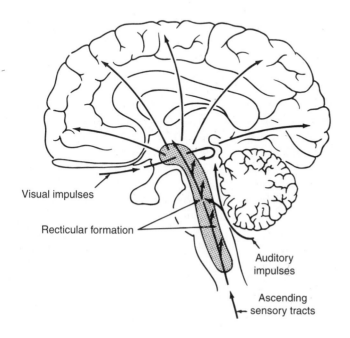

Visual impulses

Recticular formation

Auditory impulses

Ascending sensory tracts

Figure 6-11   The reticular activating system. The reticular formation (shaded area), an important part of the brainstem arousal system, receives input from all the sensory systems. In turn it activates cells (see arrows) that deliver their messages throughout the cerebral cortex. (After Netter, 1958.)

We are measuring a kind of summed, or average, activity of many millions of brain cells (Fig. 6-12A).

If we do that in a subject who is sitting at rest with eyes closed, we would see a tracing of the kind shown in Figure 6-12B. There would be a rhythmic up-and-down trace. This is the **alpha rhythm**, also called a **synchronized EEG** (see below). The pattern is characteristic of low arousal level.

If the subject opens his eyes, or if we ask him a question or otherwise alert him, the tracing will change to the kind shown in the middle part of Figure 6-12C. The wiggles are faster and of lower amplitude. This is a **desynchronized EEG**, one showing arousal.

Why does this happen? Maybe an analogy will help here. Suppose we are at a party, where many conversations are in progress. A great deal of information is being transmitted within the room as a whole; many different arguments, stories, and flirtations are going on. If we simply record the overall sound level, our recording will not change very much over time, because the peaks and valleys of individual conversations will cancel each other out. The recording will look like the middle part of Figure 6-12C.

On the other hand, suppose all the people are saying the same thing at the same time—"DEE-fence! DEE-fence!" Now the peaks and valleys of the sound level are in phase with each other. Our record will make bigger swings back and forth in the rhythm of the chant—as in Figure 6-12B. But, let's face it, not much information is being transmitted. The chant may be fun, but it simply is not terribly informative. Just so, if many of the brain cells are doing the same thing at the same time, what they are doing is unlikely to be very interesting. The cells cannot be processing complex information if they are all chanting in unison.

Perhaps one effect of the impulses coming in from the BAS is to break up this synchrony. The BAS may say to the cortical cells, "Hey, listen. Something important is happening, and we may all have to do our different jobs to deal with it." If the task of saying that is entrusted to messengers—the cells of the BAS—who must spread the alert throughout the room, then we would expect the chant to break up. Various different out-of-phase conversations—What's up? Who are you? What's happening?—will ensue as the message gets around. Our sound recording will then show rapid but low-amplitude fluctuations, again as in the middle part of Figure 6-12C. Something like that may happen when our subject opens his eyes, or hears our question, or otherwise prepares to deal with information.

What is the role of sensory input in this system? Inasmuch as our subject's EEG switches to an aroused, desynchronized pattern when we ask a question, it seems that incoming sensory messages can arouse the brain. And it turns out that the specific sensory systems do give off branches into the BAS as they ascend in the brain. The result is that sensory inputs can have two effects. They convey specific sensory information, and they arouse the brain so that it can deal with that information.

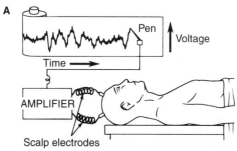

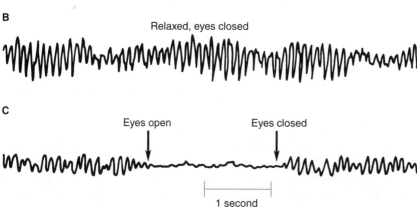

Figure 6-12   Procedure for recording EEG (A), and two typical records (B, C). (A) Scalp electrodes placed on the subject's head pick up the electrical fields generated by the activity of brain cells. These small electrical signals are magnified by an amplifier and are then used to drive a recording pen. Since the electrical signal fluctuates, the pen goes up and down, tracing a wavy line on the moving paper. The number of such waves per second is the EEG *frequency*. (From Gleitman, 1981.) (B) When the subject is relaxed with eyes closed, the record is of high amplitude (large electrical changes) and of relatively low frequency. This suggests that the many cells generating the electrical field are in *synchrony;* that is, they are all in the same state at the same time. (C) When the subject's eyes open, the wave breaks up and the record is at low amplitude and at a higher frequency, this suggests *desynchrony* of the cells' activities. (B, C: After Guyton, 1966.)

STIMULATION OF THE BRAIN   Artificial stimulation of the brain gives us further evidence for an arousing or alerting function of the BAS. When the BAS was stimulated electrically in a sleeping animal, the synchronized EEG shifted at once to the desynchronized, aroused pattern. Behavioral arousal occurred too; the animal would raise its head, open its eyes, and look around alertly.[20] Strong stimuli can waken a sleeping animal, of course, but it seems

20. Lindsley, 1960.

we can bypass the sensory system and produce the same awakening directly, by stimulating the BAS.

DAMAGE TO THE BRAIN Another set of findings shows the effects of damage to this diffuse system.[21] In a classic series of experiments, knife cuts were made through the tissue of the BAS in cats. These cuts interrupted the ascending BAS, but avoided the sensory freeways that carry sensory information up into the brain. Presumably, therefore, the cats could hear, see, and feel, but they were drowsy, lethargic, and unresponsive after the operation. They simply did not react to sensory information. The messages got through, but the brain's bureaucracy did nothing about them. And this state of somnolent unresponsiveness was accompanied by a synchronized, high-voltage, low-arousal EEG.

All this is further evidence that it is not enough for sensory messages to get to the forebrain. The forebrain must be prepared to do something about them. And that preparation can be disrupted by BAS damage.

The reference to "somnolent unresponsiveness" reminds us of another kind of unresponsiveness—the akinesia and sensory neglect produced by lateral hypothalamic damage. We looked earlier (pp. 182–84) at the evidence that a non-specific system may run up through that area of the brain, one that says, "Isn't that interesting!" to incoming stimuli. As we have described it, damage to the BAS seems to interfere with an "Isn't that interesting!" reaction.

AROUSAL AND EXTERNAL STIMULI When we say that the system is aroused, what exactly do we mean? An aroused brain might be one in which response systems—movements—are primed directly. Or its aroused activity could be a *response to* movements, rather than a cause of them.

Or, yet another possibility, an aroused brain might be one in which the effect of *external* inputs is increased. In one experiment, tiny wires were implanted in the brainstem while the rats were anesthetized. These made it possible to record the electrical activity of single neurons in the BAS, later when the animal was awake and freely moving. It was found that some cells showed very *low* activity when the rat was eating or grooming, even though these are very vigorous actions. But when the animals were attending to *external* stimuli rather than (as it seemed) focusing on what they were doing, these cells became very active indeed. The researchers suggest that *vigilance* might be a better term than *arousal* to describe the latter state.[22]

In yet other experiments, the effect of BAS activity on response to external signals has been shown directly. In Figure 6-13, we see that electrical stimulation of the visual pathway, in an anesthetized cat, caused a small electrical response in the visual receiving area of the forebrain (A). But when the BAS

21. Moruzzi and Magoun, 1949.
22. Aston-Jones, 1985.

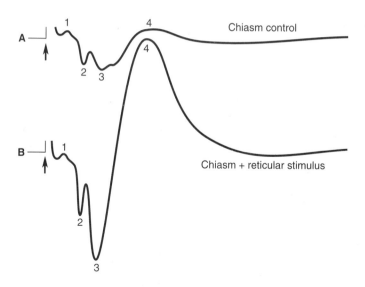

Figure 6-13 In an anesthetized cat, electrical stimulation of the optic tract—the bundle of nerve fibers running from the eye into the brain—causes an electrical response in the visual receiving area of the cerebral cortex. As with the EEG, this "evoked response" reflects the summed activity of many thousands of cortical cells. Note the much greater response in the lower tracing, especially at 2, 3, and 4. The difference is that in the lower tracing, the brainstem arousal system was stimulated as well as the optic tract. (From Singer, 1979.)

was stimulated along with the visual pathway, the effect was very much greater (B). In all this, it seems as if the BAS is acting, not so much as an "engine" of behavior, but as a "volume control" for inputs from the environment.

Finally, these operations—priming responses, or registering responses that have already occurred, or vigilance for sensory inputs—are not incompatible. They may all be going on when the brain is aroused. What we have been calling the BAS is actually a very complex collection of subsystems, and different subsystems may well have different jobs.

A Look Backward—and Forward

As we have seen, the sympathetic nervous system is designed to arouse the body. The BAS and related systems are designed to arouse the brain, to make it vigilant and responsive.

Sensory input may have two different effects on the brain. It may go to its specific sensory receiving areas in the brain to convey specific information and call forth specific reactions. But in addition, it may arouse the whole brain by way of the diffuse BAS. In this way an incoming report from the sensory systems could say two things to the brain: (1) "Here is the specific information I have to convey," and (2) "Something is happening! Isn't that interesting! Pay attention! Prepare to investigate and perhaps do something about it!" The latter is the arousal reaction.

All this looks backward once again to the very important notion that we saw earlier when we talked about hunger and sex. Internal and external influences on motivation and behavior are not independent; they interact with each other. An external event can contribute to internal changes—in blood chemistry for example or, as here, in an internal state of arousal. Conversely, internal states can affect how external signals are reacted to. In the last section, we saw that internal changes in BAS activity can affect the sensory pathways that register external events.

OPTIMAL AROUSAL THEORY

For Hull, some state of need or deprivation—drive, or *D*—is necessary for any behavior at all to occur. Total absence of drive should produce an organism that does nothing whatever—like a car with the engine switched off.

Very different is the notion of *optimal arousal*, to which we now turn. It says this: The ideal state is one in which there is an *intermediate* level of arousal—not too much, not too little. That state is best for effective behavior, it is most pleasant, and it is the state that organisms seek to attain or maintain (Fig. 6-14).

Sources of Optimal Arousal Theory

Various ideas converge to support this theory. First, there are the results of introspective studies of pleasantness and unpleasantness. For a variety of sensory modalities, pleasure tends to be evoked by stimuli of low or medium intensity; high-intensity stimuli tend to be unpleasant. Thus there is an inverted U-shaped relationship between the intensity of a stimulus and its pleasantness.[23] We can easily think of examples. Almost any stimulus can actually be painful if it is strong enough. Short of that, consider salt in scrambled eggs. A little is good. A lot is not so good!

Figure 6-14   Optimal arousal theory. Action, learning, and information processing are most efficient at an intermediate level of arousal, neither too high nor too low. (From Hebb, 1955.)

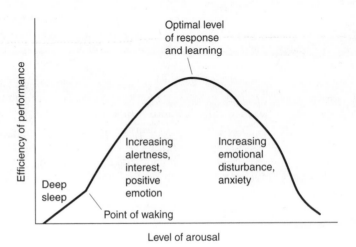

23. See for example Wundt, 1910.

Second, there are the results of some early experiments from the animal learning laboratory. One study looked at the efficiency of maze learning in mice, varying two things: the difficulty of the task, and the strength of the drive.[24] Briefly, there is an optimal level of drive for a task of given difficulty. Again there is an inverted U-shaped function, this time relating efficiency of learning to drive level. This relationship is often referred to as the **Yerkes-Dodson law.**

Finally, a number of writers have wondered how the biasing mechanisms of the brain, that push it toward negative or positive responses to stimuli, fit into the picture. Recall again the non-specific systems running up through the hypothalamus. One says, "Isn't that nice!" and one says, "That's awful!"—to a variety of inputs. Daniel Berlyne, among others, has pointed out that the inverted U-shaped curve could result from the joint action of a positive "Isn't that nice!" system and a negative "That's awful!" system if we assume three things: (1) that the "nice" system is the more sensitive one, but (2) that it quickly saturates, so that it can be activated just so much and no more, and (3) that awfulness subtracts from niceness.[25] That would mean that low-intensity stimuli activate only the sensitive "nice" system. But as stimulation gets more intense, it becomes intense enough to bring the "awful" system into play. And the more intense it is, the more the balance shifts away from niceness and toward awfulness (Figure 6-15).

Seeking Optimal Arousal

The notion of an optimal arousal level has been a popular one. Let us look at just a few of the many findings that fit within it.

TOO MUCH AROUSAL   First, this theory would agree with Freud's theory, and Hull's, that too much is too much—of anything. In both animals and humans, loud noises are aversive, and will support escape or avoidance almost as effectively as electric shock. They can also affect physiological functioning and disrupt performance.[26] For example, children whose school was in the flight path of a Los Angeles airport were found to have higher blood pressure than children from quieter but otherwise comparable schools.[27] They were also more likely to fail on problems or to give them up.

Crowding, too, can cause increased blood pressure and feelings of discomfort,[28] and it is likely to disrupt performance on complex tasks.[29] Here is the Yerkes-Dodson law in human performance.

---

24. Yerkes and Dodson, 1908.
25. Berlyne, 1970, 1971; see also Schneirla, 1959.
26. Cohen et al., 1981.
27. Paulus, McCain, and Cox, 1978.
28. Epstein, 1981.
29. McClelland, 1974; cited by Worschel and Shebilske, 1983.

Figure 6-15 How two systems, one positive ("Isn't that nice!") and one negative ("That's awful!"), could give rise to an optimal arousal level. Feeling or mood reflects the difference between the two systems (dashed line), that is, the extent to which positive exceeds negative. Mood would be most positive at an intermediate arousal level that excites the positive system, without exciting the less sensitive negative one.

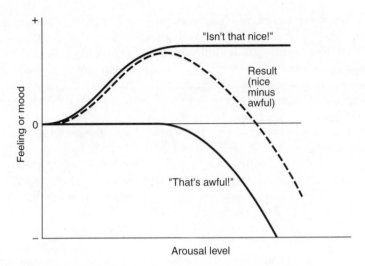

Finally, a state of too much arousal is not just aversive and disruptive. It can be life-threatening:

> Twice in the past eight months . . . the Montreal newspapers reported the behavior of a human being who, suddenly finding himself in extreme danger but with time to escape, simply made no move whatever. One of the two was killed; the other was not, but only because a truck driver chose to wreck his truck and another car instead.[30]

In such cases, one might suppose that the people simply froze in terror. Not necessarily. Hebb cites records of behavior during emergencies in which people displayed not freezing, but "a clear impairment of intelligent behavior, often with aimless and irrelevant movement." And he makes explicit the parallel with Hull's ideas: "a high [drive] arouses conflicting [habits]?"

TOO LITTLE AROUSAL   On the other hand, optimal arousal theory breaks sharply with Freud and Hull at the other end of the spectrum. Too little going on can be as bad as too much.

Consider an experiment like this:

> [The] subjects were paid handsomely to do nothing, see nothing, hear or touch very little, for 24 hours a day. Primary needs were met, on the whole, very well. The subjects suffered no pain, and were fed on request. It is true that they could not copulate, but at the risk of impugning the virility of Canadian college students I point out that most of them would not have been copulating anyway. . . . The secondary reward, on the other hand, was high: $20 a day plus room and board.[31]

30. Hebb, 1955.
31. Ibid., p. 245.

The subjects in these **sensory deprivation** experiments might lie on a cot, with opaque goggles over their eyes, earphones over their ears, and mailing tubes over their hands so that they could manipulate nothing and touch very little. Nothing bad happened to them. They were simply left there.

Notice that the subjects are in an ideal situation from either the Hullian or the Freudian point of view. Any homeostatic needs are quickly met; there are no tensions, drives, requirements, or hassles of any sort. The subjects should simply have been *unmotivated,* and they should have relaxed and enjoyed it.

> In fact, the subject was well motivated for perhaps four to eight hours, and then became increasingly unhappy. He developed a need for stimulation of almost any kind. . . . Some subjects were given [through the earphones] a talk for 6-year-old children on the dangers of alcohol. This might be requested, by a grown-up male college student, 15 to 20 times in a 30-hour period. Others were offered, and asked for repeatedly, a recording of an old stock-market report.[32]

The Regulation of Arousal

It appears then that there is something like an **optimal arousal level,** set not at zero (as for Freud) but at some moderate value. Moreover, we have seen evidence that organisms *seek* that optimal level. If arousal is too low, one seeks to raise it: If there is nothing else to see or hear, college students ask to have stock-market reports read to them. If arousal is too high, one seeks to lower it: A harassed city dweller seeks a quiet walk in the woods. That suggests that there are negative-feedback loops for arousal as there are for blood sugar level, so that we seek to decrease arousal if it is too high, or to increase it if it is too low.

Donald Hebb interprets many of our everyday behaviors as attempts to raise a too-low arousal level.[33] We read exciting stories; we go to scary movies; we ride roller coasters. And we make arbitrary responses to be able to do these things—transporting ourselves, shelling out money, and so on—so we are seeing the action of *motivational states* in these instances. We will go to considerable lengths, taking whatever action is available, to escape from boredom.

Conversely, we sometimes will escape from a situation in which too much is going on—even if it is not acutely threatening. Those are the times when we will seek peace and quiet—again by whatever action is available.

But Is There One Optimal Arousal Level?

Optimal arousal theory has a certain surface plausibility. We don't like to be bored, but we also don't like to be bombarded with too much going on. Still, on second thought, we may wonder whether there is any *one, single* level of arousal that is optimal all the time, as the theory implies.

32. Ibid., p. 246.
33. Hebb, 1955.

Consider how our bodies feel after a roller-coaster ride. Our hearts pound, our knees shake, we are in a cold sweat—and we find it pleasant. If our bodies were in the *same* state after a visit to the dean's office, would we find that pleasant? And if not, how can we say that any given level of arousal is pleasant, or optimal, in itself? We can't.

Studies of physiological arousal raise similar questions. Experiments have shown that unpleasant situations, such as stress or crowding, increase the outpouring of epinephrine and norepinephrine. A stress reaction? Perhaps, but when an exciting game of Bingo is in progress, the measure of sympathetic activity can rise just as high.[34] If we say that a given amount of sympathetic activity is *too high* when produced by crowding or threats, how can the same activity level be *just right* when produced by a Bingo game?

Indeed, even the everyday examples that make the theory seem plausible can be less supportive when examined more closely. Jean is bored, and wants some excitement. James is hassled and harried, and wants some peace and quiet. Is it really the *same* final state that the two people are seeking, from opposite sides? It seems unlikely. My guess is that they would cross over if they could, that Jean, who wants excitement, will seek a somewhat higher level of arousal than will James, who wants some peace.

Optimal Arousal and the Task

Finally, let us look again at the Yerkes-Dodson law. What the law actually says is not that there is *one* optimal level of motivation, but rather an optimal level *for the task at hand*. And that optimal level varies with the task. It seems to be lower when the task is complex (where there are many possible *H*s to compete with each other?). It is higher when the task is simple (where only one *H* is clearly dominant?).

Athletes and performing artists, and their coaches, are familiar with this idea. For finely skilled activity, one wants to be excited and "up" for the occasion, but not too much so. "Tensing up" can be fatal to good singing, and "choking under pressure" can be disastrous for the skilled golfer or billiards player. Where finely skilled movement is less important than an explosion of strength or speed, as for the sprinter, then the level of tension can be considerably higher without endangering performance. There is some direct experimental evidence for this idea.[35] Because of this, athletes and performers often deliberately take steps to raise or lower their own arousal levels toward what is optimal for the upcoming test (see below, pp. 240–41).

Notice, however, that we have shifted ground here. We are now thinking of a given level of arousal, not as something that is currently present to affect our behavior, but as a *goal*—something that is not present now, but that we seek to bring about. And the *motive* involved is not an existing state of arousal,

34. Frankenhaeuser, 1976.
35. For review see LeUnes and Nation, 1989.

but our desire to do well at the task. Achieving the right level of arousal is thus a stepping-stone toward that end.

All this moves away from the notion of arousal as the "engine" of behavior. Instead, it looks forward to the general problem of goal-directed behavior, to be considered in later chapters.

COGNITIVE FACTORS IN AROUSAL: DISCREPANCY AND SURPRISE

Thus far, we have spoken as if arousal were determined simply by the amount of sensory input an organism receives. If that were so, arousal could be seen as a direct physiological response to sensory inputs. But that is too simple, for we must also consider *cognitive* influences. We will see that arousal depends on what we *expect* to happen, and not just on what does happen.

Stimuli or Events?

If we put aside a boring novel and pick up a new and more interesting one, our eyes are not receiving any more light than they were before. Interesting conversation is not necessarily any louder than boring conversation. There is something important about the *content* of the input, not just the *amount* of it that we receive.

Further experiments with sensory deprivation make the same point. Instead of lying in darkness, a subject may wear translucent goggles which, like frosted glass, admit light but not *patterned* light. Instead of hearing only silence, he may hear continuous shooshing "white noise" through headphones. Then he is hearing sound, but not *patterned* sound.

Now if the simple *amount* of sensory input determines how much excitation is fed into the BAS, and therefore how aroused the forebrain is, then even unpatterned sensory input should prevent the disorganization of brain function and the distress associated with it. It does not.[36] Subjects find **pattern deprivation** just as intolerable as the original sensory deprivation of darkness and silence.

What Is an Event?

It appears that sensory deprivation is not just a matter of reduced physical input to the sense organs. It is deprivation of patterned sensory input, or events, or *happenings.* "Nothing happens, nobody comes, nobody goes, it's awful!" To understand this, we need to know what qualifies as an *event,* as opposed to a physical stimulus.

HABITUATION AND AROUSAL   Part of the answer comes from some classic experiments by E. N. Sokoloff.[37] In human subjects, Sokoloff recorded

36. See Hinde, 1970, for discussion.
37. Sokoloff, 1960.

various physiological measures of arousal while his subjects were sitting in a quiet room. From time to time, a tone would suddenly come on. Sure enough, subjects were aroused by the tone—at first. But if the tone came on repeatedly, for fixed durations and at fixed intervals, the arousal response gradually weakened until it disappeared altogether.

This waning of responsiveness, with repeated or continuous presentation of a stimulus, is known as **habituation.** It is responsible for the fact that you are quite unaware of the pressure of your socks against your feet, until I call it to your attention. Notice that this is not a matter of sensory adaptation. When you attend to it, you feel it all right; the sensory input is getting through. But it is filtered out by the habituation mechanism, and is not an effective input until you and I make it so.

What Sokoloff did then was to introduce various changes in the time of onset or offset of the tone. If the tone occurred on schedule, the habituated subjects' bodies simply went on about their business; no arousal response occurred. But if the tone came on too early, the arousal response at once occurred. It also occurred if the tone stayed on too long, or ended too soon, or *failed* to appear when it was due. Notice in particular that the arousal response could occur with *no change at all* in the external input, as when the tone failed to appear, or to disappear, on schedule.

EVENTS AS SURPRISES   What subjects find arousing, then, is not a physical input as such, but a *deviation* of the input from what was expected. If what happens is only what ought to happen, there is no discrepancy between the expected and the actual input—and no arousal. If there is a difference—the tone is too early, too late, or whatever—then that is an event. Arousal results.

In a word: to qualify as an event, an input must have some *surprise* value. Otherwise it is ignored.

Obviously there are limits to this habituation mechanism. An intense pain, even if expected, still hurts. And habituation applies primarily to *continuous* stimuli, like the socks on our feet, or *regularly repeated* ones, like the tones in Sokoloff's experiments. Distinct events, like the arrival of someone we have waited for, are still events when they occur even though we expect them.

The important fact remains, though, that relatively few of the stimulus inputs we receive are treated as events. And a good thing, too, or we would be swamped with information. The fact that the sun is up or down as it should be, that the chair under me is still solid—these are not events and can be ignored. Even an act that requires close attention, like the reading you are doing now, ignores most of what is going on. There are all sorts of things about this text that you are not aware of; but if I change one of them, dann sind Sie erstaunt, nicht wahr? It is very much an event if I start writing in German, but I'll bet you had no awareness at all of the fact that I was writing in English before.

In summary, arousal level is affected by *events*—by surprises—as distinct from sensory inputs. And if there is an optimal level of arousal, this may mean that there is an optimal level of surprises to deal with.

Finally, here is yet another point at which these ideas make contact with sports psychology and the performing arts. Skilled actors, at the moment when their skills are about to be tested, may perform a stereotyped series of movements, a kind of ritual. A baseball player about to bat, or an ice skater about to skate, may insist on taking a few seconds to do this. Such rituals may serve the purpose of warming up or shaking loose certain muscle groups; but it may also be important that the ritual, because it is stereotyped, is *utterly predictable*. There are no surprises in it. It may, for just that reason, be one way of lowering arousal or anxiety to a level that is closer to optimal for the task at hand (compare pp. 238–39).

AROUSAL: A LOOK BACKWARD

The concept of arousal, as we have elaborated it, can be schematized as in Figure 6-16. The basic idea is that specific effects of causal factors on behavior are superimposed on a background of higher or lower general arousal, produced by non-specific influences like the four Ss: stimuli, stimulant drugs, stresses, and surprises. This idea is still very much with us.

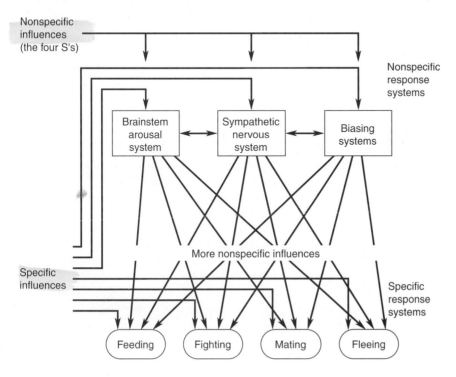

Figure 6-16 Hierarchical organization of specific and non-specific influences on action. See text for explanation.

Arousal versus Drive

Students of arousal have been interested in different problems from those that engaged Clark Hull, and they made little or no use of Hull's algebraic formulation. Still, the arousal concept has some points in common with Hull's generalized drive, or D.

First, as Hull saw it, tissue imbalances or needs arising from *any* source (food deprivation, water deprivation, sexual deprivation)—*all* converge to increase the motivational multiplier D. Similarly in the case of arousal. A creature may go into emergency or alertness mode for any of a number of reasons—the approach of a predator, or a rival, or a forest fire, or an experimenter, or the big long drop coming up on a roller-coaster ride. *Any* of these can throw the actor into the *same* emergency mode of operation.

On the output side, Hull saw D as multiplying, indiscriminately, *all* habits (Hs) that exist in a situation. Similarly, a state of arousal has multiple manifestations, all called into play at once. There are changes in the circulation, in the digestive system, in respiration—and in the brain, which becomes alert and engaged, ready to take in the situation and translate what it finds into action. Finally, a number of different actions—not all, as with Hull, but a number—may be primed together. An animal can be ready to fight *or* flee *or* freeze in fear—to do, that is, any of a number of specific things as the situation requires.

So arousal, like drive, may arise from any or all of a number of sources. And it may enhance any or all of a number of reactions or reaction tendencies, both physiological and behavioral.

Arousal and Motivation—Are They the Same?

Is this all there is to motivation, then? Will it help us to think of arousal as the motivating "engine" of behavior, and of other influences as non-motivational? Probably not.

In the first place, Figure 6-16 is drastically oversimplified in a number of ways, and one of these is that it omits *inhibitory* interactions among sub-systems. We saw earlier (pp. 207–8) that dehydration, which promotes drinking, can actually inhibit feeding. Stress can augment feeding behavior (pp. 224–25); but stress can also inhibit feeding under other circumstances.

By the same token, whereas an irrelevant stress (like mild pain) *can* enhance feeding or sexual activity, it doesn't follow that all influences have that generalized effect in all circumstances. We've seen that an especially tasty food can trigger a bout of eating that would otherwise not occur, without having any detectable effect on other motivational systems such as courting or mating. Perhaps we should think of the non-specific effects shown in Figure 6-16 as influences that *can* occur, not as ones that always and automatically do occur.

The same is true of physiological response systems. Heart rate can increase under some arousing circumstances, but it can decrease under others. It is affected by the sympathetic nervous system, but it is affected by more specific influences as well.

We might sum it up this way: Various response systems may all be driven in the same direction—upward—by non-specific arousal. But at the same time, they may be driven in *different* directions by *specific* influences, internal and external: thus dehydration may inhibit feeding, and a sexual gesture, in some species, may inhibit attack. Whether the end result is enhancement or depression of a given sub-system (like feeding or fighting) will depend on how strong these competing influences are, relative to each other. It surely is not true that everything automatically enhances everything else.

A FINAL LOOK BACKWARD

At the beginning of this chapter, we embarked on a search for the "engine" of behavior—the part that makes it go. Have we found our engine? No. Should we continue to search for it? I think not.

Hull's generalized-drive concept was certainly an idea worth checking out. But psychologists did check it out, and found it wanting. Not all drives promote all behaviors, and not all behaviors are evoked by drives.

Freud's theory, in attempting to reduce the engine of action to a handful of drives, faces some of the same problems as Hull's theory does. It is simply too limiting. Even many of Freud's early associates parted with him on this point. Few psychoanalysts, and fewer research psychologists, take this aspect of his theory seriously now.

More generally, modern researchers wonder whether Freudian phenomena, even if we grant their occurrence, really require the energy metaphor at all. Some of them at least may reflect "cold," dispassionate operations of our cognitive apparatus, rather than the "hot" passionate clash of opposing forces We will return to this matter in Chapter 11.

The notion of *arousal,* we have emphasized, is still very much with us. But we no longer think of it as an engine, with other influences relegated to a guidance or steering function. Activity in the arousal systems is simply one, among many, influences on behavior. As to its mode of action, recall that we changed the metaphor in our previous discussion (pp. 232–33), comparing arousal level to the setting of a volume control. There is something compelling about the notion that the engine is the "motivating" part of a car. It is much less compelling to think of the volume control as the "motivating" part of a hi-fi system!

The notion of *optimal arousal* again moves us away from the engine metaphor. There very likely is something to the idea that arousal may be too low, leading to sluggishness; too high, leading to tension or frenzy or disorganization; or just right for the problem we face. But in looking more closely, we saw (pp. 237–39) that there probably is not any one "optimal" level, that the system regulates in a homeostatic way. Rather, there may be a level that is optimal *for the task on hand;* and in such case, we may take action to raise or lower arousal as needed. But then the optimal level is not an engine but a destination; not a present state, but a goal or way station.

Finally, it is not clear that we gain anything by speaking of non-specific influences as "motivational" and calling other influences something else. If a yummy food calls forth a bout of feeding that would not otherwise occur—and does it without measurable effect on, say, sexual readiness—there seems no reason not to speak of that food, or the cues it provides, as *motivating* the feeding act. Similarly, if a situation promotes a drinking response but inhibits a feeding response, is there any point in calling the promoting influence "motivational" and the inhibiting one not? I do not think so.

All told, the attempt to make a hard-and-fast distinction between motivational and other influences was once a popular indoor game, but it has lost its popularity in recent years. Behavior is subject to many influences, and all of them need to be understood. Arousal level may be an important such influence, but it is only one, among many.

SUMMARY

Some early theories about behavior held that only one motivational concept, analogous to energy, was required. This would determine how vigorous or persistent behavior would be, whereas more specific influences determined what direction the behavior would take. By this account, motivation is like the engine of a car, whereas non-motivational factors are like the steering mechanism.

One such theory was Clark Hull's. His *generalized drive* (D), a kind of motivational energy, was assumed to energize all stimulus-response connections, or *habits* (H), indiscriminately. Thus actual behavior was assumed to reflect a multiplicative relationship between a motivational influence D and an associative or learning-based influence H.

This theory has some interesting implications. For example, it predicts that high drive should aid performance if the best response is the dominant one, but should hinder performance if an incorrect response is dominant; and there is some support for that prediction in learning experiments with human subjects.

Other experiments, however, do not fit the theory. Animals that are not deprived of anything (hence, presumably, in no drive state) can learn, and persist in, complex activities. And we cannot say that all drive states facilitate all responses; for example, thirst can inhibit feeding or food-getting responses. Nevertheless, the notion of a non-specific arousal mechanism is still with us, as is the notion of joint control by motivational factors on the one hand and learning-based and cognitive ones on the other. And the failure of the theory is a case study in how we test our ideas, and so learn when they are wrong.

Another energy-like concept was Freud's theory of drives or instincts. These were conceived as engine-like forces all having their origin in biological energy. Drives have different *sources* in different parts of the body, and different *objects* by which they may be satisfied, but all have the same *aim*—the reduction of discomfort, which reduction is felt as pleasurable. To Freud, all behavior is ultimately directed toward that aim. That is his *pleasure principle.*

Tendencies to think or act can come into conflict with each other; one may be opposed or blocked by another or redirected because of such opposition. Complexities can arise here, the more so because some person or object may come to represent, or symbolize, another. In this way, drive energy may be directed toward an object that is only a symbol of the object originally desired. Thus much of our behavior can be seen as disguised expressions of primitive impulses. Freud saw this principle as most clearly visible in dreams, where the disguises may be most easily seen through.

Much of this goes on below the level of consciousness, so that the disguised expression of wishes may be as incomprehensible to the person as to anyone else. Often the wishes, and the need to disguise them, date back to early childhood, so that adult behavior becomes a kind of re-enactment of childhood conflicts. Some writers believe, however, that the kinds of conflicts that arise can depend a great deal on the culture within which one is raised. Conflicts that are common within a culture may be reflected in its myths and legends as well as in the thoughts and actions of individuals.

Freud's work has been severely criticized. A cornerstone of his theory, that material may be actively thrust out of mind, or *repressed,* has never been demonstrated convincingly. How much was he reading into what his patients said? And how much of what they said was in response to the theoretical ideas that Freud forced upon them? Might they have *created* false "memories" in response to his insistence? Finally, because the theory is complex enough to give an after-the-fact explanation of anything that happens, it really cannot be tested. Despite all this, Freud was certainly addressing a vitally important question: Why do we so often do things, or think things, that we ourselves do not understand? Freud's answers are not widely accepted, but his question was fundamental.

Yet a third engine-like conception in motivational theory is the concept of *arousal.* Certain conditions can affect, not just this or that action, but a variety of actions; mild pain, for example, may induce an animal to feed or to mate. Such findings suggest a generalized arousal state, in which the organism's whole repertoire of actions is primed and energized or, perhaps, in which it is more vigilant and alert to incoming information.

Certain systems within the body also have widespread effects on a variety of systems all at once. Activation of the *sympathetic nervous system* affects a number of organs in preparing the body for "fight or flight." Within the brain, the *brainstem arousal system,* which includes the *reticular formation* of the brainstem, transmits its activity diffusely through the forebrain so that it, too, seems to activate a number of systems all at once. Damaging that system can produce a state of sluggishness, somnolence, and unresponsiveness to a variety of sensory inputs.

Much evidence suggests that there is something like an optimal level of arousal for the task at hand—not too high, not too low. Intermediate stimulus intensities tend to be judged pleasant; and the *Yerkes-Dodson law* states that an intermediate level of drive leads to most-effective functioning. At one extreme, intense arousal can lead to life-threatening panic. At the other, *sensory deprivation* is a severe stressor. Subjects may seek to regulate their arousal levels, reducing them if too high, augmenting them if too low. In such cases, however, optimal arousal becomes a goal that is sought, not something that is acting to cause the behavior now. Moreover, we must remember that different levels of arousal may be best for different tasks. There probably is no one single optimal level of arousal.

Level of arousal is affected, not just by internal and external sensory inputs, but by violations of expectations—in a word, by surprises. A stimulus to which we have become *habituated* may no longer arouse us. So cognitive factors (such as expectations) can affect arousal. This gives us four ways of arousing a subject: stress, stimuli, stimulant drugs, and surprises. We can remember these as the four Ss.

Like Hull's *D,* arousal can be augmented in a variety of ways, and can activate a variety of behaviors. But it is clearly not true (as Hull supposed) that *all* response systems, behavioral or physiological, are automatically and indiscriminately augmented by any increase in arousal. Different systems have their own, specific determinants as well as these more general ones like drive or arousal. All of these need to be understood. The attempt to divide these determinants into motivational and non-motivational ones has not proved very fruitful.

CHAPTER 7

Acquired Drives and Rewards

Motives are learned

In previous chapters, we have referred to the impact of learning on how, and whether, we express even basic biological motives. This chapter will focus on cases in which the motives themselves are learned.

These cases are clearly of great importance. Biologically based drives and incentives obviously account for only a minute fraction of human and animal behavior. We act, and act persistently and vigorously, when we are not hungry, thirsty, angry, or sexually aroused, and when no delicious food or attractive partner is in prospect. If biological motives fall far short of explaining here-and-now actions, then non-biological motives must fill the gap. Learned motives are prominent among these; and relatively simple learned motives, of the kind we consider here, might provide building blocks for more complex ones.

ACQUIRED DRIVES AND REWARDS

We will consider two such building blocks: acquired drives, and acquired rewards. As an example of an *acquired drive,* suppose you and I are afraid of hornets, because we learned about them the hard way. Then the sight of a hornet will evoke an unpleasant state that motivates action. We might call it *fear.* It can motivate an arbitrary response such as opening a car window to let the hornet out. It is true that we also have a goal or incentive—relief from fear, or avoidance of pain. But we didn't have to learn to seek freedom from fear and pain. What we learned is that creatures that look like *that* are to be feared, and so *that* stimulus evokes the drive of fear.

As an example of an **acquired reward,** consider a person drinking coffee. Now the odds are that that person did not like coffee at all when he first tasted it. Put a bit of coffee on an infant's tongue, and she will make a nasty face and reject it. It is a curious fact that *most* people, in cultures all over the world, learn to seek and enjoy commodities that at first are disliked.

Access to a cup of coffee, in this society, supports arbitrary responses that make it available: We make our way to the coffee shop, plunk down money, and so on. Yet there may be no internal state that motivates this action. We may not be thirsty at all; or if we are, we didn't have to learn to be. We did have to learn to seek coffee.

In summary, an acquired drive is an internal impetus to action—a push from within—that we have learned. An acquired reward is something we seek—a pull from without—because we have learned to seek it. This chapter will explore both of these cases.

AVOIDANCE LEARNING

Pain is a powerful motivator. So is the *threat* of pain; we may go to great lengths to escape that threat, as in taking any action available to get that hornet out of here.

How do threats become motivators? Here we will follow our usual tactic of beginning with simpler cases. Then we will see how the resulting ideas may bear on more complex problems.

Avoidance Conditioning

Consider this experiment. A rat is placed in a long narrow box, divided in half by a partition. The floor of the box is a grid of steel rods that can be electrified to provide a painful shock (Fig. 7-1A).

After a few seconds, a buzzer comes on. Now the rules of the experiment are this: The rat has, say, 5 seconds to cross the barrier over to the other side of the box. If the rat does this, the buzzer goes off and all is well; nothing else happens. But if the rat fails to cross in time, then shock comes on and continues until crossing does occur.

In either case, there will be an interval of time after the rat makes the crossing-over response; then the buzzer comes on again, and the rat must again cross the partition. Over a series of such trials, therefore, the rat must shuttle back and forth from one side of the box to the other, and so this apparatus is called a **shuttle-box.**

What happens in such an experiment? On the first few trials, the rat is likely to make no crossing response when the buzzer comes on. The shock comes on 5 seconds later, causing the rat to run and scramble and, before long, cross over the barrier. Crossing turns the shock off, and we say that the rat has *escaped* the painful shock (Fig. 7-1B).

A

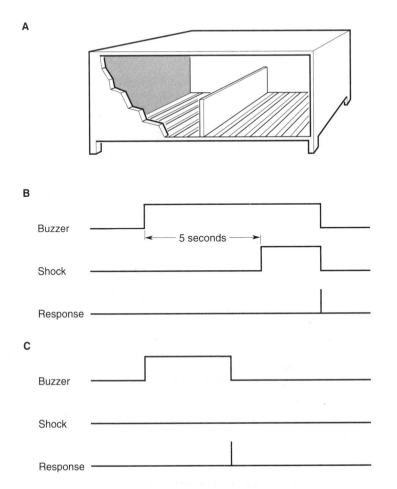

B

Buzzer

← 5 seconds →

Shock

Response

C

Buzzer

Shock

Response

Figure 7-1 (A) A shuttle box. The floor is made of metal rods that can be electrified. (B) An escape trial. The response terminates the buzzer and the shock. (C) An avoidance trial. A response made before the onset of shock turns off the buzzer and prevents the shock from occurring.

Over successive trials, we usually will see a progressively more prompt escape response. That is, the rat will freeze or crouch when the buzzer comes on, but after the shock begins the rat will quickly make the crossing-over response that turns it off. But eventually most rats will begin to make *avoidance* responses, crossing during the warning interval between buzzer onset and shock onset. That prevents shock from occurring (Figure 7-1C). Eventually, a well-trained animal may go on trial after trial, day after day, crossing over on signal and never receiving a shock.

Now a rat's escape response—running to turn off shock after it has come on—poses no particular problem and involves no acquired drive. We can see it as maintained by the law of effect: The shock is painful, running turns it off, and so running is rewarded and strengthened. Running, as we say, is *reinforced* by escape from pain. The problem comes when we ask what reinforces the *avoidance* response, which prevents the shock from coming on at all. Does the absence of shock keep responding going? But how can the *absence* of an event be a reinforcer? How can a non-event strengthen and maintain behavior?

One answer is the cognitive answer.[1] The rat expects shock if it does not make the response, and expects not to get shocked if it does make it. It prefers no shock to shock, understandably enough. And it makes the response that has the most preferred expected outcome.

Behaviorists will have none of that. We simply do not know, they point out, what if anything a rat expects. We know the response that occurs, so let us speak so that we know what we're talking about. Can we show that avoidance behavior is really a response to a stimulus, not to a non-stimulus, after all?

We can try. It is an instructive exercise in what early behavioristic theorizing was like. And it will show us the relations and the contrasts between two points of view—the behaviorist and the cognitive ones. So let us work through it.

The Two-Factor Theory of Avoidance Conditioning

The theory we now consider says that avoidance learning involves two stages, or **factors.** First, the rat acquires a conditioned response—fear—to the buzzer or other warning stimulus. Second, the avoidance response reduces the fear. What reinforces avoidance responding is not a non-event—the absence of shock. It is an event—fear reduction—that is the reinforcer. Let us look more closely.★

Consider what happens on early trials. The buzzer comes on and, 5 seconds later, the painful shock. Now the shock will produce many responses: muscles tense, heart rate increases, breathing rate increases, the adrenal gland pours forth secretions, and so on. This happens in the presence of the buzzer, and so we have the situation under which *classical conditioning* occurs. These stress responses begin to occur in response to the buzzer, just as, in Pavlov's dogs, salivation occurred in response to the bell (Fig. 7-2A). This is the first of the two factors in two-factor theory.

Now let us assume that these responses, of muscle tension and the like, in turn produce stimuli and that these stimuli are unpleasant. We might think of them as comprising an emotional state, *fear. Fear, in this analysis, is the acquired drive.* It is not a mental state but an internal stimulus situation. It is the set of internal stimuli produced by the conditioned stress responses. It is also unpleasant or, as we say, *aversive,* just as the shock itself is. Therefore, any response that terminates fear will be reinforced and strengthened (the law of effect). Well, if the rat crosses over before the shock comes on, that turns the buzzer off; the stimulus for fear is taken away, and so the fear state ends. That is the reinforcement for the avoidance response (Fig. 7-2B). The avoidance response is strengthened by reinforcement—fear reduction—and that is the second of the two factors.

Putting these two factors together, we have our familiar negative-feedback loop. A stimulus (the buzzer) produces fear, which in turn calls forth an action

1. See for example Seligman and Johnston, 1973.
★For fuller discussion see Mowrer, 1950.

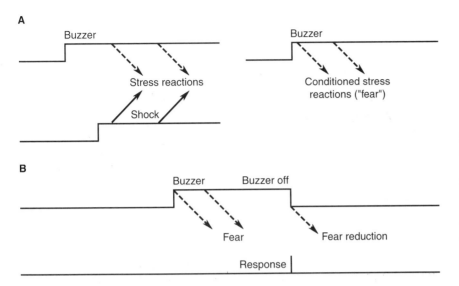

Figure 7-2 The two-factor theory of avoidance learning. (A) Early in training, stress reactions are conditioned (dashed lines) to the buzzer or other warning signal. (B) Once that conditioning has taken place, any response that turns off the warning signal will be reinforced by reduction of fear.

(running) that removes the fear by removing the stimulus that causes it. Fear reduction also reinforces the response, making it more likely to occur the next time.

The analysis is an ingenious one. It treats the avoidance response, not as a foresightful response to something that hasn't happened yet, but as a response to something that *has* happened—fear produced by the buzzer. And it treats the avoidance response as reinforced, not by something that doesn't happen, but by something that does—reduction of fear. No expectancies, forethoughts, or cognitions are required.

Two-Factor Theory and Human Fears

Despite the problems with two-factor theory (see below), it has been an enormously influential one—and not just for rats or dogs in shuttle-boxes. It has been extended in fascinating ways to explain some human behavior.

Many ineffective and even irrational forms of human behavior may be seen as avoidance responses. They may be motivated by fear, and maintained by fear reduction; and the fear itself may be traceable to certain experiences that created them, just as shock creates fear of the buzzer in the rat. And if this is so, what we learn about the principles of avoidance conditioning may suggest ways of dealing with troublesome fears.

SYMPTOMS AS AVOIDANCE BEHAVIOR: COMPULSIONS   As an example, perhaps the behaviors known as *compulsions* can be seen as habitual avoidance responses, reinforced by anxiety reduction.* Freud thought so.[2] So did many behaviorist writers.[3]

Compulsions are repeated, stereotyped, ritualized actions. The patient feels *compelled* to perform them, and unable to control the urge to do so. They often go along with **obsessions,** which we may think of as *compulsive thoughts.* These are thoughts that persist in coming into consciousness; often they are frightening or abhorrent, but the patient finds them difficult or impossible to dismiss.

The effect of these compulsive rituals is not trivial. They can make life an unending misery for patient and family. Listen:

> One of our patients . . . feared contamination by germs. As a result she engaged in prolonged and intensive washing and cleaning rituals. Her young child was restrained in one room of the four-bedroom house, as it was the only one that she could keep satisfactorily free from germs. Three of the rooms were kept permanently locked because she was incapable of ensuring that they were sufficiently sterile. . . . The patient's fear of contamination made her virtually housebound, and her child was not permitted to leave the house except on a very few essential occasions. On returning from work each day, her husband was obliged to go through a series of decontaminating-cleaning rituals. Their sexual relationship, never satisfactory, had been abandoned because of her fears of contamination. Their social life was damaged beyond repair, and they had lost all but one of their friends; even the members of their families could neither visit them nor be visited by them.[4]

All that cost, all that pain, because of intense and irrational fear of germs. The behavior seems as bizarre as—well, as the behavior of a rat compulsively shuttling back and forth in a two-compartment box. Of course, if we know the rat's conditioning history, its behavior makes sense. So might the patient's if we knew enough about *her* conditioning history. So the behaviorist would say.

However, the suggestion that these rituals are avoidance responses came originally not from behaviorists, but from Freud! The obsessive thoughts and the actions that come from them are seen as defenses against really terrifying thoughts. Abhorrent wishes threaten to break into consciousness; this causes intense, though unconscious, fear. The patient unconsciously transforms his thoughts into ones that symbolize the forbidden wish but are less threatening. These are the obsessive thoughts. And so fear, though it may persist, is still reduced; it is much less intense than it would otherwise be.

There is evidence, from both the clinic and the laboratory, that fear or anxiety does underlie these symptoms.[5] If a patient is prevented from performing

---

*Many writers would distinguish *fear* from *anxiety,* treating the first as realistic and evoked by some definite stimulus, the second as diffuse and less definite as to its object. The distinction is not critical for the argument here, however; for discussion of it in this context, see Schwartz, 1984.

2. Freud, 1917.
3. Dollard and Miller, 1950.
4. Rachman and Hodgson, 1980, pp. 58–59.
5. Rosenhan and Seligman, 1984.

the compulsive act, he may experience overwhelming anxiety. Moreover, some patients report that they do experience anxiety before performing the compulsive act, and lose it when the action is performed. It may be just this that makes obsessions and compulsions difficult to treat. They work! They reduce anxiety, just as the rat's avoidance response turns the buzzer off and reduces fear.

THE TREATMENT OF FEAR: RESPONSE PREVENTION IN BEHAVIOR THERAPY   As the theory of avoidance conditioning may help us understand where some problematic behaviors come from, so it may help us do something about them.

The class of treatment methods that incorporate behaviorist theories is known as **behavior therapy.**[6] It draws directly upon the laboratory analysis of behavior, especially learned behavior.

Behavior therapists believe that compulsive actions are avoidance responses. Think again about the well-trained rat, shuttling back and forth in the box. Now suppose that the shock apparatus has been turned off. Then crossing the barrier when the buzzer comes on is no longer necessary. The behavior no longer serves any purpose. But the rat, as long as it goes on responding to the buzzer, cannot learn that.

One way to bring the rat to reality is to *prevent the avoidance response from occurring*. Place a barrier between the sides of the boxes. Let the buzzer come on; and the animal, unable to make an avoidance response, must discover that shock no longer threatens. If that happens several times, the fear response will undergo extinction. Then, when the barrier is removed again, the animal should sit placidly when the buzzer comes on. And that is what happens.[7]

Exactly the same logic has been used in the clinic, where it is called **response prevention.** Let a patient, who fears contamination by dirt, touch a contaminated object, and prevent her from performing any cleaning or other rituals that otherwise would compulsively ensue. When this is done a number of times, and when nothing bad happens, the fear should weaken—or, as we say, it should undergo extinction—and the compulsive behavior it motivates should stop. This direct approach has been used to treat compulsions, with some success.[8] Some patients are unable or unwilling to tolerate the stress of such treatment, but when the patient can do it, it often helps.

THEORETICAL ISSUES IN AVOIDANCE CONDITIONING

Although the two-factor theory has been influential in both human and animal research, there are some problems with it.[9] It may tell part of the story of what happens in avoidance conditioning, but it does not tell it all.

6. For an excellent introduction see Rimm and Masters, 1979.
7. Solomon, Kamin, and Wynne, 1953.
8. Reviewed by Rachman and Hodgson, 1980.
9. Discussed by Rescorla and Solomon, 1967; Schwartz, 1984.

Difficulties with the Two-Factor Theory

Everything in two-factor theory hinges on the idea that a **warning stimulus,** such as the buzzer, produces the fear that motivates the avoidance response. Running across the barrier turns the buzzer off; offset of the buzzer takes the fear away, and that reinforces avoidance behavior. So the theory goes.

AVOIDANCE CONDITIONING WITHOUT A STIMULUS In fact, however, one can see avoidance behavior maintained in a stimulus situation that *does not change when the response occurs.*[10] In one such method, the rat is in a box, with lever-pressing the avoidance response. At regular intervals—every 10 seconds, let us say—automatic apparatus delivers a brief pulse of shock through the box floor, unless the animal makes an avoidance response. The rat can avoid these short shocks by pressing the lever. Every lever-press *postpones* the delivery of the next shock for a period of time—say, 10 seconds. If the rat presses, and then waits a full 10 seconds, then shock will occur after 10 seconds. But if the rat presses the bar at 9.9 seconds, then that shock will not occur and the next shock will not come due for a full 10 seconds more; and it too can be postponed if the rat presses again. Thus, if the rat presses the bar at least once every 10 seconds, shock will never occur.

Failures to learn this difficult task are not uncommon, but some rats do learn it, and work away at the lever *even though no stimulus change follows the lever-press.* There is no buzzer to go silent and take the fear away. How can *fear,* as a response to a warning stimulus, be reduced if there is no warning stimulus? And if fear is not reduced, what reinforces lever-pressing?

IS FEAR MAINTAINED? An even worse problem for two-factor theory is this: If we measure the effects of fear in other ways, fear simply does not seem to have the properties the theory requires.

We can measure fear of a buzzer, for example, by seeing how much it suppresses some other, ongoing activity. When we do so, we find that early in avoidance training, the buzzer does indeed provoke fear. Later, however, a well-trained rat may show little evidence of fear—but it continues to make the avoidance response when the buzzer sounds. It is as if the well-educated rat knows just what to do about buzzers, and does it placidly, without fear, when occasion arises.

This particular behaviorist theory, then, has its problems. That would seem to leave us with the cognitive theory:[11] The rat expects shock if it does not respond, no shock if it does respond; it prefers no shock to shock, and so it responds.

That theory fits comfortably with common sense; but it too has its problems, as we will see. In particular, neither of these theories addresses the issue of

10. Sidman, 1953; see also Herrnstein and Hineline, 1966.
11. Seligman and Johnston, 1973.

instinctive influences on escape and avoidance learning. We now turn to that topic.

To this point, we have considered the learning of motives as if it occurred against a blank background. Early discussions of the nature-nurture issue often were posed that way: Is this or that action innate *or* acquired? Is it provided by heredity *or* environment? We have come to see that the question cannot be asked that way. Rather, there are complex interactions between what we teach an actor and the untaught repertoire she or he already has available. We will explore three such cases: instinctive defensive reactions in avoidance learning, taste-aversion learning, and fear of strangers in human children.

Defensive Reactions and Avoidance Conditioning

In setting up an avoidance experiment, the response we choose as the "correct" one is arbitrary. For a rat it may be running, lever-pressing, or rearing up on the hind legs. For a pigeon, it may be pecking an illuminated disk mounted on the wall, called a *pecking key;* or it may be wing-flapping, or jumping on a treadle to press it down. We can choose any response we like, and arrange matters so that it will escape, or avoid, something unpleasant.

We can choose any response we like. But the animal may or may not be able to learn it. Some responses are learned much more easily than others. These constraints were part of laboratory folklore, tricks of the trade of teaching animals to avoid shock, but they played no role in our theories until Robert Bolles pointed out their great importance.[12]

A pigeon, for example, readily learns to jump on a treadle to avoid shock, but it learns to peck a key only with great difficulty or not at all. That is not just because key-pecking itself is more difficult, for if the reinforcer is food rather than shock-avoidance, then the key-peck response is rapidly learned. Similarly, rats learn to run in avoidance situations much more easily than they learn to press a lever.

Why? Bolles suggests this: An animal comes to the experiment equipped with certain ways of responding to danger. These form a hierarchy of instinctive action patterns, analogous to the stickleback's hierarchy of sexual responses (pp. 112–14). But this time, the instinctive system is not reproductive, but *defensive*. Various action patterns are components of the system—freezing, attacking, running away, flying away if one can fly, or withdrawing into a shell if one has a shell. What actions are included in the system depends on the species. Therefore, Bolles calls these action patterns **species-specific defensive reactions,** or SSDRs (Fig. 7-3).

12. Bolles, 1970.

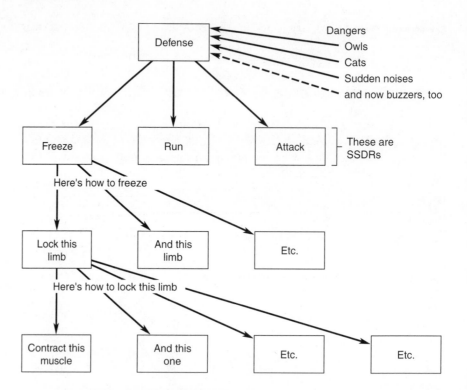

Figure 7-3 The hierarchy of species-specific defensive reactions (SSDRs). An avoidance conditioning experiment does not provide new defensive responses, but a new situation in which to use defensive responses already available.

When the experiment begins, it is these instinctive responses that the animal uses. If one of them is effective, then that response will be learned quickly. If none of these SSDRs will work, then, and only then, will the animal try something that is not an SSDR. It will be learned slowly, laboriously, or not at all.

Thus pecking is *not* an SSDR for the pigeon. Jumping, however, is part of a flight or attack system of responses that pigeons instinctively use when threatened. For the rat, freezing is an SSDR. Faced with danger, a rat is likely to freeze. If freezing does not work, the running-away SSDR may be tried; and that will be effective in a shuttle-box situation, but not in a box where a lever-press is required. If running does not work either, biting the pain source may be tried; and a lever-press response is often made by biting the lever, thus depressing it by accident. But a lever-press response with the paws is not part of a rat's instinctive repertoire of reactions to danger. If that is made the correct response in an avoidance experiment, it will be learned very slowly, if at all.

This conception of avoidance is very different from the one we have dealt with up to now. It says this: The successful escape or avoidance of shock does not *strengthen* a new response, such as running from one place to another. The rat already knows how to run; and more than that, it already is inclined to run if danger threatens. The learning that goes on teaches the rat, first, that *this* situation is dangerous, and second, that *this* member of the class of SSDRs is effective. It does not, we might say, teach the rat a new trick. It teaches the rat which of the tricks it already knows is the one to use.

Conditioned Taste Aversions

We have seen that the response one tries to reinforce, in an avoidance experiment, is not as arbitrary as we had supposed. A species-specific defense reaction is easy to condition; others may be very difficult or impossible to condition in this way.

Similar specificities, it turns out, are to be found on the stimulus side. Some stimuli make it easy to learn to avoid certain consequences; others make it very difficult indeed.

DEMONSTRATIONS OF TASTE-AVERSION LEARNING   Allow me a personal example here. When I was nine years old, I wrongfully ate an entire bag of jelly beans, and got violently sick while playing baseball on the lawn some time later. From that day to this, I have had an utter detestation for the sight, sound, smell, or mention of jelly beans. I am reluctant even to write about them!

Now why? I have no particular aversion to baseball, or to lawns, even though the sickness was most closely paired with baseball on the lawn, and the jelly beans had been eaten quite some time before. Moreover, the pairing of jelly beans with sickness happened only once, whereas avoidance conditioning is often a slow and gradual process requiring many trials, even in humans.

Apparently there is something special about *illness* as an aversion state that makes it particularly easy to associate with *tastes* and perhaps smells—very quickly and across remarkably long time intervals. A clear demonstration of this is provided by the work of John Garcia and his colleagues.[13]

Briefly, rats were permitted to drink a novel and normally preferred saccharin solution. After that, they were exposed to X-irradiation, a treatment that produces nausea in humans and appears to do so in rats as well. In subsequent tests, the rats showed a clear avoidance of the novel taste, whereas rats that received the taste without the irradiation, or the irradiation without the taste, showed no such avoidance. And this was true after *one* taste-illness pairing, and even though the illness was separated from the taste by a full half-hour—and later experiments showed that the interval could be much longer than that and still be effective. No rat would ever learn to avoid shock so quickly and with such a long delay.

This rapid learning seems to be specific to *taste paired with illness*. If a rat is shocked for drinking saccharin after a similar delay, it does not learn so rapidly to avoid saccharin. If it is made ill after hearing a buzzer and seeing bright flashing lights, it does not avoid those. In other words, neither taste nor illness by itself leads to especially rapid learning, but if we pair taste with illness, then learning is very fast indeed.

The phenomenon has also been demonstrated experimentally in humans.[14] The subjects were children who were undergoing radiation treatment for

13. Garcia, Ervin, and Koelling, 1966.
14. Bernstein, 1978.

abdominal cancer, a treatment that often produces nausea. Briefly, subjects who were given a novel ice cream flavor (Maple Toff) before undergoing their treatment liked that flavor less afterward (Fig. 7-4). Control subjects, who received the treatment *or* the ice cream but not both, did not show this effect.

It is worth noting too that this avoidance of Maple Toff occurred even in the face of the subjects' cognitive apparatus. These children *knew perfectly well* that their nausea was caused by the treatment they were receiving, not the ice cream. But the ice cream was rejected anyway. Conscious knowledge, it seems, was no match for the biological "knowledge" that says to us: "If you feel sick, it's probably something you ate. Whatever you ate recently—avoid it."

And it is that biological knowledge that makes this case an example of the interaction between learning and instinct. Apparently, if they get sick, rats and children will avoid any new food that they have recently eaten. They need not learn to do that. What they learn in the experiment is that *this particular food—* a saccharin solution, or Maple Toff ice cream—is to be avoided.

Fear of Strangers

Let us turn to a quite different example in humans. Children at around nine to fifteen months of age, in many different cultures, go through a period in which the approach of a *strange adult* causes face aversion, crying, and other signs of intense fear. This is not just a response to novelty or surprise, for an unfamiliar child causes no such reaction.[15] It has to be an adult. And the fear response is an unmistakable action pattern, universal among human children, including the deaf and blind.[16]

The fear stage may develop and decay at different rates in different soci-

Figure 7-4 Conditioned taste aversion in human children. Offered the choice between the new ice cream and a game, children were less likely to choose the ice cream if its taste had been paired with nausea. (Data from Bernstein, 1978.)

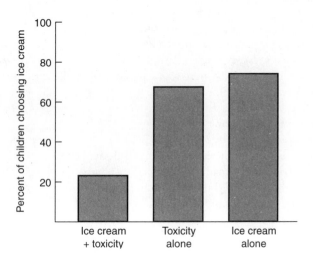

15. Brooks and Lewis, 1976.
16. Eibl-Eibesfeldt, 1972.

eties, so culture can influence its time course.[17] But why does it develop at all? Is it instinctive or acquired or both? It is both—it is an interaction of the two.

Suppose little Bill cries when his Aunt Sara—whom he has not seen since the day he was born, when he wasn't paying attention—approaches. Obviously Aunt Sara is not a releasing stimulus; the brain did not evolve a recognition mechanism for Aunt Sara herself. Little Bill had to *learn* who is a familiar figure in his life. But little Bill probably has never been threatened or hurt by an adult; or if he has, it has probably been by a familiar one, not a strange one. Experience was needed to teach the child who is familiar and who is not. But *experience did not teach him to fear unfamiliar adults.* That fear response must be untaught.

A Look Backward: How Instinct and Learning Interact

What is common to all these cases—SSDRs, taste aversion, and fear of strangers—is this: In each of them, the learning experience teaches the animal what kind of situation it faces. But it does *not* teach it what to do about that situation. That part, it seems, is instinctive, or untaught. Thus we see that experience does not *teach* a child to fear strange adults, though it does teach the child which adults are familiar and which are not. Similarly, avoidance conditioning does not *teach* a rat to run when threatened. It does teach the rat that the experimental chamber, or the onset of the buzzer, is a threat. Rats and humans need not learn to avoid novel foods paired with illness. They do learn *what* foods to avoid on those grounds.

INSTINCTIVE RULES   We might say it this way: A human or animal brings to the learning situation certain *rules* about what to do in certain situations. The rules are ones that a human could express in words: "In danger, it's a good idea to freeze or run (for a rat) or to fly and jump (for a pigeon). Try it!" Or: "If you feel nauseous, it's probably because of something you ate. Remember it and avoid it!" Or: "If you see an adult who matches none of your memories, it's fearsome! Fear it!" We need not learn these rules. Experience teaches us when to apply a rule of this kind, but it does not give us the rules themselves. In some biological sense, we already know them.

THE CONCEPT OF PREPAREDNESS   Now it is much easier to learn something if we already know something about it. Thus, if what we are to learn—these two stimuli belong together, or this is the response that the problem requires—fits in with rules we already have, the learning task is greatly facilitated. We are, in Martin Seligman's words, already *prepared* to learn certain things about the world.[18] We are prepared to learn to avoid foods whose ingestion is followed by illness, for example. Learning to avoid foods followed

17. Konner, 1972.
18. Seligman, 1970.

by shock is much harder; it is *unprepared*. We bring with us no rule that relates foods to external pain.

Does the notion of **preparedness** help us understand more complex human problems? It may. Here is an example.

A Case Study: Phobias

A **phobia** is a persistent fear reaction that is out of proportion to the reality of the danger. It is an irrational or unjustified fear. One speaks of claustrophobia, or a fear of being enclosed; agoraphobia, or a fear of open and exposed situations. Quite a few people are afraid of spiders or snakes, but some, *phobics,* are terrified of them, terrified even of photographs of them. And as anyone knows who has experienced severe anxiety at exam time or before speaking in public, even mild phobias can be truly debilitating.

Now we assume that these fears are learned. Yet the *content* of the fears does not suggest that an unfortunate experience with just any object can evoke fear of it. Certain objects are feared by a great many people who have never been hurt by them—spiders and snakes, for instance, or exposure before groups of people as in public speaking. Other objects are seldom the focus of a phobia; few people are afraid of lambs, shoes, or electric sockets, though the latter at least is more dangerous than any spider. Why?

PREPAREDNESS AND PHOBIA   Perhaps, Seligman has suggested, because we are *prepared* to learn to fear certain things and not others.[19] These may be things that, in fact, were dangerous to our evolutionary ancestors: Small, crawly things can deliver painful bites; snakes can kill; speaking before a group could draw the attention of enemies or predators. Perhaps we have become prepared to associate these with negative consequences as we associate tastes with illness; and so it takes only minimal negative experience with certain stimuli to make us fear them, with an intensity that may be out of all proportion to the experience itself. It is as if we had a rule that says, "Crawly things are likely to be dangerous." Then we might quickly learn, with only one mild bad experience: "Yes, crawly things *are* dangerous!"

There are some data that support this idea. The fears expressed by a large number of phobic patients were classified with rating scales, constructed independently, of "the extent to which the [feared] object or situation was . . . dangerous to pretechnological man."[20] Such things as predators, blood, thunderstorms, and darkness were rated high on this scale; such things as flowers were rated low.

As it happened, the majority of patients' fears *were* of things that once would have been dangerous. Not all of them were, but then the theory does not say

19. Seligman, 1971.
20. deSilva, Rachman, and Seligman, 1977.

that all phobias are prepared. It only says that prepared ones are most readily acquired and so ought to be most frequent—as, in fact, they are.[21]

In an even more dramatic demonstration, a fear response was directly conditioned in *nonphobic* human subjects by presenting certain stimuli along with electric shock. The stimuli were either snakes and spiders, or houses and faces. After conditioning, the experimenters told the subjects that no more shocks were coming; they even removed the shock electrodes. Fear of houses and faces disappeared at once, but fear of snakes and spiders persisted full-blown.[22]

VICARIOUS LEARNING AND PHOBIA   There remains a difficulty with all of this. We might be prepared to learn to fear (say) snakes after a minimum of bad experience with them. But some people are afraid of snakes who have not, as far as they or we can determine, had *any* bad experiences with them. What sets the phobia going in such a case?

Of course it is hard to be really sure just what experiences a person has or has not had; memory is fallible. With animals, we can introduce (or rule out) certain learning experiences experimentally. In an especially elegant series of experiments, Susan Mineka and her colleagues have shown (1) that a Rhesus monkey, that we *know* has never encountered this or that object before, can develop a fear of it just by watching another monkey react fearfully to it, and (2) that the preparedness concept applies to such *vicarious learning* too.[23]

In these experiments, the "teacher" monkeys were monkeys that had been born and reared in India; they were captured in the wild as adults, and brought to the laboratory. They reacted with intense fear to the sight of a snake—a sensible way for a monkey to react in the jungle (Fig. 7-5)!

The "learner" monkeys, in contrast, were laboratory-born and -reared. They had never seen a snake before these experiments. And, in fact, they showed no fear of snakes—*unless* they had watched one of the teacher monkeys

Figure 7-5   A wild-reared monkey grimaces in fear and retreats to the back of the cage on seeing a snake. After watching this happen, laboratory-reared monkeys also develop a fear of snakes but not of other objects such as flowers. (Courtesy of Susan Mineka)

21. For further discussion see Rachman and Hodgson, 1980.
22. Hugdahl and Öhman, 1977.
23. See for example Cook and Mineka, 1990.

react fearfully to one. If they had, then they reacted fearfully themselves. They acquired the fear "vicariously"—just by seeing a fellow monkey's fear reaction.

But did the feared object have to be something (like a snake) that would be dangerous in nature? Would any old "object" work equally well? No, the "object" cannot be just anything. "Learner" monkeys who watched the "teachers" reacting fearfully to an arrangement of dried flowers, developed no fear of flowers themselves.

(And how, one may ask, does one get a "teacher" monkey to react with fear to flowers, and how does one know that the reaction is equally intense for snakes and flowers? The study was a masterpiece of experimental control. The researchers first showed that the learner did not have to watch the teacher in the flesh; he could watch a videotape of the teacher's panicked reaction to a snake, and learn to fear snakes that way. Then for other learners, the videotape was dubbed so that it showed flowers where the snake really was. Thus the teacher's fear reaction was exactly the same, for the snakes and the flowers. But the fear was picked up by the learner only for the snake, not the flowers.)

At least one species, then, (1) can learn an intense fear vicariously, and (2) can be predisposed or "prepared" to learn to fear certain objects, but not others, under otherwise identical conditions. In such cases it is the predisposition, not the fear itself, that we might call instinctive or untaught.

Theoretical Issues Revisited

Before leaving this topic, we should note the theoretical problems it raises. Our original behaviorist two-factor theory, which treats the "threat" signal as arbitrary (e.g., a tone or a buzzer), makes no provision for these SSDRs, untaught predispositions, and "instinctive rules". But neither does cognitive theory, in its simple commonsense form. If the Maple Toff eaters know that the ice cream did not cause their illness, they ought not to avoid it thereafter. But they do.

Look again. Cognitive theory (and common sense) says: If a rat expects shock if it does not make Response X and no shock if it does, and prefers no shock, then of course it makes Response X. But then any action the creature can perform should be learned as fast as any other. Not so, says Bolles: If the action is an SSDR, learning will be rapid, otherwise not. Similarly, if we can teach an animal that a buzzer (say) is a signal for shock, any such signal should work as well as any other. Again, not so: Avoidance or fear of some "signals" is learned rapidly, of others not. Animals are predisposed to learn certain responses (but not others) to certain signals (but not others). And to know what to expect of a given species in an escape or avoidance experiment, we must know what that species' predispositions are.

Cognition, in the sense of rational expectations, may have very little to do with all this. Perhaps the irrationality of phobics is like the irrationality of the Maple Toff eaters. These subjects knew that the ice cream had nothing to do with their illness, just as phobic subjects know that a garter snake is harmless. But our biological preparednesses or predispositions may be among the many things that can override our intellects.

CONDITIONED REINFORCEMENT

To this point, we have talked mostly about bad things—shocks and spiders and the like. In this section and the next, we turn to nicer things.

Many, probably most, of our actions are performed not only with no bio-logical drive to motivate them, but also without any biologically relevant rewards to maintain them. Obviously, many of the things we work for and strive for have value only because we have learned to value them. The acqui-sition of such value has been studied in the laboratory, in particular through the investigation of **conditioned reinforcement.** This is the process by which a stimulus that has no reinforcing power of its own, acquires such power through learning. The stimulus becomes an *acquired reward*. *(seek something)*

Experimental Demonstrations

Actually, there are two kinds of experimental demonstrations that have been called conditioned (or secondary) reinforcement, and it is unfortunate that they have been called by the same name. They are quite different.

In one, a response is reinforced by something that has no value in itself, but is exchangeable for something that does. Chimpanzees, for instance, have been allowed to work for poker chips which, some time later, may be exchanged for grapes. Chimps are much attracted to grapes, whereas they show little interest in poker chips per se; but if the poker chips are a means to grapes, the animals will work avidly to obtain the chips (Fig. 7-6).[24]

Humans, of course, will go through some high-level cerebration to obtain poker chips, too—especially if the chips are exchangeable for green pieces of paper that are in turn exchangeable for worldly goods. Obviously, money itself can be a conditioned reinforcer in this sense.

More puzzling is the second kind of conditioned reinforcer, in which the reinforcing stimulus is of no use to the subject whatever. It is not *exchangeable* for anything. Suppose, for instance, that a rat is trained to press a bar for food reinforcement, and that the delivery of a food pellet is accompanied by a loud click. Then the food-delivery apparatus is turned off; no food is delivered any more. For some of the rats, pressing the lever now produces nothing at all. For other rats, it produces no food, but it does produce the click of the pellet dis-penser. The latter group will go on working at the lever much longer.[25] As someone has said in one of the worst puns on record, the rats press the lever "just for clicks."

Why? You can't eat a click, or even exchange it for food. Objectively it has no value, never had and never will. But it will maintain behavior for a while; and such a stimulus may even support the acquisition of a new response, for which it is the only reinforcer.

24. Wolfe, 1936; Cowles, 1937.
25. Bugelski, 1938.

Figure 7-6 Conditioned reinforcement. The chimp has been trained to work for poker chips that can be used to obtain food.

A more recent example shows the role of conditioned reinforcement in selection among foods. Anthony Sclafani and his co-workers showed that an arbitrary, non-nutritive, non-preferred flavor can become a preferred one if its ingestion is paired with nourishment.[26] Over a series of training days, the hungry rat is offered one or the other of two distinctive flavors. As the rat licked at the drinking spout, a sensing device was triggered which operated a pump, so that liquid was infused into the rat's stomach without being tasted. For one of the two flavors, the liquid so infused had nutrients in it. For the other flavor, plain water was pumped into the stomach. Thus one of the two flavors (but not the other) was paired with, or predicted, the arrival of nutrients into the body. Later, when the rats were offered a choice between the two flavors, they strongly preferred that solution over the other. An initially non-preferred flavor, then, can become a sought-after one through conditioning.

The Establishment of Conditioned Reinforcers

There have been several suggestions about what happens here. One is that the click becomes a reinforcer, not just because it is *paired with* a natural or primary reinforcer, but because it *predicts* the occurrence of one. Thus the click says to the rat: Food is coming soon.[27]

26. For example, Sclafani, 1990.
27. For discussion see Fantino and Logan, 1979.

The other possibility is that a conditioned reinforcer need not *predict* a primary reinforcer, but need only be *paired with* one. It may be that a stimulus acquires reinforcing properties simply by occuring along with a stimulus that already has such properties. This view is close to the *associationism* of Hobbes (see Chap. 2). Hobbes might have said that the conditioned reinforcer acquires *pleasantness* through being associated with something already pleasant.

In the human case, there is evidence that stimuli acquire reinforcing power simply by being paired with reinforcers,[28] apart from what they predict or can be exchanged for—*if* we are willing to assume that reinforcing power and *pleasantness* are related.★

In one experiment,[29] human subjects were repeatedly exposed to two flavored solutions, one of which had table sugar as an added flavorant. Later on, the subjects tasted and then rated the pleasantness of both solutions, *without* the sugar. It turned out that the taste that had been associated with sweetness, even though it no longer was, was rated more pleasant than the other taste. Perhaps the pairing of new tastes with familiar and pleasant ones may be one way that humans develop likings for new tastes.

Functions of Conditioned Reinforcers . . .

Behavior theorists have assigned a variety of important functions to conditioned reinforcers, especially in complex human behavior. Here are some of the things conditioned reinforcers might do:

1. They can *provide information*. They tell the actor that he has done the right thing. The chimp earns tokens, the rat earns clicks, but only for appropriate responses.
2. They can *provide stimuli that guide subsequent behavior*. If the chimp has a token available, it can exchange the token for food.
3. They can *bridge gaps in time*. If conditioned reinforcers are important in human behavior, it is likely that this is their most vital function. If writing a book, or writing a paper, were reinforced only by its final payoff, the reward would probably be too long delayed to have any effect. The behavior would extinguish before the job was done. As it is, our telling ourselves, "One more page done!" might be a conditioned reinforcer if one has been reinforced before for completing writing assignments. A chimp might never learn to make a response for food if thousands of responses were required for each morsel. But it may do so if it collects tokens along the way.

---

28. See Martin and Levey, 1978.
★The definition of reinforcement does not require that assumption, as we will see in Chapter 8.
29. Zellner, Rozin, Aron, and Kulish, 1983; see also Warwick and Weingarten, 1994.

4. They may simply *become pleasant in their own right*. Chimps may come to *like* poker chips, as human subjects come to like a flavor that was paired with sweetness before.

. . . And a Note of Caution

The discovery of conditioned reinforcers was exciting to early behavior theorists. Such learned reinforcements could go a long way, it appeared, toward accounting for the variability and individuality of human behavior, and for the maintenance of behavior, such as studying or writing a book, that is far removed from any natural reinforcer such as food or warmth.

The key, once again, is the *arbitrariness* of the stimulus that acquires reinforcing properties. The rats pressed the bar just for clicks, but they could have pressed just for tones or flashing lights if the experiment had been set up that way. Chimps worked for chips, but marbles could just as well have been used instead. Presumably, *any* stimulus could become a conditioned reinforcer—like the pieces of paper we call money, or the sound of praise in a familiar language or marks on paper that constitute a high grade—depending on the actor's conditioning history, which has made those stimuli reinforcers for his actions.

There is a danger, however. Because the principle *might* explain so much, we may *assume* that it does when evidence is lacking. In discussing conditioned reinforcement, one writer gives these examples:

The student earns an "A" only for appropriate responses. . . . When the instructor says "Good backswing!" to her tennis pupil, the "good" provides feedback about having performed correctly . . . it may also make the pupil feel good.[30]

Now these stimuli—an A, or praise from an instructor—are indeed reinforcers, if they lead us to repeat the actions that preceded them (the law of effect). And obviously their reinforcing value is learned. But was it *conditioned* in the way I've described? Are the stimuli reinforcers *because* they were paired with food or sex or even cuddles? There is no evidence that this is so, and it seems rather unlikely.

Or think again about money. Money is clearly a learned reinforcer, and in adults, its value depends on its exchangeability for other things. This is demonstrated dramatically when money loses its value in an inflationary economy. But when little children first learn to value money, is it because of this exchangeability? Possibly, but possibly not. It may have much to do with the fact that coins are pretty and bright. Or it may be important that money is given to the child by an adult (e.g., a parent) who obviously values the money and who is valued by the child (see *contagion,* below). In view of how important money is to adults, we know surprisingly little about how that value is first acquired.

30. Schwartz, 1984, pp. 185–186.

A Look Backward: Pavlovian Conditioning and Acquired Motivation

It is now time to pause and take stock. There is a single principle that could underlie *all* the diverse instances of acquired motivation we have summarized this far. And it is the principle that Ivan Pavlov first explored experimentally.

Let's look again at his experiments. Food, for a hungry dog, already triggers salivation and other positive reactions. For short, we will call it an **unconditioned stimulus** or US. Now a bell or a tone does not initially call forth salivation; but if it is paired with food a number of times, then it does. We call such a stimulus, that calls forth a reaction only as the result of conditioning, a **conditioned stimulus** or CS. Thus a bell (CS) comes to trigger salivation if it is paired repeatedly with food (US).

Now consider how general the idea is. (1) Shock (US) calls forth fear reactions; and a buzzer (CS), if paired with shock, comes to evoke them too (or so two-factor theory proposes). (2) To a trained rat, food (US) already calls forth lever-pressing and other approach responses; a click (CS), if paired with food, comes to do so as well. (3) A load of calories delivered into the stomach (US) may have positive effects, and an initially neutral flavor paired with such loads (CS) may become positive in turn. (4) A flavor that is not attractive in itself (CS) may come to be attractive after it is paired with a flavor that already is (US).

Finally, we might *speculate* that (5) even vicarious learning might fit the framework. Assume that seeing another species member behaving fearfully evokes a "sympathetic" fear in ourselves (US). We also see the object that evokes the fear (CS). Since the object is paired with the fear, it might itself come to evoke the fear through conditioning. And this could happen after only one pairing, if the actor is prepared to associate fear with certain CSs such as snakes. Or, if seeing an adult enjoying food triggers a "sympathetic" pleasure in a child (US), that pleasure might be transferred by conditioning to the food the child sees the adult enjoying (CS).[31]

What is common to all these cases is this: A stimulus takes on positive or negative properties, that it wouldn't otherwise have, by being presented along with some other stimulus that already has such properties. Perhaps, in Hobbes's terms (pp. 32–33), the originally neutral stimulus (CS) becomes *associated with* the nice or nasty one (the US), and so takes on niceness or nastiness in turn. Sometimes the learning is very rapid (prepared), sometimes not, but the conditions for its occurrence seem to be the same throughout.

In short, a single set of principles—the principles of classical or Pavlovian conditioning—could help us make sense of a quite impressive variety of cases in which objects or stimuli *acquire* motivational properties.[32]

However, all this is still far short of the whole story. There are some other cases in which positive or negative motives are clearly acquired, and in which

31. Rozin, 1990.
32. For further discussion see Rozin and Zellner, 1987.

the notion of *association* is clearly relevant, but which do not fit the Pavlovian conditioning framework at all. Let us look.

CONTAGION, SIMILARITY, AND MAGIC

Magic? That seems a strange concept to introduce into a discussion of motivation! But there just might be certain "rules of thought" that (1) are highly important sources of acquired motivation, (2) have been neglected until quite recently by research psychologists, but (3) have been identified by students of folklore, myth, and magic.[33] They may be seen in the beliefs and practices of many societies, most definitely including our own.

Everyone has heard of the malicious sorcerer who, wishing to injure a victim, makes a doll that resembles the victim; adds to it a bit of the victim's person, such as nail clippings or a lock of hair; and then burns the doll or sticks pins in it. This image incorporates two principles of magical thinking—two implicit beliefs, so widespread that we may see them operating in cultures all over the world. These principles have been called *contagion* ("once in contact, always in contact") and *similarity* ("similar things have similar properties"). The sorcery image includes both. The doll resembles the victim (similarity). And the hair or nail clippings, having once been part of the person, remain connected with the victim through some substance, spirit, or essence (contagion). On both counts: Harm the doll, and you harm the victim. Let us look more closely.

Contagion

Among the Hindus of India, high-caste people may eat raw foods purchased from lower-caste people, but not cooked food. Since cooking involves more contact with the food, cooked foods are thought to retain more of the essence of their low-caste preparers, which remains part of the food itself ("once in contact, always in contact") and "contaminates" that food. Notice that health considerations, which are often suggested as explanations for food taboos, will not explain this one. Cooked foods are objectively *less* likely to be contaminated (by germs) than raw foods are; yet raw foods are permitted, cooked ones not.[34]

An example from our own society? American college students refused to drink from a glass of fruit juice after a dead cockroach had been dipped in it and removed.[35] Fear of germs, do we say? But the subjects were assured, and believed, that the cockroach was guaranteed sterile and germ-free—this was, after all, a psychological laboratory! It didn't matter. Because "once in contact,

33. For example, Frazier, 1959.
34. Rozin, 1990.
35. Rozin et al., 1986.

always in contact," the juice remained contaminated by the essence or, so to speak, the *idea* of cockroach, and was unacceptable.

Now in this case, one might still think of a conditioning process: a cockroach is disgusting (US), and we see it come in contact with the juice (CS) which then itself triggers disgust. There are other cases, though, where a conditioning interpretation simply does not fit. Some examples:

1. Among the Hopi of the American Southwest, the umbilical cord of a newborn male is attached to an arrow shaft so that he will grow up to be a good hunter.[36] The cord is no longer connected to the boy and never will be again; but "once in contact, always in contact," and so the boy's spirit or essence can be affected by what happens to the cord now. There is no CS or US here—and what is the response?

2. A few weeks ago (as this is written), I read in the newspaper that a perfectly ordinary used wallet, nothing special *qua* wallet, was sold for several thousand dollars. Why? Because Elvis Presley had once owned it! In this case too, a conditioning model will not work, for it is likely that neither the buyer nor the seller had ever met Elvis in the flesh—so what was the US? The mere *knowledge* that an admired figure had once owned the wallet was enough to "contaminate" the wallet with positive value—thousands of dollars' worth!*

Other examples from our society abound. "Shake the hand that shook the hand of John L. Sullivan!" one boxing fan would cry to another in the Boston saloons of the 1880s. The legendary champion could transfer some of the adoration in which he was held to another man's hand, just by shaking it. Or consider how a crowd may reach and shove, expending much energy, to touch a celebrity (Fig. 7-7). What makes the touch worth all that effort? Contagion! These examples, by the way, show that contagion can operate in the positive as well as the negative direction.

Similarity

The underlying idea here is that "like produces like"—that things that are superficially similar are similar at some deeper level of essence or spirit. Among the Hua of New Guinea, soft or reddish plant products are considered to resemble female genitals—and pubescent males are forbidden to eat them, because the males could be feminized by doing so.[37]

Does this happen only among superstitious, "primitive" folk? In our own society, perfectly good chocolate—known to be just that and nothing else—was refused if it was shaped to *resemble* an insect or a bit of dog-do.[38] If dog-do

---

36. Rozin and Nemeroff, 1990.

*A committed Pavlovian, it is true, could argue that the *name* Elvis Presley might call forth pleasant emotions, and that these might transfer to the wallet by conditioning. This seems unlikely. I doubt that I could make my wallet worth several thousand dollars by showing it to a Presley fan and chanting "Elvis Presley, Elvis Presley, . . ." over it. I wish I could!

37. Rozin, 1990.

38. Nemeroff and Rozin, 1992.

Figure 7-7 Why are they doing that?

is disgusting, so is anything that looks like it, whether "rationally" it ought to be or not.

The similarity principle may underlie another set of concepts that is widespread among cultures: the concepts of *homeopathic medicine*.[39] Homeopathic medicine seeks cures that resemble the symptoms of the illness, or the state of health that is desired. Respiratory disorders may be treated with powders or potions made from the lungs of a fox, an animal supposed to have very strong respiratory powers. Like produces like!

A Look Backward

These laws of magic or magical thinking—like goes with like (similarity) and once in contact, always in contact (contagion)—are so widespread that they just might represent universal, though perhaps non-rational, laws of human thought. They have received surprisingly little attention, perhaps because the role of conditioning has dominated our thinking about acquired motivation until quite recently. Interest in them is increasing, however, and we may expect to learn much more about them in coming years.

NON-ASSOCIATIVE MECHANISMS IN LEARNED MOTIVES

As we noted earlier, even if conditioning principles do not fit them very well, the laws of magic do include something like the notion of *association*. Value, positive or negative, is transferred *from* some object that already has it, *to* some-

39. Nisbett and Ross, 1980.

thing else that resembles that object (similarity) or has been in contact with it (contagion).

Even this is not the end of possibilities. Objects or events can acquire motivational properties in ways that even the broader notion of association does not cover. We turn to that topic next.

Imprinting

In certain species of birds, including domestic chickens and ducks, an intriguing and powerful form of *learned reward* can be demonstrated. Experimentally, let a very young, previously isolated chick or duckling encounter any large, moving object. That object then becomes the focus of approach behavior of a variety of kinds: The little bird will follow the object around, or make an arbitrary response to be brought into contact with it, and emit distress calls when it isn't there. This early and rapid learning is called **imprinting**.[40]

In the normal course of events, the large moving object will usually be the parent. Then all will be well; thereafter, the little bird will stick with its parent, and later approach other members of its species, as it should. But if it imprints on a member of the wrong species, the consequences for its social life can be catastrophic. In later life it may prefer the company of the wrong species (Fig. 7-8). It may even court the members of that wrong species. The ethologist Konrad Lorenz found that his adopted jackdaws made perfectly normal, jackdaw-like action patterns of courtship toward *him!*

Imprinting is most likely to occur during a certain sensitive period, early in life. Let the large object appear too late, and imprinting will not occur.

Figure 7-8 Imprinted ducklings follow a member of the wrong species—Konrad Lorenz.

40. Lorenz, 1965.

953-2001

Now the stimulus upon which the animal imprints must have certain characteristics: it must be fairly large, and it must move. Beyond that, it may be perfectly arbitrary. A chick can be imprinted on a human being or, for that matter, upon a block of Styrofoam. Such a useless object would be rejected with contempt by a chick or duckling that had not been exposed to it during the sensitive period. Thus the imprinting phenomenon is related to some ideas we are familiar with, but it also is different, and may provide us with a new principle to consider.

The object—a Styrofoam block or a green wooden cube or whatever—does become a reinforcer, for the little bird will make an arbitrary response to obtain commerce with it.[41] It acquires that reinforcing power through learning. But it is *not* a conditioned reinforcer, because conditioned reinforcers acquire their rewarding power through being paired with, or predicting, a natural or *primary* reinforcer such as food. In imprinting, there is no primary reinforcer.

This is an important difference. We might think of conditioned reinforcement as a *transferring* of reinforcing power from a stimulus that already had it (such as food), to a stimulus that did not (a click or a poker chip). Similarly, we can think of the stress reactions to electric shock as *transferred* to a buzzer paired with shock, by the conditioning process.

But imprinting is not like that. Value is not transferred *to* the Styrofoam block *from* something else. There is no *something else*. The Styrofoam block does not offer the little bird anything of value—and it does not predict, and is not paired with, anything else that does. Apparently the bird does not so much transfer, as *assign,* positive value to the imprinted stimulus when it appears. That stimulus becomes a reinforcer, not because it is paired with a natural reinforcer, but simply because it appears at the right time—during the sensitive period—and has the right properties—it is large and it moves.

How many other such *assignments* of reinforcing power are there? The imprinting phenomenon itself may turn out to have considerable generality as a component of parent-to-young attachment in a variety of species, humans included.[42] But the process of assignment, as opposed to transfer, of reinforcing power has not been much discussed in other contexts. It seems unlikely that it is restricted to parent-child attachment situations.

Mere Exposure

Another case of non-associative learning in motivation is the effect of *mere exposure* to a stimulus complex. Both small children[43] and big college students[44] like a flavor better if they have experienced it before than if they haven't. Robert Zajonc, one of the few who have studied the matter in detail, finds that Chinese characters, nonsense syllables, and photographs of faces, all become more positive as subjects are repeatedly exposed to them. He summarizes other data

41. Hoffman and Ratner, 1973.
42. Bowlby, 1969; Hoffman and Ratner, 1973.
43. Birch et al., 1982.
44. Pliner, 1982.

showing that paintings or music in unfamiliar styles become more pleasing with mere exposure of the material, not paired with anything.[45]

Why? We are not sure. The effect does not seem to depend on conscious recognition; it occurs even if subjects do not recognize the material as having been presented before.[46] Zajonc suggests that it may reflect the disappearance of an initial tense reaction to anything new—a kind of cognitive SSDR that says, "Is it dangerous?" As the stimulus is repeated and nothing bad happens, that reaction drops away.

The mere-exposure effect may be of great importance. It is too bad that we know so little for sure about how it works.

THE OPPONENT-PROCESS THEORY

Now we are ready to look at a more complex process in the acquisition of motives. This theory deals with both nice things and nasty things, and it includes both associative and non-associative mechanisms. Let us begin with an example, and look again at imprinting.

When hungry, cold, or otherwise stressed, baby ducks emit characteristic high-pitched distress calls, over and over. Figure 7-9 shows the frequency of these distress calls over blocks of time in a warm, unstressed duckling, in a comfortable environment. At the beginning of the session there are no distress calls (left panel). An imprinted object—a Styrofoam cube—is introduced; still no distress calls (middle panel). The cube is removed; and *then* distress calls begin (right panel). If we take distress calling as an indication of a duckling's misery, then we conclude that the *withdrawal* of the object evokes substantial misery when its simple *absence* did not.

We empathize with this reaction. We would react the same way if some-

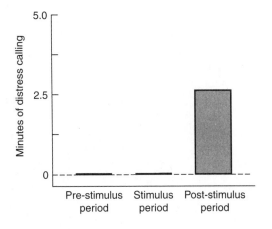

Figure 7-9 Distress calling by ducklings, before an imprinted object is introduced (prestimulus period), while it is present (stimulus period), and after it is withdrawn (poststimulus period). (From Hoffman and Ratner, 1973.)

45. Zajonc, 1968, 1980 (pronounced *Zah*-yonss).
46. Moreland and Zajonc, 1979; Bornstein and D'Agostino, 1994.

thing nice were taken away. But why should it be that way? Objectively, the situation at the end of the session is the same as it was in the beginning: no Styrofoam cube. Why is the duckling's misery so much greater after the object goes away?

Richard Solomon and John Corbit have developed a theory about the *time course* of positive and negative feelings that may shed light on the psychology of disappointment—and on much else besides. The basic idea is: If a situation generates a state of liking or disliking, of happiness or misery, then that state will in turn trigger its opposite—the **opponent process.** Happiness generates its opposite. So does unhappiness.[47]

The theory is diagrammed in Figure 7-10. A situation has as its first component (Process A) a hedonic reaction; enjoyment or pleasure, let us say. That evokes the opponent process B, a state of displeasure or lack of enjoyment. Since B is opposite to A, it subtracts from it, and the resulting enjoyment levels off at some value below the original one.

Suppose now that the happiness-evoking situation goes away. Since B is evoked by A, not by the situation itself, it lags behind A. As a result, there will be a rebound—a swing toward negative feelings, because of the unopposed action of State B.

This theory is, in a sense, a *homeostatic* theory of emotion or mood. We see our familiar negative-feedback homeostatic system as developed in Chapter 3: An input (Process A) triggers an action (Process B) that reduces the input. The effect is that neither pleasure nor displeasure is allowed to be very intense for very long. That obviously brings good news and bad news; our moments of intense misery will be short-lived, but so will our moments of intense joy. And we can expect a rebound, either way. Solomon calls it a Puritan's theory: Joy must be paid for with grief later, but pain now promises better to come.[48]

We can see, too, that there are certain advantages to such a system. If distress is always moderated by its opposite, this may allow organisms to keep going in the face of pain, or disappointment, that could otherwise be immobilizing. On the positive side, we can *speculate* that even here there may be advantages to moderation. It might not be to our advantage to be too ecstatic for too long. In the wild where we evolved, our ancestors had many tasks and faced many dangers, and needed to keep their wits about them even in moments of joy. Perhaps a joy-moderating system evolved out of that necessity.

Now let us apply the theory to the duckling case. When the cube arrived, let us assume that it was greeted with a swing toward pleasure. That pleasurable reaction may have decayed with time—no measure of that is provided here—as a result of the modulating action of Process B. Then when the cube went away, Process B was unopposed, and the duckling went into a rebound mood of misery and distress. The resulting disappointment was expressed long and loud.

47. Solomon and Corbit, 1974.
48. Solomon, 1980.

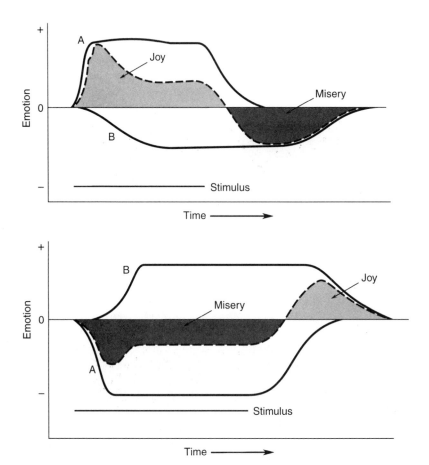

Figure 7-10   The opponent-process theory. The shaded area represents the *difference* between the primary A process and the opponent B process. Top panel: Joy (A) produced by a stimulus is quickly reduced by the opponent process (B), which also produces a rebound toward misery when the stimulus ends. Bottom panel: The converse case; misery (A) is alleviated by the opponent process (B), which produces relief when the unpleasant stimulus ends.

The Generality of Opponent Processes

What this theory does is to bring motivational/emotional states into line with what seems to be a general principle of nervous system function: Push the nervous system in one direction, and it will push back in the other. One example is the effect of drugs. Amphetamine is a nervous system *excitant.* The symptoms of amphetamine withdrawal, after prolonged and heavy use, are the symptoms of nervous system *depression:* lassitude, slowness, and somnolence. Conversely, alcohol is a nervous system *depressant.* And the symptoms of alcohol withdrawal, after prolonged and heavy use, are the symptoms of nervous system *hyperexcitability:* exaggerated reflexes, irritability, and (in extreme cases) convulsions and hallucinations. In each case, removal of a drug that causes one set of effects triggers the opposite effects.

The Dynamics of the Opponent Process

Thus far, States A and B can be considered more or less fixed processes underlying our hedonic states. Complications come in with Solomon's further suggestions about the properties of the opponent process B. It changes over time, and in two ways. First is a non-associative change: Process B is *strengthened by use*. Second, there is associative change: Process B is *conditionable*. Let us look at these complications in that order.

THE GROWTH OF OPPONENT PROCESSES   The opponent process B, but not the initial state A, is assumed to become faster and bigger if it is evoked repeatedly and often. In this respect it is like fatigue. Lift a weight once a second, and we will quickly get tired; lift the same weight once a week and we won't. In a similar way, if Process A is evoked often enough, with only short times between, the B process will increase over successive episodes. Since the A process doesn't change, this means that (1) the difference between them will diminish—the first emotional reaction will get smaller and smaller—and (2) the rebound swing to the opposite mood will become more and more severe.

Here is an example. Parachutists, during their first jump, often experience utter terror. Their hearts race, their breathing is spasmotic, their bodies are curled and stiff. After landing safely, they may appear stunned for a few minutes, stony-faced and silent. Then they go into a period of elation, with smiling and rapid excited talk. A mild euphoria has replaced the misery of fear.

After a number of jumps, matters are different. The fear is much reduced, and the parachutists may look forward to their jump with excitement. After landing, activity level is very high, and there may be leaping, shouting, and back slapping. Their success at jumping, we might say, has taught them that they can jump safely; perhaps that is why the fear is lessened. But why should the euphoria after the jump become even greater than before?

It makes sense if one assumes that the opponent process leading to euphoria has been strengthened by use (Fig. 7-11). We assume that Process A, the fear response, doesn't change, but that the opponent process B gets bigger and bigger with repeated jumps. Thus, on the first few jumps, the opponent process mitigates fear somewhat and overshoots to produce mild euphoria. But after many jumps, Process B is greater in magnitude. It neutralizes fear (Process A) almost entirely; moreover, when danger is over, it rebounds into an even greater euphoria than it did originally.

On the negative side, it appears that a duckling's misery is also strengthened by repeated evocations. When the Styrofoam cube is introduced and then withdrawn the first time, distress calls are evoked, as we have seen. As such episodes are repeated, distress calling becomes more and more prolonged (Fig. 7-12). A new source of misery is thus added to the duckling's existence. The first disappointment is bad enough. Repeated ones get worse and worse.

Some Applications of Opponent-Process Theory

The opponent-process theory may help us make sense of a wide variety of behavioral phenomena that we see in daily life. Let us look at just a couple of examples.

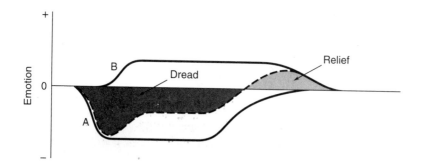

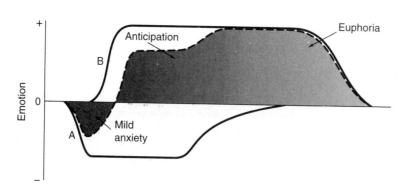

Figure 7-11 Effects of strengthening the opponent process by repeated use. Top panel: Over the first few experiences, the weak B process alleviates parachutists' dread only slightly and leads to only a mild rebound after the jump. Bottom panel: On later experiences, the strengthened B process may quickly overcome the A process, producing anticipation instead of dread, and a large rebound into elation and euphoria after the jump.

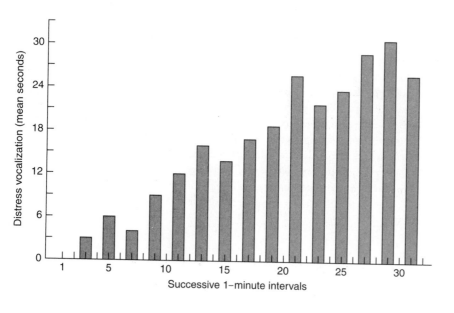

Figure 7-12 Strengthening of disappointment by repeatedly evoking it. As an imprinted object was repeatedly presented and withdrawn, the distress calls which followed the withdrawal became more and more prolonged. (From Hoffman et al., 1974.)

HOW LUXURIES BECOME NECESSITIES   Barry Schwartz points out that many objects, appliances, etc., that start out as "special treats" in our lives, may come to be seen as necessities rather than luxuries. Why? Because of the operation of opponent processes.[49]

Consider this scenario. It is summertime, and you are living in an apartment that gets uncomfortably hot. So you buy an air conditioner, plug it in, and turn it on. Within a few minutes the apartment is pleasantly cool. Wonderful! What a relief! You are very happy indeed (the A process). But of course the joy is temporary, and after a while you forget about it and go on with your daily life (A process lessened by the opponent B process).

As the days go on, you experience less and less joy and gladness when you turn the air conditioner on. The comfort is taken for granted now; it's routine (B process strengthened by repeated evocations). But now, suppose the air conditioner breaks down. Picture your misery! That hot apartment, once merely uncomfortable, is now intolerable. It is much more unpleasant than it was before you ever bought that air conditioner, just as a duckling is more miserable when the imprinted object is withdrawn than before it arrived at all. Earlier on, air conditioning was a luxury, a present for yourself that gave you pleasure. Now it seems more like a necessity—not much pleasure in its presence, but severe *displeasure* in its absence.★

DRUG TOLERANCE AND WITHDRAWAL   Here is another example of how luxuries may become necessities. It seems quite unrelated to the air-conditioner story, but in fact it just might reflect the same underlying process. Consider addictive drugs.

The self-administration of heroin is followed by a rush of pleasure, which some people compare to orgasmic feelings (Process A). This initial thrill soon settles down into a state of pleasant euphoria (pleasure partly neutralized by Process B).

After frequent and repeated use, however, the picture changes. Even if Process A stays the same, the rebound process B gets bigger and bigger. This has two consequences. First, the pleasure produced by the drug is much reduced, and higher doses are required even to approach it. This is known as **tolerance.** Second, the discontinuance of the drug results in distressing physical symptoms, known as **withdrawal symptoms.** At this stage, the person, now physically dependent on the drug, may seek it, not for pleasure but for relief of the discomfort of withdrawal. A positively reinforced response has now become an escape or avoidance response, motivated by withdrawal symptoms. One seeks to prevent their onset (avoidance) or end them if they do occur (escape).

49. Schwartz, 1986.
★For other examples see Scitovsky, 1976.

How tolerance and withdrawal work at the cellular level is not known. But many of our theories, including the opponent-process theory, see the two as reflecting a single underlying principle. It is the principle we saw earlier: Push the nervous system and it will push back. Thus tolerance may occur in part because the opponent process B, strengthened by repeated elicitations, neutralizes the pleasurable process A. And withdrawal may occur in part because the strengthened process B results in progressively greater rebound as the drug leaves the body.★

Conditioning of Opponent Processes

We have seen that the opponent process B begins as a response to the initial process A. However, there is evidence that Process B also can be conditioned, so that *external* stimuli can cause it to occur.★★

Dramatic instances of such conditioning have been obtained by the use of drugs. In a classic series of experiments, Shepard Siegel examined the effect of morphine, a powerful pain-reducing drug, on pain sensitivity in rats.[50] He and his co-workers measured rats' sensitivity to pain by placing their feet on a metal surface, hot enough to begin hurting after a few seconds. The more sensitive the rat is to pain, the faster he removes his paws from the surface. If morphine reduces sensitivity, then rats treated with morphine should delay longer before withdrawing their paws, and they do.

Now this effect of morphine also shows tolerance; that is, repeated treatments with the drug gradually become less effective, even though drug and dosage remain the same. Here the experimenters gave the rats repeated injections of morphine, and sure enough, the effect of the drug grew less and less. Finally, to test for conditioning, the rats were given an injection as usual—but this time, the injection had no morphine in it. It consisted only of physiological saline.

Before going on, let's think about what ought to happen here. Among morphine's effects (it has many) is to reduce sensitivity to pain. If that effect gets less and less with repeated doses (tolerance), that must mean that the body is doing something to oppose the drug. So the effect of that "something" (the opponent process) must be to *increase* sensitivity to pain. Finally, suppose that the opponent process can become a conditioned response to the situation in which it has occurred, so that the handling and the injection now evoke the opponent process, just as Pavlov's bell evoked salivation.

But now, on the test trial, the conditioned opponent process should kick in when there is no morphine in the body for it to oppose. The result ought to be

★"In part," because other physiological processes also contribute to tolerance and withdrawal. For discussion see Jaffe, 1990.
★★Opponent-process conditioning has been demonstrated experimentally in the effects of a familiar drug—caffeine. See Rozin et al., 1984.
50. Siegel, 1975.

an *increase* in sensitivity to pain. And that is exactly what happened: The morphine-tolerant animals were actually *more* sensitive to pain than animals that had had no morphine experience.

Conditioned opponent processes could be very useful in some situations, but they also could introduce potentially lethal dangers. Morphine can have yet another effect: At high enough doses, it can kill! And that effect too shows tolerance: Animals, or humans, that have developed tolerance to morphine can survive doses of the drug that would be fatal to non-tolerant users. So, with repeated exposures to morphine, the body does something (the opponent process) that opposes its life-threatening effects. By itself, that is good news.

But suppose the compensatory reaction is also conditioned as a response to certain environmental cues. Then it will be weakened if those cues are changed. Suppose, for instance, that a heroin addict injects the drug at a dosage she has learned is safe—but does it in a novel environment. Then the body's compensation could be less than usual, because environmental conditioned stimuli for that compensation are lacking. A fatal overdose could result. There is evidence that this can and does happen in drug users. And it has been shown by direct experiment that it can happen in animals: A dose of morphine that was safe for addicted rats, if given in an environment associated with its use, was life-threatening in an environment where it had not been given before.[51]

The Status of the Opponent-Process Theory

What are we to make of the opponent-process idea? Certainly it has made sense of data obtained in a variety of species and settings—orphaned ducklings, parachutists, and human drug users.

It is obviously a very flexible theory, and that is what makes some writers, including me, uncomfortable with it. Solomon himself has expressed some misgivings about its flexibility. It could easily be tailored so as to explain any possible finding. For example, why does Dad's apple pie never lose its attraction? If it is because we don't eat it that often—often enough to build up a strong opponent process B—well, how often is *that often?*

The theory's account of addiction leaves similar loose ends. Morphine or heroin *can* produce intense pleasure on first usage. But many users find the first few experiences very unpleasant. For them, heroin is an acquired taste. Are we to say that an opponent process leads from displeasure to pleasure early on, and *another* opponent process later swings the other way to produce tolerance and withdrawal? Obviously, if we are allowed to stack opponent processes end to end like that, we could explain anything whatever.

None of this is intended to dismiss the opponent-process theory. It only says that we are not yet sure how to evaluate it. We need to test its many implications, and to work out the laws that the processes can be expected to follow—how strong is strong enough, how often is often enough, and whether

51. Siegel, et al., 1982.

the occurrence of separate early and late opponent processes can be demonstrated with independent evidence. Then we will be able to judge whether the theory is on the right track, or only ingenious.

A LOOK BACKWARD: ADDICTION

By way of reviewing these ideas, let us look at a topic that combines a large number of them—and has to do with a serious social problem. There is an acquired motive that can come to dominate an individual's existence, causing severe disruption to both the individual and the community. Let us consider *addiction*. And, to keep the discussion both concrete and manageably short, we will focus on one addictive drug: alcohol, for alcohol is a drug, and it is definitely addictive, or can be so.

For most people (though not all), alcohol is very much an acquired taste. Most babies detest it, as do most young children on first exposure. Children or adolescents may continue to experiment with it, however, until they come to like it—to the point where they will make arbitrary responses, like going to bars and paying money, to obtain alcoholic beverages. Now such beverages meet our definition of acquired *rewards.*

There are many factors that could contribute to experimentation with alcohol. These include simple curiosity or peer pressure or both. Then again, if the big folks drink alcohol, it must be a big-folks' drink, so we will be big folks if we drink it ourselves *(contagion).* Could something like this underlie the value of drinking as *symbolizing adulthood* and autonomy?

As to a person's acquiring a taste for alcohol, again many factors could contribute. *Mere exposure* could make it more palatable (pp. 272–73). And many beginning drinkers begin with sweet, heavily flavored mixtures such as whiskey sours; thus the taste of the alcohol is mixed with something already palatable, and may come to be more palatable in itself through *conditioning* (compare p. 265). And, of course, the person will discover that alcohol's actions on the brain may produce positive effects—mood elevation in some persons, reduced anxiety and inhibition in others. These changes may in themselves reinforce alcohol drinking; and the taste of alcoholic drinks, because it is reliably followed by these effects, may become a *conditioned reinforcer* (pp. 263–66).★   / *association*

Thus, there are a number of reasons why people might develop a taste for alcohol, and drink it on occasion and in moderate amounts. We can look at drinking of this sort as guided by the *incentive value* of the taste of the drink (compare pp. 87–88) and of its physiological effects.

However, in some drinkers, the picture changes—usually very gradually, but sometimes abruptly—into something quite different. At this point, *opponent processes* become important. With repeated large doses of alcohol, the drinker becomes less sensitive to the drug, and so requires larger and larger

★For further discussion of acquired tastes see Rozin, 1990.

amounts to achieve the desired effect *(tolerance)*. And if drinking then stops abruptly, the "rebound" may produce *withdrawal symptoms*. These may be relatively mild, though still unpleasant: trembling, restlessness, and insomnia. At the extreme, if the person has drunk very heavily for long periods of time and then stops abruptly, the symptoms may progress to terrifying hallucinations and even to potentially fatal convulsions. It is entirely possible to die of alcohol withdrawal.[51]

And—an important point—these symptoms can be relieved, totally and very rapidly, by further drinking. Our drinker soon discovers this (or is told it), and may now continue drinking, not for the positive effects of the drug, but to make the withdrawal symptoms go away. The sequence has become a negative-feedback loop: The symptoms appear (input), and drinking alcohol (output) takes away that input (negative feedback).

Notice how drastically this changes matters. Earlier on, the person could take a drink, available "out there" in the environment, if she wished to experience its pleasant effects. Nothing bad would happen if she didn't have a drink. But now, something bad is already happening—the withdrawal symptoms— and these will go on happening *unless* she drinks. Moreover, the symptoms are not "out there" but "in here," within her body; she cannot walk away from them. Thus the response of drinking, once a positively reinforced response, now is an *escape response* (p. 248). As a rat can turn off shock by jumping over a barrier, so the person can turn off withdrawal symptoms by drinking. Or, to say it another way, alcohol is no longer just an external acquired *reward;* the need for alcohol is now an acquired internal *drive* (pp. 250–51).

But now there is a further problem. A drink or two will end the discomfort of withdrawal, yes. But it also strengthens the physiological process that leads to the discomfort in the first place (the opponent process intensified by repetition). Before very long, the symptoms will crop up again more unpleasant than before, requiring further drinking for their suppression, thus strengthening the addiction yet more, . . . A vicious cycle has set in (Fig. 7-13). It is at this point that we may begin speaking of the person as *chemically dependent* or as *addicted,* and, if alcohol is the drug of concern, as *alcoholic*.★

We can take it yet another step. The drinker will discover (or be told) that drinking can not only end the unpleasant state once it has begun. If one drinks *before* the symptoms begin, one can prevent them from occurring at all—just as a rat, if the experiment is set up that way, can prevent shock from coming on at all by jumping the barrier during the warning period. Now we have drinking, not as escape, but as an *avoidance response* (p. 248). Of course this also means that drinks must be taken more frequently still, and the vicious circle draws tighter.

51. Jaffe, 1990.

★The use of these terms is inconsistent and somewhat arbitrary (see Jaffe, 1990); so the present usage reflects the author's choice, not a consensus.

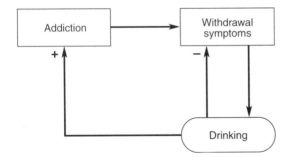

Figure 7-13   In an addicted person, drinking (or other drug use) relieves the withdrawal symptoms (negative feedback), but it also strengthens the dependence that produces those symptoms.

What happens then? If the person is successful at concealing her drinking (as many alcoholics are), such "relief drinking" can go on for years. Indeed, there is no way to know how many people manage it indefinitely, never coming to our attention and so not appearing in the statistics.

It is certain, however, that for many addicts something will fall apart sooner or later and call attention to the disorder. Prolonged alcohol abuse has a variety of physiological effects, the symptoms of which may lead the person to seek treatment. Alcohol-related accidents or arrests may bring the person to the attention of authorities. Or decreased performance on the job, or changes in behavior at home, will become unmistakable to a boss or a spouse.

If a severely addicted person does seek treatment, this may begin with a period of hospitalization for detoxification. There, tranquilizing or muscle-relaxant drugs can be given to suppress the withdrawal symptoms over the 5 to 7 days that they last. Once they have subsided, the vicious cycle *may* be broken, and the person can refrain from drinking without discomfort.

This, however, is only the first phase of recovery from alcoholism. In a sense, now that the escape-avoidance cycle is broken, the person is back at an earlier stage in which the *positive* effects of alcohol are available. But the person will be strongly advised, by clinicians and by other former addicts (e.g., through Alcoholics Anonymous), not to seek these effects, but to stop drinking and stay stopped. If a person drinks who has once been addicted to alcohol, the odds of re-addiction are very high. And what we have learned in this chapter might help us understand that too.

First, we recall that the opponent B process is thought to grow stronger with repeated elicitations. Thus if the person resumes drinking, (1) a reduction in the effect of the drug (tolerance) is likely from the outset, so that more-than-normal doses are required to produce even the positive effects. And (2) if the drinker does drink herself into dependence again, the rebound is likely to be greater and produce more severe withdrawal symptoms this time. It has been shown in animals that *repeated* addictions and withdrawals give rise to more and more severe withdrawal symptoms, even if the amounts of alcohol involved are held constant. Many alcoholics report a similar experience.[52]

52. Jaffe, 1990.

Second, we recall that the B process can be *conditioned*. This means that tolerance and withdrawal symptoms may be greater than before, because of the *external* stimuli that accompany drinking—the setting (e.g., a bar) and, of course, the taste of the beverage. Even the setting itself, without the drug, can have powerful effects. Consider this case study:

> The patient was a 28 year old man with a 10-year history of narcotic addiction. He [was arrested and] reported experiencing severe withdrawal during the first 4 or 5 days in custody, but later . . . felt like a new man, and decided he was finished with drugs. . . . On the way home after release from prison, he began thinking of drugs and feeling nauseated. As the subway approached his stop, he began sweating, tearing from his eyes and gagging. [These are characteristic withdrawal symptoms.] This was an area where he had frequently experienced narcotic withdrawal symptoms while trying to acquire drugs. As he got off the subway, he vomited onto the tracks. He soon bought drugs, and was relieved. . . . The cycle repeated itself over the next few days and soon he became readdicted.[53]

In a word, withdrawal symptoms can occur as *conditioned responses* to a setting in which drug use has occurred. Alcohol use may be affected in similar ways.[54] This may be one reason why recovering alcoholics and drug users are advised to avoid not only the drug, but also "slippery places"—settings associated with drinking or use.

As we see, there are a number of processes that may be operating at the same time, all supporting the *acquired motive* that leads to seeking and using addictive substances. Perhaps this is why addictive disorders are so difficult to treat, and so distressingly subject to relapse.

SUMMARY

Acquired drives are internal states that motivate action, and that occur as a result of learning. Acquired rewards are stimuli or situations that become incentives as a result of learning. Since biological drives account for only a fraction of behavior in humans and animals, we look to acquired motives to explain the rest.

A case of acquired drive is *avoidance learning*, in which an animal learns to prevent the occurrence of a painful stimulus such as shock. Since the response prevents the stimulus from occurring, there is the question of what maintains it—how can a non-event reinforce responding? The *two-factor theory* is an early behavioristic theory designed to answer that question. It proposes that an animal first learns to be afraid of a warning stimulus, such as a buzzer or tone. The conditioning of that *acquired drive* is the first of the two factors. Second, a suc-

53. O'Brien, 1976.
54. Ludwig and Wikler, 1973.

cessful avoidance response turns off the warning signal and reduces the fear. That is the second factor: Fear reduction reinforces avoidance responses. This theory has been applied in the clinic, for example, in understanding and treating compulsive behavior through response prevention.

But there are problems with the theory, for avoidance responding can be maintained with no warning stimulus and no stimulus change following the response. And there may be no evidence of fear, especially in well-trained rats. To some writers, such data argue for a cognitive interpretation of avoidance condition: We must consider not only what the rat's environment is like but what it expects and perceives. But this theory too has its problems, which become apparent when we look at the interaction of learned and instinctive behavior.

There are instinctive constraints on avoidance learning. Animals and humans come to a learning experience already *prepared* to try certain responses to threat (Bolles's *species-specific defense reactions,* or SSDRs); to associate certain events with others, as mammals quickly associate taste with illness; and, in human children, to fear unfamiliar adult faces. In such cases, learning experiences tell the animal when to apply its biological rules—that *this* situation is a threatening one, or that *this* taste goes with illness, or that *this* face is not a familiar one. The rules themselves are untaught. And we apply them even when we know better.

Perhaps the prevalence of certain kinds of phobias reflects a *preparedness* to fear certain kinds of objects. Mineka's work shows that fear may be acquired *vicariously:* by seeing someone else's fearful reaction to an object, we may come to fear it ourselves. And this kind of learning, too, seems to involve preparedness for learning to fear certain objects but not others. Monkeys can acquire a fear of snakes, but not of flowers, in this way.

Like acquired drives such as fear, acquired rewards were first studied as instances of conditioning. *Conditioned reinforcers* can be established in two ways: (1) by making some neutral object, like a poker chip, *exchangeable* for a natural or *primary* reinforcer such as food and (2) by simply presenting a neutral stimulus, such as a click, along with the primary reinforcer. Often in such cases, the neutral stimulus must predict the occurrence of the primary reinforcer; but there also is evidence that simple pairing will sometimes do, at least in humans. Such conditioned reinforcers can provide information, telling the actor that the right response has been made; they can guide subsequent behavior; they can bridge gaps in time, maintaining behavior even when the reinforcement is long delayed; and they may become pleasurable in their own right. However, there is the danger of *assuming* that a conditioning process is operative in all cases of learned rewards. This is unlikely.

In many of these cases, acquired drives or rewards involve *association* of one stimulus with another, perhaps through classical or Pavlovian conditioning. Thus shock triggers fear reactions, and a signal (such as a buzzer) that is paired with the shock comes to trigger such reactions too. Magical thinking shows us other such cases. An implicit belief in *contagion* (once in contact, always in contact) can make an ordinary wallet very valuable if a celebrity had owned it, or perfectly good food unacceptable if a person of low caste has prepared it. Again, the *similarity* principle (like produces like) may lead us to reject perfectly good chocolate if it is shaped to resemble something disgusting. Thus, an implicit and perhaps unconscious belief in these magical principles can be shown in our own society as well as others.

However, some acquired rewards clearly do not involve conditioning in the usual sense. They are not stimuli that are paired with, or that predict, natural rewards. Rather, they seem to be *assigned* positive values if they occur under certain conditions. In the case of *imprinting,* which occurs in some animals including ducks and geese, an arbitrary object becomes a reinforcer if it appears during a sensitive period when the animal is young. Or a stimulus may be assigned higher value simply because it has occurred before, the *mere-exposure effect.*

The *opponent-process theory* combines many of these ideas. A swing toward pleasure or displeasure (the A process) causes another process (the B process) that opposes it and outlasts it. Therefore, either happiness or unhappiness will be moderated by the opponent process; and when the mood-arousing circumstances are removed, a rebound will follow. It is assumed that the B process, but not the initial A process, is strengthened by repeated use, and can be conditioned as a response to environmental cues.

Similar opponent processes may operate in the nervous system. Addictive drugs have less effectiveness with repeated use; this is *tolerance.* When the drug is discontinued, the rebound reaction may be intense, producing *withdrawal symptoms.* Both tolerance and withdrawal could occur because the opponent process, which opposes the effect of the drug, is strengthened with repeated, frequent drug use. Moreover, tolerance may be in part a conditioned drug-opposed response to the situation, making drugs more potent and potentially dangerous in an unfamiliar environment.

In fact, the phenomenon of addiction allows us to review many of these ideas. Alcohol, for example, is an acquired taste; and acquiring the taste may involve mere exposure, conditioning (alcohol is often mixed initially with something tasty), and even contagion (it's an adult drink, so it will confer some adulthood on us if we drink it). Then there are the positive effects of alcohol itself, such as relaxation or reduced inhibition.

Once a person comes to enjoy alcohol, it may be a trouble-free pleasure. For some, however, a dangerous process sets in. If alcohol is taken frequently and in large amounts, tolerance develops, requiring still higher intake. If intake is high enough long enough, its cessation brings on unpleasant withdrawal symptoms, which can be relieved by further drinking. Drinking has now become, not a positively reinforced response, but an escape response—a way of removing the withdrawal symptoms. The trouble is that drinking also strengthens the physical addiction that gives rise to the symptoms, so they will soon return at even greater strength. A vicious cycle has set in. A similar progression can be seen with many other addictive drugs.

The cycle can be broken by treatment of withdrawal symptoms, but even a symptom-free alcoholic is well advised to remain abstinent. Otherwise, the rebound opponent process, strengthened by repetition and perhaps now a conditioned response, is likely to lead to re-addiction. Thus the acquired motive of seeking and using alcohol is a multiprocess one, incorporating many of the concepts this chapter has surveyed.

PART 3

Purposive Behavior

CHAPTER 8

Reinforcement Theory

> I have but one lamp by which my feet are guided, and that is the lamp of experience. I know no way of judging of the future but by the past.
>
> —PATRICK HENRY

M ost voluntary behavior appears to be **purposive.** It is forward-looking and directed toward a goal. Attainment of that goal—finding food or a mate, escaping or avoiding fear or stress—is the **consequence** that directs behavior this way or that.

In this chapter and the next, we will look at contrasting theories about what makes behavior purposive. This chapter will focus on **reinforcement theory,** a cornerstone of modern behaviorism. Briefly, the theory says: *The behavior we call purposive is behavior that is maintained by its reinforcing consequences.*

REINFORCEMENT AND PURPOSE

From very early on in this book, we have distinguished between a stimulus-bound reflex or action pattern on the one hand, and a purposive, goal-directed motivational state on the other. A motivational state, we have seen, is one that can be expressed by an arbitrary response. If we see that the subject *does whatever is available* to obtain a goal, then we say that a motivational state exists. Now in practice, when we show that an animal will make an arbitrary response to obtain a goal, we almost always use a reinforcement procedure.

The Use of Reinforcement to Diagnose Purpose

Think again about a rat pressing a lever to get food. We may train the rat to press a lever, but we could just as well train it to turn left at a choice point or dance around the cage. We select an arbitrary response—pressing or turning left or dancing—and then *reinforce* it with a bit of food. If the experiment is successful, then we have shown a motivational state.

In such a case the reinforcer—food—is an *environmental* object or stimulus. But it is easy to see how internal factors, as discussed in Chapters 3 and 4, can affect behavior by way of these environmental events. To a food-deprived rat or human, food is a reinforcer; to a sexually motivated one, access to a mate is a reinforcer; and so on. Internal factors can affect behavior by *setting the reinforcing value of environmental commodities.*

This is similar to the idea we developed on pages 95–97: that drive states can determine the *pleasantness* of an object such as food. But the notion of reinforcement is more general than that, as we will see in a minute.

Reinforcement Theory: Purpose Means Reinforcement

Thus we use reinforcement *procedures* as a way of deciding whether or not an action reflects a motivational state. But we also speak of reinforcement *theory*. This is the modern behaviorist's theory about the nature of purposive behavior, and it offers a solution to the great paradox with which such behavior confronts us.

The paradox is this. We speak of behavior as influenced by its consequences. But when the behavior occurs, those consequences haven't happened yet. They lie in the future. And if there is one thing we insist on, it is that causes precede their effects; they don't follow them. Hence the problem: How can future events cause present actions? How do we get the future into the present?

Reinforcement theory says: We don't. The action is affected not by its *future* consequences, but by what the consequences of such action have been *in the past.* If in the past an action has been reinforced, then the organism is changed in such a way that that action is more likely to occur thereafter.

Reinforcement theory asserts that we can understand all purposive behavior this way. The causes of action are not in the future; they are in the past where they belong. And the *consequences* that control action are not future ones, but past ones.

That is the theory. Before we examine its accomplishments, let us review where it came from.

DEVELOPMENT OF THE REINFORCEMENT PRINCIPLE

In Chapter 2, we saw some forerunners of the reinforcement principle. There was Hobbes's *hedonistic* theory of action: We perform acts that are *associated with pleasure,* and refrain from ones associated with displeasure. Why are they associated with one or the other? Because they have led to one or the other in the past.

The modern statement of the idea began with Thorndike's *law of effect*. Thorndike saw the attainment of satisfying consequences as connecting the response more firmly to the stimulus situation. For him, the *association* was between the stimulus situation and the response. Reward strengthened that association; punishment weakened it.

Skinner's System

During the 1930s, B. F. Skinner presented a different way of looking at the law of effect.★ His formulation is the one that is most influential at the present time.

OPERANTS AND RESPONDENTS   Skinner begins by distinguishing two kinds of actions. Responses that are *elicited by a stimulus* are called **respondents.** This class of responses includes built-in reflexes; for example, a pinprick *elicits* leg withdrawal. It includes classically conditioned responses; for example, after an appropriate conditioning history, Pavlov's bell *elicited* salivation in dogs. It also includes action patterns evoked by releasing stimuli. In short, respondents are any acts that are *stimulus-bound* (pp. 112–15).

Operants are responses that are *not* elicited by stimuli. These are the actions that we speak of as voluntary rather than reflexive. Bar-pressing in the rat does not bear any fixed relation to an eliciting stimulus. Thorndike saw such a response as becoming attached to the stimuli provided by the situation; but Skinner saw no need to talk that way. The responses occur, but no specific environmental events *make* them occur; they surely have causes, but those causes are not environmental stimuli. Hence, Skinner speaks of such responses as *emitted* by the organism, rather than as elicited by stimuli. And it is these responses that are related to their consequences.

REINFORCEMENT AND EXTINCTION   The heart of Skinner's system is his restatement of the law of effect. He presents his **law of conditioning** for operants: "If the occurrence of an operant is followed by presentation of a reinforcing stimulus, the strength [of the operant] is increased." And there is the converse **law of extinction:** "If the occurrence of an operant already strengthened through conditioning is not followed by the reinforcing stimulus, the strength is decreased."[1]

And what is a reinforcing stimulus? It is one that does strengthen the response that precedes it. If Response R is followed by Stimulus S, and if Response R increases in strength, then Stimulus S is a reinforcer by definition.

★There is a great deal of confusion about this, because careless writers have lumped Skinner with the Thorndike-Watson "stimulus-response" or S-R tradition within behaviorism. Skinner himself has made it very clear, however, that he is not an S-R psychologist (he does speak of stimulus control, but he means something quite different by it); and his views on behavior are fundamentally different from Thorndike's.

1. Skinner, 1938, p. 21.

Strictly speaking, therefore, the law of conditioning is not a law at all in the usual sense. Rather it is the definition of a reinforcing stimulus.

Notice that a reinforcer, so defined, is not assigned any specific properties. In particular, nothing in the definition says that the reinforcer must be pleasant or satisfying, or even that it must be perceived by the subject. It is a reinforcer if, and only if, it reinforces. Skinner's system specifies nothing else about it.

DISCRIMINATIVE STIMULI AND STIMULUS CONTROL   Although operants are not *elicited* by external stimuli as reflexes are, external stimuli can come to control them in another way. Think again about a rat in a box, pressing a lever for food. Let there be a light in the box that can be turned on or off. When it is on, lever-pressing will be reinforced with food; when it is off, lever-pressing will not be reinforced. The rat will eventually come to press the lever only when the light is on. When it is off, lever-pressing will weaken—undergo extinction—and cease to occur. When that has happened—when the rat presses the lever if the light is on, and not when it is off—we say that the light has acquired **stimulus control** over the emission of the response.

A case of stimulus control in humans is our behavior at traffic lights. If the light is green, we drive on; if red, we hit the brake. Other examples abound—whether to dress formally or casually, whether to use the formal or the familiar form of address in French. In all such cases, what we learn is not the behavior itself, but what behavior is appropriate in what situation. When we have learned it, then we say that the situation exerts *stimulus control* over the behavior.★

This role of the stimulus is quite different from the eliciting or releasing function of the stimulus in the case of respondents. There is nothing about the light that causes a bar-press from the rat; there is nothing about the red light that causes brake-pressing in humans. Look at it this way: In both cases, the conditions of reinforcement could just as well be reversed. The light could signal the *unavailability* of food, not its availability. Then the rat would learn to press when the light was off, not when it was on. We could have set up the rule that green means stop, and red means go; then drivers would learn that.

In short, discriminative stimuli are not eliciting stimuli. Rather, they provide *information*. The stimulus tells the organism that the situation is one in which that operant will be reinforced.

The Terminology of Reinforcement and Punishment

If a rat is allowed food after pressing a bar, and bar-pressing increases as a result, then we speak of the food as a **positive reinforcer.** It is something the animal will work to obtain. On the other hand, if bar-pressing serves to turn off a

---

★The human cases are more complicated because, in most cases, the stimulus control is not developed by reinforcement and extinction, but by *instruction*—we are *told* what to do when. Still we can say that the situation exerts stimulus control over our actions if, in fact, we emit different operants in different situations.

painful shock, then shock is a **negative reinforcer.** Its *offset,* rather than its *onset,* reinforces the bar-press; it is something the animal will work to get rid of. Finally, if we follow a response with the *onset of a negative reinforcer* such as shock, then we are employing **punishment.** Punishment is the *onset of a negative reinforcer, dependent on the occurrence of a response.* Thus punishment and negative reinforcement are not the same; don't confuse them.

Notice also that what is reinforced or punished is the response, not the actor. We don't reinforce rats; we reinforce lever-pressing. We don't punish a child, we punish its misbehavior. This sounds picky perhaps; but on the other hand, if we are careful about what we say, it may help us be careful about what we do.[2]

Suppose we have a child who snitches cookies between meals, and we wish to suppress this. We see it happen, call the child to us, and administer a punishment. Now the child has been punished, all right. But the *response* that has been most immediately punished is not snitching cookies but coming to us. The child may come to inhibit approaches to us—the punished response— rather than snitching cookies.

We have introduced the most important concepts used by modern reinforcement theorists: The operant-respondent distinction, the concept of reinforcement, and the concept of stimulus control. Now let us look more closely at some of the ways in which these concepts are investigated. Then we will see some ways in which they are applied.

METHODS IN THE STUDY OF OPERANT BEHAVIOR

The phrase **operant conditioning** covers any experiment in which a reinforcer is delivered if, and only if, a specified response occurs. The famous maze, in which the rat must make a correct turn or series of turns to collect its reward, is technically a case of operant conditioning.

There is a problem with mazes and related methods, however. The rat, let us say, reaches the goal and eats its food. The experimenter must corral the animal and, at some later time, return it to the apparatus for another trial. The animal's stream of behavior is broken up into a series of distinct events called **trials,** whereas real-world behavior is a continuous flow.

The Free Operant

Because it preserves that continuity of behavior, the **free operant** method has become the most popular way of studying operants. Here we encounter the famous Skinner box (Fig. 8-1).

The subject is enclosed in a small chamber, with some well-defined response available at all times: a lever for a rat to press; a disk or *pecking key*

2. See Catania, 1979.

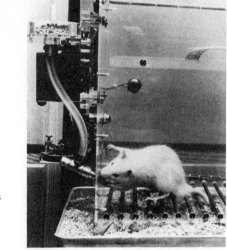

Figure 8-1 Experimental chambers for the study of reinforcement. (A) A rat pressing a lever for small pellets of food. (B) A pigeon pecking a lit pecking key for food reinforcement.

A   B

mounted on the wall for a pigeon to peck; or a button to be pressed by a human subject. When the response is made, reinforcement is delivered. A pellet of food may drop into a food cup for the rat. A hopper full of grain may be brought up so that a pigeon can feed from it for a few seconds. Or a counter may record points earned by a human subject.

After reinforcement occurs, the situation does not change. The subject need not be removed and replaced, and there need be no trials. The rat can simply emit the operant again, and earn another pellet. The lever is always available, and the rat is free to press it at will, so to speak, over and over again. That is why this procedure is called *free operant*.

In such an experiment, the most obvious measure of the strength of an operant is its frequency, or **rate of occurrence.** A bar-press response that occurs more rapidly, over time, is presumably stronger than one that occurs only at a low rate, with long delays in between. More generally, one can think of the rate of a response as an estimate of its *probability*—that is, its frequency of occurrence relative to other responses that the situation allows. Obviously, the greater the rate at which a rat presses the lever, the less time it is spending doing other things; and, therefore, the greater is the probability that it will be bar-pressing at any given instant.

With this method, one can watch the rate of a response change *continuously* over time, without interruption. Reinforce key-pecking with food, and a hungry pigeon will very shortly come to peck at a high rate. Stop reinforcing the response and its rate goes down again; this is *extinction* of the response. If we reinforce key-pecking only when a tone is sounding, or only when the key is illuminated with green light, then the response will undergo extinction at other times, and the tone or the color of the key will acquire *stimulus control* over the rate of emission of the operant.

Schedules of Reinforcement

Of course, there is no law that requires *every* emission of the operant to be reinforced, even when reinforcement conditions are in effect. Instead, one may use **partial reinforcement,** in which only some occurrences of the response are reinforced. Very often, a **schedule of reinforcement** is imposed; that is, some rule relates the occurrence of reinforcement to the passage of time or to number of responses.

In an **interval schedule,** reinforcement is made available by a timing device. For example, a 5-minute fixed-interval schedule would be one in which, after each reinforcement is delivered, 5 minutes goes by before the next reinforcement is available. After 5 minutes is up, then the next response is reinforced. Responses made during the 5-minute period are recorded, but not reinforced.

Or one may impose a **ratio schedule,** where the ratio is number of responses to number of reinforcements. On fixed-ratio 10, for example, every tenth response is reinforced (that is, responses/reinforcements = 10).

Partial-reinforcement schedules such as these may lead to remarkably persistent responding. It is possible to generate an enormous amount of behavior for very few reinforcements—a point, reinforcement theorists would say, that has not been lost on owners of slot machines and similar devices. The large literature on reinforcement schedules is discussed in books on learning; we simply lack space to consider it further here.

APPLICATIONS OF REINFORCEMENT

The use of reinforcement extends far beyond the laboratory. In recent years, psychologists dealing with personal, academic, and industrial problems have paid close attention to the possible role of reinforcement in complex human behavior. Many of the behavior therapist's techniques depend upon the identification, and modification, of the conditions of reinforcement that operate in natural settings. Stated briefly, these interventions revolve around the attempt to see that appropriate behaviors get reinforced—and that inappropriate behaviors do not.*

In the Hospital and Clinic

One of the best examples of reinforcement therapy is also one of the earliest.[3] In mental hospitals, severely disturbed patients all too often receive little more than custodial care. Their needs are met, things are done for them that they cannot or will not do for themselves, but they may receive little attention or

---

*For an excellent survey of both the rationale and the findings of these methods, see Rimm and Masters, 1974.
3. Ayllon and Michael, 1959.

social interaction unless their behavior becomes bizarre, assaultive, or self-destructive. In that case, nurses and attendants may flock to calm them down.

This caring, helping behavior is of course understandable and its intentions are admirable. But what if attention and soothing actions serve to reinforce disruptive behavior? What if doing things for the patient reinforces his not doing them for himself? Quite possibly we are reinforcing, and thus maintaining, the very kind of behavior we would like to get rid of—for the patient's benefit even more than our own.

Two therapists recognized this situation and attempted to turn it around— to *stop reinforcing inappropriate actions*. They began by training, not the patients, but the psychiatric nurses at the hospital where they worked. The concept of reinforcement was explained to the nurses in ways like this:

> Reinforcement is something you do for or with a patient, for example, offering candy or a cigarette. Any way you convey attention to the patient is reinforcing. . . . When we say "do not reinforce a behavior," we are actually saying "ignore the behavior and act deaf and blind whenever it occurs."[4]

Training the nurses was not easy. Yet the results showed some dramatic changes in the patients' behavior. One female patient persistently entered the nurses' office and distracted them from their work. Previously, this behavior had been reinforced! The nurses would take the patient by the hand and lead her away. When they ignored her instead, her intrusions underwent extinction and occurred much less often (Fig. 8-2). This shows that the nurses' previous reaction was in fact a reinforcer for the disruptive actions. In other words, what was maintaining those actions was not the patient's illness alone, but also the *environmental consequences* of the actions—that is, the nurses' reactions to them.

Two other psychotic patients refused to feed themselves, and had to be spoon-fed by the staff. In seeking an effective reinforcer for self-feeding, the

Figure 8-2 Declining frequency with which a patient entered the nurses' office and disrupted it when the nurses stopped reinforcing these intrusions. (From Ayllon and Michael, 1959.)

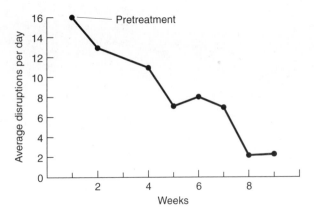

4. Ibid., p. 325.

investigators looked carefully at these patients' likes and dislikes. It turned out that both patients were concerned about the neatness of their clothes, and didn't like to get stains on them. So the nurses were instructed as follows: The patients would be spoon-fed if they insisted, but it was to be done without conversation, and carelessly, so that drops of food would fall on a patient's dress. If the patient fed herself, then the nurse was instructed to remain with her and talk with her. Here again we see social attention used as a reinforcer, this time combined with an *avoidance* procedure (Chap. 7): To avoid spots on her dress, the patient must feed herself.

The result was a dramatic increase in self-feeding by both patients. Indeed, one of the patients, who initially weighed only 99 pounds, gained more than 20 pounds over the next 8 weeks.

Does this sound like a cold and heartless procedure—deliberately staining a patient's dress, and refusing to converse with her unless she behaved "properly"? One could argue that it is. On the other hand, is it kinder to keep a patient indefinitely in a state of helpless, spoon-fed passivity? The nurses' previous actions were doing just that, as shown by what happened when those actions were changed.

The use of such procedures is not limited to institutions. Family members at home also may be powerful sources of reinforcement—for better or for worse. For example, there is the case of a woman who went into a deep depression following the death of her mother.[5]

The actions typical of depression—lassitude, weeping, expressions of helplessness—met with sympathy and consolation from the woman's husband and children. This is understandable, but shortsighted too, if these attentions were acting as reinforcers for the unproductive and miserable depressive actions.

On the advice of the therapists, the woman's family members agreed to change their reactions. As in the hospital study, the family members forced themselves to ignore depressive behaviors, but to respond with attention and support when positive coping behaviors took place.

Figure 8-3 shows the results. Depressive behaviors were high, coping behaviors low, over a 1-week baseline period. When the new reinforcement conditions were put into effect, these two classes of behavior promptly changed places. When the initial conditions of reinforcement were reinstated, depressive behaviors again began to climb, but then, when reinforcement for coping behaviors was applied again, coping behaviors rose again, and depressive behaviors fell to low levels and remained there. We see again the reinforcement of appropriate behaviors combined with the extinction of inappropriate behaviors.

In the Classroom

Experiments much like the hospital one have been conducted in schools, to reduce disruptive behavior in the classroom.[6] But my favorite example is the

5. Liberman and Raskin, 1971.
6. See for example Hall, Lund, and Jackson, 1968.

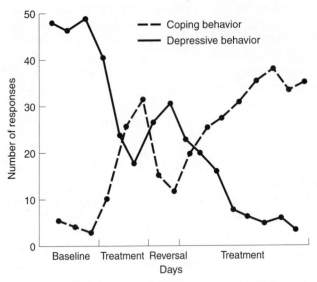

Figure 8-3 Frequency of depressive and of coping responses. Before treatment (Baseline), when the family reinforced depressive responses, coping responses were few and there were many depressive responses. The relative frequencies reversed when treatment (the new reinforcement conditions) was imposed (Treatment). They reversed again when the family returned to its previous reactions (Reversal), but depressive responses fell once again and remained low when the new program was restored and left in effect (Treatment). (From Liberman and Raskin, 1971.)

delightful study in which a class of junior high school students had a mean, snarly teacher to contend with. The students were given a cram course in reinforcement theory, and it was pointed out to them that they could increase the number of pleasant contacts between the teacher and themselves by reinforcing pleasant behavior on the *teacher's* part. They could reinforce it by smiles, sincere efforts to learn, and discussions before and after class.[7] But these reinforcers were to be delivered only when the teacher was pleasant. They were not "free" reinforcements; the teacher had to earn them.

As Figure 8-4 shows, pleasant student-teacher contacts were greatly outnumbered by snarly ones, at the beginning—but not after 6 weeks of teacher modification by students.

In the Workplace

For the next example, recall our discussion of *conditioned reinforcers*. A poker chip, or similar token, can be made exchangeable for some more natural reinforcer, such as grapes for a chimp or privileges for a hospital patient. The token then becomes a reinforcer—a conditioned reinforcer.

7. Gray, Graubard, and Rosenberg, 1974.

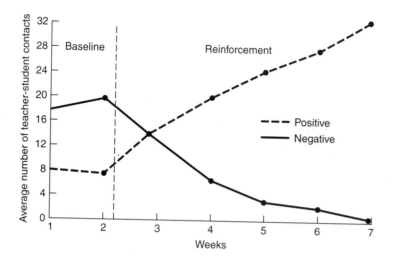

Figure 8-4 Teacher-student contacts were more often negative than positive during the preexperimental baseline period. Positive reactions were much more frequent when students reinforced the teacher's friendly behavior. (From Gray et al., 1974.)

Because they are cheap and portable, such tokens can be used when it would be difficult to follow up desired behavior with a natural reinforcer right away. In some hospitals, whole **token economies** have been set up, based solely upon tokens.[8] Even short of that, they can be highly effective.

In a factory in Mexico City, there was a severe problem of worker tardiness. Seven hundred fifty instances were accumulated in 1970 alone. So a team of researchers tried a program of token reinforcement: Arriving for work on time was reinforced with tokens, each exchangeable for a small amount of money. What happened? The incidence of tardiness fell from about 10 percent to about 2 percent, and stayed there.

These findings are all the more striking when we consider that the workers could earn the equivalent of about $40 a year with the extra bonus system—and that the company had already been paying an *annual* bonus of $40 for consistent punctuality, with no effect at all! It sems that *frequent* and *immediate* reinforcement has an impact of its own, apart from long-term gain.[9]

Here's another example, which highlights some other characteristics of the reinforcement approach.

Injuries were becoming frequent at a wholesale bakery, and management, alarmed, called in consultants who instituted a program in two of its problem departments to promote safe working practices. First, the desired behavior was specifically defined—not in vague terms like "be careful" or "be conscientious," but in terms like "walk around conveyor belt" or "look toward knife being sharpened." Then the environment (not the workers) was modified so as to support desired behaviors. Safety scores were presented on a graph so workers could see at a glance how they were doing and how their records compared with previous ones, and with those of other departments. Here,

8. See Rimm and Masters, 1979.
9. Herman et al., 1973.

improvement itself and, perhaps, out-doing the other department, were the reinforcing consequences of working in a safe way.

Results? From performing safely 70 and 78 percent of the time—not good enough!—performance in the two departments improved to 96 and 99 percent. Within a year the number of injuries went from 53 to 10.[10]

On the Playing Field

In sports psychology too, reinforcement methods have found a place. A team of consultants tried "behavioral coaching" as a way of teaching young football players how to block.* "When the athlete executed a blocking motion properly, a coach blew a whistle and told the player 'Great, way to go.' . . . Furthermore, the player was given explicit instruction using the coach as a model and later was asked to imitate the proper techniques. This behavioral method contrasted with the standard method [in which] the coach did not often provide encouragement and when verbal rewards were given they were not enthusiastically offered."[11]

Figure 8-5 shows the effects of the shift to behavioral coaching in four players. Note that in each one of them, after the shift was made, the percentage of correctly executed blocks more than doubled.

A Look Backward: The Operant Philosophy

In running through these examples, we see not only the power of reinforcement, but also a definite point of view about the nature of behavior, its causation, and its problems. This operant philosophy, a product of the behavioristic approach, has certain emphases and assumptions that characterize it.

THE FOCUS ON THE ENVIRONMENT   In all our examples, we see behavior therapists addressing a problem *behavior,* and attempting to modify *the behavior itself.* And this is done by modifying the *environmental conditions that affect that behavior.* One does not ask what the behavior means to the actor or refer it to an underlying anxiety or personality trait. The operant philosophy assumes that conditions *outside the person*—stimulus control and the reinforcements the environment provides—provide the answer to the question, "Why does she do that?"

Allow me a personal example, which brings the point home to me each semester. I routinely set up class demonstrations of operant conditioning in rats. Of course, few things run smoothly for very long, and often I find my rats

---

10. Komaki, Coombs, and Schepman, 1991.

*For readers unfamiliar with American football, to "block" means to protect a teammate who is carrying the ball from a defender who wishes to stop him from doing so, by interposing one's body between the two. It takes considerable skill: If you try to block by just standing there, you will be ineffective because you will become horizontal, very quickly.

11. LeUnes and Nation, 1989, p. 72.

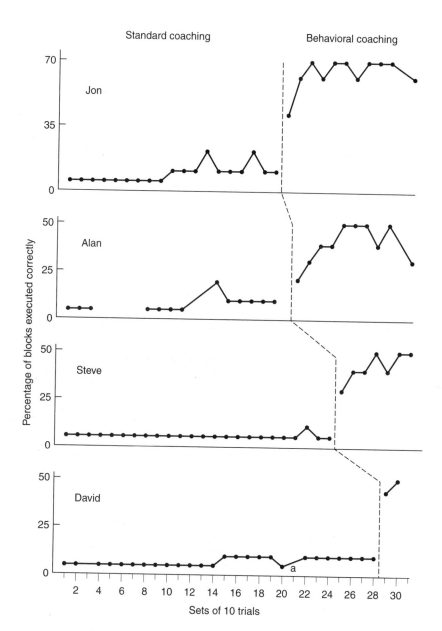

Figure 8-5 Percentage of trials on which blocks were performed correctly, by four individual players. The dashed line indicates the point at which the coaching method changed from "standard" to "behavioral." Notice that the percentage rose abruptly, and remained higher, after the change. (From Allison and Ayllon, 1980.)

behaving improperly—not displaying the behavior I wish to show my students. Something is wrong, and I must find it and fix it. And, invariably, what I find and fix is not in the rats but in the apparatus. The fault in behavior is a fault in the environmental conditions, set up by the apparatus, that produce that behavior. "The organism is always right," Skinner has said; it does what it ought to do under the conditions imposed upon it. That is the operant philosophy in a nutshell.

A behavior therapist would address problematic human behavior in the same way. He does *not* assume that "people are like rats"; no sane person does. He does assume that behavior, in people or in rats, occurs in the environment and is responsive to that environment and will change if the environment does.

Of course, especially in the human case, other people are a major part of one's environment. That is why a behavior therapist so often has to begin work with the nurses, teachers, or family members who provide reinforcements for people. This can present great difficulties of its own, for apart from the natural reaction "Why are you talking to *me? He's* the one with the problem!", one may have to combat very strongly entrenched attitudes, habits, and vested interests in those who interact with the "problem person."

THE FOCUS ON CONSEQUENCES   Reinforcement theory pays careful attention to what happens after an action, that is, to its reinforcing *consequences*. It looks at what the consequences of action are now, and at how consequences might be arranged, or rearranged, so as to support effective action.

IDENTIFICATION OF BEHAVIORAL GOALS   To produce the desired behavior, we must set up the environmental conditions that will in turn produce it. This means that we must think about the behavior we wish to bring about, at least as carefully as we think about the problematic behavior we wish to change. And we will think of the goals in terms of specific actions. A consultant or therapist who emphasizes reinforcement techniques will also try to specify the behavioral goals concretely: What *specific* responses do we want to promote?

An insightful paper written for business managers points out "the folly of rewarding A, while hoping for B" and describes case after case of it.[12] In politics, we *hope* that candidates will have in mind clear and specific solutions to problems, but we *reward* statements that "may be relied on to offend absolutely no one"[13] and wonder why we have few statesmen. Businesses *hope* that administrators will consider costs and opportunities over the long term, and initiate programs that will pay off some years down the road. But if they *reward* only short-term sales or profits, they virtually ensure that only the short term will affect the actions actually taken. Many firms *hope* for performance but *reward* attendance, and attendance is what they get. And schools—at all levels? What is hoped for? What is rewarded? In your experience, how does the one match up with the other?

The Operant Philosophy and Common Sense

If any reader is inclined to say, "Well, all that is just common sense," I invite that reader to think again. First, if these methods are all that commonsensical,

12. Kerr, 1975.
13. Ibid., p. 769.

why hadn't these intelligent and experienced managers, coaches, and hospital personnel been using them all along? They hadn't.

Moreover, reinforcement theory does differ from common sense on just about every point we've discussed. Consider:

Common sense is unlikely to explain problematic behavior by reference to the *environment*. We tend instead to explain it by internal characteristics of the actor: "He's a klutz." "She's compulsive." "That teacher is a real sourpuss."

Common sense tends to focus on what happens *before* the action in question, not after. Thus in the case of the snarly teacher, common sense might advise: "Be smiling and alert, and then the teacher will be pleasant to you out of happiness or gratitude or something." It was much more effective to turn it around: First pleasantness on the teacher's part (the operant), then the students' response (the reinforcing consequence).

Again: We tell people in advance (and often in vague terms), "Work carefully," or "Try harder." And these exhortations are vague because they do not refer to *specific* behaviors; "trying harder" is not a specific action, so it cannot be a specific behavioral goal.

Perhaps the greatest difference is that common sense focuses on behavior that is *not* wanted, rather than behavior that is. Coaches who do not reward good performance will roast their players for bad performance. In the workplace, Dale Carnegie saw the paradox over half a century ago. How does a supervisor typically behave? "If he doesn't like a thing, he raises the Old Harry; if he does like it, he says nothing."[14]

No, the "operant philosophy" represents a distinct change in mind set from the commonsense approach to behavior and its problems. As to whether the change can make a difference—well, the cases we've run through are just examples from an impressive array of evidence that it can.

THE COST OF REWARD

To this point, we have examined a series of success stories in the application of reinforcement techniques. There are stories of another kind too, however, and it is time to look at them.

Undermining Intrinsic Reinforcement

Consider this experiment. Nursery school children were reinforced with tokens for drawing. The reinforcement was effective: The children worked vigorously at drawing while the reinforcement conditions were in effect. But when the tokens were no longer given, the children stopped drawing, and actually did *less* drawing, later, than children who had never been reinforced for doing so.

14. Carnegie, 1936.

The *intrinsic* rewards of drawing—that is, the satisfactions that the activity itself provides—no longer maintained the children's drawing activity.[15]

Note that this finding is not a failure of reinforcement theory. The reinforcers did just what they ought to do; they increased the amount of drawing that occurred, *as long as they were delivered*. The problem was the weakening of **intrinsic reinforcement**—the rewards of drawing for its own sake.

Why should this happen? We are not sure. It might have to do with how the children interpreted the situation, reflecting a labeling or attribution process (Chap. 11). Drawing for tokens may have been labeled by the children as work rather than play, and everybody knows that work is no fun. Or it may have to do with how the children interpreted their own behavior. The children may have said to themselves, during the reinforcement phase, "I'm drawing to get tokens." Then when tokens were withdrawn, they may have said, "Well, if I'm drawing to get tokens, and there are no more tokens, why draw?" Both of these ideas imply that we must consider not only the effects of reinforcement on behavior, but also how the person *interprets* the reinforcements and the behavior.★

The weakening of intrinsic motivation by reinforcement has been seen many times. It is a troublesome finding. If one wants to strengthen some desired behavior, one's first thought is to support it with a powerful reinforcer. But suppose that the powerful reinforcer cannot be maintained indefinitely, and one must eventually turn the behavior over to other, more natural but less powerful reinforcing consequences? In such cases, we may actually leave the behavior *weaker* than it would have been if the powerful reinforcers had never been applied.

More troubling still is this possibility: In providing external rewards for behavior that otherwise would reward itself, we may not only weaken the intrinsic rewards, but change the behavior itself into something different. One writer tells a story that she finds quite saddening (as do I):

> I recently read a newspaper article about an 8-year-old boy who found an envelope containing more than $600 dollars and returned it to the bank whose name appeared on the envelope. The bank traced the money to its rightful owner and returned it to him. . . . As a reward, the man . . . gave the boy $3 . . . A simple "thank you" [would have been] adequate . . .
>
> But some of the teachers at the boy's school . . . took up a collection for the boy . . . they presented the good Samaritan with a $150 savings bond . . .
>
> What does this episode say about our society? . . . A young boy . . . finds money that does not belong to him and he returns it. He did the right thing. Yet doing the right thing seems to be insufficient motivation for action . . . we rely on external "stuff" as a measure of our worth . . .

15. Lepper, Greene, and Nisbett, 1973.

★Both these explanations may be more complex than necessary; see Schwartz, 1982, for discussion.

We call these things incentives, telling ourselves that if we can just reel [the children] in and get them hooked, then the built-in rewards will follow.★

But will they? Or will the exact opposite happen: will the "built-in rewards" be prevented from ever taking hold?

The writer goes on to say that "like so many things, kindness and honesty have succumbed to inflation," but I don't think it's inflation that bothers her. It is that kindness and honesty are assigned a cash value at all. If external rewards are placed on kindness and honesty, then these, once their own reward, may well *become* just another set of hoops to jump through or chores to be endured, for the goodies we obtain at the end.

Will we, as a society, develop the habit of asking the icy question "What's in it for me?"—in part *because* we attempt to let there be "something in it" as an external incentive, where the built-in rewards could be more than enough?

Responding versus Understanding

There is another kind of cost to the use of reinforcement procedures. They may promote certain aspects of behavior at the expense of other ones that may be more important.

In one experiment, college students were placed in an operant situation, in which a series of responses would produce reinforcement—points exchangeable for money. And any one of a number of such sequences would work, for there was a rule that determined which sequences would be reinforced and which would not. But the subjects were not told the rule. They were simply told after each trial that they had succeeded (if they had used a response sequence that followed the rule), or that they had failed (if they hadn't).

Some subjects were not told that there was a rule, but were just told to earn as much money as they could. They did not discover the rule; rather they would find a sequence that worked, and stick with it. This was not because the rule was too difficult to discover; other subjects, who were *told* to find the rule, did so with little trouble.

Worst of all, when the original subjects were asked to find the rule, *after* a period of just working for reinforcements as above, they had great difficulty doing so. They tended to repeat particular sequences, though they could learn nothing new by doing so. Or they would return to hypotheses about what the rule was that they had already ruled out earlier. It appeared that working for reinforcement alone had actually switched off part of the subjects' rule-finding, hypothesis-testing apparatus—and that they did not find it easy to switch it on again![16]

Here again, the findings do not imply a failure of reinforcement theory. The reinforcers worked. If a sequence was reinforced, that sequence was likely to be repeated. The problem is that sequences were strengthened *at the expense*

★Arguelles, 1991. For a thoughtful discussion of this and related problems, see Schwartz, 1986.
16. Schwartz, 1982, 1993.

of cognitive operations leading to rule discovery. That may not be the outcome we want:

> [S]uppose that our educational goals include developing the ability to discover general rules, as scientists do, and fostering an interest in learning so that the rewards [of] acquiring knowledge are an inherent part of the learning process itself. The [rule-discovery experiment] suggests that operant contingencies are not an effective tool for developing rule discovery. Indeed, they might even interfere with the development of this ability. And the [intrinsic motivation] experiment . . . suggests that operant contingencies may take control away from the rewards inherent in an activity, rather than promoting them. Thus, for people who view these educational goals as significant, the lesson of these two experiments may be that operant contingencies can interfere with effective education rather than facilitate it.[17]

The Reinforcement Theorist Replies

Now a reinforcement theorist would not accept that criticism. He might reply:

> Look, it is well known that weak reinforcers—intrinsic reinforcers, for instance—become weaker still when they are contrasted with more powerful ones. Behavior therapists are well aware of this problem. Some have stated it as a rule: Never reinforce a response unless the natural environment will continue to reinforce it.
> As for rule-finding and other forms of comprehension, we know that it's folly to reinforce A while hoping for B [see p. 304]. If we want subjects to find rules and principles, and not just settle on a response sequence that works, then we must identify and reinforce the behavior that leads to rule-finding.

Such a reply may make good theoretical sense, but the critic of reinforcement procedures is not likely to be satisfied with it. The problem is whether the theory can be implemented in practice. It is easy to say, "Don't reinforce a response unless the natural environment will reinforce it." That, however, may be more a wistful hope than a practical principle. In the classroom, reading and studying can be promoted by reinforcement.[18] But what happens when the child leaves school, if she returns to a home and a peer group in which reading and studying are not reinforced? Just how do we get that natural environment to reinforce reading, studying, and the like? And if we do not yet know just what the behaviors are that lead to comprehension rather than rote performance, maybe we should wait until we do know before we rush in with our reinforcement-based interventions.

As for the weakening of weak reinforcers (like intrinsic ones) by more powerful extrinsic ones: Yes, perhaps. Then again, as we think about this, we see a bigger question looming on the horizon: Is it best to think of the intrinsic rewards of "doing the right thing" as matters of reinforcement at all? Here again is the writer we quoted earlier:

17. Schwartz and Lacey, 1982, p. 250.
18. See for example Hall, Lund, and Jackson, 1968.

I don't know how many times my 13-year-old son has told me about classmates who received $10 for each A they receive on their report cards—hinting that I should do the same . . . forget it! This is not to say that I would never praise my son for doing well in school. But my praise is not meant to reward or elicit future achievements, but rather to express my genuine delight at the satisfaction he feels at having done his best. Throwing $10 at that sends out the message that the feeling alone isn't good enough.[19]

A Look Backward: The Risks of Reinforcement

These findings about the costs of reward do not pose a challenge to reinforcement *theory*. But they certainly do pose a challenge to its simple-minded *application*. And precisely because operant techniques have been used so successfully in schools, factories, and hospitals, some writers fear that we may adopt them with an enthusiasm that does not consider their dangers.

THEORETICAL ISSUES IN REINFORCEMENT

We have seen examples of how reinforcers affect behavior in a variety of settings. Now we need to take a closer look at just what we are doing when we reinforce a response. What is a reinforcing event, anyway? What does it do and how does it do it?

What Is a Reinforcer?

Skinner defines a reinforcer by its effects. A reinforcer is something that reinforces. It may indeed turn out that that is the best we will be able to do. But it is natural to wonder whether different reinforcing events have something in common. If they do, and if we knew what it is, we would be able to specify in advance whether a given event will be a reinforcer or not. There have been several suggestions.

THE HEDONIC HYPOTHESIS   The notion that *we seek what brings us pleasure* is a venerable one, dating back through Hobbes to the Greeks and probably much farther than that (Chap. 2). One might suggest that the reinforcement principle is just a special case of that commonsense axiom. Food is pleasant to a hungry rat, attention is pleasant to a disruptive patient (is it?), and so these organisms act in ways that produce these pleasures.

There are some obvious difficulties here. First, we cannot ask an animal what is pleasant.★

---

19. Arguelles, 1991.

★We can ask a human, it is true; but even then we must wonder what the answer means. Do you mean by pleasure what I do? Is my red the same as your red?

And if we infer pleasure from behavior, we end up arguing in a circle. Why does a hungry rat work for food? Because food is pleasant. How do we know it is pleasant? Because the rat works for it. We must do better than that.

THE DRIVE-REDUCTION HYPOTHESIS Clark Hull's theory of behavior (see pp. 202–8) included the reinforcement principle explicitly, and he linked that principle to the concept of *homeostasis*. The idea is this: If a biological drive exists and if a response results in a reduction of that drive—thus reducing the homeostatic disturbance as well—then that response will be reinforced. In other words, *reinforcement occurs when a drive is reduced*. That way, the animal learns to do what meets its body's needs.

The **drive-reduction hypothesis** was a plausible and attractive theory. Unfortunately, there are many powerful reinforcers that cannot be shown to have anything to do with meeting physiological needs.

Rats, for instance, will repeatedly run down an alley for an opportunity to copulate, even if ejaculation—the presumed drive reduction—is not allowed.[20] Rats will drink a saccharin solution avidly—that is, the solution will support the operants of going to where the bottle is and lapping from it—even though the rats are not deprived and the saccharin has no food value.[21] Monkeys will take apart a mechanical puzzle, time after time, for no reward but the opportunity to do it again.[22] And teachers become more friendly if their students are pleasant and attentive; what drive does that reduce? The conclusion is clear: Drive reduction characterizes some reinforcers, but not all.★

RESPONSE FACTORS AND THE RELATIVITY OF REINFORCEMENT A quite different approach to the nature of reinforcement shifts the emphasis from the reinforcing stimulus or event, to the *response* that such an event permits. We present food to a hungry rat, and the food permits the rat to eat. What if the actual reinforcing event is not the food itself, but the *opportunity to eat?*

Strong evidence for such an idea was provided by an ingenious experiment by David Premack. Consider a rat that lives in a cage, with food, water, and a running wheel available. The rat spends a certain amount of time drinking, a certain amount running, and a certain amount eating.

Now we impose some rules. The running wheel is locked, so that the rat cannot run in it—unless he drinks some water first. Now drinking is the oper-

---

20. Sheffield, Wolf, and Backer, 1951.
21. Ernits and Corbit, 1973; Sheffield and Roby, 1950.
22. Harlow, Harlow, and Meyer, 1950.
★Of course we could hypothesize drives to be reduced as the case requires—for example, an exploratory drive for the monkeys, reduced by exploring; or an affiliate drive for the teachers, reduced by the students' sociability. And it must be said that some writers have played that game of pseudo-explanation with enthusiasm. Some suggested, for instance, that Harlow's monkeys were anxious in the presence of a mechanical puzzle, until it had been thoroughly explored and found safe. Harlow's answer was eloquent: "It is not the monkeys that are anxious, but the drive-reduction theorists."

ant, and opportunity to run is the reinforcer. Sure enough, under these conditions the amount of drinking rises. Opportunity to run will reinforce drinking behavior.

Now we reverse the situation. Water is withheld from the rat, unless it runs in the wheel. Running in the wheel makes water available for a short time, and then the rat must run some more to obtain more water. Sure enough again: The amount of running increases. Opportunity to run will reinforce drinking; but also, opportunity to drink will reinforce running.[23]

This demonstration makes the important point that we cannot think of reinforcers just as events of a particular kind. It is not that some *stimuli* are reinforcers and others are not. Instead, the reinforcing event may involve the relation between one response and another. One response is reinforced because it permits another response to occur.

This takes us to the **response-deprivation hypothesis,** which says: If a response is prevented from occurring as frequently as it normally would, then the opportunity to engage in that response is a reinforcer.[24] Thus, opportunity to run will reinforce drinking, but only if the rat has first been prevented from running. Opportunity to drink will reinforce running, but only if the rat has first been prevented from drinking.

Thus we see that the operant-reinforcer relation is not fixed but relative. Under some conditions, A will reinforce B; but under others, B will reinforce A. Reinforcers cannot be defined independently of the response they reinforce, the constraints on the emission of that response, and the frequency with which it would occur if those constraints were not there.

This idea explains how drive states produced by deprivation set the reinforcing power of various commodities. Food deprivation, we say, makes food a reinforcer. But a better way of saying it might be: Deprivation of opportunity-to-eat makes opportunity-to-eat a reinforcer. The deprivation need not be tied to homeostatic needs. Deprivation of opportunity-to-run makes opportunity-to-run a reinforcer, though there is no homeostatic *need* to run.

The idea may also make sense of some well-known phenomena that at first glance look problematic for reinforcement theory. For instance, food is often a good reinforcer, and a child could be rewarded with food for performing some chore. However, eating food can also be an operant that gets reinforced, rather than a reinforcing event. Consider how children may be persuaded to finish their dinners by allowing them to play only after they have done so. In the first case, opportunity to eat is denied until the chore is done; so opportunity to eat is a reinforcer. In the second case, opportunity to play is denied until the meal is eaten; so opportunity to play becomes a reinforcer, and eating becomes the operant.

Or consider a child doing poorly in school, who plays with friends a lot but seldom reads a book. A counselor, parent, or behavior therapist might pre-

23. Premack, 1962.
24. Dunham, 1977.

vent the child from playing until after a period of reading. On the other hand, what about a bookish child who seldom plays with others, and so is not picking up the social skills he needs? For such a child, it might be best to turn the situation around: Access to a book could be denied until the child has played with other children for a while.

As a final example (a real one), the response-deprivation idea was put to effective use by a sales organization. Salespersons, it was found, preferred to make renewal calls to old customers rather than new service calls to prospective ones. Solution: Employees were allowed to make five renewal contract sales, but only after they had made one new service sale. New service sales increased substantially.[25]

The response-deprivation hypothesis has much to recommend it. We still have to wonder, though, whether it can really encompass *all* instances of reinforcement. What about the teacher's actions reinforced by students' behavior? Was there any response the teacher could then make, that she was otherwise prevented from making? We could speculate about that, but certainly it has not been demonstrated. So, although this idea fits many cases of reinforcement, we cannot say that it fits all.

Moreover, there can be real difficulties in establishing just when one is deprived of this or that response. We speak of response deprivation if the response is restricted below its spontaneous rate of occurrence. Well, suppose we go to a movie once a week, on the average. Suppose an experimenter wants to deprive us of movies, and doesn't let us go. At what point do we become "movie-deprived"? After the *average* inter-movie interval? After the *longest* time without a movie that we have let pass spontaneously? Or what? The concept of response deprivation is less precise than it sounds.

THE EMPIRICAL LAW OF EFFECT   We have seen three answers to the question: What is a reinforcer? One is hard to evaluate (the hedonic hypothesis); one clearly won't do for all cases (the drive-reduction hypothesis); and the third may or may not apply to all cases (the response-deprivation hypothesis). In practice, most reinforcement theorists have fallen back on the **empirical law of effect.** An event is reinforcing if it reinforces.

This simply means that the reinforcing properties of an event are demonstrated by the effect of that event. For example, if we find that a child shakes a rattle that makes noise and goes on shaking it, stops shaking it if it stops making noise and goes back to shaking it if it begins making noise again— then we have discovered that the noise is a reinforcer for her rattle-shaking operant.

That conclusion leaves open the possibility that different events may reinforce for different reasons. And, after all, there is no particular reason why all reinforcers should work in the same way. Consider three people who emit the operants of walking to the coffee shop and paying for coffee. For Anne, the

25. Komaki, Coombs, and Schepman, 1991, pp. 91–92.

reinforcer might be the taste of the coffee. For Brad, it might be the lift that the caffeine provides. For Carol, it might be the opportunity to engage in conversation with the other two.

Here are three different reinforcers for the same operant. And these *are* reinforcers, in the strict technical sense of the term. They maintain coffee-shop-going behavior, and if they were no longer forthcoming the behavior would extinguish. If the shop began serving bad-tasting coffee, Anne would stop going. If it began serving coffee with no caffeine in it, Brad would stop going. And if Anne and Brad stopped going, Carol would stop going. The reinforcers are very different, but they all reinforce.

In this sense, the reinforcement principle is somewhat like the Darwinian conception of **fitness.** One form of a species is fitter than another, by definition, if its reproductive success is greater. But one form may reproduce more than its cousins because it is stronger, or because it is smarter, or because it is more cowardly and thus escapes predation better, and so on. Fitness can take many forms. Perhaps *reinforcement* has many possible mechanisms.

What Do Reinforcers Do?

As we have seen, a reinforcer is defined as a stimulus that increases the strength—that is, the probability—of a response that it follows. However, there are several ways that a stimulus could have that effect.

The theories here fall into two classes. One, the original behavioristic view, holds that a reinforcer does something to the *response* that immediately precedes it. It may strengthen that response directly, changing the organism in some way so that the response becomes more likely to occur in the future. That was Skinner's view. Or we could think of it as strengthening a bond, or association, between the situation and the response, so that that situation is more likely to trigger that response in future. This was Thorndike's view, and Hull's.

The other view is the cognitive one. Reinforcers don't *strengthen responses;* they *provide information.* More specifically, they set up an association between the response and the reinforcing event. We might as well call that association an *expectation:* the rat expects food to follow a lever-press. This of course is also the view most congenial to common sense. We find it natural to say that the rat presses the lever because he *wants* food, and *expects* the lever-press to lead to food.

But which view is right (if either)? There is an enormous literature on this problem. It provides some good examples of how psychologists attempt to decide among competing theories. They do it by setting up an experiment in which different theories make different predictions as to what should happen. Then, when we see what does happen, we have evidence in favor of the theory that made the right prediction, and against the theory that made the wrong one.

One research team built an apparatus in which a rat could make either of two responses: pressing a lever or pulling on a chain.[26] Each of these produced food, but the food was quite different in the two cases; a lever-press led to one kind of food, a chain-pull to another kind. (Which food was associated with which response, of course, was counterbalanced across different rats, so that differences in, say, effortfulness of response could not affect the overall data.)

In the first, or training phase of the experiment, the rats were trained until both responses had been reinforced equally often and were being emitted at about equal, and high, rates. Then came the test phase, in which the important observations were made. The experimenters changed the conditions in two ways.

First, they *devalued* one of the foods (call it Food 2), by conditioning an aversion to it. A bout of eating that food was followed by injection of a mild poison that made the rats sick for a while. As we recall from Chapter 7, a single such experience is enough to make rats avoid the food in question thereafter (pp. 257–58).

Second, both food-delivery systems were disconnected, so that neither response produced food any more. The question was how long and vigorously the rats would work at each response in the absence of any further reinforcement, or, as we say, "in extinction." We can think of this as a measure of the "strength" of the response in question.

Before we look at what happened, let us see what the two theories say *ought* to happen (Figure 8-6). The response-strengthening theory says that the two responses should have equal strength. Why? Because they have received equivalent reinforcement, and that is what determines their strength. True, one of the foods would no longer be an effective reinforcer if it were presented now, but that doesn't matter; it is the *past history of reinforcement* that determines response strength. So, since the responses are equally strong, the animal should persist equally in emitting the two of them.

The expectancy theory says: The animal has learned to expect Food 1 if he makes Response 1, Food 2 if he makes Response 2. But Food 2 is no longer attractive to the rat, so he ought not make the response that has led to it. He should persist only in emitting Response 1, not Response 2.

Well, what does happen? In Figure 8-7, we see that the two responses are emitted at very different rates. The animals worked long and hard at the response that had led to the still-valued Food 1, but very little at the response that had led to the now-devalued Food 2.

We cannot account for this difference by looking at the rats' histories of reinforcement. In the training phase, the two responses had received equivalent reinforcement. And in the test phase, reinforcements were again equivalent, at zero; no further reinforcements were given for either response. Clearly the original view—reinforcements strengthen responses, period—will not do.

26. Colwin and Rescorla, 1985.

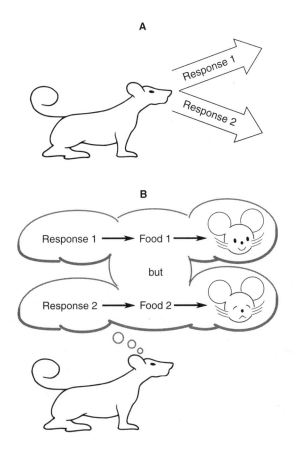

Figure 8-6 Two theoretical conceptions of what should occur in the Colwin and Rescorla experiment. (A) is based on the response-strengthening interpretation of reinforcement; (B) is based on the cognitive interpretation.

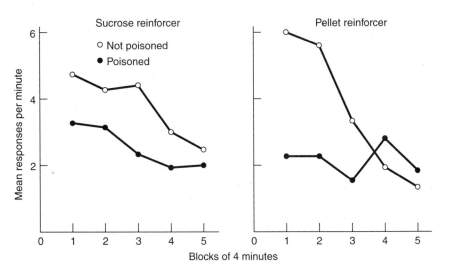

Figure 8-7 Responses in extinction (no reinforcers delivered). Responding was higher and persisted longer for the response that led to Food 1 ("not poisoned") than for the response that had led to Food 2 ("poisoned" for short, though the rats were made only mildly ill). This was true whether Food 1 was a sucrose solution and Food 2 was pelleted food, or the reverse. (From Colwill and Rescorla, 1985.)

But the data are exactly what cognitive theory would lead us to expect. If Response 2 is associated with Food 2 in the rat's little cognitive apparatus, and if he no longer wants Food 2, why should he work hard at making that response? And in fact he does not.

A Look Backward—and Forward

Now, no single experiment overthrows a theory. It takes a considerable body of evidence to do that. But we looked at only one experiment, taken from what is in fact a very considerable body of evidence. Overwhelmingly, the evidence says this to us: Reinforcement does not just increase the probability of a response. It provides information that the animal can incorporate into a set of expectancies, telling it what outcomes to expect from what actions.[27] Through this literature, the study of reinforcement makes contact with the study of expectancies and other cognitive processes, including ones we'll examine further in the next chapter.

As noted earlier, such a cognitive view of the reinforcement process is also the one that fits most naturally with common sense. However, there is another side to that coin. If there are data that make trouble for a response-strengthening theory, so there are data that make trouble for cognitive theory *and* for common sense. Let us turn to them.

BIOLOGICAL CONSTRAINTS ON REINFORCEMENT

Characteristic of early experiments in operant conditioning was the arbitrariness of the relation between response and reinforcer. Pressing a lever has no necessary connection with food. But we can train a rat to make such an arbitrary response to obtain food. We can train it to press a lever, or to pull a chain, or, for that matter, to dance around the cage if we so choose. Granted, we can't train a rat to fly, but we ought to be able to take any response of which the animal is capable and, by reinforcing it, make it more frequent.

The choice of reinforcer should be similarly arbitrary. If we can reinforce a response with food, we ought as well be able to reinforce it with, say, shock termination. So the theory goes. Or went, for matters turned out not to be so. What happened can best be made clear by turning at once to some examples.

Top-Down Constraints: The Misbehavior of Organisms

The first set of examples was also among the first to be discovered. Briefly, what they show is this: If we activate a higher level of a lattice hierarchy, we may end up activating many, or all, of the lower-down components that are

27. Gallistel, 1990.

linked with it. And this can happen whether the reinforcement conditions specify it or not, and whether we like it or not.

THE CASE OF THE HAMMERING CHICKEN   The research that led to this discovery began as an exercise in applied learning theory. Keller and Marian Breland were training animals for commercial purposes: advertising displays in store windows, television commercials, and the like. Trained animals can make effective, eye-catching displays (Fig. 8–8).

In some cases, the training, based on operant-conditioning principles, proceeded smoothly. In other cases, it ran into unexpected difficulties. The Case of the Hammering Chicken is illustrative of the snags that can arise:

> The observer sees a hopper full of oval plastic capsules which contain small toys, charms, and the like. When [a light] is presented to the chicken, she pulls a rubber loop which releases one of the capsules onto a slide. . . . The capsule rolls down the slide and comes to rest near its end. Here one or two sharp, straight pecks by the chicken will knock it forward off the slide and out to the observer, and the chicken is then reinforced by an automatic feeder. . . .
> However, a good 20% of all chickens . . . fail to make the grade. After they have pecked a few capsules off the slide, they begin to grab at the capsules and drag them backwards into the cage. Here they pound them up and down on the floor of the

Figure 8-8 The piggy that went to market. The pig was trained with operant techniques to push a market cart. In this case, the experiment was successful; "misbehavior" did not intrude.

cage. Of course, this results in no reinforcement for the chicken, and yet some chickens will pull in over half of all the capsules presented to them.[28]

Obviously, the dragging-and-hammering behavior was not what the hungry chicken was reinforced for doing. It was not part of, and it interfered with, the food-getting operants. It is an example of what the Brelands happily call the **misbehavior of organisms.**[*] The animal simply does not do what it is reinforced for doing. It does something else instead.

We can understand this intrusive hammering action as a response that already is a component of chicken feeding behavior. The chicken that hammers capsules is exhibiting instinctive behavior having to do with breaking open seed pods and killing insects, grubs, and the like.

The Brelands provide several other examples of the misbehavior of organisms. The general principle seems to be that when a motivational system is aroused, the sub-units of that system will occur—not because they are reinforced but because they *are* components of that system (Fig. 8-9). Here, hammering is a component of the food-getting hierarchy that was activated in the conditioning situation. We might think of all those components as being primed, or facilitated, by higher levels. And the little capsules, which the bird was supposed to knock toward the observer, were enough like seeds or grubs to release the hammering action pattern instead. And so that action drifted into the bird's behavior, to the detriment of the response that the reinforcement conditions required.

AUTOSHAPING   Another example is a phenomenon known as **autoshaping.**[29] Pigeons are placed in a Skinner box where a response key is available. From time to time the key will be illuminated for a few seconds, and then food is delivered. The food is free. The pigeons don't have to peck in order to get it. But they begin to peck at the key anyway, and they will persist indefinitely in this useless behavior. That is autoshaping.[**]

Autoshaping does require that food be offered from time to time, and that its approach be signaled to the bird. Pigeons do not peck keys if they are not fed in the apparatus, so they are not pecking just for the fun of it. Further experiments showed that pigeons would persist in pecking, under such conditions, even if pecking *cost* them food.[30] In these experiments, each peck at the key would actually postpone the next delivery of food. To get fed, the pigeons had to *refrain* from pecking when the key illumination came on. But the birds would not or could not refrain. They persisted in pecking.

28. Breland and Breland, 1961.
[*]The phrase is a takeoff on Skinner's classic book *The Behavior of Organisms.*
29. Brown and Jenkins, 1968.
[**]The name comes from the practice of carefully training, or "shaping," the key-peck response for food reward in pigeons. It seems that the careful training is unnecessary after all. The pigeons will "shape" the key-peck themselves—hence, autoshaping, or "self-shaping"—even if reward does not depend on it.
30. Williams and Williams, 1969.

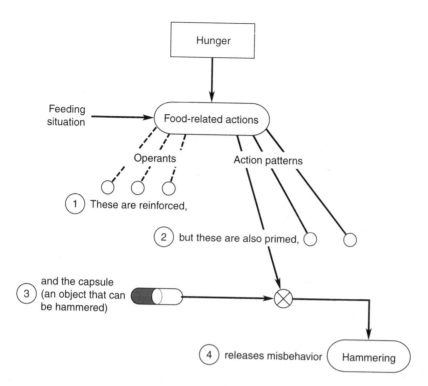

Figure 8-9 How instinctive action patterns can intrude into operant-conditioning experiments, producing such misbehavior as the hammering pattern even though quite different responses are reinforced.

To make any sense of this, we must suppose that pecking is a strong component of a pigeon's feeding system. Pigeons peck in situations where food is forthcoming, whether or not they are reinforced for doing so, and even if they are punished for doing so by postponement of food. The pecking component of the hierarchy of pigeon feeding behavior is extremely difficult to suppress, even if it costs the bird food.

Bottom-Up Constraints: Recruitment

There is another kind of interaction among levels that has received remarkably little study, though it is potentially of great importance. It appears that under some circumstances, the activation of components can bring into operation, or **recruit,** the higher-order system of which the components form a part.

A dramatic example of this sort of thing has been observed in pigeons.[31] The investigators were studying the operant conditioning of aggressive behavior. To obtain food reinforcement, their experimental pigeon was required to peck at another pigeon. The experimenters had no trouble training a bird to peck another bird, but the interesting thing was this. Once it had begun pecking the target bird, the experimental pigeon began launching full-blown attacks on that bird, with jumping and vigorous beating with the wings. These latter

31. Azrin and Hutchinson, 1967.

responses, *which were not required to produce reinforcement,* are naturally-occurring components of a pigeon's attack pattern. It appears that the act of pecking another bird was able to recruit the attack pattern as a whole, so that all its components were expressed.

In people as in pigeons, it seems that the activation of low-level components can bring whole systems into play. Many people have found, and it can be shown by direct experiment, that pretending happiness can actually improve one's mood. Pretending anger, as in a stage play, can increase one's self-reported feelings of anger (see Chap. 12).

A more involved and grimmer phenomenon *may* be another example of this kind of recruitment. This is the simulated-prison study conducted by Philip Zimbardo and his colleagues. They built an artificial prison in the basement of the psychology department building at Stanford University. Of the experimental subjects—normal, healthy, mature young men—half were assigned at random to play the role of prisoners, half the role of prison guards.

The subjects began playing the roles assigned to them. They began, of course, by just going through the motions—literally, by deliberately activating the specific responses that characterize guard-like and prisoner-like acts. But in a very short time, their emotions and their spontaneous behaviors were recruited into the roles they played.

> It was no longer apparent to us or most of the subjects where they ended and their roles began. . . . We were horrified because we saw some boys (guards) treat other boys as if they were despicable animals, taking pleasure in cruelty, while other boys (prisoners) became servile, dehumanized robots who thought only of escape, of their own individual survival, and of their mounting hatred of the guards.[32]

The role-playing marathon had been planned to run 2 weeks. In fact, Zimbardo stopped the experiment early, for fear of his subjects' physical and mental safety. How long did this take? Just 6 days.

Implications of Constraints

It is clear from all this that if we set out to reinforce some arbitrary response with an arbitrary reinforcer, we may get more, or less, than we bargained for. Other, related responses may be strengthened in addition to—or instead of—the one we reinforce. And a reinforcer that is effective for one response may not be effective for another.

Can we make sense of these findings? Once again, we can try. But once again, the attempt must be very tentative and speculative. We are scouting new territory here.★

32. Zimbardo, 1971, p. 131.

★The ideas proposed here are similar to those advanced by Shettleworth, 1983, and Timberlake, 1983. For discussion and alternatives see Rozin and Schull, 1988.

RESPONSE HIERARCHIES REVISITED   Suppose that an animal comes to us with its instinctive response patterns organized into different hierarchies depending on which motivational system is activated (compare pp. 113–15). There will be a class of food-getting responses, and another class—with different responses in it—of danger-avoiding responses.* These classes may represent untaught hierarchies, as in the stickleback (pp. 113–15), or the results of previous learning, or some combination of both. Finally, there seems to be "cross-talk" within a class, so that activating one of its members can activate the whole class (recruitment).

Now, suppose we train the animal to learn a food-getting response to get food in *this* situation, as when we require a pigeon to peck to get food in an operant chamber. It will learn quickly. But what if we ask it to use a non-food-getting response (like not pecking) to get food, or a food-getting response to avoid danger? Then it will have great difficulty, and will learn slowly or not at all.

This idea is very much like the one we encountered in the previous chapter, when we discussed Bolles's analysis of avoidance conditioning (pp. 255–56). Training in avoidance, Bolles argued, does not teach the rat new tricks; it teaches it which of the tricks it already knows is the one that works. Just so: Pecking is a "trick" that the pigeon "already knows" is a good one to use in food-getting (but not shock-avoiding) situations. So a pigeon quickly learns to peck to get food—but not to avoid shock (pp. 255–56). *Refraining from pecking* is not a food-getting trick, and the pigeon has great difficulty learning to use it for food-getting purposes.

CONSTRAINT AND COGNITION   These instinctive constraints are yet another problem for the original, response-strengthening conception of reinforcement. But it is also important to see what a blow they are to the commonsense cognitive view of reinforcement. A bird pecks a key for food, we're inclined to say, because it believes that pecking the key will lead to food, and it wants the food. So it pecks. What a smart bird the pigeon is!

The problem is: Why can't the bird just as well learn that *refraining from pecking* will lead to the food that it wants? Or that pecking will avoid the shock that it doesn't want? But it learns these tasks poorly or not at all. What a stupid bird the pigeon is!**

Smart bird, stupid bird, which is it? Obviously, it depends. A pigeon may be very smart at some tasks, and appallingly stupid at other tasks which, considered only as intellectual problems, look just as easy. And not just pigeons, of

---

*No doubt there will be other classes as well, as for young-protecting, mate-attracting, and so on. And the classes may subdivide as well; vervet monkeys, for example, use different classes of responses for snake-avoiding, leopard-avoiding, and eagle-avoiding (Cheney and Seyfarth, 1991.)

**Of course we could wave our hands and say, "Well, some expectancies are harder to learn than others." That easy reply, however, begs too many questions to be acceptable. Is it that the bird can't form the right expectation, or forms it but doesn't know what to do about it, or knows what to do but can't do it? Or what?

course. We can expect an animal to be smart at doing (and learning!) some things and stupid at doing (and learning!) other things; and what those "things" are depends on the species and what its instinctive repertoire is like—what "tricks" it "already knows" for dealing with the problems we present it with.

A Look Backward: Conditioning, Cognition, and Instinct

The phenomena we have surveyed—misbehavior, recruitment, and the like—have important implications for the theoretical questions we looked at in the previous section. Keeping in mind what we have learned, let us ask again: What does a reinforcer do?

PIECES OF THE PUZZLE   The original behaviorist conception was that reinforcement strengthens responses, and that's all that need be said. Some behaviorist writers still hold to that view, but most writers (including this one) do not think it can be maintained. The experimental evidence against it is simply too strong. We do need to understand the internal cognitive operations by which, for example, animals form specific expectancies about the consequences of their actions (pp. 313–15).

But this does *not* mean that we can heave a sigh of relief and lapse back into common sense. A commonsense cognitive view—the bird believes that pecking leads to food, it wants food, so it pecks—will not do either. It has trouble with the data on biological constraints, as we have just seen. We must also come to understand how cognitive operations interact with instinct (compare pp. 255–62), that is, with the untaught "bag of tricks" our subjects come prepared with.

PUTTING THE PIECES TOGETHER: CONVERGING VIEWPOINTS Conditioning, cognition, instinct—scientists investigating these three problems used to be indifferent to each other if not downright hostile. That is changing fast. The techniques of operant conditioning are being used to study cognitive processes—not just to show that they're there, but to investigate how they work.[33] The methods of ethology—observation and field experiments in natural settings—also are being applied to the study of cognition.[34]

And, to complete the circle, the constraints-on-learning literature reflects a mutual borrowing of concepts and methods by operant conditioners and ethologists. Since we have just discussed this topic, let us look at this convergence more closely.

Take the hammering chicken, for example. As we saw, the hammering can be understood as an action pattern used in nature to break open seeds or kill grubs. But in order for us to know that, someone had to have watched enough chickens, long enough and in natural environments, to identify that pattern

33. For example, Premack, 1988.
34. For example, Ristau, 1991.

and its function. This kind of careful observation and classification is characteristic of ethology. So is the emphasis on hierarchically organized behavioral systems (pp. 113–15).

So, too, is the emphasis on the *evolution* of a species' behavioral repertoire, along with its fur or its feathers (pp. 34–40). The untaught "bags of tricks" we have spoken of, are "tricks" that have evolved in response to the problems faced by a species over its evolutionary history. And—a final line of convergence—these may include cognitive "tricks" as well as behavioral ones. Cognitive mechanisms, or ways of processing information, are themselves products of evolution. They may differ from species to species and, for a given species, in the use to which the information is put.[35] For example, the *conditioned taste aversion* mechanism (pp. 257–58) is an information-handling "trick" of just this kind.

For now, what is important is that we see how seemingly very different approaches to the study of learning are coming together. What were once distracting squabbles are now turning into productive discussions.

REINFORCEMENT THEORY IN PERSPECTIVE

Finally, in pointing out new links between reinforcement theory and other views, we shouldn't forget the valuable contributions reinforcement theory has made in its own right. Its technology—its procedures for shaping new responses and teaching subtle discriminations—has had impact in the clinic and the workplace, in the school and on the playing field, besides permitting us to ask questions about the animal mind at a level of sophistication we would once have thought impossible.

Perhaps most important, it has properly emphasized the role of the *environment,* and especially the environmental *consequences* of actions, in maintaining disordered or ineffective behavior—or ordered and effective behavior, for that matter. Even cognitive psychologists caution us: Let's not get so caught up in what is going on in the actor's head that we neglect what is going on outside his head, in the situation.[36] Such writers freely acknowledge their—or rather our—debt to behaviorism.

SUMMARY

Reinforcement *procedures* are used to train animals to perform arbitrary acts. We use them to diagnose motivational states, as opposed to stimulus-bound reflexive or instinctive actions. Reinforcement *theory* holds that all purposive

35. See, for example, Rozin and Schull, 1988; Gallistel, 1990.
36. For example, Ross and Nisbett, 1991.

behavior is maintained by its reinforcing consequences. To call an act *purposive* is to say, not that future consequences are anticipated, but that such an act was established and maintained by reinforcement in the past. Internal states such as food deprivation affect purposive behavior because they set the reinforcing value of environmental events; for example, food deprivation makes food a reinforcer.

Modern reinforcement theory uses concepts developed by B. F. Skinner. It distinguishes between *respondents,* which are elicited by stimuli, and *operants,* which are emitted by the organism without stimuli that cause them. If an event increases the strength of a response that it follows, then that event is defined as a reinforcer. Positive reinforcers are those whose onset is reinforcing. With negative reinforcers, the offset of the event is reinforcing; termination of painful shock is an example. If a response is followed by the onset of a negative reinforcer, we speak of *punishment.* These events are defined by their effect on a response; it is responses, not organisms, that are reinforced. If a response is reinforced in the presence of a stimulus and not reinforced in its absence, then it will come of occur only when that stimulus is present. We then call the stimulus a *discriminative stimulus* and say that it has acquired *stimulus control* over the emission of the operant.

Operant behavior is frequently studied in a chamber (operant chamber or Skinner box) with some defined response available, such as pressing a lever for a rat or pecking a key for a pigeon. Reinforcements can be delivered and rate of response measured without changing the situation and without interrupting the continuity of behavior.

Reinforcement procedures have been applied in a variety of settings—hospitals, homes, schools, workplaces, and the playing field—to increase the frequency of effective behavior. Often *conditioned reinforcers,* such as money or tokens, can be used where natural reinforcers would be difficult or inconvenient to use.

These methods reflect a definite point of view—an operant philosophy—about the nature and causes of behavior. They center on identifying reinforcing conditions, identifying the behavior that is desired and/or problematic, and arranging that the one be reinforced and the other not. Thus they focus on the *environmental* determinants of behavior. Much of this may seem at first like just good common sense, but in fact it is at odds with common sense on a number of points. Common sense tends to explain actions by referring to conditions inside the organism, such as personality traits; to deal in vague exhortations ("try harder" or "work carefully") which do not refer to specific actions and which precede the behavior rather than follow it, as reinforcers do; and to focus on behavior that is not wanted rather than behavior that is.

Reinforcement procedures may have unintended consequences, so they do have their dangers. Powerful reinforcers may undermine the intrinsic motivation for an activity—the reward of performing the activity for its own sake. They may encourage the rote performance of successful actions as opposed to the discovery of principles, rules, and concepts. Both these effects are compatible with the theory of reinforcement; still, they show that the use of reinforcement has its dangers.

What makes a reinforcer reinforcing? The hedonic hypotheses—reinforcers are pleasant—is hard to test. The drive-reduction hypothesis may cover some cases of reinforcement, but not all. The response-deprivation hypothesis says that opportunity to make a response, when such opportunity is otherwise restricted, is reinforcing. That idea explains the fact that Response A may reinforce Response B under some conditions, but B may reinforce A under others. However, not all reinforcers depend on response restriction in any obvious way, nor is it always clear what responses are restricted and how much. We are left with the *empirical law of effect:* An event is a reinforcer if it reinforces. Perhaps different reinforcers have that effect for different reasons.

What exactly do reinforcers do? The original behaviorist view, held by Thorndike and by Skinner, is that they strengthen responses: A pigeon pecks a key because key-pecking has been strengthened by the food reinforcement that has followed it in the past. The cognitive view is that they set up internal expectancies: The bird pecks because it expects to obtain food if it does. A large literature attempts to decide between these two views, and of the two, it favors the cognitive one.

However, the research on biological constraints suggests that both these theories are inadequate. For a long time it was assumed that reinforcement conditions can take hold of any response, at any level, and cause just that response to become more frequent. More recently we have realized that reinforcement taps into the hierarchical structure of behavior systems. Food reinforcement, for instance, brings an animal's repertoire of food-getting behaviors into play. Unwanted components of that system may occur, even at the expense of the reinforced response. Autoshaping is an especially vivid example: In a situation where food is predicted, pigeons peck, even if it costs them reinforcements (food). Besides these top-down effects, there may be bottom-up effects: Strengthening one component of a hierarchy can recruit the entire system, with its other components. In pigeons and perhaps in people, if one goes through the motions of behaving aggressively, aggressive motivational states may follow.

All this means that if we reinforce one response, we may increase other, quite different responses—a problem for the response-strengthening view. But it also means that not all response-reinforcement combinations are learned with equal ease—a problem for the cognitive view. If a pigeon can learn to expect that pecking leads to food, and so pecks, why can it not learn to expect that *not* pecking leads to food, and so *not* peck? Apparently it is easy to condition a response with food reinforcement if it is already part of the species's repertoire of food-getting actions, but not otherwise. Similarly for its repertoire of danger-avoiding actions (Bolles's SSDRs). We need to learn more about what these repertoires are in a given species and how reinforcement (or the formation of expectancies) interacts with them. Thus behaviorists, cognitive psychologists, and ethologists are increasingly coming to share their ideas and methods.

In its own right, however, the behaviorists' work on reinforcement has taught us much. It has found direct application in a variety of settings, and it has reminded us of the important role of *environmental consequences* in molding and guiding action.

CHAPTER 9

Images, Plans, and Schemas

Reynolds talked about how much soda pop he was going to drink the rest of his life. Cherry couldn't think about anything but chocolate ice cream. As I listened to the thirsty talk between the rafts, my own mind slowly filled with visions of chocolate malted milk. I could actually taste it, to the point where my tongue worked convulsively. The strange part is that I hadn't had a chocolate malted milk in nearly 25 years.

—EDWARD V. RICKENBACKER[*]

In the last chapter, we looked at the behaviorist account of goal-directed behavior. In the present chapter, we will look at it from the cognitive point of view.

We saw that the basic question of purposive behavior is: How can we get the future into the present? How can our actions be affected by things that haven't happened yet? The reinforcement answer is: They are not. What look like effects of future events are really effects of past ones, that is, of our histories of reinforcement.

The cognitive theory takes a different approach. Its answer to our question is: In a sense, we do get the future into the present, because we can imagine it now. Future outcomes affect what we do because we expect, or want, or hope for, imagined future events.

IMAGES

Let us begin by asking what images are, and how they can be used.

A few minutes ago, a student wandered unsuspectingly into my office. Just so I could write this section, I asked a minute of her time to do some strange-looking favors for me.

"Close your eyes," I requested. She did. "Now, do you know where the clock on my wall is?" She nodded. "Point to it, please." She did, quite accu-

[*]Quoted by Wolf, 1958, p. 435.

rately. "Now suppose it were lowered three feet. Point to where it would be." She did, again quite accurately I thought—I did not measure the error, though I could have. "Thank you," I said, and she replied, "You're . . . uh . . . welcome."

Now let us look at what she was able to do. She pointed to an unseen object, much as she would have done if it were seen. She used a *memory image* as the target of her pointing. Then she *manipulated* the image. Having moved the clock in her mind to a new location, she could point to it as if it had actually been moved—but without the effort and danger of actually moving it. That is what makes such capabilities so valuable, as we will see.

Thus we have a preliminary conception of what an image is. It is an internally generated process that can provide some of the same information, and guide our actions in some of the same ways, as externally generated stimuli can. We can shorten that by saying that an image is an internal *representation* of some state of affairs. We can represent an actual state or, by manipulating the image, a potential or possible one.

A word of caution, however. This does *not* mean that an image is a "picture in the head" of the external event. An image may or may not be visual, and it may or may not be conscious. And it can *represent* an external state of affairs without in the least having to *resemble* one. A picture can represent an actual scene, and resemble that scene; but a verbal description can also represent a scene, yet the speech sounds or the words on paper do not resemble the scene at all. Our internal representations—or our open-eyed perceptions, for that matter—may be much more like descriptions than like pictures.[1] We do not know how images are formed or maintained in the brain; but that there are no pictures in the brain, we may be certain.

Let us say, then, that an image is an internally generated process that represents, without necessarily resembling, some state of affairs. And we can generate and manipulate images voluntarily, as my student did, to provide information about what *would* be the case if such and such were done.

IMAGES AND GOAL DIRECTION

Now let us see how useful images can be in initiating and guiding purposive behavior, in both animals and human beings.

Efference Copies

Even at the level of simple movements, images play a role in the guidance of action. What happens is this: When we act, we also imagine what the sensory consequences of action will be. This image, the *efference copy,* is normally quite unconscious, but no less important for that. Here's an example.

When a singer holds a note, her voice actually wobbles a bit over time, above and below the pitch intended. What the singer does is make continuous

1. Pylyshyn, 1973.

little corrections, comparing the note she hears herself sing with the image—the efference copy—of the note she expects to hear herself sing (Fig. 9.1). If we open the feedback loop, as by preventing the singer from hearing her voice, she will drift off pitch to a surprising degree.[2]

In this case, the singer's corrections are guided by the *difference* between the note imagined and the note actually heard. The singer changes the tension on her vocal cords (output) so as to reduce or eliminate any such difference (negative feedback). In other words, we have again a negative-feedback loop. And the input to the loop is a *mismatch* between the actual state of affairs and the desired one. That is a simple model of goal-directed, purposive behavior as the cognitive theorist views it.

Images as Guides: Search Images and Cognitive Maps

Consider what happens when a goal is not at hand. If an animal wants something but hasn't got it, we are inclined to say that it *searches for* what it wants.

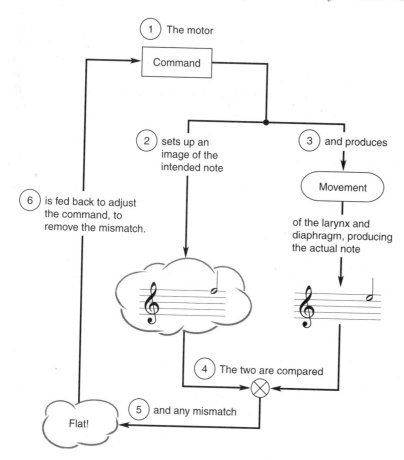

Figure 9-1 An efference copy as a goal.

2. Deutsch, 1960.

But if an animal can do that, then it must be able to represent or specify the desired object, even before it encounters that object. Can an animal do that? Can it know what it is looking for before it finds it? Can it know where the desired object ought to be—again, even before it finds it? For at least some animals, the answer is clearly yes.[3]

In an early demonstration, a chimpanzee was trained to open a box, within which it would find a bit of banana. After this training, the experimenter craftily introduced a test trial, in which a bit of lettuce was placed in the box instead.[4]

Now lettuce is a perfectly acceptable food for a chimp. One might expect the chimp to accept this reward as readily as any other—if a reward is just a reward. Instead, the chimp rejected the lettuce with every appearance of contempt and outrage; and, the picture of a disappointed ape, it searched all around the box and environs. The lettuce, presumably, was not what it *expected* to find. And if we admit that, then we must admit that the expectation—the *search image* specifying banana—was present somewhere in the chimp, even if there was no banana in the environment.

Let us relate this idea to more familiar ones—but let us also see how it takes us further. Earlier (pp. 91–93), we saw how motivational states prime the actor's responses to certain environmental stimuli. In a hungry chimp, we might imagine that the hunger general tells the officers in charge of eating, "Take action if you encounter food stimuli" (Fig. 9.2A).

That would account for a hungry chimp's grasping and eating food *after* the food was found. But the search image adds a new dimension. It adds a process of *comparison* between what is seen and what is expected, and a process of *search* if the two do not match. The chimp was not just passively ready to eat food *if* it found it—it was actively looking for banana even *before* it found it (Fig. 9.2B). Such capabilities enable chimps—and people—to look for what they want, and not just accept it when they happen to encounter it.

Finally, the mismatch between the stimulus and the search image led to searching behavior which might well have turned up the banana if it had been around. Once again, the search, like the singer's corrections, was driven by a mismatch between the sensory input and the image.*

But there is yet more. The chimp was not just looking for the banana; it was looking (at first) for the banana *in the box,* where the banana should have been. Clearly it had an internal representation of the spatial layout of the situ-

---

3. For discussion see Gallistel, 1990.

4. Tinkelpaugh, 1928.

*There is, to be sure, a problem here. As shown, the system has the chimp returning to its search whenever it finds no banana; and, if there were no banana anywhere around, the chimp might search and search forever. There must be *stop rules* that eventually inhibit search if it remains unsuccessful. Some writers have suggested that fatigue and habituation (pp. 239–41) evolved as stop rules to break just such infinite loops (see Gould, 1982).

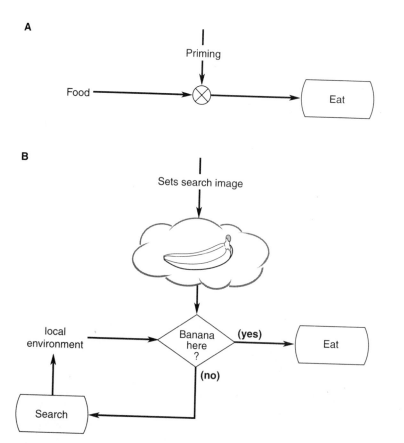

Figure 9-2 (A) If the hunger state primes responsiveness to food, the actor can respond to food only when food is encountered. (B) The search image permits active food search, which modifies the stimulus situation until food is found or the search is terminated.

ation, not only of what things there were in it, but also of where they were. Such a representation is called a *cognitive map*.[5]

Such internal cognitive maps can be enormously useful. Some species of birds, for example, will hide away seeds when food is abundant; they retrieve the seeds and eat them later. Are they *remembering* where the seeds are and guided to them by the resulting cognitive map? Yes.

In one study, an experimental "habitat" was built that contained landmarks (shrubs, plants, and the like), and also a large number of places to hide seeds— tiny seed-sized holes, covered with flaps of felt.[6] There were 100 such hidey-holes. Each bird was allowed to hide twelve seeds, wherever it wished. Then the bird was removed from the habitat, and, 2 hours later, returned to it. By then the bird was hungry, for these birds (marsh tits, *Parus palustris*) are very small and use up their energy reserves quickly.

Twelve seeds, remember, were hidden with 100 holes to choose from. If the birds visited the hiding places at random, they would make on average

5. Tolman, 1948.
6. See Shettleworth, 1987.

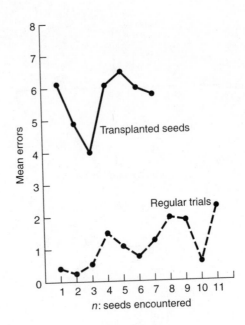

Figure 9-3 Average number of errors made by marsh tits before recovering each *n*th seed (that is, the first seed [1], the second seed [2], and so on). When the seeds were where the birds had put them (regular trials), the birds made many fewer errors than would occur by chance. This was not so if the seeds were "transplanted" by the experimenters after the birds had hidden them. (From Shettleworth, 1987.)

about 7.4 errors, or visits to empty holes, for each seed recovered (88/12 is about 7.4). However, as Figure 9.3 shows, they made very many fewer errors than that (dashed lines). But were the birds really remembering where they had put the seeds? Or were they sensing them in some other way, smelling them perhaps? No. If, during the hours while the bird was away, the experimenters sneakily moved the seeds to new hiding places, then the birds made very many "errors"; they went to the places where the seeds should have been, not to where they were.

Now the brain of a marsh tit is comfortably smaller than the last segment of your thumb. Yet out of a hundred possibilities (at least), it can remember where it has put (at least) twelve seeds, for at least 2 hours and probably much longer than that. Even a very tiny brain can hang onto a very impressive amount of information.

Internal Modulation: Making Images Goals

In discussing hunger in Chapter 3, we saw that internal states can modulate responsiveness to external stimuli. Food is a more effective stimulus to a hungry rat than to a sated one. It might even taste better to a hungry rat (pp. 94–96).

Internal states can modulate the effects of images, too. They can make images into goals—in rats as in humans. Let us look at another classic experiment that shows us yet another example of the rat's capabilities.

SALT-SEEKING IN RATS: MEMORIES AS GOALS Salt-deficient animals, we remember (pp. 75–76), develop an appetite for salt. They will seek salt solutions vigorously and ingest them avidly. A team of experimenters took advantage of this specific hunger to show that salt-deficient rats do not just react to salt when they find it; they can search for it before they find it, and they know what they are looking for.[7] They can have an image that *becomes* a goal when salt is needed.

The experiment was done in the following way. First, rats that were *not* salt deficient were trained to press a lever in a Skinner box for fluid reinforcement. For half the rats, the fluid was plain water; for the other half, it was a solution of salty water. The rats worked at about the same rate for these two fluids. This was the first phase of the experiment.

In the second phase, there were two changes. First, half the rats in each group were made salt deficient. Second, the apparatus was turned off; no reinforcements were delivered to any rat in this second phase. The question was: How long would the rats persist in responding during this extinction session?

Figure 9.4 shows the design and the results of this experiment. The rats in Group 1, that had received salt as reinforcement for bar-pressing *and* were salt deficient now, made about twice as many responses before quitting as did any of the other groups.

As with the selective-devaluation experiment (pp. 313–16), there is simply no way that these results can be attributed to effects of reinforcement history. Groups 1 and 3 had identical reinforcement histories: salt-solution reward for lever-pressing in Phase 1, and no reward in Phase 2. Why then were they so different in Phase 2?★

We must suppose (1) that the rat remembered what a bar-press had brought in the past and (2) that salt deficiency affected the goal properties of that memory image. If the memory was of salt, *and* if the rats were salt deficient now (Group 1), then the memory became a goal. The rats *wanted* the taste they remembered and worked hard in the attempt to get it. If the rats remembered the salt taste but had no need for salt, then the memory was only a memory. It was not a very potent goal, and the rats didn't try very hard to bring it about.

And if that is so, it means that the animal's internal state—here, salt deficiency—can somehow modulate a memory so that it becomes a goal, calling forth persistent and vigorous attempts to produce the remembered state of affairs.

FANTASIES AS GOALS If specific memory images can serve as goals, so can fantasized images. Think about the quote that begins this chapter. Thirsty men were tormented by images of tasty drinks. And, had there been any way of

7. Krieckhaus and Wolf, 1968; Wolf, 1970.

★The other groups were controls. Group 3, as compared with Group 4, shows that a history of salt reinforcement does not by itself lead to more persistent bar-pressing. And Group 2, as compared with Group 4, shows that salt deprivation by itself does not lead to greater persistence.

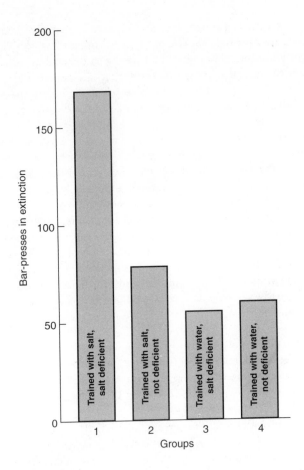

Figure 9-4 Results of the salt-seeking experiment in rats. See text for explanation. (Data from Krieckhaus and Wolf, 1968.)

obtaining these longed-for commodities, we can be sure that those images would have become the targets of vigorous goal-directed actions.

A Look Backward: Images and Goal-Seeking

We have discussed only a few examples of an active research area. Many animals, it seems, are perfectly capable of imagining a set of conditions that does not exist at the time. An animal may go looking for a particular kind of food or a particular place in the world, specifying the properties of the commodity that is sought, even before the commodity is encountered.[8] Cognitive maps specify *where* it is. Search images specify *what* it is. And states of the body can make these specifications into goals, so that what was merely remembered or imagined now is actively *sought*.

Just how this happens—how images are formed in the brain, how they are made into goals—we do not know. Maybe if we understood the simpler cases

8. See Gallistel, 1990.

better, we would better know what questions to ask about how more complex goals are formed and sought.

Finally, before leaving this topic, we should note that some of the ideas and findings discussed in the previous chapter are relevant here. Consider, for example, the research on response-reinforcer expectancies (pp. 313–16). We could think of an *expectancy* as a kind of image: something that is not yet present to be perceived is nonetheless represented within the system.

IMAGES AND ACTION: GOALS, SUB-GOALS, AND PLANS

We have seen that images can act as goals. They can trigger and guide actions directed at obtaining the imagined state or commodity. Now let us ask: How do they do it? How do images produce actions? Suppose a chimp (or a person) has a cognitive map and knows where the gravy lies. How does that knowledge drive the leg muscles to get the chimp to the gravy? As the behaviorist Edwin R. Guthrie once quipped, a cognitive map seems to leave the animal "buried in thought." How do we get it moving?

Plans

Let us consider a case study, to see one way in which a purposive sequence of action might be organized.

In driving home from work, I must turn the engine on, back the car out of its parking space, drive to the top of a ramp and turn left, . . . , and so on, until I reach the intersection at which a right turn brings me to my goal, my home.

Such a sequence is often called a *plan.* It is a hierarchically organized sequence of actions (see below), directed toward a goal. George Miller, Eugene Galanter, and Karl Pribram have offered an influential theory about how plans work, a theory that relates such sequences to concepts we are now familiar with.[9]

The Organization of Plans

To illustrate their theory, let's look more closely at driving home. It is, first of all, a well-integrated and well-practiced plan; I know how to drive home. We might suppose that the plan is represented in my brain as something equivalent to a series of instructions, a *cognitive program,* by analogy to a *cognitive map:*★

    1. Start car.
    2. Drive to top of ramp.

9. Miller, Galanter, and Pribram, 1960.

★As with images, we need not suppose that plans are necessarily conscious. In fact, the role of unconscious processes in plans and thought is a venerable controversy in psychology; for a discussion of the early literature see Humphrey, 1951.

3. Turn left.
. . .
20. Drive to intersection.
21. Turn right.
22. Drive to driveway.
23. Drive into driveway. End.

Each of these actions in turn breaks down into components. The first command, for instance, can be expanded:
a. Open door.
b. Sit in seat.
c. Insert key in ignition.
d. Turn key. . . .

And so on. And each of these sub-commands breaks down into a pattern of muscle contractions. We have our familiar *hierarchical organization*.

The Activation of Plans

This set of instructions represents my *knowledge* of how to get home. How do we execute the program; how does it lead to action? Miller et al. answer that question with two familiar ideas, plus a new one.

First, complex systems operate by calling simpler components into play. Here, our list of instructions translates into the familiar military analogy: The general gives orders to the officers who give orders to the sergeants, and so on down to the muscle-cell foot soldiers who move the body.

Second, the components that are called into play are responses to the present environment. This too is familiar; it is like the case in which the feeding sergeants are told, "Take action!" when food is perceived (pp. 91–93).

The third idea is the new one. It says: These responses are called into play by *setting the goals* that they are to attain. The general's orders, in this theory, do not say "Make this or that response." They say, "Act until this or that goal is achieved." In other words, the overall goal sets *sub-goals* for the component sub-systems.

Thus, each component of the plan is a negative-feedback loop, which acts to reduce the difference between the existing situation and the sub-goal set for it. Compare the case of the singer (pp. 328–29). As we saw, singing an F on pitch is controlled by its own negative-feedback loop, which corrects deviations from the intended pitch—the goal. But singing that F is only a sub-goal in the plan for singing the whole song. The image of the F becomes a goal only when it is time to sing the F.

Now let us go back to driving home, and see how these ideas apply there (Fig. 9-5). Superficially, we might represent the driving-home plan as a simple negative-feedback loop (Fig. 9-5A). Being not home leads me to drive until I *am* home. But that obviously won't do. I do not *always* drive home when I'm

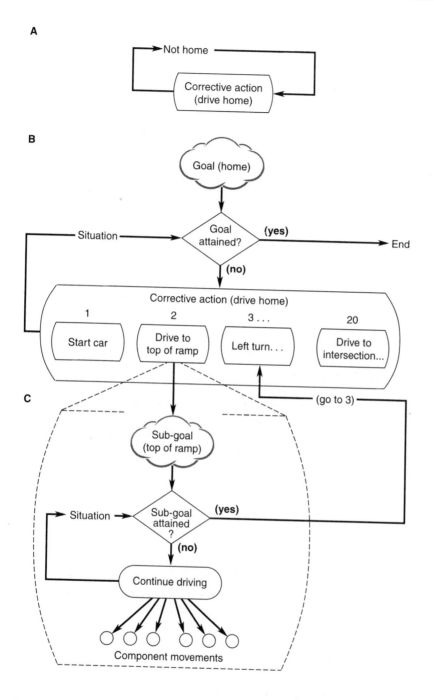

Figure 9-5 Plans as negative-feedback loops. (A) An overly simple loop, which would cause the actor to drive home whenever he is not at home. (B) A more realistic plan compares the external situation with the goal situation and, if the two do not match, takes corrective action to modify the situation. It is still a negative-feedback loop, driven by the difference between the situation and the goal until the difference disappears. (C) Expanded view of the "drive to top of ramp" component. This is also a negative-feedback loop, operating until the situation matches the sub-goal for that component.

not home, and my employers wouldn't like it if I did. We must consider both the situation and the intention or goal: (1) I'm not home, and (2) my goal is to get home. I act until the difference between the goal and the present situation is no longer there (Fig. 9-5B)—again, just as the singer does.

But the plan is actually a hierarchy of feedback loops (Fig. 9-5C). The whole system continues to operate until I am home, and then it shuts down. But each component is also a negative-feedback loop, whose goal is set by the overall plan. I manipulate the ignition key until I feel it slip into the lock—an *efference copy* as sub-goal. I turn the ignition key until I hear the engine start—another such sub-goal. I drive down the street until I reach the intersection—an external situation, specified by a *search image,* as sub-goal. And so on. At each stage, the action continues until the sub-goal is attained.

A system organized this way has great advantages. It might seem as if the existing situation—say, my car at the bottom of the ramp—could trigger the response directly—drive to the top of the ramp. The trouble is if that were so, any variation in the response would require a separate command to correct it. If I drive fast, the command must specify a shorter duration to the response; if slow, a longer one. If I stop to give right of way to a squirrel, a new response command must be issued to start me going again. But if the goal is specified—"get to the top of the ramp"—then I can drive fast or slow, straight or swerving to avoid potholes, braking for animals as needed, and *no further commands need be issued.* I need only compare where I am with the goal, and drive until they match.

An analogy may make this clearer. Think again about using a furnace to bring the room to a desired temperature. We could do it by turning on the furnace directly; that is like commanding a movement directly. But then we have to turn it off when the temperature is high enough, turn it on again next time the temperature drops, . . . and so on. That takes a lot of time, trouble, and attention.

How much easier if the furnace is controlled by a thermostat. We can set the thermostat, establishing the goal that the system is to seek, and forget about it. The control system automatically turns on the furnace if the goal is not attained, and stops the furnace when the goal is attained, with no further commands from us. In a similar way, once my plan sets the top of the ramp as a sub-goal, well-practiced habits and skills get me there—fast or slow, with or without interruptions, as necessary—without requiring any further orders.

Purposive behavior, in Miller et al.'s theory, is organized by commands like that—commands that specify goals, not movements. Much of the flexibility of our behavior results from this.

Internal Organization in Plans

But all this is still too simple. We have treated plans as a series of goal-directed actions, each triggered by an *external* state of affairs. But for many plans and sub-plans, we must also consider the *internal* organization of the controlling system. The steps may be organized and put in the right sequence by commands from higher levels within the system, rather than by the changing environment outside it.

Motor skills provide good examples. Consider a skilled pianist playing a fast passage. Her finger movements cannot be triggered individually by the corresponding note in the score, or by stimuli that in turn trigger the next one, from the previous movement. They are too rapid for that. So the phrase as a whole must be played by an internally programmed sequence of operations that imposes the necessary interval between each output and the next, and diverts each output to the appropriate finger.

Think once again of the military analogy. Imagine that the officer's orders were: "Platoon A, take action at 0600. Platoon B, take action at 0800. Platoon C, take action at 0900." That would cause each platoon to begin operations at the right time, as set by the overall plan, without reference to the external situation.

A Look Backward: The Organization of Plans

Let us review what we have learned about plans.

A plan is a hierarchically organized set of represented (imagined) goals and sub-goals. The system specifies some goal state—as an image, because it hasn't happened yet. It compares that internally generated goal state with the present external state of affairs, as registered by the perceptual apparatus. And if the two do not match, the system will operate to reduce the difference between what is and what ought to be. This gives us our familiar *joint control by internal and external influences*.

This can happen at each level of the controlling system. The system may seek its goals by specifying sub-goals that the component actions seek in their turn. We have our familiar *hierarchical organization*.

In some cases, such as driving a familiar route, each component of the plan is activated by attainment of the previous sub-goal. Here we see again our familiar joint control by internal and external influences, now operating on the components of a plan rather than the plan as a whole. In other cases the plan may have its own internal organization, as in skilled action (like piano-playing), so that a sequence of actions is imposed without reference to the environment.

Finally, a lower-level sub-unit can be a component of any of several higher-order systems. We could put the key in the ignition as part of a plan to drive home, to drive to work, to drive to the store, or to drive from New York to San Diego for that matter. And so we have another familiar idea, the *lattice hierarchy*. A given sub-goal may be sought, or a given sub-plan may be executed, in the service of many higher-order purposive sequences.

A Look Forward: Constructing Plans

Before leaving this topic, we should note that we still have considered only simple cases—ones in which plans are well-learned and habitual. Obviously there are times when we must *construct* plans on the spot, to meet a new situation.

Suppose we find that the usual route home is closed. What then? We consider various possible sequences: If we turn right to Appletree Road and then left, will that get us home? Or would it be faster to go back to Ridge Street? . . . And so on. Here we move into the topic of imagining the outcomes of possible actions—modeling the world in our heads—which links the study of plans with the *theory of decision-making.* We will address it in the next chapter.

MOTIVATIONAL APPLICATIONS OF IMAGERY

We have sketched out some of the ways in which images can guide behavior in animals and humans. Now let us look at some ways in which this knowledge has been put to use.

Systematic Desensitization Therapy

First, let's look at a therapeutic technique called *systematic desensitization therapy,* often used to combat troublesome fears, or *phobias* (pp. 260–62). It applies the principles of classical conditioning (pp. 46–48), but uses an *imagined* stimulus as CS.

First, the patient with a phobia is given training at total, deep-muscle relaxation until he can relax his entire body on command. After that, there follows a series of conditioning trials on which the patient *imagines* the feared situation—an examination perhaps, or a snake, depending on what he is afraid of. The person forms a clear and vivid mental image of the feared object or situation, while maintaining a state of deep-muscle relaxation. Extensive practice at this is given. The idea is this: If one can establish relaxation as a conditioned response to the image, then the relaxation will inhibit fear and the fear will be reduced. Notice that this is a conditioning situation, with this difference: The conditioned stimulus is not in the environment but in the person's imagination.*

One therapist, for instance, has used this method to treat college students who reported intense fear of snakes. He found, first, that the method was highly successful and, second, that its success did depend on a specific condi-

---

*There is the further assumption, justified by the success of this method, that the relaxation response will generalize from the image of the feared object to the object itself (e.g., a real snake). One may also try to condition relaxation to actual feared situations rather than imagined ones; but, interestingly enough, it is not clear that this method works any better than the one described, done in the patient's head.

tioning procedure.[10] Just learning to relax, and just getting used to thinking about snakes, did not help. The two had to be paired with each other, so that relaxation responses could become *conditioned* to the thought of snakes and thus reduce fear of them (Fig. 9-6).

Systematic desensitization is one of a number of techniques known collectively as *cognitive-behavioral therapies*. Such techniques draw ideas from both cog-

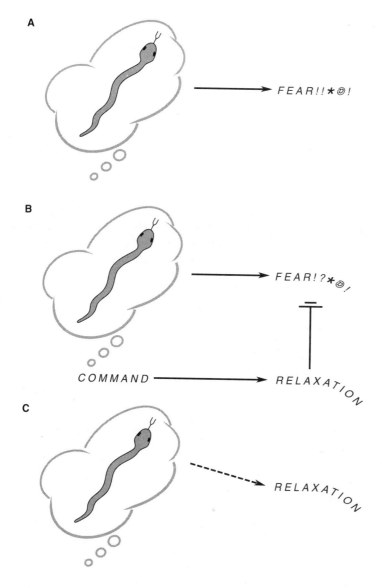

A

FEAR!!★⊘!

B

FEAR!?★⊘!

COMMAND ⟶ RELAXATION

C

RELAXATION

Figure 9-6 (A) In a severely phobic person, even the thought of a snake can generate fear. But (B) if the person has extended practice imagining a snake while following instructions to relax, then (1) the relaxation inhibits the fear, and (2) the relaxation comes to occur as a conditioned response to the thought of a snake.

10. Davison, 1968.

nitive and behaviorist theories, and ask each theory to give a bit of ground. It asks cognitive theorists to admit that such cognitive operations as thinking, wishing, and image formation are *responses* and provide *stimuli*, and that these follow the same laws as any other responses and stimuli—in particular, the laws of conditioning. It asks behaviorists to accept, for their part, that thoughts, wishes, and images can be important influences on behavior. This statesman-like compromise seems to be gaining popularity among clinicians.

Goal Setting

Both in the workplace[11] and on the playing field,[12] extensive research indicates that performance can be improved if specific *goals* are set—if, in other words, one imagines the standards of performance or attainment that are to serve as goals from now on. A survey of research has suggested some general principles:

1. Specific goals lead to better performance than vague goals. We are speculating now, but we wonder: Does *specific* mean something like *concretely imaginable?*
2. Short-term goals can facilitate the achievement of long-term goals. Perhaps (though again we're speculating) it helps if the steps toward achievement—the plans and sub-goals—are concretely imaginable.
3. Goals must be accepted if they are to affect performance. An image by itself is just an image; it must become a goal (pp. 332–34).

As so often, there is much more to it than this. As one example, it makes a difference how, and by whom, the goals are set. They may be more effective if the worker or athlete has a voice in setting them; and they should be tough, but realistic. These complexities look forward to topics such as self-determination and self-efficacy (pp. 563–64).

But even with just this much, we notice an interesting parallel: Both the behaviorist emphasis on reinforcement, and the cognitive emphasis on imagined goals, include the same advice: Be specific. In the one case, the advice is: Decide *specifically* what response is desired. In the other it is: Decide *specifically* what goal is to be attained. And in both cases, we are warned that the usual non-specific pep talk—"try harder," "do your best," "work carefully"—is likely to be resoundingly unsuccessful.

Plans in the Mind: Mental Rehearsal

"Practice makes perfect," we say—but it doesn't. We might better say that practice makes *habits*. And it turns out that imagined practice can do the same. There is now substantial evidence that practicing skills "in our head"—imag-

11. Latham and Locke, 1993.
12. LeUnes and Nation, 1989.

ining ourselves performing them—can lead to improved performance when the time comes to do them for real.

If this technique is to work, it is important that we practice, or "rehearse," doing the task *right*. All too often, we do the exact opposite! Consider: In a few minutes we must get up before all these people and do whatever—make that free throw, give our speech, sing the song without cracking on the top F. And we worry and fret and suffer, imagining *all the ways we might do it wrong*. We are, in effect, rehearsing mistakes! It would be much better to push these thoughts of ineptitude out of our minds and, in the few minutes we have, concentrate firmly on thinking about doing the job well.

A Look Backward

In these examples, we have seen how imagined events can have many of the motivational properties of real, environmental events of the kind we've explored in previous chapters. Take conditioning, for example. Pair a bell (CS) with food (UCS) many times, and the bell begins to trigger salivation as a conditioned response. Well, in this section we see how the thought, of snakes for example, can be treated as a CS, and we condition a relaxation response to it (desensitization).

Or we can point to analogues of operant conditioning. Imagined outcomes, like real ones, can serve as incentives (goal-setting). Finally, just as real practice at responses or response sequences can improve our skills, so can imagined practice (mental rehearsal).

But not all images serve us as well as these. A moment ago, we mentioned the kind of troublesome thoughts that make us worry and fret and suffer. Such thoughts are a topic in their own right.

UNWANTED IMAGES

Let us try an experiment now, Reader, you and I. Your task is a simple one: Don't think of a white bear. Easy enough. You weren't thinking of one before, after all. So put down this book and look away and, for a minute, don't think of a white bear.

Did you try it? How did you do? If you're like most of us, you found the thought of a white bear returning despite your best efforts. After all, to keep the task going you had to say to yourself, "I mustn't think of a white bear"—but if you do that, then you *are* thinking of a white bear, right?

Unwanted images—images that we wish would not come to mind, but do—are not rare, at least in this society. Sometimes the intrusion of these thoughts is only mildly annoying or even humorous. I'm having a bit of trouble right now, in fact, thinking about what I'm writing because a line of music keeps running through my head (the march from Act II of *La Boheme,* if you're

Trouble is, a guy tries to shove it out of his head. That don't work. What you got to do is kind of welcome it.

—JOHN STEINBECK,
The Winter of Our Discontent

curious). But the consequences are not always trivial. For one who has "quit smoking," the *thought* of smoking may come to mind with such pesky insistence, again and again, that it becomes unbearable and leads to relapse. (Your author knows!) Persistent thoughts of a broken romance may escalate to a severe depression. In the extreme, such thoughts may be so upsetting or interfering as to be called *obsessions,* which we may think of as compulsive thoughts analogous to compulsive actions (pp. 251–53).

Now the natural thing to do, when an unwanted thought intrudes, is to try to make it go away directly by pushing it out of mind. But Daniel Wegner, who has studied this kind of thought control extensively, cautions us that such thought suppression may *not* be a good idea.[13]

Before looking at Wegner's work, we must make a distinction. It is tempting to identify such "pushing out of mind" with Freud's concept of *repression* (pp. 214–15). We should resist the temptation, for several reasons. First, if the notion of a white bear were repressed in Freud's sense, this would mean that it would be pushed entirely out of consciousness, so deep that it would never come to mind spontaneously. But it does—that's the problem! Second, Freud thought of repression as itself an unconscious mental act, so that we would not only forget about white bears, but also forget that we had forgotten about them. Clearly that is not so. And third, there is some dispute about whether Freudian repression really occurs at all. But that we push thoughts out of mind—surely there is no dispute about that. So we use the term *suppression* to distinguish what we are talking about now from *repression* in the Freudian sense.

The White-Bear Experiments

But how do we study the process of thought suppression? Wegner and his colleagues approached the problem quite directly: Set up an unwanted thought to be suppressed, and see what happens to it.

In one experiment, each subject was isolated in a laboratory room, with a microphone and a button which, when pushed, rang a bell. For the first 5 minutes, the person was asked to speak into the microphone whatever thoughts came to mind—something like Freud's free association. Then, the person was asked to talk aloud as before, but *not* to think of a white bear. If the thought came to mind anyway, the person was to ring the bell and go on. Finally, the subjects were told that it was now okay to think about white bears, but to continue ringing the bell each time they did.

Of course, not to think of white bears proved a difficult task. Here is part of one subject's transcript (each asterisk shows a bell ring):

> Of course now the only thing I'm going to think about is a white bear. Okay, I mean it's hard to think that I can see a bell★ . . . and don't think about a white bear. Ummm, what was I thinking of before? See, if I think about flowers a lot★ . . . I'll

13. Wegner, 1989, 1992.

think about a white bear, it's impossible.★ I could ring this bell over and over★ and over★ and over★ and . . . a white bear★ . . . and okay . . . so, my fingernails are really bad, they . . . need to be painted because they . . . they're chipping at the ends . . . it's like I have to force myself to not think★ about the white bear. So, I also have this little brown freckle on my finger and I also have little sparklies★ all over my hands and neck from Halloween last night 'cause we got all dressed up. . . . And I'm trying to think of a million things to make me think about everything★ but a white bear and I keep thinking of it over★ and over★ and over★ and over. So . . . ummm, hey, look at this brown wall . . . I'm upset but . . . because (pause) but all I think about is white bear.★

In fact, though, subjects did have some success at thought suppression. They did ring the bell less than control subjects, who were told just to go ahead and think about white bears (Fig. 9-7). More interesting was what happened after the prohibition was lifted and the subjects were free to think about white bears. The thought showed a "rebound;" they actually thought about white bears *more often* than subjects who were free to think about them from the outset. Indeed, they appeared to think about such creatures more and more, not less and less, as time went by.

This rebound has been demonstrated many times; but why does it occur? One's first thought is again a Freudian one: The forbidden thought, denied access to consciousness, gathered more and more energy and pushed for expression all the harder, and so whooshed out in a rush when permitted to do so. Wegner takes a different view, a cognitive rather than a psychodynamic one. He sees it not as a matter of energy, but of *association*.

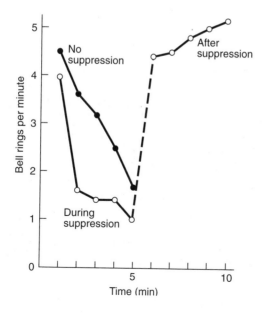

Figure 9-7 The white-bear experiment. Subjects succeed in suppressing white-bear thoughts ("suppression"), as compared with control subjects who are allowed to think about white bears ("no suppression"). But notice the lasting increase in white bear thoughts after the instructions to suppress are removed ("after suppression"). (Redrawn from Wegner, Schneider, Carter, and White, 1987.)

To see why, let us look more closely. What we have in this situation is—again!—our old friend the negative-feedback loop. When the forbidden thought is detected (input), some system is called into play (output) to make the unwanted thought go away (negative feedback). So we need an input device to detect the forbidden thought, and an output device to get rid of it.

Suppose then that the subject splits his mind, so to speak, into two parts, which we may call the "lookout" (to detect the thought) and the "bouncer" (to send it away). The bouncer does the actual pushing out when the forbidden thought occurs; at other times, the bouncer can relax. But the lookout must detect the forbidden thought whenever it does occur, so as to summon the bouncer; and so the lookout must be vigilant *all the time,* ever watchful for an appearance of the dreaded white-bear image.

But to be vigilant is to know what one is watching for—one has a kind of internal *search image* that represents the forbidden thought. The lookout must be forever asking, "Has a white-bear thought appeared?"—and that, of course, *is* a white-bear thought. In a word: If one is actively suppressing the thought of a white bear, one is only keeping it from the front of one's mind. In the back of one's mind (Freud's preconscious), where the lookout is posted, the thought is there all the time—precisely *because* the lookout must watch for it in order to suppress it.

What about the bouncer? To move the thought out of the focus of consciousness, he replaces the thought with something else—e.g., the chipped fingernails, the Halloween costume, the brown wall. But, because the white bear is always prowling in the back of the mind, each of these "distractors" can become *associated with* the white-bear image. Each becomes, so to speak, a reminder of white bears. So, when the ban is lifted, the subject may think of the costume and be reminded of the bear, see the fingernails and be reminded of the bear, see the brown wall and be reminded of the bear, . . . No wonder the bear comes so often to mind!

But how can we test this idea? It has been tested in many ways, but let's look at two examples.

First, think again about the lookout. That part of the mind, we said, must be on the alert for white bears all the time. If we increase the amount of work the mind must do, then less cognitive capacity (or psychic energy?) should be available to the lookout, and suppression should fail more often. This happens. In one study, subjects were asked either to suppress or not to suppress a particular word (e.g., *house*) while performing some other task as well. If they performed that second task under time pressure (increasing the cognitive load), then the unwanted word popped into mind more often than if time pressure was absent (Fig. 9-8).[14] So, if the "backs of our minds" are kept busy with something else, they can't be as vigilant about white bears!

What about the bouncer? The argument, again, is: (1) If the bear image does come to mind, the bouncer boots it out by replacing it with other

14. Wegner and Erber, 1992.

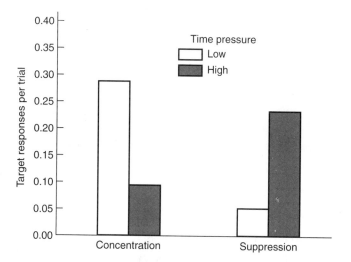

Figure 9-8   Left bars: In subjects concentrating on a class of target words, high cognitive load (high time pressure) interfered with concentration. However (right bars) in subjects trying to *suppress* the thought of those words, high cognitive load interfered with the suppression! (From Wegner and Erber, 1992.)

thoughts; but (2) such "other thoughts" will then become associated with white bears; and (3) the other thoughts are usually drawn from stimuli in the immediate environment (e.g., a brown wall). It follows that such a simple matter as *moving to a different room,* before the last phase of the experiment, should reduce the rebound that otherwise occurs then. And it does. Notice that the Freudian theory of rebound—a buildup of pressure behind the white-bear image itself—does not predict this result and cannot easily explain it.

The Red-Sports-Car Experiment

The idea can be tested in another way. The suggestion, again, is that rebound occurs because a variety of irrelevant cues (fingernails, brown walls) are now associated with white bears—because subjects switch now to one, now to another, such cue when the bear comes to mind. If so, then we ought to be able to reduce the rebound if only *one* irrelevant idea is substituted for the bear image. To test this idea, the original white-bear experiment was repeated, but with a difference. In one condition, the subjects were asked not to think about white bears as before. In another condition they were told that if the white bear did come to mind, they should switch their mental focus to the image of a red sports car.

Focus on the red sports car did not much affect the frequency of white-bear thoughts while subjects were suppressing (Fig. 9-9, middle bars). But it did greatly reduce the rebound increase in white-bear thoughts after the period of suppression (Fig. 9-9, right-hand bars). Presumably, by focusing on a red sports car and nothing else, these subjects were prevented from linking the white-bear idea to a variety of cues.

There may be some everyday parallels to this finding. "Items that children seek for 'security' [such as "security blankets"] could have the same palliative influence we found with the [red sports car]. . . . Some people report . . . that

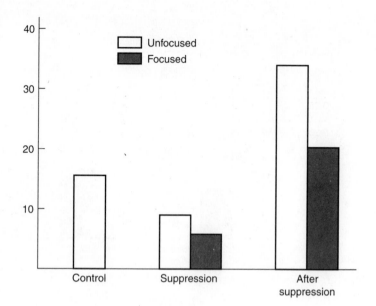

Figure 9-9 The red sports car experiment. See text for explanation. (Data from Wegner, Schneider, et al., 1987.)

when they have an unwanted thought, they pray or think of God. This . . . like turning to thoughts of a [red sports car], may produce long-term advantages in the avoidance of the unwanted thought."[15]

Secrets

Wegner has extended these ideas to another domain that at first looks quite different, but turns out not to be—the domain of keeping secrets.

If the white bear is a *thought* to be suppressed, a secret is *speech* to be suppressed. Someone tells us something interesting, X, but also says, "Now, that's a secret. You mustn't tell anyone else—especially Waldo!"

What should happen? We now give the lookout an assignment: "Are we about to speak of X? If so, we must inhibit that act—especially if Waldo is around!" But then the thought that we *might* say X will be always in the back of our minds, especially in Waldo's presence. And that thought will become associated with all the features of each situation in which it occurs—especially Waldo's presence! The very act of suppressing that speech increases the danger that it might pop out accidentally.

Let us see what havoc this could play. Suppose Mary has a relationship with Harry. Suppose it must be kept secret, for whatever reason—maybe she has a spouse, Barry, who would not be pleased about it. So she must be constantly on guard against speaking of her relationship with Harry—which means that Harry will be ever in the back of her mind, triggering the lookout.

15. Wegner, 1987, p. 69.

Now suppose Mary takes one further step: Realizing that Harry is always in the back of her mind, she draws a conclusion from this. She says to herself, "Gosh, I find that Harry comes to mind over and over again. I want to tell everyone about him—but of course I can't. But I keep thinking about him all the time. You know . . . I must be just wild about Harry!" She may, in a word, conclude that she's madly in love with Harry, because he's on her mind all the time—when in fact he is on her mind all the time only because he must be kept secret.★ Without the secrecy, Mary might not be much interested in Harry at all. Indeed, she might even see that he's kind of a Jerk (p. 356). Wegner calls this sort of thing a "synthetic obsession."

In the extreme case, Mary might divorce Barry and marry Harry. And *then,* now that he isn't a secret any more, she may find that she seldom gives him a thought. She may even recognize his jerkhood now, as she didn't before. The result could well be that Mary, Barry, *and* Harry are all less happy than before— and all because of a "mustn't tell." One wonders how often it happens.

Does all this sound farfetched? It turns out that at least a mild case of it can actually be created experimentally. In one study, mixed-sex couples (assigned so that the partners were strangers to each other) competed in a card game with other couples.[16] These experimental couples were asked to "engage in non-verbal communication with their feet and ankles under the table,"[17] that is, to play "footsie." But in one condition, the game of footsie was kept a secret; in the other, it was not. Just that much was enough to make a difference! At the end of the game, the secret-footsie players reported themselves more attracted to each other than did non-secret players or couples who did not play footsie at all. Secrecy itself, in other words, enhanced how attracted the subjects felt toward each other—even after only a very brief acquaintance with, shall we say, minimal contact.

A Look Backward

Looking back over these ideas, what advice can we give a person who is in the grip of recurrent unwanted thoughts? Let us suppose a romance has broken up. Harry is obsessed and depressed about his lost one, and painful thoughts of his loss well up again and again. In part, that's because Mary is embedded in a rich and dense network of *associations.* Mention of a coastal town where the two spent a weekend, sight of the telephone on which he used to chat with her, hearing a word that they used as a private joke—any of these may bring all the memories crashing back. If the relationship was secret, it might be that the

---

★This may sound very strange. Can't Mary just look inside herself and *see* whether she's in love with Harry or not? There are complications here (pp. 484–88), but the short answer is: Not necessarily. We do draw conclusions about our own mental states from observing our own behavior, just as we draw conclusions about others' minds from observing theirs (Bem, 1967).

16. Wegner, Lane, and Dimitri, 1992.
17. Wegner, 1992, p. 198.

obsession is so haunting in part *because* it was secret (a synthetic obsession). But that's little comfort to Harry now.

If Wegner is right, one thing we can say is: To suppress the thought directly, replacing it with whatever comes to mind each time, is not a good idea. It will likely prolong the sadness, (1) by keeping Mary around in the back of Harry's mind, because the lookout must look out for her continuously, and (2) by adding still more everyday cues that now become associated with Mary, because the bouncer switches to each of them in turn when she does come to mind.

Instead, Harry might try the red-sports-car technique: Fix on some *one* distracting thought, and think of that every time Mary comes to mind. One trouble is that Harry may find it unpleasant to treat such warm memories in such a mechanical way. And that may be just as well. As Wegner says, "We can become mean and heartless" if thoughts of another person are flipped out of mind like empty soda cans—even (especially?) if the flipping is effective.[18]

In the end, the best thing for Harry to do might be to "kind of welcome it," in Steinbeck's words: to go ahead and think about Mary when she comes to mind. Eventually there will be a certain habituation (pp. 239–41) which will reduce the sadness of the thoughts. (Time heals, we say, and perhaps that is how it does it.) Meanwhile, it will hurt, that's true; but the alternatives might hurt even more, as we have seen. And even the pain is not all bad. If Harry can feel that strongly about another human being, well, perhaps it can please him to know that.

One final point. At the end of the last section, we spoke of pushing out of mind our worries about how we might do something poorly, and focusing instead on rehearsing doing it well. Are we now taking back that advice?

Not really, for there is a difference. We mentally rehearse a good performance in the few minutes we have, and then we go out and make the free throw, or give an eloquent speech, or sing the song well. After that, we may indeed have rebound thoughts of how we *might have* messed up; but so what? It's over and we didn't mess up, and that's what counts. In short, active thought suppression might be very good for getting troublesome thoughts out of our way until a job is done. It is over the long term, as a way of dealing with *recurring* unwanted thoughts, that it is likely to boomerang.

SCHEMAS

Earlier, we mentioned that an image need not be a picture in the head. Indeed, we can go further: We use inner representations of events or things, or classes of such, that *could not* be as specific as that.

18. Wegner, 1987, p. 74.

For example, we know what a cat is. Seeing some animal for the first time, we have no trouble deciding whether it is or is not a cat. Do we do this by checking it against a "picture" of a cat in our heads? We couldn't—because no such picture could match both a white cat *and* a black cat. But we can easily judge the catness/non-catness of either a black or a white candidate.

Our knowledge of what a cat is, therefore, must leave many details (like color) unspecified. An abstract bit of knowledge of this sort is called a *schema*.

Plans, too, can be schematic rather than specific. Consider how someone can say, "Let's go eat!" We may agree to the suggestion even before we decide just what to eat or where. We have no specific images in mind, but only the abstract framework: Somewhere or other, we shall seek something or other to eat. The details are unspecified.[19]

Let us look more closely.

Schemas and Movements

Consider a basketball player taking a shot. He can throw the ball at the basket from any of an indefinite number of positions on the court; and each position requires a different set of movements if the shot is to succeed. The farther the player is from the basket, the harder he must throw the ball, and the more arch—angle of the toss relative to the floor—he must put into the throw.

Now a very experienced player *could,* perhaps, learn the specific throwing movements to be associated with each possible position on the court. But that obviously would entail a very long period of training and a formidable load on memory. It would be more efficient for the player to learn a set of *relationships*—for example, ones that specified the relation between distance from the basket and (1) the force and (2) the amount of arch, required for success. Knowing those relationships, and knowing one's distance from the basket right now, one could *compute* the needed force and angle and, in turn, establish these as goals for the muscle-control systems lower in the hierarchy. The internal representations of these relationships would constitute the schemas that in turn make up the higher-order motor schema, "skill at sinking baskets."

That one may learn such relations has been shown many times.[20] In one experiment, children practiced tossing bean bags at a target with their eyes closed. Some children practiced at a distance of 3 feet from the target. Another group of children practiced sometimes at 2 feet and sometimes at 4 feet away. Then on test trials, everybody threw from 3 feet away. Of the two groups, the variable-practice group performed more accurately, even though they had had *no* practice at throwing from that distance before!

How could they do so well at a task they hadn't practiced? The practice they did obtain, at throwing from a variable distance, must have allowed them to learn the *relation* between distance from the target and the kind of tossing

19. Mook, 1990.
20. For review see Mazur, 1994.

movements required to hit it. It is as if they had learned an equation—the schema—which related distance from the target to the required force of the toss, for example. Then, for the new distance, they solved the equation to compute the force required now (Fig. 9-10). Or if they did not do exactly that, they did something that had the same effect. And they did it on the spot, rapidly, and quite unconsciously—the odds are that the kids could not have told us, if asked, just how they had accomplished this feat.

If all this seems like an impossibly difficult cognitive achievement, be assured that feats of computation as difficult, or more, can be accomplished by much smaller brains than ours. Honey bees, for example, can navigate by taking their bearings from the sun. Having found a food source and returned to the hive, the bee can find the food again by flying off at the appropriate angle relative to the sun. This means that at minimum, the bee must note the sun's angle (so many degrees to my left) on the homeward flight, and from it compute the appropriate angle (so many degrees to my right) for the outward flight. (The bee does not fly home backward!)

But the navigational achievement is even more remarkable than this. The sun's position in the sky (as seen by an earthling) changes over time. What if time goes by between coming home and flying out again—and if during that time the bee is inside the hive, in darkness? (If this does not happen spontaneously, an experimenter can make it happen.) What happens is that the bee *corrects* the angle for its departure, so that it is appropriate to the sun's new position given the time that has elapsed.

Figure 9-10 Practice at throwing from 2 feet and from 4 feet enables a child to learn the relation between distance and force required. The necessary force for 3 feet can then be calculated.

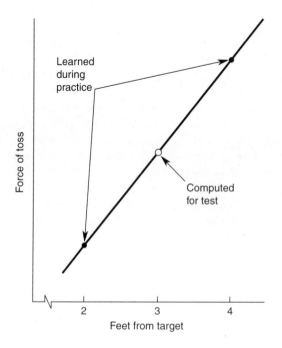

Of course the bee does not literally solve equations the way you or I would—we give it no pencil and paper, and it has not had the math prerequisites—but something happens in the brain of the bee that has the same effect. And when we consider that the entire bee is substantially smaller than the brain of a rat, much less a human, we must be impressed yet again with how much Nature can do with how (relatively) little.

Higher-Order Schemas: Lattice Hierarchies Revisited

Schemas, including how-to schemas or plans, may exist at various levels. For example, as members of this society, we have a sandwich-making schema; that is, we know how to make a sandwich (a cheese sandwich, a roast-beef sandwich, or whatever). That schema breaks down into lower-order ones (plans) that set specific goals and fill in the details: Find the bread and extract two slices of it; find the spread and spread it on the bread; find whatever-it-is to put in the middle; find the lettuce—cancel; this is to be a grilled-cheese sandwich, so no lettuce—and so on.

But we could do all these things for any of a number of reasons. We may of course "run" the sandwich-making schema in response to our own hunger. Or, suppose a Significant Other calls to us, "Would you make me a sandwich, please?" Then we may run the same schema as a sub-unit within a quite different higher-order schema, one that says, "Be nice (within reason) to Significant Others." Or if we are restaurant workers, again we make the sandwich, but this time within a "doing our job" schema, which may in turn be part of a "breadwinner" schema, and so on. We have our familiar lattice hierarchy (Fig. 9-11).

Even with just this much, there is room for a formidable degree of complexity. Consider this scenario:

The breadwinner comes home, tired from a hard day at the office. She calls to her spouse, "Honey, would you make me a sandwich, please?" But the spouse is tired too, from cleaning and feeding the baby and changing diapers and shopping and preparing dinner. . . . What shall he do?

Well, the sandwich-making schema is a sub-routine within the "Be nice . . ." schema, and also, perhaps, within the "homemaker's duties" schema. For these and other reasons, the husband may say "Sure," and do it. But all this may clash with another schema, "Chores should be divided equally between spouses," which in turn is nested within "People should treat each other equitably." If that pathway is the more available one right now, the spouse could well react with "Hey, make your own sandwich!" with escalation a distinct possibility.

Interviews with American homemakers (all female in this case) show that they can feel pulled both ways by just such conflicting schemas:

There have been times when I felt it was very unfair . . . Before we got our washer and dryer we had so many arguments over the laundromat . . . Because he didn't

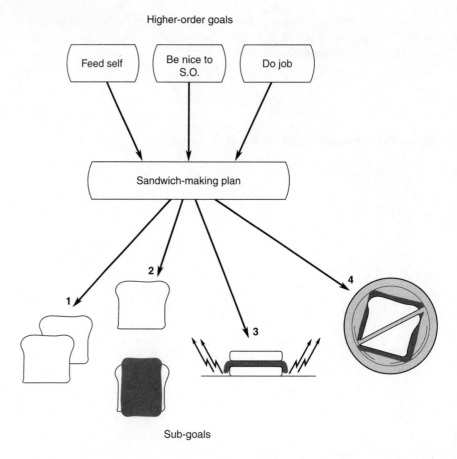

Figure 9-11 The sandwich-making plan may be called into play by different higher-order goals on different occasions.

want to go do laundry with me . . . [So] I left his laundry and I took mine. I said, "You wash your own. If you can't go with me to help me do it then you can wash your own." And that changed right away.[21]

But on another occasion, the same woman said:

But I do it because I know if I don't do it, it won't get done. . . .[22] And somebody at work's going to say, "God, his wife must not care about his clothes." Because people naturally assume that the wife does these things. . . . I just don't want them to think I'm not doing what I should. Again it's doing my wifely duties.[23]

One other point. Did you notice, Dear Reader, how the crafty author introduced a half-twist into the sandwich-making scenario? Did you do a men-

21. Quinn, 1992, p. 96.
22. Ibid., p. 97.
23. Ibid., p. 100.

tal double take while reading it? We will return to such matters when we talk about default values and schema-driven inference (pp. 409–11).

Scripts and Players

Our schemas extend beyond actions and things or classes of things, to events, sequences, and characters. Schemas that sketch out sequences of events are sometimes called *scripts*.[24] For example, suppose we have decided to go to a restaurant to eat. We have a schema—a restaurant script—that tells us, in general, what to expect. We will enter, order food, eat it, pay for it, and then leave. Details are unspecified; we might pay the waiter or waitress, or a cashier; but the general sequence of events is blocked out in our minds in advance.

And scripts are performed, or otherwise acted out, by *players* that we can identify using Player schemas. Thus in the restaurant script, we know that we might encounter either a Waiter or a Waitress, though possibly neither (it might be a cafeteria), and perhaps, but not necessarily, a Host or Hostess. Of course we can readily identify a player who plays a more specific role—the Surly Waiter, for example—just as we can identify the Bad Guy in a Western movie. And we know how to deal with surly waiters (speak firmly and skimp on the tip), just as we know that a Bad Guy, somehow or other, will get his comeuppance in the end. Many of our stereotypes or slang terms identify Players: the Bookworm, the Sexpot, the Male Chauvinist, the Man-hater, the Crusty Old Country Doctor, ...

Or: Suppose we meet a professor we have never encountered before. Still, we know a great deal about her, because we know about professors and she is cast in the Professor role (Fig. 9.12). She will probably lecture or lead discussions, suggest readings, and turn in some evaluation of students' performances at term's end. She will probably not write us a speeding ticket, or jump up on a table and sing *Melancholy Baby*. In short, we know quite a lot about a professor before we observe anything about her. The Professor schema gives us that information.

Scripts and players, like other schemas, may have the familiar hierarchical organization. This stranger we've just met clicks into the schema Professor, and also the schema Woman; and both of these are components of the schema Person. There are more restricted sub-schemas in turn; if someone tells us, "Professor Bunzoff teaches a really stiff course," that triggers the Hard Professor schema, and tells us a great deal right there.

But let's look at an actual Script with real Players. Anthropologist Dorothy Holland followed the college careers of a number of women, with particular attention to their adventures within romantic relationships.[25] Her data suggested that there was in fact an identifiable Script that such relationships followed. In the case of heterosexual relationships, we have a Guy and a Girl (the Players). The script goes like this (as seen by the Girl):

24. Shank and Abelson, 1977.
25. Holland, 1992.

Figure 9-12 By classifying persons or events—that is, by assimilating them to schemas—we make available our prior knowledge about persons or events of that kind.

1. The Guy and the Girl are drawn to one another.
2. The Guy learns and appreciates the Girl's unique qualities.
3. Sensitive to her desires, the Guy shows his affection by treating her well; for example, he takes her places she likes and shows that he appreciates her uniqueness as a person.
4. She in turn shows her affection and interest and allows the relationship to become more intimate.

The motives and rewards also are schematized. The relationship provides the rewards of intimacy, and it validates the attractiveness of both Girl and Guy.

Since the details are unspecified, this Script leaves room for ad-libs. For example, if the Guy's attractiveness or prestige is lower than the Girl's, he compensates by treating her especially well.

But even with a well-crafted script, performances do not all run smoothly. Some actors flub their lines, or simply can't handle their parts. Consider the female who is so unfortunate as to meet up with a Jerk—or the unfortunate male who is one. A Jerk is

a type who is neither attractive *nor* sensitive to women. He cannot compensate for his low prestige by treating the women especially well. He's too stupid or too "out of it" to discern her special qualities and anticipate her desires. . . . He may be so insensitive, in fact, that he cannot even tell that she dislikes him. Because he cannot "take the hint," he will not leave her alone and thus he becomes more and more irritating as time goes by.[26]

26. Holland, 1992, p. 66.

Now this description of the Jerk comes from interview data with women at two colleges in the American South. But at a third college on the East Coast, the present author has replicated parts of Holland's study, and finds the Jerk a sadly familiar player at that institution too. Indeed, my informants are divided as to whether a Jerk is even worse than a Creep. But he's pretty bad, either way.

Schema-Driven Affect

Jerks are unpleasant to deal with—they can't help it, but neither can we. We don't like them. Schemas, then, may call forth emotion or *affect,* in which case we speak of *schema-driven affect.*★

If we are told that Harry is a jerk, we may dislike Harry before we have even met him; the schema ("He's a jerk") drives the affect ("I don't/won't like him").

Such things as accidental resemblance can bring a schema to mind, triggering its emotional component. We may take an instant dislike to a professor because she reminds us of old Miss Phacemask whom we so hated in the second grade. A trivial matter, do we say? President Harry S Truman, who was not usually the most trusting of men, placed a great deal of trust in the leader of the Soviet Union, Josef Stalin. His private correspondence tells us why: Stalin reminded Truman of a man who had befriended Truman when he was younger! Stalin's appearance triggered the schema for the old friend, and its affective component—"trustworthy"—was then applied to the Russian dictator.[27]

Attitudes, Values, and World Views

Schemas can be even broader than in these examples, and they can be linked together in even more complex networks. Indeed, the schema concept may help us understand how specific actions make contact with the attitudes and values that characterize both individuals and cultures.[28]

Among orthodox Hindus in India, for example, it is taboo for a widow to eat fish. We can suppose that such a widow has a fish-eating schema—she knows how to eat fish—and that this schema is a member of a higher-order schema, "ways of feeding oneself." But now her status as a widow places that plan within another abstract schema, "actions that are forbidden." So the plan will be inhibited and not expressed.

For people raised in American society, it may be hard to realize just how strong the taboo can be. Part of what makes it so strong is that the "taboo" schema links this action with very many others, to generate a dense and emo-

---

★Fiske, 1982. The term *affect* (a noun when used this way; accent on the first syllable) refers to emotions or feeling states, as of pleasure or displeasure.

27. May, 1973.

28. D'Andrade and Strauss, 1992.

tion-laden network of associations. It is instructive to compare the answers of Americans and Indians to a series of questions about that taboo, asked by a team of anthropologists, Richard Shweder and his colleagues.[29] First, an American respondent:

> Q. Is the widow's behavior wrong? A: No. She can eat fish if she wants to.
>
> Q. Is it a sin? A: No.
>
> Q. What if no one knew this had been done? Would it be wrong then? A: It is not wrong in private or public.
>
> Q. Would it be best if everyone in the world followed the rule that it is all right for a widow to eat fish? A: Yes. People should be free to eat fish if they want to. Everyone has that right.
>
> Q. In India, it is considered wrong for a widow to eat fish. Would India be a better place if it was considered all right for a widow to eat fish if she wants to? A: Yes. That may be their custom but she should be free to decide if she wants to follow it.
>
> Q. What if most people in the United States wanted to change the rule so that it would be considered wrong for a widow to eat fish? Would it be okay to change it? A: No. You can't order people not to eat fish. They have a right to eat it if they want.
>
> Q. Do you think a widow who eats fish should be stopped from doing that or punished in some way? A: No!

For a typical Indian respondent, the dialogue might go like this:

> Q. Is the widow's behavior wrong? A: Yes. Widows should not eat fish, meat, onions or garlic, or any "hot" foods.
>
> Q. Is it a sin? A: Yes, a great sin. She will suffer greatly if she eats fish.
>
> Q. What if no one knew this had been done? Would it be wrong then? A: What difference does it make? It is wrong. A widow should spend her time seeking salvation—seeking to be united with the soul of her husband. Hot foods will distract her. They will stimulate her sexual appetite. She will lose her sanctity. She will want sex and behave like a whore.
>
> Q. Would it be best if everyone in the world followed the rule that widows should not eat fish? A: That would be best. A widow's devotion is to her deceased husband—who should be treated like a god. She will offend his spirit if she eats fish.
>
> Q. In the United States, widows eat fish all the time. Would the United States be a better place if widows stopped eating fish? A: Definitely, it would be a better place. Perhaps American widows would stop having sex and marrying other men.

29. Shweder, Mahapatra, and Miller, 1990; adapted here.

Q. What if most people in India wanted to change the rule so that it would be considered all right for widows to eat fish. Would it be okay to change the rule? A: No. It is wrong for a widow to eat fish. Hindu dharma—truth—forbids it.

Q. Do you think a widow who eats fish should be stopped from doing that or punished in some way? A: She should be stopped. But the sin will live with her and she will suffer for it.

Looking over these dialogues, we see at once that we are dealing with larger issues than fish-eating here. The Hindu schema network links eating fish with sexual matters, the nature of marital obligations (e.g., toward the husband's spirit), the nature of the marital relationship itself (see below)—and much besides. One schema is linked closely with many others, both within and across levels.

For an American, many misfortunes "just happen." They are seen as matters of chance. For the Hindu, events are caused and the universe is just.[30] A misfortune (such as becoming a widow) is a punishment for sin—if not in this life, then in a previous one—and a chance to expiate it. And sins will be punished (the widow will suffer greatly if she eats fish), again in another life if not in this one.

Look again. At first glance, another fundamental difference in outlook between the two cultures seems to be this: The American sees the taboo as a matter of *social convention*—a widow's eating fish is considered wrong because a society calls it wrong. It would be okay, nay better, for society to change that rule. To the Hindu, for a widow to eat fish *is* wrong, and that is a *fact*—no matter what any society says. Would it be okay for society to change the rule? No. For a society to call it right would not make it right, any more than we can make a circle a square by calling it one.★

But if we look more closely, we see that the difference is more subtle than that. Some Americans, too, insist that certain actions are wrong *in fact,* whatever society's rules may be; some object to abortion on such grounds, for example. And even in the above dialogues, the American answers imply that certain moral rules hold as matters of fact, though these are unstated because they are taken for granted. It is assumed that individuals have a "natural right" to do as they please, provided they treat others fairly and do not hurt them. And this "right" articulates with the American marriage-and-family schema. Marriage is something like a contract: Two people freely enter into a relationship between equals, retaining their "natural rights" as individuals.

For Hindus, the taken-for-granted moral principles do not center around the *rights* that individuals possess, but around the *obligations* that fall on them as members of a group. Now in fact, that kind of schema is not unfamiliar to

30. Shweder, 1991.

★A legislative body in the United States, not so long ago, solemnly passed a bill fixing the value of *pi* at 3.0.

Americans. Shweder et al. suggest this interesting analogy: Compare the Hindu marriage not to a contract between equals, but to a military organization.*

Most Hindu marriages are arranged by the parents, just as a soldier may be drafted into the military with little to say about it. As a soldier he has obligations to his group; and these, whether he likes it or not, take precedence over his individual rights—just as a Hindu wife's obligations to her husband (even to his departed spirit) supersede her own likes and dislikes. Punishment for shirking one's obligations may be very severe. If a Hindu woman leaves the house without her husband's permission, he may think it quite proper to beat her— just as a soldier who leaves his base without his superior's permission risks a very unpleasant experience. Finally, the relationship between soldier and officer is *not* a relationship between equals—far from it! Each has obligations to the other, as do a Hindu wife and husband. But in both cases, who gives the orders, and who takes them, is not in question.

That explanation may not lead my Western readers to *like* the Hindu outlook any better, but it may convince them that it is not bizarre or unintelligible. It's a matter of what model, or metaphor, or schema, one applies to marriage: is it like a contract, or like a soldier's duties? It makes a great difference.

All that, from a "simple" taboo against widows' eating fish? Yes; that is the point. As we trace lines of association and embeddedness, we find the taboo embedded in a rich and dense network that takes us to very abstract and general schemas indeed. These are schemas that specify attitudes, values, even world views: the nature of morality and of the soul, what a family is, even what it means to be a person within a society.

Looks Backward and Forward: Schemas and Motives

Let us review what we have learned about schemas, and let's also see more explicitly how they may have *motivational* properties.

Schemas are structures of general knowledge—knowledge about *kinds* of events, persons, and things. Our professor schema tells us something about professors—not just this or that professor, but professors in general. Similarly for restaurants in general, Jerks in general, generals in general, and so on. Schematic knowledge would also include our knowledge of how to make a sandwich or change a tire (any tire), and of the relation between (say) distance from a target and force required to hit it, so that from any particular distance we can estimate the force we need to apply. And it would include, if we are orthodox Hindus, our knowledge that it is wrong for a widow to eat fish—not this or that widow, but widows in general.

But how do schemas take on motivational properties? How do they affect not just what we know or believe, but what we do?

---

*Shweder et al. draw this analogy only in passing; the present elaboration of it is my own, and it is my fault if I misunderstand it.

It obviously is not automatic. You and I may know how to make a sandwich, without being inclined to make one right now. A group of American workers agreed that, in general, "getting ahead" is a good thing. The decisions they actually made, however, had little to do with "getting ahead"—they might actually work against this—but they did fit the schema, "being a good breadwinner."[31] Some schemas, in other words, are more closely coupled to action than others.

But how are they coupled to action at all? Well, some schemas specify consequences—analogous to reinforcers and punishers—directly: This is what will happen if we do such and such.[32] "A sandwich would taste good right now." "My friends and/or in-laws will look down on me if I let my husband's clothes go unwashed." "The widow will suffer if she eats fish, in this life or a later one." In all these cases, the imagined consequence is affectively or emotionally charged (schema-driven affect): *"Wouldn't that be* [nice or awful]!"

Actions also can be linked not to consequences, but to other emotionally laden schemas. One may believe in general that *fairness* is a good thing. Then, moving from that general schema to the specific instance, we may get to "It's unfair for her to ask me to make her a sandwich on top of everything else," and thence down to the specific plan, "Here's how to refuse"—and doing it! Or, a belief such as "Good spouses accept certain duties" may be in control at the moment; and by way of "Sandwich-making is one such duty," we could work down to activation of the sandwich-making plan. Here we look forward to the relation between motivation and cognition (Chap. 11) and between motivation and emotion (Chap. 12).

All this aside, cognitive theories of motivation point to a close interaction between *motives* and *beliefs* in determining action—and schemas are important determinants of beliefs. If we ask our motivational question, "Why did he do that?" a cognitivist's reply will often be of this sort: "He did X because he believed Y. And why did he believe Y? Because . . . ," and the schema concept will figure in the explanation that follows. All this will be clearer after we have had a look at *decision theory* (Chap. 10).

Thus, schemas can affect action in ways we might consider not motivational, but cognitive—but this is a difficult line to draw (Chap. 11). For example: Do we believe that we are competent at handling romantic relationships? Whether we seek such relationships can depend on the answer.[33] This looks forward to such issues as self-efficacy (pp. 563–64) and helplessness (pp. 564–65). Or: what alternatives do we consider when deciding what action to take? Do we consider alternatives at all? If we believe that some one action is necessary or inevitable or both, we may "just do it" without consideration. That looks forward to such topics as the framing of decisions (pp. 395–97).

31. Strauss, 1992.
32. D'Andrade, 1992.
33. Holland, 1992.

All told, the schema concept is a busy interface among three broad domains of psychological inquiry: motivation, cognition, and action. We shall meet it again many times.

SUMMARY

The basic question of purposive behavior is: How can we get the future into the present? The cognitive answer is: We represent, or imagine, the future state now. An image can be thought of as an internal process that represents, without necessarily resembling, some state of affairs.

Images can guide goal-directed behavior in a number of ways. Actions can be corrected by correcting a mismatch between the actual effect of the action and its intended, or imagined, effect; the imagined effect is sometimes called an *efference copy.* Or one can imagine an object that is (or could be) located in the environment, even though it is not there to be perceived now. *Cognitive maps* specify *where* it is. *Search images* specify *what* it is. The literature shows overwhelmingly that even sub-human animals are capable of such cognitive feats; this literature includes the work on response-reinforcer expectancies, described in the previous chapter.

Plans are organized, hierarchical sequences of goal-directed actions. We can think of them as *cognitive programs,* analogous to cognitive maps. They may take hold of behavior by specifying sub-goals, so that the resulting sub-plans are activated in sequence, each until its goal is met as registered by the perceptual systems; this gives us our familiar joint control by internal factors (the plan) and external ones (the present situation). In other cases, though, the sequence and the timing of actions may all be "pre-programmed" within the plan, and run off without reference to the external environment.

Imagery has been put to practical use in a variety of contexts. In desensitization therapy, a way of treating phobias, an image of the feared object or situation is made a CS for a relaxation response. Or we can represent (imagine) the intended outcomes of actions, as in goal-setting. We can also practice responses in our imagination rather than in the real world, with good effect (mental rehearsal).

Some images are unwanted. Obsessive thoughts, fears, and regrets may intrude insistently into our minds, to distress us or distract us from the task at hand. The natural tendency is to try to push them out of mind; but, ironically, this can make them persist all the more, for two reasons. First, some part of our minds must be on the lookout for them; and so, by this very watchfulness, they are held in the backs of our minds. Second, if we think the unwanted thought, and banish it by thinking of something else, that "something else" may become associated with the unwanted thought and so be added to the cues that can trigger it. Thus active thought suppression, or active speech suppression as in keeping secrets, can backfire.

Schemas are internal representations of *kinds* of things, persons, places, or events; they are skeletal knowledge structures, in which details are left unspecified, to be filled in by particular situations. Thus, because we know something about what professors in general are like, we know something about a particular professor even before we meet her if we know that she is one.

In the case of movements, a schema may consist of our knowledge of certain relationships. For example, we may have learned by experience how much force must be applied to a basketball, from varying distances, to get it to the basket. Then, given a specific value of one variable (here is where we are on the court right now), we solve the schematic equation to calculate how much force this throw requires. This may sound overly complicated, but even a tiny brain can do something like it, as when a honeybee corrects for the sun's apparent movement over time in plotting its course to a supply of nectar.

Schemas exist at various levels and can enter into complex lattice hierarchies. Thus our knowledge of how to make a sandwich—our sandwich-making plan or schema—can be called into play in the service of any of a number of higher-order goals: feeding ourselves, earning a living, being nice to someone else, etc. Conflicts can occur at various levels, too; our schematic wish to treat others nicely may clash with our schematic wish to be treated fairly ourselves.

There can also be schemas, or *scripts,* for kinds of events or sequences and for kinds of persons *(players).* The script for a heterosexual romance, for example, involves two players, a Guy and a Girl, in our society; and we know certain things that, in general, are expected of each. Unfortunately, we have also some idea of what to expect from a Guy who plays his part ineptly—a Jerk.

Schemas can be linked in turn to emotion or *affect,* and activation of a schema may activate its emotional component (schema-driven affect). If we don't like professors and we learn that Joe is a professor, we may be prepared to dislike Joe before we ever meet him.

The network of associations among schemas may be extraordinarily rich. Our analysis of a "simple" orthodox Hindu taboo against a widow's eating fish showed that the taboo is related to very general conceptions of what marriage is, what a family is, and even what the universe is like—whether misfortunes just happen, or are just punishments when they do.

How do schemas influence action? Some specify rewarding or punishing consequences directly. Or they may be linked to other, emotion-laden schemas, such as our belief that fairness is a good thing or that acceptance of certain duties is part of being a good spouse. We see that an intimate relationship between motivation and cognition—between what we do and what we believe—is beginning to take shape.

Decision Theory

In the last chapter, we talked about how goal-directed actions are implemented once a goal has been decided upon. Now let us ask: How do we
decide what action to take, or what goal to seek?

Any action requires a decision (Fig. 10-1), if only between doing something and doing nothing. In this chapter, we will examine the *theory of decision-
making*.

If reinforcement theory is the heart of modern behaviorism, decision theory
is the mainstay of the cognitive approach to motivation. It is fundamental to
economic theorizing, too, so that it provides a point of convergence between
psychology and economics (pp. 369–71). It first arose from the mathematical
analysis of gambling games, so it has close historical ties to statistics and probability theory. And, as we shall see, it can be applied to a surprisingly wide range
of psychological phenomena.

A rich and important theory! Let us see how it works.

OVERVIEW OF DECISION THEORY

Consider how chess is played.* We examine the board and, for each move we
consider, we imagine the resulting position and our opponent's possible replies.
"If I go here and then here, he will counter with that and I'm busted"—that is,
I lose. That's no good. However: If I check *there* with the knight, his only legal

*If you don't play chess, think of checkers or tic-tac-toe; the principle is the same.

HAMBURGER	$2.35
CHEESEBURGER	$2.95
TUNA SALAD	$2.75
EGG SALAD	$2.65
OMELETTE	$3.10
BEEF STEW	$3.45
FISH FIL'	$3.1⁰

Figure 10-1 Any action involves a decision.

move is to put the king in the corner. Then my rook slithers down to the last rank, and it's checkmate. Isn't that nice! Do it.

Here we have decision theory in a nutshell. We imagine each possible action, consider its consequences, and perform the action whose expected or imagined consequences we most prefer.

We can do this on any of several levels. Given a goal, we can ask: Which of the possible actions is the best way to attain that goal? Here is a rat in a maze, and its goal is finding food: Should it turn left or right? Here we are in a strange town and our goal is to find our hotel: Should we turn left or right? My goal is to win this chess game: Shall I take the knight he offers or will it give him too strong an attack? In each case the question is: Which of the available actions is the best route to the goal?

Or, at a higher level, we can face the problem of comparing goals with each other. Stay home or go to a movie? Accept John's proposal of marriage, or George's, or neither? Become a psychologist, or go to law school?

But let's look at some specific examples.

Case 1: Outcomes Certain

Suppose we are in the presence of a very rich experimenter, whom we trust not to have any tricks up his sleeve. He says, "Would you like me to give you a dollar? Yes or no?" We will probably say "yes," for we get something of higher value for saying "yes" than for saying "no."

Similarly, if he says, "I'll give you either $10 if you shrug your shoulders, or $20 if you scratch your nose," we would of course scratch our nose. We choose the action whose outcome we most prefer. Simple.

Of course, in real life, choices can be very difficult even if outcomes are certain. Shall we take this apartment, with its pros and cons, or that apartment with *its* pluses and minuses? The problem is that each apartment is a mixed bag of the good and the bad. Indeed, it might be a good idea to "decompose" these alternatives, listing the features of each apartment, assigning positive and negative values to each feature, and adding them up to *calculate* which is the better choice.[1]—Or it might *not* be such a good idea, as we will see (pp. 394–95)!

But back to the rich experimenter.

Case 2. Outcomes Uncertain

Suppose he says this: "If you say 'yes,' I'll give you a dollar. If you say 'no,' either I'll give you $10 or I won't." Now we hesitate. We would rather have $10 than $1, so saying 'no' has higher possible value. But how likely is it that we will get that higher value? We would ask for more information; we need to know the *probabilities* of the outcomes, not just their values.

So the experimenter says, "Okay. If you say 'yes,' you get the dollar. If you say 'no,' I'll toss a coin: Heads I give you $10, tails I give you nothing." Do we take the dollar or go with the gamble? Probably we'd gamble. It might occur to us that a fifty-fifty chance at $10 would give us an *average* payoff, if the gamble were repeated many times, of $5 a game. That is the *expected value* of the gamble. Notice that it is not a matter of what we "expect" to happen, in the cognitive sense. It is a mathematical "expectation," and it means the *average* value that would result from a given choice if it were made many times in identical situations.

As exercises, let's consider some more things the experimenter might say. For each one, you should stop to calculate what your choice should be, before looking at the bottom of the next page for the correct choices.

1. "If you say 'yes,' you get $2. If 'no,' the odds are 1 in 10 that you'll get $5, and 9 in 10 that you'll get nothing."
2. In the previous example, make it $100 instead of $5.
3. In example 1, suppose the odds of getting $5 were fifty/fifty rather than 1 in 10.
4. "You can have $10 with probability 1/4, or $100 with probability 1/100. Which gamble would you prefer?"

---

1. See for example Dawes, 1988.

5. "If you like, you can play this game: Toss an honest die, and if it comes up 1 you get $30, otherwise nothing. Will you pay me $10 to play the game?"★

Rational Choices and Good Outcomes—Don't Confuse Them!

One more point before we move on. Suppose our friend Chris did accept the foolish gamble described in Choice 5. She paid her $10, rolled the die, and it did come up 1—so she received $30 on the deal. We're tempted to say, "Well, it wasn't such a dumb choice after all, right?"

Wrong. It was still a dumb thing to do. Look at it this way: If it were a smart thing to do, Chris should go on doing it, no? But if she did, she would become a money tree, paying on average $50 for every $30 she took in.

This may seem obvious, but in fact we do tend to judge decisions by their outcomes rather than by the rationality of the thought processes that entered into them. There may be important psychological reasons for this (compare the "representativeness heuristic," pp. 408–09), but it still is a mistake, and many injustices occur because of it. In an uncertain world, even a sound decision can turn out badly, while remaining sound.★★

A Case Study: Of Crime and Punishment

Now let's leave our experimenter and look at the real world. A few years ago, the New York legislature was outraged, as many legislatures are today, at the traffic in illegal drugs that was sweeping the cities. The lawmakers responded by greatly increasing the penalties for such trafficking, so that long, long prison sentences awaited those convicted of drug dealing.

What was the effect on the drug trade? Virtually none.

Why not? Probably because the penalties, harsh as they were, had little chance—low *probability*—of actually being imposed. Only a few dealers were arrested; of these, only a few were convicted and sentenced. And even a very high penalty, or *cost,* becomes a very low *expected cost* if it has a very low probability of occurring.

It is for reasons like this that many criminologists suggest that we try to increase, not the severity, but the certainty—the *probability*—of punishment for crimes. That would entail, not longer sentences, but such things as more police,

---

★Here is what you should have done:
 1. A return of $5 with probability 1/10 gives an expected return of $5 × 1/10 = $0.50. That is less than $2, so take the sure thing; say "yes."
 2. A return of $100 with probability 1/10 gives us an expected value of $10, much greater than $2. Take the gamble and say "no."
 3. The expected values are $5 × 1/2 = $2.50, as against $2. Again we should take the gamble.
 4. $100 × 1/100 = 1, whereas $10 × 1/4 = $2.50. Take the $10 gamble.
 5. Since the odds of rolling a 1 are 1 in 6, the expected return from the game is $30 × 1/6 = $5. Since that is much less than $10, you should refuse to pay $10 to play.

★★For discussion see Dawes, 1988; Redelmeier, Rozin, and Kahneman, 1993.

more courts (to reduce the clogging of the court system which encourages plea bargains), and the like. To do that, it is argued, would increase the *expected cost* of crime much more than would an increase in penalties that probably won't be imposed.

The Maximization Principle

Now let us generalize these ideas.

Decision theory assumes that we perform the action whose imagined outcome is of highest value to us, or, as we say, highest *utility*. Saying it another way, we choose among actions so as to *maximize utility*.★

Now for many decision problems, since the outcomes haven't happened yet, we cannot be certain what they will be. Then we have to consider how *likely* we think the various possible outcomes are. What we do, the theory says, is maximize the mathematically *expected utility*. For each action we might perform, we consider all the possible outcomes; for each outcome, weight (that is, multiply) its utility by its probability; and add the resulting products to get the *expected utility* of that action. Then we take the action whose expected utility is highest.

In many real-life situations, it is not clear that we do the kinds of explicit *calculations* that our earlier exercises permitted. Even then, however, decisions do depend on two factors that we feel could be represented by numbers: the utilities—how much do we like or dislike each possible outcome?—and the probabilities—how likely is it that a given outcome will follow a given action? If these probabilities are known, then numbers can represent them. When they are not known, still one usually has some idea of the likelihood of various events, and so we can speak of estimated probabilities—or, as they are called, *subjective probabilities*—as entering into our calculations. Multiplying the utility of each outcome by its subjective probability gives us its *subjective expected utility,* and we can choose so as to maximize that.

A Look Backward

The important thing to see is how our decisions are affected jointly by the *likelihoods* of outcomes (probabilities or subjective probabilities, a cognitive factor), and their costs or values to us (their utilities, a motivational factor). Increasing one has the same effect as increasing the other (when two numbers are multiplied, increasing either one will necessarily increase the product). There can also be trade-offs between the two; increasing one can compensate

---

★The term *utility* is borrowed from economics. We need such a term to describe the value to us, the "niceness," of various outcomes. Words like "niceness" or "preferredness" are awkward. We don't want to call it "value," for that connotes monetary value, which may not be what we mean. Nor do we want to call it "pleasantness," for if we must decide between raking the leaves and cleaning the sink, pleasure may have very little to do with it. The term "utility" sounds strange, but at least it is neutral.

for decreasing the other. In the above set of problems, we made different decisions in Cases 1 and 2, because the utilities were different, and in Cases 1 and 3, because the probabilities were different.

Finally, I wonder if the reader is experiencing a tingle of recognition here. Our theory bears a distant family resemblance to Hull's algebraic theory of behavior (pp. 202–08)! As with Hull, our tendency to take a given action is seen as dependent on the two factors. One is motivational—*D* (Drive) for Hull, utility here. The other is non-motivational, but based on learning or cognition—*H* (Habit) for Hull, subjective probability here. And the theories even agree in treating the two factors as multiplying to determine the final outcome! The difference is that Hull's reaction potential (*E*) is seen as driving behavior directly. In contrast, the subjective expected utility of an action is a quantity that is *considered*—compared with those of other possible actions—before the choice among actions is made.

A Look Forward: The Problem of Risk Perception

Perhaps this is the place for a word of caution. The fact is that human beings do not always behave in the crisply logical way that describes our experimenter's hypothetical subject—or the real-life drug dealer! For example, we may worry very seriously about risks that are actually minor—refined sugar in our diet, for instance—while ignoring such risks as driving without seat belts, a practice whose effects on our well-being are much more likely (probability) to be very severe (utility).[2] This looks forward to the problem of *availability* in decision-making—a problem for any logical, rational theory of human behavior.

EXTENSIONS AND APPLICATIONS OF DECISION THEORY

Decision theory and its offshoots have provided a wealth of ideas to explore. In what follows, we will look at how it can be applied in a number of different contexts. That can give some feeling for its richness.

Utility Theory

First, let's look more closely at the notion of value or utility.

THE UTILITY OF MONEY   In many economic situations, decisions involve the exchange of money or of commodities with monetary value. Can we use the monetary value of a commodity as a measure of its utility? Not

---

2. Rozin, 1989.

really. It is easy to show that the *value* of money, its utility, is not related to the *amount* of money in any simple way.

Suppose we were in the presence of a *really* rich experimenter, who said to us: "I will give you $5,000 outright, as a gift. Enjoy." Let us agree that that would make us happy.

Now imagine that he said, "No, better still, I'll give you $10,000." That would please us even more—of course! But would it make us twice as happy as the $5,000 gift? Happier, yes; but *twice* as happy? Most people think not.

In fact, when this thought experiment is actually done, a typical reply is that the gift would have to be *quadrupled* in order to double the value of the happiness it would bring.[3] In other words, utility increases as the square root of the dollar value. People differ to some extent in these judgments, of course, but this much is consistent: *The utility of money increases less rapidly than the dollar amount does.*

To show this idea and its consequences, Figure 10-2 presents a graph of the utility of money—its value to us—against the amount of money in dollars. Such a plot is called the *utility function* of money. Notice that it is concave downward, so that as the dollar amount rises, the increase in utility gets less and less. If the increase in utility drops off rapidly, then $10,000 will be less than twice as valuable to us as $5,000 is, as shown.

This bent utility function shows the well-known economic principle of *diminishing marginal utility.* Presumably it applies to any commodity; more of anything brings us less added happiness or utility, when we have more of it to begin with. This simple idea illuminates some important human actions.

UTILITY FUNCTIONS AND EXCHANGES   Suppose we buy a loaf of bread from a grocer for a dollar. What makes this exchange possible is that it produces a gain in utility for both participants. We would rather have the bread than the dollar. The grocer would rather have the dollar than the bread. So we swap, and everyone is happier.

Figure 10-2   A utility function for money. The value or utility of money increases more slowly than its dollar amount does, and the increase in value gets less and less as the dollar amount increases.

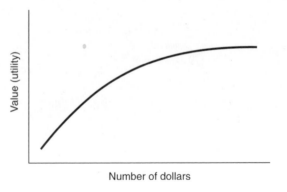

Value (utility)

Number of dollars

3. Galanter, 1962.

But why? A loaf of bread is not *always* more valuable to us than a dollar is. What determines whether it is or not? How much of each commodity—bread and money—we already have. That determines where, on the utility function for each commodity, we and the grocer find ourselves.

Suppose we have plenty of money in our pocket, but little or no bread in the house. Then our position is high on the utility function for money, where the slope is small and a dollar gained or lost doesn't mean much. But we are low on the utility function for bread, so a loaf gained means a lot. In that case, we would buy the bread, accepting a small loss in utility (the dollar) for a big gain in utility (the bread).

But now suppose the converse case. We have plenty of bread in the house, but little money. Now we are low on the utility function for money, where the curve is steep; a dollar lost is a substantial loss in utility. We are high on the utility function for bread, where the curve is shallow; one more loaf wouldn't give us much satisfaction. Under those conditions we would not pay a dollar for a loaf of bread. We might even sell one of our loaves ourselves.

The grocer of course is in a different position. He, we assume, always has more bread than he wants for himself; that's what makes him a grocer. For that reason, a sale is always a gain in utility for him.

The important point to see is that the bent utility function—the principle of diminishing marginal utility—underlies many cases of sale or barter. If we consider how much of human affairs depends on such exchanges, we begin to see just how important a principle it is. It makes the world go round—or so it has been said.

Signal-Detection Theory

To this point, we have considered outcomes that follow actions with probabilities that are fixed. But suppose that the outcome of an action depends on something else—some X that may or may not be true, and we are not sure whether it is true or not. Such decisions are the province of *signal-detection theory*.

Examples abound. Consider:

1. The nation on our border is mobilizing its armies. Does it intend to launch an attack on us? Shall we mobilize our own forces? If we do, and if our neighbor does intend to attack, we will be ready to meet the attack (good). But if it doesn't, we will have gone to needless expense and been needlessly provocative (bad).
2. In dim light, a robber takes your wallet at gunpoint. At the police station, you are shown a photo of a known holdup person, and the police say to you, "Is this the robber?" If you say yes, and you are right, you have helped to catch a robber and you might even get your wallet back (good). But if you are wrong, you will have fingered an innocent person (bad).

3. Suppose the accused person is brought to trial, and each juror, having heard all the evidence there is, must now vote "guilty" or "not guilty." Same dilemma: A vote of guilty, if the accused *is* guilty, is a vote to punish the guilty (good); but if he is not, then it is a vote to condemn the innocent (bad).

4. We are chatting with a fellow student whom we do not know. Shall we invite him or her out for coffee? If we do, then if the stranger is receptive, we will have a new friend, perhaps a new relationship (good); but if not, we will be rejected (bad).

5. Suppose we are sitting in an experimental chamber with headphones on, and a constant white noise (a kind of shooshing sound) is being fed into our ears. On each trial, we get a cue that tells us to listen carefully; and a "signal"—perhaps a very, very faint tone—either is, or is not, added to the noise. On each such trial, we must decide whether the signal was presented or not. If we say "Yes, there was a signal on that trial," and there was, we are correct (good); but if there wasn't, then we are incorrect (bad).

It is from that kind of experiment that signal-detection theory gets its name. So let us look at that experiment more closely.

On each trial, there are four possible outcomes, because there are two possible states of affairs (a signal was presented or it wasn't), and two possible responses: "Yes, I think there was a signal," or "No, I don't think there was a signal" (Fig. 10-3). We assume, remember, that the signal is so faint that the subject *cannot be sure* whether it is there or not, and so she will make mistakes. And there are two kinds of mistakes she can make: She can say no when the answer is yes (a "miss"), or yes when the answer is no (a "false alarm").

Now, presumably the subject wants to perform accurately, and would rather not make mistakes. She places some positive value on right responses and some negative value on wrong ones. Suppose we take experimental control over these values, by explicitly paying her for right responses and fining her for mistakes. We set up what is called a *payoff matrix* (Fig. 10-4). In the first of

Figure 10-3   Possible outcomes for a signal-detection trial.

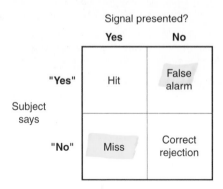

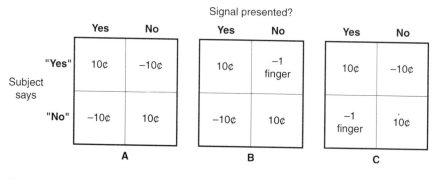

Figure 10-4 Three possible payoff matrices in a signal-detection experiment. As compared with the symmetrical payoff matrix A, matrix B strongly encourages a "no" response, and matrix C strongly encourages a "yes" response.

these (Fig. 10-4A), the payoffs are symmetrical: a mistake of either kind carries the same cost.

But we could just as well set up the payoffs as in Fig. 10-4B). A miss carries only a trivial cost of 10 cents. But if the subject ever makes a false alarm—saying "yes" when she should say "no"—we chop off a finger, then and there! (Note to human subjects committees: This experiment is imaginary.) What will happen? Obviously, the subject will almost never say "yes." The cost of being mistaken in doing so is simply too great. So, over a series of trials, she will have very few false alarms (good), but also very few hits (bad).

Now, after a series of trials like that, suppose we change the payoffs—and tell the subject we are doing so. Suppose we set them as in Figure 10-4C. Now it is a false alarm that carries only a small penalty, but a miss—failing to say "yes" when she should—now costs a finger each time it happens. Obviously, the subject will now say "yes" on nearly every trial. She will have many hits (good), but many false alarms too (bad).

So, by changing nothing but the payoff conditions, we can induce the subject to say "yes" on every trial, or on none of the trials. It would seem likely that less extreme variations in the payoff conditions could produce less extreme response strategies, so that we could place the likelihood of saying "yes" at intermediate values. And that is exactly what happens when such experiments are done (Fig. 10-5).

Notice that all this has nothing to do with how *accurately* our subject is performing. It has to do only with how inclined she is to say "yes" as opposed to "no" when in doubt. But we can get from the experimental data a measure of the subject's accuracy, too. That will be shown by *how much the hit rate exceeds the false-alarm rate* (Fig. 10-6). To the extent that the subject more often says "yes" when she should than when she shouldn't, she is performing accurately. Notice that the frequency of "hits," by itself, does not give us that information. A high hit rate—even 100 percent—might reflect accurate performance; or it might mean only that the person is saying "yes, yes, yes" a lot, whether the signal is there or not. False-alarm data will allow us to distinguish these.

It is for reasons like this that in the robbery scenario, the police ought not show us a *single* photo and ask, "Was that the criminal?" Our answer depends too much on our inclination to say "yes" when in doubt, and thus too little on

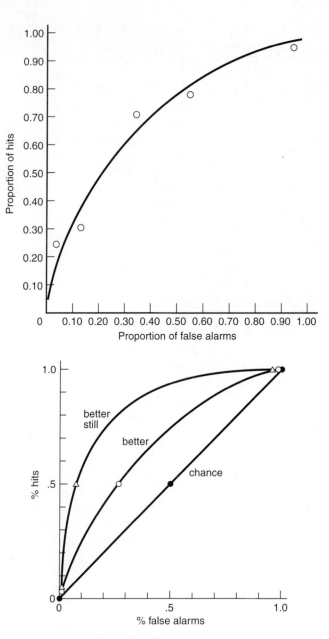

Figure 10-5   Hit rate plotted against false–alarm rate. Each circle represents the outcome of a series of trials under a given payoff matrix. Payoffs that favor a "yes" response—high reward for hits, low cost for false alarms, or both—will lead to high rates of both hits and false alarms, as in the circle high to the right. Payoffs that discourage a "yes" response—low reward for hits, high cost for false alarms, or both—will lead to low rates for both, as in the circle low to the left. Less extreme payoff conditions will lead to less extreme performance, as for the remaining circles. (Data from Green and Swets, 1966.)

Figure 10-6   Data for hypothetical signal-detection experiment. Notice that the hit rate may be the same (here, 50) for data points on all three curves, but differences in the false-alarm rate allow us to distinguish between very poor, chance-level performance (filled circles) and a high level of performance (triangles).

whether the photo really does or does not show the criminal. The purpose of police lineups and the like is to give the viewer a chance to make mistakes (false alarms), and thus allow the police to distinguish an accurate witness from a yes-person.

   And that example allows us to take these ideas back to the real-world scenarios with which we began this section. We see that in every one of them, our decision problem comes down to this: What are the payoffs for various outcomes? More specifically: *Of the two kinds of mistakes we could make, which is worse, and how much worse?* Is it worse to mobilize our armies when we don't have to, or to fail to mobilize when we're about to be attacked? To punish the innocent, or to let the guilty go free? To miss an opportunity to make a friend, or to be put down and rejected?

As an exercise, the reader should apply this kind of analysis to the various scenarios with which this section began. Let's look more carefully at Scenario 4, for example. Which would be worse, to miss an opportunity for a friendship, or to be rejected? If we are very much hurt by rejections, then to ask and be rejected (a "false alarm") might be the worse kind of mistake, carrying a high cost (Fig. 10-7A). That would make it likely that we'll refrain from asking. Our decision would be different if we're not bothered by a turndown (Fig. 10-7B) *or* if the other person is the person of our *dreams,* so that a missed opportunity would be even worse than a rejection (Fig. 10-7C). In either case we would be likely to go ahead and make the offer, with high hopes.

(A question for the interested student to ponder: How much of what we call "personality characteristics"—shyness, for example, or introversion, or sensitivity to rejection—can be seen as depending on the costs and values we assign to various outcomes of our social decisions?)

Finally, in this example we have focused on the *motivational* component of the theory—the payoffs for various outcomes—for that, after all, is our topic. But the *cognitive* component will be just as important—how *likely* do we think we are to be turned down? This will depend on our beliefs about other people: do we think most people are friendly, or cold or hostile? It will also depend on our beliefs about ourselves: Do we think that we are reasonably attractive and acceptable, or that we are unattractive and likely to trigger rejection? A lot of ideas come together in this "simple" analysis!

Before going on, readers should pause to convince themselves that all this does make sense. The numbers in Figure 10-7 should not be taken literally— we made them up, after all—but our decisions do consider "quantities" that represent probabilities and the costs and values of various possible outcomes. Which outcomes are likely or unlikely? What outcomes are good, and how good? Bad, and how bad? That is true of our social decisions as of any others (Fig. 10-8).

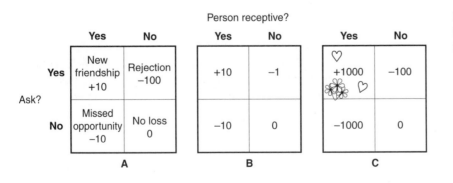

Person receptive?

Figure 10-7   To ask or not to ask? Three possible payoff matrices.

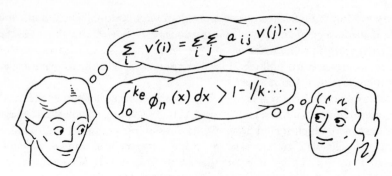

Figure 10-8 Social decisions require some quick intuitive calculations.

These examples can only give you the flavor of an extensive literature on signal-detection theory. Whole books have been written just on the psychology of eyewitness testimony, as in Scenario 2 above,[4] and in them, the concepts of signal-detection theory figure very prominently indeed.

The Costs of Rationality

We mentioned earlier that a rational, utility-maximizing decision is not to be confused with a good outcome. So it is only right to note that there are cases in which strict, utility-maximizing rationality can take us places we would not wish to go. It can, in a word, lock us into decisions whose outcomes are not good for us or for anyone else.

THE TRAGEDY OF THE COMMONS   In 1968, economist Garrett Hardin published a thoughtful article entitled "The Tragedy of the Commons." Imagine a pasture that everyone in a community can use as a place where his cattle can graze. That pasture is a *commons,* shared by all the herdsmen.

Now it is only rational for each herdsman to try to maximize profits. How many animals should he have? Well, he may ask at any point: What is the utility to me of adding one more animal to my herd?

Adding another animal involves both gain and loss. The gain is the profit from the animal that is added. We assume that the herdsman gets all of that. There is also a long-term cost, which results from the effects of overgrazing. But that cost is *shared by all the herdsmen there are.* The cost to each individual herdsman is divided by the total number of herdsmen; and so, for each individual, it is low.

Thus it may be to the advantage of *every* herdsman to add another cow, and another, ... Each herdsman gets all the profit, and only a fraction of the penalty, by doing so. "Each man is locked into a system that compels him to increase his herd without limit—in a world that is limited."[5] And this happens, not out of wickedness or even shortsightedness, but simply because each herdsman rationally seeks to maximize utility.

4. Loftus, 1979.
5. Hardin, 1968, p. 1244.

As another example, consider the problem of pollution. "The rational man finds that *his share* of the cost of the wastes he discharges into the commons [for example, the rivers and lakes] is less than the costs [which fall on him alone] of purifying his wastes before releasing them."[6] If so, it is rational for him to pollute rather than purify.

So, by behaving as a rational decision maker, each person perpetuates a system in which everyone loses in the long run. There ought to be a law against such decision situations! And, in fact, there are such laws: legislation about pollution or about land use is an attempt to break up just such traps as these. Stiff fines for pollution, for example, are costs imposed on *individual* manufacturers rather than spread over all of them. They are intended to make it *rational* for each individual to refrain from polluting.

THE PRISONERS' DILEMMA GAME   A "game," in decision-theory parlance, is any situation in which the outcomes depend jointly on what two or more actors, or "players," decide to do. And there's a particularly nasty kind of game known as the "prisoners' dilemma." It gets its name from the following scenario:

Two players, Smith and Jones, are arrested and charged with (say) bank robbery. At the police station, they are separated from each other, and each is told the following:

> "Look, Smith [or Jones], we don't have enough evidence to convict you of the robbery. We need a confession. If you each confess, you'll get ten years in prison. If neither of you confesses, we'll convict you of a minor charge and you'll each get one year. But if one of you confesses and the other doesn't—then we'll grant immunity to the one who confesses, and he'll get off scot free. But we'll throw the book at the other—thirty years in prison. And we're telling your partner the same thing, in another room, even as we speak."

What should the prisoners do? Figure 10-9 presents the payoff matrix for the game. As we look it over, we recognize a horrible truth: *No matter what Jones does, Smith is better off confessing!* To confess, therefore, is clearly his optimal strategy. And the same is true for Jones. So if both play rationally and confess, they'll each get 10 years in prison, where they could have held it to 1 year for each by remaining silent.

Imagine Smith's agony, even if he is an honorable thief:

> "It would be best for us both to keep silent; a year in prison isn't so bad. But what a reward I might get for confessing, if Jones doesn't! Worse still: What a risk I'd be taking if I didn't confess! If I don't confess and Jones does, I'll spend my best years in durance vile [Smith is a literary thief as well]. Moreover, Jones has the same pressures to confess as I do; and I know that, which adds to my fear that he'll confess; and he knows *that,* which adds to his fear that *I'll* confess, and so he has all the

6. Ibid., p. 1245, my italics.

Smith

	Confesses	doesn't confess
Jones Confesses	Smith 10 years Jones 10 years	Smith 30 years Jones free
doesn't confess	Smith free Jones 30 years	Smith 1 year Jones 1 year

Figure 10-9 A prisoners' dilemma payoff matrix.

more reason to protect himself by confessing. No, I'd better play it safe and confess."

Jones, we may be sure, is saying the same things to himself.

In short, logic inexorably leads to a joint decision whose consequences—10 years in prison for each—is far from the best possible outcome for either player.

We might suppose that it would be a good thing if the two prisoners could agree, beforehand, not to confess. But that would only bounce the problem back a step, for then each must decide: Shall I keep the bargain or break it? By the same logic, to break the agreement is necessarily more rational than to keep it.

Real-world examples of the prisoners' dilemma are very much out there. Watching a ball game, we would all be more comfortable sitting than standing. But if other people stand, why, we ourselves must stand as well in order to see at all! Everyone ends up standing in self-defense. Hardly the most comfortable outcome—but even worse, for us, would be to remain sitting while others stand. (President Jimmy Carter once pointed out that exactly the same considerations can drive inflation. No one likes inflation. We'd prefer it if prices and wages were stable. But if other people get higher wages and we don't, then prices will rise and we'll end up behind; so we'd better press for higher wages too. And if others reason the same way, ...)

Or consider arms races. Two nations are wasting enormous sums of money on armaments, each to protect itself from the other. Each would prefer to disarm and spend its wealth on something better. But either nation could be in deep trouble if it disarms and the other does not.

A LOOK BACKWARD—AND FORWARD   Like the tragedy of the commons, prisoners' dilemma–type payoff matrices can make the rational choice a very bad choice—even for the actor himself. The important thing to see is that these unfortunate choices do not result from malice or shortsightedness. They result from the simple logic of utility maximization.

From a theoretical point of view, it is significant that people do not, in fact, always do the coldly rational thing in such situations. We refrain from despoiling nature, out of respect for posterity—even though, as the saying goes, "What did posterity ever do for us?" People do, under some conditions, cooperate (with the other player, not with the police!) in prisoners' dilemma games.

In short, there may be times when (1) we do not in fact behave as purely rational maximizers, and (2) it is just as well that we do not! Keep that idea in mind; we'll return to it.

DECISION THEORY AND EVOLUTION

Animals, like people, face choices. A stickleback, faced with a rival, must fight or run away. A ram must court this mate—or not. A bird can look for food right *here* or right *there*. Can decision theory help us understand these cases too? Yes, in a way. It can help us understand how motivational mechanisms evolved—how they came to be the way they are.

Evolution and Maximization: The Progeny Payoff

The basic idea is that how a creature spends its time and energy will affect its *reproductive success*—the number of descendants it has (pp. 34–37). What evolution is all about is: Who gets to be an ancestor? If, within a population, those with long necks are ancestors to more descendants than those with short necks, then there will be more long-necked descendants in later generations. Presently living animals bear the genes of those, and only those, who succeeded in becoming ancestors.

Thus, the number of descendants a creature has, its reproductive success, represents a kind of utility—a progeny payoff—for allocating its resources in the way it does. A present organism's repertoire of action patterns, releasing stimuli, unconditioned reinforcers, and other inherited behavior mechanisms can therefore be seen as ones that led to high reproductive success on the part of its ancestors. We can ask: What payoffs in progeny led our ancestors to evolve *these* mechanisms rather than others?

Before we get into examples, however, we must pause to get one thing clear. To this point, we have been using decision theory as a *cognitive* theory of choice. We've assumed, in other words, that the actor is in fact doing the relevant calculations (utility $\times$ probability) and basing choices on the results—or, at least, doing something very much like that.

In this section, we will use the theory in a different way, a purely descriptive one. If we say that Actor A is maximizing utility, we will mean by it only that Actor A is doing something that *has the effect* of maximizing utility—whether the actor knows anything about it or not. In other words, we will be describing the *outcomes* of actions, not their causes—and often the "actions" will be those of ancestors long dead, not those of any actors who are onstage now.

But even when used in this descriptive, behavioristic way, decision theory can give us a handy way of describing what goes on. Let us look.

Foraging and Food Selection

What should an animal do about eating? Where is it most likely to find food? How much of each prey type should a predator eat? These are decisions an animal must make, or behave as if it made.

Consider the shore crab. These creatures feed on mussels, whose shells they must break open to get at the morsel of meat inside. The meat, when eaten, provides energy. But breaking open the shell *costs* energy. Actual calculations (by humans, not by crabs!) show that mussels of intermediate size will maximize the benefit/cost ratio for the crab. Smaller mussels yield too little energy; larger ones cost too much. The benefit/cost ratio is shown by the solid curve in Figure 10-10. And the bar graph below shows that the food selections actually made by crabs, when offered a choice, fit that curve quite well.[7]

Figure 10-10 An example of optimization. Shore crabs *(Carcinus maenas)* prefer to eat the size of mussel that gives the highest rate of energy return. *(A)* The curve shows the calorie yield per second of time used by the crab in breaking open the shell. *(B)* The histogram shows the sizes eaten by crabs when offered a choice of equal numbers of each size in an aquarium.

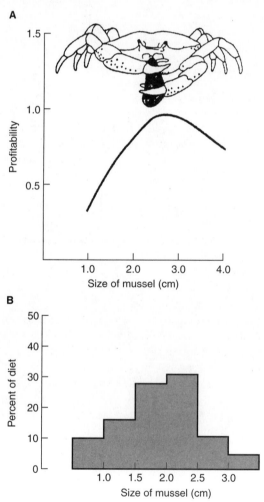

7. Adapted from Rozin and Schull, 1988.

But we see at once that the *cognitive* theory of decision-making does not apply at all to this case. No one is suggesting that the crabs do the relevant calculations in their heads—crabs are lousy at arithmetic. Rather, what presumably happened is this: Over the generations, ancestral crabs left more descendants if their nervous systems were "calibrated" so that prey of near-optimal size were the most potent releasing stimuli for feeding, because crabs so calibrated wasted as little energy as possible in feeding themselves. And today's crabs are so calibrated because they *are* those descendants.★

Mate Selection

Back in Chapter 5, when we discussed the Coolidge Effect (pp. 125–31), we pointed out that the way for a male to have the most descendants—to maximize his progeny payoff—is to mate with as many females as possible.

Not so the female. She has only so many possible children, whether she stays or strays. And in some species such as most mammals and birds, she has a substantial investment in each one; she eats for it before it is born and feeds it after it is born. The way for the female to maximize reproductive success, with the limited number of offspring she can have, is to see that as many as possible of her few children survive to adulthood after they are born.[8]

All this is not so bad if the female can raise infants by herself. She can then have about as many surviving children if the male deserts her as if he stays around to participate with her in child care. But what if raising children really requires both adults? In many birds, for instance, keeping a nestful of babies fed is a full-time job for both parents. Unless both parents participate, the young will die.★★ And in many such species, monogamous male-female pairs are formed. All the babies would die if the male did not do his share—and neither male nor female would leave any descendants.

But if there is *any* reasonable chance that the female can do the job of child-rearing by herself, then the male might still do better to desert! Even if most of the offspring die, still, a male can father so very many children that his mathematically *expected* number of descendants—number of babies times survival rate—could be higher if he mates with many females than if he stays to raise the young with one.

Now the female is not helpless in the face of this vicious payoff structure that favors male fickleness. What she can do—and in many species does do—is *refuse to mate* unless the male shows that he is likely to stay around to raise the young with her. She might, for instance, require him first to build an elaborate house for her, a nest or bower, before she will accept him as a mate. Or she

---

★For simplicity, we assume that selection is instinctive in this case, though in fact, recent experience affects it as well. For discussion and further examples see Rozin and Schull, 1988.
8. Trivers, 1971.
★★Notice that successful ancestry requires not only our having children, but also having them survive to give us grandchidren and thus keep us going as ancestors.

might insist that he first establish and defend a territory, driving other males away (pp. 112–13).

Notice that setting such tasks for the male is doubly to the female's reproductive advantage. First, they make it more likely that the male she mates with will be healthy and strong. Second, they *reduce the expected utility of desertion for the male*. If all the females of the species behave like that, then the male cannot just fertilize when he feels like it. If he leaves his mate to seek a new one, he will have to begin the whole business of courtship all over again with her. This being so, it may now maximize his progeny payoff to have fewer babies, with one mate, and work hard to make sure that those few survive.

The female's finickiness about mates, in such species, must have evolved because finicky females had more descendants than non-finicky ones. And, in a population of finicky females, faithful males had more descendants than the non-faithful ones, who were forced to waste too much time and effort in multiple courtships. We can say that finickiness and fidelity, for females and males respectively, maximized reproductive success among such birds' ancestors.

But notice that again we use *maximize* in a strictly descriptive sense. No one is suggesting that the birds reason all this out. Rather, these courtship rituals evolved simply because the successful female ancestors were those who did require them as releasing stimuli for their own sexual receptiveness. Thus they acquired faithful mates, and a higher grandchild tally as a result; and the multi-great-grandchildren are those that are with us now.

These brief glimpses of an active research area should further emphasize the broad domain of the maximization concept and the theory of decision-making. As a way of looking at the problems an animal faces, and as a way of describing how it solves them, the idea has applications far beyond the cognitive domain in which we first encountered it. In the next section, we will see still more.

CHOICE AND REINFORCEMENT

In the last section, we saw the convergence between decision theory and the study of instinctive repertoires by ethologists. But what about learned repertoires? In this section, we will again see convergence, this time between decision theory and the laboratory study of operant behavior.

Concurrent Schedules

Consider a pigeon in a Skinner box, confronted with a pecking key (pp. 295–96). Suppose that at irregular intervals, food reinforcement is set up on a given key so that the next peck on that key is reinforced with food. This is a *variable-interval* (VI) reinforcement schedule. Nothing indicates to the bird when reinforcement is available; any peck could be reinforced as far as the bird can tell, and so the pigeon pecks away at a steady rate.

Let us add a complication: another pecking key. Now there are two response keys, and reinforcement can be programmed at variable intervals independently on each response key. The availability of reinforcement on one key has nothing to do with whether or not it is available on the other. And there is still no signal to tell the bird when either key is set up to deliver reinforcement. Now we have *concurrent variable-interval schedules* of reinforcement.

The Matching Law

Now let us ask: What is the effect of different rates of reinforcement on the distribution of pecking behavior? Richard Herrnstein ran a series of sessions using concurrent VI schedules with pigeons.[9] The total number of reinforcements available in an hour-long session was held constant at 40; but Herrnstein varied the proportion of reinforcements that could be obtained by pecking each key. For example, on some sessions each key might be programmed to yield 20 reinforcements per hour. In other sessions, one key might be programmed to offer 10 reinforcements per hour and the other key 30 reinforcements per hour; in yet other sessions, the two keys might offer 5 and 35 reinforcements per hour. And so on.

Figure 10-11 shows some striking findings. The bird's allocation of pecks exactly matches the ratio of reinforcements available on the two keys.

It doesn't have to be that way. A pigeon could obtain all the reinforcements available, with *any* distribution of pecking behavior over the two keys, as long as it pecked each key at least occasionally. In fact, however, the bird distributes its pecks to match the relative frequencies of reinforcement, and with

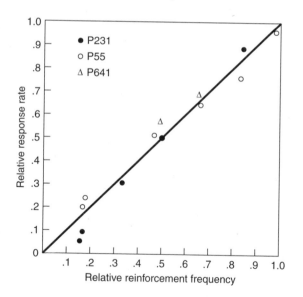

Figure 10-11 Pigeons distribute pecks between two keys to match the relative rates of reinforcement on the two keys. Each symbol represents an individual pigeon. (From Herrnstein, 1970.)

9. Herrnstein, 1970.

remarkable precision. If one key pays off three times as often as the other, the bird pecks that key three times as often as the other; if twice as often, twice as often; and so on. That is the *matching law*.

The matching law turns out to have considerable generality. It holds for key-pecking in pigeons under a variety of conditions. It is also seen in bar-pressing experiments in rats, and with button presses or even eye movements in human beings.[10]

The Law of Relative Effect

What the matching law says is this: The effect of a reinforcer on response rate is not absolute. Rather, its effect is relative to the effects of other reinforcers available in the situation. A given reinforcer, on a given schedule, will have strong effects if few other reinforcers are available. If many are available, it will have weaker effects. For that reason, the matching law is sometimes called the *law of relative effect*. It turns out to have some intriguing implications.

For example, it follows from the law that we could reduce responding to Key A in either of two ways: (1) by reducing the rate at which we reinforce it, or (2) by *increasing* the rate at which we reinforce some alternative, such as pecks at Key B. This is exactly what happens.

The same idea has been extended to behavior therapy in humans (pp. 297–99). For example, there is the case of a mildly retarded male who showed outbursts of assaultive behavior. Extinction of the behavior would have been too slow and dangerous; and the man's parents were reluctant to use punishment. Instead, the man was reinforced by tokens, exchangeable for money, for various activities having to do with personal hygiene, chores, and the like. Reinforcing these actions, *which had nothing to do with the problem behavior,* resulted in a prompt and substantial reduction in that behavior.[11]

Examples of the principle in everyday affairs are easy to find. Suppose we live in a community where there are few or no good eating places. We try a new restaurant, and—surprise!—we get an excellent meal. Our likelihood of going back to that place will become very high, so the good meal is a potent reinforcer. But if there already were many good places to eat in the neighborhood, we could try the *same* new restaurant and get the *same* excellent meal—but our likelihood of going back would not increase as much. The reinforcer is the same, but it has less effect if other reinforcers are available.

Or: Consider the horrible change that comes over the most pleasant, civilized people when they get behind the wheel of a car. They bully; they jockey; they cut each other off; they risk disaster to get one car length ahead of the other guy. Why? One possibility is: the matching law:

> In these contexts, people have little to reward them besides the minor victories of the bus or the road. The relative reward is therefore large, so it provokes a rich flow of action.[12]

10. Schroeder and Holland, 1969.
11. McDowell, 1982.
12. Brown and Herrnstein, 1975, p. 84.

In other words, the small reinforcement of getting one car length ahead of another driver can become a potent reinforcer if no other reinforcers are available. And when we're stuck in a car in rush-hour traffic, few reinforcers *are* available. Getting a bit ahead is about the only reward we can obtain. So we may work hard, and risk much, to obtain it.

Melioration

Okay, but how does it work? How does distribution of responses come to match relative rates of reinforcement?

For concurrent reinforcement situations, there are different theories about just what the pigeon is doing. Many of them assume that in matching response allocation to reinforcement frequency, the bird's behavior is maximizing something, e.g., the momentary probability of reinforcement[13] or the rate of reinforcement over short periods.★

Herrnstein's view is different. As he sees it, the process that produces matching, called *melioration,* is just a restatement of the reinforcement principle: Other things equal, a response that is reinforced more often than another will come to occur more often than that other. And if the pigeon comes to peck either key more than the matching relationship says it should, then *rate* of reinforcement (reinforcements per response) will be greater for the "neglected" key when it does get pecked, and the bird will therefore drift toward pecking it more. Thus deviations from matching are corrected by differences in average rate of reinforcement.★★

Notice a few things about this idea. First, the process is assumed to be continuous over time. Decision theory, as we developed it earlier, suggests that a decision is a distinct *event:* The actor calls "Time out!" and considers her

---

13. See for example Shimp, 1975; Platt, 1979.

★In fact, a great deal of attention has been paid to the relation between matching and maximizing. This literature has become very technical; the reader who is interested, and comfortable with mathematics, must be referred to original sources (for example, Herrnstein and Vaughan, 1980; Herrnstein, 1993; Staddon, 1993).

★★To see this, let's work through an example. Suppose a pigeon can emit 1000 responses in an hour's session. It can distribute these in any way it likes between two alternatives, say Key A and Key B. Suppose there are a total of 90 reinforcements available in that hour, 60 from Key A and 30 from Key B, but that reinforcements on both are available at unpredictable intervals.

Suppose that at first, the bird responds equally at the two keys. Over the session, its total return from Key A would be 60 reinforcements per 500 responses, or on average, 0.12 reinforcements per response. Its return from Key B would be 30/500, or 0.06 reinforcements per response. And, because the rewards are delivered at variable intervals, those two *average rates* of return would be present from the outset of the session. But wait! The bird is getting more reinforcements per response from Key A. If rate of response increases with rate of reinforcent, the bird ought to begin directing more of its responses toward Key A.

Suppose that it does, and that it overshoots; it begins pecking 90 percent of the time at Key A. But then its rate of return from Key A would be 60/900, or 0.07, whereas from Key B it receives 30/100, or 0.3. So now it should drift back toward spending more pecks on Key B. Let the process continue, and response distribution should settle down to *match* reinforcement distribution over the two keys. That, we recall, is exactly what happens.

options, calculates her expected utilities, chooses the best course of action, and then steps back into life and implements it. But melioration is an ongoing process in which an actor keeps a kind of running track of relative payoffs, drifting from Action A toward Action B whenever B's *rate* of return (payoff per unit time or effort) exceeds A's.

Second, this account does not speak of the subject as *maximizing* anything. The bird simply responds to rates of reinforcement. Indeed, Herrnstein argues that melioration is a more important psychological process than maximization, in that it better describes how animals (including humans) actually behave most of the time. In many cases, it is true, melioration and maximization predict the same actions, or close to them. But there are cases where they make different predictions; and in such cases, there is indeed evidence that animals and humans are more likely to match than maximize.[14]

Third, this theory does not try to specify the cognitive *mechanisms* that produce the actions we see. Thus this kind of theorizing—like theories about progeny payoffs—is descriptive, not cognitive.

It does, however, put the behaviorist-cognitivist debate in a new light. Let us see how.

A Look Backward

With the concept of melioration, we come to the cutting edge of modern behaviorism. And an interesting thing has happened in this research area: Behaviorism and cognitive psychology, once fierce rivals in debate, have become complementary.

As I see the current situation, few writers would deny that cognitive mechanisms operate even in animal behavior. The experimental evidence for cognitive maps, search images, response-reinforcer expectancies, and the like, is simply too strong (Chap. 9). The fact remains that we know little about how these processes work, or just how they take hold of overt behavior in any given case. And, for some purposes, we do not have to know.

Consider melioration. The animal's behavior, we say, tracks the average rate of return for each of the response alternatives. But surely the pigeon does not *literally* count reinforcers, count responses, and then whip out its calculator to divide one sum by the other! We can say, descriptively, that it behaves *as if* it did *something* like that; but what that "something" is, further research must unravel. We don't know.[15]

Meanwhile, however, we can try to specify more precisely the relation between behavior and environment, e.g., whether the animal is maximizing or meliorating or what. In doing so, we can leave the underlying cognitive processes unspecified, just as the cognitivist can leave underlying physiological processes unspecified. We can, in other words, try to state more clearly *what*

---

14. See Mazur, 1994; Herrnstein, 1990.
15. Gallistel, 1990.

the system is doing. Questions about *how* it does it can wait (compare pp. 23–24).

And, recognizing that, cognitive and behaviorist theorists find themselves with little left to argue about. Perhaps we can all live in the same house after all.

A LOOK BACKWARD: THE THREE FACES OF DECISION THEORY

In applying decision theory to a number of contexts—eyewitnesses, coffee dates, grocery stores, and even foraging and key-pecking—we see that the theory has a number of quite different uses. It really is not one theory, but three. It is time to look over these three faces, and distinguish them.

The Cognitive Theory: Maximizing as Mechanism

First, decision theory can be a cognitive theory about *how* decisions get made. That theory is the one we explored first: The actor anticipates the outcomes of possible actions, and chooses the action leading to the highest expected utility. This implies that the actor is actually performing the cognitive operations that calculate expected utilities, or, at least, doing something very much like that.

The Descriptive Theory: Maximizing as Outcome

Second is the descriptive, or behavioristic, use of decision theory. We might say that Subject Y is maximizing X, and mean by it simply that what Subject Y does *has the effect* of maximizing X. This need not imply anything whatever about what, if anything, the subject is thinking or calculating or anticipating. It says nothing about the mechanisms that caused the actions we see.

For example, in Darwinian theory (pp. 34–37), evolution is a matter of maximizing fitness, where fitness is defined simply as reproductive success—leaving descendants. But a given creature, making its living in the world, is not calculating its reproductive success. With some human exceptions, it is not even trying to leave descendants—not all humans know what makes babies, and it is unlikely that any other animal does. The behaving animal is only trying to find food or a mate, avoid dangers, and the like.

This means that fitness and reproductive success, though important concepts, are not *motivational* concepts in Darwinian theory. Reproductive success is not part of what causes a living creature to do what it does. It is a term that we, the observers, use to describe the *outcomes* of its actions—or the actions of its ancestors, long dead.

The Normative Theory: Maximizing as Best Choice

Finally, decision theory can be a *normative* theory. That means that it describes, not what we do, but what we ought to do. It gives us a way of calculating the *best* selection from the options we are confronted with.

For example, suppose we are playing poker, blackjack, or any game of chance in which various events occur with fixed probabilities and in which fixed gains or losses—say, monetary payoffs—attend the various outcomes. Now it can be shown that if we actually do the decision-theory calculations, and play the game according to those calculations, then in the long run we will win more money (or lose less) than if we play it any other way.

If we do play that way, then we might say that we are playing *rationally*. We are logically calculating what is the best thing to do, and then doing it.

The normative theory is not the same as the cognitive one. If we calculate wrong, or if we don't know how to do the calculations, then we cannot play the game rationally in the strict normative sense. We can still play it cognitively. We may decide to stay in the hand because we believe that our hand is strong, and so we expect to win. But if we are operating on hunch, not on calculation, then we will not—except by accident—consistently make the normatively correct decision. And we will lose out, over the long run, to a player who does.

The Three Faces Compared

It is easy to confuse these uses of the term "maximizing." They can shade into each other to such an extent that the theorists themselves may have trouble distinguishing them on occasion.[16]

What makes things so confusing is that, very often, all three apply. Consider again the expert poker player, who calculates that her best action is to throw in her hand. She is doing the necessary calculations in her head and basing her decision on them; the cognitive usage applies. She is also doing what is in fact the best thing to do if she wants to make money; the normative usage applies. And we can describe her behavior by saying that it maximizes expected utility, even if we don't know whether she is actually doing the calculations or not; the descriptive usage applies.

But the three uses do not have to coincide. Where they don't—as in mate selection or foraging, for example—it is important not to confuse them (compare pp. 379–82).

SOME COMPLICATIONS IN DECISION-MAKING

In introducing decision theory, we considered the decision maker as weighing alternatives, calculating expected utilities, and choosing an action on the basis of those calculations. But that *is* a theory; it may or may not describe how decisions are made by real-world actors. When we look at what actually happens, we find that matters are not so simple as we have supposed.

16. See for example Mazur, 1983a, b; Staddon and Hinton, 1983.

The Problem of Capacity

Thinking and planning, like courting or eating, take time and effort. And certain constraints will be imposed by time limitations—we have only so much time and energy to devote to any activity.

Consider this: We encounter a tiger. The tiger has no cage around it, and somehow looks as if it has not eaten recently. What do we do? Do we stop to consider all possible actions—we might try to pet the tiger, we might sing a song to sooth its savage breast, we might try to hypnotize it—and carefully calculate expected utilities? Of course not. There isn't *time*. We must do something *now,* even if it is not a carefully calculated maximizing action.

Indeed, in extreme cases, time constraints make a truly maximizing strategy quite impossible. Take the problem of selecting a marriage partner. Obviously, it is out of the question to interview *all possible* marriage partners before selecting one. So that decision—an important one—must be made in some other way.

Conversely, suppose we are deciding where to go for lunch. Do we sit down to consider all possible places, calculating quality, price, cost of getting there, . . . ? Probably not. It simply *isn't worth it.*

Fully rational decisions, then, could take too much effort or too much time—more than we have, or more than they are worth. So we turn to shortcuts—ways of simplifying the decision process—so as to reduce the time and effort it takes.

Alternatives to Maximizing

Suppose we were deciding where to go for lunch. We could go through a careful, maximizing decision process; but is there time? Is it worth it? No? Well then, how else might we decide?

SATISFICING   We could begin by setting up a standard: What outcome would be *good enough*? Then we consider various possible actions one by one and pick the *first* one whose expected outcome is good enough.[17] That strategy is called *satisficing.*

Satisficing differs from maximizing in several important ways. First, satisficing may require much less time and effort, since we need not consider all the alternatives; we stop when we find one that is good enough. That is the good news. The second is not such good news: when we satisfice, we pick the first alternative that is good enough, so we may well miss another that is better still. Finally, in maximizing we can consider the possible actions in any order, since we're going to consider them all anyway. But if we satisfice, the order in which we think of alternatives makes a great difference. If we consider restaurants in alphabetical order, we might decide that Archie's Place is good enough, and go

17. Simon, 1976.

there. If we considered them in reverse alphabetical order, maybe Zorba's Place would be good enough and we'd go there instead.

Satisficing may be far more commonly used than maximizing. Shoppers often satisfice. Rather than insisting on the very best necktie or hamburger in town for the money, one may choose the first that is *satisfactory* in quality and price. Obviously the time and effort saved is considerable.

BETTERING   Another kind of decision strategy goes by various names, such as *incrementalism* or *muddling through*.[18] *Melioration* (pp. 385–86) is a special case of it. Let us call it *bettering*. The decision rule is as follows: Whatever you're doing now, if an option comes along that has higher expected utility than that, switch to it. Otherwise go on with what you're doing.

This strategy differs from the other two in that it is a continuous process. Maximizing or satisficing requires that one take time out, step back from life to make a decision, and then step back into life and implement it. Bettering, on the other hand, describes an actor who is going on with the routine business of living, but always alert to the possibility of making life better for herself, and changing from one action to another if it has that expected outcome.

Examples abound. We might put our savings in a bank, leave them there, and forget about them, until we see that another bank offers higher interest rates. Then we switch banks.

Or think again about where to eat lunch. Suppose our group goes to Gary's Grill for lunch every day. We don't really *decide* to go there, we just go; it's routine. But today someone says: "Let's all go to Francoise's Fine Filet and Frogs' Legs Place. My treat." We all agree—of course! The food is much better there than at Gary's, and for us it's free. Our lunching strategy is a bettering one: We just do the usual thing, unless a better option is put before us. If one is, we take it.

Bettering is a fine strategy for reducing the time and effort allocated to decision-making. No decision is required at all unless a better alternative comes along. It has its dangers, however. If the actor never steps back to decide on long-term goals, she will be alert only to immediate short-term ones. It will be difficult to take one step back to go three steps forward, to take a loss now for a bigger gain later.

Then there is the converse danger: A series of small, bettering changes can lead step by step to a destination that would not have been chosen had one foreseen it during a moment of thoughtful decision. "A stepwise increase in commitment can end up locking the person into a career or marriage without his ever having made a definite decision about it."[19]

Thus, some writers picture the human actor as operating mostly on habit and inertia—they even refer to him as a "reluctant decision maker." He goes about his routine by rote, unless he sees risks or costs in doing so, including the

18. Herrnstein and Vaughan, 1980; Janis and Mann, 1977
19. Janis and Mann, 1977, p. 35.

"cost" of passing up something better. That placid existence may be punctuated with minor decisions—where to go for lunch, which necktie to buy, and the like. These are probably decided by a *satisficing* strategy.[20] Indeed, it is just such trivial decisions that the satisficing concept was designed to account for.

AH, BUT WHICH STRATEGY?   The recognition of alternative strategies does make decision theory more flexible and, perhaps, more realistic. But if we wish to develop it into a theory of purposive behavior, these options pose a problem. We can make decisions in more than one way, we say. But then which strategy shall we use? Must we first decide *that?* And if so, on what basis?

Thus it has been suggested that satisficing, as a way of choosing a necktie or a lunch, really is an optimizing strategy if one figures in the costs of acquiring all the information we would need in order to use a maximizing strategy. That sounds fine, but in practice, it could trap us in an infinite regress. Must we *decide* whether to consider these costs? Must we first consider just what information we would need in order to consider them? What information do we need in order to know what information we need? We seem to have a formula for paralysis here (Fig. 10-12).

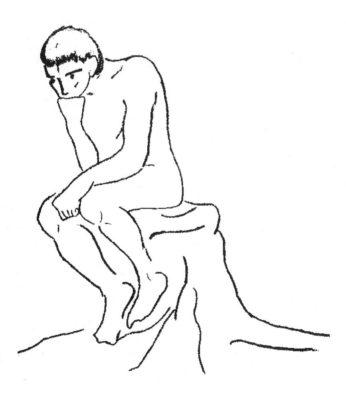

Figure 10-12   *"I'm deciding whether to decide whether or not it would be worthwhile to gather all the information I would need in order to decide whether. . . . Don't bother me!"*

20. Simon, 1976.

Of course, research can be, and is, directed toward the question of strategy selection: What determines when we use one strategy and when another? The problem is that we don't have a normative theory that tells us when we *should* use one strategy or the other. And that could land us in big trouble because, lacking that, we have no solid criterion for determining when a decision is *rational* and when it is not!

In short, we see theoretical storm clouds on the horizon. They are about to get darker.

The Problem of Availability

There was once a king who died of a fever, brought on by sitting too close to a hot brazier. He continued to sit there, literally roasting to death, because the servant whose job it was to move the brazier couldn't be found. Apparently it never occurred to His Majesty to move the brazier himself. It wasn't the sort of thing that kings do for themselves—and so he simply did not *consider* doing it. It was not, as we say, *cognitively available* to him.[21]

We too may fail to solve problems because certain ideas are not cognitively available to us. Consider the following riddle:

A boy and his father were in an automobile accident. The father was killed instantly. The boy was alive but badly injured, and was rushed to the hospital and prepared for emergency surgery. But the surgeon, on seeing the boy, said, "I can't operate on that boy. He's my son."

How can that be? (No, it has nothing to do with adoption or reincarnation.) If you see the solution right away, try the riddle on your friends and see how long it takes them to find it. If you don't see it right off, think about it until you do. Then think about the implications of the fact that the solution—a perfectly obvious one—has a way of being cognitively unavailable to many people in this society.

Then again, if some actions don't occur to us, this is not necessarily a bad thing. Consider this example. A popular view of moral behavior—dating back to Thomas Hobbes if not earlier—is that we refrain from stealing or lying because of fear of disapproval or punishment. Sometimes, no doubt, self-control does depend on these expected outcomes; but it can also depend on what options we consider at all. In one study, children of Mennonite and of neighboring non-Mennonite families were interviewed as to what behaviors should or should not be performed. The Mennonite children seldom even mentioned the moral values of their community that prohibited stealing, lying, and the like. It seems that those well-internalized values placed these actions outside the range of options to be considered.[22] Such actions were not cognitively available; they simply did not *occur* to the children.

21. Tuchman, 1984.
22. Radke-Yarrow et al., 1983.

IMPLICATIONS OF AVAILABILITY   No strategy of decision-making—maximizing or any other—will lead us to choose a response that is never considered. Nor does decision theory tell us what responses we *should* consider. It only specifies ways of choosing among the options we do consider. So our strategies for decision-making, such as the maximization of utility, come in only after we "list" in our minds the options that we will consider. They provide no guidance as to how to make the list.

And what *that* means is that decision theory is incomplete as a cognitive, descriptive, or normative theory of action. To its logic about how to make rational decisions, we need to add considerations that are not *logical* but *psychological*: What alternatives are, or are not, even considered in a decision situation?

WHAT DETERMINES AVAILABILITY?   What exactly does it mean to say that an option is "available" or that it isn't? In some cases, it may have to do with how readily a response—or a goal or a plan—can be called into play by a higher-order system. This might reflect untaught properties of a creature's cognitive apparatus.

For instance, Bolles's concept of species-specific defense reactions (pp. 255–56) could be restated this way: Certain actions, but not others, are readily available as ways of coping with danger. Conversely, consider again the fact that pigeons have trouble *refraining from pecking* as a food-getting response (pp. 318–19). The utility-maximizing response is simply not readily available to the actor, for whatever reason. In humans too, there is some evidence that certain cognitive actions are readily available for some problems, but not for others that are logically, but not psychologically, equivalent.[23]

Second, one's learning history may make certain options readily available, others not. The culture in which one is raised may have a decisive influence here: To a Mennonite child, stealing is not cognitively available as an option, whereas to an inner-city American youth it may well be. Indeed, society's learning curriculum may try to short-circuit the decision-making process altogether, by making only *one* alternative cognitively available as the only right or possible thing to do. If this is successful, an actor may "just do" the socially approved thing, "mindlessly" if you wish, without really making a decision at all.[24]

Finally, what we might call "local," situational events may promote or discourage the availability of certain thoughts over the short term. We speak of "hints" that jog certain ideas into availability, perhaps by association (shades of Thomas Hobbes!).

For example, think again about the riddle of the surgeon's son (p. 392). Suppose you tried the riddle out on a friend, and she was unable to solve it. Now, if she had just come from a discussion of the problems faced by profes-

23. Barkow, Cosmides, and Tooby, 1992.
24. Quinn, 1992.

sional women in this society, then the solution might have come to her mind at once.

And, Gentle Reader: If *you* failed to solve the riddle, does that reference to "professional women" enable you to solve it now? If so, then you see how a situational influence—the text you are reading, right this minute—can jog your mind to increase the *availability* of an idea! (Do not feel bad. An incredibly high proportion of college students, women as well as men, fail to solve that riddle. Think about that.)

The Availability of Reasons

We may make poor decisions, then, because too little information is cognitively available to us. We may also do so because too much is! Irrelevant considerations may throw us off the track of sound decision-making.

That at least is one way of interpreting a disturbing series of studies by Timothy Wilson and his colleagues.[25] In one experiment, college students were allowed to make selections from a number of posters. They could take home the ones they selected and put them up on their walls. Some were asked to make careful decisions, "decomposing" the various prints into their pluses and minuses and weighing these against each other.[26] Later on, these subjects were significantly *less* satisfied with the choices they had made than subjects who had simply gone with their overall impressions. Similar results were found for a variety of other products, and even for how much dating couples liked each other!

Why should this be so? Wilson and his colleagues suggest the following: When we sit down to list pros and cons, we do it verbally, in a kind of internal conversation with ourselves. (This is all the more true, of course, if we list the pros and cons in written words.) The problem is that some of the pros and cons will be easy to put into words. Others—our intuitions, emotional reactions, and gut feels—will not be. So, when we make our lists, they will likely include those pros and cons that are easiest to put into words. Those that are hard to put into words will likely be omitted or downplayed.

But in fact, these hard-to-describe reactions may actually be among the most important determinants of our true preferences. If so, then to omit or downplay them is to omit or downplay the most important influences on what we like and how much we like them. In that case, a careful listing of *verbalizable* pros and cons could lead us away from, not toward, a clear appreciation of what our own likes and dislikes really are. It's the sort of thing we mean when we say, "I talked myself into it," especially when we add or imply, "And I wish I hadn't!"

Wilson does not of course claim that this always happens, and that a careful decision will necessarily be a bad one. But his studies show that it can be.

25. Wilson et al, 1993; Wilson and Kraft, 1993.
26. Dawes, 1988.

Therefore, as so often, the question is: When does this happen, and when not? And why?

The Framing of Decisions

As a normative theory of rational decision-making, decision theory assumes that the possible actions, and the expected utilities of their outcomes, are established. We know what we want, what our options are, and what is likely to happen if we do each.

But it just is not that simple. Amos Tversky and Daniel Kahneman have investigated this matter in an ingenious series of thought experiments. And they have shown how the *same* decision problem can have very different rational solutions, depending on how one looks at it—where more than one way of looking at it may be quite legitimate.

In one of their studies, all subjects read the following "stem":

Imagine that the U.S. is preparing for the outbreak of an unusual Asian disease, which is expected to kill 600 people. Two alternative programs to combat the disease have been proposed. Assume that the exact scientific estimate of the consequences of the programs are as follows:

Then half the subjects read the following continuation:

If Program A is adopted, 200 people will be saved.
If Program B is adopted, there is a 1/3 probability that 600 people will be saved, and a 2/3 probability that no people will be saved.
Which of the two programs would you favor?

The other half saw the following:

If Program C is adopted 400 people will die.
If Program D is adopted there is a 1/3 probability that nobody will die, and a 2/3 probability that 600 people will die.
Which of the two programs would you favor?[27]

Looking over the whole business, we see that the two possible decisions are identical in the two cases. Programs A and C describe the same outcome; Programs B and D describe the same outcome. If A is preferred to B, then C should be preferred to D. But in fact, of the subjects who had the A-B choice, 72 percent preferred A; whereas of those given the C-D choice, 78 percent preferred D!

There is no way we can resolve this wild inconsistency without elaborating our theory of decision-making. The choices change, depending on how subjects are invited to look at the problem.

27. From Tversky and Kahnemann, 1981.

Why? Because A and B treat the problem in terms of *lives saved.* C and D treat it in terms of *lives lost.* Let's examine the utility functions that characterize these scenarios (Fig. 10-13). We assume that the diminishing-returns principle applies to lives saved and lost, as well as to money. Then we see that saving 200 lives for sure has higher expected utility than a 1/3 chance of saving 600 lives (Fig. 10-13A). If we look at the problem in terms of lives saved, we should take the sure thing—as most subjects did.

But what if we look at it in terms of *lives lost?* Then a 2/3 chance that 600 people will die has less *negative* expected utility than 400 deaths for certain (Fig. 10-13B). If we look at it that way, we should go with the gamble. Most subjects did.

But the only difference is in how one states the problem! To save 200 lives *is* to lose 400 lives. By looking at it one way or the other, we can make either decision the rationally correct one.

Now we see why the notion of "framing" is appropriate here. It is as if each subject were looking at the problem through a window that showed one utility function or the other. Different window, different decision—even for the same outcome.

Well, which frame is the correct one to use? How ought we to look at the problem? *Decision theory does not tell us how we ought to look at it.*

As a normative theory, decision theory tells us what we ought to do if we want to maximize expected utility of lives saved. It tells us what we should do if we want to minimize expected cost of lives lost. But if we can look at the same problem in either of those two ways, the theory is simply no help. It applies only *after* the utilities have been framed. Framing them is up to us.

Figure 10-13   The framing problem. (A) If one considers lives saved, then 200 saved for sure has higher positive utility than the expected utility of the gamble (1/3 the utility of 600 lives saved). (B) If one considers lives lost, then 400 lives lost for sure has lower utility—or greater *negative* utility—than the expected utility of the gamble (1/3 the utility of no lives lost).

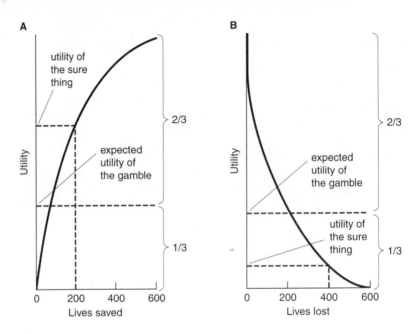

The framing effect operates in real-life decisions, too. Surgery for lung cancer was seen as less attractive, relative to radiation therapy, when the two were compared using mortality (lives lost) rather than survival (lives saved) figures. The effect was just as large with physicians as with lay people.[28]

Other examples? Consider two merchants, who accept both cash and credit cards. One gives a *discount for cash*. The other charges a *surcharge for credit cards*. These could amount to exactly the same charges, but doesn't one sound like a bargain and the other like a rip-off?

Then there is a personal experience of the author's, and you have my solemn word that this actually happened. In a course I taught, I gave students the option of writing a term paper, to be worth extra points toward the course grade. On an anonymous course-evaluation questionnaire, one student complained that such a policy was unfair. It would be more fair, said she or he, to require a term paper of everybody—and then deduct points for those who didn't write one!

As we look over these last sections, we notice that our concept of rational decision-making is becoming much less clear than we might have thought it would be. We saw, for instance, that two quite different solutions to the same decision problem could be considered normatively optimal, depending on how the problem is framed.

It is important to see just how troublesome this is. What it means is that in cases where utilities can be framed in different ways, we have no criterion for rational behavior! That's because we have no normative theory for the framing process itself. We can try to construct descriptive theories about how people do frame problems, and cognitive theories about the mental operations by which they do so.[29] But no theory tells us how they *should* go about it.

A Look Backward: Some Problems for Decision Theory

Historically, decision theory emerged from the analysis of games of chance; and for that purpose, it did very well. The alternatives, probabilities, and payoffs all are fixed and are known; and the mathematics of decision theory do tell us how best to play poker, blackjack, and the like.*

To extend the theory to choices of all kinds seemed natural enough. And it fit well with common sense: The actor does what he *believes* (subjective probability) will get him what he most *wants* (utility). Simple!—or so it seems at first.

As a general theory of decision-making, however, we have seen that the theory faces some problems.

28. Redelmeier, Rozin, and Kahneman, 1993.
29. See Tversky and Kahneman, 1981, 1983.
*Though even in that domain, non-logical factors may enter in, as when an adult intentionally loses a game to a child.

RATIONAL DECISION-MAKING: DO WE DO IT? There is a wealth of experimental evidence that humans do not, in fact, behave as fully rational decision makers.[30] To give just one example: A collection of professional scientists, mathematicians, and philosophers played a simulated prisoners' dilemma game. Now, as we saw earlier (pp. 377–78), one's rational "move" in the game is necessarily to "confess." But among these professionals, all thoroughly familiar with the logic of the game, the plain fact is that only some chose "rationally." Some did, some did not.

Even where rational calculations do seem to describe our decision processes, they may come in after the decision, not before. As Robert Zajonc points out:

> We sometimes delude ourselves that we proceed in a rational manner and weigh all the pros and cons of the various alternatives. But this is probably seldom the actual case. Quite often "I decided in favor of X" is no more than "I liked X." Most of the time, information collected about alternatives serves us less for making a decision than for justifying it afterward.[31]

Other writers too have suggested that we may use the maximization idea not to guide a decision, but as a *reason* by which we explain the decision, to others and to ourselves.[32]

COULD WE DO IT? If we do not always make coldly rational decisions in practice, could we do so if we tried? It is not clear that we could.

Sometimes a maximizing strategy is impossible in principle, as in selecting a marriage partner. And even a careful maximizing decision about where to go for lunch would obviously be more trouble than it is worth. But then, how do we decide whether that is so? An infinite regress looms: Must we rationally decide whether to rationally decide . . . ? Do we take time to decide whether we have time . . . ?

Finally, even where maximizing is possible in principle, we may lack the necessary capability. A really good poker player may do the mental arithmetic necessary to figure the probability that drawing another card will lead to a winning hand and, knowing that, the size of the pot, and the cost of staying in the hand, calculate that dropping out is the correct choice. But most of us, the author definitely included, usually cannot do that; we don't know how, or we lack the necessary skill and concentration for such mental arithmetic, or both. I might make the same decision—to drop out—but base it not on calculation but on a vague intuitive feeling that it would be best to do so.

Let us stay with that example for a minute, for it may help bring the problem into sharper focus. If good poker players calculate expected utility and maximize it, what do poor players do? Whatever it is, (1) it is *not* identical to the process that decision theory describes, and (2) it is probably the more usual

30. See for example Nisbett and Ross, 1980; Kahneman, Tversky, and Slovic, 1981.
31. Zajonc, 1980, p. 155.
32. See for example Shafir, Simonson, and Tversky, 1994.

mode of human decision-making. There are, after all, more poor poker players than good ones.

Well, what does a poor poker player do? If he throws in his hand, it is because of a vague hunch that his hand isn't very good and the cost of staying in is high and, well, it doesn't seem worth the risk. Most of us make most decisions by habit or hunch or gut feel. In experienced poker players, these hunches may be "calibrated" by the player's history of successes and failures in situations like this one. In other words, they may be calibrated by their *environmental consequences,* somewhat as reinforcement theory would have it (see the previous chapter). Or they might depend on rules of thumb, or *heuristics,* which guide our decisions (see the next chapter!).

Either way, decision theory will have to be expanded before it can become an adequate theory of human behavior. It will have to consider the habits, heuristics, and hunches that do not flow from its arithmetic, but that do describe most of the decisions we make, most of the time.

SHOULD WE DO IT?   As a cognitive theory, we see that decision theory has its limits. What about as a normative theory? *Should* we maximize expected utility? It is not clear that we should.

There clearly are cases in which to be *rational* might not be, well, *sensible.* We don't have much time to calculate when faced with an uncaged tiger; and tigers aside, choosing a lunch place rationally could leave us no time to eat! And even if we do have time, careful, thoughtful decision-making does not always work out well in practice, as we have seen.

Finally, there are cases where we do not maximize and are glad of it! In the prisoner's dilemma game, a maximizing strategy leads inexorably to an unwanted outcome. But as we have seen, even knowledgeable professionals did not, in fact, all play the game rationally. And one of the players, a philosopher, gave his reason: "I would rather be the person who buys the Brooklyn Bridge than the person who sells it."[33] This looks forward to the role of emotion in decision-making, and the strategic uses of emotion (Chap. 12).

The Bottom Line

The conclusion we reach is simply this. If the behaviorist approach to purposive behavior—reinforcement theory—is incomplete (Chap. 8), well, so is the prototype of the cognitive approach—decision theory. And if neither one will do, that means that at this point we simply do not have an adequate theory of purposive behavior. Such a theory, when it comes, will probably borrow ideas from both of the other theories; but it may well look quite different from either one.

33. For discussion of this experiment and related issues, see Hofstadter, 1985.

MODELS IN THE MIND

Since the last two chapters have been concerned with the cognitive approach to motivation, it is worth pausing to make clear the relations between the two chapters.

We get the future into the present, cognitive theory says, as an image of a potential state of affairs. Thus such images can represent the *imaginary* consequences of actions we *imagine* taking.

Here is where decision theory comes in. The decision maker is assumed to imagine possible actions and their consequences in deciding what to do. Thus the actor creates an internal model of the world. Then she runs the model faster than the world runs, and, from what happens in the model, she predicts the consequences of actions before they are performed. And she decides what action to take, based on those predictions. Specifically, she calculates the subjective expected utilities of the various actions and chooses the action whose subjective expected utility is highest.

The process reminds us of the use of computer models to simulate the world. Such models allow us to calculate what *would* happen if such and such were done. The advantages of this are very great. We can ask such questions as: If we made this or that design change, would the airplane be likely to crash? And we can ask the question without actually trying the experiment, risking a valuable real-world plane and a valuable real-world pilot. In a similar way, we can consider the costs and benefits of an action without the risk and effort of actually performing it in the real world. Decision theory as a cognitive theory is a simplified, first-pass attempt to describe how we do that "considering."

SUMMARY

As reinforcement theory is basic to modern behaviorism, so decision theory is basic to cognitive theories of action. It treats our decisions as guided by two factors: the utilities, or values to us, of the possible outcomes of an action (a motivational factor), and the probabilities of the various outcomes (a cognitive factor). The utilities, weighted (multiplied) by the probabilities, of the possible outcomes of each action sum to give us the *expected utility* of the action in question. Then we choose the action with the highest expected utility (or, where probabilities are unknown and must be estimated, the highest *subjective expected utility*).

The theory can be elaborated in a variety of ways. In *utility theory*, the principle of diminishing marginal utility shows that the value of a commodity to us is likely to decrease as the amount we already have increases. This simple psychological principle makes possible much of our economic activity, even such a simple matter as buying bread from a grocer. Often we must make a decision in which the outcome depends on whether some condition, *X*, is true or not when we are not sure whether it is true or not. Our decision then will depend on how likely we think it is that *X* is true (the cognitive factor) and the costs or benefits of possible outcomes (the motivational factor). *Signal-detection theory* applies decision theory to such cases. But rational decision-making does not always lead to the happiest possible outcomes, as shown by the *tragedy of the commons* and the nasty *prisoners' dilemma.*

Decision theory can also shed new light on the evolution of behavior. Species evolve because some forms leave more descendants than others, and so we can think of number of descendants as an outcome—a "progeny pay-off"—for "deciding" to evolve certain anatomical structures *and* tendencies to behave in certain ways. Thus shore crabs are "calibrated" so as to select prey that maximizes the benefit/cost ratio (energy gained/energy lost) in handling the prey. The Coolidge Effect (Chapter 4) can be seen as increasing the reproductive success of the male, though the female may increase her own reproductive success by behaving in ways that oppose it. In all this, however, decision theory is used descriptively, not cognitively. No one suggests that the animals do the calculations. If they behave as if they did, it is because ancestral animals that behaved that way left more descendants than those that did not; so modern animals, who *are* those descendants, have inherited the corresponding instinctive tendencies.

Reinforcement theory also makes contact with decision theory, as in the analysis of concurrent reinforcement schedules. The *matching law*—organisms divide their choices so as to match the relative amount of reinforcement for the various actions—gives rise to the *law of relative effect:* The effect of a reinforcer is relative to what other reinforcers are available. This work also has led to the notion of *melioration* as an alternative to the principle of maximizing expected utility. These ideas are yielding new points of convergence between behavioristic and cognitive theories.

Looking over these developments, we see that decision theory can be used in at least three quite different ways. It can be a *cognitive* theory, describing the calculations an actor performs before making her decision. Or it can be purely *descriptive,* describing the outcomes of a decision while making no assumptions about how the decision was made. Finally, it can be a *normative* theory, showing us what we ought to do in a given situation if we wish to maximize utility. These are quite distinct uses of the theory; in discussing evolution, for example, we use the theory as a descriptive one, but not as a cognitive one.

Decision theory is, after all, a theory. In real life, we may not behave as the theory suggests we do. First, we have only so much time and effort to devote to decision-making (we could not possibly consider *all possible* marriage partners, for example); and a careful, utility-maximizing decision strategy could take too long in emergencies or be too much trouble for trivial decisions. There are alternatives to maximizing, such as *satisficing* or *bettering.* But how do we decide among strategies? Do we decide how to decide? Do we decide how to decide how to decide? . . . An infinite regress threatens, and decision theory does not tell us how to avoid it.

Then too, much depends on what options we consider—which ones are cognitively *available* to us. Again, decision theory is no help; it tells us how to weigh the options we do consider, but not which ones we should consider.

Conversely, we may give more weight to certain considerations—those most easily verbalizable, for example—than these considerations ought to have.

Yet another complication is the problem of *framing*. Do we think in terms of lives saved or lives lost? What is the optimal decision may depend on how we look at a problem, and again the theory may be silent about how we ought to look at it.

All told, decision theory has limitations as a theory of action. Humans do not in fact always behave as rational decision makers. In some cases—perhaps many—we could not do so if we tried. And that is perhaps just as well, for it is not always clear that we *ought* to behave in a strictly "rational," payoff-maximizing way. The crisp logic of decision theory must come to grips with the fuzzy "psychologic" of actual decision-making, which includes considerations of what we do or do not think about (the problems of capacity and availability), of how we think about it (the problem of framing), and of what we really want.

PART 4

Human Motivation

CHAPTER 11

Motivation and Cognitive Processes

Reasoning does not *happen* to us; we *do* it.

—C. S. LEWIS

Over two thousand years ago, Socrates argued (pp. 27–28) that humans inherently *want* to do the right thing and will *decide* to do it, if only they *know* what it is. At least since that time, questions about action and questions about knowledge have been closely interrelated. Think again about decision theory: Choice is governed jointly by utilities (motivational), and subjective probabilities—what we know or believe (cognitive). This partnership is one reason why a book about motivation must say something about cognition as well.

There are other reasons. We have noted repeatedly that thinking, remembering, judging, and other cognitive operations are actions in their own right. "Reasoning does not *happen* to us; we *do* it." Perhaps what we have learned about overt actions may help us understand cognitive "actions" as well. The first part of this chapter will explore that possibility.

Second, are motivation and cognition really independent of each other? In decision theory, they can in principle vary quite independently. We may want something very much (high utility). But we may see our chances of getting it (subjective probability) as anything from zero (no chance at all; that's awful!) to unity (a sure thing; isn't that nice!). But wait: If we want something very much, may that very desire make it *seem* more likely to happen? Do we tend to believe what we want to believe, remember what we like better than what we don't, and so on? Do motivational influences affect and perhaps distort our cognitive actions? The second part will consider such questions.

Finally, motives and cognitions cooperate so intimately that they can be hard to disentangle. One may easily be mistaken for the other. At the end of the chapter we will look at some examples of this difficulty, and at the controversies to which it has led.

COGNITIVE ACTIONS: STIMULUS-BOUND AND GOAL-DIRECTED

Back in Chapter 5, we distinguished between *stimulus-bound* actions and *goal-directed* ones (pp. 113–15). The former, which include reflexes and certain action patterns, are controlled by their antecedents. The latter, which have the flexibility of motivational states, are controlled by their consequences; one does *whatever is available* to attain a goal.

Well, a similar distinction has been made among cognitive operations. It has become customary to distinguish two kinds of these: *automatic,* and *goal-directed.* The former tend to occur effortlessly and, well, automatically; we need not try to perform them, and, indeed, they may run themselves off even if we try to inhibit them.

An example? Look at the following array of lines, but *do not read it:*

WALL

We can't; it is impossible. The act of reading a word is so well learned and habitual that it seems to happen all by itself, not only with no effort but despite any effort to hold it in check. That example, by the way, shows that an "automatic" cognitive action—like an instinctive action pattern—need not be a simple one. *Reading* obviously is a fantastically complicated process; but in experienced readers, it is automatic just the same.

As an example of an effortful, goal-directed process, think of trying to prove a geometric theorem. Or consider the *tip-of-the-tongue* phenomenon. We try to remember: What was the name of that Russian composer who wrote *Night on Bald Mountain?* Was it Malenkov? No, he was a politician. Malinsky? No. . . . Gosh, it's on the tip of our tongue! We may remember that it begins with M, and has three syllables with the accent on the middle one. We have what William James called a word-shaped hole in our memories, a kind of schematic *search image* of the word we seek, but we don't have hold of the word itself. And we do what a rat seeking water might do, trying one thing and, if it doesn't work, trying another. . . . When we get to the "goal," we know it.

And, Reader, if *you* can't remember who the composer was and are feeling frustrated, take note of that frustration, for that, in a way, is my point. (It was Moussorgsky.)

Of course, real-life action (overt or cognitive) may have components of both kinds. As just one example, consider a *dichotic listening* experiment. A subject sits with headphones on, and a stream of words is fed simultaneously into his two ears—different words to each ear (Figure 11.1). The subject may be

A list of words, or (as here) a passage of connected discourse, is fed into one ear . . .

. . . while at the same time a different list or a different connected passage (as here) goes to the other ear . . .

. . . and the subject is instructed to attend to one or the other.

Figure 11-1 An experiment in directed attention.

instructed to attend to only one ear, the left or the right. He can do this, directing attention as requested (goal-directed), so as to ignore the information that comes to the unattended ear. And when questioned later, he may have little or no memory for what was fed into that ear. But let a very loud word be fed into that ear, or the subject's own name—and that will be remembered. Certain signals, in other words, can preempt attention in an automatic, stimulus-bound way—a kind of "misbehavior of cognition" (pp. 316–19)!

COGNITIVE CONSTRAINTS AND COGNITIVE SHORTCUTS

Especially when our cognitive operations are effortful, we face again the problem of *capacity* (pp. 288–89). We can think of only so many things at a time, and have only so much energy to expend in cognitive work. The Scarecrow's problem was that, lacking a brain, he had limited cognitive capacity indeed.

As we saw in the last chapter, a fully rational, careful, maximizing decision-making strategy may not be a sensible strategy to use; it may be more effort than it is worth for trivial decisions, and take too long for emergencies. Exactly the same can be said for *thinking* in a careful, fully rational way, basing our beliefs and judgments on a thorough gathering and weighing of the evidence. It could take too long, and it might not be worth it.

In everyday life, our decision-making makes heavy use of shortcut, labor-saving strategies such as satisficing and bettering (pp. 389–91). In a similar way, our everyday thinking makes extensive use of cognitive shortcuts. We use ways of making judgments and forming beliefs that are quicker and more efficient, even if less accurate, than a careful scientific approach would be.

"If this road goes in, it must come out," said the Scarecrow, "and as the Emerald City is at the other end of the road, we must go wherever it leads us."

"Anyone would know that," said Dorothy.

"Certainly, that is why I know it," returned the Scarecrow. "If it required brains to figure it out, I never should have said it."

—L. FRANK BAUM,
The Wizard of Oz

Heuristics

A **heuristic** is a rule of thumb. It is a principle which, while not guaranteed to work every time, will work well enough for practical purposes most of the time. We use certain cognitive rules of thumb in deciding what to believe, or what to do. Let us look at some of these.*

THE AVAILABILITY HEURISTIC   In forming beliefs, we depend heavily on what we can remember about cases like the one that confronts us. So we search our memories for relevant information. The **availability heuristic** is a rule of thumb that says: Deal with the first few things you can remember. In other words: Use the information that is most readily *available* in memory.

What affects the availability of items in memory? It depends on how *noticeable* and *memorable* they are—how likely we were to notice an event when it happened, and how likely we are to recall it now. These in turn depend on a number of things—how recently or how often we've encountered such an event, and how noticeable or salient it was relative to other events.

As a specific example, *events* themselves are likely to be noticed and remembered. Non-events, things that do *not* occur, are not likely to be noticed or remembered—even if their non-occurrence is informative.

Even this simple mechanism can wreak havoc. Consider a scenario:

> P and O are roommates. P has the annoying habit of leaving his socks on the floor for O to pick up. After the two discuss the matter, P agrees to deal with his own socks. Usually he does; and when he does, O hardly notices, for it is only what is expected (compare *surprises,* pp. 239–41). But occasionally P forgets and leaves his socks on the floor, and O picks them up—noticing, resenting, and remembering. The confrontation is easy to imagine. O says to P, "My goodness, P," or words to that effect, "you *always* throw your socks on the floor!" For in fact, the only socks-related episodes O has available in memory are of just that kind. Whereas P, who remembers all the times he might have thrown his socks on the floor, but didn't, replies: "I most certainly do not!" Escalation is likely.

THE REPRESENTATIVENESS HEURISTIC   Another rule of thumb is that *similar things belong together.* That is the **representativeness heuristic.** For instance, we assume that actors resemble their actions. We assume that causes resemble their effects.

One example of this is the **halo effect,** the tendency for persons high in one "good" attribute to be rated high in others as well. Good qualities, we assume, go with good people; bad qualities, with bad people. In an experimental demonstration, a child's misbehavior was judged as a milder offense if an attractive child committed it. And the child was judged less likely to misbe-

---

*For an excellent and highly readable treatment of the issues touched on here, see Nisbett and Ross, 1980. The following sketch draws heavily on their discussion.

have again if he was shown as attractive than if he was shown as ugly. Thus predictions—subjective probabilities—are affected as well as judgments.[1]

Conversely: If bad things happen to us, we must be bad people. In the days after World War II, a group of German civilians was taken through a nearby Nazi death camp. One was heard to say, "What terrible criminals these prisoners must have been to get such punishment."[2]

Schemas

We encountered the notion of a *schema* back in Chapter 9 (pp. 350–62). Schemas represent our knowledge and beliefs about *kinds* of things, or kinds of persons *(players)* or events *(scripts)*. Examples are the knowledge we have about cats-in-general, eating-at-restaurants-in-general, Jerks-in-general, generals-in-general, and the like.

It is likely that every event or person we encounter is immediately classified, or, as we say, *assimilated* to a schema. Once that happens, our actions are affected not just by what we observe, but by what we know—or think we know—about that kind of thing. And our prior knowledge and theories about the world are vitally important, for they tell us what to expect, and what to do, even where we have no observations to draw on, as when we meet a professor or enter a restaurant we have never encountered before.

Schema-Driven Inference

What schemas tell us comes as a kind of logical inference: I know these things about *X*s, *this* is an *X*, therefore I know these things about *this* too. Hence we speak of *schema-driven inference:* we use the knowledge we have about the general case to make inferences about this particular one.

Often our inferences are quite correct, of course. Trouble can arise, however, when we depend too much on schemas and not enough on the specifics of the case before us. We say in effect: "I know all about it. Who needs facts?" It is interesting that we have a special name for schemas when used that way; we call them "preconceptions." Let us see examples of what can happen.

THE FALSE SCHEMA.   First, we may depend on a schema that is simply wrong. History abounds with examples of schematic thinking that seem quaint to us now. Consider the fate of one Rodrigo de Jeres, who sailed with Columbus to the West Indies and picked up the smoking habit there. He brought the habit back with him to Spain; but when he began breathing smoke from his nostrils, the authorities thought he was demon-possessed and tossed him in prison!

A contemporary example is the *false stereotype*. Consider the belief, widely held by both men and women, that women-in-general are no good at math.

1. Dion, 1972.
2. Gleitman, 1981, p. 558.

The belief may be quite false; but if a woman's math professor, or the woman herself, believes it, this can have unfortunate consequences. The woman may avoid math courses or, if she takes one, give up and not study. The professor may be reluctant to help her; or he may look at her papers in a cursory way, their fate already sealed.

THE MISAPPLIED SCHEMA.   Then there are cases where a schema is quite accurate in itself, but is triggered where it does not apply (Fig. 11-2).

> I'm always amazed at the number of people who fire off flashbulbs when photographing a sunset. If you ask them why they do it, they say, "Because it's getting dark, and when it's dark you need flash." These two statements are correct. At sunset, general illumination is decreased, and flash adds light when it is dark. Unfortunately, flash has no appreciable effect beyond ten feet. The sun is some 93 million miles away . . .
>
> —MICHAEL CRICHTON,
> *Electronic Life*

Well, let's look at that instance. What kind of problem do we face?—that is, to what schema do we assimilate it? One answer is: *The problem is to take a picture in dim light.* And how do we solve that problem? Use a flash—obviously! But if instead we see that the *problem is to take a picture of the sun,* then we will pocket the flash bulb and save its cost.

There can be room for disagreement as to which schema properly applies to a given instance. Consider this case study:

> Professor Y told Sarah that he liked her hairstyle, that it looked less severe than when she first got it cut. I was there when he said it, and I watched her expression. Once he left the room I tried to calm her—he meant well, he was trying to be

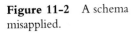

Figure 11-2 A schema misapplied.

friendly in his awkward way—but she was outraged. What makes him think he can say that to me? she asked. That is sexual harassment.[3]

Attempt to be friendly, or harassment? I can't resolve that, of course, but note that the question is: Which schema applies? The example reminds us, too, that schemas can be heavily charged with emotion (*schema-triggered affect*, pp. 357–60), and thus have motivational significance—as here![4]

DEFAULT VALUES.   Schemas, we recall, are items of belief about general cases; specifics are unspecified. But certain specifics may be *assumed* when a schema is activated, unless information to the contrary is offered—and used. Schemas, as we say, have *default values.*★

An example? Think of the riddle—the one about the surgeon and her son (p. 392). What makes it so hard to solve? The fact that our surgeon schema has "male" as its default value for the (unspecified) gender. Unless we are given some hints, the sub-schema "female surgeon" tends not to occur to us—it tends to be cognitively unavailable. And note again: My unpublished studies show that this is just as true for female college students as for male ones.

Combining Shortcuts

We are not restricted to one or another cognitive shortcut. Often we combine them. Then, if used appropriately, they save us all the more time and effort; if inappropriately, they can get us even deeper into trouble. To see this, and to review these themes, let's consider a case that combines several of them.

A few years ago, a judge (a certain Archie Simpson) acquitted a fifteen-year-old male who had raped a high-school female. The judge thought the girl's dress had been so short that she had excited the boy's passions to irresistible levels!

What we have learned might help us understand this reaction. Our account will of course be speculative—we can't look inside His Honor's head, or the boy's—but let's look at what *might* have happened.

The crime occurred, the male was brought to trial, and the judge looked for a plausible cause for his behavior. Well, the crime was sexual, so the judge assumed that its cause lay in an excess of sexual motivation. Here is the *representativeness heuristic*—effects resemble causes. But what produced the excess? The girl's short skirt was readily *available* as an explanation, especially if it triggered this *schema:* Revealing dress (in general) excites males (in general)! That schema may have some truth to it, but it may well have been misapplied here. His Honor may also have believed that women secretly want to be raped, and

3. Roiphe, 1993, p. 118.
4. D'Andrade, 1992.
★The term is borrowed from computer jargon. In many computer programs, the computer will automatically assign certain values to certain variables, unless it is told specifically to do otherwise. These "assumed" values are the default values for those variables.

"ask for it" by dressing provocatively—another schema! So he made the *schema-driven inference* which no doubt drove disapproval in turn *(schema-driven affect):* It was all the girl's fault! The victim had suddenly become the offender.

It is unlikely that Judge Simpson thought much beyond these conclusions, which reflected *default values* in his schematic thinking. Had he thought the matter through more carefully, he might have seen that a quite different explanation was possible. Many males in this society still accept schemas like these: A woman's "no" may (in general) mean "yes;" and to sweep a woman off her feet is (in general) a daring, macho, and masculine thing to do. If these schemas were in the male's head, he might have been acting, not from irresistible sexual passion, but out of a set of beliefs—i.e., schemas. We might, in other words, better understand his action in *cognitive* than in *motivational* terms. If so, this example also shows how easily the one may be mistaken for the other.

It should be made very clear that we are trying to understand what the boy did, not to excuse it. (The old saw that "to understand is to forgive" is, obviously, quite false.) When offered the idea that such an action could come from "cold" cognitive sources rather than "hot" passions, many people are incensed. It's as if such an explanation made excuses for rapists, or invited us to think of rape as somehow less bad.

But that's the representativeness heuristic again! Effects should resemble their causes; bad effects should have bad causes. And, if we say that rape may reflect cognitive operations that are not bad in themselves, we may seem to be saying that the act itself is not such a bad thing.

But that is *not* what cognitive writers are saying, and their analysis does *not* make such behavior any more tolerable or any less severe a social problem. It does, however, suggest that there may be ways of combating it that would be more effective than trying to redirect the passions. We might do better to combat the misconceptions instead.

A Look Backward: Shortcuts and Decisions

This discussion, like much of the literature on this problem, has emphasized the errors that heuristic and schematic thinking can produce. Yet the use of these cognitive shortcuts is not an inherently foolish way to proceed.

THE VALUE OF SHORTCUTS   We operate under constraints. We can handle only so much information at a time, and we have limited time for thinking. Heuristics and schema serve us well, most of the time, by reducing the amount of information we have to deal with.

Take availability, for instance. If we encounter a tiger, we really don't want to run through *all* we know about tigers—tiger begins with "t," tigers are mammals, tigers live in Asia but the *Tarzan* books got it muddled and put them in Africa—before deciding what to do. We have time to think of only a few things, and they might as well be the most noticeable and memorable ones. After all, noticeable and memorable things do tend to be important, most of the time.

As for schemas, it is inconceivable that we could function without them. We would have to forget all we knew and start from scratch in investigating every situation, an intolerable cognitive burden. Then too, letting our acts be guided by a causal theory is not necessarily irrational even if the theory is wrong. Suppose we lived in a society that does a communal rain dance in the spring; then the rains come and the crops grow. Now, a simple experiment would show that the rain dance has nothing to do with it; the rains would come anyway. But the community is not about to omit the rain dance just to see what will happen! The crops are too important, and the present practice is good enough. As we say: If it ain't broke, don't fix it (another heuristic!).

Thus heuristic and schematic thinking are not automatically bad thinking. They can be seen as a kind of cognitive *satisficing,* a set of cognitive operations which work well enough, most of the time, for us to make sense of the world and get around in it. Trouble arises because we may substitute these shortcuts even when better information is available, and even when the judgment is important. We satisfice, so to speak, when we could and should maximize instead.

SHORTCUTS AND SATISFICING   There is still another old idea that arises in a new context here. When we discussed *satisficing* in decision-making, we saw that the order in which alternatives are considered makes a great difference. In deciding where to go for lunch, either Archie's Place or Zorba's Place might be good enough; and we'd go to whichever place we thought of first. So whenever we use a satisficing strategy—and that is very often—we could reach different solutions to the same decision problem, depending on which options we think of first.

Well, what will we think of first? We will think of the options most available in memory, and those that are most typical solutions to the *kind* of problem we see the decision problem to be. In other words, heuristics and schemas affect our decisions by affecting whether an option will come to mind early or late. When we satisfice, if we don't think of an option early, we probably won't consider it at all.

HEURISTICS, SCHEMAS, AND HUNCHES   Finally, let us again look back to Chapter 10. There we saw that most humans operate most of the time on hunches, intuitions, and habits—not on rational calculations. Well, heuristics and schemas sound a lot like hunches and habits—habits of thought, if you like. These ways of making decisions work well enough, most of the time, to produce satisfactory and even rational-looking results, by not-quite-rational means.

THE COGNITIVE-COHERENCE MOTIVE

In the previous section, we looked at shortcuts designed to save us cognitive work. Now let us look at the other side of the coin. We may also *spend* cognitive time and effort, when at first it would seem that we don't have to. We do it in order to keep our ideas simple, coherent, and intelligible.

We began this book by noting that the itch to understand things, to make sense of them, to perceive the world as orderly and coherent, is a powerful motive for human beings. It is the driving force behind science itself. We *want things to make sense,* and we are willing to do some cognitive work to make them do so.

Coherence in Perception

This work occurs even in the perception of simple figures. Take a look at Figure 11-3, a simple cube. We have some options as to just how we see the cube. We can see it with the northwest face forward, or with the southeast face forward. But we cannot, without a great deal of effort, see it as a two-dimensional array of lines with nothing forward of anything else—which is what it is! As an array of lines, it is just too complicated to perceive as a unit. We do the cognitive work of creating a non-existent third dimension. Then the complex array of lines snaps into a simple, coherent figure—a three-dimensional cube.

Actually, that bit of mental work probably *saves* us work in the long run. As a result of it, we don't have to contemplate a complex, puzzling figure. It's a cube, that's all, and we know all about cubes. That saving in mental effort may well be the basis of the cognitive-coherence motive.

The principle operates in time as well as space, to affect our perception of events and actions as well as of simple pictures. We try to perceive these too as simple, complete, well-organized wholes. We don't like it when events don't make sense, or when actions are left up in the air.

Figure 11-3 A two-dimensional array of lines that is seen as a three-dimensional cube.

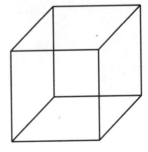

Here is a demonstration that I use in lecturing. While talking, I take out a cigarette and put it in my mouth. I begin to light it, but then remove it from my mouth as if struck by a thought, and say a few words. I put it back in in mouth, begin to light it, remove it again and say something more, ... I seldom have to do that more than three or four times before the tension becomes unbearable, with shuffling of feet and perfectly audible mutters of "Will you *light* that thing?"

In both cases, the cube and the cigarette, the reaction is more or less automatic. But we can see similar tensions generated by effortful, goal-directed attempts to make sense of the input. For example, Reader: What does the following say?

YOU   JUST   ME

Word salad! It makes no sense. As we stare at it, we try different ways of interpreting it (whatever is available); but we know that what we try is wrong if it doesn't relieve the tension, if we don't feel that click of comprehension: "Oh, I see! Yes, that does make sense." And that cognitive click is unmistakable when it does occur—as when, stymied, we look at the bottom of the page.★

Coherence and Memory

We do cognitive work, then, to make our perceptions coherent and simple. We work on our memories, too, to produce coherence and simplicity over time. In a word, we rewrite them.

REWRITING OUR HISTORIES   In one study, after having given their opinions on a topic, students were induced to write essays opposing their own opinions. Later on, the students' attitudes showed a shift in the direction of the essays' positions (see cognitive dissonance, pp. 424–29).[5] More surprising, the students then remembered their previous attitudes—expressed only a week earlier—as similar to their present ones, rather than as they actually had been.

In another study, a group of adults was surveyed in 1973 and again in 1982 as to their opinions on a variety of issues—aid to minorities, equality for women, legalization of marijuana, and the like. In addition, they were asked in 1982 how they had responded in 1973. The subjects' recall of their 1973 attitudes was actually more closely related to their present attitudes than to their actual past ones![6]

We may also rewrite our memories so that old memories are made coherent with new inputs—new questions, for example. In one study, if subjects

---

★What it says—of course!—is "just between you and me."

5. Bem and McConnell, 1970; see also Wixon and Laird, 1976.
6. Marcus, 1986.

who had watched a videotaped auto accident were asked "How fast were the cars going when they smashed into each other?" the subjects "remembered" higher speeds than if the word "hit" was used instead of "smashed into."[7] Asked, "Did another car pass the red Datsun while it was stopped at the stop sign?" many subjects later "remembered" a stop sign that simply hadn't been there.

This sort of question-induced rewriting of memory raises some serious practical concerns.

EYEWITNESS TESTIMONY   On May 15, 1975, the assistant manager of a store was kidnapped at gunpoint and driven to the store where he worked. He was told to open the safe, but he convinced his two kidnappers that he could not do so. They took $35 from his wallet and let him go.

The victim described the kidnappers' car, but all he could say about the men was that one of them looked Hispanic, and looked like a man who had recently applied for a job at the store. On the basis of his memory, a composite sketch was made by the police.

Three days later the police stopped a car that looked like the one described, and arrested the driver and passenger. Neither one looked like the sketch; neither had applied for a job; and both had several witnesses to their being elsewhere when the crime took place. Nevertheless, the manager positively identified them as the kidnappers, and the jury convicted them. Only when one of the real kidnappers confessed were they released, and then only because of a pardon issued by the governor. The courts refused to re-try them![8]

This miscarriage of justice occurred because the jurors placed too much confidence in the manager's identification of the two men. "Seeing is believing," we say (a heuristic!). The jury discounted the clear fact that the composite sketch, made on the basis of the manager's more recent memories, looked quite different from either suspect. But then why should the manager have identified one of them as one of the kidnappers? A possible answer, though speculative, is: For the same reason that experimental subjects, asked about a stop sign that wasn't there, "remembered" one now. As memory for the past can be rewritten so as to be coherent with a question asked now, so it can be rewritten to fit a person presented now.

(Incidentally, the story does have a happy ending in that the prisoners were released; but the episode cost the two impoverished men many thousands of dollars.)

THE FALSE-MEMORY SYNDROME   In the fall of 1988, Mr. Paul Ingram was accused by his two daughters, now young adults, of having abused them sexually when they were little. Mr. Ingram first denied the charges, but later, at the urging of detectives and of his pastor, began to produce memories that

7. Loftus and Palmer, 1974.
8. Baddeley, 1990.

supported them. It appeared that he, as well as the daughters, had repressed those horrifying memories until careful probing allowed him to recover them.

As time went on, the daughters' accusations spread to the mother and to two male friends of the family, and were elaborated into "memories" of ghastly Satanic rituals involving torture and the sacrifice of animals and human babies. Eventually, the stories became too bizarre and contradictory for even the prosecution to believe; but by that time, Mr. Ingram had already pleaded guilty to the original charges of abuse and had been imprisoned; and the two men friends had been held in custody for quite a long time. Clearly a family had been destroyed.

It may well be that none of it had ever happened. But if so, why had Mr. Ingram confessed? A psychologist, Richard Offshe, tried an experiment: Could he actually *implant* in Mr. Ingram a memory for something that had never occurred, by insisting that it had occurred, and that Mr. Ingram would remember it if he allowed himself to do so? Yes, he could, and did.[9] The experimental implantation of such false memories has been demonstrated by others too, including Elizabeth Loftus, a prominent memory researcher.[10]

The implications of these findings for law enforcement are horrendous. What they imply is that *even a confession is not proof positive of guilt*. It has now been shown by direct experiment that an accused can "remember" an episode that simply did not take place. That is the *false-memory syndrome*.

In the past few years, literally thousands of persons have come forth with memories ("memories"?) of sexual or ritual abuse, many years earlier, by parents, teachers, or religious counselors. There are two ways of interpreting this recent flood of accusations. One is that very many people, encouraged by society's awareness of the problem and acceptance of its victims, are bringing their memories out of the closet of repression and calling their victimizers to account. But the other is that many of the charges are false memories, triggered by the *availability* of child-abuse scripts in today's society, together with the well-intentioned encouragement of therapists to "remember" such episodes—and that the lives of quite innocent people are being destroyed by the false-memory syndrome. Certainly some of the "memories" would strain credulity to the breaking point, absent an atmosphere of hysteria.★

In 1992, a number of accused parents founded the False Memory Syndrome Foundation in Philadelphia, to aid and support parents falsely accused by their children. Within a year, more than 3700 people so accused had come forward!

Make no mistake: Child abuse by adults can and does occur; and when it does, we are right to insist that something be done about it. But the false-mem-

---

9. Offshe, 1992.
10. Loftus, 1993.

★Consider a woman who had come to remember sexual abuse by her uncle. She recalled the exact date. Her horrified mother showed her that in fact, the uncle had been in Korea at the time. Responded the woman: "I see, Mother. Yes. Well, let me think. If your dates are right, I suppose it must have been Dad" (McHugh, 1992).

ory syndrome can and does occur, too. Whether it happens only in highly suggestible people, or could happen to anyone under the right conditions, is an open question. At the very least, it implies that accusations dredged up from "memory" need to be bolstered with independent evidence, and this requirement, where the crime is private almost by definition, will seldom be easy to meet.

Finally, we recall that the false memory syndrome may have contaminated the very core of the initial evidence that Sigmund Freud put forward for his theory of motivation: episodes of childhood seduction remembered or fantasized by his patients (pp. 41–42). It now appears that Freud was far from being a passive, objective observer. Rather he was quite capable of concluding that this-or-that must have happened, and forcing his guesses insistently on his patients. Many of these patients never did remember the early episodes Freud insisted upon. Even when they did, the resulting memories might have been false ones of just the kind we're discussing. It would be the height of irony if Freud were remembered as the discoverer, not of infantile sexual urges persisting in the unconscious, but of a quite different, powerful, and dangerous unconscious mechanism: the false memory syndrome.

A LOOK BACKWARD   The important thing to remember is that when we "call up" a memory, our minds are doing something *now*. And what we do includes *cognitive work*—something we do to our memories that changes them, making them less complicated but less accurate too. As we transform a two-dimensional figure into three dimensions, so we transform a memory for a previous attitude into one that agrees with our current one, or a memory for a previous event into one that is coherent with the questions to which, much later, we are now responding.

This too may save us cognitive work in the long run.[11] Perhaps "I've always thought *X*" is just easier to remember than "I thought not-*X* before, but I think *X* now." So we lighten our memory load, even at the cost of inaccuracy.

The question is how much inaccuracy, and of what kinds, we can accept. We need to be aware that distortions of memory are very real, and, as in the false-memory syndrome, are capable of doing enormous damage.

Coherence and Causal Understanding

A special case of the cognitive-coherence motive is so important that it rates a section of its own. In our efforts to make the world intelligible, finding **causal explanations** for events plays a central role. We may do a formidable amount of cognitive work to answer the question: Why did that happen?

11. Greenwald, 1980.

The Goal of Causal Understanding

The search for causal understanding is not always just idle wondering. It can have all the properties of purposive, goal-directed behavior. For example, Shelley Taylor has examined this process in cancer patients, cardiac patients, and others faced with life-threatening events. In people's reactions to such events, she finds that a *search for causal explanation* is prominent. People ask themselves: What caused the event to happen?[12]

And they find, or construct, answers. The true cause or causes of cancer are unknown. Nevertheless, almost all cancer patients (95 percent in Taylor's sample) adopted some explanation for their disease: stress, diet, heredity, or *something*. Interestingly, far fewer (63 percent) of the patients' *spouses* adopted such explanations. This difference suggests that the patients' search for explanation was an *active, goal-directed process;* the patients were not just parroting the explanations offered by folklore. If it were only that, such explanations should have come as readily from the spouses as from the patients.

Even more revealing is what happened when a causal explanation was disconfirmed. Most patients would quickly pick up another one to replace it. One patient, for instance, blamed her cancer on a recent car accident and wanted to sue the other driver. Assured by her doctor and her lawyer that that causal theory was unfounded, she promptly switched to another cause instead. The whole process reminds us of our definition of a motivational state. The actor takes *whatever means is available* to reach a goal—here, the goal of feeling that one understands why one is ill. And a patient does take any cognitive means available to attain that goal; if one explanation won't work, she will try another.

The urge to understand may be yet another universal characteristic of the human mind. Every culture we know of has invented *myths*—causal stories, or causal theories, about why the world is as it is and where it came from. Inasmuch as these include some of the world's finest literature, it is evident that the cognitive work put into them is very considerable.

Cognitive Conservatism: The Stubbornness of Schemas

If cognitive work may be done to keep our perceptions, memories, and self-concepts *simple*, it is also done to keep them *stable*. This has been called **cognitive conservatism**—a disposition to keep existing knowledge structures the way they are.[13] In a word, we resist changing our minds.

> One of the authors, in his first years of teaching, was amazed and disturbed by the tendency of many of his female undergraduate students to maintain negative stereotypes of their mathematical abilities even though their successes belied such stereotypes. Often, a student would succeed admirably in a statistics course that, on the first day of class, she had tearfully predicted she would fail. Such a student usually

12. Taylor, 1983.
13. Greenwald, 1980.

proved capable of readily assimilating her unanticipated success to her previous view of herself, assigning credit to the lucidity and patience of the instructor, to her strenuous efforts, or to the "easiness" of the course. It was quite difficult to get such a student to entertain the possibility that her previous theory about herself was simply wrong.[14]

Such a student's self-concept, or self-schema, contains the item "I can't do math." And the schema is defended against contrary data. In the example, such data were dismissed by a *schema-driven inference:* The woman inferred her success was due to luck and effort, and not to ability. And she did that, not because the data required such an inference but because her self-schema did.

The process has been demonstrated experimentally as well. In one such study, subjects were given false information about how well they were doing at a novel task. Some were told they were doing well; others, that they were doing poorly.

Then the experimenter "debriefed" the subjects, telling them—truthfully— that they had been *assigned* to receive bogus evaluations, good or bad, by a random-number table. They were even shown the experimenter's instruction sheet, assigning them to one or the other condition before the task had even begun. Surely, this total discrediting of the evidence should have convinced the subjects that the information they had received was worthless, and that it implied nothing about their ability at the task.

Not so. When asked how likely they were to do well at such a task in the future, subjects receiving a bad initial report continued to rate themselves lower than those who had received a good initial report. What the subjects were told at the outset—"You're doing well" or "You're doing poorly"—seemed to set up a theory in the subject's mind about his own ability at the task. And the theory persisted *after the evidence for it was totally discredited.*[15]

How Are Schemas Defended?

We defend our opinions, theories, and concepts—our schemas—against data that challenge them. How do we defend them? There are several ways.

SELECTIVE INFORMATION PROCESSING   In the first place, schemas serve as organizers of information, and so new information, as it comes in, is assimilated to them. For instance, subjects watched a videotape of a woman having dinner with her husband. Some were told she worked as a waitress; they remembered seeing that she drank beer and owned a television. Others were told she worked as a librarian; they remembered that she wore glasses and owned classical records.[16] In a word, memory was **selective.** What was

14. Nisbett and Ross, 1980.
15. Ross, Lepper, and Hubbard, 1975; see also Ross and Anderson, 1982.
16. Cohen, 1981.

remembered was what fit the stereotype; and, therefore, what was remembered supported it.

CREATIVE INFORMATION PROCESSING: THE "ILLUSORY CORRELATION" In evaluating our ideas, we may not only select confirming information, but also manufacture it! In a word, we may "see" evidence that simply isn't there. In one study, subjects read a series of fictitious protocols which presented descriptions of patients' symptoms along with their responses to Rorschach ink blots. These responses were paired *randomly* with symptoms, so that there could be no correlation between one and the other. Nevertheless the subjects, having read over the material, reported having "seen" the symptom-response relationships that theoretically should have been there. The subjects, by the way, were not college students. They were experienced clinicians.[17]

ELASTIC ATTRIBUTION   The *attribution* process selects among many possible causal explanations for any event. Since there are so many options, it is likely that *some* explanation can be found that is consistent with the schema, and so allows us to hang on to it. We saw this earlier in the case of the woman who did well on a statistics exam. By attributing success to luck or effort, rather than to ability, she defended her theory of herself: "Nevertheless, I can't do math!"

Similar mechanisms can allow a prejudiced person to defend her prejudices against any assault by the facts. Suppose we believe that members of Group X are incompetent. We meet a member of Group X who has done well at a demanding job, and therefore seems highly competent. Is he evidence against our belief? No; we simply attribute his success to an external cause—he was lucky, or people smoothed the way for him. But if we see a member of Group X who is not in fact doing well, we attribute it to *him*—he is incompetent—and that too fits our prejudice! A person of Group X is compatible with our prejudiced schema whether he does good things or bad things, succeeds or fails. Research has shown the process in action (Figure 11-4).[18]

THE SELF-FULFILLING PROPHECY   The surest way of guarding a theory from contrary data is not to let the contrary data arise. If our theory says that X ought to happen, we may act in such a way as to assure that it will. The theory becomes a **self-fulfilling prophecy.** The student convinced that she can't learn statistics may not study—and so never learn statistics.

WOODEN-HEADEDNESS   Finally, there is what historian Barbara Tuchman has called **wooden-headedness.**[19] This is a failure, or refusal, to lay our

17. Chapman and Chapman, 1969.
18. Pettigrew, 1979.
19. Tuchman, 1984.

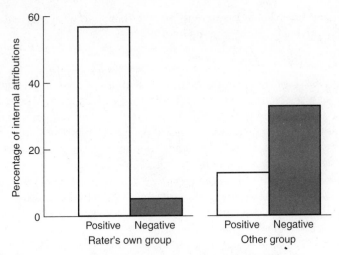

Figure 11-4 Elastic attribution. These data were collected in India, at a time when hostility among religious groups was intense. Subjects were given descriptions of actions—some good actions, some bad ones—and were asked to choose the most likely cause of each action. For each kind of action, some were described as carried out by a member of the rater's own group; others, as carried out by a member of the other group that the rater disliked. Positive actions by one's own group, and negative actions by the other-group members, were more likely to receive *internal* attributions—the acts were attributed to characteristics of the actor. Bad actions by one's own group, and good actions by the other group, usually received *external* attributions—the acts were assumed to be caused by the situation. (Data from Pettigrew, 1979.)

theories alongside the facts at all. We might call it the pure case of schema-driven inference; it says, "My mind is made up. Don't confuse me with facts."

Gordon Allport, in his classic book *The Nature of Prejudice,* reported the following dialogue:[20]

> X: The trouble with the Jews is that they only take care of their own group.
> Y: But the record of the Community Chest campaign shows that they gave more generously . . . to the general charities of the community than do non-Jews.
> X: That shows they are always trying to buy favor and intrude into Christian affairs. They think of nothing but money; that is why there are so many Jewish bankers.
> Y: But a recent study shows that the percentage of Jews in the banking business is negligible, far smaller than the percentage of non-Jews.

20. Allport, 1954, pp. 13–14.

X: That's just it; they don't go in for respectable business; they are only in the movie business or run night clubs.★

Striking in this dialogue is how Mr. X's mutually incompatible and totally wrong beliefs never confronted either the facts or each other. So, neither their falseness nor their contradictions (there are so many Jewish bankers/they don't go into respectable business) were recognized. The "facts" lived in logic-tight compartments, impervious to evidence.

Refusal to acknowledge facts has a long history, as Tuchman shows. "No matter how often a campaign that depended on living off a hostile country ran into want and even starvation, as in the English invasions of France in the Hundred Years' War, campaigns for which this fate was inevitable were regularly undertaken."[21]

About some things, we just don't learn.

Why not? Perhaps, in such cases, we simply do not do the cognitive work of relating the data to the theory at all. We do not detect the clash of the data with the theory, because we don't compare them. If we "mindlessly" follow a theory without checking it, then it goes uncorrected, however often it is disconfirmed.

A LOOK BACKWARD: CONSERVATISM AND COGNITIVE CONSTRAINTS   The stubbornness of our theories is yet another cognitive complication that is not, in itself, foolish or maladaptive. A scientist may hold on to a well-supported theory, even in the face of contrary evidence; it is not necessarily irrational to trust the theory more than the evidence. And our opinions of others and ourselves should not be expected to drift with every exception or inconsistency. "[I]f you changed your mind about your integrity every time you let a parking meter run out, you would never be sure of exactly who you were."[22] Cognitive conservatism can be justified, then, on the grounds that proceeding any other way is simply too *expensive* in the time and effort it would take to keep updating our opinions and theories as life went on around us.

Conservatism becomes a problem when it is *too* conservative. But this happens often; we are likely to have much more confidence in our opinions, and cling to our theories much more stubbornly, than is rational or even sensible.[23] In the extreme case, no data can shake our theory, because we make no use of data at all—and we have wooden-headedness.

★Allport's book was written in 1954, and it would be comforting to think that our society has outgrown that sort of thinking. But the following was said in 1974: "Jewish influence in Congress . . . is so strong you wouldn't believe it. . . . They own, you know, the banks in this country, the newspapers. Just look at where the Jewish money is." The speaker was chairman of the Joint Chiefs of Staff.

21. Tuchman, 1984, p. 8.
22. Fiske and Taylor, 1990, p. 20.
23. See for example Einhorn, 1982; Slovic et al., 1982.

When Are Schemas Defended?

Obviously, cognitive conservatism operates within limits. We don't *always* resist changing our minds. We have even been known to admit that we were wrong. When do we do that, and when do we defend our theories?

Some writers have suggested that we follow a least-effort principle here.[24] If a belief is weak and the disconfirming evidence is strong, we are likely to change our minds. If the reverse is true, we don't; we reject the weak evidence instead. But when strong evidence meets a strongly held contrary belief, we have a dilemma. Something has to give; and it may require less cognitive work to bend the data to the theory, or ignore the data entirely, than to modify a theoretical view of the world. By this argument, cognitive conservatism minimizes the allocation of effort to cognitive processes.

We could summarize these ideas with two principles: (1) we are willing to do cognitive work to attain the goal of keeping things simple in our minds—cognitive coherence. But (2) we want to do as little work as possible to achieve *that* goal too; and once the job is done, we will return to re-do it only if we must—cognitive conservatism.

These ideas show how cognitive conservatism is related to earlier topics. Recall our earlier discussion of decision-making, which says that careful, rational decision-making is most likely when (1) the problem is serious and (2) we have time for careful thought. Similar principles may apply here. There is evidence that we do think more carefully about causal attribution if the issue is important.[25] And we are more likely to notice and remember information that does *not* fit a stereotype, if we have time to think about that information.[26]

Perhaps rational beliefs are likely to be formed under the conditions that promote rational decision-making in general. The trouble is that careful thought, like careful decision-making, may not occur unless risks are recognized. To think through our beliefs, we must recognize the risks of routine, habitual, heuristic-driven, and schema-driven thinking.

COGNITIVE DISSONANCE: HOW ACTIONS AFFECT VALUES

With this topic, we reverse the causal order in decisions. These, we have said, are affected by our beliefs—subjective probabilities—and our desires or preferences—utilities. But now we will see how these variables are themselves affected *by* the decisions we make.

The Concept of Cognitive Dissonance

The basic idea, first stated by Leon Festinger, is this. We feel that our actions *ought* to be consistent with our beliefs and values. We ought to behave like

24. Alloy and Tabachnik, 1984; Fiske and Taylor, 1984.
25. Chaiken, 1980.
26. For review see Fiske and Taylor, 1990.

rational decision makers. If our cognitions seem to go one way and our behavior another, something is amiss; something doesn't make sense. We will try to bring the behavior and the cognitions into line with each other.

Finally, if the behavior itself has already occurred, it cannot be modified now. So what can be modified? Our attitudes and values! We may modify these so that they are no longer inconsistent, or as Festinger says, *dissonant,* with what we have done.

Cognitive dissonance, then, is a perceived inconsistency between our attitudes and our actions, which causes us to change our attitudes so that they become consistent with our actions.

Experimental Demonstrations

Here is the classic demonstration of this effect.[27] Each of the subjects was brought to the laboratory and was given some tasks to perform. These were purposely made dull, useless tasks—packing spools in a tray and dumping them out and then packing them in again, for example. After that, the subject was released into the waiting room, and here the real experiment began.

The experimenter said, in effect: "Look, another subject is waiting to do the same things you did, and it's important that she think the task she's about to perform is interesting and enjoyable. Tell her it was, will you? I will pay you . . ." And then some subjects were offered a dollar, but others were offered twenty dollars, to tell the lie. An ingenious cover story made all this sound quite plausible.

Now let us try to empathize with the subject after he has complied. Let us assume that we have a self-schema that says: "I'm a reasonably good person. I'm OK." But as subjects, we now have another item of knowledge: "I just told a bare-faced lie." Those two items do not fit together. Our self-image has lost coherence; it doesn't make sense any more.

Or does it? It does if we can say, "Well, for twenty dollars who wouldn't tell a harmless lie? I did it, but I'm still OK." The large external reward lets the items of knowledge fall into a coherent pattern (Figure 11-5A).

But what if there was no large external reward? A mere dollar doesn't justify a bare-faced lie. We are stuck with the dissonant cognitions: "I'm OK," but also, "I lied" (Figure 11-5B).

Then, says the theory, some cognitive work must be done. A subject could recover a coherent image of himself, *if* he could change one of the two cognitions so that they no longer clashed. Well, the lie is already told; the subject can't change that. But he *can change his attitude about the boring task itself.* If he can convince himself that it really wasn't so boring—that packing spools is a relaxing break from study, actually—then he would *not* have lied! And he could have a perfectly coherent view of himself, incorporating two quite com-

27. Festinger and Carlsmith, 1959.

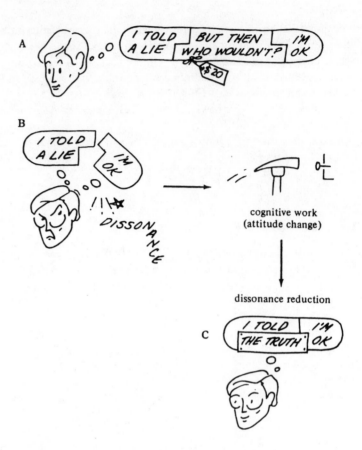

Figure 11-5 Shift in attitude caused by cognitive dissonance. See text for explanation.

patible cognitions: "I'm OK," and "I told the truth about the task" (Figure 11-5C).

Therefore, the subjects who had told a lie for only a little money should later rate the task itself as more interesting and enjoyable than did the subjects who were paid well for their lie. And that is exactly what happened.

Another demonstration shows the generality of the idea.[28] It was shortly after a riot in New Haven, Connecticut, in which it was alleged that the police had behaved in a quite brutal manner. Students at Yale were incensed at their actions. Now, some students who held strongly anti-police opinions were asked to write essays *supporting* the police. As in the other study, some were paid highly, others were paid only a little, for doing so.

The results paralleled the spool-packing study. Students paid only a little for their pro-police essays actually developed a more favorable attitude toward the police, as measured after the essays were written. This is the dissonance condition: "I mis-stated what I believe. I wrote a lie, and for a lousy fifty cents!

28. Cohen, 1962.

How could an OK person like me do that? Well, maybe it wasn't a lie; maybe the police were right after all."

Students paid highly had less reason to experience dissonance. "Yeah, I misstated what I believe, but for ten dollars who wouldn't, and what's the harm anyway?" And their anti-police attitudes remained strong.

Extensions of Dissonance Theory

The ramifications of this idea go far beyond such trivial matters as essays and spool-packing tasks. Let us look at just a few.

BLAMING THE VICTIM   There was a time when our nation, along with others, used the natives of other countries as sources of cheap labor. We forced other people to work for us, and we backed up the system with force—the police at home, the military abroad. This is the system of slavery that existed in early America, and the colonialism of American and European powers that persisted into the present century.

But how could we, the dominant group, treat other people in this way? We believe in humane and respectful treatment of other human beings. How can we reconcile those values with our actions?

Easily. We can convince ourselves that slaves are not people, but property; they are not fully human. Being lazy, they have no right to expect good pay. As for the use of force, well, slaves are childlike and, like children, must sometimes be punished for their own good.

Dissonance theory predicts that if we mistreat another person, we ought to think less of him or feel anger toward him afterward. Thus we bring our attitudes into line with our action: the action, already performed, of harming someone. We can even justify beating or killing a fellow human, if we convince ourselves that he deserves no better—that it is *his* fault! And if he deserves it, then that justifies our going on to mistreat him some more.

This example should start us thinking. It may start us thinking about the Nazi death camps of World War II. It may start us thinking about the unarmed and unresisting men, women, and infants gunned down by American soldiers at My Lai. Unspeakable barbarities have been committed by people who, in other aspects of their lives, are perfectly normal and decent—*and continue to regard themselves as such.* Dissonance theory might help us to understand how this can be.

Laboratory models of this situation have shown that the predicted attitude shift can and does occur. In one study, volunteer students were assigned to watch another student being interviewed and then, after the interview, tell him that he seemed a dull and untrustworthy person. After that, the volunteers privately rated the student as actually less worthy and likable—even though they had delivered the insults specifically at the experimenter's request, and not on the basis of their observations at all![29] Perhaps, having said things that were cer-

---

29. Davis and Jones, 1960.

tain to hurt the student's feelings, the subjects had to justify the action by convincing themselves that it was deserved.

THE PSYCHOLOGY OF COMMITMENT   The dissonance phenomenon may also make it hard to abandon a course of action once we embark upon it. A decision to change to a new action may be dissonant with our knowledge that we have devoted time and effort, perhaps expense and risk, to the old action.

In an analysis of the Pentagon Papers, which documented America's ever-deeper involvement in Vietnam, journalist Ralph White points out that many of the decisions made by political and military leaders during the Vietnam War were based not on evidence that they would be effective, but on the need to justify actions already taken. For instance, the decision to escalate the bombing of North Vietnam was described as our "trump card," an action that would break the will of the North Vietnamese. It didn't. But the bombing continued anyway. The cognition, "We committed all that effort, resource, and danger to the bombing raids" would have clashed with the cognition, "Bombing raids don't weaken an enemy's morale." As White put it, "There was a tendency, when actions were out of line with ideas, for decision-makers to align their ideas with their actions.[30]★ That is cognitive dissonance.

A dramatic demonstration of the effects of commitment is one we have met before—the group who predicted the approaching end of the world.[31] The predicted day of doom came and went, and nothing happened. In the face of this clear disconfirmatory evidence, did the group members abandon their beliefs? Not a bit of it. They adopted such wild rationalizations as, for example, that their faith had saved the world from disaster. Indeed, by every outward sign, their beliefs grew stronger rather than weaker! They began publicizing their views and actively seeking converts, things they had never done before.

Why? Quite possibly because any other action would have been inconsistent with their prior actions. Most had quit their jobs, stripped themselves of possessions, and settled into a house to await the day of doom. To say "We were wrong" would have made all these prior actions seem irrational and senseless. Instead, the group concluded: "We were right, but doom was withheld"—and then their prior actions, and the failure of doomsday, made perfect sense together.

Interpretations of Cognitive Dissonance

Let us turn from this sampling of cases that the dissonance mechanism might help us understand, to the question: How does it work?

30. White, 1971, p. 50.
★Historian Barbara Tuchman (1984) has shown how this pattern—action taken not for reasons of effectiveness, but to justify actions already taken—reverberates down through the ages, from the Greeks at Troy to the Americans at Vietnam.
31. Festinger, Reicken, and Schachter, 1956.

Festinger's original theory was that the clash of dissonant cognitions produces tension and discomfort. We don't like it when things don't make sense. This discomfort is what motivates attitude change, so that we reduce the discomfort—negative feedback once again!

There is some evidence that a dissonance condition does in fact produce discomfort, though the evidence is indirect and weaker than we might wish.* If we grant that it does, still there is dispute about what produces the discomfort.

It might, as Festinger suggested, reflect simple incompatibility between two ideas: the subject in a dissonance experiment says, "I said X when I believe Y. That doesn't make sense, and I'm uncomfortable when things don't make sense." But some writers argue that what produces discomfort is not just incompatibility between any two cognitions, but incompatibility between a cognition and our positive images of ourselves. By this theory, the person does not say, "I said X when I believe Y and that makes no sense," but rather: "How could an honest, OK person like me do that?"

The matter remains controversial.** There are other possibilities too, and it might be that the effect occurs for different reasons rather than just one.[32]

A LOOK BACKWARD   We may not have to think of cognitive dissonance as an independent mechanism. It may take its place as a special case of some more general one: perhaps the coherence motive, or perhaps our desire to maintain our good opinions of ourselves as OK people. In the latter case, dissonance phenomena would be closely related to what Freud called *rationalization*.[33]

If cognitive dissonance is a special case of something else, however, it may be a very important special case. Certainly it has offered us a new way of looking at a wide variety of phenomena. People who ask "Why did he or she do that?" will find these ideas coming to mind with surprising frequency.

THE POLLYANNA PRINCIPLE: PLEASURES, PAINS, AND COGNITION

We have looked at cognitive coherence as a goal that our cognitive mechanisms may seek to attain. And we have seen that to attain that goal, our cognitive apparatus will accept some cost in accuracy, distorting reality here and there—rewriting our memories, for instance.

But we have long suspected that our motives may distort our thinking in another way, too. Is cognition biased by our pleasures and pains, our likes and

---

*It turns out, for example, that "stress-reducing" drugs such as tranquilizers or alcohol can reduce dissonance effects. But who can say what other effects they might have besides stress-reduction?

**For review see Sabini, 1992.

32. See for example Baumeister and Tice, 1984.

33. Sabini, 1991.

dislikes? Do we believe that X is the case because we *want* X to be the case? Do we believe that Y is false because it would be terrible if Y were true? Do we refuse to take Z into account, even if it is important, because it simply is too unpleasant to think about?

If so, then our minds operate on a Pollyanna Principle: Accentuate the positive; eliminate (or discount) the negative.[34] And to the extent that this is so, rational decision-making, which assumes that beliefs reflect reality, is compromised from the very start.

But is it so? Let us look at some of the evidence.

Motivation and Perception

Beginning after World War II and continuing to the present, an important question for experimental psychologists has been whether motivational influences on cognition can be demonstrated under controlled laboratory conditions. These experiments deal with relatively simple phenomena, and they seem to take us a long way from complex human irrationalities. With simpler cases, however, we have a better chance of seeing what is going on. If motives can be shown to influence simple perceptions, we could study how they do so, and then work up to more complex cases.

THE BETTER THE BIGGER? An early and influential study was conducted by Jerome Bruner and his co-workers.[35] They asked children to adjust the size of a spot of light until it matched the size of a coin (for some children) or of a cardboard disc (for other children). The matches showed that the coins were seen as larger than discs of equal size. Moreover, the effect increased with the value of the coin. And it was greater in children from impoverished homes, who presumably valued the coins more. Value of the stimulus, in other words, increased its perceived size. The better the bigger, it seems!

Such effects are small and not everyone has been able to produce them, but on balance the evidence is that such distortions do occur.[36] It is a delightful literature. Children have been found to draw larger pictures of Santa Claus, but not of more neutral objects, as Christmas approaches. And before the election of 1960, between John F. Kennedy and Richard Nixon, more Kennedy supporters than Nixon supporters judged Kennedy to be the taller of the two—which he was, by half an inch.

In short, there may be a kind of perceptual exaggeration of stimuli that are important to us. It may serve to make them more noticeable, increasing their availability as cues.

34. Matlin and Stang, 1978.
35. Bruner and Goodman, 1947.
36. See Baker, Rierdan, and Wapner, 1974; Matlin and Stang, 1978.

PERCEPTUAL DEFENSE   Freud saw the person as actively pushing threatening memories and thoughts out of consciousness, that is, repressing them. If so, is there a similar gatekeeping operation on the input side? Can we refuse not only to remember threatening material, but also to perceive it in the first place?

There is a large literature on this topic, asking, for example, whether subjects take longer to recognize nasty words than nice words when these are presented briefly. Some writers believe that such *perceptual defense* does occur, but if so, the effect is not a reliable one.

On the other hand, perhaps the notion of *perception* is being used too restrictively here. After all, if we want to defend ourselves from perceiving a threatening stimulus, we can always just close our eyes, as people sometimes do during horror movies. For that matter, we can just refuse to go to horror movies in the first place.

Do people avoid exposing themselves to unpleasant stimuli? Unfortunately there is no simple answer. It depends on what the information is *for*. And salient or surprising information may grab our attention even if it is unpleasant. We are biased toward noticing what is *interesting*, more than toward noticing what is *nice*.

One idea, however, may help bring some order to this area. There may be important individual differences in the use of such defenses. Some people, it has been claimed, are *repressors;* they avoid criticism, avoid thinking about the initial symptoms of illness, and are likely to forget information that contradicts their attitudes.[37] Other people may be more vigilant in noticing threats, dangers, and challenges to their beliefs. Similar differences have been noticed among surgical patients: some seek, and others avoid, knowledge about what to expect. Perhaps it is only some individuals who refuse to confront the unpleasant side of life.

There is experimental evidence for this idea, though it also shows that the matter is not simple. In one study, subjects read a series of adjectives which, they thought, were descriptions of themselves based on personality questionnaires. It was found that repressor subjects (but not others) spent less time scanning the information if the overall evaluation was negative than if it was positive (Figure 11-6, left panel). They also remembered the information less well later.[38]

Intriguingly enough, the repressors remembered even *neutral* items less well, when these were embedded in an overall negative evaluation. So it seems that the cognitive shutdown was a more global one than the notion of perceptual defense (or Freud's theory) would lead us to expect. It was not that the repressors were saying, "I reject *just this* item of information, because it displeases or threatens me." Rather, they were tuning out the situation altogether, as if to say, "I don't want to know *anything* about what is going on right now." We are reminded of the mythical ostrich, burying its head in the sand.

37. Olson and Zanna, 1979; Zanna and Olson, 1982; see also Baum and Singer, 1982.
38. Baumeister and Cairns, 1992.

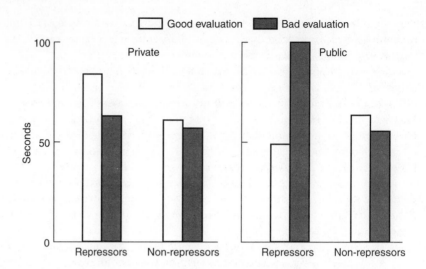

Figure 11-6 Average time spent by subjects in scanning purported information about themselves. Subjects were either repressors or non-repressors; the evaluation was either good or bad; and in each case, it was known to others ("public") or not ("private"). (Data from Baumeister and Cairns, 1992.)

To repeat, however, matters were not so simple even as this. The findings just described fit the subjects who believed that the evaluations were being shown to them only. There were other subjects who believed that other people, with whom they would have to interact, were also seeing the evaluations. For *these* subjects, the pattern was reversed (Figure 11-6, right panel). Negative material received *more* scanning time, and was remembered *better* than positive material, by repressors. Perhaps under these conditions, the subjects took time to consider how to rebut the negative information that, as they thought, others were receiving about them.

Thus, once again, much depends on what the information is to be used for. Therefore, the cognitive shutdown found in the "private" condition is not an automatic defensive reaction; it can itself be shut down, in a purposive goal-directed way, if the information must be dealt with.

Motivation and Memory

Analogous questions can be asked about our memories. Do we remember the things that please us better than the things that do not?

Unfortunately, again the answer is not clear. Very happy occasions may be very well remembered; but so may very unhappy or scary ones. Again, vividness may be more important than niceness or nastiness per se.[39]

Even where results are positive, we may not be seeing *motivational* effects on memory. We may instead be seeing the influence of *arousal* (pp. 223–34), whose effects on memory may be very complex.[40] Or again, sometimes it may have to do with the simple *availability* of pleasant items in speech, thought, and memory. Pleasant events may be remembered better than unpleasant because

39. For review see Schwartz and Reisberg, 1992.
40. Baddeley, 1990; Schwartz and Reisberg, 1992.

they are rehearsed more often. In other words, we may have more practice at remembering pleasant things because we call them to mind more often.

Similar sorts of things may be said about the "self-enhancing bias" in memory. It is very clear that people in this society are likely to remember their successes better than their failures, and also to attribute the former to their own skill and effort, and the latter to external factors that were "not their fault." We may also have unrealistically high conceptions of our social competence. One study compared people's ratings of themselves with other people's ratings of them, after a group interaction. The subjects tended to rate themselves higher than they were rated by others in the group.

But are these motivated distortions? Perhaps not. We might instead see ourselves as relating events to causal schemas that usually are quite accurate: Our achievements usually *are* produced by our own efforts, and our failures usually *are* the result of external circumstances that thwart us. How often do we try to make bad things happen? As for social skills, courteous people will respond to us as if we were likable and interesting, whether we are or not; if I bore you, you will try to conceal it. Why shouldn't I conclude that you are more impressed with me than you are, if you send me signals to that effect? Once again, we see how difficult it can be to separate motivational and cognitive influences.

Finally, before moving on, we should inject a word of caution: These self-serving biases may be more specific to Western society than we have supposed. People in Western societies are, as we noted, likely to take credit for success and blame failures on something or someone else. But recent findings in other societies—in Japan, for example—find that such biases may be absent or even reversed. Perhaps they reflect, not a universal wish for self-enhancement or to "feel good about oneself," but a set of schematic beliefs that Western society inculcates in most of its members.*

Pollyanna Predictions

Let us turn from the picking-up and retrieval of information to the *use* of information in beliefs, predictions, and subjective probabilities. Here we meet another form of the Pollyanna Principle: If it's good, it's probable. If it's bad, it probably won't happen. And in this domain, the evidence for Pollyanna-style distortion is very strong.

PROBABILITY JUDGMENTS   One experimenter used a card-drawing game with school children, in which some of the cards were worth "points" and others not. The children knew how many point cards were in each deck. Nevertheless, asked before each draw how likely it was that they would draw a point card, the children consistently overestimated the likelihood that the next draw would be a favorable one. In fact, a pleasant outcome that had an actual

*For review and discussion, see Markus and Kitayama, 1991.

probability of 10 percent was predicted almost as often as an unpleasant event that had a probability of 90 percent![41] The results were similar with college students.[42]

THE ILLUSION OF CONTROL   Many people, then, have objectively unjustified beliefs that good things are going to happen.* Not only that; they may also have objectively unjustified beliefs that they can *make* good things happen.[43] In a situation in which events occurred irrespective of what the subjects did, subjects overestimated their degree of control over favorable outcomes, and underestimated their control over unfavorable ones. "If it's good, I can make it happen," they seemed to say; and "If it's bad, it's not my fault."

Consider a classic study by Ellen Langer. Subjects received lottery tickets, prior, of course, to the drawing. Of these, some subjects selected their own tickets; others simply had their tickets handed to them. Later (but still before the drawing), the experimenter offered to buy back each subject's ticket. On average, subjects who had selected their own tickets asked nearly *twice as much money* for the ticket as ones who had not.

Now the tickets *qua* tickets were slips of paper, worth nothing. A ticket was valuable only because it might win. So, if the "selecting" subjects assigned greater value to their tickets, they must have had a higher estimate—unconsciously of course, for it makes no objective sense at all—of the ticket's chances of winning. They behaved as if their *act of selection* had increased the ticket's chances!

The Pollyanna Principle leads to a pervasive optimism, at least in this society.[44] The average person believes she will live longer than average. She believes that smoking is a health hazard, but not for her. Indeed, even if we carefully ask people to compare themselves only with other people in similar circumstances, the average person thinks she is better off than average!

Again: The vast majority of Taylor's cancer patients (pp. 418–19) believed that they, or their doctor, had some control over the course of their disease. Once again, the spouses' beliefs in the controllability of the cancer was less strong; this suggests that such beliefs were actively constructed by the patient and not just picked up from our culture's folklore.

The Price of Pollyanna

Then there is the other side of the Pollyanna Principle: If it's bad, it's unlikely. A study of women with unwanted pregnancies revealed a distressing amount of ignorance on the women's part, but also a distressing amount of Pollyannaism.

41. Marks, 1951.
42. Irwin, 1953.
*I say "many people" here, because there are some intriguing exceptions to all this (pp. 561–62).
43. Taylor, 1983, 1989; Taylor and Brown, 1988.
44. Vallone et al., 1990.

The most common reason given for the pregnancy was "I thought it was during the safe period" (35 percent), but 27 percent said "I thought it couldn't happen to me."[45]

Or consider the case of Stephanie Mencimer, a journalist in Washington, D.C. She is, she tells us, sexually active; fully aware of the dangers of infection by the deadly HIV virus; but unwilling to take precautions against such infection. She wrote a newspaper article to ask herself and us: Why is she behaving that way?[46]

She says: "[T]he primary reason heterosexuals aren't using condoms is . . .: We just don't think we're going to get AIDS." That of course is a Pollyanna prediction, loud and clear.

Mencimer mentions some other reasons too, ones that look backward over several ideas we've encountered in this chapter. "Women at the homeless shelter where I volunteer seem to use condoms regularly, and I suspect it's because they have friends and family members with AIDS"—the *availability heuristic* (pp. 408–9). And: "If you can trust a man enough not to laugh at you when you take your clothes off, he's probably not going to give you a terminal disease either"—the *representativeness heuristic* (pp. 409–10). If a person is nice enough to make love with, he's surely nice enough not to give you a fatal disease!

(If that idea strikes you as too irrational to be plausible, consider the experience of Carol Nemeroff, a student of *contagion* [pp. 268–69]. She was asking subjects how they would feel about finishing a portion of ice cream that someone else had started. It turned out that subjects would have trouble with that, even if the "someone else" were a loved one—but not if it were Albert Schweitzer! One woman said, "Oh, he wouldn't have any germs, or if he did, they'd be good germs." Then she stopped herself short and said, "I can't believe I said that!")

Then again: Taking time out for precautions may violate the schema, or *script,* for a passionate encounter. As the author says, there is conflict between "paranoia and passion." (A revealing turn of phrase! The word "paranoia" implies that fear of infection is objectively ill founded, whereas the point of the article is that it isn't. Why didn't she say "between prudence and passion"? Pollyanna again?)

"Stupid—I know. And that's the point." Yes, it is. That nice guys wouldn't have HIV, that Albert Schweitzer would only have good germs, that the act of selecting your lottery ticket makes it more likely to win—none of these ideas, *if we stop to think about it,* makes any rational sense at all. But that's a big *if.* What is so sneaky about heuristic, schematic, and Pollyanna-style thinking is that we typically *don't* stop to think about the quite irrational assumptions they lead us to make.

Mencimer concludes her article: "Now what we need is safe-sex indoctrination smart enough to recognize how dumb we really are." Exactly so.

Even so, safe sex to me just means sex that won't make you pregnant. As for disease, I am willing to take the risk.
—*journalist Stephanie Mencimer*

45. Reported by Petit, 1975.
46. Mencimer, 1993.

The Pollyanna Principle might underlie many tragedies. Consider how a person will drive when he knows he has had too much to drink. He risks terrible consequences—a fatal collision, or hitting a child. Question: Do we do these things, not in spite of the risks, but because of them? Maybe the Pollyanna Principle makes us discount their likelihood: "That would be so terrible that it must be very unlikely." Think about it.

A Look Backward

The Pollyanna Principle does, on the face of it, lead to irrational beliefs. If people on the average think they're better off than average, then it's just a cold fact of arithmetic that people on the average are mistaken.

WHY POLLYANNA? Why does this happen? It is especially puzzling because, in general, wishful thinking is not good thinking. A mouse might be displeased by the sight of a hawk, but mice that refused to acknowledge hawks would leave few grandchildren. In our own society, even short of disaster, an exaggerated sense of control can lead us to set unrealistic goals and make ill-advised commitments.[47]

On the other hand, it may be to an actor's advantage to be *optimistic when in doubt*—not the same thing as being foolhardy when disaster is certain. Cold, clear judgment is not always optimal. Perhaps it is just as well if the bride and groom on their wedding day do not have it clearly in mind that their odds of divorce are about even. And Taylor notes that her patients seemed to function better if they had even an illusory sense of control.[48]

In short, a certain optimism could foster perseverance, initiative, and a necessary willingness to risk.[49] That may be a prerequisite for risk-taking, which in turn is prerequisite for action, survival, and progeny payoffs.

A NOTE OF CAUTION: THE REVERSE-POLLYANNA PROBLEM Before moving on, we ought to introduce a note of caution in all this. If our predictions and self-descriptions are often unrealistically optimistic—sometimes they are just the reverse. We may do cognitive work to defend sharply *negative* cognitions. Consider:

1. What about the student who persists in the belief that she can't do mathematics, despite clear evidence to the contrary? It is not obvious that there is any food for self-esteem in math anxiety.

2. Obesity is negatively valued in our society. People put down fat people; even other fat people do. If we always bent our beliefs in a positive direction, we ought to deny being fat even if in fact we are. Quite the contrary: The number of people (especially women) who think they are overweight is *much* greater than the number who, by objective standards, really are.

47. Baumeister, Heatherton, and Tice, 1993.
48. Taylor, 1983; Taylor and Brown, 1988.
49. See Alloy, 1984.

3. Think about this:

[C]onsider the plight of a person who has persuaded a visiting relative to take a later flight than originally planned so that they could enjoy a relaxed dinner beforehand. The relative agrees, takes the later flight, and . . . dies in a horrible crash. Inevitably, the grieving survivor would express guilt and anguished self-castigation over "causing" the death. This would not be surprising . . .[50]

But why wouldn't it be? Certainly if anyone *else* were to blame the survivor for the death, "[w]e would label him a fool or a madman." Yet we think it reasonable, we even empathize, when the survivor accepts a *clearly irrational and sharply negative self-attribution*—"It was my fault," when obviously it wasn't.

So it is clear that the question is not: Does a Pollyanna Principle operate to affect our cognitions? Rather it is: *When* does it operate, and when not? And why?

THE FREUDIAN DEFENSE MECHANISMS

In psychoanalytic theory, the cognitive systems that make up the ego—the perceiving, judging, decision-making executive—develop so as to satisfy that bundle of uncomfortable urges, the id. Remember that for Freud there is one and only one motive—relief from discomfort, the pleasure principle (pp. 209–10). Cognition is only a means to that end.

But how do cognitive mechanisms work in Freudian theory? Let us look.

Cognition begins (pp. 42–43) with the *primary process*. Tensions arising from the body are experienced as discomfort. The infant forms an image or hallucination—nowadays we might say a *search image*—of the source of gratification. That is the primary process. The child then learns ways of finding the real object that matches the image (compare pp. 329–31). That is the *secondary process,* the beginning of rational thought, planning, and decision-making.

However, there are discomforts from other sources too. First, the immediate gratification of wishes might simply be dangerous. The person must inhibit the expression of urges until it is safe to express them. The ego, thinking ahead as the id cannot, produces such inhibition by opposing the urge with another one—anxiety, which blocks the expression of the wish. This *reality anxiety* is the anxiety produced by real external dangers.

Another source of discomfort is the fear of disapproval. Indiscriminate wish gratification brings disapproval from others, especially parents. The resulting expression of disapproval, perhaps mild from the parent's perspective, may be terrifying to the child. So there arises another source of anxiety, and this blocks actions that would lead to disapproval. Anxiety from that source Freud called *moral anxiety.* It is the basis of the superego, the internalized commands and prohibitions of the parents and society.

50. Nisbett and Ross, 1980, p. 289.

Thus the decision-making, planning ego operates under constraints; it has, as Freud put it, three harsh masters. It must (1) plan effective action to gratify id urges, while (2) suppressing impulses if they lead to danger, *and* (3) suppressing them if they lead to moral anxiety or guilt.

Now, a final and important complication. Like behaviorists, Freud emphasized that *cognitive operations are actions*. They may not be distinguished from actual behavior; especially to a child, thinking about doing something is not so different from actually doing it. If performing an action is dangerous, so is thinking about performing it. And if performing it would bring guilt, thinking about it also brings guilt—moral anxiety.

Here is where motivational effects on cognition come in. The ego must find ways of modifying thoughts, as well as actions, so as to avoid anxiety—even if the thoughts are distorted as a result. These ways are the **defense mechanisms**. Defense against what? Against anxiety. Let us look at some examples.★

Repression

The mechanism of repression—an active pushing of thoughts and wishes out of consciousness—was Freud's most important defense mechanism, and all the others depend on it. We can think of it as a kind of cognitive avoidance response; thoughts are inhibited, and denied access to consciousness, because it would be too anxiety-arousing to think them.[51]

But when pushed out of consciousness in that way, the original impulses do not go away. They are still striving for expression, but even the thought of expressing them generates so much anxiety that the person must disguise them from himself, as well as from others, and express them in symbolic form (pp. 210–11).

Clinical case histories often focus on the motivated forgetting of traumatic events. Here is a patient of the French physician Pierre Janet, a contemporary of Freud:

> Irene was a girl of 20 years, who was greatly disturbed by the long illness and death of her mother . . . When finally her mother did die, Irene became very much disturbed emotionally. She tried to revive the corpse, to call the breath back again . . . Yet in a little while Irene seemed to have grown forgetful of her mother's death. She would say: "I know very well my mother must be dead, since I have been told so several times . . . but I really feel astonished by it all. When did she die? What did she die from? Was I not by her to take care of her? . . . I feel as if her absence was nothing to me, as if she were travelling and would soon come back."[52]

★For discussion see Fenichel, 1945.
51. Dollard and Miller, 1950.
52. Quoted by Baddeley, 1990, pp. 379–380.

Reaction Formation

Another way of not thinking dangerous thoughts is to think opposite thoughts. If the thought of anger at our parents threatens to intrude and make us anxious, we can focus on the opposite thought—how much we love our parents. And we can do this at the level of thought or of overt behavior or both. That is *reaction formation*.

If a person makes repeated and vigorous protestations of love for her children, especially if she treats them with indifference in other ways, a psychoanalyst would suspect reaction formation. The mother may use these verbal declarations to hide, from herself as well as others, an unconscious hostility toward the children.

Projection

To *project* an emotion is to defend against the anxiety it causes by attributing it to another person, not oneself. One says: That terrible thought or feeling is not part of *me,* it's part of *him* instead. Thus, a person who sees other people as hostile and vicious may be concealing his own hostility from himself.

There are other defense mechanisms, but these are enough to give us the flavor. The important point is this. To Freud, intellect can operate in violently irrational ways in order to minimize the tensions of anxiety or guilt. Freud saw it ignoring logic, blocking memory, refusing to acknowledge aspects of ourselves that are plainly there. Cognition for Freud is servant to our motives—not their partner, much less their master—and only as rational as their demands permit it to be.

A Look Backward: What about Freud?

For about the last century of its history, psychological theory has developed over a repeated, ominous figure in the bass: What shall we say about Freud? Was his thinking a great leap forward or a century-long wild goose chase? The defense mechanisms, the Oedipus complex, and other Freudian ideas have entered our everyday speech; but do they give us insight, or only the illusion of insight?

FREUD AND COGNITIVE PSYCHOLOGY   In the last few years, partly under the urging of Matthew Erdelyi, we have seen yet another convergence of ideas, this time between Freudian psychology and modern cognitive psychology.[53] Many of Freud's ideas, with little revision or none at all, could be translated into contemporary cognitive terms. Thus one commentator notes:

> The new cognition was described in terms of *filtering* and *selectivity,* rather than censorship. Proponents of the new cognition talked of *executive processes;* Freud had

53. Erdelyi, 1985, 1992.

talked of the *ego*. There were now *decision nodes* (rather than conflicts); there was *working memory* (rather than the conscious) . . . Suddenly the very idea of unconscious processes was not only noncontroversial but was an 'obvious and fundamental feature of human information-processing' . . .[54]

In light of what cognitive psychology has taught us, how do Freudian ideas fare?

First, are there unconscious mental processes? Of that there can be no doubt whatever. Consider the tip-of-the-tongue phenomenon: We know the word we're looking for, for we recognize it when we do get to it; but we cannot get to it now.

May these processes operate irrationally? Not much doubt of that either. Consider the implicit assumption that our selecting our lottery ticket increases its chances of winning, or that Albert Schweitzer's germs, if any, would be good ones. These assumptions have to be implicit and unconscious, because they won't stand conscious examination for two seconds. But there they are, in the data that are right in front of us. And they do not affect only trivial decisions, either; consider safe sex (pp. 434–35).

Is there an "economic" distribution of energy among different psychic actions, so that performing one steals energy from another? Well, we have seen that idea even in non-Freudian theorizing. Recall Chapter 9 (pp. 346–47): To be on the lookout for an unwanted thought does tie up some cognitive capacity, so that one is all the more likely to think of a white bear (or let slip a remark about Harry) if one's mind is engaged in something else at the time. By the same token, that theory implies that we can divide our mind into parts, forming a kind of committee in our heads (recall the lookout and the bouncer). That too is a recognizably Freudian notion.

THE "DYNAMIC UNCONSCIOUS"   But all this leaves out of account what is really the cornerstone of Freudian psychology—the notion of the mind as a cauldron of urges, striving, doing, pushing ideas out of mind, condensing them with others, symbolically expressing wishes, and replaying conflicts that date back to early childhood. How has this *dynamic unconscious* fared? Less well.

Take repression, for instance. There is a whole body of experimental attempts to demonstrate repression under controlled conditions (this means simply: under conditions where we know what is going on). To be brief, but not, I think, unfair: Nothing has come of it.[55] There have been no reliable experimental demonstrations of repression.

Now some authors take these experimental failures as an indictment of the experimental method, not of Freud's ideas. Thus: "The clinician shakes his head in disbelief at the experimental psychologist, whose paltry methodology cannot even demonstrate a phenomenon as obvious and ubiquitous as repres-

54. Loftus, 1992, p. 762; italics in original.
55. For reviews see Baddeley, 1990; Schwartz and Reisberg, 1992.

sion."[56] And: "From the clinical standpoint, the evidence for repression is overwhelming and obvious."[57] But we could turn that argument right around: Psychologists *have* demonstrated by experiment that what is "obvious" can also be dead wrong—e.g., that a confession is proof positive of guilt! And if repression is in the beholder's eye, might it not be in the eye of the clinician? This is what has been called the Achilles' heel of psychoanalytic thought: In whose head are these defenses, disguises, and symbols? The patient's, or the analyst's?

We seem to be thrown back on clinical case material for our evaluation of that question. The problem here, of course, is that when looking over material as complex as that, we will have no trouble "seeing" the patterns we are looking for. We have the illusory correlation (pp. 420–21), and the false-memory syndrome (pp. 416–17) too, to worry about. And remember that when an analyst makes an interpretation, even the patient's assent gives us no guarantee that the interpretation is correct! The patient too is trying to make sense of her own behavior and experience (the *coherence motive*), and an interpretation may be accepted as a plausible story, right or wrong.

After all this, we seem to be left only with proof-of-the-pudding evidence for psychoanalytic theory: Does it lead to effective therapy? No more so than other approaches, based on quite different assumptions. Even Freud's own track record as a therapist is not a very impressive one.[58]

COGNITIONS HOT OR COLD?   Finally, let us grant that repression, projection, and the like do occur. Still it is a separate question whether such things happen for the reasons Freud gave. Modern cognitive psychology has given us some new and different perspectives on these phenomena.

As an example, let's look again at *projection* (p. 439). In a neat experimental demonstration, male college students were recruited for an experiment in which, they were told, they were to be assigned a blind date. Some of the men were given sexually arousing material to read while waiting for the experiment to begin. Other men were controls, given non-arousing material. Then each man was shown a picture and a description of an attractive woman whom, he was told, he was about to date.

Sure enough, the sexually aroused men rated the woman more attractive (compare pp. 123–24). But they also rated her more uninhibited, amorous, and sexually available than non-aroused men did.[59]

Now on the face of it, this is distorted thinking. Certainly it is illogical for a man to infer that a woman is sexually available just because *he* is aroused. A Freudian interpretation would be: The men's sexual arousal produced unconscious guilt feelings; and so, rather than recognize the arousal in themselves, they projected it onto the woman.

56. Erdelyi, 1985, p. 105.
57. Ibid., p. 258.
58. See Crews, 1993.
59. Cited in Berscheid and Walster, 1978, pp. 153–154.

But there is another possibility. If the men were sexually motivated, that should call to mind the images of women who would provide gratification. The schema—attractive, sexy woman—was cognitively available. And here is a woman who partly fits the schema—she is an attractive woman. The subjects may have applied the more inclusive schema—attractive *and* available woman—to her, simply because that schema was on their minds. We have spoken of *schema-triggered affect* (pp. 357–58). It is tempting to regard this experiment as an instance of *affect-triggered schema!* If a schema has both cognitive and emotional components, it is not surprising that a person fitting either component might trigger the whole schema.

The important thing to see is that this account makes no appeal to unconscious forces, urges, or anxieties. It is a motivational theory at all, only in that it speaks of sexy feelings bringing schemas to mind. Beyond that, it is a theory about how our thought processes work—not about how motives affect thinking.

Or consider *repression* again. Forgetting of important and traumatic events occurs; but it may not occur because an active suppressing force pushes the material from consciousness. Here is an example of the evidence that leads us to look beyond Freud:

In 1968, presidential candidate Robert Kennedy was shot to death by a man named Sirhan Sirhan. After that:

> Sirhan had absolutely no recollection of the actual murder . . . Sirhan carried out the deed in a *greatly agitated state* and was completely amnesiac with regard to the event. . . . Under hypnosis, as Sirhan became progressively more *worked up and excited,* he recalled progressively more, the memories tumbling out while his excitement built to a crescendo leading up to the shooting.[60]

Now it is most unlikely that the memory of the murder caused intolerable guilt or anxiety in Sirhan. The murder was political and was planned in advance. It is much more likely that the amnesia is an instance of *state-dependent memory.* This is a well-documented phenomenon: Events that happened during one psychological state—a state of high arousal here—are best remembered when one is put back in the same state, as Sirhan was under hypnosis. Perhaps many of the highly traumatic events Freud's patients recalled, that were forgotten in everyday life, were of that kind—assuming that they occurred! And perhaps the fading and blunting of memory in the case of Pierre Janet's patient (p. 438) reflected something of the sort as well.

We will not pursue this topic, for it is not really a motivational one.[61] But that is the point! Repression may not be motivated at all, but in at least some cases may reflect the "cold" cognitive phenomenon of state-dependent memory.

60. Bower, 1981, p. 129; my italics.
61. See Bower, 1981.

There we have the controversy. Do our irrationalities reflect active, distorting, "hot" motivational forces—psychodynamics? Or do they reflect the quiet, "cold" operation of our cognitive apparatus, which follows rules that are not always quite rational—psychologic? Do they show motivational intrusions on our thinking, or do they only reveal the way our thinking works?

My own guess is that as our knowledge develops, Freudian concepts will be replaced with cognitive ones and that Freud will be remembered, not as a man who gave us concepts of fundamental psychological importance, but as one who presciently anticipated some of them. But that *is* a guess, and your author's crystal ball is cloudy. If we've learned anything, it is that it is risky to prejudge such matters.

SUMMARY

Motivation and cognition are closely related. In decision theory, for example, our actions are affected both by what we want, which sets utilities (motivational), and by what we believe, which sets subjective probabilities (cognitive). Then too, thinking and judging are themselves actions, so we need motivational concepts to explain our doing these things. And we must ask whether motivation and cognition really operate independently.

As actions can be characterized as stimulus-bound or goal-directed, so can cognitive operations. Even some very complex cognitive events, like reading, may occur in an automatic, stimulus-bound way. Others are effortful and goal-directed; for example, attending to one stimulus input to the exclusion of another, or searching for a word that is on the "tip of our tongue."

We have only so much time and energy to devote to assessing our situation and forming beliefs about it. So, as we may satisfice rather than maximize in making a decision, so we may call on cognitive shortcuts as time- and energy-savers. These include *heuristics,* or rules of thumb, such as the representativeness heuristic (like goes with like) and the availability heuristic (use what first comes to mind). *Schemas* also are valuable cognitive labor-savers, bringing to bear what we know (or think we know) about situations *like* the one we now face. These labor-saving devices work well enough for most purposes, but they can lead to serious errors when misapplied or when better information goes unused because of them.

The tendency to perceive the world as orderly, coherent, and stable seems to reflect a motive in its own right—the *cognitive coherence* motive. To achieve the goal of a coherent view of the world, we do cognitive work—rewriting our memories or actively seeking causes for events. We seem to take whatever means is available to achieve this end. This we know to be characteristic of motivated action, and here we see it in cognitive action. These processes can also lead to serious distortions and even tragic errors, as in eyewitness testimony and the false-memory syndrome.

In addition to keeping our world view simple, we do cognitive work to keep it stable. We may resist changing our minds, even in the face of evidence (*cognitive conservatism*). We may do this in a number of ways: failing to note contrary evidence, creating illusory confirming evidence, finding an explanation that fits our preconceptions, not allowing contrary data to arise (the self-fulfilling prophesy), or simply refusing to confront preconceptions with the evidence at all (wooden-headedness).

Preferences and values affect actions, but they can also be affected by them. *Cognitive dissonance* arises when we perceive inconsistency between our actions and our opinions or attitudes. If we can't change the action, we can perhaps change our opinions or values to make them fit the action. A person who has mistreated a victim may decide that the victim must deserve it—and mistreat him some more. Having committed ourselves to a course of action, we may feel it inconsistent to back off from it—and so we commit ourselves further.

As to how the process works, there is dispute. Some writers believe that discomfort or tension can arise because of *any* inconsistency, i.e., that it reflects the cognitive coherence motive. Others argue that it requires a more specific inconsistency between our actions and our good opinions of ourselves.

Do we perceive, believe, and remember what pleases us rather than what does not? There is some evidence for such a Pollyanna Principle in perception and memory, but it is strongest when we move to *predicting* what is likely to happen. Here it is very clear that we are likely to overestimate the likelihood of favorable events and underestimate the likelihood of unfavorable ones. We may also overestimate the degree of control we have over outcomes, that is, our ability to *make* good things happen. There may sometimes be benefits to these distortions, but they can also be extremely dangerous, in contexts ranging from unsafe sex to driving while impaired. If a possible outcome would be very bad, its badness may lead us to discount its likelihood.

Freud's *defense mechanisms* were seen as attempts to reduce anxiety associated with dangerous thoughts, even at the cost of cognitive distortion. More recent work suggests that these defenses may reflect, not the "hot" clash of instinctive forces, but the "cold" operation of our cognitive machinery. Such theorizing is building new bridges between Freud's motivational theory and modern concepts in cognitive psychology.

CHAPTER 12

Motivation and Emotion

Then Fingolfin beheld (as it seemed to him) the utter ruin of the Noldor, and the defeat beyond redress of all their houses; and filled with wrath and despair he mounted upon Rochallor his great horse and rode forth alone, and none might restrain him. He passed over Dor-nu-Fauglith like a wind amid the dust, and all that beheld his onset fled in amaze, thinking that Oromë himself was come; for a great madness of rage was upon him, so that his eyes shone like the eyes of the Valar.

—J. R. R. TOLKIEN,
The Silmarillion

Throughout this journey, we have noted the close ties between motivation and emotion. The two concepts are so closely related that, in some cases, they may be hard to distinguish at all. Let us look at some of these relations, by way of preview.

EMOTION AND MOTIVATION: HOW ARE THEY RELATED?

In the simplest case, we may say that emotions *are* motives, somewhat analogous to drive states (pp. 56–60); thus one writer speaks of the "central motivations we call emotions."[1] Anger may lead us to strike, fear may lead us to flee, and we may feel that an appeal to an emotion is all the answer we need to our question, "Why did he do that?" That is what first leaps out at us from the quoted passage: Fingolfin rode off against his enemy *because* he was in a rage.

Closely related is the view that if emotions are not identical with motives, they *accompany* them. An early instinct theorist, William McDougall, proposed that the activation of an instinct, by what we would now call a "releasing" situation (pp. 112–13), also activates the corresponding emotion. Thus the instinct of aggression is accompanied by the emotion of anger. Modern writers too have argued that emotion is characteristic of motivated behavior.[2] It is a plausible idea. When we learn that the octopus engages in sexual intercourse

1. Izard, 1991, p. 3.
2. See for example Epstein, 1982.

with no change whatever in its heart rate, we do feel that we are dealing with a pretty cold-blooded beast in both senses, and we wonder whether the octopus can possibly experience sexual motivation or sexual pleasure in anything like the way we do.

There are other views. Anger and fear are specific emotions perhaps, but they have in common a certain state of *arousal* that provides much of their force. Thus we will need to look back at arousal theory (Chap. 6) in discussing emotion.

And, of course, the reactions of the body that accompany emotion or arousal are just that—reactions. This reminds us of the behaviorist outlook: Emotions are *behavior,* and these forms of behavior have their own explanations. Fingolfin's blazing eyes expressed the rage he felt. So, for that matter, did his headlong and hopeless ride to assail an unbeatable foe. We will look at the physiological concomitants of emotion, and at emotional expression, in this context.

Yet another way of looking at the matter is this: Emotions may act to set the reinforcing properties of events or the utilities of anticipated outcomes. Emotions may set the goals of complex *plans*. Literature is rife with examples of long, multistage action sequences by which an actor hopes to achieve revenge *(The Count of Monte Cristo)* or union with a lover *(Romeo and Juliet)*. Fingolfin knew what his enemy had done to his homeland, and could imagine how happy the world could be without that enemy's malice. Perhaps he had in mind a vague and foolish plan for slaying his enemy—for he was not, in his hyper-aroused state, thinking clearly about the likely outcome of his act.

There are still more possibilities. If emotions can set goals, they can also *be* goals. If we're feeling sad, we may try to make ourselves feel happier. Or we may do the opposite: we may try to feel sad, as at a funeral for example.

Finally, emotions are tightly intertwined with cognitive operations, as discussed in previous chapters. Thoughts and images can evoke emotions: "Every time I think about that episode, I (laugh/cry/grind my teeth) all over again." Conversely, our feelings and reactions may set complex cognitive operations in motion: "Just why am I feeling so tense and jittery?" Our minds may bounce back and forth from emotion to cognition to emotion again: "What an annoying remark! Did he mean that as an insult? Yes, I think he did; I'm going to get angry!" How we *think* about a situation has a great deal to do with how we *feel* about it.

By now, the reader will see why we have deferred the topic of emotion until now, rather late in this book. We will find that we need all the background we now have, to understand current research and thinking in this complex area.

EARLY THEORIES OF EMOTION

It seems obvious enough that emotions can be among the causes of action. If one person lashes out at another, we say it is because she is angry; if she weeps, it is because she is sad.

The James-Lange Theory

William James took a different approach. Emotions often accompany important actions, yes. But what if they are *results* of action rather than causes?

> Common-sense says, we lose our fortune, are sorry and weep; we meet a bear, are frightened and run; we are insulted by a rival, are angry and strike. The hypothesis here . . . is that we feel sorry because we cry, angry because we strike, afraid because we tremble. . . . Without the bodily states following on the perception, the latter would be purely cognitive in form, pale, colorless, destitute of emotional warmth. We might then see the bear, and judge it best to run, receive the insult and deem it right to strike, but we should not actually *feel* afraid or angry.[3]

This theory says that what we feel as emotion is simply our perception of our own *responses to arousing stimuli*. These could include skeletal movements such as running, but James emphasized responses of the autonomic nervous system, which in turn produce sweating or a pounding heart and, especially, states of tension in our abdominal organs. We feel these, and that feeling *is* the emotion.

A similar theory was offered at about the same time by Carl Lange, who emphasized arousal-induced changes in the circulatory system—for example, increases in blood pressure—and our perception of those. The theory that emotion is our perception of our body's responses is now called the **James-Lange theory of emotion.**

Notice what a radical departure from the commonsense viewpoint this is. It is remarkably close to the behaviorist view. Emotion is not a cause of action. Rather, it is our perception of a coping reaction that has *already occurred,* and whose cause is in the environment. Seeing a threat, our internal machinery goes into emergency mode, and perhaps we begin to run away. The emotion does not *make* these things happen. Rather it is our awareness that they *are* happening or *have* happened.

Cannon's Critique

Walter Cannon criticized the James–Lange theory severely.[4] He had many reasons for doing so, but perhaps the most important were these:

3. James, 1890, v. II, p. 449.
4. Cannon, 1929.

First, people continue to feel emotion even after the nerves are cut that connect the abdominal organs with the brain. The sensations from these organs are then lost, but emotional experience is not. Second, the response of the body's organs is simply too slow to account for the immediate emotional experience we perceive in threatening or anger-arousing situations. Third, although our emotions vary widely, the response of the autonomic nervous system to all kinds of arousal is pretty much the same. Fear and rage both activate the sympathetic nervous system, producing the global effects of such activation everywhere in the body. If an emotion *is* autonomic arousal or our perception of its effects, how can we tell one emotion from another?

That objection, it develops, may not be a serious one. In recent years, some investigators have found that different patterns of heart-rate changes, skin temperature, and other autonomic signs do accompany different emotional states.[5]

However, we need to be careful in interpreting these findings too. If these physiological changes occur under various emotional states, it doesn't follow that different emotions are experienced *because* they occur. They could just as well be reactions to events elsewhere in the body, such as changes in posture and facial expression, that in turn accompany various emotions. Indeed, there is some evidence for this. Quite a few writers have found that when subjects *pose* various emotions—simply adopt an angry posture and make an angry face, for example, at the experimenter's request—the changes in skin temperature or conductance follow. So these physiological reactions could be causes of emotion or consequences of emotion—or they could be consequences of other consequences, such as facial and bodily adjustments.

Direct experimental test of the James-Lange theory also raised problems for it. In one study, subjects were injected with epinephrine, to produce directly the effects of sympathetic activation. The subjects experienced the symptoms all right, but reported feeling no emotion except, perhaps, a "cold" emotion—a feeling "as if" they were afraid or angry. But no subjects mistook the cold emotion for the real thing.[6]

Cannon's Theory

Whereas James and Lange put emotional experience in the periphery of the body—the autonomic nervous system and the structures it controls—Cannon put it in the brain. As he saw it, emotion-provoking stimuli activated brain circuits concerned with emotion. These circuits were built around focal points in the brainstem, in the thalamus and hypothalamus. Once activated, these emotional centers sent messages downward to the spinal cord, to evoke autonomic arousal and emotional behavior; and upward to higher brain systems, to evoke emotional experience.

5. See for example Levenson, 1992; Ekman, 1992.
6. Landis and Hunt, 1932.

The idea is quite similar to Stellar's theory of drives (Chap. 5). It suggests that there are specific circuits in the brain for different emotional states, and that these are activated selectively by different emotion-arousing situations. To this, later writers added generalized arousal.[7] This might contribute an intensity dimension to the emotional state, or to the behavior that expresses it, or both.

BRAIN MECHANISMS AND EMOTIONS

Cannon's theory implies that different circuits in the brain underlie different emotions. In this, emotions could resemble *drives* of the sort we discussed earlier (Chaps. 3–5).

Indeed, some of the examples used earlier in our discussion of the brain could just as well be considered examples of emotional behavior. We saw that a cat's attack reaction consists of bits and pieces if the hypothalamus is taken out of the system, but is organized and coordinated if it is left in (pp. 164–67). Lesions in the ventromedial hypothalamus produce overeating in rats, but they also produce in *some* rats (not all) a shift toward aggressive, even vicious behavior.[8] Do these animals experience the *emotion* of anger or rage? We cannot be sure, but it is possible.

However, again thinking back to Chapter 5, we realize that emotions are no more likely than drives to be "localized" in specific "centers." We should not expect to find anger simmering in some one cluster of cells, fear trembling in another, and happiness peacefully asleep in yet a third. Any emotion, like any drive, is far more likely to involve the coordinated activity of many structures at many levels of the brain. Remember that a map of the brain will look like a map of a freeway system, not like a map of Europe (p. 179).

An Aggression Circuit?

Let's stay with aggression and anger for an example of this multilevel control.

ANGER, AGGRESSION, AND THE AMYGDALA   We noted a minute ago that hypothalamic lesions can produce a vicious, aggressive animal. Now, it has also been found that the effect can be reversed by further damage to the brain, in an area called the *amygdala*. This is a complex collection of cell clusters that lies under the cortex of the temporal lobe, in the forebrain. On the one hand, it reaches up to connect with the cerebral cortex, and on the other it reaches down to connect with the hypothalamus. Anatomically it is well suited to translate complex cortical interpretation of stimuli into activity of the brainstem mechanisms controlling motor reactions.

Why should a disorder produced by brain damage be corrected by more damage? One possibility is this: Suppose the amygdala (or some portion of it) is

7. See for example Lindsley, 1960.
8. For reviews of these and other related findings see Izard, 1991; Carlson, 1994.

a place whose activation can organize and trigger a rageful response. Suppose further that input from the hypothalamus holds that area under inhibitory check. Then, with hypothalamic damage, the amygdala might be released from inhibition, so that a hair-trigger temper results. With further damage to the amygdala itself, still there is no inhibition, but now there is nothing that needs to be inhibited. Result: calmness.

But we should emphasize that this is a *possibility,* not a demonstrated fact. And of course we are still wondering what, if any, emotions the animal actually *feels* while all these things are going on. Humans can tell us; what do they say?

AGGRESSION AND THE AMYGDALA IN HUMANS   Consider the case of Thomas, a young engineer who suffered extensive brain injury. His behavior thereafter was characterized by uncontrollable anger. He would fly into a rage at even minor incidents. For example, if another car cut in front of him, he would take it as a personal insult, speeding after the car and forcing it to the side of the road, then assaulting the driver. He would rage at his wife or children because of some innocuous remark. After tissue in his amygdala was destroyed surgically, the violent attacks ceased.[9] It is as if the extensive damage to the brain had removed an inhibitory brake on aggressive actions, which in turn were primed by a system involving the amygdala.

This case shows us an emotional system that has many points in common with systems controlling simple *motives* such as hunger (compare Chap. 5). In particular, it shows us yet another case of joint control by internal and external influences. Thomas's rage did not occur in a vacuum, but was triggered by *environmental* events—a remark, or being cut off by another driver. The syndrome may reflect a system in the brain that primes aggressive reactions, and accompanying anger, to *external* provocations.

Electrical stimulation in the amygdala can also cause anger—or something like it—in humans. One woman, receiving electrical stimulation there, reacted as follows:

> SUBJECT: I feel like I want to get up from this chair! Please don't let me do it! Don't do this to me. I don't want to be mean!
> INTERVIEWER: Feel like you want to hit me?
> SUBJECT: Yeah, I just want to hit something. I want to get something and just tear it up. Take it so I won't. [She hands over her scarf; interviewer hands her a stack of papers which she tears to shreds.] I don't like to feel like this! . . . Don't let me hit you![10]

When the electrical current was reduced or turned off, there was immediate relief.

Several things about this episode are striking. First, the woman wanted to hit the interviewer—but she didn't. This tells us at once that the brain stimu-

9. Mark and Ervin, 1970.
10. King, 1961.

lation was not just triggering attack *movements*. It seems to have evoked a motivational/emotional state, but inhibitory control over aggressive action itself was still operative. Again, as in hunger and thirst, we see the interplay of excitation and inhibition.

Second, the desire to strike could be modified by presenting a target—the papers—which offered the opportunity for a different kind of forceful or destructive response—tearing. This again sounds like a motivational state; the woman would *do whatever was available* to express that state.

Third, in this case the woman did not refer the urges to any external provocation. She did not over-react to some innocuous stimulus in the environment or invent an insult which might have justified attack, as Thomas magnified minor traffic episodes. Whatever was evoked was experienced as coming from within, not from without.

SOME PROBLEMS OF INTERPRETATION   Then, however, there arises the question: Just what *was* evoked? What was the experience like? After the session was over, the woman had some trouble describing just what had happened:

INTERVIEWER: Did you feel any pain?
SUBJECT: No, it's just a feeling in my body. No pain.
INTERVIEWER: Would you like to go through that again?
SUBJECT: No. It didn't pain, but I don't like the feelings.
INTERVIEWER: Can you describe them?
SUBJECT: I can't describe it, just can act it . . .[11]

The experience seemed to have had a strange, unreal quality to it. If the patient had simply felt angry, it should have been easy for her to say so. But apparently the experience was not quite like natural anger or assaultiveness, and the woman had trouble saying just what it was like. Perhaps the experience was not one of anger at all. Or it may be that in natural anger, identifying the *situation* that produces the anger is an important part of the experience, and that without a provoking situation the experience itself is different. This looks forward to the role of cognition in emotion.

In Thomas' case, too, it is not clear just how to interpret the findings. Surgical destruction of amygdala tissue does not always reduce aggressiveness. In animal studies, it may reduce it or enhance it! In one classic study in monkeys, the effects of such damage depended a great deal on how *other* monkeys reacted to brain-damaged ones. If the other monkeys were challenging, the experimental subject was likely to cower and flee; if submissive or placating, the experimental monkey might become dominant and bullying.[12] It has been suggested that what such damage actually does is interfere with the processing of social signals—or, indeed, of biologically important signals generally.

11. Ibid., p. 485.
12. Rosvold, Pribram, and Mishkin, 1962.

Thus, for example, Tom might have been disposed to interpret innocuous signals as aggressive ones, even before the injury; we do not know. Prior to the brain damage, such reactions might have been dampened or held in check, but were released from inhibition after the accident. If so, then a man who reacted differently to those social signals in the first place might have shown no increase in aggression after equivalent brain damage, and further damage to the amygdala might not have been beneficial or indeed required. Certainly there is no reason to think that surgery of the amygdala will provide a magic bullet against aggressiveness.

In short, it may be that there is a brain system for aggression in humans, and *perhaps* its activity generates the emotion of anger as well. The emotional state may not be quite the same as true anger, however. Whether this means that the mechanism is not the same either, or that anger without some external provocation does not feel normal, is an open question.

An Anxiety Circuit?

Stimulation effects on other emotions have been less well explored. There have been scattered reports of *fear* produced by brain stimulation, for instance; but whether these are responses of a fear system or simply reactions to a terrifyingly strange experience is uncertain.[13]

However, the opposite tack—interruption of brain function to break up an emotion—has been explored. The results suggest that there is a specific brain system mediating *fear* or *anxiety*. This idea is supported by two lines of evidence. First, certain drugs that affect the brain do appear to reduce anxiety specifically, without depressing other emotional reactions. Second, in patients suffering from severe and debilitating anxiety, brain surgery has been used as a treatment of last resort, with some success.[14] The effective operations again involve interruption of communication lines that link cortical, subcortical, and hypothalamic cells into a single interacting system.

Mood Circuits?

One of the (very few) things nearly all researchers on emotion agree about, is that emotional states can be classified as pleasant or unpleasant. And these states can last for some time, shading into what we call *moods,* happy or unhappy, good or bad.

But does this difference reflect a single underlying dimension, so that our mood changes from nice toward awful as we move, so to speak, from left to right along it? Or are there two systems, one for niceness and one for awfulness? Studies of the brain bear on this question, and they suggest the latter answer: The two are separate.

13. Valenstein, 1973.
14. For review and discussion see Powell, 1979; Gray, 1982.

One line of evidence comes again from the study of drugs. Certain drugs are quite effective in treating severe *depression;* and one of the symptoms of this serious disorder is, of course, a chronically sad and pessimistic emotional state. Some of these drugs, including the best-known one, fluoxetine hydrochloride or Prozak, appear to act by blocking the re-uptake of a neurotransmitter called *serotonin.* Blocking re-uptake, we recall (pp. 186–88) prolongs the activity of a neurotransmitter and thus makes it more effective. In short, we can relieve depression by increasing the effectiveness of serotonin as a neurotransmitter.

But this does not mean that serotonin can be thought of as a "happiness chemical," nor can antidepressants be thought of as "happy pills." If the effect of an antidepressant like Prozak were simply to shift mood from low toward high, then it ought to act as a mood elevator even in non-depressed persons. It doesn't. Conversely, drugs that do act as mood elevators, like amphetamine and cocaine, ought to be effective antidepressants; but again, they are not.★

There is evidence of quite another sort that high moods and low moods may reflect separate systems in the brain. There is some evidence for *lateralization* of high- and low-mood systems. (When we speak of lateralization, we simply mean that one side of the brain plays a greater role than the other.) The pop-psychological notion that intellect lives in the left brain, and emotion in the right brain, is *not* supported by the evidence. Some findings do suggest, however, evidence that the left frontal portion of the cerebrum is more active in positive emotional states, and the right frontal portion in negative states.

In one study, EEGs (see pp. 229–31) were recorded from both frontal areas as subjects were shown film clips designed to produce either amusement or disgust. The EEGs showed greater right-side activation for the negative emotion. The same result was found in newborn infants, when either a sweet taste (nice) or a bitter taste (awful) was presented. The difference extends to long-term mood differences, as well as to these brief bursts of pleasure or displeasure. Thus depressed subjects had less left-side frontal activation than their non-depressed controls.[15]

A Look Backward: Emotions and Drives

In this quick survey, we find that there are indeed many parallels between brain mechanisms of emotion and of drives. We see familiar principles: internal and external control, the priming of responses to the environment by internal state, multiple-output systems, and the interplay of excitation and inhibition.

★Another reason we ought not to think of serotonin as a "happiness chemical" is that there is a paradox about the antidepressants that affect serotonin. Their effects on the re-uptake of this neurotransmitter can be demonstrated almost immediately after they are injected. Yet their therapeutic effect typically requires 4 to 6 weeks of daily ingestion before it kicks in. Obviously, these effects of brain chemistry on mood cannot be direct, but must reflect a process that the effects set in motion and that in turn has therapeutic value down the road. The details of this process are not clear.
15. Davidson, 1992.

In both cases, too, we see how physiological investigations can clarify the organization of behavioral systems. The niceness and awfulness of mood states are accompanied by the activation of different parts of the forebrain. And studies of the *chemical coding* of mood states—for example, that antidepressants are not good mood elevators and vice versa—suggests further that niceness and awfulness are separate systems, not just two extreme states of a single one.

Then again, this smattering of findings also reminds us of some of the cautions we raised earlier, in discussing Stellar's theory and theories like it. It is most unlikely that there is any single center or circuit in the brain that "does" hunger, all of it and only it. It is just as unlikely that there is any center or circuit that "does" anger or joy. Emotional response involves registering the situation. This may involve specialized mechanisms for, e.g., recognizing significant events; but these mechanisms are specialized for a specific kind of recognition, not a specific kind of emotion. Again, emotional response may require interpreting a situation; that may involve memory, and so require the participation of systems concerned with memory.

In short, any emotional reaction involves a variety of specific functions. It is these functions that systems in the brain "do," and they likely combine in different ways to generate many different kinds of emotional reactions.

EMOTION AND AROUSAL

Strong emotions are often characterized by states of high physiological arousal, including, for example, a storm of activity in the sympathetic nervous system. And emotion can trigger the characteristic *consequences* of high arousal.

Emotion and Behavioral Disruption

Recently a group including some very attractive men walked into a restaurant. As the waitress described the day's specials, she focused her attention in turn on each member of the party. By the time she had made eye contact with each, she had totally lost her routine and could not remember a thing. One interpretation was that her feelings of attraction had her completely flustered. (This was actually borne out later by her sending over a carafe of wine.)[16]

We saw in Chapter 6 that a state of high arousal can disrupt performance, especially if we are doing something complicated—the *Yerkes-Dodson law*. Emotional arousal can also do that. Surely we all have had the experience of being too upset to work or think. But the effect is not confined to unpleasant emotions; the waitress in the above example was probably not displeased.

16. Fiske and Taylor, 1990.

Emotion and Cognitive Disruption

We also saw in Chapter 6 that under high arousal, behavior tends to become more simple and stereotyped. Parallel effects occur in the sphere of cognitive action. People in very good moods have been shown to depend more often on simple and obvious actions, decision strategies, and habits of thought, than people not so happy. They are likely to satisfice when they could maximize, or to think heuristically rather than carefully.[17]

Emotional Spillover

The parallel goes even further than that. Again in Chapter 6, we saw how arousal even from an irrelevant source can promote a variety of actions. A pinch on the tail can trigger feeding or mating in rats. In emotion, similar effects have been found; arousal from one source can "spill over" into the expression and experience of a seemingly irrelevant emotion.

For example, people who had just exercised and were in an aroused, hard-breathing state responded more angrily to provocation than people who had not exercised.[18] Such effects can happen even in people who do not realize that they are aroused.

An especially ingenious study took advantage of a pair of bridges over a river. Of these, one was a 5-foot-wide, 450-foot-long bridge made of wooden boards attached to wire cables. It swayed over a 200-foot drop to rocks and shallow rapids beneath, and its low wire handrails intensified the crosser's impression that he was about to be pitched over the side. The other bridge, upriver, was solid wood and only 10 feet above a shallow rivulet. It was assumed—and subjects' self-reports confirmed—that crossing the former bridge was a highly anxiety-arousing experience.

Male subjects, men who happened to cross one or the other bridge, were met by a female experimenter who asked them to help her with a psychology project. The men filled out a questionnaire, and responded to a test that later was scored for sexual imagery. Finally, the female experimenter gave each subject her phone number, with the excuse that she would be willing to discuss the experiment with the subject if he wished.

The question was: Would physiological arousal, caused by the frightening high bridge, enhance sexual arousal? If so, then the high-bridge subjects should be more attracted to the experimenter. They should (1) show more sexual imagery in their test responses and (2) be more likely to call the female experimenter later.

Both predictions were confirmed. Of the men interviewed on the high bridge, fully 50 percent telephoned the experimenter. Of those interviewed on the safe bridge, only 12 percent did so.[19]★

17. Isen et al., 1982.
18. Cacioppo, 1979.
19. Dutton and Aron, 1974.
★There is of course the possibility that the men who chose the high swaying bridge were simply more enterprising to begin with than those who chose the safe one, and therefore more likely to telephone a woman they didn't know. However, a replication of the experiment makes this

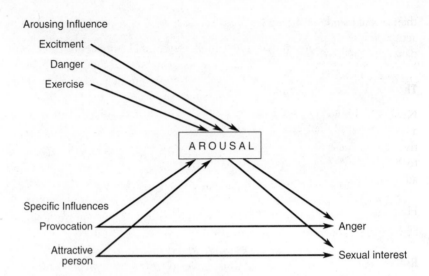

Figure 12-1 Arousal as an intensifier of emotional reactions to emotion-evoking circumstances.

A Look Backward: Arousal and the Emotions

We can represent the situation as in Figure 12-1. The excited state may intensify emotional reactions, both positive and negative. In addition, various exciting conditions such as exercise can contribute to that excited state.

Notice that this conception is again exactly parallel to the role we assigned to *arousal* in governing biological action systems, back in Chapter 6. Arousing stimuli, like mild pain, can contribute to a diffuse arousal that in turn enhances feeding reactions, mating reactions, and so on. In a similar way, arousing stimuli, like those that crossing a high bridge provides, can enhance social or sexual responsiveness.

THE EXPRESSION OF EMOTION

Let us turn now to look at the expression of emotion. Here we focus on emotion as behavior in its own right. Once again we will meet some old friends along the way; we will find ourselves looking back, for example, to our discussion of sex and aggression in Chapter 4 and to the concepts of *ethology* (pp. 112–13).

The ethological study of emotional expression began with Charles Darwin, author of the theory of evolution. Darwin recognized clearly (1) that mechanisms of behavior must evolve along with the structure of a species and (2) that

---

unlikely. In that study, the control subjects were not men who crossed the safe bridge. They were men who *had* crossed the risky bridge, but were interviewed some time later after physiological arousal had dissipated. The results were the same. A full 65 percent of the men interviewed while crossing the bridge called the experimenter later; only 30 percent of those interviewed *some time after* crossing the bridge did so. Even so, other interpretations of this finding are possible, as we will see later (pp. 468–71).

the mechanisms evolve because they enhance *reproductive success*. Any instinctive action, therefore, is there because ancestral animals that had it left more descendants than those that didn't.

The Value of Communication

Now one way an action pattern can enhance reproductive success is by serving a *communicative* function. It is to an animal's advantage to communicate effectively with other species members. If Animal A is disposed to mate, or is ready to fight, it is to its advantage to convey that fact to Animal B; and it is to B's advantage to get the message.

Therefore, as Darwin saw, behavior can evolve *because* it communicates. His studies of emotional behavior (Fig. 12-2) anticipated what modern writers call *ritualization*.

Ritualization

If any behavior serves as a signal to another animal, evolution may select animals in which that behavior is especially conspicuous and easy to interpret.

A

B

Figure 12-2   (A) A dog expressing what Darwin called "hostile intentions" as it approaches another dog. Note the forward stance with forelegs straight, and forward ear position. (B) Here these signs are reversed (Darwin's "principle of antithesis"). The ears are back, forelegs are bent, and the back is curved down; the dog is expressing a "humble and affectionate frame of mind." (From Darwin, 1872.)

This is so even if that behavior originally served a quite different purpose. Behavior that has evolved in exaggerated form, sending a loud and clear signal to another animal, is said to be **ritualized.**

Many ethologists believe that emotional expressions are ritualized forms of behavior. For example, opening the mouth and exposing the teeth prepares a creature to bite, but it can also signal an *intention* to bite, and thus serve as a threat gesture. Similarly, lowering the brows, while also widening the eyes underneath them, will protect the eyes in a fight and also allow one to see more of what is going on. But such gestures also signal aggressive intent to a fellow creature. Put all these bits together and we have the **open-mouth threat display** (Fig. 12-3).

Conversely, an intention *not* to attack can be signaled by exaggerated preparations *not* to fight (Darwin's *principle of antithesis;* see Fig. 12-2). Showing *closed* teeth can signal that one does not intend to bite—how can you bite with your teeth closed? Turning the head to one side is incompatible with a head-on charge and can signal an intention not to make one. Combining these gestures, we get a stance and expression that signals a readiness *not* to do battle (Fig. 12-4).

Fragments of these patterns can be blended together to form complex mixtures, communicating subtle differences among emotions.* Figure 12-5 shows an example. In A, a model is portraying *disgust,* shown by contortion of the mouth—perhaps a ritualized spitting-out gesture—and *narrowing* of the eyes. In B, she is portraying *surprise;* in that emotion, the eyebrows are raised high and the eyes are widened. That may be the ritualized response of getting the brows and eyelids out of the way, the better to see what is happening. If we cut the photographs and combine the surprised eyes with the disgusted mouth (C), we get a blend that we can clearly recognize: "That's disgusting, but it's fascinating!"

Figure 12-3 Open-mouth threat display in two primate species, red uakari and human. (From Jolly, 1972.)

*This is true in animals as well as humans; see Hinde, 1970.

Figure 12-4 Grinning with teeth closed and head averted is a non-aggressive display in some primates. (From Wallace, 1979.)

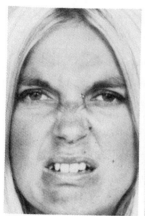
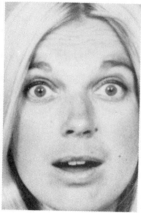
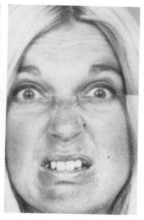

Figure 12-5 A mixture of expressive actions. Part A shows a posed expression of disgust; B shows surprise. Combining the surprised top of the face with the disgusted bottom half gives us an expression of mixed surprise and disgust (C). (From Ekman and Friesen, 1975.)

This is not to suggest that animals, or humans, plan these signals and send them deliberately. Rather, modern species have these ritualized action patterns and the nervous-system mechanisms that program them, for the same reason that they have fur or feathers. Animals that communicated their intentions effectively had more descendants than those that did not. And the animals living today *are* the descendants.

Human Facial Expressions

It may be that human facial expressions, and certain other non-verbal communicative gestures, evolved as ritualized signals.[20] We saw some examples above.

Certainly facial expressions have some of the properties of action patterns. They are sent and interpreted in the same way by cultures that have been sep-

20. See for example Andrew, 1965.

Figure 12-6 Some human facial expressions are recognized across cultures that have had minimal contact with each other. (A) A man of the Fore of New Guinea poses this expression when asked to imagine that a friend has arrived. American college students have no trouble recognizing it as expressing happiness. (B) Conversely, the Fore have no trouble recognizing this expression, posed by an American, as expressing happiness. (From Ekman, 1973.)

arated from each other by many thousands of years, so in that sense they are characteristic of the species (Fig. 12-6).[21] And they are, at least initially, untaught. They are displayed by people who could not have learned them in any obvious way—for example, children born blind and deaf (Fig. 12-7).[22]

THE ROLE OF EXPRESSION IN EMOTION   On the other hand, there is a distinct difference between human facial expression and the action patterns of, say, the stickleback. The *response* may be species-wide and untaught, but the eliciting or releasing *stimuli* are not.

We saw in Chapter 4 how the external conditions evoking anger vary with the society in which one lives. More than that, almost any emotion we can think of can be evoked by *words,* which means that the stimuli must be interpreted by the language-processing apparatus before they evoke emotion. What role, then, does expression play in the emotional state itself? It is not, except perhaps in infants, a pattern evoked by an untaught releasing stimulus.

Well, we might think of it as an untaught indicator of the emotional state itself—released perhaps by the internally felt emotional state rather than by an external releaser (Fig. 12-8A). Some writers do take such a view.[23] Others suggest that expressive actions, and emotion, are parallel effects of the *situation* that

21. Ekman and Friesen, 1971.
22. Eibl-Eibesfeldt, 1972.
23. For example Izard, 1991; Ekman, 1977; Tomkins, 1962, 1963.

Figure 12-7   A seven-year-old girl, born both blind and deaf, smiles and laughs in a familiar way, throwing back her head, opening her mouth, and narrowing or closing her eyes as children who are not handicapped do. (From Eibl-Eibesfeldt, 1970)

arouses both (Fig. 12-8B). This has been suggested both by behaviorist writers, who emphasize the situation itself,[24] and by cognitive writers who emphasize the situation *as interpreted*.[25]

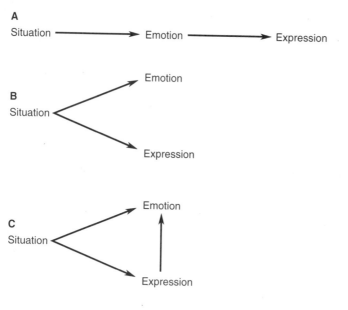

Figure 12-8   Three views of the role of expression in emotion. (A) This is the commonsense view: Emotion leads directly to its expression. Alternatively (B), expression may be a reaction to the situation that also produces the emotion. Or (C) the expression may affect the emotion rather than the other way around. This is the facial-feedback hypothesis.

24. Skinner, 1971.
25. Mandler, 1984.

DISPLAY RULES Finally, we remember that *untaught* doesn't mean *unteachable*. If facial expressions are untaught, still they can be modified or suppressed by what Paul Ekman calls **display rules**—rules taught by the culture about what expressions are appropriate, when.[26] In our society, we hear things like "Don't give me that angry look," or "Look happy now when your aunt gives you a present." In Japan, one is taught to mask any negative emotion with a polite smile. It is these rules, Ekman says, that differ from one society to another and make for frequent misunderstandings. Here is an example both amusing and sad:

> The class was basic English for foreign students, and an Arab student, during a spoken exercise, was describing a tradition of his home country. Something he said embarrassed a Japanese student in the front row, who reacted the proper Japanese way: he smiled. The Arab saw the smile and demanded to know what was so funny about Arab customs. The Japanese, who was now publicly humiliated as well as embarrassed, could reply only with a smile and, to his misfortune, he giggled to mask his shame. The Arab, who now likewise felt shamed, furiously hit the Japanese student before the teacher could intervene. Shame and anger had erupted in a flash, as each student dutifully obeyed the rules of his culture. Neither could imagine, of course, that his rules might not be universal.[27]

All this has a familiar ring. It sounds like our discussion of human sexuality—cultural training selecting from, and adding to, a perhaps instinctive core of arousing stimuli and expressive responses. Thus we are taught to react emotionally to stimuli, including arbitrary ones such as speech sounds; and we are taught how to express the emotion, facially and in other ways too.

Facial Feedback

There may be yet another thread to this tangled web. The *facial-feedback* hypothesis is a variation on the James-Lange theory which says: When we adopt the expressions that characterize an emotion, we feel the movements of the facial muscles; and these sensations contribute to our experience of that emotion (Figure 12-8C).

Some data suggest exactly this. Subjects who are instructed just to put on a sad or happy face, or just to arrange their muscles so as to mimic sadness or happiness, report *feeling* sad or happy.[28] In one experiment, differenct facial expressions actually produced different autonomic reactions:

> For example, when the actors made the muscle movements on their face for anger and those for fear (and . . . they weren't told to pose these emotions but instead just

26. Ekman, 1985.
27. Tavris, 1982.
28. See for example Laird, 1974; Lanzetta, Cartwright-Smith, and Kleck, 1976.

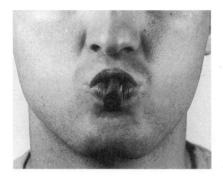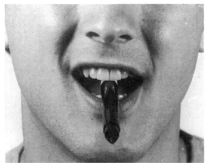

Figure 12-9   The experimental manipulation in the experiment testing the facial-feedback hypothesis wherein subjects were asked to hold a magic marker in their mouths. Holding it with their teeth but not their lips produced a smile; holding it with their lips but not their teeth produced a pout. (From Strack, Martin, and Stepper, 1988, p. 771.)

to make specific muscle actions) . . . [their] skin became hot with anger and cold with fear.[29]

An especially ingenious demonstration is the procedure shown in Figure 12-9. The experimental subjects were told nothing about emotions, or expressing them, or posing them. They were simply asked to hold a pen, (1) with their teeth or (2) with their lips. And it's virtually impossible to do (1) without making a grinning face or (2) without making a pouting face. Sure enough, "grinning" subjects were more amused by cartoons than "pouting" ones were.

The facial-feedback hypothesis is highly controversial.[30] And at best, it can be only one of several influences on emotion; obviously we can smile without feeling happy and we can feel happy without smiling (multiple inputs again!). However, its role may not be trivial. It has been claimed that keeping a stoic face, rather than expressing pain, can actually make the pain hurt less. There may be a definite point to the proverbial "stiff upper lip."

EMOTION AND COGNITION: DISCREPANCY AND INTERRUPTION

The ideas we have considered focus on the mechanisms and effects of emotion. We now turn to the conditions that produce it. Specifically, we will look at the role of cognition in mediating the situation-to-emotion chain of events. What we *feel* can depend on what we *expect* or what we *think*.

29. Ekman, 1985, p. 119.
30. See Buck, 1980; Tourangeau and Ellsworth, 1979; Izard, 1991.

Discrepancy, Surprise, and Optimal Arousal

We have already seen how emotion is related to *arousal*. Now from our earlier discussion of arousal, we recall the idea that moderate levels of arousal—some, but not too much—are pleasurable. From the work on habituation and surprise, we have the idea that arousal is produced not by stimuli per se, but by their deviation from what is expected. Where do we get if we put these two ideas together?

We arrive at the **discrepancy hypothesis,** which says this: *A moderate discrepancy from the input we expect is pleasurable. A large discrepancy is aversive.* In other words, we tend to like mild surprises; we tend to dislike severe ones. Therefore, to please another organism and hold his attention, we should surprise him—but not too much.

The idea is like the notion of optimal arousal, except that the arousal is produced not by the stimulus itself, but by its surprise value. If there is no surprise, there is too little arousal, and we are bored. Too much surprise is too much arousal, and we are shocked and disoriented. Somewhere in between is just right.

Data that support this idea have been obtained in many situations and many species—especially in young species members, who presumably are only beginning to form expectations against which stimulus inputs can be compared. For instance, young chicks are most likely to try to approach a stimulus that is *slightly different,* but not *very different,* from a stimulus that is thoroughly familiar.[31] Data from human babies have been interpreted in the same way. Thus Jerome Kagan found that very young babies were about equally likely to inspect the "face" and the "scrambled-face" pictures shown in Figure 12-10. Older babies, however, preferred to look at the "face" picture.[32] Presumably the older babies had learned something about what a human face looks like, and so were intrigued by the "face" card; this looks almost but not quite like a

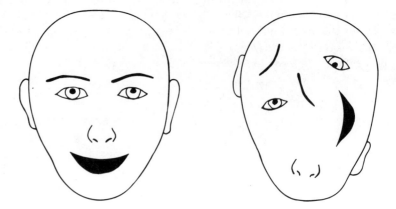

Figure 12-10 A face and a scrambled face, examples of face-like stimuli presented to infants. (From Kagan, 1970.)

31. Bateson, 1966.
32. Kagan, 1970.

real face. By that time, the scrambled-face card was too much surprise; it looked all wrong, and represented too great a mismatch between stimulus and image. Older babies tended to look away from it.

Extreme surprises are clearly unpleasant even to babies. In another experiment, the baby saw the mother in one location, but—because of a crafty arrangement of microphones, speakers, and soundproof glass—heard her voice coming from a different place. Three-month-old babies were very much upset by such a shocking change in the nature of the world. Younger babies, who presumably had not formed the relevant expectations yet, were unperturbed.[33]

Let us see what light this idea can shed on some topics discussed elsewhere in this book, and on some new ones.

Theme and Variation

In speech, drama, and music, we see the discrepancy principle put to use to maintain interest and attention. The trick is to set up an expectation of what is to come, and then violate it, but not too much. Then the discrepancy between expected and actual input is arousing, attention-getting, and pleasing.[34]

For instance, one may present material (the theme), and then repeat it—but not quite (the variation). One way is to begin the repetition in the same way as the theme, but then go somewhere else with it each time. Thus the sequence is A, B; A, C; A, D. Arthur Sullivan does this in the following two phrases:

The second time around, Sullivan could have repeated the whole passage exactly. But notice how much more interesting it is when the second phrase is changed, although the first phrase is the same both times: A, B; then A, C.

In oratory, Winston Churchill used this device very effectively:

A	B	A	C	A
We shall fight	on the beaches;	we shall fight	on the landing grounds;	we shall fight

D
on the fields and in the streets . . .

Another such device is to turn the sequence around. From different starting points (the variation), one comes home to the same ending (the theme). The sequence is then B, A; C, A; D, A; and so on. Thus Abraham Lincoln:

---

33. Aronson and Rosenbloom, 1971.
34. See Berlyne, 1971.

<u>   B   A   C   A   D   A   </u>

And that government of the people, by the people, for the people . . .

In poetry we have Alfred Noyes:

<u>   B   A   C   A   D   A   </u>

Look for me by moonlight; watch for me by moonlight; I'll come to thee by moonlight . . .

At the level of individual words, of course, this tactic is called *rhyme*.

Still another device is sequence reversal: A, B; B, A. Here it is the elements themselves that provide the theme, and the reversed order is the variation. Thus John F. Kennedy:

<u>   A   B   B   A   </u>

Ask not what your country can do for you, but what you can do for your country.

Thus Shakespeare:

<u>   A   B   B   A   </u>

What is Hecuba to him, or he to Hecuba?

Thus Franz Schubert:

We see that the discrepancy hypothesis has wide ramifications indeed. It may be a large part of what keeps us interested, involved in situations, and intellectually and emotionally alive.* If life is full of surprises, that's all to the good within limits—but may all our surprises be little ones.

Exposure, Familiarity, and Discrepancy

Consider this story:

A mysterious student has been attending a class at Oregon State University for the past two months enveloped in a big black bag. Only his bare feet show. Each Monday, Wednesday, and Friday at 11:00 A.M. the Black Bag sits on a small table near the back of the classroom. . . . Charles Goetzinger, professor of the class, knows the identity of the person inside. None of the 20 students in the class do. Goetzinger

*It even has ramifications within economics; see Scitovsky, 1976.

said the students' attitude changed from hostility toward the Black Bag to curiosity and finally to friendship.[35]

It seems as if simply *being there* for a while is enough to make a stimulus more positive. Robert Zajonc has shown that what he calls "mere exposure" increases subjects' liking even for such biologically inert material as nonsense syllables and Chinese characters![36] Advertisers make extensive use of this: How many times a day do we see the Coca-Cola logo?

Compare the Black Bag episode with this one: When Igor Stravinsky's ballet *The Rite of Spring* was first performed in 1913, it nearly caused a riot. The outraged audience demanded their money back, complaining, "This isn't music!" The *Rite* violated so many musical conventions of the time that it was simply too discrepant from audiences' expectations to be accepted. Nowadays, people may or may not like Stravinsky's music, but they don't riot about it. They have heard music like that before.

What these vignettes have in common is a negative reaction to the unfamiliar. It is as if the child, developing his conceptions of how things are, also develops the assumption that *the way things usually are is the way things ought to be.* This takes us back to the *discrepancy hypothesis.* The idea is that small deviations from what we expect may be interesting and pleasurable, but large deviations are unpleasant and bewildering.

In these terms, it is easy to see how *negative reaction to discrepancy* could be a powerful socializing influence. Cultures may transmit their norms to their children partly because those very norms determine what will be familiar to the child and what will not.★ We don't eat ants. Men in our society don't wear cotton frocks even in blazing heat. Why not? Because we don't! And if anyone does, it is so severe a violation of expectation that we are uncomfortable.

Discrepancy and Cultural Change

If we humans do tend to assume that the way things are is the way things ought to be, then it follows that a society's values, attitudes, and customs will have considerable inertia. Change is likely to be quite slow. On the other hand, it also suggests how change can be brought about: Just keep the new idea in the air, long enough so that our expectations expand to include it. In other words, let it become familiar. Then, whether or not people like it any better (the mere exposure effect), at least they will no longer be shocked by it (the discrepancy effect). Stravinsky's music hasn't changed; audiences' schemas have. As another

---

35. Zajonc, 1968.
36. Zajonc, 1968, 1984.

★This sounds a great deal like Zajonc's "mere exposure," and one may wonder whether the two hypotheses amount to the same thing. Zajonc doesn't think so. He has found that "mere exposure" may increase the pleasantness of stimuli, even if subjects don't recognize them as familiar (see pp. 272–73). The "mere exposure" effect does not, therefore, imply a conscious recognition of familiarity or discrepancy. The discrepancy hypothesis does.

example, today there are plays, articles, and open discussions about homosexuality. Even thirty years ago, the very subject was unmentionable. It was just too discrepant from the culture's norms. Now that we've gotten used to the idea, we can discuss it.

EMOTION, ATTRIBUTION, AND LABELING

LADY JANE: [Love is] a transcendentality of delirium—an acute accentuation of the supremest ecstasy—which the earthy might easily mistake for indigestion.

—W. S. GILBERT, *Patience*

Discrepancy theories point to *situational* causes of emotion. Cognitions are involved in them because the situations violate our expectancies. But recall that we also seek *explanations,* or *causal attributions,* for events. How we explain an event has a great deal to do with how we feel about it.

Labeling Symptoms: Schachter's Theory

Stanley Schachter and his colleagues have advanced an enormously influential theory of emotional experience. They propose that our experience of an emotional state depends·on how we explain that state to ourselves.[37]

We begin with the state of autonomic arousal that an event may provoke. We perceive that state of arousal (as in the James-Lange theory). Then, the theory goes, we look for the cause of the aroused state. The causal attribution we make—how we interpret or **label** the arousal—determines the emotion we experience.

THE SCHACHTER AND SINGER EXPERIMENT   Schachter and Singer performed an ingenious experiment to test this idea. They placed some of their subjects in a state of physiological arousal, by injection of the sympathetic hormone epinephrine. This produces the signs of physiological arousal, and the subject experiences some of them directly—he feels his heart pounding, his hands shaking a bit, and the like. Now these subjects did not know they were receiving this hormone—the purpose of the experiment was disguised throughout—and they did not expect these bodily reactions to occur. What would they make of them when they did occur?

It depended on the situation. After receiving the injections, the subjects were put in a room, ostensibly to fill out a questionnaire. And in the room was a stooge, pretending to be another subject but actually a role model for the real subject.

In one condition, this stooge acted like an utter giddy idiot. He bounced around the room, laughing, making paper airplanes out of the questionnaire sheets, and generally acting euphoric and full of fun. What happened? A hormone-treated subject was more likely to join in the fun and describe himself as happy, than control subjects were.

37. Schachter and Singer, 1962; Schachter, 1971.

In another condition, the stooge portrayed anger. He scowled, griped about the experiment, and swore at the questionnaire, finally tearing it to pieces.★ What happened? The subject himself was more likely to act angry, and report himself as angry, than control subjects.

In short: In a situation designed to promote euphoria, the subjects were euphoric. In a situation designed to promote anger, they were angry. But there was more. These reactions happened only in subjects who experienced the physiological arousal, *and did not expect to experience it*. If the subjects were led to expect the tremors, the pounding heart, and so on, as an effect of the injection they were getting—then they were much less affected by the stooge's giddiness or griping.

Schachter and Singer interpret the findings as follows. If a subject feels himself in an aroused state, he seeks an explanation for it. If he is told to expect those symptoms, then he can say, "Okay, my hands are shaking and my heart is pounding. That's the drug; they told me that would happen. Why is this other guy acting so sour [or silly]? Oh well, nothing to do with me."

But suppose the subject feels this arousal *and* has no explanation for it? Then he will seek an explanation, and the environment provides one. He may say, "Boy, that guy is mad. And my heart is racing, and I'm shaking. Maybe I'm mad too! And, come to think of it, this questionnaire is pretty infuriating . . ." Having decided he is furious—having *labeled* his state of arousal that way—he will act accordingly. A similar but happier train of thought will occur in the subject whose partner is having fun.

In short, the emotion did not depend on the physiological arousal. That was the same for happy-stooge and angry-stooge subjects. It depended on how the arousal was labeled. The emotional experience was not the physiological state per se, but the result of a judgment made about that state.

At first glance, Schachter's theory sounds very strange. Surely we know whether we're angry or euphoric; surely we don't *really* confuse love with indigestion. But then, we usually know what the situation is. Perhaps we label our emotions appropriately, most of the time, because we interpret the situation appropriately. If we didn't, could we actually confuse love and indigestion? Read on.

There were some difficulties with the Schachter and Singer study, and the investigators were well aware of them.★★ It is a landmark study, not because the data were definitive, but because the study launched a whole series of further investigations. And an impressive body of evidence supports the main idea: Self-attributions—the causes we find for our bodies' actions—affect the emotions we experience.

★The angry act was plausible, because the questionnaire itself was designed to be offensive. As just an example of what the subjects had to put up with, one item asked the subject how many extramarital affairs his mother had had. The permitted answers were 0–4, 5–9, and 10 or more!
★★For example, not all of the findings met conventional levels of significance, and subjects were discarded on grounds that were reasonable but unorthodox. Some writers have had difficulty replicating the findings, and Schachter and his colleagues have found difficulties with their difficulties. See Maslach, 1979; Marshall and Zimbardo, 1979; Schachter and Singer, 1979.

IS AROUSAL NECESSARY? Schachter's theory gives us another way of interpreting some of the emotional spillover data (pp. 455–56). We suggested, you recall, that the arousal produced by crossing a dangerous, swaying bridge enhanced the subjects' attraction to a female experimenter, much as a tail pinch may arouse a rat to eat or mate. It could also be, however, that the arousal was *mis-labeled* as attraction. These two theories sound similar, but there's an important difference. A mis-labeling theory implies that the subjects *mistook* their arousal for attraction, and concluded that they were more attracted than they really were. By the spillover theory, the subjects were making no mistake. Because of their general arousal, they really *were* more attracted to the female.

Many of the findings could be interpreted either way. It is clear, however, that a "pure" mis-labeling can occur. In one ingenious experiment, male college students looked at pictures of women while listening to what they thought were the sounds of their own heartbeats, fed back through earphones. With some slides, the subject was made to hear a change in the heart rate that he thought was his own. The subjects rated those slides as most attractive. And when they were invited to take some of the pictures home with them as reward for participation, it was the pictures they *thought* had made their hearts go pitty-pat that they were most likely to choose.[38]

In other words, one may not need physiological arousal to produce the labeling effect. If a subject *believes* that his body is aroused, he will seek an explanation for that. And if an emotional state such as sexual attraction is available as an explanation, then that explanation will be accepted—and the emotion will be experienced. Do we confuse love with indigestion? We don't know; but attraction with heart palpitations, yes.

CLINICAL IMPLICATIONS If emotions result from labels, a great deal of confusion and unhappiness could result from the labeling, and might be alleviated if the label were changed. A case study makes the point well:

A woman was so concerned about her recent irritability and jumpiness that she feared a nervous breakdown. It turned out that she had recently been drinking eight to ten bottles of diet cola per day. The therapist pointed out that the caffeine being consumed was quite enough to produce jitters and jumpiness. This relabeling of the jitters gave the patient a much better outlook on life, though the jitters were the same as before.[39]

A LOOK BACKWARD: LABELING AND SCHEMAS Schachter's theory can easily be linked with the discrepancy theory discussed earlier. Discrepancy or interruption produces arousal. Cognitive evaluation labels that arousal.[40]

There remains dispute about how important a process this is. Despite the success story of the caffeine drinker, more systematic research on re-labeling in the clinic has yielded mixed results. Not all the findings are easily replicable,

38. Valins, 1966.
39. Rimm and Masters, 1979.
40. Fiske, 1981.

and the process may operate within more severe limits than at first appeared.[41] The evidence that labeling *can* affect how we experience an emotion, however, is quite strong.

Finally, notice that the label given to the bodily state, in all these studies, is closely related to the *causal explanation* that was given for it. *How* we label a feeling depends on *why* we think we feel it. Thus Schachter and Singer's subjects were led to infer that the insulting questionnaire was what led to the arousal, and therefore that the arousal must be anger. The label for the arousal depended on the causal attribution. Similarly for the jumpy patient. She perceived a symptom—trembling, perhaps. She labeled the symptom, "I'm jittery," and attributed a cause to that state: "I'm going to break down." A more accurate label, "I'm reacting to caffeine," would entail a more accurate causal attribution: "Well, that's because I drink too much cola, don't I?"

Or we could say the same thing in a different way. In attributing our symptoms to causes, we assimilate them to a causal *schema*—that is, we say, "This is the kind of thing that causes such symptoms." Then the emotion experienced is the result of a *schema-driven inference,* which leads us to draw a conclusion—right or wrong—about what we are feeling.

Attributing Causes: Weiner's Theory

Schachter's theory of emotion is an *attributional* one. It argues that we assign or, as we say, *attribute* causes to the symptoms we experience. Bernard Weiner's theory of emotion is not incompatible with Schachter's, but extends it from the symptoms to the situation.[42] We ask, not just "What am I feeling and why?" but also, "What has happened and why?"

As Weiner sees it, our attributions of causality vary along three dimensions. First is *external versus internal:* Did I cause this situation (internal), or did someone or something else (external)? Second is *stable versus unstable:* Is the cause likely to continue to be there (stable), or is it something that could come and go (unstable)? Third is *controllability:* Is (or was) the event under someone's control, or not?

Emotional reactions can be triggered by the event itself, but also by the causes to which we attribute it. Suppose we have failed an important exam. That, let us agree, would cause displeasure (the first emotional reaction). But now we think about it: Why did that disaster happen?

Suppose we decide that we have the necessary ability, and that the exam was fair, but we just didn't study very hard. That's an internal attribution (the failure was our own doing), and the cause was unstable (we won't, or at least we needn't, make that mistake again), and under our control. As a result, we are likely to feel the emotion of *guilt.*

41. For discussion see Fiske and Taylor, 1990.
42. Weiner, 1989.

But suppose instead we attribute our failure to lack of ability. That changes matters. Now the cause is still internal (within us), but it's stable and not under our control. We are likely to feel, not guilt, but *shame*. That is a different emotion, and it's different precisely because our attributions have different implications in such a case.

Finally, what if we decide that we have the ability and we studied hard, but the exam was unfair—the questions were too hard, ambiguous, or picayune. That makes a difference! The cause is now external—it's the professor's doing, not our own. It may or may not be stable, depending on what we think his intentions are for the future. But it is certainly controllable—the slimy fellow could have written a fair exam if he had chosen to do so. We will feel *anger*, and must then decide what to do about it.

Thus Weiner sees emotional experience as embedded in a network of cognitions—thoughts about what happened and why it happened—leading in turn to action (Fig. 12-11). In support of these ideas, he has conducted a series of thought experiments, in which he asked his subjects what they would think, feel, and do in a series of hypothetical situations.[43] In one such study, subjects read the following scenario:

> At about 1:00 in the afternoon you are walking through campus and a student comes up to you. The student says that you do not know him, but that you are both enrolled in the same class. He asks if you would lend him the class notes from the meeting last week, saying that notes are needed because he skipped class to go to the beach.

For other subjects, the last sentence read ". . . because of a severe eye problem." The relevant dimension here is *controllability:* going to the beach is presumably under the other student's control, whereas a severe eye problem is not.

Subjects did indeed rate the beach-going as controllable, the eye problem as not; they felt pity for the student with the eye problem, but anger at the beach-goer; and they rated themselves more likely to help (by lending the notes) in the case of the student with the eye problem.

Thus all three of the measured variables—how controllable students thought the problem was, how they felt about it, and what they thought they

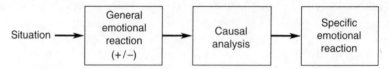

Figure 12-11   Weiner's attributional theory of emotion. A situation or event may give rise to an initial, global reaction of pleasure or displeasure. But the actor also seeks an explanation of the situation or event (causal analysis). The causal explanation then determines a more specific emotional reaction, as of anger, shame, etc.

43. Weiner, 1986.

would do—all varied together as the description of the problem was varied. But what was most important in determining what the subjects would do— what they thought about controllability, or how they felt about the situation? To tease these apart, Weiner's group used a statistical technique known as *partial correlation*. That allows us to ask this question: Given that variables A and B are correlated with each other, and with another variable C: How closely would A and B be correlated with each other if C were held constant? It turned out that the actions students would take (helping or not helping) remained strongly correlated with the emotions they would feel, even if their attributions were statistically held constant. Their actions were *not* correlated with their attributions if emotion was statistically held constant.

From this, Weiner concludes that what affected the subjects' (hypothetical) actions were not the attributions themselves, but the emotions resulting from these. In other words, it was not what they thought about the situation, but what they felt after thinking it, that shaped their decisions as to what to do about it.

Appraising the Situation: Lazarus' Theory

Richard Lazarus has constructed a theory of emotion that combines many of these themes, and enlarges upon them.[44] As he sees it, emotion results from a kind of labeling, or cognitive *appraisal,* of the whole situation. This may (but need not) include labeling our symptoms (Schachter) or assigning causes to events (Weiner), but in any case it includes more than that.

When something happens, we ask ourselves what kind of event it is, and what implications it has for our well-being. Does it mean that something nice is likely to happen, or something awful? Is it likely that we will be helped, or hindered, in the fulfillment of our goals? Our answers to these questions make up our appraisal of the situation.

Note that for Lazarus, an emotion is a response to an event (as for Weiner and Schachter). Something has to happen, to trigger the appraisal process. And the emotion is accompanied by a tendency to act in response to the situation, for Lazarus as for McDougall and other early instinct theorists—and Freud. Finally, we distinguish those "happenings" that help us from those that hinder us. Thus Lazarus speaks of *goal-congruent* and *goal-incongruent* emotions.

The prototype of a goal-congruent emotion is *happiness,* an emotion whose variants range from *joy* (an acute reaction to a specific event) to the "mild and unarousing" state of *contentment*. It results, of course, from a positive appraisal of our future prospects. It produces in turn a tendency toward expansive and out- going behavior: "We usually want to share the positive outcomes and approach others."[45]

44. Lazarus, 1991.
45. Ibid., p. 269.

A clear example of a goal-incongruent emotion is *anger*. It is accompanied by a tendency to attack (which may of course be inhibited). It occurs when someone is accountable for a harmful action—where "harm" means specifically a threat, insult, or assault on our self-esteem, and "accountable" means that the "someone" controlled the action and could have refrained from it (compare Weiner). If the "someone" is another person, the anger is directed outward; if ourselves, then the anger is directed inward upon ourselves.

At first glance, this looks like an overly restrictive conception of anger. We are angered when we see someone hurting a child, for example; there is no threat to our self-esteem. But perhaps there is, Lazarus replies; an assault on a child is an assault on certain cherished values of fairness and kindness to which we feel committed, so that we are threatened when we see them violated.[46]

Well then, what about anger at an inanimate object? We kick a stone on which we have tripped—do we hold the stone accountable? No, says Lazarus; but we may unconsciously let the stone represent a person whom we do hold accountable, or at whom we are angry for other reasons.—At about this point, however, this author at least begins to see red flags rising. If we are allowed to appeal to unconscious (and unverified) symbolic processes to bring the facts (like stone-kicking) into line with the theory, then this theory, like Freud's (pp. 219–22), risks becoming so flexible as to be untestable.

But then, in fairness, perhaps Lazarus' theory is not intended to be tested all in one fell swoop.★ Rather, it may be intended to help us organize our thinking and put pieces together. Is it useful for that purpose? Let us see.

A Look Backward: Labeling, Attribution, and Appraisal

As a way of putting together these ideas, consider an example that touches on all of them. Suppose we wake up one morning with those unmistakable aches and pains that lead us to say, "Oh, boy. I'm coming down with the flu." What emotion(s) are we likely to feel?

We label the aches and pains as disease symptoms (a la Schachter). We realize that we will be uncomfortable and slowed down and robbed of energy, so all our goals will be a little harder to attain for the next few days; and we are displeased about this (a la Lazarus). Why is it happening? Because we contain some flu germs, that's why. This is a temporary and external cause, and it's uncontrollable in the sense that we did not decide to get sick, nor did the germs decide to make us sick. They are just doing what germs do. So we don't get angry at them—at least my informal survey suggests that we do not—a la Weiner.

The emotion that results from all this is hard to classify. It is a kind of resigned melancholy, with perhaps a dash of resentment at the implacable universe that permits germs to exist.

---

46. Ibid., p. 220.
★Bits and pieces of it can be tested individually; see Lazarus, 1991, for review.

Now, let us change things. Suppose we live in a society that does not know about germs, but considers illness to result from a spell cast by a sorcerer. Our symptoms may be the same as before, but how different the emotion will be! We label the symptoms (a la Schachter) as an injury done to us. And done to us *by someone;* we see the cause as external and under the control of the sorcerer, who could instead have chosen to let us alone. We will probably be angry at the sorcerer (a la Weiner). But is our condition temporary or not, and what does it portend for us? These depend on how we appraise the sorcerer's intentions (a la Lazarus). If we believe that our symptoms are but the first stage of a life-threatening magical assault, then real terror may quite overshadow our anger.

Culture: The Label Shop

We have seen how the emotions we feel are influenced by the labels we attach to the feelings or the situation or both. To a large extent, *the labels themselves are provided by the culture we live in.*

THE AVAILABLE SCHEMAS   We saw an example earlier, when we discussed waking up with the flu. Our society makes the germ schema, and the flu label, readily available to its members. Applying that label, we conclude that *we* contain flu germs—and we feel miserable and frustrated (Fig. 12-12).

A culture that lacks the germ schema may instead make the magic-spell schema available. Applying that schema, we may go on to the schema-driven inference that we are bewitched and in deadly danger—and feel terrified. Our society's store does not stock the sorcery T-shirt, and so that label and that emotion are unlikely to occur.

FEELING RULES   Our labels for symptoms and situations—our scripts and schemas—often contain explicit rules for what to feel about them. These too are taught to us by the culture we live in.

We saw examples of this earlier, when we talked about cultural differences in anger and aggression. In some societies, for a man even to speak to another man's wife could be extremely dangerous. The husband could interpret it as a deadly insult, feel enraged, and take violent action. In our society, there would be much less danger. And this is not because the husband in our society refrains from expressing his anger, as with Ekman's *display rules* (see p. 462). He doesn't feel any anger. The point is: In very many situations, we feel what our culture teaches us we ought to feel. These are the **feeling rules.**[47]

Some feeling rules are mandatory. In some societies, if another man spoke to his wife, the husband would be *obligated* to be furious. A bride on her wedding day is obligated to feel happy in this society. It is as if some schematic T-shirts were like uniforms; if we dress symptoms or situations in one of those, we accept certain expectations and obligations about what we ought to feel, when.

47. Hochschild, 1979.

Figure 12-12 Our culture provides the labels for our own symptoms and actions, determining what explanations will be cognitively available and likely to occur to us.

AGAIN THE PROBLEM OF INTERNALIZATION   How does all this work? In some cases, we may do explicit cognitive work to make our feelings conform to the feeling rules. If we felt jolly at a funeral, we might try deliberately to feel sad as well as to act sad. A bride who feels miserable on her wedding day might work hard—and perhaps successfully—to convince herself that she is in fact happy.

But in the earlier example, the outraged husband does not have to try to feel rage. He just feels it. We meet the problem of *internalization* (pp. 533–34): In some way that we do not understand, we make society's rules our own. As a result, we not only do what we are expected to do, but also feel what we are expected to feel. How that happens, we simply do not know.

STRESS AND COPING

Any threat to the smooth progress of an organism's life can be considered a *stressor*. And the emergency reaction to such a threat, especially if it is prolonged, we call *stress*.

Why do we take up this topic under emotion? For two reasons. First, stress does typically have emotional components or correlates; and typically these are negative, so we try to make them go away. Second, the concepts we've introduced in this chapter are directly applicable to the topic of stress and coping.

Stress

The physiologist Hans Seyle, who did much to pioneer the study of stress, found that a variety of physiological stressors—cold, heat, injury, food deprivation—all had effects in common.[48] Later, other stressors were added to the list. These included psychological stressors, ranging from threat of electric shock to loss of a loved one. Any or all of these can trigger a stress reaction.

In this, the notion of stress resembles the *arousal* concept (Chap. 6): A variety of stimuli, quite different from each other, can all call forth a single constellation of reactions. Indeed, the stress constellation has much in common with the "emergency mode" of physiological functioning that we discussed earlier in connection with the sympathetic nervous system. (pp. 225–26). It would not be far off the mark to think of stress as a prolonged emergency mode.

The body reacts to emergencies in a number of ways, two of which are most important for our purposes. One we are familiar with from Chapter 6: the activity of the sympathetic nervous system and, accompanying this, the outpouring of epinephrine (adrenalin) from the medulla of the adrenal gland. These have the effect of increasing heart rate (among many other things), and that's good news in the short run, for it increases the supply of fuel to muscles that may have to act vigorously. But it also increases the work load on the heart, and that, if prolonged, could be not such good news.

The other reaction is the outpouring of hormones, called *glucocorticoids*, from the outer covering, or *cortex*, of the adrenal gland. These too increase the availability of fuel to the muscles (good news). But they also suppress the body's *immune system*, by which it fights off diseases (bad news). And there is a variety of evidence that the risk of illness—from common colds on up—does increase with the stressfulness of one's life (Fig. 12-13).

Coping with Stress

Prolonged and severe stress, as we see, is not only unpleasant but actually dangerous to health. It is not surprising that for both emotional reasons (we don't like it) and cognitive ones (we know it's bad for us), we try to lessen the impact of stress—in other words, to *cope* with stress.

How do we do this? In what ways can we cope? To get a picture of what our options are, let's consider that stress, as any emotional reaction, typically begins with a situation or event. We have learned, however, that often it is the

48. Selye, 1956.

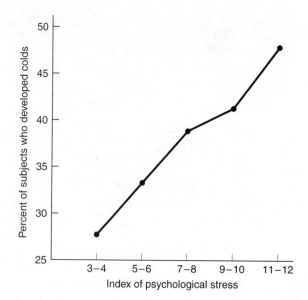

Figure 12-13 Percent of subjects with colds as a function of an index of psychological stress. (Adapted from Cohen et al., 1991.)

situation as interpreted by the actor that is the immediate cause of the emotion. The same, of course, can be true of stress.

Thus we have a multistage causal chain from situation, through interpretation, to symptoms of emotion or stress. Figure 12-14 shows this multistage process, and it shows how the stages set our coping options. To "cope with" stress means to reduce it or make it go away. So we greet our old friend, the negative-feedback loop! But there are three possible negative-feedback loops—long, medium, and short. We could cope by changing the situation itself (problem-solving), by changing our interpretation of the situation (cognitive restructuring), or by dealing directly with the symptoms (Richard Lazarus calls this "palliation").

Let us look more closely.

PROBLEM-SOLVING   Dealing with stress by removing its causes needs no prolonged discussion here. Our earlier discussion of *escape* is relevant, for what we are talking about is in fact escape behavior (compare pp. 248–49): taking action that has as its goal, or is reinforced by, getting rid of an unpleasant state

Figure 12-14   Three possible ways of coping with stress.

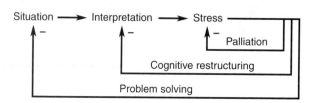

of affairs. This way of coping, then, probably follows the same principles as any other goal-directed action on the environment.

COGNITIVE RESTRUCTURING   If stress results from a situation *as interpreted,* then another way to alleviate the stress is to change the interpretation! That is what is called "cognitive restructuring."

Perhaps the purest form of cognitive restructuring is the psychotherapeutic technique known as *rational-emotive therapy,* developed by Albert Ellis.[49] Ellis believes that many of our problems in living stem from things we say to ourselves, that are irrational in the strict technical sense: They are illogical. The premise simply doesn't entail the conclusion. Examples:

I *must* succeed at such and such or I'm totally worthless. (Ellis calls such thoughts "musturbations.")

I've been rejected by so-and-so; therefore I'm unlovable.

I've violated my diet; therefore, it has failed and I might as well give it up. (Compare pp. 101–5.)

Rational-emotive therapy confronts the illogic of these beliefs, by challenging the client to prove, logically, that the conclusion follows from the premise. Of course the client can't, because it doesn't. The intended result is a change in these self-defeating beliefs—that is, a *restructuring* of one's *cognitions.*

All this doesn't mean that a change in appraisal will necessarily be for the better. *Denial* could be considered an instance of cognitive restructuring; but if its effect is to leave a danger unheeded, it is a shortsighted way to reduce stress. Lazarus notes, for example, that some heart-attack patients will embark on a vigorous exercise program, running long distances and doing pushups, to "prove" that their hearts are not damaged. But if they *are* damaged, that coping strategy could be a terminal one.

PALLIATION   Finally, we can cope with stress symptoms (including their emotional component) directly, by taking steps to suppress them. Means of doing so would include alcohol and other drugs, meditation, biofeedback and related relaxation techniques, or a Charlie Chaplin movie.

At first glance, palliation sounds like a shortsighted and superficial coping strategy, dealing as it does with symptoms rather than causes. Indeed, it may be. To drown our problems in alcohol, rather than trying to do something about them, will be an effective coping strategy only over the shortest of terms.

At other times, however, it may be the only sensible thing to do. An example: Suppose we must undergo surgery. The surgery is in fact necessary, and we know, correctly, that it is; so neither problem-solving nor cognitive restructuring avoids that necessity. So we are offered anesthesia to *palliate* the pain it would otherwise cause. Of course we accept! It would be foolish to reject the offer on the grounds that it addresses "only" the symptoms, not the cause.

49. Ellis, 1990.

Before moving on, we should emphasize once again that this framework *is* a drastic oversimplification, on several counts. First, it begs some questions. Should we distinguish between stress and the emotional reaction, or do they amount to the same thing? Not only the situation but also the symptoms may be appraised or labeled, as in Schachter's theory (pp. 468–69). So cognitive restructuring could be applied at that stage too, and with benefit ("It isn't a breakdown, it's caffeine poisoning!"). And suppressing the symptoms may sometimes allow us to think more clearly about the situation; so is that palliation or cognitive restructuring or what?

Second, we have been assuming that coping is brought to bear only after the stress is encountered. But these devices may be used proactively rather than reactively, to head off stress before it is upon us. An extensive literature is developing on "stress inoculation" and related techniques.[50]

Finally, no law says that a coping device may not operate in more than one of these ways. Sometimes one might, for example, restructure and palliate at the same time. An example is this story, told by a government official in Thailand:

> It seems that two experienced hikers, a Thai man and an American man, were hiking in the woods and got lost. The longer they searched for a way out, the darker and deeper the woods seemed to get. In the midst of the search, the Thai man broke into a grin, then began to laugh out loud, at the silly predicament these two seasoned hikers had gotten themselves into. The American turned to him and said, "Why are you laughing? Don't you see how lost we are?" The Thai hiker replied, "Oh—If I stop laughing will we find our way out?"[51]

Of course both men were *problem-solving,* or trying to. But the Thai hiker was also *restructuring* his appraisal of their dilemma, making it a joke rather than a grim predicament—*and* palliating his distress with laughter, all at the same time.

And which hiker do you think was the less stressed by the situation? I think so too.

THE STRATEGIC USE OF EMOTIONS

Most of us would not want to be Vulcans like Mr. Spock, reacting with cold unfeeling logic to life's viscissitudes. Imagine what life would be like if we had no emotions—no joy at a sunrise or at a baby's gurgle, no feeling of tingling anticipation before a wedding. We would certainly consider it a juiceless, joyless kind of existence.

50. For review see Fiske and Taylor, 1990.
51. Weisz, 1990, p. 140.

True enough; but there is more to the story than that. Emotions may benefit us in many ways besides the spice they add to our lives. Let us see why.

Payoffs from Passions

You might check out how your friends respond to the following scenario. This one brings the psychology of emotions into the domain of *decision theory*.

THE BENIGN EXPERIMENTER REVISITED   Suppose you and I are once again in the presence of the benign experimenter, who says to us, "Let's play the following game." He hands me $10, and he says to me: "Your task is to offer a division of this $10 between yourself and your partner [that's you]. You can make only one offer, and your partner must accept it or reject it. If your partner accepts, then you divide the money as you have suggested. If your partner rejects the offer, then neither of you gets any money at all. [To me:] Go ahead; make your offer!"

What should I do?

If you and I are both out to maximize monetary payoff, and we both know it, then it is quite obvious what I should do. I should offer to give you a penny, and keep $9.99 for myself.

Why? Because I know that you, as a rational person, will accept my offer if it gives you any money at all. That's because if you refuse the offer you get nothing. Well, a penny is clearly better than nothing. And of all the offers that give you something, a penny for you leaves the maximum possible payoff for me.

Case closed, no? No.

What that argument leaves out, Gentle Reader, is your "irrational" capacity for anger! You would very likely react with outrage if I made such a selfish offer—and we'd both end up with nothing. And I know that. So I must somehow estimate what offer I could make to you that would avoid triggering your anger. It might even occur to me to offer a fifty-fifty split. You would surely accept such an equitable division as that, and so I would guarantee a $5 payoff for myself. Thus I try to be rational about your irrationality!—or, better, your emotionality.

At first glance, these considerations seem to pose yet another serious difficulty for decision theory itself. Certainly my thought processes—trying to predict your emotional reactions—are a far cry from the cold economic analysis that should lead me to offer you a penny. That analysis does not describe my cognitive operations, so it fails as a cognitive theory. Nor does economic analysis predict the offer I will actually make; it fails as a descriptive theory. And it fares no better as a normative theory. If I know that you would explode with anger at my offer of a penny, then I will make a more generous offer and you will have more money for yourself. But then how can we say that a coldly rational willingness to accept a penny, as better than nothing, is the *optimal* stance for you to adopt? We can't.

In fact, however, we can continue to think of the matter in decision-theoretic terms after all. Consider that your outrage at my selfishness would add a high *cost* to the option of accepting my penny. The thought of my walking away with $9.99 in my pocket and a satisfied smile on my face might be so unpleasant for you to imagine, that you would gladly accept some monetary loss to keep it from happening. In that sense, your refusal would be rational and normatively correct. That still means, though, that in our decision-theoretic analysis we cannot consider only money gained and lost. We must also consider the positive and negative values that our *emotional* reactions place on the various outcomes.

PASSIONS WITHIN REASON Economist Robert Frank has written a book about the "strategic use of emotions," one that elaborates ideas like these.[52] It can be a very good thing, he argues, that we do react emotionally rather than, as it were, economically, and that we let our fellows know that we will do so.

Suppose you steal a briefcase worth $100 from me. Suppose further that if I have you arrested and take you to court, it will cost me $200 in time lost from work in order to testify against you—and I know that, and you know I know it. Then you might figure that since a prosecution would cost me more than the briefcase is worth, my rational decision would be to let the theft go unpunished even if I detected it—a strong incentive for you to go ahead with the theft.

But not so fast! If I am outraged by your action, I might well go ahead and prosecute even if it costs me money. The "cost" of seeing you get away with such dastardly behavior could be a greater cost to me than the $200 I'll lose. If I am inclined to such "irrational" indignation, and if you know that, then you will decide (let's hope) that the theft would not be a good idea—and I keep my briefcase *and* lose no time from work. Thus, because of my "irrational" capacity for anger I come out ahead.

Thus our emotional reactions may not be rational in the economic sense, but they can nonetheless have an effect that benefits us. In short, we face a wild paradox: it can be *rational to be irrational!* That's enough to make our heads spin. It is the stuff of which cartoons are made (Fig. 12-15). And yet it does make sense. We'll bet that our conspicuously "irrational" cartoon character sells a lot of pencils!

Then there is the darker side of that analysis. The cartoon in Figure 12-16 is not at all funny, and is not intended to be. It depicts a grim scenario that may be acted out repeatedly on our cities' streets (compare pp. 152–53). If young men will "irrationally" risk their lives in an exchange of bullets rather than be treated with disrespect—and if they let others know that—then, in fact, they may be less likely to encounter disrespect. Again, "irrationality" can work. It can also fail, with tragic loss of life as a result.

52. Frank, 1988.

Figure 12-15 The Extortionist (Drawing by Modell, *New Yorker,* © 1971.)

Or consider a case in which a United States President made explicit use of such logical illogic. During the war in Vietnam, Richard Nixon tried it in an attempt to make the North Vietnamese capitulate. "I call it the Madman The-

Figure 12-16 (*Washington Post,* August 2, 1993.)

ory," he said to a subordinate. "I want the North Vietnamese to believe I've reached the point where I might do *anything* to stop the war. We'll just slip the word to them that, 'for God's sake, you know Nixon is obsessed about Communists. We can't restrain him when he's angry—and he has his hand on the nuclear button'—[the North Vietnamese] will be in Paris in two days begging for peace." In this case, the strategic emotional display failed of its purpose. The North Vietnamese were not intimidated.[53]

Looks Backward and Forward

To blame the savings-and-loan boys for being greedy is like blaming cats for having claws.
—SYNDICATED COLUMNIST
JAMES KILPATRICK

We are outraged, we have said, at selfishness or injustice. And when we describe such a feeling as *irrational,* we do not mean that it is foolish. It may be, as in the pencil-seller case. But more often, it is just one more line of evidence that we do not, in fact, behave like economic calculating machines, maximizing dollars-and-cents payoffs to ourselves.

Nor is it at all clear that we should (pp. 397–99). Imagine a person contemplating a theft. Suppose he realizes that if he is caught, he will face (a) a prison term *and* (b) the lasting contempt of his fellows. That (b) factor, which rests on just the sort of outrage we're discussing, could be a strong added deterrent to this and other kinds of destructive behavior. We'll touch on this again when we discuss attitudes, values, and the problem of crime in the next chapter.

If we discount such emotions, on the grounds that they are "irrational" or "naive" or "like blaming cats for having claws," we could lose a powerful force for honesty and civility.[54]

EMOTION AND SELF-AWARENESS

We have looked at the processes of inference and attribution that, we said, permit us to decide how we feel. Thinking about these data and theories, we experience a certain bewilderment. Don't we *know* how we feel? Can't we look inside ourselves and *see* what our emotions are and what produced them?

One writer who answered "no" was Sigmund Freud. We cannot, he said, see what is going on in our unconscious minds. Some of it simply is not available to consciousness and never was. Worse still, we may expend a great deal of effort to *keep* some items from entering consciousness—the mechanism of *repression*. We can look inside ourselves, but we cannot trust what we see; we see only a bit of it, and what we do see may disguise what is really going on.[55]

53. Zuckerman, 1984, p. 191.
54. For discussion of these and related issues see Schwartz, 1986, 1993.
55. Freud, 1949.

More recently, and for entirely different reasons, some cognitive writers have reached the same answer. Much of what happens in our own minds cannot be observed directly. As a result, we literally may not know how we feel, or why we feel that way. This is not because the knowledge is pushed out of consciousness, as Freud argued. It simply *is not* conscious, and never was.

There really is nothing surprising or revolutionary about this idea. After all, we know that we have information-processing mechanisms that cannot be watched while they work. When we look at a page, we are not aware of the activity of cells in our optic nerve. We are aware of the *result* of that activity—seeing the page—but not of the activity itself. At the other extreme of complexity, we have it from Mozart himself that he simply did not *know* how his melodies and themes came into his mind. He generated them somehow, but he was unable to watch the process in operation.[56]

Telling More Than We Can Know

Richard Nisbett and Timothy Wilson have suggested that the same invisibility extends to higher-level cognitive and emotion-generating operations as well. We cannot always see them at work; and often when we think we can, we are "telling more than we can know."[57]

In support of this conclusion, they report a series of experiments in which subjects were asked to give reasons for their actions or feelings, and in which the answers given were simply and demonstrably wrong. Here are just two examples.

SEEING WHAT ISN'T THERE   What determines our emotional state, or *mood,* over a day? What sorts of things affect it?

There is a widespread belief that *amount of sleep* the night before has a great deal to do with it. Lots of sleep, good mood; not enough sleep, bad mood. To see whether this is so, a sample of college students kept a diary over a period of several weeks, recording amount of sleep, mood of the day, and a number of other things. From the data, it was clear that the mood of the day was virtually unrelated to amount of sleep obtained the night before.

But *the subjects insisted that the two had been related.* After completing the diary, subjects were asked to judge how important each of several factors had been in determining a day's mood, over the time they had kept their diaries. Overwhelmingly, they rated sleep as an important determinant of mood—even though their own data, which they themselves had recorded, showed no such relationship. The subjects "saw" the relationship that was *supposed* to be there,

56. Dennett, 1978.
57. Nisbett and Wilson, 1977.

in the very data that showed it was not there. (Compare the *illusory correlation,* p. 421.)

MISSING WHAT IS THERE   It seems, then, that we can "see" effects on our moods that simply are not there if we believe that they *should* be there. Conversely, we may fail to see an influence that *is* present if we believe that it shouldn't be.

In one study, passersby in a shopping mall were invited to examine an array of consumer goods (for example, a rack of nightgowns) and rate their quality—how good each one was, and how much the subject liked each one.

Now we have some knowledge about how one rates the quality of clothes. We have a clothes-judging schema: One considers the fabric, the stitching, and so on. Does one consider the *position of the garment on the rack?* Of course not! And when the subjects in the study were asked if position on the rack had affected their ratings, they reacted with concern about the experimenters' sanity.

But it had. There it was in the data: a clear tendency for the nightgowns on the right to be preferred to the ones on the left.★ Position affected preference, but our theory of clothes-judging says it shouldn't, and the judges vigorously denied that it had.

Introspection versus Inference

Clearly, there are times when (1) we do not know what has affected our moods or preferences, but (2) we think we do know. Why? Nisbett and Wilson answer: If we do not see these influences directly, then we can only *infer* what they must have been. And sometimes these inferences are wrong.

More specifically: When we explain an action or a feeling, we are not really seeing inside ourselves and reporting what is going on there. We are reporting a *theory* about what the cause was. We make a quick trip to the schema store. We select an explanation that is prominently displayed—that is, one that our culture makes readily available. That will be the explanation we will offer to anyone who asks—an onlooker, an experimenter, *or ourselves.* The actor will explain her own behavior to herself, using the explanations the culture makes available.

This doesn't mean that the explanation will necessarily be wrong. But if it is right, it's often because the actor's theory is right, not because she see the causes of her behavior directly.

It need hardly be said that this analysis is controversial.★★ But the evidence is clear that subjects *can* be unaware of the causes of what they do, even when they think they are aware. The controversy is about whether this is the excep-

---

★Actual positions of the different nightgowns, of course, were counterbalanced among different subjects.
★★For discussion see Nisbett and Ross, 1980; Fiske and Taylor, 1990.

tion or the rule, and about just when we can, and when we cannot, observe the causes of our actions directly.

A Look Backward: Labeling, Attribution, and Schemas

As we see, Nisbett and Wilson's theory is a self-labeling theory somewhat like Schachter's. We look for explanations of our feelings, because we do not see their causes directly. Having performed an action, we ask, "Why did I do that?" Because we do not see the causes of action directly either, we infer from the action and the situation what the cause must have been.

In a later paper, Timothy Wilson extended the argument in a way that relates it to other familiar ideas.[58] He begins by distinguishing two systems. One is a system of cognitive and motivational processes that directs overt behavior. This system is partly, perhaps largely, unconscious.

The other is a conscious *verbal explanatory system,* which seeks and reports explanations for actions. It attempts to identify feelings and motives, or the reasons for them. But it does it by going to the schema store, in search of an explanatory T-shirt that fits the action or the feeling. The verbal explanatory system does not, and we do not, directly observe the actual causes of our emotions and actions. These are not available to consciousness; and so, in Wilson's phrase, we are "strangers to ourselves."

Wilson's two-systems approach does not just offer a new look at the problem of self-awareness. It also provides some bridges between the cognitive theory of emotions and other points of view that at first look quite different.

First, compare Wilson's ideas with the behaviorist approach. Back in Chapter 1, we saw that to a behaviorist, asking the reasons for an action only confronts us with a new bit of behavior—verbal behavior—to explain. We have to ask why the actor did what he did, and we have to ask why he said what he said about it. Wilson's analysis, starting from a cognitive rather than a behavioral perspective, has ended at a strikingly similar place. Action is produced by one system. The explanation we give for the action is produced by a different one.

Wilson's view is not identical with behaviorism. A behaviorist would have little interest in the cognitive mechanisms we have been discussing—schemas, self-attribution, and the like. He would deny the importance of these internal operations, insisting that the causes of action are in the environment. Cognitivists such as Wilson believe that mental operations do play an important role in the causation of behavior. But they include things the actor cannot talk about—things that are not accessible to his introspections.

Does this mean that they are *unconscious* in the Freudian sense? Once again there are similarities and differences. Like Freud, Wilson believes that we are unaware of much of what goes on in our minds. Unlike Freud, he does not see the unconscious as a cauldron of urges seeking expression in action. Rather than a source of "hot" instinctual drives and wishes, Wilson's unconscious is a

58. Wilson, 1985.

place where "cold" information-processing goes on. It is a machine shop, not a steam kettle.

All told, Wilson's analysis presents an intriguing model of the differences among approaches to motivation, emotion, and cognition. It also urges a healthy skepticism about actors' explanations for their actions—even if we are the actors and the actions are our own. We simply do not know ourselves nearly as well as we think we do.

SUMMARY

The relation between motivation and emotion is a close one, but there is disagreement as to just what it is. To some writers, emotions *are* motives; to others, they always accompany motives; to others, they are actions in their own right. Emotions may set the reinforcing properties, or values or utilities, of the outcomes of action. Or they may themselves be goals; we may try to feel this or that emotion. Finally, like motives, they make close contact with cognitive operations.

The James-Lange theory treats emotion not as a cause of action, but as the perception of action that has already occurred—especially the action of internal organs to prepare the body for fight or flight. Walter Cannon criticized the theory, partly on the grounds that internal responses are too slow, and too similar to one another as between one emotion and another, to account for the swiftness and variety of emotional experience. More recent research has questioned these criticisms, especially the latter ones: various emotions may be associated with different patterns of autonomic reaction.

Instead, Cannon saw emotions as produced by the action of systems in the brain, as drive states may be. There may be specialized systems for anger and fear, though the evidence is hard to interpret; and there is evidence that positive and negative emotions are mediated by different parts of the brain.

Arousal may affect emotion, as it affects other actions, in a non-specific way. Arousal produced by one means can "spill over" to enhance the emotion produced by something else.

The expression of emotion may serve a definite purpose. It is to an animal's advantage to communicate its intentions, and to be sensitive to such messages from others. Therefore, expressions of emotions may have evolved as action patterns. In addition, evolutionary selection pressures may have operated to make them conspicuous and easy to read; so we have *ritualized* emotional displays, which have evolved in exaggerated form. Some writers believe that human facial expressions evolved in such a way. Though learning can modify them, at least some facial expressions are apparently untaught; blind-deaf babies show them, and they are recognized from one society to another very different one. However, learning does modify emotional expression; different societies have different *display rules,* telling their members what expressions are appropriate and when.

Besides expressing emotion, the signals may contribute to it. The *facial feedback* hypothesis states that facial expressions appropriate to an emotion may enhance, or suppress, or perhaps even induce, that emotion.

Cognitive processes also contribute to emotion: how we think about an event has much to do with how we feel about it. Some cognitive theories of emotion rest heavily on the notion of a discrepancy from what is expected. The *discrepancy hypothesis* holds that mild surprises are pleasant, intense ones unpleasant. The theory can be extended to make contact with artistic, literary, and musical devices for maintaining pleasure and interest, and with familiarity as a mechanism of cultural change.

These theories emphasize the role of the *situation* in producing emotion, but perhaps what is important is the situation *as interpreted* by the actor. Schachter has argued that emotion results from the labeling of one's actual or perceived state of arousal. Such labels are closely related to the causes to which we attribute our perceived states of arousal. Weiner sees emotion as resulting from a causal analysis, not just of our symptoms, but of the whole situation; and Lazarus adds the idea that we also appraise what the situation implies for our future well- or ill-being. In all such cases, much depends on what labels are made available by the culture we live in. If we wake up sick in Western society, it probably does not occur to us to label our illness as the work of a sorcerer, and feel afraid; but in some societies, it would. And our culture often teaches us what we *ought* to feel in certain situations. We may label our own emotional states—appropriately or not—in accordance with these *feeling rules.*

Stress is usually accompanied by negative emotion, and in light of what we have learned, we can see it as arising from a three-stage process: The situation (1), as we interpret or appraise it (2), gives rise to symptoms of stress, perhaps including emotional ones (3). This gives us three ways of coping with stress (negative feedback). We can change the stressful situation (problem-solving) or our interpretation of it (cognitive restructuring); or we can suppress the symptoms themselves (palliation). Each of these has its place in certain circumstances; then too, coping strategies may use more than one at the same time.

Sometimes a coldly rational approach to problem-solving would not serve us well. We may, consciously or not, make "strategic" use of our emotions, as when our outrage at an offense might make us ready to punish it even if the costs to us are high. Another person, knowing that, might then refrain from the outrageous act. To lose our capacity for outrage and other emotional reactions, on the grounds that they are irrational (or childish or naive), might be to lose an important instrument of social control.

Do we know directly what we feel and why we feel it? Freud said not; often our emotions are repressed, so that we do not allow ourselves to be conscious of them. Some modern cognitive writers give the same answer for different reasons. It is not, they say, that we don't *allow* ourselves to see the sources of our emotions. We just *don't* see them. Rather we infer them, as we infer anything else: by finding a causal schema that fits them. In other words, we describe our feelings and their causes by describing our *theories* about what feelings ought to be in such situations, and about what causes them. This line of work provides a point of convergence—though differences remain—among psychoanalytic, behaviorist, and cognitive approaches to emotion.

CHAPTER 13

Social Motivation

> From the moment of his birth the customs into which [an individual] is born shape his experience and behavior. By the time he can talk, he is the little creature of his culture.
>
> —RUTH BENEDICT

Social influences affect *all* human motives. Sexual and aggressive actions, of course, are directed toward fellow species members; but even feeding and drinking, as we saw, can be as much social actions as homeostatic ones. As we moved to more complex issues, we saw how the culture we live in provides us with the skills to implement plans, imposes display rules for emotional expression and feeling rules for emotional experience, and stocks the schema shops that provide our knowledge and theories. Social influences have never been far from our minds.

In this chapter we will discuss some motivational influences that are specifically social, where the action directly affects and is affected by other people. We will look at the formation and maintenance of social bonds between individuals—first the process of adult-infant attachment, then the bonds of liking and loving among adults. Then we will look at what modern research has to say about an old, old problem: How are we inclined "by nature" to treat our fellow creatures? Are we naturally selfish, out for Number One? Or are we naturally pro-social creatures, inclined to help and nurture each other? This is the problem of *altruism*.

After that, we will consider how motives are related to the *attitudes* and *values* that we learn as members of a society. These, we will see, can guide our actions in many ways and at many levels.

ATTACHMENT

Let us begin with the first and perhaps most important social motive of all. This is the bond that typically forms between an infant and its primary caretaker, usually the mother. We could say that this is the baby's earliest expression of that powerful motive, *love*. Where does that first love come from?

The Conditioned-Reinforcement View

To early behaviorist writers, a child's attachment to a caretaker presented no unique problems. The adult caretaker, from the child's point of view, could be seen simply as a *conditioned reinforcer*.

THE CUPBOARD THEORY   Food is a potent reinforcer for a hungry animal, and surely for a hungry infant as well. Now we know that even in the rat, a stimulus paired with food reinforcement can become a reinforcer in its own right—a conditioned reinforcer. Well, here is an infant who gets hungry quite often. And here is the caretaker, repeatedly paired with food because she provides it. What is more natural than that she should become a reinforcer in her own right—a conditioned reinforcer, like any other stimulus that is paired with food?

Here we have what has been called the **cupboard theory.** The caretaker acquires positive value (or reinforcing power) because she is the cupboard from which need-satisfaction comes. She is associated with the primary reinforcement of hunger-reduction or discomfort-reduction.

Around the 1950s, it began to be clear that the cupboard theory had problems. One line of evidence, in particular, made real difficulties for it.

OF MONKEY MOTHERS   That evidence came from the now classic studies by Harry Harlow, using rhesus monkeys as subjects.[1] These studies are, in fact, an excellent example of how research with animals can turn around our thinking about the human case.

Harlow raised baby monkeys in his laboratory, in a setting designed to test the cupboard theory directly. The original question was: Which do babies really care about—the food a mother provides or the warm, clingable fuzziness—Harlow called it "contact comfort"—that she also provides? The first of these satisfies a physiological need. The second, in an adequately warmed lab, does not.

So Harlow built two foster monkey mothers—the only mothers his baby monkeys had (Fig. 13-1). One was made of bare wire mesh, with a built-in bottle of milk to which a nipple accessible to the baby was attached. She was pure cupboard. The other was covered with fuzzy terry cloth, and warmed by a light bulb suspended inside her—but she had no milk. She was a homeostatic nonentity, offering pure comfort, but no food.

1. Harlow, 1958; Harlow and Zimmerman, 1959.

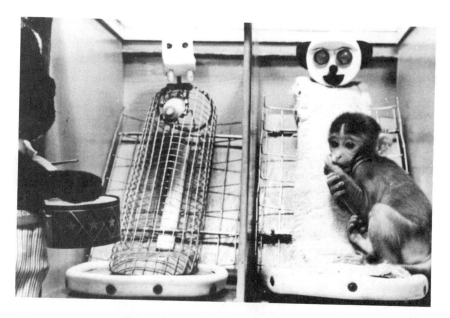

Figure 13-1 The wire mother and the cloth mother. Terrified by a teddy bear, the infant monkey rushes to the cuddly terrycloth mother. From that home base he examines the intruder. (From Harlow, 1976.)

But she offered pure delight to the babies. The little monkeys would cling to the terry-cloth mother, 12 to 18 hours a day. When they got hungry, they would climb down, nurse from the wire mother, and at once leave her again, to go back to the contact comfort of the terry-cloth mother. They cared much more for comfortable mothers than for food-associated ones.

By itself, that might imply only that we must add contact comfort to the list of primary reinforcers. But the two mothers affected their little wards in other ways, where it's hard to see how reinforcement applies at all.

For example, if unfamiliar objects were placed in the cage, the monkey would rush to the terry-cloth mother and cling to her for several minutes. After apparently calming itself this way, the baby would venture forth to explore the novel objects, sometimes running back as if for reassurance (Fig. 13-1). If there was only the wire mother, the baby would be likely to ignore the new objects *and* the mother, huddling terrified in a corner instead. The terry-cloth mother seemed to provide a home base of comfort, security, and reassurance. Given these things, a baby monkey is free to explore his world. Lacking them, he is insecure and frightened.

In short, healthy, active, exploring babies—even monkey babies—need much more than homeostasis. These findings paved the way for a quite different view of infant-parent relationships, in monkeys and in humans as well.

Bowlby's Theory of Attachment

Attachment theory in its present form comes largely from the writings of psychiatrist John Bowlby,[2] but it has been advanced and extended by the work of

2. Bowlby, 1969.

many investigators.[3] It has drawn ideas from psychoanalysis and cognitive theory, but most especially from *ethology* (see pp. 112–13).

First an overview. The baby, in humans as in many other species, is a powerful source of *releasing stimuli* that affect adults. These elicit care-taking responses from adults, ones that provide the baby what he requires.

Both babies and adults are programmed that way by evolution, Bowlby says. They have to be, because human babies are totally dependent on adults for survival. If the baby is to survive infancy, and if the adult is to have descendants, babies must be programmed with instinctive responses that will signal their needs; and adults must be programmed to respond to these signals by meeting those needs.

To speak of "meeting the baby's needs" makes the theory sound a bit like the old cupboard theory, but it is not. Parents are seen as responding to the baby's *signals,* not directly to his needs. And his needs for optimal development go far beyond the physiological requirements for food, warmth, and the like. They include his needs for security and a safe home base, for contact comfort, and for trust in his own ability to influence the world he lives in.

Early interactions between child and caregiver, then, form a back-and-forth chain of stimuli and reactions to them, a dance of signals and acknowledgments. Out of this grows a strong emotional bond between infant and caregiver—and that is **attachment.**

Let us look more closely.

RELEASERS AND RESPONSE   There is good evidence that babies' behavior, and even their anatomy, can affect adults powerfully.[4] In some species of monkey, strangers introduced into a group are likely to be attacked if they are adults, but not if they are infants.[5] If a human baby smiles at an adult, the adult is likely to smile back—and if he does not, the baby may begin to cry. And crying is a very powerful stimulus for adult action; a baby's cry elicits increased blood pressure and expressions of distress even in adults who are not parents.[6] It even upsets other babies![7]

Conversely, adults have powerful effects on babies—and not just by feeding them. A crying baby can be soothed simply by picking her up, jiggling her a bit in the process. When the baby is older, the *sight* of an approaching caretaker can be enough to quiet her, perhaps through conditioning (see below).

We also remember, though, that chains of action and reaction are not all there is. They set the stage for the development of an emotional bond. Just how that bond is formed, we do not know; but many writers have suggested that something like *imprinting* may begin the process.

3. For example Ainsworth et al., 1974, 1978; see also Lamb and Campos, 1982.
4. Bell and Harper, 1977.
5. Southwick, Pal, and Siddiqui, 1972.
6. Frodi et al., 1978.
7. See Hoffman, 1981.

In our earlier discussion of imprinting (Chap. 7), we saw that if a chick or duckling sees any large moving object under the right conditions, it *assigns positive value* to that object. Later the object is approached, and its appearance acts as a positive reinforcer. This is true even if the baby bird is punished for its approach. Well, babies too may persistently approach even punishing parents[8]—another difficulty, by the way, for a cupboard theory of attachment.

Now this matter of *assigning* positive value to things or people has not been much discussed by psychologists. Perhaps it is because we tend to think of learning as forming a *connection* between something and something else. So, in talking about learned values or desires, we think of the *transfer* of value to something from something else. But imprinting is not like that. There is no "something else." An imprinted duckling simply *gives* value to an object that appears under certain conditions.

Perhaps attachment begins that way. Maybe adult figures and, later, *familiar* adult figures are assigned positive value by children of the right age range, much as large moving figures are assigned positive value by ducklings of the right age.

In any case, while it is clearly something learned, early attachment does not sound much like the traditional conceptions of learning that emphasize connections or transfer from something to something else. It does, however, sound a bit like what Freud called *cathexis*. Freud spoke of "investing psychic energy" in a desired object; he may have meant something like what we call here the assignment of value. That still does not tell us how it works, but Freud may have had a finger on something vitally important, and something that research psychologists have neglected.

SIGNS AND STAGES IN ATTACHMENT   The process of attachment, then, may begin with something analogous to imprinting. But it does not stop with that.

Jerome Kagan lists three signs of attachment. First, the infant is more easily calmed down or placated by his caretakers than by other adults. Second, it is the caretakers he approaches for play or for consolation. Third, he is less distressed by unfamiliar events when in the presence of the caretakers.[9] To these three signs, we probably should add a fourth: The infant can be very distressed if the caretaker goes away. This **separation** anxiety appears at around 6 to 9 months of age and lasts until around 2 or 2 1/2 years of age—it follows roughly the same time course even in very different cultures (Fig. 13-2).[10]

In all of this, we are reminded of how Harlow's baby monkeys behaved, when the terry-cloth mother—but not the wire mother—was available. Attachment theorists conclude, as Harlow did, that a comforting attachment

8. See Rajecki et al., 1978.
9. Kagan, 1984.
10. Kagan et al., 1978.

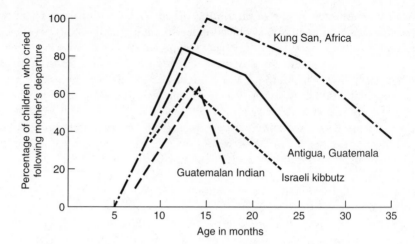

Figure 13-2   The time course of separation anxiety in different societies. In all of them, it peaks at around 15 months of age. (From Kagan et al., 1978.)

figure provides a secure base from which unfamiliar events can be inspected and unfamiliar objects and people explored.

The development of this attachment is a gradual process. It goes along with a progressive *widening* of the infant's social repertoire, coupled with a *narrowing* of the people to whom she directs it.

For example, at first, the baby has only crying to depend on; this has the effect of *bringing an adult near* to attend to the baby's distress. Later, smiling is added to the repertoire; this *keeps the adult near* for further interaction. But at this stage, any adult will do. Then, as the child develops through the sixth or seventh month, some people—familiar ones, such as the caretaker—can soothe the child, or elicit smiles and coos, more readily than others.

Motor and cognitive growth add to the ways a child can interact with adults. Games become important; the baby sticks out her tongue, the adult does the same, and the baby does it again.[11] From games of turnabout like that, many writers believe, the baby is already beginning to learn some important things about the social world: Reciprocity (one takes turns), trust (adults will respond to what one does), and, especially, **effectance**—that one can influence the behavior of other people; one can make things happen. But if adults fail to react to the baby's signals, refuse to keep the games going, and the like, then a baby may learn that he *cannot* make things happen, that he is unable to influence what others do. This, the opposite of effectance, is **learned helplessness,** which, some writers believe, may set in even this early in life (see Chap. 14). In all this, the baby is moving away from stimulus-bound reactions, to the formation of *beliefs* about the consequences of actions.

In the third phase, the child continues to smile at familiar caretakers, but stops smiling at unfamiliar adults. *Fear of strangers* may occur instead. About this time, too, we see *separation anxiety*. And, as the baby begins to crawl, he

11. Kaye and Marcus, 1981.

attempts to establish or re-establish proximity on his own initiative. This is now a goal-seeking *motivational state,* rather than an instinctive reaction to stimuli.

FROM ACTION PATTERNS TO SYSTEMS   Finally, we again meet a familiar principle in a new setting. As the child develops, individual action patterns become organized into *hierarchical systems.* Now, each system controls a *set* of component behaviors, any one of which can serve as a means to a single goal. And the entire system can be evoked or inhibited as a unit. This is our familiar *motivational hierarchy.* We can identify several of these systems:

1. One such system consists of the **attachment behaviors** proper; these actions are directed toward obtaining or maintaining proximity to a caregiver. Approaching, following, and calling are examples.
2. The **fear/wariness system** avoids proximity to unknown and potentially dangerous objects or persons. It calls into play such acts as crying, escape, and cautious immobility (compare Bolles's SSDRs, pp. 255–56) as components.
3. The **affiliative system** does not promote contact with a person or object, but permits social exploration and interchange at a distance. Smiling, and the prolonged gaze with which strangers are inspected once the fear is gone, are components.
4. Finally, when exploration is directed toward the physical environment, we have the **exploratory system.** Manipulation of objects is a prominent component of this system. Inspection of objects is another.

Attachment theorists see these systems as interdependent, each affecting the others *as a unit.* Thus, the appearance of a stranger can trigger both an attempt to avoid interaction with the stranger (fear/wariness) and attempts to achieve closeness to the parent (attachment). At the same time there is abrupt cessation of exploration and all its components, as if that system were inhibited by activation of the others.

Perhaps that is why baby monkeys—and baby people—are unlikely to explore their environments, or to learn much about them, when confronted with a strange situation *in the absence of the attachment figure.*[12] If the attachment figure is available, the attachment system need not be activated, for its goal has been attained. Then the exploratory system is released from inhibition, and the child can go about the business of exploring the world. Maybe that is how the secure-base phenomenon works.

A Look Backward

At every step of this development, we see familiar concepts in yet another context. Bowlby drew heavily on the concepts of *ethology,* for he saw attachment

12. Ainsworth and Wittig, 1969.

behavior as very much a product of evolution. The term refers to any behavior that has the "predictable consequence" of bringing child and attachment figure (e.g., the mother) closer together. This in turn has many benefits, but perhaps the greatest of these, in the evolutionary pre-history of humankind, was protection from predators. A human or proto-human baby is relatively defenseless for a very long time. Parents who came to protect their babies from danger were more likely to have surviving offspring. Babies who could bring their parents close in times of distress were more likely to *be* surviving offspring. Thus evolutionary selection pressures favored babies who sent distress signals, and parents who responded to them by approaching.

Turning from the origins of these functions to their organization into systems, we have the "lattice hierarchy": The same behavior may serve different systems at different times. Thus a child may approach an adult, not because she is attached to that adult, but as an exploratory action.

And we have, as so often, the possibility of interaction among higher-level systems. The "secure home base" phenomenon is an example. When the environment is safe and the mother is nearby, the exploratory system is activated. But if threatened with danger or with the mother's unavailability, the child seeks contact with the mother and stops exploring. This happens even in securely attached children (see later), in whom it is thought to reflect, not a failure of self-reliance, but a condition that favors its development. Conversely, an attempt to push the child into independence by rebuffing it, is likely to lead only to further attempts at attachment *and* unwillingness to explore.

Attachment Styles

There are substantial individual differences, from one child and from one parent to another, in attachment-related behaviors. In a classic series of studies, Mary Ainsworth and her collaborators have described some of these differences and their relations to other variables.

AINSWORTH'S "STRANGE SITUATION"   The Strange Situation is a method of assessing a child's "attachment style" at 12 to 18 months of age. It consists of a 20-minute sequence of events played out in a laboratory playroom. On two occasions, the parent leaves the child. Once she leaves him with a stranger, and once she leaves him first alone, and then briefly with the stranger prior to her return.[13]

In their response to this little skit, some children (roughly two-thirds) show *secure attachment*. They use the mother as a secure base from which to explore. In her absence they tend to reduce exploration and show distress, but they greet her return by smiling, vocalizing, perhaps waving.

Babies classed as *insecure-avoidant* (about 20 percent), in contrast, are little distressed by the mother's departure and tend to ignore or avoid her on her

13. Ainsworth and Wittig, 1969.

return. Ones classed as *insecure-ambivalent* (about 14 percent) stick close to the mother, exploring little or not at all; they are highly distressed when the mother leaves, and tend to stay distressed even when she returns.

CORRELATES OF ATTACHMENT STYLES   These attachment styles seem to be related in consistent ways to certain kinds of family experiences and patterns in relationships. Ainsworth has long held that the quality of maternal care, especially the mother's sensitive responsiveness to the child's signals, has a major effect on attachment security. There is plenty of evidence that attachment security is indeed related to ratings of maternal sensitivity, warmth, and responsiveness. There are reports that the insecure-avoidant pattern is related to intrusive, overstimulating maternal behavior, whereas rejection is related to unresponsive, uninvolved caregiving.[14]

Now nearly all these data are correlational, and so we cannot make causal conclusions. After all, if some mothers are responsive and others not, the two kinds of mothers probably differ in all sorts of other ways too, and any or all of these "other ways" could cause differences in their children's behavior. However, there is at least one study in which caregiving style was actually manipulated experimentally, with mothers in the Netherlands. Here the mothers were randomly assigned to a control group, or to a group in which there was actual intervention to *teach* maternal responsiveness to the child's signals. Not only did this training lead to substantial differences in maternal behavior; it also dramatically increased the proportion of children classified as "secure" in the Strange Situation (Fig. 13-3). These data put us on firmer ground in conclud-

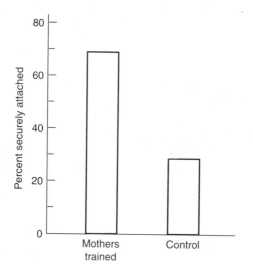

Figure 13-3 Experimental intervention, training mothers in responsiveness, produced about a twofold increase in the proportion of children scored as "securely attached." (Data from Van Den Boom, 1990.)

14. For review see Belsky and Cassidy, 1994.

ing that differences in mothering style can *cause* differences in attachment style.[15]

However—and this is worth emphasizing—it cannot be the only causal factor. For example, different toddlers in a day-care center were found to vary greatly in the security of their attachment to the very same caregiver. Obviously, factors other than the characteristics of the caregiver and his caregiving style must be responsible for these inconsistencies.[16]

Attachment style can also be related, not to what preceded it, but to what follows it. Again the data are correlational, so they do not establish what causes what. But it is a consistent finding that school-age children with secure attachment histories tend to score higher on a variety of measures of peer relationships, e.g., empathy toward peers, popularity with them, and absence of conflict with adults and siblings. Curiously, there is no consistent evidence that they are more sociable with strangers; so whatever is happening may be specific to intimate relationships, and not merely a matter of sociability or social skill.

Working Models

We have seen something about where attachment styles may come from, and where they go. But why? How does it work? How do these continuities come about?

Bowlby's thinking was heavily influenced by ethology, as we have seen. But he also made use of ideas borrowed from cognitive psychology. He thought of children as constructing internal "working models" of their situations—models in their minds, as it were—based on their experiences.

These working models are what we have called *schemas* (pp. 350–62)—schemas that provide general information about oneself, other people, and relationships in general. Thus a securely attached child may schematize others as responsive and trustworthy, himself as deserving, efficacious, and lovable. Conversely, consistent rejection fosters schemas of other people as unavailable and untrustworthy, and of oneself as helpless and, perhaps, undeserving of love and attention. These internal models should in turn affect how the children respond to others, what they expect from them and how they relate to them.

These schemas, of course, are theoretical entities, not something we observe directly. Not everyone is convinced that we need to think of attachment in these terms.[17] Maybe it's just that different children acquire different social skills. And if children's behavior at one developmental stage is related to their behavior at others, perhaps it is something *in the environment* that remains stable over time.

And once more we find ourselves on familiar ground! Here again we see an old controversy in a new context. It is very much like the controversy about the reinforcement process (pp. 313–16): Do developing kids learn actions and

15. Van Den Boom, 1990.
16. Goossens and van IJzendoorn, 1990.
17. See for example Hinde, 1989.

skills—the behaviorist view? Or do they develop schemas, mental models of the world—the cognitivist view? If behavior is stable over time, does this reflect stability of the environment—the behaviorist view—or of the children's mental models—the cognitive view?

It is quite remarkable how the same concerns surface again and again within psychology. And the issue has implications for intervention. Where insecure attachment is problematic, should we train children in appropriate skills, or should we try to modify their concepts and expectations? The controversy is unsettled.[18]

A Look Backward

Child-to-adult attachment was once dismissed as a rather uninteresting special case of conditioned reinforcement (the cupboard theory). Today, it is one of the most active research areas within psychology. The description of different attachment styles developed hand in hand with the invention of methods for assessing them (the Strange Situation). These led in turn to new questions about (1) where these differences come from, (2) what consequences they have, and (3) why—just how it all works. And these issues are yet another meeting ground for ideas from ethology, psychoanalysis, reinforcement theory, and cognitive psychology. The topic is a dramatic case study in how, and how much, our ideas change.

ATTACHMENT IN ADULTHOOD: LIKING AND LOVING

Love is surely the most talked about, sung about, thought about, and worried about of all the emotional/motivational complexes we have addressed in this book. We wonder: How can I tell if I'm in love? Is loving the same as liking, only more so; or is it something different? How do you distinguish love from infatuation—or can you?

Until recently, most research psychologists shied away from the study of love, or dismissed it with a wave of the hand as *conditioned reinforcement*—a cupboard theory of adult attachment.[19] But times are changing. More recently, researchers have made serious attempts to come to grips with this baffling condition. Let us see what is happening.

Love and Attachment

Attachment to adult figures may set the stage for our first loves of all. Again until recently, though, most writers doubted that the concepts of attachment theory would take us far in understanding adult relationships. The response systems involved seemed much too complex and variable.

18. For review see Belsky and Cassidy, 1994.
19. Sidman, 1960.

Some writers, however, are not so sure. There are similarities between attachment relations and adult intimate ones. There is a specific attachment figure or figures; the bond endures over time; one may seek closeness, especially in times of trouble; and there is distress at involuntary separation.[20]

In addition to these parallels, there are reasons to expect a certain continuity between early and later relationships. If, during attachment, one does form schemas, or internal models, about oneself and about other people and relationships with them, we might expect different schemas to develop along different lines that in turn would lead to differences in adult "attachments." In one investigation, Cindy Hazan and Phillip Shaver checked this possibility. Their provocative data support it.[21]

In two studies, questionnaires were published in a newspaper or administered to college students, asking about the most important love relationship each subject had had.[22] The questions included some key ideas in attachment theory, translated into adult terms. Also queried were subjects' attitudes about romantic relationships, and their memories about their parents' relations to each other and to the subjects themselves when they were little.

First, it did prove possible to classify subjects as secure, anxious/ambivalent, or avoidant in their reactions to adult relationships. And these classifications were systematically related to how romantic experiences were described. Secure lovers described their experiences as happy, friendly, and trusting; in addition, their relationships had tended to last longer than for the other two categories. The others reported emotional highs and lows, and jealousy, in their relationships. This also suggests, as the authors note, that "love is a multidimensional phenomenon and that individuals differ in more ways than the intensity of their love experiences"[23] (see later).

Were these differences in turn related to differences in concepts, or schemas, concerning romantic relationships in general? Yes, they were. Secure lovers tended to believe that romantic feelings wax and wane, but sometimes return to their original intensity. Avoidant lovers were more likely to believe that the head-over-heels romantic love depicted in movies and novels is a myth; it doesn't exist in real life. Anxious/ambivalent subjects, in contrast, frequently felt themselves falling in love, but doubted that they would find what they would call "true love."

Were these differences related to early attachment history? Of all the variables that were measured, the best predictor of adult attachment style was the memories of relationships with parents; secure subjects reported warmer relationships with both parents, and of the parents with each other.

Now all these data are correlational only, so the question of what causes what is, *as always* with such data, up for grabs. For instance, it could simply be

20. Belsky and Cassidy, 1994.
21. Hazan and Shaver, 1987.
22. The researchers decided to ask only about one relationship, to keep the questionnaire from getting too long; so it might as well be the most important one.
23. Ibid., p. 515.

that the more "upbeat" people remember more positive things about their romances *and* about their relations with their parents, whereas more "downbeat" people remember more negative things about both. Many of the data we've described could result from that alone.

So the most we should say is that the data are *compatible with* the suggested line of causation: Early attachment experience affects the development of schemas, or attitudes about relationships, that carry over into adult romantic encounters. The statistical relations were not particularly strong, but that is not surprising. Obviously, a loving relationship in adulthood is not *just like* attachment in infancy; if nothing else, the adult case is much more a two-way street, involving reciprocal effects of each partner's attachment style on the other.

This means that no one is *condemned,* by having had this or that kind of experience with parents, to avoidant or anxious/ambivalent relations later on. The point is a theoretical one: Our developing schemas, or internal models, may be encouraged to develop in one direction or a different one, depending on one's relationship with attachment figures early on. Thus the lasting effects of early social experience might be one, among many, influences later in life.

It is instructive to compare this account with the Freudian one.[24] In Freudian theory, adult relationships are likely to be re-enactments of relations with parents—especially if there is the "unfinished business" of unresolved Oedipal conflicts (pp. 215–17). The adult concerned (the spouse or lover) symbolizes the parent—in a sense he or she *is* the parent in the actor's unconscious mind. Thus the effects of relations with parents are likely to be decisive in later life. The view we're considering now is much softer. It sees the *cognitions* formed early in life—the attitudes and schemas that tell us what people are all about—as influenced by relations with parents, yes. But then these mental models develop as any other cognitions do, and they are very much subject to elaboration, and perhaps correction, as one grows and learns.

Liking and Loving

Okay, but the term "attachment" is still pretty general. What about liking and loving? Are they the same, or is loving liking only more so, or what?

Ellen Berscheid and Elaine Walster have offered an intriguing suggestion about this: *Liking* is determined by the rewards one receives from the partner now. *Loving* involves fantasies—the rewards one *imagines* receiving, or recollections of joys experienced in the past.[25] If this is so, we could line up liking and loving with Chapters 8 and 9, respectively, of this book! Liking is supported by actual experiences; loving, by imagined ones, both past and future.

Related to this is a way of separating the two states that many writers have endorsed: the "separation test." "If a typical friend whom one likes goes away . . . one may miss the friend, but one does not tend to dwell on the loss. One can

24. Freud, 1949.
25. Berscheid and Walster, 1978.

pick up a friendship some years later . . . without even having thought much about the friendship during the intervening years. When a close relationship goes beyond liking, however, one . . . actively misses the other person and tends to dwell on or be preoccupied with that person's absence . . . [Then] it is best to classify the relationship as going beyond liking . . ."[26]

In other words, two familiar and contradictory folk precepts could both be right—depending. If separation means "out of sight, out of mind," we should probably call our emotion liking only. But if "absence makes the heart grow fonder," then it sounds like something more. A word of caution, however: Especially if the relationship is a secret one, beware the "synthetic obsession" (p. 349)![27]

A Triangular Theory of Love

Beyond this, there is a very extensive literature on love—of course!—and we cannot try to survey it here. Instead, let us look at just one attempt to put our thoughts in order, a theory that allows us to fit some familiar ideas into this new context. Robert Sternberg and his co-workers have advanced a three-factor, or "triangular," theory of love.[28]

As Sternberg sees it, how we experience love (or, perhaps better, what we mean by the word) reflects a combination of three factors:

1. **Passion.** This is the component that leads to romance, sexual attraction, and the like. One is usually quite aware of this component, but one has relatively little control over it; passionate attraction either happens or it doesn't. If it does, it often (not always) begins with the first encounter between the two people concerned.

Clearly, physical attractiveness—the *external* evocation of motivational states—ought to be a major factor here. It is. In one study, students were assessed on a variety of measures—personality characteristics, social skills, and the like—and on physical attractiveness. Then they were randomly matched for blind dates. After the date, the experimenters asked them how much they liked each other, and checked later to see whether the couple dated again. It turned out that the *only* variable that predicted how well the couple liked each other—whether *we* like it or not—was simple physical attractiveness. Personality, social skills, intelligence—nothing else had any appreciable effect.

But there is more to the matter even for this single component. However attracted X may be to Y, X must still *decide* whether to pursue a relationship. So, at least after the first encounter, we should expect the concepts of *decision theory* to apply. And they do.

Consider: X finds Y stunningly attractive. But X himself is not all that attractive, and he knows it. He may think it unlikely that Y will accept his advances. And here we are on familiar ground: The *utility* of a relationship with

26. Sternberg, 1986, p. 124.
27. Wegner, 1992.
28. Sternberg, 1986.

Y would be very high, but the *subjective probability* of establishing such a relationship is very low. So the *subjective expected utility* (utility times subjective probability, pp. 366–68) of pursuing the matter may be very low too, and *X* may not even make the attempt.

More generally: As the potential partner is more attractive, the utility of a relationship rises, but its subjective probability declines (Fig. 13-4). We can show that subjective expected utility will be highest for a potential partner who is about equal to oneself in attractiveness. It follows, then, that dating partners, who in fact have established a relationship, should be of about equal attractiveness (as defined, of course, by the culture in which they have been raised; pp. 120–22). Just this has been repeatedly observed.

What about the time course of the passion component? Passion is, we might say, not an event but a process; and it does have a predictable time course. Sternberg suggests that this is best described—unfortunately—by the *opponent-process* theory of Richard Solomon (pp. 273–81). The giddy, wild, wonderful intoxication of passionate love will generate an internal process that opposes it, and so subtracts from it. And that opponent process grows stronger as it is repeatedly evoked. So the resultant experience (the primary emotion minus the opposing one) gets less and less positive as time goes on.

What then if the relationship breaks up? Now the unopposed opponent process will give rise to intense negative emotion. The person might then rush to reinstate the relationship or, if this is impossible, to find a new one that will, if not restore the original joy, at least mitigate the pain of loss. The whole scenario reminds us of the process of *addiction* (pp. 281–84); and indeed, popular

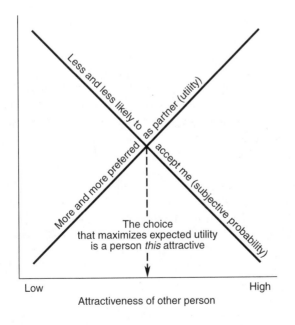

Low — High

Attractiveness of other person

Less and less likely to accept me (subjective probability)

More and more preferred as partner (utility)

The choice that maximizes expected utility is a person *this* attractive

Figure 13-4 Decision analysis of date selection. If the chooser sees himself or herself as unattractive, the descending subjective-probability curve will shift toward the left, so that the maximizing choice will shift toward a less attractive partner.

writers have suggested that love may *be* an addiction for some of us. The idea is less implausible than it might at first appear.

2. **Intimacy.** The intimacy component refers to feelings of closeness, warmth, and "connectedness" in a close relationship. It includes trust, mutual understanding, and reciprocal emotional support. It occurs across a wider array of relationships than the passion component; for example, a parent's love for her children will be very high on this component, very low on the passion component.

As to the time course of the intimacy experience, Sternberg brings to bear a variant of the *discrepancy hypothesis* (pp. 463–66). One experiences emotion when expectations are violated, or (a special case of this) when one's goal-directed actions fail or are interrupted unexpectedly. Now as an intimate relationship progresses, people learn what to expect of each other, and become more skillful at meshing their activities when they cooperate in pursuit of a goal (getting the kids off to school, for example, or perhaps just mutual support and sympathy in late-night conversations between roommates).

After a while, then, when there are few surprises in a relationship, there may be little *experienced* emotion. However, this surface placidity may conceal a barrel of dynamite: actual emotion may be rare, but the potential for emotion very high. If a partner fails to provide the right input at the right time, the sequence is interrupted; and unless it can be picked up again easily, an unpleasant emotional reaction is likely: "*Me* bring the ice? You said *you'd* bring the ice!"

Ellen Berscheid has shown how these ideas might make sense out of some seeming paradoxes.[29] First, even relationships that seem like wars can be stable ones. Many of us know couples who bicker, snipe, seem to make each other miserable—and stay together. Are they masochists? Or is it that the squabbling has become a predictable sequence in its own right, with no surprises to provoke *real* negative emotions?

Second, we can understand why people are so often bewildered when a seemingly emotionless relationship breaks up. Before, there were no surprises; but now, the old, familiar, habitual sequences don't run themselves off any more, because the other person is no longer around to contribute to them. Only then may we become aware of all that we have lost. "A perfectly good relationship may be destroyed for lack of knowledge about the nature of intimate involvement in close relationships." And that knowledge should include the realization that "the worst enemy . . . is stagnation."[30] "Hence it is always necessary to introduce some elements of change and variation—to keep the relationship growing."[31]

3. *Commitment.* The third component is the most purely cognitive one. It results from a *decision* to maintain the relationship. This decision may be made

29. Berscheid, 1982.
30. Sternberg, 1986, p. 126.
31. Ibid., p. 134.

privately to oneself, or announced to the loved one, or announced publicly to society at large as in a wedding ceremony.

So once again, decision theory should shed some light on the matter. And it does; but so do some other cognitive concepts we are now familiar with.

Consider selecting a marriage partner. First, what decisional *strategy* should we employ (pp. 389–91)? A maximizing one? Out of the question. No way are we going to explore *all possible partners* so as to select the very best one. More likely, we will adopt a *satisficing* strategy: Pick the first potential partner who is "good enough," or who exceeds "the lowest level of outcomes a member [of society] will accept in the light of available opportunities."[32]

And then what? We may stick with our commitment come what may. Or we may switch to a *bettering* strategy, staying with one relationship unless and until a better one comes along. Here, however, our judgment of "better" must include costs as well as benefits.

A changeover will have costs in many societies, including our own. First, breaking a relationship in which we have invested much time and effort may produce *cognitive dissonance* (pp. 424–29). And the surrounding culture may exact substantial costs to our reputation and self-esteem. Not so long ago in the United States, divorce was considered a stigmatizing action, so much so that a potential presidential candidate (Nelson Rockefeller) was widely discounted as unelectable because he was divorced. (The culture has changed: More recently, Ronald Reagan's being divorced was seldom even mentioned.)

The prospect of hurting our partner's feelings must be considered, too. Whatever society says, we ourselves may experience guilt as a result of our hurting another's feelings by our own, controllable action (recall Weiner's theory, pp. 471–73).

Faced with the prospect of such conflict, we, or the society in which we live, may take deliberate steps to make a changeover *unavailable* as an alternative. This would include what we might call "practical availability"—what options are in fact open to us. A society might simply forbid divorce, for example, or it might sequester some of its members, as women are confined to the home, or veiled and chaperoned outside it, in some societies. Or we ourselves could make attractive alternatives unavailable, as by breaking off interactions with people who might threaten an established relationship.

But it would also include *cognitive availability*. If an option never occurs to us, we might as well not have it at all. And it may be that in times past, romantic relationships outside of marriage were less likely to *occur* to people than they are today. The greater fragility of modern marriages has been attributed in part to this widening of the "window" of cognitively available options.

A TYPOLOGY OF LOVE   Since there are three components in Sternberg's theory, we can imagine eight possible combinations of presence or absence,

---

32. Thibaut and Kelly, 1959, pp. 21–22.

Table 13–1   Kinds of Love

Kinds of love	Component		
	Intimacy	Passion	Decision/Commitment
Non-love	−	−	−
Liking	+	−	−
Infatuated love	−	+	−
Empty love	−	−	+
Romantic love	+	+	−
Companionate love	+	−	+
Fatuous love	−	+	+
Consummate love	+	+	+

When two people are under the influence of the most violent, most insane, most delusive, and most transient of passions, they are required to swear that they will remain in that excited, abnormal, and exhausting condition continuously until death do them part.

—GEORGE BERNARD SHAW

corresponding to different "kinds" of love, near-love, or semi-love. These are presented in Table 13-1.★

Let's run through these quickly. *Non-love* (nothing there) needs no comment; nor does *consummate love* which has everything. (Perhaps it is this state that "detached" lovers tend to regard as mythical.) *Liking,* as we see, has the intimacy component only: one feels closeness, warmth, and caring, but not passion or long-term commitment. If one or both of the latter is present, Sternberg suggests, the relationship goes beyond liking. *Infatuated love,* supported by passion only, can strike like a thunderbolt ("love at first sight")—and it can dissipate as quickly. *Empty love,* supported by committment only, we think of as characterizing the end stage of a long-term relationship that offers nothing but security and stability to both parties. However, again as with arranged marriages, it *can* be a beginning rather than an end, and develop into a more fulfilling kind of love.

In the remaining kinds of love, two of the three components are there. *Romantic love* is liking plus passion—it is the liking (intimacy) component that moves it beyond infatuation. *Fatuous love* occurs when one makes a long-term commitment based only on the passions of first acquaintance, to someone one hardly knows. It is "the kind of love we sometimes associate with Hollywood, . . . in which a couple meets on Day X, gets engaged two weeks later, and marries the next month."[33] And it is what George Bernard Shaw described, without joy and gladness, in the passage quoted above.

Finally, *companionate love* combines intimacy with commitment. It may be the basis for a rewarding relationship even after the physical attraction (passion) has died down.

★Of course in real life the components would be present to varying degrees, not just present or absent; but Sternberg simplifies for ease of presentation, and so shall I.

33. Sternberg, 1986, p. 124.

A LOOK BACKWARD   Like Lazarus' theory of emotion (pp. 473–74), Sternberg's model of love is perhaps not designed to be "tested" all at once, but to help us put our thoughts in order. So used, it may be helpful.

If nothing else, the theory helps us keep in mind the multiple determinants of human relationships. If we think of love as having an element of attachment, Bowlby's theory implies a biologically based component. Well, there are surely biological determinants of passion (Chap. 4), and perhaps too in the interactions among systems that provide the "secure home base" condition (pp. 492–93)—a form of intimacy?

Yet the theory also provides a framework within which different cultural conceptions of love and marriage may be compared. In societies where marriages are arranged, of course, a commitment (made by others) comes first. If then intimacy and even passion develop between the principals, well and good; but if not, still the commitment is assumed to hold. In our society, the Myth of the Movies, prevalent until (say) around the 1950s, held that passionate love would lead more or less automatically to intimacy, commitment, and happiness ever after.

Today in our own society, the prevailing attitude seems to be that commitment follows a certain level of intimacy as well as of passion; but also that the commitment is conditional. If intimacy and passion fade, one can always correct the "mistake" and separate. But we recall from the theory that passion, and the emotional experience of intimacy, are very likely to fade with the development of opponent process and predictability, respectively.

In the United States today, the odds that a marriage will end in divorce are about even.

A Look Backward and a Note of Caution

Our discussion of love has been very tentative and incomplete—but then, serious research on the topic has only recently begun. What little understanding we have, however, has re-introduced some old friends: stimulus arousal of motivation, reinforcement, and the concepts of decision theory. These basic ideas may come together to clarify even this murkiest of motives.

However, before we leave the topic, a word of caution is appropriate. Our conceptions of liking and loving are, like other schemas, pulled off the rack of our culture's schema shop. Other societies might make very different distinctions and assign very different *roles* and *feeling rules* to the states they identify. An anthropologist writes:

> All societies recognize that there are occasional violent emotional attachments between persons of the opposite sex, but our present American culture is practically the only one which has attempted to capitalize on these and make them the basis for marriage. The hero of the modern American movie is always a romantic lover, just as the hero of an old Arab epic is always an epileptic. A cynic may suspect that in any ordinary population the percentage of individuals with capacity for roman-

tic love of the Hollywood type was about as large as that of persons able to throw genuine epileptic fits.[34]

We must consider the possibility that our analysis of loving and liking is a catalog of the T-shirts in this particular shop. We are looking for the mechanisms that underlie different states that we distinguish from one another *in this society*. That could teach us a great deal about this society's views of loving and liking. Whether it identifies states that are species-wide, however, remains to be seen.

Unrequited Love

Thus far, we have assumed that a friendship or romantic relationship will be reciprocal, and something that both parties want. But what if that is not so? Suppose that there is a would-be lover (WB for short). He seeks a romantic relationship with a person who does *not* return the feeling—a rejector (call her R for short), who does not want that kind of relationship with WB.★ What happens then? Noting that this matter had received surprisingly little study, Roy Baumeister and his colleagues explored it.[35]

WB's options are either (1) to give up the relationship, or (2) to try to win R's heart. The former offers the certainty of disappointment. The latter offers a range of possible outcomes from extreme happiness to humiliation and heartbreak. For R, the possible outcomes are less extreme, but they are *all bad*: annoyance, frustration, and perhaps the unwelcome need to cause someone pain. She may, it is true, be flattered at WB's attentions, but if he is unattractive to her this will count for little.

So WB, in pursuing the matter, is taking a high-stakes gamble. Not so for R; she is put in a no-win situation through WB's pursuit of her. (Notice that a bad outcome, produced by the controllable action of another, is the trigger for anger in Weiner's theory of emotion [pp. 471–73]. So R's annoyance and resentment would make eminent sense from his perspective.)

R's position is difficult for another reason, too: She has very little guidance from cultural "scripts" (pp. 355–57). Novels, plays, movies, and paperback books are filled with advice about how to win one's beloved. But for how to get rid of a non-beloved, there's not much guidance out there.

Still another difference is that in this situation, WB's self-esteem is on the line. If rejected, he will probably feel (and probably rightly) that he simply was not desirable enough for R. R, for her part, will have suffered no blow to self-esteem, but she may well feel guilty for causing pain.

---

34. Cited by Berscheid and Walster, 1978.

★For simplicity, we'll assume in what follows that WB is male and R female. Obviously there are other possibilities; but in fact, Baumeister's results were much the same no matter who played which role.

35. Baumeister, Wotman, and Stillwell, 1993.

(Notice something about that, too. In a commonsense way, we usually think of *guilt* as arising from our breaking some moral dictate. But let's again look backward to Weiner's theory of emotion (pp. 471–73). As Weiner sees it, guilt arises if a bad outcome arises from one's own, controllable action, whether a moral principle is involved or not. That of course fits R's behavior, even though she has violated no moral code in rejecting an unwanted would-be. That she does feel guilt, as Baumeister et al. show, must be counted a point in favor of Weiner's analysis as opposed to our commonsense one.)

To look at what actually happens, Baumeister et al. collected stories from college students about two unrequited romances, one in which the student was the WB, and one in which he or she was R. (That way, one avoids the possibility of personality differences between WBs and Rs; any differences between the stories must be attributable to the WB versus the R role.) Then judges, blind to the main hypotheses, coded the stories on a variety of dimensions.

Sure enough, students describing their experiences as WBs tended to report roller coasters of feelings, from glorious highs to crushing lows. Rs reported more negative emotions associated with the episode, and fewer positive ones, than the WBs did. In line with this, Rs were much more likely than WBs to wish that the whole affair had never happened. WBs, but not Rs, reported lower self-esteem; in addition, they often included self-enhancing statements as if trying to raise their own self-esteem. Rs rarely did so, tending instead to make self-justifying statements, presenting themselves as unable to prevent the situation. "Stereotypes of [Rs as] aloof, casual, teasing, or sadistic heart-breakers may correspond to what novelists and would-be lovers imagine, but they do not correspond to our data"[36] (Fig. 13-5).

More than this, the stories tell of wildly ineffective communications. Most Rs felt annoyed; but few WBs knew that they did. Many WBs feared rejection, but very few Rs knew that they did. A strong majority of Rs felt reluctant to deliver rejections, and about a third felt guilty about doing so; but only a handful of WBs realized that the Rs felt that way.

Now that is not surprising. In trying to be kind, Rs often would try to soften their rejections, and to give reasons for them that were *external* and *unstable*. That is, R would suggest that her rejective behavior was because of the situation (external), not because of her feelings about WB (internal), and that her reaction might be different at another time (unstable):"Sorry, I can't go to a movie with you tonight; I have to stay home and rearrange my sock drawer."

(And this time let's pause to look forward. When we discuss achievement motivation in the next chapter, we will see that an *external, unstable* explanation for WB's failure—his failure, that is, at the task of winning R's heart—is exactly the kind of explanation that should lead him to intensify his efforts rather than give up the task. If R really wishes he would give up, she would do far better to give him straightforward *internal and stable* reasons—"WB, I'm sorry, but I

36. Ibid., p. 391.

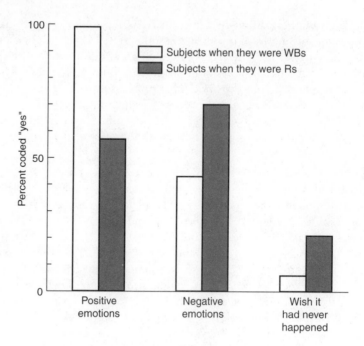

Figure 13-5 Positive and negative emotions expressed about unrequited-love experiences, when the subjects were would-be lovers (WBs) and when they were rejectors (Rs). (Data from Baumeister et al., 1993.)

simply don't want a romance with you and I don't see that changing." But of course that would hurt the feelings of this well-intentioned guy. It is a cruel dilemma for R—cause pain, or keep the unwanted pursuit going. No wonder she feels resentful!)

As a result, Rs were likely to believe that they had delivered clear messages of rejection, which the WBs had irrationally and obnoxiously refused to hear. WBs, in contrast, were more likely to believe that they had received mixed messages from a mysterious and capricious person. They were more likely than Rs to believe that their attraction had at first been reciprocated (compare the Pollyanna Principle, pp. 433–34) and that they had been led on.

Finally, Baumeister et al. wondered how their data fit Bowlby's observations on the breaking of attachments in young children. They did indeed see some parallels. Bowlby had suggested three responses to loss of an attachment "object." First was *protest,* with vocal emotional distress and refusal to accept rejection. "These reactions were amply observed in this research, particularly in accounts by rejectors who reported how would-be lovers complained, cried, made further demands, requested explanations, persisted unreasonably, occasionally went berserk, and generally refused to accept the message of rejection."[37] Second was *despair,* seen in the sadness, depression, and hurt self-esteem of the WBs. The third was *defensive detachment,* in which a child may reject the attachment figure even if she returns. So here, some WBs put down the R

37. Ibid., p. 391.

who had rejected them, and said that they would now refuse a relationship with her even if it were offered.

One final note: It may seem to you that we are painting a rather depressing picture here. Remember, though, that in writing their stories, the subjects wrote only about cases in which WB's love was unreturned *and remained so.* Not considered were the cases in which WB did eventually win R's heart, so that then she was an R no longer. Magazines and the movies give us many instances of that scenario too, and surely it happens in real life as well.

A Look Backward

Baumeister et al. sum it up this way: "To give love without receiving it in return causes pain, sorrow, and often a profoundly humiliating blow to one's self-esteem. To receive love without giving it in return causes uncertainty, awkwardness, guilt, and sometimes extremes of resentment and annoyance. It is perhaps the mutuality of love, rather than either the giving or the receiving, that makes it a pleasant, desirable, fulfilling experience."[38]

Good luck to you.

THE PROBLEM OF ALTRUISM

This happened: On October 17, 1989, an earthquake in the San Francisco Bay area caused the top level of the Nimitz Highway in Oakland to collapse onto the lower level, trapping commuters in the rubble. Residents picked their way into the rubble to try to rescue those trapped. This they did at terrifying risk to themselves; the highway was still quivering from aftershocks, and the rescuers surely knew that they risked being killed themselves. Later, interviewers asked these people why they had risked so much for *total strangers* whom they never expected to see again. One man replied simply, "There might have been people in there who needed my help" (Figure 13-6).

In ways large and small, people—*many* people—will put forth effort and inconvenience, even risk their lives, to try to help a *total stranger* in trouble. The question is: Why do they do it?

Let's try to see the problem more clearly by comparing some different approaches to it.

First, there is the view that selfishness is primary, and generosity or self-sacrifice is derivative, tacked on to human nature by training and situational constraints. This idea dates back to the hedonism of Thrasymachus and Thomas Hobbes (Chap. 2), and it remains a popular view in our society today. Look out for Number One, for if you don't, it's for sure that no one else will. It's a jungle out there. There's no such thing as a free lunch. Nice guys finish last.

38. Ibid., p. 393.

Figure 13-6 Rescuers trying to keep a car from going over the edge of the collapsed bridge.

And anyone who doubts it is, quite simply, naive, and will be devoured by those who do understand how the world works.

Why then do people sometimes go to such lengths to help each other? Because there's something in it for them after all; the altruism is only on the surface. As one writer puts it, "Scratch an altruist and watch a hypocrite bleed."

Such a vision of human nature makes contact with some recent points of view in psychology. Freud's *pleasure principle* implies that at base, a person seeks *his own* pleasure and nothing else. Fortunately, we can turn the pleasure principle around on itself. If we act generously, we may receive pleasurable rewards from others; if selfishly, unpleasurable punishments and reproofs. As our cognitive apparatus develops, we are affected too by the internal rewards and punishments that come from our internal representations of adults' rewarding or punishing voices and actions—the *superego*. But our own rewards and punishments, internal or external, are the name of the game.

Again, some writers articulate this point of view with reinforcement theory. We are rewarded (if we are!) for acts of generosity and helpfulness, and we may perform such acts because of this. Even when reward is not forthcoming, our history of rewards may make the actions persist anyway. Or such acts, because associated with rewards, may become *conditioned reinforcers* (pp. 263–64). But here again, it is the rewards and punishments we receive *for ourselves* that support acts of kindness or helpfulness. Their selflessness is only apparent. And they must be instilled by extensive training; it is no more "natural" for us to behave altruistically than it is "natural" for a dog to sit up and beg.

Now not everyone agrees. Socrates, we recall, didn't buy this idea; nor did Kant (Chap. 2). Socrates held that we are possessed of an untaught moral sense, which—if we heed it—impels us to deal justly and generously with our fellows. That point of view has been argued in our own time too, as we'll see.[39]

Then there are various compromise points of view. One goes like this: We are capable of feeling "sympathy" or "empathy" for other human beings. So, if someone else is in trouble and is unhappy, our sympathy for her may lead us to be unhappy too, and therefore to take action to relieve her distress. In this case, one can argue that such action is still selfish, because its real intent is to relieve our own distress. (That argument, which seems to me misguided, will be discussed shortly.) Or another person's happiness may make us happy, and so we may seek that person's happiness because it does. And this capacity for sympathy or empathy may be an inherent part of human nature.

For this view, we *could* bring the concepts of ethology to bear. Perhaps the sight of another's distress releases certain imitative or emotional reactions. Perhaps we are "wired up" to respond with distress at another's distress, much as a baby of a certain age is "wired up" to be upset in the presence of a stranger (p. 258).

But if these reactions are inherent parts of our untaught repertoires, they must be products of evolution—and that would appear to pose a difficulty. Evolution, it seems at first glance, ought to promote ruthless selfishness. The very history of life is one of competition for limited resources, and the ancestral forms who stayed around to have descendants (us) were the winners. It is a Hobbesian battle of all against all ("nature red in tooth and claw"), and extinction take the hindmost. Instinctive repertoires that led to acts benefiting *another*, not the actor herself, could only be a handicap. They should have been bred out of our ancestors long ago, no?

No. Recent developments in evolutionary theory suggest that a repertoire including such other-directed actions could confer a distinct advantage in the only race that matters: the race for progeny payoffs. Let's see why.

39. Wilson, 1993.

The Sociobiology of Altruism

We may define **altruism** as any action that benefits other species members, but does not benefit the actor as an individual. Such an act may even work very much to the individual's detriment.[40]

Do animals' instinctive repertoires include altruistic actions in that sense? Definitely—and the best example is so obvious that its implications were missed for a long time. Consider the behavior of parents toward their young.

PARENTAL BEHAVIOR   In many species of birds, the young cannot look after themselves for some time after hatching. What happens? The parents fly themselves to frazzles finding food and bringing it back to the nest. A parent bird may defend its nest against a predator—a fox perhaps—at great risk to itself, when it could just fly away to safety. These acts do not benefit the parent and may cost a parent its life. They benefit the young instead. Therefore they are, by our definition, altruistic.

A word of caution here. No one claims that the parent bird *feels* altruistic. We do not know what, if anything, the parent feels. We call the *behavior* altruistic if it benefits someone else and not the actor.

And, throughout this discussion, we will be speaking strictly about behavior. Altruistic *feelings* are another matter; in humans, they probably are as complex as any other emotional experience. We will have nothing to say about them here. Our topic is the evolution of altruistic *behavior mechanisms*.

Now let's return to the parent birds. Why do they accept such labor and such risks? It's obvious why. If they didn't react to the young by feeding and protecting them, the young would die. The parents would leave no descendants. Therefore, surviving species are those—and only those—whose ancestors did have the necessary action patterns, coupled to appropriate releasing stimuli, to produce nurturant and protective behavior toward their offspring if their offspring require these.

WHO IS AN ANCESTOR?   The modern theory of altruism is an extension of this simple principle. It takes only a single further step: The modern theory expands the definition of *ancestors* and *descendants*. From this, there follow some surprising consequences.

Consider two brothers, Marley and Arly (Fig. 13-7). If Marley has children, and they have children in turn, Marley's genes will be represented in future generations. That is his progeny payoff. But Arly has no children, though his brother does. Well, Arly and Marley got their genes from the same parents; Marley's daughter got half her genes from Marley; and so Arly and his

---

40. Of course I do not offer this as *the* definition of altruism. Obviously we could define the term in other, quite different ways (see for example Patterson, 1984). In defining altruism in terms of behavior and its consequences, I am only establishing ground rules for this discussion: When we talk about altruism here, this is what we shall mean by it.

Since Marley and Arly got their genes from the same parents, they have characteristics in common.

And since Karla got half her genes from Marley,

she has some of Arly's characteristics, too.

Figure 13-7 The reproductive success of all one's relatives, not just one's children, affects how much one's characteristics will be represented in later generations. Karla is Arly's niece, not his daughter; but her descendants will have some of Arly's characteristics because she has some of them.

niece have some genes in common too. So if Arly's niece, Karla, in turn has children, she will pass on some of Arly's genes to future generations.

To speak of Karla as having some of Arly's genes may sound confusing. Arly didn't actually *donate* any of his genes to make Karla, as Marley did when she was conceived. But look at it this way: Marley and Arley can resemble each other, without literally passing any of their genes back and forth. They resemble each other because they got their genes from the same parents, and so their genes produce similar characteristics. That is what we mean when we say in Figure 13-7, that the two brothers share some characteristics. In the same way, Karla will resemble Arly more than she does a non-relative. Because of their genetic relatedness, their genes produce similar characteristics. And, of course, it is *characteristics* on which evolutionary selection pressure operates. It selects for characteristics that are well-adapted to the environment—long necks perhaps, or long teeth, *and* effective repertoires of instinctive behaviors.

In a sense, therefore, *Karla is one of Arly's descendants,* as well as one of Marley's. To the extent that she resembles Arly, she will pass on his characteristics to future generations.

So, even if Arly has no children, he can increase his number of descendants by helping and protecting his nephews and nieces. But if so, it follows that he should help and protect his brother too, so that Marley can go on *having* nephews and nieces. Work it all out and we reach this conclusion: A person can increase his reproductive success—the number of his characteristics that survive in future generations—by helping, protecting, and nurturing *anyone who is related to him.*

All that has changed is this: The theory recognizes that Arly has inherited characteristics in common not only with his children and grandchildren (if any), but also with the children and grandchildren of his brothers, sisters, and cousins.

Their reproductive success will affect how much his characteristics are passed on, and that is *his* reproductive success. Uncles are ancestors, in this scheme; so are aunts and great-aunts; and a duck, to have some measure of reproductive success, doesn't *have* to be somebody's mother.

SELECTION FOR ALTRUISM Now, given this extended concept of ancestry, let us see how altruistic behavior could be *selected* by evolutionary pressures.

We assume the following:

1. There can be inherited, instinctive characteristics of the brain that "program" nurturant or protective behavior toward other, related species members. That's a big assumption, as applied to humans, but there is nothing implausible about it. It is no more mysterious than the "programs" for parental behavior toward the young.
2. For reasons given above, animals that have those programs will have more "descendants" in the broad sense—children and grandchildren, nieces and grandnephews—than those that don't. Therefore, their characteristics will be passed on to a greater proportion of subsequent generations.
3. Those characteristics will *include the altruistic "programs" themselves.* Altruistic ancestors will tend to have altruistic descendants. As a result, the inherited altruistic "programs" will be more and more prevalent in the population as the generations go by.

Therefore, sociobiologists conclude, altruistic behavior—behavior that benefits *relatives,* even at cost to the actor—could have evolved as part of the instinctive repertoire of certain species. Which species? Those that lived together in groups so that relatives could benefit from each other's efforts—a description that surely applies to humankind's ancestors.

That is the sociobiological theory of altruism. As we see, the idea is just an extension of the concept of parental behavior and how that may have evolved. Among animals that lived together in groups, ancestral forms whose instinctive repertoires led them to nurture and protect *all* their relatives—not just their children—would have more descendants. Living animals *are* those descendants. Therefore, living animals should have such instinctive repertoires.

Possible Mechanisms of Altruism

We have seen how a system might evolve, by which animals' brains are programmed for altruistic actions—toward relatives. But how might it work? How would all this affect behavior? What would such a program cause the brains to do?

MECHANISMS OF ACTION First, altruistic behavior may be wholly or partly instinctive, like sex in the stickleback, or the parental behavior of some birds. If so, the brain will be programmed to respond with certain action patterns in the presence of certain releasing stimuli. A fellow-creature showing distress might be a releasing stimulus for certain action patterns of protection or nurturance.

Second, perhaps a fellow-creature's expression of pleasure is a positive reinforcer. Or it might simply have untaught positive properties ("Isn't that nice!"), so that we seek it by any means available. Or the sight of a fellow-creature's distress could be a *negative reinforcer* (p. 295), which we will seek to remove—by whatever means are available.

Of these two possibilities, the second seems more likely to be important for complex creatures, because it provides the necessary flexibility of action. It is a long way from action patterns to, say, explaining differential equations to a friend, or donating a kidney. But both are possible. Then too, a basic repertoire of stimulus-bound action patterns could be elaborated by learning, as in attachment theory.

MECHANISMS OF SELECTION   In short, evolution could program brains for altruism by setting either the releasing potency, or the goal properties, of certain situations or emotional expressions. But there is a refinement needed here. As we saw earlier, selection pressure favors altruistic behavior toward relatives—not toward everybody. But there is no way that evolutionary selection could program an animal's brain to be nice to its second cousin. There is no way of knowing what the second cousin will look like. Therefore, some signals that are (1) detectable by the animal and (2) *correlated with* genetic relatedness must act to promote or inhibit altruistic behavior.

Familiarity might be one such signal.★ Our pre-human ancestors probably lived in small, highly inbred groups. In such a group, the chances were good that any person one knew personally, and saw often, would be a relative.

Therefore, one might enhance reproductive success by helping *familiar* people. Then a program might evolve in the brain that would say to the altruism officer: "If you see a *familiar* person in distress, then help him or her."

That mechanism does require a sophisticated system, but it is not at all implausible. The fear of strangers phenomenon is equally complicated, and we *know* that that occurs. It reflects an untaught program that says, "If you, small child, see an *unfamiliar* grown-up—fear it!" Perhaps there is also a program that says, "If you see a *familiar* person—why, isn't that nice! Treat it well."

A Look Backward: The Evolution of Altruism

Now we have the sociobiological theory of altruistic behavior. Creatures can enhance their reproductive success by helping their relatives, even at some risk. As a result, instinctive programs could evolve in the brain that could promote such altruism, as by making a fellow-creature's distress a releasing stimulus for

★There are other possibilities too; see Dawkins, 1976; Trivers, 1971.

protective or nurturing actions, or a negative reinforcer whose removal reinforces such actions. Finally, an animal doesn't know for sure who his relatives are, but he could increase the odds of helping only relatives by such devices as helping *familiar* species members.

Studies of Animal Altruism

Now all this so far is strictly theory. Is there any evidence that such altruistic motivators—releasing stimuli, unconditioned reinforcers, and the like—have actually evolved?

First, we can take it for granted that *parental behavior* in simple creatures, like fish and birds, is untaught altruism by our definition. But what other examples are there? And what about more complex creatures?

Well, chimps can be philanthropic. One chimp may hold out his hand to another who has, say, a bit of food, with a gesture that to humans looks like begging. The other chimp will often comply with the request and hand over the bit of food. True, a chimp will be generous only if it doesn't cost him anything important. But even then, why should he do it at all? It gains him nothing.

Giving can even transcend species boundaries. There is the case of Lucy, a young chimpanzee living with psychologist Roger Fouts, who was teaching her to use sign language. "As she has matured, Lucy has become more generous; often as she requests food for herself, she gives food to Roger and tells him to eat."[41] This behavior is described in passing, with no comment on how remarkable it really is. Giving food to Roger Fouts costs Lucy nothing, but it also gains her nothing. Why does she do it?

What about the *reinforcing* effects of another creature's distress or relief? Will they maintain arbitrary responses? Yes. Monkeys trained to pull a chain for food, will refrain from doing so if it also gives a shock to another monkey that they can see and hear.[42] Here, the arbitrary response is to refrain from action and forego food. Monkeys will do that if necessary, to avoid a fellow-creature's expressions of distress.

But far more convincing than these anecdotes are the cases in which the implications of the theory can be tested directly. As just one example, a researcher studied the alarm calls given by ground squirrels (Fig. 13-8). These animals give off shrill alarm calls when a predator such as a coyote approaches. It turns out, first, that such calling *is* altruistic in our sense. It increases the risk to the caller; a squirrel that calls attracts the predator's attention, and is more likely to be eaten than one that keeps quiet. Second, squirrels who have living relatives in the area—sisters or mothers, not necessarily offspring—are more likely to call than ones without relatives nearby.[43] Apparently evolution has

41. Linden, 1976, p. 115.
42. Masserman, Wechkin, and Terris, 1964.
43. Sherman, 1977.

Figure 13-8   Belding's ground squirrel gives an alarm call, and so endangers itself but benefits its relatives. (From Drickamer and Vessey, 1982.)

modified the conditions that release the call, so that calling requires not only the predator but the presence of relatives (or, more likely, just *familiar* squirrels) as well. Thus, calling is restricted to cases where it would benefit *relatives*. Such findings are pretty strong evidence that benefit to one's relatives *can* exert selection pressure on the behavior of a species.

We looked at these cases of animal altruism in order to show what is possible—even in simpler creatures. Monkeys and chimps will refrain from causing each other pain, or give away food when not compelled to. The significance of these findings does *not* depend on generalizing them to humans. I do not say: "Monkeys will do it, therefore people will do it." What I say is: *"Even* monkeys will do it. Reactions that complex can occur even in non-human species." Now let us turn to humans.

HUMAN ALTRUISM

We have seen evidence that altruistic *actions* (feelings are another matter) sometimes occur even in animals, and sociobiological theory tells us that it makes good sense that that is so. But what about humans? Theory aside, can we demonstrate altruistic motivation in our own species?

The Issue

Unfortunately, the issue is often stated in a way that hopelessly obscures it. The question is often asked and answered in such terms as these:

> What humankind inherits is the potential or possibility of learning a wide variety of social behaviors. But what is actually learned depends on the social situation. Socially adaptive cooperative and altruistic behavior are the products of learning and not biological evolution.[44]

Such remarks are true, but they miss the point of what the theory is saying.

In order to get the issue clear, let us focus on an extreme case. Consider a person who donates a kidney to another person.

Is that behavior learned or instinctive? We see at once that the question is naive. Even to call it "learned" does not do it justice; no one trained the donor in kidney-donation techniques. It is a decision based on a tremendous fund of organized knowledge. The donor must know what a kidney is, that he has two and can get along with one, and how to go about donating; he must consider the effects on himself, the effects on the recipient, and on and on. We *can* say this much: There is no way that his making the donation could be an instinctive action pattern. If that were what the argument is about, there would be no argument.

But that is not what it's about. The question is: What are the motivators? What untaught *mechanisms* contribute to the learning and the decision in such cases? If reinforcement is involved—what are the unconditioned reinforcers? Is one of them a fellow-human's well-being? Or if the donor is maximizing utility—are there untaught processes that give positive utility to a fellow-human's well-being, or negative utility to her distress?

In other words: Do humans have untaught tendencies to comfort or nurture other humans, and do these *motivate* our learning how to achieve these goals? The sociobiologist argues that there are such untaught processes. The critic argues that our untaught mechanisms do not include them.

If that is the question, let us turn to the evidence. There isn't much—not yet—but what there is is suggestive.

At first glance, case studies—such as the one we began this discussion with—would seem to answer the question. People do put forth tremendous effort and risk their lives to come to the aid of total strangers who need help. Doesn't that in itself demonstrate altruistic motivation? No, for the reasons we gave at the outset. These actions might occur for quite selfish reasons, such as an attempt to gain praise or avoid condemnation, by others or by oneself (pp. 514–15).

44. Mussen and Eisenberg-Berg, 1977, p. 45.

The Experimental Study of Altruism

Some modern writers, especially C. Daniel Batson and his colleagues, have attempted to show by experiment that a more purely altruistic motive can be demonstrated.[45] Take a look at Figure 13-9, and consider first the upper pathway. We see someone in distress, it makes us unhappy ("personal distress'), and we act to help the other person. That is not true altruism, says Batson, for it is our own distress, not the other person's, that is really our concern. But now look at the lower pathway. If we act out of "empathic concern," then it really is the other's distress that motivates us, not our own. Then, and only then, is the action altruistic.

These two sequences have both the situation and the action in common. How then can we distinguish them? One way is to manipulate how easy it is to relieve one's own distress by other means. Suppose seeing someone in trouble does make us unhappy, and we offer help only to relieve our own distress. But suppose also that it is easy for us to get out of the whole situation. Then we could relieve our distress just as well or better by leaving the scene, so we don't have to witness it any more.

Figure 13-10 shows the results of such an experiment. Some subjects, who showed low "empathic concern" as measured separately, were much more likely to escape than to help if they could escape easily. These, presumably, were following the "egoistic" branch of Figure 13-9 when they did help. But subjects high in empathic concern stayed to lend assistance whether escape was easy or not. So it is likely that their doing so was truly altruistic.

The reader may find this argument unconvincing. So does the writer. If we escape from the situation, it is true that we need not *see* the other person's distress any more. But we can *imagine* it; we know that it is still going on; and the images may be enough to keep our own distress active. For all we know, "high empathic concern" may reflect vividness of imagery as much as anything else.

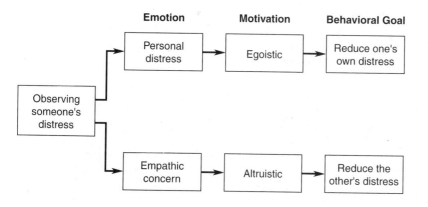

Figure 13-9 Two paths to helping behavior. Batson regards only the lower one as altruistic.

45. See Batson and Shaw, 1991.

Figure 13-10 Subjects high in empathic concern attempted to help a person in distress, whether it was easy or difficult to escape the situation. Subjects low in empathic concern offered help when escape was difficult, but when it was easy, most of them took the easy way out and left the situation.

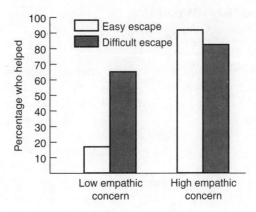

Moreover, some commentators, including the present author, feel that the argument is overly stern in its definition of altruism.[46] To count as altruistic, Batson claims, an act must be performed because it benefits another *and for no other reason.* If the person acts because it makes him feel good to help someone, or because he would feel bad if he didn't, then he is not really being altruistic. He is out to benefit himself after all.

This argument blurs some important differences. Suppose that Mary helps someone in distress, because it makes her feel good to do so. Does that make her action selfish? I do not think so, not necessarily, at least. The question is: *Why* does it make her feel good? If she does it because she expects a reward, and *that* would feel good, then we might say that the action was selfish after all. But if helping someone is enough *in itself* to make her feel good, then I think we are quite justified in calling her action altruistic. It isn't necessarily a selfish action just because she enjoys the outcome.

Similarly on the down side. John helps someone in distress because he'd feel bad if he didn't. Does that mean he is out for himself after all? Perhaps, if he feels bad because he expects to be punished or scolded. But not, I think, if someone else's distress is enough *in itself* to make him feel bad. The mere fact that John is distressed by another's distress is enough (I think) to qualify his helping as a generous and altruistic action.[47]

But even if we accept that argument, it doesn't answer the deeper question: Do we humans have altruistic tendencies "by nature"? Suppose we do feel happy at another's happiness, or unhappy at his unhappiness. Is that reaction an intrinsic part of human nature? Or does it have to be carefully taught? The question thus becomes: *What is the role of experience in generating sympathy, empathy, and the like?*

That question concerns the learning histories of the actors involved. And because human adults have extremely long and complex learning histories, our question as we see it now—what is the role of experience?—becomes extraor-

46. Mook, 1991.
47. Wallach and Wallach, 1983.

dinarily difficult, perhaps impossible, to study in them.[48] An alternative is to turn to humans who have less extensive histories—i.e., to children.

Altruism in Children

Expressions of distress, such as a baby's cry, seem to have the status of action patterns, as we saw when we discussed attachment. They also provide releasing stimuli for other humans.

One of the few well-studied cases shows that the sound of babies' cries is highly distressing to other babies. A baby, hearing another baby cry, is likely to begin crying himself.[49] Computer-generated synthetic cries, mimicking the loudness and frequency of cries, are not nearly so upsetting. It is *cries* that upset babies, not the noise they make.

Is a learning interpretation possible here? Some have suggested that a baby hears another baby's cry, associates it with his own cries when he is in pain, and becomes upset because of that association. Not so. A baby is much more upset by another baby's cries than by tape recordings of his own!

Let us expand that example a bit, for it shows how untaught altruistic motives might work. If Baby A is upset by Baby B's cries and if he could act to turn them off, then we could say that his behavior is purely selfish. But he has evolved in such a way that those cries *are* upsetting. They could motivate the child to take action to remove the distress that produces the cries—later, when he is old enough to take such action. We need not suppose that young children *feel* altruistic, any more than ground squirrels do. The point is that motivators can evolve that promote nurturance or protection of others, perhaps even at some risk or expense to oneself.

There is evidence for such *motivational states* in slightly older children. Expressions of distress can support motivated behavior directed toward reducing them:

> Recently two mothers whose 15- and 13-month-old sons frequently play together related how the 15-month-old inadvertently knocked down his 13-month-old playmate to get a toy. When the younger child began to howl, the 15-month-old first hugged him to get him to stop. He then tried to pick him up. Finally, everything else having failed, he located the younger child's bottle and handed it to him.[50]

Was the child *taught* to comfort others, in the first 15 months of his life? We cannot rule it out, but it doesn't seem likely.

Laboratory investigations of such motives are beginning to appear. In one study, kindergarten children watched a film showing another child's sadness when his marble collection was stolen. After that, children could work at turn-

---

48. Wallach and Wallach, 1991; Mook, 1991.
49. See Hoffman, 1981.
50. Rheingold, Hay, and West, 1976, p. 1157.

ing a crank—an arbitrary task—to earn marbles for that child, not for themselves. Subjects whose faces were saddest when they watched the movie, worked hardest for the reinforcement of relieving another's distress.[51]

In another, fully 50 percent of children only 18 to 21 months old would spontaneously retrieve a doll and return it to the mother, after she had pretended to lose it where the child could see it but she could not. The children were much less likely to help a strange adult in similar difficulty.[52]

As for *giving,* Harriet Rheingold and her colleagues found that giving things to mothers was a very frequent behavior in children as young as 15 months. They did it persistently and repeatedly, "without prompting, direction, or praise." In another study of children 18 to 36 months old, about half of them spontaneously offered to share things with others. Even younger babies would offer a toy or a pacifier to another person (Figure 13-11).*

Also instructive are the answers children give when we ask them *why* they share. Sometimes the reasons are self-serving—the child doesn't want to be punished, or says, "Then he will give me something back." But more frequent were replies suggesting that someone else's welfare was the immediate goal: "It makes the other kid feel happy," or "I don't want my friend to cry."[53]

51. Cited by Hoffman, 1981.
52. Johnson, 1982.
*Further evidence is cited by Hoffman (1981), Murray (1979), and Wallach and Wallach (1983).
53. Wilson, 1993, p. 44.

Figure 13-11   Even young children will attempt to comfort one another.

To speak of innate altruistic motives does not commit us to a naive, Pollyanna-ish view of the social world. If we do have natural tendencies toward altruism, they are fragile ones. Other influences can easily swamp them—for *an* influence need not be *the* influence, and *untaught* doesn't mean *unteachable*.[54]

This leads us to consider the other side of the coin: how situational factors can oppose, inhibit, indeed overwhelm, whatever generous and empathic tendencies we may have. Let us turn to examples.

The Role of the Social Situation

Our concern up to now has been with the evidence for untaught urges or tendencies to help and comfort one another. But even if we have such tendencies, it is very clear that in any given instance, we may or may not express them. It depends—and it depends powerfully on the *situation*.

Situational factors that promote altruism on the one hand, and indifference or even cruelty on the other, are so powerful that their effects have surprised us again and again. As a result, the experiments that document these effects include some of the best-known studies in psychology.

Consider the following scenarios:

1. John is a seminary student (which implies, among much else, that he has dedicated his life to helping others). One morning he is told that he is to give a practice sermon on the parable of the Good Samaritan. On his way to give his sermon, he sees a man slumped in a doorway, head down, coughing and groaning, asking for help. Does John stop to help him? He does not; he goes on walking. Joe, in a similar situation, does stop to offer help.

2. John has reported for his appointment to participate in an experiment. He is greeted by a female "assistant" who then excuses herself and leaves the room to get the materials she needs. A few seconds later, John hears from the next room the sounds of a chair being climbed, sounds of the chair tipping over, and the pained and frightened cries of the assistant who has hurt herself in the fall. What does John do? He just sits there! Joe, in the same situation, at once rushes to the door to offer assistance.

3. John again is a participant in an experiment, this time dealing with learning. John is the "teacher," and he is assigned the task of punishing the "learner," Jerry, for mistakes. As the task goes on, John is told to deliver electric shocks of greater and greater intensity, as indicated by voltage markings on the shock generator. (Actually, of course, Jerry is playing a role and receives no shocks at all—but John doesn't know that.)

I'm going to slow down and describe in detail how this scenario *typically* played itself out. You've heard it before, I know, but we ought not let familiarity blunt the horror of what took place, with perfectly normal, decent human beings—people like you and me—in the "teacher" role. It should scare the living hell out of all of us.

54. Wilson, 1993; see also Dawkins, 1976.

At first, with low-voltage shocks, Jerry (whom John can hear but not see) does not complain about the shocks. But at 75 volts Jerry begins to grunt with the pain. At 120 volts (roughly the voltage found in wall sockets in the United States) Jerry shouts that the shocks are very painful and that he wants to quit the experiment. At 270 volts his shouts become screams. At 300 volts, Jerry screams that he will no longer make the responses his learning task requires. And he doesn't; but the experimenter instructs John to treat non-responding as an error, and to continue delivering shocks—even though neither John nor the experimenter can tell, any longer, whether Jerry is even conscious. There is only an ominous silence. But the shocks continue.

It is not that John mindlessly obeys. He protests; but the experimenter says, "Please continue." He says, "We ought to see if Jerry's okay." The experimenter replies, "The experiment requires that you continue." If John insists, he is told, "You have no choice; you must go on"—all this in a calm, passionless, bureaucratic tone.

What does John do? He follows orders, to the very end—delivering, as he believes, the highest possible voltage to a now-silent, unresponsive victim. That is what most of the subjects did (about 68 percent) who participated in the original experiment.

Joe's behavior is quite different. Told that he "has no choice," he replies that yes, he jolly well does, and quits the experiment. John, of course, could have done the same at any time.

What do we make of these episodes? Looking back over the three scenarios, we're inclined to think of Joe as a kind, caring person. John, we conclude, is cold and uncaring if not downright vicious, and is badly in need of a humanity transplant.

We'd be wrong.

In every one of these cases, the most important difference between Joe and John is the *experimental condition to which each was assigned*—in other words, the external *situation*. In each case, different groups of subjects were assigned *at random* to the various situations—which means that personality variables, like altruism, empathy, and caringness, should on average be about the same from one experimental group to another. What differs is the situation—and in each case, its effect is decisive.

In the first case, John thought he was late for his sermon and had to hurry. Joe thought he had plenty of time. Of the actual subjects, 63 percent offered help in the "plenty of time" condition, only 10 percent in the "late" condition.

In the second, the mere *presence* of other people in the situation was enough to inhibit help-giving dramatically. Joe was alone in the room when the emergency occurred, and he (like 70 percent of the subjects in that condition) offered help. John was in the room with two other people who also just sat there. Of the people in that condition, only 7 percent offered help.

In the third, John was the only "teacher," alone with the experimenter who gave him his orders. Joe was with the experimenter *and* another "teacher," who was actually a confederate of the experimenter, with his own part to play in the drama. As the shock level began to rise, this second "teacher" told the experimenter exactly where to put his experiment, and quit. In this condition, most subjects behaved as Joe did: They quit too. Only 10 percent of them followed orders to the bitter end—still an amazingly high percentage, if we think about it, but dramatically less than the 68 percent of the single "teachers" who did so.

But why, in all these cases, should the situation have had such powerful effects? There are a variety of reasons, but some ideas cut through them all. And these are ideas that we are familiar with.

Consider that an adult human being must *decide* whether to offer assistance in an emergency. Now, if there are natural altruistic tendencies, these will contribute to the utility of offering help, and/or the utility cost of not doing so. But other factors, too, must be plugged into the decision equation.

In the first case, the altruistic satisfaction of helping must we weighed against the costs of being late. Reduce the threat of those costs, and we tip the decision toward helping.

In the second scenario, the presence of onlookers may discourage helping in several ways. For one thing, it may lead to what the investigators call "diffusion of responsibility." This is a kind of social "tragedy of the commons" (pp. 376–77). When there are all these onlookers, whose responsibility is it to offer help? If I offer help, then I assume *all* the risks of doing so. If I don't, then if anything bad happens the responsibility is shared by *all the onlookers there are*. Therefore, the potential cost *to me* may be much greater if I come forward than if I don't.

In the case of the obedience studies, again it is likely that a number of things were going on.[55] But all of them—the slippery slope of early, safe compliance, the authority of the experimenter, his quiet insistence on the subject's obligation to continue the experiment, and that he (the subject) had no choice but to do so—conspired to make the option of quitting the experiment *cognitively unavailable* to the subject. Saying it another way, the subject accepted the experimenter's *labeling* of the situation as one in which quitting was simply not an option.

If this is so, then seeing another person refuse to continue may have increased the cognitive availability of that non-compliance option. It said to Joe, in effect: "You do have a choice, you know. You can refuse; and in case you've forgotten, here's how to refuse." Most subjects in that condition took the hint.

Notice that in all of this, we have not had to judge the issue—are we naturally inclined to help each other?—one way or the other. We have only said that *if* we are, then such inclinations are not the only influences going. Their effects must we weighed along with those of other factors—situational ones—which may simply be more powerful in a given instance.

55. For discussion see Sabini, 1992.

A Look Backward

What about this, then? Are we creatures who, "by nature," look out for Number One and no one else? Must we be carefully taught to consider others, to care how they feel, to help them in distress? Or is it the tendency to do just these things that is ours "by nature," and is it indifference and cruelty that have to be carefully taught? Which is the doughnut and which is the hole?

This much we can say with confidence: *If* we have an untaught tendency to help our neighbors, it by no means follows that we shall do so on any given occasion. *Untaught* doesn't mean *unteachable;* and an untaught *tendency* to do thus-and-so is just that—a tendency. It may be inhibited or overriden by other tendencies. And if anything is clear from what we have learned, it is that here-and-now situational factors *can* overwhelm whatever altruistic tendencies, from whatever source, we may possess.

So, looking backward over this controversy, we can see the issue of untaught altruistic tendencies more clearly. And we see that it is much like the question: Are males "wired up" to be more responsive to sexual variety than females are (pp. 129–30)? It is a theoretical issue, not a practical one. *If* there are untaught altruistic tendencies, they are just that—tendencies—which other factors can override. And in most instances, situational factors are likely to be far more potent than any whisperings from our genes.

Of course, the theoretical question is an interesting one in its own right. My guess is that the answers we will get will come from analyses of the mechanisms of behavior—releasing stimuli, action patterns, reinforcers, and goals—across cultures, in babies, and, yes, in animals too, to show us what is possible even in simpler systems than our own.

There is one more thing we can say with confidence. People who wave their hands and say that it's "just human nature" to be selfish, haven't kept up with this controversy. We cannot say that the theory of evolution demands that conclusion. It doesn't. We cannot say that logic requires it. It doesn't; sociobiology can be a highly formal and intensely logical exercise in calculating progeny payoffs. Nor can we say that the data support it. They call it into serious question, as we have seen.

Above all, we cannot say that it is naive to raise the question. Quite the contrary: It is naive to suppose that we have answered it. We have not.

ATTITUDES, VALUES, AND ACTION

Some of us value helpfulness, and are willing to work hard in order to help others. Surely another way of saying the same thing is that we have a positive *attitude* toward helpfulness. Attitudes are cognitive structures which we often think of as having motivational force. Let's ask: What is the relation between attitudes and motives?

Well, what is an attitude? Most writers would point to two, and perhaps three, defining characteristics. First, attitudes can be about *individuals, classes,* or *general cases* of persons, places, or things. If we are speaking of Jane Smith, we might say that we have a favorable or unfavorable attitude toward her. Or we could speak of our attitude toward some group of which she is a member—i.e., of our attitude toward women (in general), or Democrats (in general), or stockbrokers (in general), and so on. In short and in our terms: Attitudes can be about *schemas*.

Second, attitudes have an evaluative or emotional component. Suppose I believe that stockbrokers (in general) tend toward conservative political views; that is, the conservative label is part of my stockbroker schema. But we wouldn't call that an attitude, unless I go on to realize that I *like* or *dislike* political conservatives in general. Then we would say that I have a positive or negative attitude toward conservatives, and hence (other things equal) toward stockbrokers as falling within that category. Without oversimplifying too much, we could say that an attitude is a *schema that drives affect* (p. 357)!

The third characteristic is a tendency to behave in certain ways toward the object of the attitude. If we have a favorable attitude toward, say, Dutch people, then we ought to be disposed to treat a Dutch person well when we encounter one. It is this characteristic that makes the psychology of attitudes relevant to our topic.

This, however, is also the characteristic we need to be cautious about. An attitude may, or may not, be reflected in our behavior.★

In light of what we know now, there is nothing at all surprising about that. If an attitude is a schema, it will be linked with other schemas—including plans, or schemas for action (pp. 351–53)—in a very complex network, and the strengths of the "links" will vary from one link to another over the long term. And over the short term, the cognitive *availability* of schemas will vary. In short, we may have a very strong attitude toward X, but (1) we may not be inclined to do anything about it, (2) we may not know what to do about it, or (3) even if we do, what we know may or may not come to mind.

Attitudes and Values

If we are willing to speak of (some of) our attitudes as motivators, maybe we should also speak of our *values* as having motivational force. Suppose, for example, that we place a high value on freedom of speech. This may well be taken to imply that we would take action in defense of free speech—opposing legislation that infringes on it, perhaps demonstrating in its support, and so on.

Indeed, we may wonder whether the two are really any different. If we say we value freedom of speech or honesty or kindness, is this any different from saying that we have positive *attitudes* toward these things or that we are *motivated* to promote them?

David McClelland has argued, along with others, that there are in fact distinctions to be made here. Values "represent the usually conscious conceptions

★For review and discussion see Sabini, 1992.

in terms of which people organize their experiences and preferences." They determine what people tell us is important to them. Motives, on the other hand, set goals and subgoals for action. Thus, "motives are more important for predicting what people *will spontaneously do,* whereas values are more important for determining what they will cognitively decide should be done."[56] And he notes elsewhere, "[T]he whole starting point of the inquiry was the common observation that what people said they valued was not a good index of what they would do."[*]

It does seem that we need to make that distinction. For example, anthropologist Claudia Strauss interviewed a sample of American working men in Rhode Island. She found that the American ideal of "getting ahead," or rising as high in one's career as one can, was strongly valued by these men. They would say things like:

> It's like, you know, whatever your mind can conceive, you can achieve. But you only get out of anything what you're willing to put into it.

Or:

> I believe if you put an effort into *anything,* you can succeed. . . . If I want to succeed, I'll succeed.[57]

However, though "getting ahead" was highly valued in the abstract, the career decisions made by these men had little to do with getting ahead. They had a great deal to do with being successful in the "breadwinner" role, providing for their families. Thus an opportunity to get ahead—a promotion perhaps, or a chance to switch to a higher-paying job—might be declined if it threatened job security or took more time away from loved ones.

In other words, both getting ahead and being a good breadwinner were valued; but of the two, only the breadwinner schema seemed to function as a goal. In McClelland's terms, therefore, we would speak of being a good breadwinner as a motive and of getting ahead as a value.

Why was this so? Strauss's data suggest that, in part, it was because the good-breadwinner schema had preemptive status for these men. In a conflict between fulfilling that goal and seeking any other, the "other" was not really considered at all. The need to be a good provider was seen, not as an option, but as a fact of life—*of course* one seeks that goal when it is relevant. Alternatives, we might say, are not *cognitively available,* so one "just does it." (Compare pp. 392–94).[58]

---

56. McClelland, 1985, p. 536.
*McClelland, 1986, p. 193. We shall follow McClelland's suggested usage here, but we ought to note that there is nothing like consistency in the way the term "value" is used by different authors.
57. Strauss, 1992, p. 206.
58. Strauss, 1992.

That is one way of looking at it. As Strauss recognizes, there is another way as well. Many of her men felt that with their skills, and in the economic climate of the time, there really were not many routes to getting ahead—not for them. In other words, they did not see any plans they could implement, or any sub-goals they could activate, to take them toward that long-term goal. Getting ahead was a fine idea, but they saw no way to get there from here. So the *cognitive availability* of plans and sub-plans may make the difference between something that is valued only, and something that is sought.

Either way, we see that the idea of getting ahead was what McClelland would call a value. So was being a good breadwinner; but the latter was a motive too, whereas the former was not.

The Problem of Internalization

We *internalize* society's attitudes and values—that is, we make them our own (Fig. 13-12). This, we recall, is the basis of Freud's *superego* (pp. 214–15). The question is: How do we do it?

It clearly is not an automatic process—what has been called the "fax model" of internalization. Some of society's attitudes acquire motivational force; others do not. But how is it that *any* of them do?

Consider an example from an earlier chapter, (p. 105). We were invited, you recall, to sit down to a nice breakfast of cockroaches; and we declined, with considerable emotion even at the thought!

This month, the *New York Times* profiled 15-year-old Shaul Linyear [who] felt his three-month-old basketball sneakers "was messed up." He said, "I'd walk down the block and people who knew me would start laughing." So, to get money for a new pair, he robbed and killed a . . . man who was delivering candy bars . . .

—H. PEARSON, "Black America's silent majority, *New York Times*, May 26, 1994

"*I'd* know. That's who would know!"

Figure 13-12 We internalize society's values, so that our actions must be acceptable to ourselves as well as to others.

Now why? It is clearly learned; a very young child might pop down a cockroach with no qualms. But learned how? Have we ever been punished for eating cockroaches, or do we know anyone who has? (We have already disposed of the cockroaches-carry-germs argument [p. 105]—sterile cockroaches are no more acceptable than ones on the hoof.)

And just what is it that is learned? It is easy to see how society could teach us to *express* disgust. Adults could teach us to *say* any or all of these things: (1) "It is the case that cockroaches are unacceptable as food," or (2) "It is the case that cockroaches for breakfast is a disgusting idea," or (3) ". . . disgusts *me.*" They could even teach us to say (4) "Yech!" The question is: How do we get from the saying to the feeling? How do we come, not just to say we're disgusted, but to *be* disgusted at the idea?

We can look at many other examples, for this internalization of attitudes and values is everywhere to be seen. In many societies (not all), for another man to make love with one's wife, under any circumstances whatever, may trigger a murderous rage in the husband. This, we might say, is one of society's "feeling rules" (pp. 475–76). But the husband does not consult a rule book that tells him he ought to feel anger. He just feels it. How do we get from *saying* "that action angers me," to *feeling* angry?

The short and honest answer is: We don't know. As I see it, it is one of the most important problems in the psychology of motivation; and it is unsolved.[59]

Attitudes and Action: The Hierarchy Revisited

When we first discussed plans (pp. 335–40), we saw that these too are hierarchically organized; and we saw that a plan is translated into action by the setting of *sub-goals* within the overall plan. This, presumably, is how any schema can have long-term motivational force for us: It sets the immediate sub-goals of our here-and-now actions.

Thus a high-level motive may set a long-term goal, like love or success. These schemas may be activated by a wide range of inputs. At lower levels are more specific schemas or plans, as for joining a dating service or attending a job fair. These direct action only when they are activated by higher-level goals.[60] And of course they break down further into plans for walking, taking a bus from here to there, or whatever.

But now we must once again add a complication that we've avoided up till now. If schemas (including plans) are hierarchically organized, then affect or attitude could be associated with a schema at *any* level of the hierarchy. We have attitudes toward potential long-term goals, but also toward short-term subgoals, and toward here-and-now actions.[61]

This makes a very great difference. To see why, let's go back to the basics of the cognitive approach to motivation. We imagine taking this or that action,

59. Schweder, 1992.
60. D'Andrade, 1992.
61. This discussion is adapted from Fishbein and Ajzen, 1975.

and the consequences of doing so and the value (or utility or niceness) of the outcome—and, if there are several possible outcomes, we weight each of these by its associated probability. But—and this is the new complication—we may assign positive or negative values, not only to the *outcomes* of the actions we contemplate, but also to the *actions themselves*.

Suppose we agree that there's nothing wrong with buying a new pair of shoes (the goal). Most of us—but not all!—would not rob or kill a person to get money to buy shoes (the sub-goal). Of course, the penalties for getting caught might enter into our calculations of expected utility (but see below). But more than that, we feel that the act itself is wrong, whatever the consequences. We make the same distinction when we ask: Does the end justify the means?

In short, the selection of action is affected both by the imagined outcome of the behavior (expected utility) and by our attitude toward the behavior itself. The end may be acceptable, but the means may not be.

All this looks backward to familiar ideas. In Chapter 4, we applied just this kind of analysis to cultural constraints on sexual and aggressive behavior. At every level, action is filtered through the constraints of the society in which it occurs. Of these, many are *internalized* constraints, which we could just as well call *attitudes*.

Thus, even when sexually motivated behavior is approved, only certain means may be. In some cultures, sexual behavior directed toward a same-sex person may be punished by condemnation or criminal penalties (expected utility), but it also may be repugnant to the actor (attitude toward the action itself). Again, even toward an "acceptable" partner, asking for a date may be okay, but a direct sexual proposition may not—first because the actor judges that it wouldn't be well received and might be punished (expected utility), but also because the actor would consider it a boorish thing to do (attitude toward the action itself).

A Look Backward: Thinking about Crime

We began this section with a criminal act; let us end it by looking at the general case. Political scientist James Wilson has discussed the problem of crime in a way that brings out many of the ideas we have surveyed.

Most of our thinking about crime, and our public policies toward it, place it squarely within a decision-theoretic framework. As Wilson summarizes it:

> No doubt, very severe penalties will deter many people from stealing, *if* those who consider stealing believe the penalty is likely to be exacted; *if* the penalty, discounted by the chances of avoiding it, is of greater value than the proceeds of the crime, discounted by the chances of not getting away with it; and *if* there is another source of income (such as a job) that would produce greater net gains.[62]

62. Wilson, 1975, pp. xiii–xiv.

Thus, harsher penalties are designed to add to the utility cost of (say) theft; hiring more police is designed to increase the subjective probability that the cost will be incurred; and provisions of jobs, job training, and the like are designed to increase the subjective probability of attaining the ultimate goal (having money) by non-criminal means.

But something must be missing from this cost-benefit analysis, because criminal behavior simply does not vary with these decision factors as the theory says it should. "Crime rose the fastest in [the United States] when the number of persons living in squalor or poverty was declining. . . . The United States has, on the whole, the most severe criminal penalties in its lawbooks of any advanced Western nation; it also has the highest crime rate of most advanced Western nations."

Many criminologists conclude from this, not that a decision analysis doesn't apply, but that we have neglected important influences on the decision. First, we leave attitudes toward the action itself out of account. Most law-abiding people condemn *criminal acts*—apart from their outcomes—and pass the condemnation on to their children, who internalize it:

> It is my experience that parents do not instruct their children to be law abiding merely by pointing out the risks of being caught, but by explaining that these acts are wrong whether or not one is caught. I conjecture that those parents who simply warn their children about the risks of crime produce a disproportionate number of young persons willing to take those risks.[63]

We need, in other words, to instill some negative attitudes about criminal *actions,* not just fear of their negative expected utilities. But there is yet another factor, and again it is a familiar one:

> [A] hundred persons may confront equal prospective benefits (say, having $1,000 stolen from a bank) and equal prospective costs (say, a one in five chance of imprisonment), but ninety-five *will not seriously consider* bank robbery, while five will pull a gun and march up to the cashier without a moment's hesitation.[64]

In other words, when criminal actions are not performed, it may be because they are not *considered,* seriously or otherwise. However much we needed a new pair of shoes, it simply would not *occur* to most of us that armed robbery would be one way of getting them. Armed robbery would be *cognitively unavailable* to most of us—though not all!—just as stealing was a cognitively unavailable option for Mennonite children (pp. 392–94).

But if a child grows up in a family and peer group that do consider violent theft (availability) and do not condemn it (attitudes toward actions), then important constraints against criminal behavior disappear from the controlling system. One is left with only the external penalties, which simply may not be sufficient.

63. Ibid., p. 229.
64. Ibid., p. 198; italics added.

This is not at all a new idea. Many other writers, too, believe that violent crime will not decrease until we can instill in young people the attitudes and values that make violence less likely to come to mind as an option, and more likely to be condemned by the actors themselves if it does come to mind.

Unfortunately, what is not so clear is: How do we get there from here?

SUMMARY

Human social interaction begins with an infant's attachment to its caretaker. Early behaviorists saw the mother simply as a conditioned reinforcer, because she provided food. But Harlow's monkey experiments showed, first, that a comfortable mother was more important than a nutritious one and, second, that a comfortable mother provided a secure home base for exploration and play, and not just reinforcement for approach and clinging.

John Bowlby has looked at attachment from an ethological perspective. Infant and parent provide releasing stimuli for each other; the baby's appearance and actions produce nurturant behavior from the parents; such behavior soothes the baby. This not only gets the baby's needs met; it also sets the conditions for development of an emotional bond. A process analogous to imprinting may play a role. There are several signs of this bond: the infant is more easily calmed by caretakers than by other adults, he approaches the caretaker for play or consolation, he is less distressed by strange events in the caretaker's presence, and he may be distressed if the caretaker goes away.

Isolated responses of approach to caretakers or avoidance of strangers become integrated into systems, which form a lattice hierarchy. There is now a whole system of attachment behaviors, one of fear/wariness, and one of exploration. Whole systems can be evoked or inhibited as units.

There are substantial individual differences in attachment-related behaviors, and these seem to be correlated with other variables in reliable ways. *Securely attached* children are likely to have sensitive, responsive caregivers and better peer relationships than *insecure/avoidant* ones. Most of these data are correlational, but some experimental data support a causal relationship here. Bowlby suggests that the effects are mediated by the kind of internal model of the world, and the people in it, the child forms—that is, by schemas.

Adult liking and loving may be compared to attachment processes; and one's beliefs about loving relationships, and successes at forming them, may be correlated with earlier experience during the attachment phase (though as always, causation is another matter). Loving and liking—adult attachment— are now topics of intensive investigation after long neglect. A powerful factor in first-impression formation, date satisfaction, and the like is simple physical attractiveness. However, date selection also is affected by the likelihood of rejection. This may balance off against the role of attractiveness—a more attractive person is more desirable, but also more likely to reject an advance—so that people are likely to end up with partners about as attractive as they themselves are.

Beyond the initial stages, *liking* becomes a factor. It may be affected by the reinforcements one has obtained from the relationship to that point. Some writers believe that *loving* differs from liking just here: It involves preoccupation, with fantasies and expectations about future gratifications, not just the effects of past ones.

Finally, a loving relationship may lead to a commitment. This is a decision, and the concepts of decision theory apply to it. But so do other cognitive complications, which may help maintain the commitment: dissonance produced by the thought of dissolving the relationship, perhaps, or the culture's framing of acceptable alternatives. Robert Sternberg and his co-workers offer a typology of adult loves, based on three underlying factors: passion, intimacy, and commitment. Direct evidence for his ideas is meager, but the ideas do offer us a way of thinking about the processes and may help resolve some seeming paradoxes. However, as so often, it may also be more bound to Western culture than we might suppose.

What if the love is unrequited? Some research on this topic suggests that it is a more consistently negative experience for the rejector, who must choose between an unwanted pursuit and the infliction of pain, than for the rejectee, who will likely experience a roller coaster of high and lows. Miscommunication is common. Now-familiar ideas from previous chapters help us understand why these things should be so.

Are humans and other animals utterly selfish by nature? Philosophers have held that they are, and evolutionary theory was misinterpreted to imply that they have to be. Actually, they obviously are not always selfish, as the behavior of a parent toward its offspring shows. By feeding or protecting its young, even at the cost or danger to itself, a parent bird demonstrates *altruistic* behavior— behavior that benefits another organism, and not the actor as an individual.

In species whose young require it, parental caretaking evolved because ancestral forms that had the needed instinctive repertoires out-reproduced those that did not. Modern sociobiologists extend this idea by pointing out that all an actor's relatives share characteristics with the actor; therefore, their reproductive success contributes to the actor's own. Instinctive tendencies to help, protect, or nurture others could have evolved just as parental behavior did: Animals who behaved in such ways out-reproduced those who did not. Signals of distress might release nurturant action patterns. They might be negative reinforcers, whose removal would reinforce the nurturant responses that removed the distress. Or, indications of another creature's well-being could have positive value for the actor.

There is evidence for this at the animal level. In humans, the question is not whether *acts* of helping and caring are instinctive—obviously many are not— but whether they are *motivated* by untaught tendencies to protect or nurture. The evidence is framentary here—attempts to settle the matter experimentally are fraught with difficulty—but there is some. Small children are distressed at another's cries; older ones take action to quiet another's distress, or give things to others, in cases where it is unlikely that they were taught to do these things.

Finally, it is (I think) a mistake to quibble about whether an unselfish action is "really" altruistic if it makes the actor herself feel good. If she feels good only because she has helped another person, and she gains nothing else for herself, then the good feeling is itself altruistic, not "selfish" in the usual sense.

Thus this question—are there untaught altruistic motives?—will surely be pursued vigorously in the future. We cannot prejudge it any more. We do have to realize, however, that any such motives, even if they exist, may be overcome by other influences in the situation. The actions of other people, sometimes their mere presence, can inhibit helpful actions.

Attitudes have cognitive, emotional, and sometimes behavioral components. If I have a positive attitude toward (say) Fomorians, I mean that I know what Fomorians are, enjoy their company, and am disposed to treat them well. On that last point, however, we know that attitudes do not always predict our behavior very well. This is not surprising: Attitudes, like other schemas, may or may not spring to mind (availability); they may conflict with each other; and even strong attitudes may not take hold of actual behavior if the necessary plans and sub-goals are lacking. Perhaps we should distinguish between attitudes that motivate action, and *values* which may not, however highly regarded they may be in the abstract. Running through all this is the problem: How do we *internalize* the feelings, positive or negative, that our society teaches us to hold toward various persons or things? How, for example, do we go from *saying* that cockroaches are disgusting to actually *feeling* disgust? We do not know.

In moving from attitudes to actions, we meet yet another complication: We will have attitudes not only toward the goal of our action, but also toward the action itself. As an extreme example, shooting a person to get money to buy shoes would be an action many of us would very strongly disapprove—so much so, indeed, that it would be cognitively unavailable and so unlikely even to occur to us. But for others, even in Western society, such disapproval might not have been internalized. And where it has not, external punishments may not be sufficient deterrents. That may be one reason why crime is such an intractable problem in this society.

CHAPTER 14

Long-Term Goals

I'm bound to be rich!
BOUND TO BE RICH!
　　　—JOHN D. ROCKEFELLER

"This is the best of all possible
worlds!" cries the optimist.
Sighs the pessimist, "I know."
　　　SOURCE UNKNOWN

T o be *motivated*, we have suggested, is to be ready to take any means available to attain an imagined goal. If so, our goals may literally be as complex as our imaginations permit—and as far in the future. Some of us want to be rich, some to be President, some to be world-class singers or figure skaters. In this chapter, we will look at research and thinking about that kind of *achievement motivation*, and at the related (converse?) case of hopelessness and help-lessness.

Then, we will consider the motive to expand our capabilities and actualize our potentials—to be all that we can be. Some writers suggest that this is the proper goal of life itself—and that this need for *self-actualization* is present in all of us, though latent in some.

In all these domains, but especially the last, we will find that we are asking some pretty fundamental questions about human nature. In a final look backward over the journey we have taken, we will try to see more clearly how scientific investigations can be directed at such questions as these.

ACHIEVEMENT MOTIVATION

The modern study of achievement motivation began with the work of David McClelland. He has devoted a long and productive research career to its complex ramifications.

McClelland's Studies of Achievement Motivation

McClelland began with a conception of motivation very much like the one we have developed in earlier chapters. One seeks goals that haven't happened yet. Therefore it is the expectation of a goal—the image—that affects behavior now. So, to study people's goals, McClelland began by studying what they imagine.

PROJECTIVE TESTS AS MEASURES OF MOTIVATION   For his methods, McClelland drew upon the pioneering work of Henry Murray, who invented one of the best-known projective tests—the Thematic Apperception Test, or TAT.

A **projective test** is one in which a person is shown an ambiguous stimulus—a blob of ink, as in the Rorschach test, or a picture showing a scene, as in the TAT (Fig. 14-1). The picture could mean any of a number of things, but the person is asked to describe what *he* sees in it, or to tell a short story based on it.

The idea is that, if different people have different preoccupations, drives, or needs (Murray's term), they will *project* these inner states into their interpretation of the stimulus material. They will see in the stimulus what is on their minds—what they are preoccupied with, or what they want or what they fear.

In other words, these ambiguous stimuli are *cues for imagery.* Because they are ambiguous, they permit us to respond with whatever thoughts and images are on our minds—including goal images.

One TAT picture, for instance, shows a man at a worktable with a small family photograph to one side. Here is one story that might be written about it:

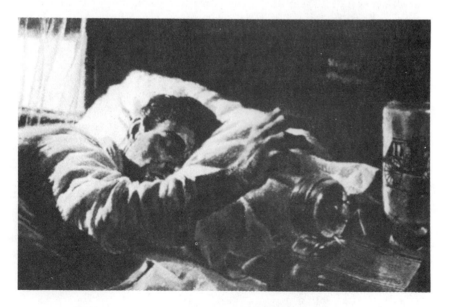

Figure 14-1 A picture from the test used by McClelland's group to measure achievement motivation. (From McClelland et al., 1976.)

The engineer is at work on Saturday when it is quiet and he has taken time to do a little daydreaming. He is the father of the two children in the picture—the husband of the woman shown. He has a happy home life and is dreaming about some pleasant outing they have had. He is also looking forward to a repeat of the incident which is now giving him pleasure to think about. He plans on the following day, Sunday, to use the afternoon to take his family for a short trip.

This story shows a person's thoughts moving toward his family and the things they would do together. Such a story would be scored very low in achievement imagery. But compare this one:

The man is an engineer at a drafting board. The picture is of his family. He has a problem and is concentrating on it. It is merely an everyday occurrence—a problem which requires thought. How can he get that bridge to take the stress of possible high winds? He wants to arrive at a good solution of the problem by himself. He will discuss the problem with a few other engineers and make a decision which will be a correct one—he has the earmarks of competence.★

Here we have a focus on a problem, and its solution by the engineer's own efforts. That story would rate a very high score in achievement imagery. If a subject told many stories like that, she or he would be considered high in **need for achievement,** or *nAch* for short.

VALIDATING THE MEASURE   The early studies using this technique were attempts to validate it—that is, to see whether or not the story images evoked by the TAT cards really could be used to measure motives. McClelland and his colleagues showed that the *experimental* arousal of achievement motivation would, in fact, increase the subjects' achievement imagery as measured by the TAT.[1] For example, if subjects were about to take an important test, and therefore had achievement on their minds, they gave more achievement-related TAT responses. The measuring instrument worked.

Some Correlates of nAch

But that was only preliminary. McClelland's interest was not in a subject's momentary desire to achieve, activated by a here-and-now challenge. He was interested in *lasting* differences between one person and another.

Some people might be concerned about achievement all the time, as a persisting long-term goal, whereas other people might seldom think about achievement. If so, and if the difference is important to the life one leads, then differences between people in *nAch* ought to be related to differences in other things. How would we expect persons who are *generally* concerned about achievement to differ from persons who are not?

★These stories are from McClelland (1964).
1. McClelland, Clark, Roby, and Atkinson, 1949, p. 243.

OCCUPATIONAL CHOICE   For one thing, McClelland reasoned, high *nAch* people might make good business executives. If they think about getting ahead, defining and solving problems, and the like, they ought to gravitate toward jobs that permit and reward these activities in real life.[2]

So McClelland and his students took samples of business executives and of people in other occupations—for example, technicians, and students at professional schools—of comparable age, intelligence, and social background. As Figure 14-2 shows, the executives did score higher in *nAch*—in the United States, in Italy, and even in a Communist country, Poland.

Now as always with correlational data like these, it is hard to know what causes what. Maybe businessmen go into business because they are high in *nAch*. Or maybe it's the other way around; maybe businessmen *develop* high *nAch* because their profession demands it.

So McClelland and his students did a longitudinal study, looking at the relationship between *nAch* scores in college students and the jobs they held 10 to 14 years later. He divided the jobs into *entrepreneurial* ones, with individual responsibility and individual risk—for example, real estate, insurance sales, private business—and other, non-entrepreneurial ones. Sure enough, people who were high in *nAch* early, when they were college students, were more often found in entrepreneurial jobs later on. It seems that *nAch* can precede career choice, and may play a role in determining it.

WHAT KIND OF ACHIEVEMENT?   One wonders: Why business executives? Isn't a concern for doing well, for achieving, necessary for success at almost anything—a scientific career, for instance?

Perhaps so; but it becomes clear as McClelland discusses this matter that *nAch* is a particular kind of achievement orientation. It is more specific than the term *need for achievement* implies.

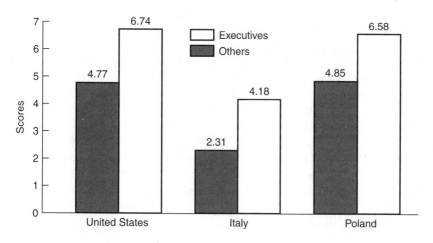

Figure 14-2   Achievement motivation as measured in business executives, as compared with other professional persons of comparable social and economic backgrounds. (From McClelland, 1964.)

2. McClelland 1965, 1978.

The high-*nAch* person, says McClelland, seeks situations in which she takes personal responsibility for solving problems. She tends to set moderate goals: not too hard, or failure is too likely; and not too easy, or success brings no satisfaction. And she wants concrete, rapid knowledge of how well she is doing. Business of course provides this kind of information in sales, profits, and production figures.

Compare these qualities with what a career in science, or in teaching, offers. A research scientist may work for a very long time, not knowing whether she is on the right track or not; she does not get immediate rewards or immediate information about the rightness of her decisions. A teacher may never be sure just how much he is getting across to his students. Concrete, rapid knowledge about how well one is doing does not occur in these professions. Such careers will not attract the high-*nAch* person. They offer other kinds of rewards, but not those that *nAch* is directed toward.

Toward a Psychology of History: Achievement and Society

McClelland is an investigator of daring imagination. Armed with his tool of *imagery* as a way of measuring motivation, he has made ingenious forays into the psychology of historical and cultural trends in whole societies.

PROTESTANTISM AND CAPITALISM   The sociologist Max Weber had suggested that the rise of capitalism in European civilization may have been accelerated by the Protestant Reformation in the sixteenth and seventeenth centuries. Briefly, his argument was this: The Protestant religions stress an *individual* relationship between persons and God, as opposed to a relationship through an institution, the Catholic Church. Martin Luther himself had spoken of a "priesthood of all believers," and Protestantism emphasized each person's seeking his own salvation. In other words, *personal initiative and effort* were valued.

Weber notes that Protestant entrepreneurs seemed to rise to the top in the emerging world of capitalistic business, despite the initial advantage in wealth that many Catholic families enjoyed. And the early Protestant businessman could not use the money he made for his own enjoyment, for early Protestantism frowned on self-indulgence. So he was likely to reinvest it in his business. Such a man "gets nothing out of his wealth for himself, except the irrational sense of having done his job well."[3]

But McClelland realized that that outlook could also describe the person high in *nAch*. Could the link between two great social movements—Protestantism and capitalism—be mediated at the individual level by the achievement motive? If it were set up as a value by the religion of a society, taught to children by that society, and expressed as individual entrepreneurship by those children when they grew up—why not?

3. Weber, 1930, p. 71.

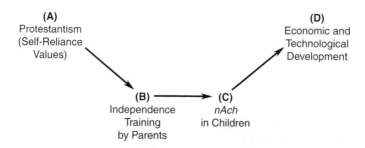

Figure 14-3   McClelland's
suggested sequence of events
relating religion, child-rearing
practices, achievement
motivation, and economic and
technological development.
(From McClelland, 1955.)

Figure 14-3 shows the idea. Protestantism, valuing self-reliance and initiative, leads parents to train their children to be independent and to take initiative. Such training builds *nAch*. That leads to entrepreneurship, which in turn leads to economic and technological development within a capitalistic society.

Now if all this happened, it happened long ago. But if the idea is correct, modern societies should still show the *process* going on. With the world for a laboratory, McClelland and his students set out to gather data.

Is there a relationship between Protestantism and economic growth? As preliminary data, McClelland divided the nontropical countries of the Western world into ones that were predominantly Catholic and predominantly Protestant. As an index of economic development, he looked at the average per capita consumption of electric power for the year 1950. Table 14-1 shows the results. By that measure, Protestant countries were indeed more heavily industrialized than Catholic ones.

What about McClelland's hypothesized steps in that relationship? First, it should be the case that Protestant families favor more and earlier independence

Table 14-1.   Average per capita consumption of electric power in Protestant and Catholic countries beyond the Tropics of Cancer and Capricorn. (For the year 1950, in kilowatt-hours, from Woytinski, 1953.)

Protestant		Catholic	
Norway	5,310	Belgium	986
Canada	4,120	Austria	900
Sweden	2,580	France	790
U.S.A.	2,560	Czechoslovakia	730
Switzerland	2,230	Italy	535
New Zealand	1,600	Poland	375
Australia	1,160	Hungary	304
United Kingdom	1,115	Ireland	300
Finland	1,000	Chile	260
Union of		Argentina	255
South Africa	890	Spain	225
Holland	725	Uruguay	165
Denmark	500	Portugal	110
Mean	1,983	Mean	457

training for their children than Catholic families do. McClelland's group tested and confirmed this prediction at least for American families.[4]

Second, independence training by parents ought to be correlated with *nAch* in children. There is evidence that this also is true.[5] When interviewed, mothers of high-*nAch* children said that they had expected their children to show independence—dressing themselves, finding their own way around the neighborhood, and the like—at earlier ages than the mothers of low-*nAch* children.★

Finally, does high *nAch* lead to business entrepreneurship and so to industrialization? Well, we recall that high-*nAch* people do in fact show a greater likelihood of choosing business occupations than do people with low *nAch*.

Thus, we have in this research program an *independent* bit of evidence for every step in the chain of events McClelland hypothesized.

ACHIEVEMENT AND INDUSTRIALIZATION   Later, McClelland came back with still more evidence.[6] Suppose high levels of *nAch* in individuals do lead to economic growth of whole societies. Can one trace a relationship between *nAch* and economic growth over the history of a nation?

What McClelland looked for here was an estimate of the interest in, or concern for, personal achievement that characterized a particular society at a particular time. To do this, he took samples of the fantasies of various time periods—their fiction! Stories, poems, songs, and plays were scored for achievement imagery just the way TAT stories would be. The frequency of such imagery does in fact change over time. The line without shading in Figure 14-4 shows the frequency of achievement themes in English literature, measured at 50-year intervals from 1500 to 1850.

Figure 14-4   Relation between achievement themes in literature and later industrial growth in England over a 350-year period. (From McClelland, 1964.)

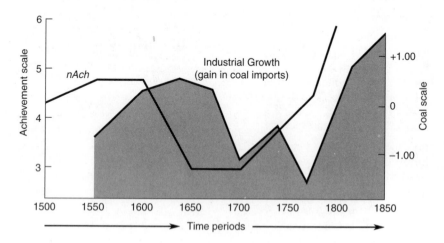

4. McClelland, Rindlisbacher, and deCharms, 1955.

5. Winterbottom, 1953.

★One can have doubts about this *retrospective* method, in which the mothers, being interviewed *now,* recall as best they can what they had done *then* when the children were younger. Winterbottom's findings are controversial (cf. Weiner, 1989).

6. McClelland, 1964.

Then, as a rough estimate of industrial growth, McClelland took the rate of increase in coal importation by the English. The changes in this rate are shown as the line enclosing the shaded area.

That measure clearly shows a big increase in industrialization around 1600 and an even bigger one after around 1800 when the Industrial Revolution began to gather steam. More important, notice that each of these jumps in industrialization was *preceded,* by about 50 years, by a surge in achievement-related imagery in popular fiction.

McClelland interprets the data this way:

> The stories tell us what is on the minds of significant elites in the country, what these influential persons tend to think about most naturally. . . . In this sense, the stories are exactly analogous to the [TAT stories] written for us by individuals. . . . Apparently, what comes most readily to the minds of these authors—whether concepts of achievement, affiliation, or power—reflects sufficiently well what is on the minds of key people in the country. . . . Thus, if the stories stress achievement, it means that an entrepreneurial spirit is abroad in the land. . . . And if the entrepreneurial types are strongly motivated to do well, they apparently succeed in getting the economy moving at a faster rate.[7]

A Look Backward: Motives and Cultures

There's much more, but these examples give the flavor. What are we to think of this line of investigation?

It has its critics. One frequent objection concerns McClelland's use of the TAT to assess achievement motivation. It is argued that studies of the TAT show it to have quite low validity. But this objection misses the point of what McClelland was trying to do. It may be true that the TAT has little validity *as a way of diagnosing an individual's personality.* But if *differences* in *nAch,* as measured by the TAT, can be related to individual differences in something else—vocational choice among individuals, economic growth among nations—then those relationships are real. They *are* validity data for that measurement technique, as used for the purpose of establishing those relationships.

Granted that the relationships are real, though, it is another matter to interpret them. Here we meet a second objection: that no system as complex as history will be amenable to the kind of direct causal analysis we have just seen. From that point of view, the parallel curves in Figure 14-4 seem almost *too* neat. After all, so many things can affect industrial growth in general and coal importation in particular—especially if we consider that the period of the study takes us from before the time of the Spanish Armada, through two revolutions in England and one in America, to just past the wars with Napoleon! With so many variables operating, how could any one of them be all that important?

But this complexity does not reduce the impact of the data. Of course a great many things were affecting industrialization besides *nAch* and the entre-

7. Ibid., pp. 44–45.

preneurial spirit. However, as McClelland points out, these other influences should act to obscure any relation between achievement themes and industrial growth, not to create one artificially. They make the data *more* compelling: With all these other things going on, we *still* see coal imports rising and falling with achievement themes in literature.

The same could be said about the arbitrary measures McClelland was forced to rely on—coal imports, kilowatt-hours, and the like—as measures of industrialization. These *were* arbitrary, true. But industrialization had to be measured somehow, and if different measures in different studies all tell the same story, the story becomes all the more compelling.

Unless we take the view that social trends like these are too complex to investigate empirically at all, it seems that we should admit McClelland's data in support of his theory. Of course, the relationships may exist for other reasons than the ones McClelland gives; we may decide that "need for achievement" might better be called something else instead; further data may modify the picture, and the theory in turn may have to be modified. But these things are true of any scientific theory; they are not criticisms of this one. At the very least, McClelland has shown us one way to gather data on the historical forces that shape whole societies—a stunning achievement in its own right.

Achievement Motivation and Task Choice: Atkinson's Theory

Whereas McClelland and his students have extended the achievement motive to the characteristics of whole societies, John Atkinson and his co-workers have focused on theory testing in the laboratory.[8] They bring the *nAch* work into articulation with *decision theory*.

THE EXPECTED UTILITY OF SUCCESS   Decision theory assumes that the person chooses, from the actions available, the one with the highest *expected utility*. Expected utility, we recall, is the value (utility) of an outcome, multiplied by the probability that it will result from the action.

Well, success at a task has positive utility, which we can think of as *pride in achievement*. Now, how does the probability of success affect matters? Suppose we could choose among tasks of varying difficulty. We could choose a very easy task, or a very difficult one, or one somewhere in between. How should we choose, so as to maximize expected utility?

In one early experiment, college students played a ring-toss game, trying to toss a ring over a post from some distance away. They could stand as close or as far away as they chose. Their choice of distance, shown in Figure 14-5, has a curious pattern. Subjects high in *nAch* tended to stand an intermediate distance from the post, neither very close nor very far away. Subjects low in *nAch* showed no such consistent pattern.

8. Atkinson, 1958.

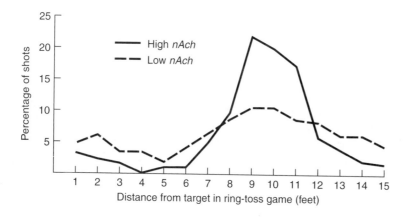

Figure 14-5 Choice of position in a ring-toss game. Students high in *nAch* tended to stand an intermediate distance from the ring, making the task neither too hard nor too easy. (From Atkinson and Litwin, 1960.)

Why should that be so? The concepts of decision theory help us to understand it.

Look at it this way. If we can perform a task that is easy to perform, then it isn't much of an achievement and success isn't very satisfying. But if we can succeed at a very difficult task, that is indeed an achievement. Thus, if the *probability* of success (P_s) is high, then the *utility* of success (U_s) is low, and vice versa. Simplifying, for a first approximation, we can let $U_s = 1 - P_s$.

Now the *expected utility* of an outcome—success, in this case—rises with the probability of that outcome, P_s, but also with the utility of the outcome, U_s. But here $U_s = 1 - P_s$. Thus the tendency to choose a task should be greatest when the product, $P_s \times (1 - P_s)$, is highest. And it is easy to show that that happens when $P_s = (1 - P_s) = .50$.

In short, a person who values success at a difficult task should seek a task at which her chances of success are about even. That is the choice that maximizes expected utility. Presumably the high-*nAch* subjects chose their intermediate distances so as to make the odds of success around .50. The low-*nAch* subjects did not do that, perhaps because success or failure mattered less to them, and so the above analysis does not apply to them.

This analysis fits the experimental data for the high-*nAch* subjects (as it was designed to do), and it fits nicely with the concepts of decision theory. Now comes a new and intriguing twist.

FEAR OF FAILURE   All the above analysis applies to persons for whom success at a task is a positive incentive—that is, those for whom *nAch* is reasonably high. But there is another influence that can also be considered a motive: the tendency to avoid failure. Call it **fear of failure** of *fF*. If we think of *nAch* as the wish to obtain the pride of accomplishment, then we can look at *fF* as a wish to avoid the shame of failure.

Intuitively, we can see the difference clearly. We all know people who work hard to prepare for a challenge—an exam, perhaps—because they want to do well. We know others who also may work hard, but in a tense, anxious way, not because they want to do well but because they are *afraid of doing badly*. Atkinson, however, describes the difference more specifically. It amounts to this: The person high in *nAch* and the person high in *fF* look at a challenge through different *frames*. The one looks at the positive utility of success; the other looks at the negative utility, or cost, of failure (Fig. 14-6).★

Variations in task difficulty will have very different effects in the two cases. To see why, consider again that probability of success, P_s, is an inverse measure of task difficulty. The higher P_s is, the easier the task is. Now if we undertake a very difficult task, and fail at it, we need not feel ashamed. But if we take on an easy task, and then fail at it—that is a failure indeed! We will be very much ashamed. In short, the *negative utility of failure*—the cost of failure, or C_f—will be directly proportional to P_s, the likelihood of success.

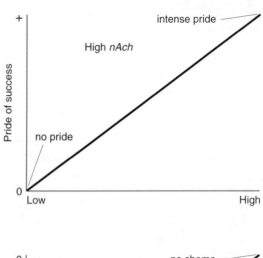

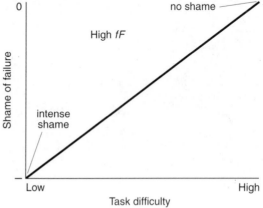

Figure 14-6 How persons with high *nAch* and high *fF* frame the utilities of success or failure at tasks of varying difficulty.

★For most of the studies in this literature, *fF* is measured by a questionnaire—for example, one or another of the many anxiety scales that have been constructed. Then the anxiety score, as an estimate of *fF*, is subtracted from the *nAch* score, which usually is measured projectively as in McClelland's work. We then know whether *fF* is greater than, or less than, *nAch*.

How then can a high *fF* person maximize expected utility—or minimize expected utility? In our decision-theory format, such a person wants negative expected utility—the probability of failure, P_f, times the cost of failure, C_f—to be as low as possible.

Well, as P_s rises, the likelihood of failure (P_f) goes down. But the cost of failure, C_f, rises. We can show this simply by letting $C_f = P_s$. So, our fearful subject should choose a task where ($P_f \times P_s$) is lowest.

But P_f is simply $1 - P_s$, so we want to *minimize* the expression: $P_s \times (1 - P_s)$.

Now we saw above that that expression is *maximized* when $P_s = .50$—that is, when the likelihood of success and of failure are about even. To *minimize* it, we should *avoid* tasks in which we have about an even chance to succeed. Instead, we should choose tasks that are either very easy or very difficult—either sure wins (P_s near 1), or sure losses (P_s near 0). Either way, we avoid the shame of failure. If the task is very easy, then we can't fail. If the task is very difficult, then we need not be ashamed even if we do fail.

Putting all this together, we get this prediction: People high in *nAch* should choose tasks of intermediate difficulty. People high in *fF* should choose very easy *or* very difficult tasks, and *avoid* tasks of intermediate difficulty.

NACH, FF, AND FRAMING   Before moving on, let us look again at the difference between *nAch* and *fF* as a matter of *framing*. It is an instructive example of how important the framing of decisions can be.

Looking again at Figure 14-6, we might say that the high-*nAch* person frames the good news, and the high-*fF* person frames the bad news. As a result, one is maximizing and the other is minimizing the same quantity—$P_s \times (1 - P_s)$! That's because the *nAch* person sees (correctly) that pride of success, which she wants to obtain, varies directly with task difficulty. The *fF* person sees (also correctly) that likelihood of failure, which he wants to avoid, varies directly with task difficulty. The optimist sees the doughnut, the pessimist sees the hole; and both are right, but what a difference it makes!

SOME IMPLICATIONS AND APPLICATIONS   We can make more detailed predictions about achievement-related choices based on Atkinson's model, and a sizable literature has developed.[9] But even this much of the theory has some interesting implications for real-world achievement situations.

For example, college freshmen who score high in *nAch,* and low in *fF,* are likely to choose major subjects intermediate in difficulty, avoiding very easy or very difficult ones.[10] This is exactly what the theory would predict.

Again: Much has been made of the importance of *challenge* in one's occupation. A challenge, we can assume, means a situation in which one may or may not succeed, that is, one in which the probability of success is somewhere around .50. Now it is true that the high-*nAch* person should find such challenges motivating, and should welcome them. But such challenges are exactly

9. See for example Feather, 1961; Weiner, 1974.
10. Isaacson, 1964.

what the high-*fF* person seeks to avoid. A person with high fear of failure may feel threatened by such a job. The result may be anxiety and poor job performance. And this will be true even if, objectively, her chances of successfully meeting the challenge are just as good as those of the high-*nAch* person. There is evidence that this pattern of reactions does happen in the workplace.[11]

There have been many other tests of the theory, but the results are not entirely consistent. People high in *nAch* do rather consistently choose tasks of intermediate difficulty, but people high in *fF* are less consistent in avoiding such tasks. Something, it seems, is missing from the theory. But what?

There are various suggestions here,[12] but they have this idea in common: It is not enough to confront a subject with the *objective* likelihood of success or failure. We must consider what success and failure *mean* to the actor—how he will interpret them. This takes us to the relations between the achievement-motivation research and the concepts of *attribution theory* (pp. 421–22).

An Attributional Analysis of Achievement Motivation: Weiner's Theory

> I will argue now that emotions are the synapses of motivational life, joining thinking with acting . . . Each affect . . . brings with it a general program for action; affects therefore summarize the past by providing an evaluation for what has occurred and suggest a prescription for the future, cueing what should be done.
> —BERNARD WEINER
> (1986, pp. 28–29.)

In thinking about achievement research, Bernard Weiner extends our line of thinking in two ways.[13] He links the outcomes of our actions (1) to what we think about them (cognition) and (2) to how we feel about them (emotion). As to the latter, he couples achievement theory to his more general theory of emotion (pp. 471–73).

CAUSAL EXPLANATIONS FOR SUCCESS OR FAILURE   In an achievement situation, a person succeeds or fails at a task and feels happy or unhappy accordingly. But he also asks himself, "Why?" And, Weiner suggests, *nAch* and *fF* people tend to give different answers.

The high-*nAch* person tends to attribute successes to his own high ability, or to his own high effort, or both. Therefore, when such a person does succeed, the success provides information that confirms his feelings of competence and encourages further attempts to demonstrate it. So he chooses tasks of moderate difficulty, because these provide the most information, to himself and others, about his competence. On the other hand if he encounters failure, he explains it in ways that are coherent with his beliefs. If his ability is high and yet he failed, then, he decides, he must not have tried hard enough. He is likely to return to the task and try all the harder next time.

Not so the high-*fF* person. This person, Weiner assumes, is likely to believe that effort is not all that important to success. Therefore, failure is attributed to low ability. Believing this, the high-*fF* person does not welcome opportunities for success—that is, tasks of moderate difficulty—for he has no control over how well he meets the challenge.

11. Steers and Spencer, 1977.
12. For review and discussion, see Weiner, 1989; Nicholls, 1984.
13. Weiner, 1989.

In short, we can see high-*nAch* and high-*fF* persons as making different attributions for failure. The high-*nAch* individual attributes it to low effort. The high-*fF* person attributes it to low ability. In the first case, failure leads to renewed effort; in the second, it leads to giving up.[14]

MANIPULATING ATTRIBUTIONS   Weiner's ideas have been applied in a wide range of contexts.[15] We will look at only one experiment that tested his basic idea directly. If accepting challenges *(nAch)* or avoiding them *(fF)* reflects the explanations one gives for success or failure, then one ought to be able to affect the response to challenging tasks by manipulating these explanations, or causal attributions, directly.

The experimenters had their subjects perform a difficult task, in which the subjects failed on early trials. Previous to that, half the subjects were given a harmless pill (a placebo) which, they were told, would slow them down and thus depress performance. The other subjects received no pill. Within each of these groups, subjects differed as to whether *nAch* was high or low.[16]

What should happen? When a high-*nAch* subject fails at a task, he usually attributes it to lack of effort and tries harder. But this time, the pill subjects are given another explanation for their failure—the effect of the pill! Then they have no reason to think that trying harder will improve matters; you can't fight pharmacology. So high-*nAch* subjects given the pill should ease up, or even give up, and try less hard after the initial failure.

What about high-*fF* subjects? They usually attribute failure not to lack of effort, but rather to lack of ability. But this time, the pill subjects have another, external explanation for their failure—the effect of the pill! So, while the subjects who did not receive a pill should be discouraged by failure and give up—"I can't do this task"—the subjects given the pill should not be discouraged. Failure carries no shame if it's the drug's fault and not the subject's. These subjects should actually be *more* persistent if given the pill.

The results are shown in Figure 14-7. They are quite striking. In the control, no-pill condition, high-*nAch* subjects worked with vigor and improved markedly in performance after the initial failure. Low-*nAch* subjects gave up and showed little improvement. But offering a strong *external* explanation for the early failure—it's the pill, not the person—actually reversed the difference: The high *fF* subjects were *more* persistent than the high *nAch* ones.*

Clearly, achievement motivation can affect the vigor with which one chooses to work at a task after failure. But now we see more clearly the difference between Weiner's theory and Atkinson's or McClelland's. To Weiner,

14. Weiner, 1989.
15. See Fiske and Taylor, 1990.
16. Weiner and Sierad, 1975.
*Notice that the logic of this experiment is very similar to that of the Schachter and Singer experiments on emotion (pp. 468–71). We seek explanations for symptoms (Schachter and Singer) or for failure (Weiner and Sierad). In both cases, a drug may provide an adequate explanation. If it doesn't, we seek an explanation elsewhere—an external explanation in the setting (Schachter and Singer), or an internal explanation in our ability or effort (Weiner and Sierad).

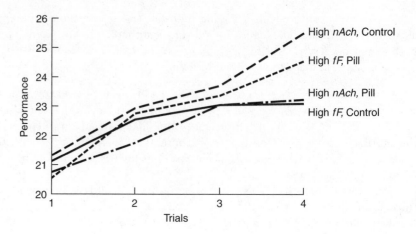

Figure 14-7 Performance on a task after early failure trials, with and without a placebo, for high-*nAch* and low-*nAch* subjects. Without the placebo pill, high-*nAch* subjects improve much more than low-*nAch* ones, but the pill reverses this difference. (From Weiner and Sierad, 1975.)

the effect of achievement motivation is not something fixed and invariable that we carry around inside us. It can depend very much on what we *think* about the situation. And manipulating what we think, as by having us swallow a placebo, can drastically change the effect of *nAch* on performance, as this experiment shows.

A Look Backward: Motive, Emotion, and Causal Analysis

Weiner's theory is a broader one than McClelland's or Atkinson's, and on three counts at least. First, he is concerned not just with what task a subject chooses to attempt on *this* occasion, but also with what the effects of the outcome will be on the *next* occasion: If a subject fails, will she try harder next time, or give up?

Second, he extends the analysis of emotional reactions to success or failure beyond the original pride/shame dichotomy. One may feel a variety of emotional reactions to a failure experience: anger at an unfair test, for example. Third, as we have seen, he links these in turn to the subject's causal analyses— why does she *think* the success or failure occurred?

Figure 14-8 shows the hypothesized sequence of events. As we see, it is an elaboration of Figure 12-11 (p. 472), and it reminds us of the three dimensions of perceived causation: locus (internal/external), stability, and controllability.

A subject attempts a task, succeeds or fails, and experiences an initial emotion positive or negative. Then she asks *why* the failure occurred. Maybe her ability is too low (internal, stable, uncontrollable). Maybe she didn't try hard enough (internal, unstable, controllable). Or maybe the test was unfair (external [to her], controllable [by someone else], and stable or not [depending on the "someone else"'s perceived intentions]). Now she will experience a more specific emotion—shame, guilt, or anger, respectively.

In addition, she will use her conclusions about causation to form expectancies about how she will do at such a task next time around. And her subsequent performance or task choice will be affected jointly by the emotions and

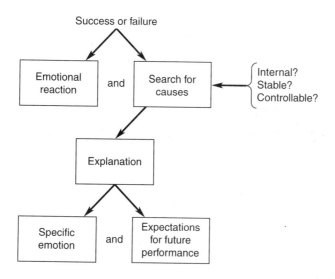

Figure 14-8   Weiner's theory of causal attribution, emotion, and subsequent performance. Compare Figure 12-11, p. 472.

the expectancies—our familiar motivational/cognitive joint influence. Looking back over this analysis, we see once again how intimate is the interaction among emotion, cognition, and motivation.

Weiner's research has extended this emotional/cognitive analysis well beyond the study of achievement motivation specifically. He has looked at how one responds to another person's failure, as a teacher might have to do when a student does poorly (compare Fig. 14-9).[17] Or, as a specific example to give you the flavor: Consider the decisions a parole board must make. Here is a

Figure 14-9   An internal, unstable, controllable causal attribution.

"Maybe they didn't try hard enough."

17. For a sampling, see Weiner, 1989.

convict, who has served X years of a Y-year sentence: Shall we release him on parole? The decision will be driven by our familiar two factors. There is the emotional one: How "bad" was the crime, and how much punishment does he deserve?—which depends largely on whether *internal* or *external* causes are seen as dominant. And there is the cognitive one: How likely is the person to offend again if we set him free?—which depends largely on the perceived *stability* of the causes. In mock parole-board experiments, it was found that by encouraging different causal conclusions about the original crime, we can influence judges' parole decisions now.[18]

HELPLESSNESS

The research we now consider began in the animal laboratory, with the study of shuttle-box avoidance conditioning in dogs. It is a fine example of (1) how animal research can give us new ways of looking at human problems and new ideas to test at the human level and (2) how different theoretical perspectives can converge.

Learned Helplessness

A shuttle box, we recall, is an experimental setup in which an animal must shuttle back and forth between two compartments of a box (pp. 248–49). The shuttling response will turn off shock (escape), or prevent it from coming on (avoidance). Either way, the animal has *control* over the situation. By escaping or avoiding, he can cause something good to happen—the shock goes off, or doesn't occur at all.

Now dogs are quite good at this task, and usually learn it with no great difficulty—*if* they begin the task from scratch, without previous laboratory experience. A particular kind of previous experience, however, can be devastating.

UNCONTROLLABLE SHOCK AND HELPLESSNESS   J. Bruce Overmier and Martin Seligman found that if dogs had been exposed to shocks that they *could not* control, *before* the shuttle-box training began, then they were much slower to learn than dogs with no such prior experience.[19] If the dogs had had that experience of helplessness before, they would often simply stand and take the shock until the experimenter rescued them. Even though this was a new experimental situation and the dogs *could* do something about the shock now, many of them made no attempt to do anything about it.

Seligman and his colleagues went on to show that the important thing about uncontrollable shock was not the shocks per se, but the fact of their uncontrollability. In one experiment, a group of dogs received shocks that they could turn off. Another group received shocks at the same intensity and pattern

18. Carroll and Payne, 1977.
19. Overmeir and Seligman, 1967.

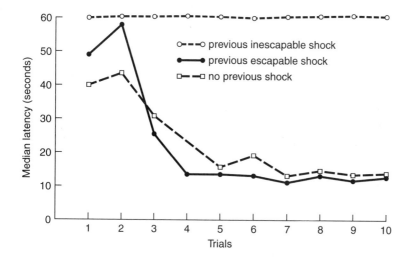

Figure 14-10   Learned helplessness in dogs. Animals quickly learned to escape shock if they had not had *inescapable* shock before, but if they had, they did not learn. On each trial, the shock was turned off after 60 seconds if the dog had not responded; therefore, a latency of 60 seconds indicates failure to make the escape response at all. (From Maier, Seligman, and Solomon, 1969.)

in time, but were not able to turn them off themselves. Later, when they were given shocks that *could* be turned off, the former group quickly learned to turn them off; the latter did not (Fig. 14-10). And this was so even when the escapable shocks were given in a new setting, that none of the dogs had experienced before.[20]

Overmier and Seligman suggested that the effect of the uncontrollable shocks was to produce **learned helplessness** in the dogs that received it. Learned helplessness amounts to a *belief* in one's inability to control a situation. The dogs came to believe that nothing they did had any effect on what happened to them. And if a dog believes that, then it may give up and lie passive even in a new situation that it could control, if only it would try.

Further work showed that learned helplessness could be produced in rats, monkeys, cats—and humans. Some human data are instructive, showing how little it takes to produce belief in one's helplessness.

In one experiment, college students were exposed to an unpleasant loud noise. Some subjects could shut off the noise by pressing a button; others could not. Then *all* subjects were given the opportunity to turn off the noise by shuttling with their fingers in a miniature shuttle box. When the obnoxious noise came on, the subject could turn it off just by moving his finger from one place to another. That's all he had to do! One would expect the subjects to discover the correct response very quickly. One group of subjects did. The others—the subjects who had had no control over the noise before—sat passively and accepted it now, and never learned the simple response that would turn it off.[21]

And, in humans as in dogs, it is the belief that counts. One study found that human subjects exposed to uncontrollable loud noise performed poorly at tasks and often gave up on them. But if the subjects believed that they *could*

20. Seligman and Maier, 1967.
21. Hiroto, 1974.

turn the noise off, even if they did not in fact do so, then these deficits were abolished.[22]

MULTIPLE EFFECTS OF HELPLESSNESS   To reiterate, the condition of helplessness can be seen as resulting from a *belief* in one's own inefficacy. One effect of this is the failure to solve problems that are solvable. Seligman calls this a **cognitive deficit.** But there are at least two other striking effects of helplessness.

First, there is **lack of initiation of action.** Perhaps that is one reason that helplessness, once established, can be terribly difficult to break up. Seligman writes:

> My colleagues and I worked for a long time without success on this problem: first, we took the barrier out of the shuttle box . . . but [the dog] just lay there. Then I got into the other side of the shuttle box and called to the dog, but he just lay there. We made the dogs hungry and dropped Hebrew National Salami onto the safe side, but still the dog just lay there . . .[23]

Second, helplessness can produce profound **emotional disturbances.** Helpless dogs may lose interest in sex, food, and play. Seligman again:

> Outside the shuttle box, too, helpless dogs act differently from nonhelpless dogs. When an experimenter goes to the home cage and attempts to remove a nonhelpless dog, it does not comply eagerly; it barks, runs to the back of the cage, and resists handling. In contrast, helpless dogs seem to wilt; they passively sink to the bottom of the cage, occasionally even rolling over and adopting a submissive posture; they do not resist.[24]

Helplessness and Depression

We see that the experience of uncontrollability can have at least three devastating effects in experimental animals: difficulty in learning, difficulty in initiating action, and emotional disturbance. Seligman was struck by the fact that each of these disturbances can also be seen in human patients suffering from **depression.**

Depression can be a terribly debilitating and dangerous disorder. Most of us go through periods of sadness and the blues, when even small tasks are just too much trouble and nothing is any fun. Usually the mood passes. But severe depression is a serious mental illness, which has been estimated to affect some 4 to 8 million people in the United States alone. A patient describes it:

> I was seized with an unspeakable physical weariness. There was a tired feeling in the muscles unlike anything I had ever experienced. . . . My nights were sleepless. I lay

22. Glass and Singer, 1972.
23. Seligman, 1975, p. 56.
24. Ibid., p. 25.

with dry, staring eyes gazing into space. I had a feeling that some terrible calamity was about to happen. I grew afraid to be left alone. The most trivial duty became a formidable task. Finally mental and physical exercises became impossible; the tired muscles refused to respond, my "thinking apparatus" refused to work, ambition was gone. My general feeling might be summed up in the familiar saying "What's the use." . . . Life seemed utterly futile.[25]

CHARACTERISTICS OF DEPRESSION   This sad description shows the characteristic symptoms of depression.

First, there is *emotional disturbance*. The state of depression is characterized by sadness, lassitude, and a hopeless outlook on life.

Second, a *reluctance to initiate action of any kind* is characteristic of severe depression:

The patient has no desire to do anything, even those things which are essential to life. Consequently, he may be relatively immobile unless prodded or pushed into activity by others. It is sometimes necessary to pull the patient out of bed, wash, dress, and feed him.[26]

Third, there is a *cognitive* deficit, difficulty in solving solvable problems or learning learnable things. One study found that even mildly depressed college students did very badly at solving anagram problems, much worse than non-depressed college students. And the more depressed they were, the worse they did.

IS DEPRESSION LEARNED HELPLESSNESS?   The symptoms of helplessness and of depression have a great deal in common. Are there common causal factors as well? Seligman, in an influential and controversial analysis, proposed that at least some depressions *are* expressions of learned helplessness. And he presented some case studies that supported the idea.

More than that, Seligman suggested that if helplessness can produce depression, other life experiences can *protect* against depression. These ideas too came from the animal laboratory. The presentation of *inescapable* shocks to dogs led to helplessness even in the face of a solvable problem later on. But if, earlier still, the dogs' *first* experience with shock had been controllable, then later inescapable shocks did not produce helplessness (Fig. 14-11). It is as if the first experience of mastery produced a belief in competence or controllability—"I can deal with this"—that later made the depressive belief—"I'm helpless" less likely. Seligman wondered whether in humans, too, early experiences of mastery and coping might immunize the person against helplessness later on.

25. Reid, 1910, pp. 612–613.
26. Beck, 1967, pp. 256–257.

Figure 14-11 Inoculation against learned helplessness. Top row: Avoidance conditioning in untrained dogs. Second row: An earlier history of uncontrollable shock leads to learned helplessness. Third row: An even earlier history of controllable shock blocks the helplessness effect.

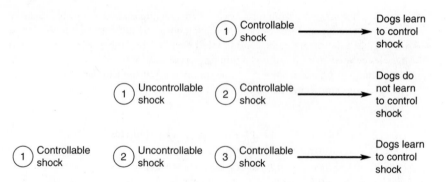

The Physiology of Helplessness

Before moving on, we should look at one more point of convergence between research in helplessness and other motivational concepts.

The helplessness theory of depression is a psychological one, founded on concepts of learning and cognition. Traditionally, it has been customary to contrast such theories with organic, or physiological, conceptions of mental illness—as if the two were incompatible. They are not.

Earlier (pp. 186–88), we looked at the brain mechanisms implicated in positive responses to stimuli—the "Isn't that nice!" system. Some researchers believe that those systems may be important in positive emotional reactions to events. Thus, certain drugs may enhance the positive effects of brain stimulation, elevate mood, *and* have anti-depressant action.

Now we have seen that Seligman identified three effects of helplessness: cognitive deficits, impaired initiation of action, and emotional disturbance. And earlier, we saw that damage to the lateral hypothalamic area can interrupt the ascending reward and/or arousal systems of the brain, producing *akinesia*—impaired initiation of action. It can also produce emotional disturbances, hard to see in rats but quite apparent in dogs:

> The dogs [with hypothalamic damage] were sad, indifferent, did not jump, did not play, did not greet their experimenters. The general look of deep sadness was very striking and reminiscent of patients during the depressive state or schizophrenia. *Nothing is worth an effort.*[27]

Thus we see deficits in initiation of movement—akinesia—and emotional disturbances, after such damage to the brain. Finally, if we look for cognitive deficits we find those too! Rats with damage to the lateral hypothalamic area are retarded in learning situations.[28] All three symptoms of helplessness and depression can be produced by lateral-hypothalamic lesions.

Do the *environmental* conditions that promote depression feed into this neurochemical system? Quite possibly. It has been found that inescapable shock

27. Fonberg, 1969; my italics.
28. Roth, Schwartz, and Teitelbaum, 1976.

caused an actual reduction of certain neurotransmitters in the brain. The same shock, if it could be turned off, had no such effect.[29] It is possible that the *immediate* cause of depressive reactions may be a disturbance in brain chemistry, but that this disturbance in turn can be caused in a number of ways—by genetic abnormalities, by drugs or hormones, *or by certain experiences.*

Again: In baby monkeys, social isolation can, under certain conditions, affect not only behavior but body chemistry as well. In one study, isolation produced an increase in cortisol secretion. (Cortisol is a hormone secreted by the adrenal gland under stress; it interferes with the immune system [pp. 476–77].) Isolation also caused abnormalities in markers for norepinephrine and, in older babies, serotonin (recall that these transmitters have been implicated in depression, pp. 452–53).[30]

Research in this area is forging new links between the workings of the body and the role of psychological factors in health and disease. For example, exposure to inescapable stress has been found to suppress the action of the body's immune system. In rats, production of lymphocytes was found to be suppressed after inescapable shocks. The same amount of shock had no such effect if the rats could turn it off. In humans, various findings suggest a similar phenomenon. For example, lymphocyte proliferation is suppressed over the 6 weeks following the death of a spouse.[31]

The fact that physical stress can affect the body's defensive systems has long been known. But now we must consider not just physical or chemical stresses, or the challenge presented by disease germs. The body's defenses can be affected by more complex psychological factors as well, such as controllability or its converse, helplessness.

Helplessness Reconsidered

Seligman's original theory was a *cognitive* one, emphasizing the belief in one's helplessness. But he saw this belief as arising from certain life experiences— experiences of actual helplessness. Similarly, immunizing experiences of mastery can block the formation of such beliefs. This fits well with a *behavioristic* emphasis on the environment as the source both of pathology and of its prevention.

Since the original statement, Seligman's ideas about depression have changed. There were many reasons, but they reduce to the same considerations that led to Weiner's reformulation of achievement theory: We need to consider not just what happens to the actor, but what he makes of it, how he explains it. This is suggested by several lines of research.

WHAT HAPPENED TO POLLYANNA? In Chapter 11, we discussed the Pollyanna Principle: our apparent belief that good things are going to happen rather than bad things, and that we can make things come out well. Now we

29. Weiss, 1968.
30. Suomi, 1991.
31. Laudenslager et al., 1983.

see depressed people convinced that bad things are coming, and that they cannot avert them—even if in fact they could. Many investigators have found that depressed persons do not show the typical Pollyanna effects.[32]

For example, some studies have found that whereas the non-depressed judged themselves to have more control than they did over favorable outcomes, depressed persons judged their lack of control quite accurately.[33] In that sense, they were wiser perhaps, but also sadder, than the non-depressed; they saw the grim reality of the situation more accurately.★

As we saw earlier (p. 436), the Pollyanna Principle may offer a kind of cognitive armor against discouragement and giving-up. Perhaps depressed people, or people at risk for depression, have holes in that armor; they lack the illusions that keep the non-depressed going.[34] But why should that be?

SCHEMAS REVISITED: BECK'S RESEARCH   Aaron Beck has emphasized the characteristic *thought patterns* of depressed patients. He sees such patients as expressing not only distorted beliefs, but also logical errors that maintain those beliefs. Such patients tend to distort what happens to them in the directions, first, of self-blame, and second, of exaggeration of the negativity of events. A random misfortune, such as a car that won't start, may be interpreted not just as a car that won't start but as one more instance of the world's hopelessness and of the person's own utter incompetence. Thus depression, Beck argues, results from faulty thinking.

Although Beck's theory is related to Seligman's, they are not identical. For Seligman, depressed persons see the outcomes as independent of their actions. For Beck, they see *negative* outcomes as resulting from their actions, but not positive ones. Depressed patients are often self-despising and self-blaming. And that is a difficulty for Seligman's original theory: If one sees oneself as helpless anyway, why should one blame oneself for failure?

Beck's ideas suggest a possible answer: the cognitive coherence motive (Chap. 11). It is as if the depressed person has a *self-schema* that says, "I'm worthless; I can't do anything right; of course bad things happen to me, and that's my fault *because* I'm worthless." The person then defends that schema as he would any other—cognitive conservatism. If something bad happens, even a random event, he can assimilate it to the schema, saying: "That figures. That's the kind of thing that happens to me." If something good happens, it is attributed to luck or to someone else's efforts, and still the schema is intact—elastic attribution. Beck's "logical errors" may be instances of the cognitive distortions that underlie cognitive conservatism (see "How are schemas defended?" in Chap. 11).

32. For review see Fiske and Taylor, 1984.
33. Alloy and Abramson, 1979.
★For further discussion of the intriguing but complex issues here, see Abramson and Alloy (1981), Alloy and Tabachnik (1984), Schwartz (1981), and Taylor (1983, 1988).
34. See Taylor, 1983.

What has happened to the Pollyanna Principle, then? Perhaps it has given way to the cognitive coherence motive. The depressed person has a sharply negative image of himself, but at least it is a stable and coherent one—he may be miserable, but at least the world makes sense. Perhaps the goal of cognitive coherence motivates defense of that self-image. Such a person is doing what the student does who says, "I can't do math," but on a more global scale—he says, "I can't do *anything.*" And, in fact, this idea of a *global* schema is a cornerstone of Seligman's revised theory.

BANDURA'S SELF-EFFICACY Both Seligman and Weiner have emphasized the role of beliefs about *events.* Albert Bandura reminds us, however, that there is another important set of beliefs: our beliefs about ourselves. Specifically: *Do we believe we are capable of performing this or that action?* If so, we believe in our *self-efficacy* with respect to that action.[35]

This is a separate matter from our beliefs about the *outcome* of this or that action, were we to perform it. If I were to go out and be a world-class singer, then the *probability* is very high that I would reap outcomes with very high *utility*: applause, appreciation, and a lot more money than I make now. So if the *expected utility* is so very high, why don't I do it? Obviously, because I couldn't—not, at least, without a talent transplant.

The problem of self-efficacy introduces a complication into a decision-theoretic account of motivation. We've been able to avoid discussing it till now, because there are many domains in which it doesn't apply. Remember that decision theory developed in the first place out of the analysis of gambling games—how much might we win, and what are the odds that we will win it, if we make this or that bet? But there is no question that we are *capable* of placing the bet (or throwing the dice, or accepting another card from the dealer).

When the question *does* come up—can we perform this action?—then we must complicate the picture. Maybe we should consider the utility of the outcome, *times* the perceived probability that the act will lead to that outcome, *times* the perceived probability that we will perform the act successfully if we try (self-efficacy). Maybe the resulting number—call it subjective expected *effective* utility—is the one to attend to.★

As Bandura sees it, many of our self-*in*efficacy beliefs may limit us quite needlessly; and certain forms of behavior therapy (pp. 340–43) may address them directly. Consider the student who is afraid of snakes, believing that he

---

35. See for example Bandura, 1989.

★Actually, we could add this complication to the original theory without changing it. Suppose we are offered a game by the rich experimenter: We toss an honest coin, heads we get $10, tails we get nothing. What is the expected utility of the coin toss? Just

$$(\$10 \times .5) + (0 \times .5) = \$5$$

Let's assume that we're fully capable of tossing a coin; i.e., that the self-efficacy multiplier is unity. Then we would have

$$[(\$10 \times .5) + (0 \times .5)] \times 1,$$

which changes nothing.

cannot tolerate them anywhere around without panic. He may be taught, by modeling, encouragement, and a gradual, fear-habituating approach, that oh, yes, he can—with benefit.

Self-efficacy (or inefficacy) beliefs are, of course, schemas—"I can't abide, not just this or that snake, but any snake anywhere, any time"—and so they too are related to Beck's ideas on depressive schemas. Returning to learned helplessness, we could see it as a kind of generalized, pervasive self-inefficacy belief—in Seligman's term, a *global* one (see below).

Helplessness and Causal Attribution

In 1978, Seligman and his colleagues,[36] taking account of these and other complexities, put forth a revised theory of helplessness and depression. The revision looked in more detail at the role of cognitive mechanisms and, in particular, the role of *causal attribution*.

In a situation where one is helpless, one can give any of a number of explanations for it. These may be internal ("It's my fault I failed") or external ("Something in the situation caused me to fail"). They can be stable ("I can't do it because I lack the ability") or unstable ("I can do it, but I was tired/distracted/unlucky this time"). Finally, they can be global ("I can't do it because I can't do anything") or specific ("I can't do it because I don't have the specific skills this task requires"). We see that, within each pair, it is the first member that would feed into a self-schema of helplessness, inefficacy, and hopelessness—just the sort of self-schema Beck describes.

This brings us to the revised theory. It says that a depressive reaction to uncontrollable stress is most likely if one makes *internal, stable, and global attributions* about the causes of the stress. If a person explains a bad event by an *internal* cause ("It's my incompetence"), if he also sees the cause as *stable* and likely to persist ("I'll never be competent"), and if he believes the cause to be *global* ("I'm not competent at anything"), then these add up to a belief in his own helplessness. And further failures, caused by the helplessness belief, will be likely to occur in a variety of situations—the *self-fulfilling prophecy*.

We see at once that this revised theory reduces the early, behavioristic emphasis on *environmental events* as the source of helplessness. The theory now emphasizes *what a person thinks* about such events. This makes a great difference, not only in theory but in its implications for treatment or prevention as well. One may attempt to modify the attribution process as well as the life experiences of the individual—what he thinks, as well as what happens to him.

More recently, Christopher Peterson and Martin Seligman discuss the revised theory more fully.[37] A depressive reaction, they say, depends on two things. First, as before, it depends on the occurrence of bad, uncontrollable

36. Abramson, Seligman, and Teasdale, 1978.
37. Peterson and Seligman, 1984.

events in the environment. Second, it depends on the person's *explanatory style,* or what sorts of explanations he tends to give for bad events.★

Peterson and Seligman present an impressive array of evidence that their idea is on the right track. The following is just a sample of the findings they describe:

1. Hospitalized patients were administered a questionnaire designed to measure depressive explanatory style. It asked what sorts of explanations the person would give for hypothetical events (e.g., a broken romance) if they happened to him. In depressed patients, responses indicating a depressive explanatory style were more frequent than in schizophrenics or medical-student controls.
2. In college students, depressive explanatory style, measured earlier, was related to depressive reactions to midterm grades that were lower than the students wanted them to be. This was true whatever the wanted grade was—that is, it was just as true for a student who wanted an A and got a B, as for a student who wanted a C and got a D. Students not adopting that depressive explanatory style were not depressed after such a disappointment.
3. In a depressed patient, depressive explanations for bad events (extracted from a content analysis of the things he said during therapy) predicted his later mood swings in the direction of depression.

Learned Optimism

In more recent work, Seligman has applied the notion of explanatory style to the positive as well as the negative side. If certain explanatory styles increase the risk of depression, others might decrease that risk and, perhaps, promote success at certain endeavors where persistence after failure is important. Weiner had implied much the same thing, in noting that people high in nAch *habitually* attribute success both to their own ability and to high effort (pp. 552–54).

In a popular book, *Learned Optimism,* Seligman summarizes some preliminary evidence that this is so; for instance, insurance brokers with optimistic explanatory styles outperformed those with pessimistic ones. Moreover, explanatory styles can be extracted from the speeches of (e.g.) political candidates; and it turns out that an optimistic style of speech is associated with political success. Indeed, Seligman claims a social-science "first": the successful *prediction* of historical events before their occurrence. Just before the United States Senate elections of 1988, Seligman and his co-workers made (sealed) predictions as to the outcomes, based on the optimism implicit in the candidates'

★Notice that Weiner said the same sort of thing about *nAch* and *fF* people; they differ in the kinds of explanations for failure they tend to give. Notice too that "explanatory style" could just as well be called a causal theory or schema. It is a theory about what the likely cause is for this or that kind of event: a bad event (Peterson and Seligman) or a failure (Weiner).

speeches. Their predictions were correct for twenty-five of the twenty-nine elections.

Another Psychology of History

Findings such as these take us to a final and intriguing idea. Depressive explanations for bad events can be extracted from a questionnaire, or simply from a tally of such explanations offered by a patient during therapy. They could just as well be derived from diaries, taped or printed interviews, newspapers—or the fiction of a period, the sort of data McClelland used to assess the level of *nAch* in whole societies.

Do certain groups within societies, or even whole societies, differ from one another in the tendency to offer depressive causal explanations—internal, stable, and global ones—for bad events? Might a given group change over time in its tendency to do that? Are differences in that tendency related to the incidence of depression within a culture?

In short, we can ask whether different societies stock different explanatory T-shirts for bad events, just as McClelland's group asked whether achievement T-shirts are more prominently displayed in some cultures' schema shops than in others'.

What a convergence of ideas! Peterson and Seligman, like McClelland, see a psychology of history emerging from the study of what schemas a culture has on its collective mind—for McClelland, its preoccupation with achievement; for Peterson and Seligman, its tendency to offer certain kinds of explanations for misfortune. And both see that a society's preoccupations or explanatory styles can be assessed from the records it leaves—books, diaries, newspapers. McClelland came to this insight from the study of projective tests in humans, Seligman from the study of avoidance conditioning in dogs. Where these two scientists came from could hardly be more different. Where they are going looks very much the same.

SELF-ACTUALIZATION

The aim of life is self-development. To realize our natures perfectly—that is what each of us is here for.

—OSCAR WILDE,
The Picture of Dorian Gray

We have looked at purposive behavior in animals and humans, seeking to understand how it works. Our examples have ranged from the immediate, like getting to the goal in a maze, to the long term and diffuse, like personal achievement in one's career.

But after our specific goals are achieved, then what?

It seems that, after our practical needs are met, there is an emergence of something else—the question, "Is this all?" and a longing for something more.

In this section we will consider the view that there is "something more" or ought to be—that there are certain *goals of life itself* that are healthy and right for the human organism to pursue. We will look at the point of view known as **humanistic psychology**, as exemplified by its most influential spokesman, Abraham Maslow (1908–1970).

Maslow's Ladder of Needs

Maslow's career began with the study of animal behavior. However, he quickly grew disenchanted with the kind of psychology to which such research seemed to be leading. He saw nothing coming from it but a conception of humankind based on animals, and selfish animals at that. As he wrote, with a dig at Freud: If we must model ourselves on an animal, why pick the wolf?

During the Second World War, the best minds in Europe were fleeing to the United States to escape the Nazis. Among these were some prominent figures in psychology: Max Wertheimer, the founder of Gestalt psychology, and the psychoanalysts Erich Fromm and Karen Horney. Maslow sought out these remarkable people and learned much from them. They showed Maslow that there was a one-sidedness even in human psychology, especially in psychotherapy and the theories, such as Freud's, that arose from it. We attempt to help unhappy people. We try to treat "mental illness." But what about *health* in the positive sense? Being radiantly healthy is more than being free of disease. If that is true of physical health, why not mental health too? Are there people who are not just *normal,* but in unusual psychological *good health?*

Positive Psychological Health

So Maslow set out to study the healthiest people he could find. As he said:

> If we want to know how fast a human being can run, then it is no use to average out the speed of a "good sample" of the population; it is far better to collect Olympic gold medal winners and see how well they can do. If we want to know the possibilities for spiritual growth, or moral development in human beings, then I maintain that we can learn most by studying our most moral, ethical, or saintly people.[38]

We will have more to say about such "abnormally healthy" people in a minute. First, let us see how, according to Maslow, one gets to be that way. This brings us to his theory of human motivation.

Maslow posited a number of human needs. We have all of these needs, he says, but some come before others; there are priorities among them. Some must be satisfied before others can emerge. They are, in order:

PHYSIOLOGICAL NEEDS These needs include such obvious candidates as hunger and thirst. These *cannot* remain unmet for very long; failure to gratify them is not a neurosis (see below) but a life-threatening emergency. When unmet, they dominate our existence; the starving man may have little interest in the esteem of others or in loving relations with them.

When these needs are met, we can forget about them. Then we begin to think about safety.

38. Maslow, 1970, p. 7.

SAFETY   Freedom from danger is the next need to emerge. This need is especially apparent in children, who are objectively less able to fend for themselves than adults. In real danger, these needs can dominate adult behavior too. Then there are adults who appear to live their lives, in Maslow's words, "like spies in enemy territory"—chronically anxious and afraid.

This is especially true because threats can arise not only to life and limb, but also to one's sense of stability and order in the world. Here we make contact with the *coherence motive* (Chap. 11) as a need for a stable conception of the world and oneself. In times of disorder and uncertainty, such as existed in the 1930s in Germany, people are likely to accept the authority of a dictator who will at least maintain order. Erich Fromm, in his *Escape from Freedom,* analyzed the rise of the Nazi movement in similar terms.[39]

LOVE AND BELONGINGNESS   When both physiological and safety needs are gratified, both drop out as motivating forces. Now we can begin to seek friends, a spouse, or a group to join. We might see *attachment* as an early expression of this need.

ESTEEM   If we succeed in meeting our needs for love and friendship, the need for esteem emerges. This includes the esteem of others, and also esteem for ourselves. Both of these can come from productive and useful work. As illustrations of what their frustration can do, consider the negative self-schemas of depressed persons.

SELF-ACTUALIZATION   If all our lower needs are met, then the highest one emerges: the drive toward self-actualization. This Maslow defines as

> ongoing actualization of potentials, capacities and talents, as fulfillment of mission . . . as an unceasing trend toward unity, integration, or synergy within the person.[40]

And elsewhere:

> A musician must make music, as an artist must paint, a poet must write if he is ultimately to be at peace with himself. What a man [he meant "person"] *can* be, he *must* be. This need we may call self-actualization.[41]

To Maslow, this drive is as biologically given as any other in the human species. Psychologists have neglected it, he says, because we have focused on animals on the one hand and disturbed people on the other. Moreover, only those people who have met their other needs *can* seek self-actualization with their full energies. Such people are few, but they exist.

39. Fromm, 1941.
40. Maslow, 1968, p. 25.
41. Maslow, 1954, p. 91.

The bottom-to-top arrangement of these needs has three important implications. First, as we ascend the ladder, the needs get progressively more complex, and more characteristically human.

Second, the needs *emerge in order;* as each is fulfilled, the next one arises. But if a need at any level is frustrated, then that need will persist, and the next higher ones will not emerge.

Third, the *frustration of these needs generates pathology.* Neurosis, in particular, represents a desperate attempt to meet an unmet need. Hence, Maslow can again draw a parallel with physical health: *Neurosis is a deficiency disease.* As he says, "we 'need' vitamin C. The evidence that we 'need' love is of exactly the same type."[42]

Self-Actualized People

Only a few people become self-actualized, but it is those people who most interested Maslow, as showing what human beings are capable of becoming.

Maslow set out to identify self-actualizing, *healthy* individuals—people who were operating at full capacity, realizing their capabilities fully, being all that they could be. Among the publicly known figures he identified were Jane Addams, Albert Einstein, Sigmund Freud, Thomas Jefferson, and the Roosevelts—Franklin perhaps, and Eleanor certainly.

These remarkable people had a surprising number of characteristics in common. An abridgement of Maslow's list is as follows.

1. **Realism.** They perceive reality accurately and fully, and they accept themselves, and others, as they are. They have little need for the Pollyanna Principle or to defend against anxiety.
2. **Spontaneity.** Having no need to wear a mask, they exhibit openness, simplicity, and naturalness. They have a well-developed, non-hostile sense of humor.
3. **External, problem-centered focus.** They tend to be concerned with problems, not with themselves.
4. **Autonomy.** They do not need other people, though they can accept and enjoy them; they tend to develop deep relationships with only a few. They have a strong need for privacy. They are autonomous, setting their own goals and values rather than depending on the opinions of others. They tend to identify with humankind as a whole, rather than with any one group. They tend to accept democratic values, paying little attention to differences among nations, classes, or races.
5. **Ethical sensitivity.** Although they set their own standards of right and wrong, they are sensitive to ethical issues and aware of the ethical implications of their actions.

42. Maslow, 1955, p. 5.

6. **Openness to experience.** This quality expresses itself in creativity and productiveness, but also in a certain freshness of experience; self-actualized people can take renewed pleasure with every sunset, every encounter with a baby. More than that, self-actualized people are likely to have mystical or "peak" experiences, which Maslow describes thus:

> [F]eelings of limitless horizons opening up to the vision, the feeling of being simultaneously more powerful and also more helpless than one ever was before, the feeling of great ecstasy and wonder and awe, the loss of placing in time and space with, finally, the conviction that something extremely important and valuable had happened, so that the subject is to some extent transformed and strengthened even in his daily life by such experiences.[43]

Not that self-actualized people are perfect by any means. Maslow saw in them a tendency toward vanity, stubbornness, and shortness of temper. Moreover, the autonomy that lets them live independent lives could lead to a remoteness or even ruthlessness in their treatment of others—what Maslow calls a "surgical coldness" in, for example, cutting off unsatisfying friendships.

A Look Backward: The Structure of Motivation

Maslow's theory of motivation can be summarized as shown in Figure 14-12.

In a way, the theory is like the ones we are familiar with: until we get to the top, it is a series of negative-feedback loops. If physical needs are unmet, we try to meet them. When they are met, the next level emerges: safety needs. And so on through the need for esteem.

But the highest motive—the need for self-actualization—is a *positive*-feedback loop. This means that fulfillment does not feed back to diminish the activity of the system; it feeds back to make it greater than before. As we eat food, we want it less and less. But as we grow and develop our capacities, we want further growth and development—not less and less, but more and more!

Critique

Maslow's notion of a stepwise progression in the development of motives has become so familiar that, like Freud's repression, it often is taken to be established fact. For both concepts, we need to step back and ask: Just how well are they established? The answer is the same for both: Not well.

THE HIERARCHY   Maslow tells us that higher needs arise only when lower ones are fulfilled, so that these must in fact be fulfilled before growth to higher levels can occur. Clearly, this need not be so. People have starved themselves to make a political point. Or think about the "code of the streets" (pp. 152–53). Young men and, increasingly, young women may literally risk their lives to

43. Maslow, 1970, p. 164.

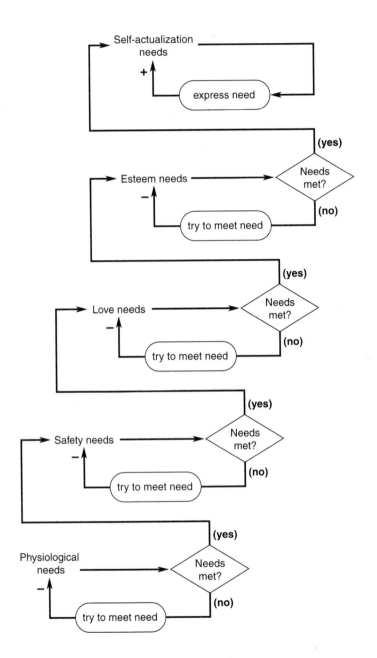

Figure 14-12   Maslow's theory of human motivation. We act to reduce needs—the motives are negative-feedback loops—except for self-actualization. That motive intensifies as we express it. It is a positive-feedback loop.

avoid or avenge being "dissed." We can say that their actions serve their needs for esteem, but then they are putting esteem needs *before* safety needs—a clear inversion of Maslow's order.

Of course it can be replied that the hierarchy is a flexible one, and Maslow himself notes that it may be possible to skip a stage, regress to an earlier one, or even (as here) bootstrap to a higher level if a lower one is unmet. That reply at first seems only to do justice to human complexity; but if we think more carefully, we see that it also makes the theory impossible to test—and of very limited use. Unless we can say something about when and how such inversions should occur, it comes close to saying, "The hierarchy holds except when it doesn't." Not very illuminating.

For the rest, it is just hard to know how much is "out there" and how much is in Maslow's head. His work does not show that self-actualizers have more peak experiences than the rest of us. It couldn't, because he included no sample of "the rest of us."

More systematic research, too, lends little support to the hierarchical structure Maslow proposes. In one study, a researcher designed a questionnaire to measure needs and their gratification in workers and managers. This questionnaire asked, for each of several categories designed to tap various needs: How much of this is there in your job now? How much should there be? How important is it?[44]

Then the extent of a person's deficiency for a given need could be calculated by subtracting how much there is from how much there should be. Now, Maslow says that the more a person is deficient in a given need, the more important it should be. And the more the needs at each level are satisfied, the more important the needs higher in the hierarchy ought to be. There was little support for either prediction in the data.

WHO IS SELF-ACTUALIZED?   Maslow selected self-actualized people to study, from among personal friends and from among public and historical figures, as showing "the full use and exploitation of talents, capacities, potentialities, etc."[45] And his data consisted "not so much in the usual gathering of specific and discrete facts as in the slow development of a global or holistic impression."[46]

There are dangers in such methods. Maslow knew this as well as anyone, but he thought the importance of the problem worth the risk. But that still means that the conclusions have to be qualified accordingly.

For example, how much have Maslow's own values intruded on his theorizing about the nature of humankind? Unkind as it may be, the question must be asked: Are Maslow's self-actualized people really the *healthiest* people, in any objective sense? Or are they just people Abraham Maslow *likes*?

44. Porter, 1961.
45. Maslow, 1970 p. 150.
46. Ibid., p. 152.

David McClelland put it well: "Who has the right to select self-actualized people: Maslow, St. Paul, or Mao Tse-Tung? . . . I feel sure that they would nominate different sorts of people and that, if psychologists analyzed the nominees, we would have some conflicting conclusions as to what the motives are which lead to maximum psychological health."[47]

THE CULTURAL CAUTION McClelland's question takes us to yet another caution about the self-actualization notion. To what extent is it an instinct-like characteristic of human nature, and to what extent is it a creation of Western culture?

Western society takes the individual person as the basic unit, the "atom" of social chemistry. Not only that, but one "atom" is often set off in opposition to others. We in this society are encouraged to excel, to be the best, to be, as we like to say, "winners." But in Japan, there is a folk saying: "The nail that sticks up gets pounded down."

The fact is that not all societies make the individual the "atom," as we do. Many Asian societies, for example, insist on the fundamental relatedness of individuals with each other. The emphasis is on being sensitive to the expectations of others and fulfilling them effectively and harmoniously—playing one's role well, as it were, rather than writing one's own script. One's identity is not something one *has* within oneself, but is defined by the network of related-nesses and expectations within the group.

For such reasons, some writers have detected a specifically American bias in Maslow's concept of actualization of oneself, free of conventions and constraints. Americans like the image of an independent, non-conforming person. But in Japan, where harmony in interpersonal relations is primary, such an attitude would be considered simply insensitive and shallow.

Where does this leave Maslow's theory? There are two things we might say. One is that he was wrong: a drive toward self-actualization is a cultural invention, not a fact of human nature. The other is that he was right: we are motivated to fulfill our potential. But then we still have to ask: Potential for what? To be independent and autonomous, or to be most effective as a participating member of one's group?

Either way, Maslow's own concept of a universal "healthy personality" might only reflect what one group of people, at one point in history, say they admire.

What shall we say, then, about the approach? Does it advance our understanding, or is it just another brand of pop psychology?

Our answer to that question does not depend on whether we agree with what is said (much less with whether we like it), but on whether the ideas are well supported by objective data. On those grounds, I myself would place

A small Texas corporation seeking to elevate productivity told its employees to look in the mirror and say "I am beautiful" 100 times before coming to work each day. Employees of a Japanese supermarket . . . were instructed to begin the day by holding hands and telling each other that "he" or "she is beautiful."★

47. McClelland, 1955, p. 33.
★Markus and Kitayama, 1991, p. 224. This paper reviews and discusses many ramifications of the issues raised here.

Maslow closer to the pop psychology end of the spectrum. That doesn't mean that what he says is wrong. It means that for now, we must return the Scottish verdict: Not proven.

This point is worth some emphasis, for some of Maslow's ideas—like some of Freud's—are heard so often that we may be tempted to think of them as established facts. The very term "self-actualization" sounds so good, presents such a flattering picture of humankind and its potential, *and* has become so familiar, that it has the sound of an idea that is generally accepted among psychologists.

It is not. It is unclear what "self-actualization" is, who (if anyone) has attained it, and how bound to Western culture it is; and the evidence that it stands at the pinnacle of a hierarchy of instinctive motives is virtually non-existent. In short, the term has received far more press than its supporting evidence warrants.

On the Other Hand

On the other hand, there is this to be said. In the 1940s and 1950s when Maslow began writing, it is true that many important questions about human nature simply were not being addressed by research psychologists. Powerfully influential were the attempts of Freud on the one hand, and behaviorists such as Clark Hull on the other, to reduce human motivation to a handful of homeostatic drives. Hence humanistic psychology was often called, by its advocates, a "third force" within psychology, to be set off in opposition to the other two—psychoanalysis and behaviorism. The "fourth force" of cognitive psychology, which by now has outgrown its parents, was still embryonic at the time.

The study of parent-infant attachment had not yet taken off; the cupboard theory, which treated it as a simple matter of conditioned reinforcement, held the day. Few people indeed were studying human love, which also was waved away as conditioned reinforcement. (You may be getting the impression that a *lot* of things were shrugged off as "just conditioned reinforcement," and you'd be right.)

It is no longer so. The systematic study of intrinsic motivation, effectance, reactance, creativity—all these are flourishing research areas now. But at the time Maslow began writing, he was one of a few voices in the wilderness who were calling, "Look at all we're neglecting!" And he had a point.

Then too, we are not confined to a sweeping evaluation of Maslow's theory in its entirety. If the theory as a whole is not well supported, still there are bits and pieces of it that may fare better.

For example, in a previous chapter, we touched on the notion of *intrinsic motivation*—performance motivated by pleasure in the task itself, rather than on external rewards offered for performing it. Think of the difference between a man who works on a car as a hobby, for the joy of it (intrinsic), rather than as a job, for the paycheck it brings (extrinsic).

Now Maslow notes that his self-actualized people were task oriented, caught up in tasks and challenges per se, and not in the extrinsic rewards of performing them—most definitely including the social "rewards" of approval by others. Might we speculate that intrinsic motivation is one characteristic of those whom Maslow called self-actualized?

There is a developing literature on intrinsic motivation,[48] and some of it has a recognizably Maslovian flavor. Intrinsic motivation has been associated with greater creativity, spontaneity, and interest in the task. And intrinsic motivation is fragile. As we saw in Chapter 8, extrinsic rewards for an activity can turn play into work, and clobber it. Anxiety about someone else's evaluation can do the same.[49]

Does intrinsic motivation reflect a more complex set of motives that cannot emerge unless simpler ones are satisfied or dormant? If so, that is reminiscent of the Maslovian hierarchy of needs.

Indeed, in thinking along these lines, we find other parallels occurring to us: think of how securely attached children will direct social exploration toward a stranger, but only if the attachment figure is around (pp. 495–97). We are speculating and perhaps straining a bit here, but are we seeing the release of social motives when, and only when, the (lower?) safety motives are satisfied? Again, a recognizably Maslovian possibility.

Or in another early study, babies were given operant control over a mobile suspended above the crib. By turning its head to one side (thereby closing a switch), the baby could make the mobile twirl for a few seconds. Babies cooed and gurgled happily when they made that happen. And this was not just a reaction to the antics of the mobile. For other, control babies, it was the experimenter who made the mobile twirl. These babies showed proper interest for a while, but little or no delight.[50]

Now, if even a little baby likes to *make things happen,* could this be a component of a more general motive toward expanding our capabilities, becoming better able to make things happen, becoming "all that we can be"? Again this is speculation, but it doesn't seem unreasonable. Suggestive too is that in hospitalized or nursing home patients, such *self-determination*—having control, being able to make things happen—can improve not only morale, but even physical health and longevity.[51]

Finally, intrinsic motivation has been associated with the experience of *"flow."* This is a perception of being totally involved in, even one with, the job one is engaged in. It involves "a 'loss of ego' and an experienced unity

48. Deci and Ryan, 1992.
49. Harackiewicz, 1992.
50. Watson, 1967.
51. For example, Langer and Rodin, 1976.

with one's surroundings."[52] Expanded to include not just a task, but a whole situation at a moment in time, could that perception contribute to the feeling of a "peak experience," with its "loss of placing in time and space"?

A Look Backward

All told, even if Maslow's theory is unsatisfactory as a general theory of human motivation, it may contain more specific ideas that will be fruitful. Moreover, Maslow called attention to problems—creativity, self-determination, and intrinsic motivation—that were in fact being neglected when his work began. If they are less neglected now, that may be in part because of his writings. Maybe we should say of him, as we said of Freud: His answers may or may not have been right, but his questions surely were.

A FINAL LOOK BACKWARD

Let's look once more at what humanistic psychology implies. If it is *good* that human beings should realize their natures and actualize their potentialities, then it follows that human nature is itself intrinsically good.

Does that have a familiar ring? It should. Back at the beginning of our journey together (pp. 27–29), we looked at the origins of motivational theorizing in Greek philosophy. And we contrasted the Freudian/Hobbesian view of Thrasymachus with the *sort of* Maslovian view of Socrates!★

So, at first glance, it appears that our journey has come full circle. It has, in the sense that we find the same problems before us now as we did way back then. But in another sense, it has not done that—and it is simply not true, as is often claimed, that we have made no progress on these issues since Socrates' time. For although the problems are the same, we see them in different ways now, and we can bring different methods to bear on them.

Is human nature fundamentally good, so that our all-too-frequent wrong actions pose a problem? Or fundamentally bad, so that the question is why we ever behave well? Which is the doughnut and which is the hole? Let's begin by looking more closely at the question.

What Does "Human Nature" Mean?

What does it mean to say that, for example, it's "human nature" to be X? (Let X be anything we wish—selfish perhaps, or aggressive.) Such a claim might mean:

52. Deci and Ryan, 1992, p. 46.

★I say *sort of* because Socrates, while anticipating Maslow in emphasizing human goodness, paid much more attention to our *intellectual* appraisal of what is good and right. For Maslow, the emphasis is on the emotional experience of *feeling* what is right for us—a big difference!

1. It is the way all people everywhere are, have always been, and must be. It is part of what being a human being means. A person who wasn't X would be like a bird without wings.

Or it might mean:

2. It is the way some, most, or all people are, under a particular set of conditions—social, economic, and environmental. These could be otherwise, may once have been otherwise, and may still be otherwise in different cultures. Where they are otherwise, some, most, or all people will probably not be X.

When we speak of "human nature," it makes a great deal of difference which of these we mean. Suppose we say "It's only human nature" about some way of behaving that is problematic—again, let it be greed or aggressiveness. If we mean this in Sense 1, we are throwing up our hands. There is nothing to do but live with it. Bees sting, cats have claws, and people are selfish (or whatever).

But if we mean it in Sense 2, there is much to be done. We will want to identify the conditions under which people are selfish and those under which they're not; and if we would reduce selfishness, we may opt to try to change the conditions under which selfish people live.

What Is Human Nature Like?—Two Case Studies

In the following paragraphs, we will look at two examples of human nature— which simply means *what human behavior is like*—under extreme conditions. These were conditions of deprivation that stressed humanness to the breaking point, conditions so severe that the mere feat of *staying alive* should have taken all that these human beings had. In one case, maybe it did, or close to it. In the other, we will see that it did not.

Be advised: You have some very rough reading ahead. But if we are to learn about human nature from the best examples we can find, as Maslow proposed, we must also learn from the worst.

CASE STUDY 1: THE IK   In 1973, the anthropologist Colin Turnbull published a powerful account of his life with "the mountain people," the remnants of a tribe in East Africa known as the Ik.[53] This tribe, before World War II, had lived a nomadic hunting-gathering existence, following the game and gathering roots, berries, and wild vegetables as they went.

As national boundaries became fixed, the Ik were excluded from their major hunting grounds, which became a national park. They were confined instead to a small, drought-blasted area that they were expected to farm. The result, quite simply, was that there was nothing to eat. To survive, the Ik had to scrounge what food they could from the land and from visitors; when this was not enough, they were reduced to theft (illegal), poaching (illegal), or death by starvation (quite legal).

53. Turnbull, 1973.

These starving people became capable of actions that seem, to us, almost inhuman in their callousness and indifference:*

> Sitting at a *di,* for instance, men would watch a child with eager anticipation as it crawled toward the fire, then burst into gay and happy laughter as it plunged a skinny hand into the coals.[54]

Even parents' concern for their children could crumble to powder under the relentless impact of starvation. Listen:

> [Nine-year-old Adupa's] parents . . . ignored Adupa, except when she brought them food that she had scrounged from somewhere. They snatched that quickly enough. But when she came for shelter they drove her out, and when she came because she was hungry they laughed that Icien laugh, as if she had made them happy . . . But that is not how she died. . . .
> She kept going back to [her parents'] compound, almost next to Atum's and the closest to my own. Finally they took her in, and Adupa was happy and stopped crying. She stopped crying forever, because her parents went away and closed the *asak* tight behind them, so tight that weak little Adupa could never have moved it if she had tried. But I doubt that she even thought of trying. She waited for them to come back with the food they promised her. When they came back she was still waiting for them. It was a week or ten days later, and her body was already too far gone to bury.[55]

It is impossible to read Turnbull's account without seeing, and sharing, his rage at what the Ik had become. And yet Turnbull reminds us that what he saw came not from any innate depravity of the Ik, but from the circumstances that were imposed on them, by their wasteland excuse for an ecology and by a government remote, indifferent, and incompetent enough to place them there. It was not always so. Among the Ik, the very old remember "a time when people were kind, when parents looked after their children and children looked after their parents."[56]

CASE STUDY 2: THE NAZI DEATH CAMPS   During the Nazi regime, the "enemies" of Hitler's Third Reich were imprisoned in concentration camps in eastern Germany and conquered Poland. These included primarily

---

*Turnbull describes the Ik in general in quite negative terms: "[H]unters frequently display those characteristics that we find so admirable in man: kindness, generosity, consideration, affection, honesty, hospitality, compassion, charity . . . [but the Ik] were as unfriendly, uncharitable, inhospitable, and generally mean as any people can be. For these positive qualities we value so highly are no longer functional for the Ik" (1973, p. 31.). These conclusions have been questioned by other field workers, whose experience with the Ik was quite different (see Wilson, 1993). The present writer is not qualified to resolve a dispute among anthropologists. Here, therefore, I present only accounts of events that Turnbull apparently witnessed directly.

54. Ibid., p. 32.
55. Ibid., pp. 131–132.
56. Ibid., p. 232.

Jews, but also political dissidents and Communists. The very names of these extermination camps, for that is what they were, are monuments to what nations are capable of—Auschwitz, Buchenwald, Treblinka.

In these camps, men, women, and children lived, and died, under conditions that stagger the imagination. Terrence DesPres has collected and commented upon accounts of death-camp experience, written later by prisoners who survived.[57]

It began in the trains—the locked boxcars—that carried prisoners eastward to the camps:

> The temperature started to rise, as the freight car was enclosed and the body heat had no outlet. . . . When dawn finally rose . . . we were all quite ill and shattered, crushed not only by the weight of fatigue but by the stifling, moist atmosphere and the foul odor of excrement. . . . There was no latrine, no provision. . . . We were to live for days on end breathing those foul smells, and soon we lived in the foulness itself.[58]

And after days in these cars without water or rest, the prisoners arrived at the camps:

> [T]he wagon doors were torn ajar. The shouts were deafening. S.S. men with whips and half-wild Alsatian dogs swarmed all over the place. Uncontrolled fear brought panic as families were ruthlessly torn apart. Parents screamed for lost children and mothers shrieked their names over the voices of the bawling guards.[59]

Prisoners were fed in amounts well below minimal requirements. Like the Ik, they were starving to death; they were supposed to. Safety was nil; one could be killed before one starved, for any reason or for no reason.

These conditions were far more extreme even than the environment of the Ik. Physiological needs were unmet; safety, moment by moment, was nonexistent. Surely all higher needs should have melted away in these prisoners. But they did not.

Little acts of generosity persisted among starving people:

> Ilse, who worked on the day shift, came back at noon. . . . She turned away from me so that I could not see what she was doing, and dug into her pocket. "I have brought you a present!" she announced triumphantly. There, on a fresh leaf, was one red, slightly mashed raspberry![60]

And larger acts of caring, requiring the last drops of energy and often the risk of immediate death—these too persisted. DesPres says:

57. DesPres, 1976.
58. Ibid., p. 53.
59. Ibid., p. 77.
60. Ibid., p. 137.

Most survivors simply found themselves helping each other, as if by instinct, as if in answer to a need. Their experience suggests, in fact, that when conditions become extreme a *need to help* arises; and there is no more terrible, nor more beautiful, instance than the way people helped each other during the days and weeks of the death marches. As the Eastern Front collapsed, camp after camp was evacuated; prisoners were driven into the winter dawn in endless columns, guarded by SS men hysterical with fear and viciousness. Whole camp populations were forced to walk across the frozen wastes of Poland into Germany, sometimes for weeks without food or even shoes. Those who fell behind or stopped for any purpose were shot, and at night many froze to death in their sleep. This last extremity pushed survivors to the limit of endurance, and here if anywhere self-interest made sense, each prisoner determined not to be dragged down now, so close to the end. But just here the testimony of survivors is full of examples of help—men and women giving a vital part of themselves, literally their last reserves, to keep each other going.[61]

One survivor reported:

My hand was frozen and the wound on it was endless torture. By now I was completely bent and dragged myself along with my two hands between my thighs. . . . A wearisome drowsiness possessed me; my knees gave way and I collapsed in the snow. . . . Someone was tugging at me and calling my name. "Let me sleep," I murmured. But the woman tugged harder, and through half-closed eyes I recognized Klari. "Please let me sleep, Klari," I begged. But she grabbed my arm and forced me to my feet.[62]

A *need to help*—in the face of starvation and immediate and ever-present danger to one's own life. What does it imply?

As with any other case study, there is the danger that we may read into the facts what we expect to find. The facts themselves, however, do tell us this much: Concern for one's fellow humans does not *have to* fall apart when homeostatic needs, and safety needs too, are unmet. Giving and helping, even at risk of one's life—these actions *can* survive, without support from the lower levels of the Maslovian hierarchy.

These are the facts. Moving on to interpret them, DesPres suggests an organization of human motives quite different from Maslow's. Physiological needs must be met to keep the body going, yes. But when we speak of actions and the motives behind them, DesPres argues, we find social motives just as basic as physiological ones. He says:

Social behavior among higher animals is very pronounced, having evolved through a process of natural selection to the present range of structures, all of which serve the cause of survival . . . in man it reaches a pitch of interrelatedness and mutual recognition which in fact constitutes, or is the prior condition for, humanness as we know it.[63]

61. Ibid., p. 132; italics in original.
62. Ibid., p. 132.
63. Ibid., pp. 143–144.

And later:

> [P]rimary aspects of the camp experience—group formation, organizing, sharing and the giving of gifts—are evidence . . . that in man social instincts operate with the authority and momentum of life itself, and never more forcefully than when survival is the issue.[64]

We have seen two examples of behavior under extreme conditions. One, the case of the Ik, shows how concern for one's fellows *can* collapse under such conditions. The other, life and survival in the camps, shows that such concern *need not* collapse even under these conditions. Which is human nature? Both are.

Studying Human Nature

But if human nature is so variable and contingent, how can we say anything about it at all? A few paragraphs ago, I suggested that we have learned to ask our questions in new ways, and bring new methods to bear on them. Let's look backward over some examples of what I mean.

NEW KINDS OF QUESTIONS   Consider some of the ways we have learned to look at our question, "Why does he/she/it do that?" First, we have learned—if we take our lessons seriously—that events need not have single causes. Multiple-input systems provide for multiple causation, and the question "Why does one do such and such?" may have many answers—even for a single such and such!

Second, we find ourselves evaluating candidates for causality in a much less either/or way than once we did. We do not ask whether we are guided by emotion *or* by reason, for we have come to see some of the ways in which emotion and cognition cooperate with each other. We do not ask whether the tendency (say) to aggress when angered is innate *or* acquired. We have learned that the taught and the untaught interact with each other, and also that *untaught* doesn't mean *unteachable*.

Third, we have come to appreciate the decisive impact of *situational* variables on behavior. The more global situation within which one lives—the culture—determines one's options at every level, from specifying what is edible and by what means (pp. 105–6), to specifying what events are grounds for anger and, where they are, how the anger may be expressed. More specific situational variables also can have decisive effects; these can make the difference between our acting like John the Indifferent, or like Joe the Caring (pp. 527–30). Time and again, we have seen them swamp the effects of personality variables like empathy—or, presumably, degree of mental health! There is every reason to think that situational factors could produce a concentration-camp guard—or a Klari.

---

64. Ibid., p. 197.

There's another way, too, in which our questions have changed. There is a certain modesty about the way we ask them now. We take smaller bites. We ask more limited questions, for which we have a better prospect of getting answers.

Thus: Are organisms inherently selfish? That is too big a question; we don't know how to design a study that would answer it. But we can ask: Are there conditions under which a creature will take steps to alleviate a fellow creature's distress? The answer is yes, as we saw in our discussion of altruism. Further studies, in babies and even in animals, suggest that such actions need not be a product of specific training.

Do humans have a need to self-actualize? That too is a big question, probably too big. But suppose we ask: Can a person get a kick out of *making things happen?* The answer is yes (pp. 575–76). And if the person is a little person, for whom culture has not yet become a major influence—then that suggests that there may indeed be an untaught tendency to enjoy having an effect. And such a tendency could certainly be a *component* of a more general tendency to enjoy exercising our capacities. Other investigations can reveal other components, as in the study of intrinsic motivation and flow (pp. 575–76).

AND WAYS OF ANSWERING THEM   Now let us turn to method. In the last chapter, we saw how both experiments and field observations in animals and humans could be brought to bear on the question: Are altruistic motives a part of human and animal nature? It is not as if the data have provided a definitive answer to that question, but they have helped us to see parts of the answer. We can be sure that more parts will be revealed by further investigation.

Look again. We have seen how the study of *attachment* has moved from the Hobbesian cupboard theory toward an almost Maslovian conception of a hierarchical instinctive repertoire: infants disposed by nature to signal their needs, adults to respond to these signals, and infants disposed to explore and investigate if a secure base is provided (effectance motives released when safety needs are met?). We have seen how a need to help can, under some circumstances, be as strong as, or stronger than, a need to eat. And speaking of eating, our understanding even of hunger has moved far beyond the simplistic way we envisioned it at first (Chap. 3).

What has made these advances possible? First, our asking researchable questions, and then, our application of systematic research methods to the questions so asked. We have turned from argument to observation and experiment, testing our understanding and learning when we are wrong (compare pp. 7–8).

In short, we are learning how to ask better questions and how to pursue investigations that can answer them. By taking small bites, asking little questions and getting solid answers, we can build up systematic bodies of data that in turn illuminate the larger issues—issues that are of fundamental importance. The issues are old, yes. But they need not be argued in a vacuum anymore.

Motivated behavior can be seen as the pursuit of imagined goals. Our goals, therefore, may be as complex as our imaginations permit, and projected as far into the future.

One such long-term goal is personal achievement. Using projective tests—cues for imagery—as his measurement device, David McClelland has asked what variables affect or are related to the striving for achievement, in individuals and in whole societies. People high in need for achievement *(nAch)* are likely to choose occupations that entail independent decision-making and rapid, concrete knowledge of results. McClelland's group has gathered evidence that across societies, and within societies over time, industrialization and economic growth are associated with the prevalence of achievement motivations.

Extending the theory, John Atkinson offers a decisional analysis of task choice. A person high in *nAch* maximizes expected utility—pride of success, times the probability of success—by choosing tasks of intermediate difficulty, where success is not impossible but is not guaranteed either. A person high in *fear of failure (fF)* should minimize expected *negative* utility—shame of failure, times the probability of failure—by *avoiding* tasks of intermediate difficulty. The first of these predictions has often been confirmed, but the second is less consistently supported. Bernard Weiner has suggested that we must also consider the individual's interpretation of success or failure—the causes to which it is attributed—and the emotions that result. The high *nAch* person may attribute failure to insufficient effort (an internal, unstable, controllable constellation of causes), feels guilt, expects success with greater effort, and tries harder. The high *fF* person may attribute failure to insufficient ability (internal, stable, and uncontrollable); she expects to fail again, and gives up. Manipulating these causal attributions changes the way people respond to failure. This kind of analysis has been extended to the study of people's reactions to the actions of others, as when a teacher must react to a student's success or failure, or a parole board decide whether to free a prisoner. In all this we see the intimate interactions among cognitions, motives, and emotions.

The study of learned helplessness began with avoidance-conditioning experiments in animals. If animals were subjected to uncontrollable stress, later on they would often fail to learn to control unpleasant events even when they could have done so. The animals appeared to develop a belief that nothing they could do would matter—*learned helplessness.* That belief interfered with learning, and it also produced emotional changes and a reluctance to take action of any kind. These three symptoms—cognitive deficits (failure to solve problems), emotional changes, and reluctance to initiate action—also characterize depression in humans. Martin Seligman suggested that human depression may reflect learned helplessness and result from the experience of uncontrollable stress.

A later version of the theory shifted the emphasis from uncontrollable stress itself, to the person's interpretation of that stress. Depression may result from a depressive explanatory style or a depressive theory about the causes of negative events. Negative events are likely to trigger depression if the person explains them as caused by his own incompetence (internal attribution) and regards this as a stable and global causal factor (the incompetence will not change and applies in many domains).

At several points, the theory makes contact with other, related ideas. Aaron Beck has pointed out the distorted belief structures (schemas) of depressed patients. Albert Bandura has pointed out that the actions we will attempt depend not only on the values of the expected outcomes, but also on our beliefs about what we can or cannot do (self-efficacy beliefs). We could see learned helplessness as reflecting a kind of stable, global belief in our own inefficacy. More recently, Seligman has explored the other side of the coin, the correlates of an optimistic explanatory style.

Depressive causal theories may characterize individuals or whole groups. And one could investigate the prevalence of such causal explanations across societies or across historical periods, much as McClelland's group investigated the prevalence of preoccupation with achievement.

Abraham Maslow has suggested that our repertoire of instinctive motives includes such complex ones as the search for esteem and love, and especially the striving for self-actualization, or the full realization of one's potential. He believes that these complex goals emerge only after our more basic needs, as for food and safety, have been met. But they are just as instinctive, just as much a part of what human nature is or ought to be, as hunger and thirst are.

There are findings that support bits and pieces of the theory. These suggest, for example, a motive for autonomy and a certain pleasure, displayed even by babies, in being able to make things happen. Intrinsically motivated activity—action performed for its own sake—has been associated with greater interest, creativity, and "flow" or task involvement, than actions performed for external reward.

However, evidence for Maslow's hierarchy of motivation is not strong. Often the priorities of motives are reversed; one may starve oneself to make a political point, or risk one's life to earn respect. His choice of self-actualized people to study may reflect his own likes and dislikes more than anything universal. Again, an autonomous, independent person may be admired in this society, but not in others in which the group rather than the individual is the social "atom." Therefore, even if we accept the notion of an inborn drive to actualize our potentials, we must ask: Potentials for what? To be independent of society, or to be sensitive and responsive to its expectations? Perhaps we could be self-actualized in either way, but the end product would clearly be different in the two cases. The notion of self-actualization may have acquired a familiarity and an aura of acceptance that it does not merit on the evidence.

Maslow's premises do ask some very basic questions about human nature, and lead us back to some of the questions with which this book began. If it is good for humans to express their nature, then it would seem that human nature must itself be intrinsically good—as Socrates argued, and opposed to the views of writers like Thrasymachus and Hobbes.

Have we, then, made no progress on such questions? I think we have made a great deal of progress. If nothing else, we see that the questions are simplistic: Human beings are capable of incredible brutality and callousness, and also of incredible unselfishness and heroism. Behavior is multiply caused, and situations are at least as powerful as any underlying "human nature" in directing behavior this way or that.

So today, rather than directing our attention to global issues of human nature, we ask more modest questions about the specific determinants of actions. We have learned a great deal, as we see when we look at how our ideas have changed about altruism, love, attachment, and even hunger.

There is much that we do not know, but we are learning how to find out. And that, perhaps, is not a bad note on which to end a book.

References

Abramson, L. Y., and Alloy, L. B. Depression, nondepression, and cognitive illusions: A reply to Schwartz. *Journal of Experimental Psychology: General,* 1981, 110, 436–447.

Abramson, L. Y., Seligman, M. E. P., and Teasdale, J. Learned helplessness in humans: Critique and reformulation. *Journal of Abnormal Psychology,* 1978, 87, 49–74.

Adolph, E. F. *Physiological regulations.* Lancaster, PA: Jaques Cottell Press, 1943.

Adolph, E. F. Urges to eat and drink in rats. *American Journal of Physiology,* 1947, 151, 110–125.

Ainsworth, M. D. S., Bell, S. M., and Stayton, D. J. Infant-mother attachment and social development: "Socialisation" as a product of reciprocal responsiveness to signals. In M.P.M. Richards (Ed.), *The integration of a child into a social world.* Cambridge, England: Cambridge University Press, 1974.

Ainsworth, M. D. S., Blehar, M. C., Waters, E., and Wall, S. *Patterns of attachment: A psychological study of the strange situation.* Hillsdale, NJ: Lawrence Erlbaum, 1978.

Ainsworth, M. D. S., and Wittig, B. A. Attachment and exploratory behavior of one-year-olds in a strange situation. In B. M. Foss (Ed.), *Determinants of infant behaviour* (Vol.4). London: Methuen, 1969.

Allison, M. G., and Ayllon, T. Behavioral coaching in the development of skills in football, gymnastics, and tennis. *Journal of Applied Behavior Analysis,* 1980, 13, 297–314.

Alloy, L. B., and Abramson, L. Y. Judgement of contingency in depressed and nondepressed students: Sadder but wiser? *Journal of Experimental Psychology: General,* 1979, 108, 441–485.

Alloy, L. B., and Tabachnik, N. Assessment of covariation by humans and animals: The joint influence of prior expectations and current situational information. *Psychological Review,* 1984, 91, 112–149.

Allport, G. *The nature of prejudice.* Cambridge, MA: Addison-Wesley, 1954.

Anand, B. K., and Brobeck, J. R. Hypothalamic control of food intake. *Yale Journal of Biology and Medicine,* 1951, 24, 123–140.

Anderson, E. *Streetwise: Race, class, and change in an urban community.* Chicago: University of Chicago Press, 1990.

———. The code of the streets. *Atlantic Monthly,* May 1994, 80–94.

Andrew, R. J. The origins of facial expression. *Scientific American,* 1965, 213, 88–94.

———. Arousal and the causation of behaviour. *Behaviour,* 1973, 48, 135–165.

Anonymous. Effects of sexual activity on beard growth in man. *Nature,* 1970, 226, 669–670.

Antelman, S. M., and Caggiula, A. R. Norepinephrine-dopamine interactions and behavior. *Science,* 1977, 195, 646–653.

Antelman, S. M., and Szechtman, H. Tail-pinch induces eating in sated rats which appears to depend on nigrostriatal dopamine. *Science,* 1975, 189, 731–733.

Arguelles, M. Money for morality. *Newsweek,* October 28, 1991, 15.

Aronfreed, J. The socialization of altruistic and sympathetic behavior: Some theoretical and experimental analyses. In J. Macaulay and L. Berkowitz (Eds.), *Altruism and helping behavior: Social psychological studies of some antecedents and consequences.* New York: Academic Press, 1970.

Aronson, E. *The social animal* (3rd ed.). San Francisco: Freeman, 1980.

Aronson, E., and Rosenbloom, S. Space perception in early infancy: Perception within a common auditory-visual space. *Science,* 1971, 173, 1161–1163.

Aston-Jones, G. Behavioral functions of locus coeruleus derived from cellular attributes. *Physiological Psychology,* 1985, 13, 118–126.

Atkinson, J. W. *Motives in fantasy, action, and society.* Princeton: Van Nostrand, 1958.

Atkinson, J. W., and Litwin, G. H. Achievement motive and test anxiety conceived as motive to approach success and motive to avoid failure. *Journal of Abnormal and Social Psychology,* 1960, 60, 52–63.

Ayllon, T., and Azrin, N. H. *The token economy: A motivational system for therapy and rehabilitation.* New York: Appleton-Century-Crofts, 1968.

Ayllon, T., and Michael, J. The psychiatric nurse as a behavioral engineer. *Journal of the Experimental Analysis of Behavior,* 1959, 2, 323–334.

Azrin, N. H., and Hutchinson, R. R. Conditioning of the aggressive behavior of pigeons by a fixed-interval schedule of reinforcement. *Journal of the Experimental Analysis of Behavior,* 1967, 10, 395–402.

Azrin, N. H., Hutchinson, R. R., and Hake, D. F. Extinction-induced aggression. *Journal of the Experimental Analysis of Behavior,* 1966, 9, 191–204.

Azrin, N. H., Hutchinson, R. R., and McLaughlin, R. The opportunity for aggression as an operant reinforcer during aversive stimulation. *Journal of the Experimental Analysis of Behavior,* 1965, 8, 171–180.

Baddeley, A. *Human memory: Theory and practice.* Boston: Allyn & Bacon, 1990.

Baker, A. H., Rierdan, J., and Wapner, S. Age changes in size-value phenomena. *Child Development,* 1974, 45, 257–268.

Baldessarini, R. J. Drugs and the treatment of psychiatric disorders. In A. G. Gilman, T. W. Rall, A. S. Nies, and P. Taylor (Eds.), *Goodman and Gilman's The pharmacological basis of therapeutics.* New York: Pergamon, 1990, pp. 522–572.

Bandura, A. *Aggression: A social learning analysis.* Englewood Cliffs, NJ: Prentice-Hall, 1973.

———. Human agency in social cognitive theory. *American Psychologist,* 1989, 44, 1175–1184.

Barash, D. *The whisperings within.* New York: Harper & Row, 1979.

Bard, P., and Mountcastle, V. B. Some forebrain mechanisms involved in the expression of rage with special reference to suppression of angry behavior. *Research Publications of the Association for Research in Nervous and Mental Disease,* 1948, 27, 362–404.

Bard, P., and Rioch, D. McK. A study of four cats deprived of neocortex and additional portions of the forebrain. *Bulletin of The Johns Hopkins Hospital,* 1937, 60, 73–147.

Barfield, R. J., and Sachs, B. D. Sexual behavior: Stimulation by painful electrical shock to skin in male rats. *Science,* 1968, 161, 392–395.

Barker, R. G., Dembo, T., and Lewin, K. Frustration and regression: An experiment with young children. *University of Iowa Studies in Child Welfare,* 1941, 18, 1–314.

Barkow, J. H., Cosmides, L., and Tooby, J. (Eds.) *The adapted mind: Evolutionary psychology and the generation of culture.* New York: Oxford University Press, 1992.

Barlow, D. H., Agras, W. S., Leitenberg, H., Callahan, E. J., and Moore, R. C. Case histories and shorter communications. *Behaviour Research and Therapy,* 1972, 10, 411–415.

Barnett, S. A. *Modern Ethology.* New York: Oxford University Press, 1981.

Baron, R. A. *Human aggression.* New York: Plenum, 1977.

Bateson, P. P. G. The characteristics and context of imprinting. *Biological Reviews,* 1966, 41, 177–220.

Batson, D. C., and Shaw, L. L. Evidence for altruism: Toward a pluralism of prosocial motives. *Psychological Inquiry,* 1991, 2, 107–122.

Baum, A., and Singer, J. E. Psychosocial aspects of health, stress, and illness. In A. H. Hastorf and A. M. Isen (Eds.), *Cognitive social psychology.* New York: Elsevier/North-Holland, 1982.

Baumeister, R. F., and Cairns, K. J. Repression and self-presentation: When audiences interfere with self-deceptive strategies. *Journal of Personality and Social Psychology,* 1992, 62, 851–862.

Baumeister, R. F., Heatherton, T. F., and Tice, D. M. When ego threats lead to self-regulation failure: Negative consequences of high self-esteem. *Journal of Personality and Social Psychology,* 1993, 64, 141–156.

Baumeister, R. F., and Tice, D. M. Role of self-presentation and choice in cognitive dissonance under forced compliance: Necessary or sufficient causes? *Journal of Personality and Social Psychology,* 1984, 436, 5–13.

Baumeister, R. F., Wotman, S. R., and Stillwell, A. M. Unrequited love: On heartbreak, anger, guilt, scriptlessness, and humiliation. *Journal of Personality and Social Psychology,* 1993, 64, 377–394.

Beach, F. A. *Characteristics of masculine "sex drive."* In M. R. Jones (Ed.)., Nebraska Symposium on Motivation: 1956. Lincoln, NE: University of Nebraska Press, 1956.

Beck, A. T. *Depression: Clinical, experimental, and theoretical aspects.* New York: Hoeber, 1967.

————. *Cognitive therapy and emotional disorders.* New York: International Universities Press, 1976.

Bell, R., and Harper, L. *Child effects on adults.* Hillsdale, NJ: Lawrence Erlbaum Associates, 1977.

Bell, S. M., and Ainsworth, M. D. S. Infant crying and maternal responsiveness. *Child Development,* 1972, 43, 1171–1190.

Belsky, J., and Cassidy, J. Attachment: Theory and evidence. In M. Rutter, D. Hay, and S. Baron-Cohen (Eds.), *Developmental principles and clinical issues in psychology and psychiatry.* Oxford, England: Blackwell, in press.

Bem, D. J. Self-perception: An alternative interpretation of cognitive dissonance phenomenon. *Psychological Review,* 1967, 74, 183–200.

————. Self-perception theory. In L. Berkowitz (Ed.), *Advances in experimental social psychology* (Vol. 6). New York: Academic Press, 1972.

Bem, D. J., and McConnell, H. K. Testing the self-perception explanation of dissonance phenomena: On the salience of premanipulation attitudes. *Journal of Personality and Social Psychology,* 1970, 14, 23–31.

Berkowitz, L. Aversive conditions as stimuli to aggression. In L. Berkowitz (Ed.), *Advances in experimental social psychology* (Vol. 15). New York: Academic Press, 1982.

Berlyne, D. E. Novelty, complexity, and hedonic value. *Perception and Psychophysics,* 1970, 8, 279–286.

————. *Aesthetics and psychobiology.* Englewood Cliffs, NJ: Prentice-Hall, 1971.

Bermant, G. Sexual behavior: Hard times with the Coolidge Effect. In M. H. Siegel and H. P. Zeigler (Eds.), *Psychological research: The inside story.* New York: Harper & Row, 1976.

Bernstein, I. L. Learned taste aversions in children receiving chemotherapy. *Science,* 1978, 200, 1302–1303.

Berscheid, E. Emotion. In H. H. Kelley et al., *Close relationships.* San Francisco: Freeman, 1983.

Berscheid, E., and Walster, E. H. *Interpersonal attraction.* Reading, MA: Addison-Wesley, 1978.

Birch, L. L., Birch, D., Marlin, D., and Kramer, L. Effects of instrumental eating on children's food preferences. *Appetite,* 1982, 3, 125–134.

Birdsell, J. B. *Human evolution: An introduction to the new physical anthropology* (2nd ed.). Chicago: Rand McNally, 1975.

Blass, E. M., and Epstein, A. N. A lateral preoptic osmosen-sitive zone for thirst in the rat. *Journal of Comparative and Physiological Psychology,* 1971, 76, 378–394.

Blass, E. M., and Hall, W. G. Drinking termination: Interactions among hydrational, orogastric, and behavioral controls in rats. *Psychological Review,* 1976, 83, 356–374.

Blass, E. M., and Kraly, F. S. Medial forebrain bundle lesions: Specific loss of feeding to decreased glucose utilization in rats. *Journal of Comparative and Physiological Psychology,* 1974, 86, 679–692.

Blass, E. M., Nussbaum, A. E., and Hanson, D. G. Septal hyperdipsia: Specific enhancement of drinking to angiotensin in rats. *Journal of Comparative and Physiological Psychology,* 1974, 81, 422–439.

Blass, E. M., and Shite, D. J. Some comparisons among the calming and pain-relieving effects of sucrose, fructose, and lactose in infant rats. *Chemical Senses,* 1994, 19, 239–249.

Blass, E. M., and Smith, B. A. Differential effects of sucrose, fructose, glucose, and lactose on crying in 1- to 3-day-old human infants: Qualitative and quantitative considerations. *Developmental Psychology,* 1992, 28, 804–810.

Bolles, R. C. Species-specific defense reactions and avoidance learning. *Psychological Review,* 1970, 77, 32–48.

Booth, D. A. Conditioned satiety in the rat. *Journal of Comparative and Physiological Psychology,* 1972, 81, 457–471.

Booth, D. A., and Davis, J. D. Gastrointestinal factors in the acquisition of oral sensory control of satiation. *Physiology and Behavior,* 1973, 11, 23–29.

Bornstein, R. F., and D'Agostino, P. R. The attribution and discounting of perceptual fluency: Preliminary tests of a perceptual fluency/attributional model of the mere exposure effect. *Social Cognition,* 1994, 12, 103–128.

Boskind-White, M., and White, W. C. *Bulimarexia: The binge/purge cycle.* New York: Norton, 1983.

Bower, G. H. Emotional mood and memory. *American Psychologist,* 1981, 36, 129–148.

Bower, G. H., and Cohen, P. R. Emotional influences in memory and thinking: Data and theory. In M. S. Clark and S. T. Fiske (Eds.), *Affect and cognition: The 17th annual Carnegie symposium on cognition.* Hillsdale, NJ: Lawrence Erlbaum, 1982.

Bowlby, J. *Attachment and loss.* Vol. 1: *Attachment.* New York: Basic Books, 1969.

Brain, P. F. Steroidal influences on aggressiveness. In J. Obiols, C. Ballus, E. Gonzales Monclus, and J. Pujol (Eds.), *Biological psychiatry today.* Amsterdam: Elsevier/North-Holland, 1979.

Breland, K., and Breland, M. The misbehavior of organisms. *American Psychologist,* 1961, 16, 681–684.

Brobeck, J. R., Tepperman, J., and Long, C. N. H. Experimental hypothalamic hyperphagia in the albino rat. *Yale Journal of Biology and Medicine,* 1943, 15, 831–853.

Brooks, J., and Lewis, M. Infants' responses to strangers: Midget, adult, and child. *Child Development,* 1976, 47, 323–332.

Brown, P., and Jenkins, H. M. Autoshaping of the pigeon's keypeck. *Journal of the Experimental Analysis of Behavior,* 1968, 11, 1–8.

Brown, R. *Social psychology.* New York: Free Press, 1965.

Brown, R., and Herrnstein, R. J. *Psychology.* Boston: Little, Brown, 1975.

Brownell, K. D. The addictive disorders. In C. M. Franks, B. T. Wilson, P. C. Kendall, and K. D. Brownell, *Annual review of behavior therapy: Theory and practice* (Vol. 8). New York: Guilford Press, 1982.

Brownell, K. D., Greenwood, M. R. C., Stellar, E., and Shrager, E. E. The effects of repeated cycles of weight loss and regain in rats. *Physiology and Behavior,* 1986, 38, 459–464.

Bruch, H. *Eating disorders: Obesity, anorexia nervosa, and the person within.* New York: Basic Books, 1973.

———. *The golden cage: The enigma of anorexia nervosa.* Cambridge, MA: Harvard University Press, 1978.

Brumberg, J. J. *Fasting girls: The history of anorexia nervosa.* Cambridge, MA: Harvard University Press, 1988.

Bruner, J. S., and Goodman, C. C. Value and need as organizing factors in perception. *Journal of Abnormal and Social Psychology,* 1947, 42, 33–44.

Buck, R. Nonverbal behavior and the theory of emotion: The facial feedback hypothesis. *Journal of Personality and Social Psychology,* 1980, 38, 811–824.

Bugelski, B. R. Extinction with and without sub-goal reinforcement. *Journal of Comparative Psychology,* 1938, 26, 121–134.

Byrne, D. Repression-sensitization as a dimension of personality. In B. A. Maher (Ed.), *Progress in experimental personality research.* New York: Academic Press, 1964.

Cabanac, M. Physiological role of pleasure. *Science,* 1971, 173, 1103–1107.

Cacioppo, J. T. Effects of exogenous changes in heart rate on facilitation of thought and resistance to persuasion. *Journal of Personality and Social Psychology,* 1979, 37, 489–498.

Caggiula, A. R., and Hoebel, B. G. "Copulation-reward site" in the posterior hypothalamus. *Science,* 1966, 153, 1284–1285.

Campbell, B. A. Absolute and relative preference thresholds for hungry and satiated rats. *Journal of Comparative and Physiological Psychology,* 1958, 51, 795–799.

Campbell, C. S., and Davis, J. D. Licking rate of rats reduced by intraduodenal and intraportal glucose infusion. *Physiology and Behavior,* 1974, 12, 357–365.

Campbell, J. P., and Pritchard, R. D. Motivation theory in industrial and organizational psychology. In M. D. Dunnette (Ed.), *Handbook of industrial and organizational psychology.* Chicago: Rand McNally, 1976.

Cannon, W. B. *Bodily changes in pain, hunger, fear and rage.* New York: Appleton, 1929.

———. *The wisdom of the body.* New York: Norton, 1939.

Carlson, A. J. *The control of hunger in health and disease.* Chicago: University of Chicago Press, 1916.

Carlson, N. R. *Physiology of behavior* (5th ed.). Needham Heights, MA.: Allyn and Bacon, 1994.

Carnegie, D. *How to win friends and influence people.* New York: Simon & Schuster, 1936.

Carroll, J. S., and Payne, J. W. Judgments about crime and the criminal: A model and method for investigating parole decision. In B. D. Sales (Ed.), *Prospectives in law and psychology* (Vol. 1: *The criminal justice system*). New York: Plenum, 1977.

Catania, A. C. *Learning* (2nd ed.). Englewood Cliffs, NJ: Prentice-Hall, 1979.

Catania, A. C., Matthews, B. A., and Shimoff, E. Instructed versus shaped human verbal behavior: Interactions with nonverbal responding. *Journal of the Experimental Analysis of Behavior,* 1982, 38, 233–248.

Chaiken, S. Heuristic versus systematic information processing and the use of source versus message cues in persuasion. *Journal of Personality and Social Psychology,* 1980, 39, 752–766.

Chapman, L. J., and Chapman, J. P. Genesis of popular but erroneous diagnostic observations. *Journal of Abnormal Psychology,* 1969, 72, 193–204.

Cheney, D. L., and Seyfarth, R. M. Truth and deception in animal communication. In C. A. Ristau (Ed.), *Cognitive ethology: The minds of other animals.* Hillsdale, NJ: Lawrence Erlbaum, 1991, pp. 127–151.

Cohen, A. R. An experiment on small rewards for discrepant compliance and attitude change. In J. W. Brehm and A. R. Cohen (Eds.), *Explorations in cognitive dissonance.* New York: Wiley, 1962.

Cohen, C. E. Person categories and social perception: Testing some boundaries of the processing effects of prior knowledge. *Journal of Personality and Social Psychology,* 1981, 40, 441–452.

Cohen, S., Evans, G., Krantz, D., Stokols, D., and Kelly, S. Aircraft noise and children: Longitudinal and cross-sectional evidence of adaptation to noise and the effectiveness of noise abatement. *Journal of Personality and Social Psychology,* 1981, 40, 331–349.

Cohen, S., Tyrrell, D. A. J., and Smith, A. P. *New England Journal of Medicine,* 1991, 325, 606–612.

Cohn, C., and Joseph, D. Influence of body weight and body fat on appetite of "normal" lean and obese rats. *Yale Journal of Biology and Medicine,* 1962, 34, 598–607.

Colwill, R. M., and Rescorla, R. A. Postconditioning devaluation of a reinforcer affects instrumental responding. *Journal of Experimental Psychology: Animal Behavior Processes,* 1985, 11, 120–132.

Cook, M., and Mineka, S. Selective associations in the observational conditioning of fear in rhesus monkeys. *Journal of Experimental Psychology: Animal Behavior Processes,* 1990, 16, 372–389.

Corbit, J. D., and Stellar, E. Palatability, food intake, and obesity in normal and hyperphagic rats. *Journal of Comparative and Physiological Psychology,* 1964, 58, 63–67.

Cowles, J. T. Food-tokens as incentive for learning by chimpanzees. *Comparative Psychology Monographs,* 1937, 14, No. 5.

Craighead, L. W., Stunkard, A. J., and O'Brien, R. Behavior therapy and pharmacotherapy for obesity. *Archives of General Psychiatry,* 1981, 38, 763–768.

Crews, F. The unknown Freud. *New York Review,* November 18, 1993, 55–66.

Curtiss, S. *Genie. A psycholinguistic study of a modern-day "wild child."* New York: Academic Press, 1977.

Damasio, H., Grabowski, T., Frank, R., Galaburda, A. M., and Damasio, A. R. The return of Phineas Gage: Clues about the brain from the skull of a famous patient. *Science,* 1994, 264, 1102–1105.

Damon, W. *The moral child.* New York: Free Press, 1988.

D'Andrade, R. Schemas and motivation. In R. D'Andrade and C. Strauss (Eds.), *Human motives and cultural models.* Cambridge, England: Cambridge University Press, 1992, pp. 23–44.

D'Andrade, R., and Strauss, C. (Eds.). *Human motives and cultural models.* Cambridge, England: Cambridge University Press, 1992.

Darwin, C. *The origin of species.* 1859.

———. *The expression of the emotions in man and animals.* London: Murray, 1872 (republished: Chicago: University of Chicago Press, 1965).

Davenport, W. Sexual patterns and their regulation in a society of the Southwest Pacific. In F. Beach (Ed.), *Sex and behavior.* New York: Wiley, 1965.

Davidson, J. M. Activation of the male rat's sexual behavior by intracerebral implantation of androgen. *Endocrinology,* 1966, 79, 783–794.

Davidson, J. M., Camargo, C. A., and Smith, E. R. Effects of androgen on sexual behavior in hypogonadal men. *Journal of Clinical Endocrinology and Metabolism,* 1979, 48, 955–958.

Davidson, R. J. Emotion and affective style: Hemispheric substrates. *Psychological Science,* 1992, 3, 39–43.

Davis, K. E., and Jones, E. E. Changes in interpersonal perception as a means of reducing cognitive dissonance. *Journal of Abnormal and Social Psychology,* 1960, 61, 402–410.

Davison, G. C. Systematic desensitization as a counterconditioning process. *Journal of Abnormal Psychology,* 1968, 73, 91–99.

Dawes, R. *Rational choice in an uncertain world.* San Diego, CA: Blackwell, 1988.

Dawkins, R. *The selfish gene.* New York: Oxford University Press, 1976.

DeCaro, G., Epstein, A. N., and Massi, M. *The physiology of thirst and sodium appetite.* New York: Plenum, 1986.

Deci, E. L., and Ryan, R. M. The initiation and regulation of intrinsically motivated learning and achievement. In A. K. Boggiano and T. S. Pittman (Eds.), *Achievement and motivation: A social-developmental perspective.* Cambridge, England: Cambridge University Press, 1992, pp. 9–36.

Dennett, D. C. *Brainstorms.* New York: Bradford Books, 1978.

deSilva, P., Rachman, S., and Seligman, M. E. P. Prepared phobias and obsessions: Therapeutic outcome. *Behavior Research and Therapy,* 1977, 15, 54–77.

DesPres, T. *The survivor: An anatomy of life in the death camps.* New York: Oxford University Press, 1976.

Dethier, V. G. Feeding behavior in the blowfly. In D. S. Lehrman, R. S. Hinde, and E. Shaw (Eds.), *Advances in the study of behavior.* New York: Academic Press, 1969.

———. *The hungry fly.* Cambridge, MA: Harvard University Press, 1976.

Deutsch, J. A. *The structural basis of behavior.* Chicago: University of Chicago Press, 1960.

———. Food intake: Gastric factors. In E. M. Stricker (Ed.), *Handbook of Behavioral Neurobiology* (Vol. 10: *Neurobiology of food and fluid intake*). New York: Plenum, 1990, pp. 151–182.

Deutsch, J. A., Young, W. G., and Kalogeris, T. J. The stomach signals satiety. *Science,* 1978, 201, 165–167.

Dion, K. Physical attractiveness and evaluations of children's transgressions. *Journal of Personality and Social Psychology,* 1972, 24, 207–213.

Dion, K., Berscheid, E., and Walster, E. What is beautiful is good. *Journal of Personality and Social Psychology,* 1972, 24, 285–290.

Dollard, J., and Miller, N. E. *Personality and psychotherapy.* New York: McGraw-Hill, 1950.

Drewnowski, A. Taste and food preferences in human obesity. In E. D. Capaldi and T. L. Powley (Eds.), *Taste, experience, and feeding*. Washington, DC: American Psychological Association, 1990, pp. 227–240.

Drickamer, L. C., and Vessey, S. H. *Animal behavior: Concepts, processes, and methods*. Boston: Willard Grant, 1982.

Dunham, P. The nature of reinforcing stimuli. In W. K. Honig and J. E. R. Staddon (Eds.), *Handbook of operant behavior*. Englewood Cliffs, NJ: Prentice-Hall, 1977.

Dunn, J. *The beginnings of social understanding*. Oxford: Harcourt Brace Jovanovich, 1988.

Dunnett, S. B., Bjorkland, A., and Stenevi, U. Transplantation-induced recovery from brain lesions: A review of the nigrostriatal model. In R. B. Wallace and G. P. Das (Eds.), *Neural transplantation research*. New York: Springer-Verlag, 1983.

Dutton, D. G., and Aron, A. P. Some evidence for heightened sexual attraction under conditions of high anxiety. *Journal of Personality and Social Psychology*, 1974, 30, 510–517.

Ebbesen, E., Duncan, B., and Konecni, V. Effects of content of verbal aggression on future verbal aggression: A field experiment. *Journal of Experimental Social Psychology*, 1975, 11, 192–204.

Eibl-Eibesfeldt, I. The interactions of unlearned behaviour patterns and learning in mammals. In J. F. Delafresnaye (Ed.), *Brain mechanisms and learning*. Oxford: Blackwell Scientific, 1961.

———. *Ethology: The biology of behavior*. New York: Holt, Rinehart & Winston, 1970.

———. The expressive behaviour of the deaf and blind born. In M. von Cranach and I. Vine (Eds.), *Non-verbal behaviour and expressive movements*. London: Academic Press, 1972.

Einhorn, H. J. Learning from experience and suboptimal rules in decision making. In D. Kahneman, P. Slovic, and A. Tversky (Eds.), *Judgment under uncertainty: Heuristics and biases*. New York: Cambridge University Press, 1982.

Ekman, P. Cross-cultural studies of facial expression. In P. Ekman (Ed.), *Darwin and facial expression*. New York: Academic Press, 1973.

———. Biological and cultural contributions to body and facial movement. In J. Blacking (Ed.), *The anthropology of the body*. New York: Academic Press, 1977.

———. *Telling lies*. New York: Norton, 1985.

———. Facial expressions of emotion: New findings, new questions. *Psychological Science*, 1992, 3, 34–38.

Ekman, P., and Friesen, W. V. Constants across culture in the face and emotion. *Journal of Personality and Social Psychology*, 1971, 17, 124–129.

———. *Unmasking the face*. Englewood Cliffs, NJ: Prentice-Hall, 1975.

Elner, R. W., and Hughes, R. N. Energy maximization in the diet of the shore crab, *Carcinus maenas*. *Journal of Animal Ecology*, 1978, 170, 103–116.

Epstein, A. N. Water intake without the act of drinking. *Science*, 1960, 131, 497–498.

———. The physiology of thirst. In D. W. Pfaff (Ed.), *The physiological mechanisms of motivation*. New York: Springer-Verlag, 1982.

———. Instinct and motivation as explanations for complex behavior. In D. W. Pfaff (Ed.), *Physiological mechanisms of motivation*. New York: Springer-Verlag, 1982, pp. 25–58.

Epstein, A. N., Fitzsimons, J. T., and Rolls, B. J. Drinking induced by injection of angiotensin into the brain of the rat. *Journal of Physiology (London)*, 1970, 210, 474.

Epstein, A. N., and Teitelbaum, P. Specific loss of the hypoglycemic control of feeding in recovered lateral rats. *American Journal of Physiology*, 1967, 213, 1159–1167.

Epstein, Y. Crowding, stress and human behavior. *Journal of Social Issues*, 1981, 37, 126–145.

Erdelyi, M. H. A new look at the new look: Perceptual defense and vigilance. *Psychological Review*, 1974, 81, 1–25.

———. *Psychoanalysis: Freud's cognitive psychology*. New York: Freeman, 1985.

Erickson, C., and Lehrman, D. Effect of castration of male ring doves upon ovarian activity of females. *Journal of Comparative and Physiological Psychology*, 1964, 58, 164–166.

Ernits, T., and Corbit, J. D. Taste as a dipsogenic stimulus. *Journal of Comparative and Physiological Psychology*, 1973, 83, 27–31.

Everitt, B. J., and Herbert, J. The effects of implanting testosterone propionate into the central nervous system on the sexual behaviour of adrenalectomized female rhesus monkeys. *Brain Research*, 1975, 86, 109–120.

Fantino, E. Conditioned reinforcement: Choice and information. In W. K. Honig and J. E. R. Staddon (Eds.), *Handbook of operant behavior*. Englewood Cliffs, NJ: Prentice-Hall, 1977.

Fantino, E., and Logan, C. A. *The experimental analysis of behavior: A biological perspective*. San Francisco: Freeman, 1979.

Fantino, M., Baigts, F., Cabanac, M., and Apfelbaum, M. Effects of an overfeeding regimen—the affective component of the sweet sensation. *Appetite*, 1983, 4, 155–164.

Fausto-Sterling, A. *Myths of gender: Biological theories about women and men*. New York: Basic Books, 1985.

Feather, N. T. The relationship of persistence at a task to expectation of success and achievement-related motives. *Journal of Abnormal and Social Psychology*, 1961, 63, 552–561.

Fedorchak, P. M., and Bolles, R. C. Nutritive expectancies mediate cholecystokinin's suppression-of-intake effect. *Behavioral Neuroscience*, 1988, 102, 451–455.

Feingold, B. D., and Mahoney, M. J. Reinforcement effects on intrinsic interest: Undermining the overjustification hypothesis. *Behavior Therapy*, 1975, 6, 367–377.

Fenichel, O. *The psychoanalytic theory of neurosis*. New York: Norton, 1945.

Festinger, L., and Carlsmith, J. M. Cognitive consequences of forced compliance. *Journal of Abnormal and Social Psychology*, 1959, 58, 203–210.

Festinger, L., Riecken, H. W., and Schachter, S. *When prophecy fails*. Minneapolis: University of Minnesota Press, 1956.

Fishbein, M., and Ajzen, I. *Belief, attitude, intention, and behavior: An introduction to theory and research*. Reading, MA: Addison-Wesley, 1975.

Fisher, A. E. Effects of stimulus variation on sexual satiation in the male rat. *Journal of Comparative and Physiological Psychology*, 1962, 55, 614–620.

Fiske, S. T. Social cognition and affect. In J. Harvey (Ed.), *Cognition, social behavior, and the environment*. Hillsdale, NJ: Lawrence Erlbaum, 1981.

———. Schema-triggered affect: Applications to social perception. In M. S. Clark and S. T. Fiske (Eds.), *Affect and cognition: The 17th annual Carnegie symposium on cognition*. Hillsdale, NJ: Lawrence Erlbaum, 1982.

Fiske, S. T., and Taylor, S. E. *Social cognition (2nd ed.)*. Reading, MA: Addison-Wesley, 1990.

Fitzsimons, J. T. Drinking by rats depleted of body fluid without increase in osmotic pressure. *Journal of Physiology, (London)*, 1961, 159, 297–309.

———. The role of a renal thirst factor in drinking induced by extracellular stimuli. *Journal of Physiology (London)*, 1969, 201, 349–369.

Fitzsimons, J. T., and LeMagnen, J. Eating as a regulatory control of drinking in the rat. *Journal of Comparative and Physiological Psychology*, 1969, 67, 273–283.

Flynn, J. P., Vanegas, H., Foote, W., and Edwards, S. Neural mechanisms involved in a cat's attack on a rat. In R. Whalen, R. F. Thompson, M. Verseano, and N. M. Weinberger (Eds.), *The neural control of behavior*. New York: Academic Press, 1970.

Fonberg, E. The role of the hypothalamus and amygdala in food intake, alimentary motivation and emotional reac-

tions. *Acta Biologiae Experimentalis (Warsaw)*, 1969, 29, 335–358.

Ford, C. S., and Beach, F. A. *Patterns of sexual behavior*. New York: Harper & Row, 1951.

Francoeur, R. T. *Becoming a sexual person*. New York: Wiley, 1982.

Frank, R. H. *Passions within reason: The strategic role of the emotions*. New York: Norton, 1988.

Frankenhaeuser, M. The role of peripheral catecholamines in adaptation to understimulation and overstimulation. In G. Serban (Ed.), *Psychopathology of human adaptation*. New York: Plenum, 1976.

Frazer, J. G. *The golden bough: A study in magic and religion*. New York: MacMillan Co., 1959 (reprint of 1922 abridged edition, edited by T. H. Gaster; original work published 1890).

Freud, S. *An outline of psycho-analysis* (translated by J. Strachey). New York: Norton, 1949.

———. *Introductory lectures on psychoanalysis* (edited and translated by J. Strachey). New York: Liveright, 1977.

———. *The Interpretation of Dreams* (edited by J. Strachey). New York: Avon, 1980.

Friedman, M. I. Body fat and the metabolic control of food intake. *International Journal of Obesity*, 1990, 14 (Suppl. 3), 53–67.

———. Making sense out of calories. In E. M. Stricker (Ed.), *Handbook of behavioral neurobiology* (Vol 10: *Neurobiology of food and fluid intake*). New York: Plenum, 1990, pp. 513–529.

Friedman, M. I., and Stricker, E. M. The physiological psychology of hunger: A physiological perspective. *Psychological Review*, 1976, 83, 409–431.

Friedman, M. I., and Tordoff, M. G. Fatty acid oxidation and glucose utilization interact to control food intake in rats. *American Journal of Physiology*, 1986, 251, R840–R845.

Frodi, A. M., Lamb, M. E., Leavitt, L. A., Donovan, W. L., Neff, C., and Sherry, D. Fathers' and mothers' responses to the faces and cries of normal and premature infants. *Developmental Psychology*, 1978, 14 490–498

Fromm, E. *Escape from freedom*. New York: Rinehart, 1941.

Galanter, E. H. The direct measurement of utility and subjective probability. *American Journal of Psychology*, 1962, 75, 208–220.

Gallistel, C. R. *The organization of action: A new synthesis*. Hillsdale, NJ: Lawrence Erlbaum, 1980.

———. *The organization of learning*. Cambridge, MA: MIT Press, 1990.

Garcia, J., Ervin, F. R., and Koelling, R. A. Learning with

prolonged delay of reinforcement. *Psychonomic Science,* 1966, 5, 121–122.

Gardner, H. *The shattered mind.* New York: Vintage, 1974.

Garrow, J. S. *Energy balance and obesity in man.* Amsterdam: North-Holland, 1978.

Gay, P. *Reading Freud: Explorations and entertainments.* New Haven, CT: Yale University Press, 1990.

Geary, N., and Smith, G. P. Pimozide decreases the positive reinforcing effect of sham fed sucrose in the rat. *Pharmacology, Biochemistry and Behavior,* 1985, 22, 787–790.

Geen, R. G., and Quanty, M. B. The catharsis of aggression: An evaluation of a hypothesis. *Advances in Experimental Social Psychology* (Vol. 10). New York: Academic Press, 1977.

Geiselman, P. J., and Novin, D. The role of carbohydrates in appetite, hunger and obesity. *Appetite,* 1982, 3, 203–223.

Geliebter, A. Gastric distension and gastric capacity in relation to food intake in humans. *Physiology and Behavior,* 1988, 44, 665–668.

Gilman, A. The relation between blood osmotic pressure, fluid distribution and voluntary water intake. *American Journal of Physiology,* 1937, 120, 323–328.

Glass, D. C., and Singer, J. E. *Urban stress.* New York: Academic Press, 1972.

Gleitman, H. *Psychology.* 4th ed. New York: Norton, 1995.

Goosens, F., and Van IJzendoorn, M. Quality of infants' attachment to professional caregivers. *Child Development,* 1990, 61, 832–837.

Gould, J. L. *Ethology.* New York: Norton, 1982.

Graff, H., and Stellar, E. Hyperphagia, obesity and finickiness. *Journal of Comparative and Physiological Psychology,* 1962, 55, 418–424.

Graham, R. B. *Physiological psychology.* Belmont, California: Wadsworth Publishing Co., 1990.

Gray, F., Graubard, P. S., and Rosenberg, H. Little brother is changing you. *Psychology Today,* 1974, 7, 42–46.

Gray, J. A. *The neuropsychology of anxiety.* Oxford: Oxford University Press (Clarendon), 1982.

Green, D. M., and Swets, J. A. *Signal detection theory and psychophysics.* New York: Wiley, 1966.

Greenwald, A. G. The totalitarian ego: Fabrication and revision of personal history. *American Psychologist,* 1980, 35, 603–618.

Griffitt, W., May, J., and Veitch, R. Sexual stimulation and interpersonal behavior: Heterosexual evaluative responses, visual behavior, and physical proximity. *Journal of Personality and Social Psychology,* 1974, 30, 367–377.

Grill, H. J., and Kaplan, J. M. Caudal brainstem participates

in the distributed neural control of feeding. In E. M. Stricker (Ed.), *Handbook of behavioral neurobiology* (Vol. 10: *Neurobiology of food and fluid intake*). New York: Plenum, 1990, pp. 125–149.

Grill, H. J., and Norgren, R. The taste reactivity test. II. Mimetic responses to gustatory stimuli in neurologically normal rats. *Brain Research,* 1978, 143, 263–279.

Grossman, S. P., Eating or drinking elicited by direct adrenergic or cholinergic stimulation of the hypothalamus. *Science,* 1962, 132, 301–302.

Grossman, S. P., Dacey, D., Haloris, A. E., Collier, T., and Routtenberg, A. Aphagia and adipsia after preferential destruction of nerve cell bodies in the hypothalamus. *Science,* 1978, 202, 537–539.

Guyton, A. C. *Textbook of medical physiology.* Philadelphia: Saunders, 1966.

Hall, R. V., Lund, D., and Jackson, D. Effects of teacher attention on study behavior. *Journal of Applied Behavior Analysis,* 1968, 1, 1–12.

Hall, W. G. Weaning and growth of artificially reared rats. *Science,* 1975, 190, 1313–1315.

Halmi, K. A., and Sunday, S. R. Temporal patterns of hunger and fullness ratings and related cognitions in anorexia and bulimia. *Appetite,* 1991, 16, 219–237.

Han, P. W., and Frohman, L. A. Hyperinsulinemia in tube-fed hypophysectomized rats bearing hypothalamic lesions. *American Journal of Physiology,* 1970, 219, 1632–1636.

Harackiewicz, J. M., Manderlink, G., and Sansone, C. Competence processes and achievement motivation: Implications for intrinsic motivation. In A. K. Boggiano and T. S. Pittman (Eds.), *Achievement and motivation: A social-developmental perspective.* Cambridge, England: Cambridge University Press, 1992, pp. 115–137.

Hardin, G. The tragedy of the commons. *Science,* 1968, 162, 1243–1248.

Harlow, H. F. The nature of love. *American Psychologist,* 1958, 13, 673–685.

———. Monkeys, men, mice, motives, and sex. In M. H. Siegel and H. P. Zeigler (Eds.), *Psychological research: The inside story.* New York: Harper & Row, 1976.

Harlow, H. F., Harlow, M. K., and Meyer, D. R. Learning motivated by a manipulation drive. *Journal of Experimental Psychology,* 1950, 40, 228–234.

Harlow, H. F., and Zimmerman, R. R. Affectional responses in the infant monkey. *Science,* 1959, 130, 421–432.

Harlow, H. F. Motivation as a factor in the acquisition of new responses. In M. R. Jones (Ed.), *Nebraska symposium on motivation.* Lincoln: University of Nebraska Press, 1953.

Harris, G. W., and Michael, R. P. The activation of sexual

behavior by hypothalamic implants of estrogen. *Journal of Physiology,* 1964, 171, 275–301.

Hashim, S. A., and Van Itallie, T. B. Studies in normal and obese subjects with a monitored food dispensary device. *Annals of the New York Academy of Science,* 1965, 131, 654–661.

Hazan, C., and Shaver, P. Romantic love conceptualized as an attachment process. *Journal of Personality and Social Psychology,* 1987, 52, 511–524.

Heath, R. G. (Ed.) *The role of pleasure in behavior.* New York: Harper & Row, 1964.

Hebb, D. O. *The organization of behavior: A neuropsychological theory.* New York: Wiley, 1949.

———. Drives and the CNS. *Psychological Review,* 1955, 62, 243–254.

Heider, F. *The psychology of interpersonal relations.* New York: Wiley, 1958.

Heiligenberg, W., and Kramer, U. Aggression as a function of external stimulation. *Journal of Comparative Physiology,* 1972, 77, 332–340.

Herman, C. P., and Polivy, J. Restrained eating. In A. J. Stunkard (Ed.), *Obesity.* Philadelphia: Saunders, 1980, pp. 208–225.

Herman, J. A., deMontes, A. I., Dominquez, B., Montes, F., and Hopkins, B. L. Effects of bonuses for punctuality on the tardiness of industrial workers. *Journal of Applied Behavioral Analysis,* 1973, 6, 563–570.

Herrnstein, R. J. Relative and absolute strength of response as a function of frequency of reinforcement. *Journal of the Experimental Analysis of Behavior,* 1961, 4, 267–272.

———. On the law of effect. *Journal of the Experimental Analysis of Behavior,* 1970, 13, 243–266.

———. Behavior, reinforcement and utility. *Psychological Science,* 1990, 1, 217–224.

Herrnstein, R. J., and Hineline, P. N. Negative reinforcement as shock frequency reduction. *Journal of the Experimental Analysis of Behavior,* 1966, 9, 421–430.

Herrnstein, R. J., and Prelec, D. Melioration. In G. Loewenstein and J. Elster (Eds.), *Choice over time.* New York: Russell Sage Foundation, 1992, pp. 235–263.

Herrnstein, R. J., and Vaughn, W. Melioration and behavioral allocation. In J. E. R. Staddon (Ed.), *Limits to action.* New York: Academic Press, 1980.

Hervey, G. R. Regulation of energy balance. *Nature,* 1969, 222, 629–631.

Hess, W. R. *The functional organization of the diencephalon.* New York: Grune and Stratton, 1957.

Hetherington, A. W., and Ranson, S. W. Experimental hypothalamohypophyseal obesity in the rat. *Proceedings of the Society for Experimental Biology and Medicine,* 1939, 41, 465–466.

Hinde, R. A. *Animal behavior: A synthesis of ethology and comparative psychology* (2nd ed.). New York: McGraw-Hill, 1970.

Hinde, R. J. *Continuities and discontinuities: Conceptual issues and methodological considerations.* In M. Rutter (Ed.), Studies of psychosocial risk: The power of longitudinal data. Cambridge: Cambridge University Press, 1989.

Hiroto, D. S. Locus of control and learned helplessness. *Journal of Experimental Psychology,* 1974, 102, 187–193.

Hobbes, T. *Leviathan,* 1651.

Hochschild, A. R. Emotion work, feeling rules, and social structure. *American Journal of Sociology,* 1997, 85, 551–575.

Hodgson, R., Rachman, S., and Marks, I. The treatment of chronic obsessive-compulsive neurosis. *Behavior Research and Therapy,* 1972, 10, 181–189.

Hoebel, B. G. Brain reward and aversion systems in the control of feeding and sexual behavior. In J. K. Cole and T. B. Sonderegger (Eds.), *Nebraska Symposium on Motivation.* Lincoln: University of Nebraska Press, 1974.

———. Neuroscience and motivation: Pathways and peptides that define motivational systems. In R. C. Atkinson, R. J. Herrnstein, G. Lindzey, and D. Luce (Eds.), *Stevens' handbook of experimental psychology* (Vol. 1: *Perception and motivation*). New York: Wiley, 1988, pp. 547–625.

Hoebel, B. G., and Teitelbaum, P. Weight regulation in normal and hypothalamic hyperphagic rats. *Journal of Comparative and Physiological Psychology,* 1966, 61, 189–193.

Hoebel, B. G., and Thompson, R. D. Aversion to lateral hypothalamic stimulation caused by intragastric feeding or obesity. *Journal of Comparative and Physiological Psychology,* 1969, 68, 536–543.

Hoffman, H. S., Eiserer, L. A., Ratner, A. M., and Pickering, V. L. Development of distress vocalization during withdrawal of an imprinting stimulus. *Journal of Comparative and Physiological Psychology,* 1974, 86, 563–568.

Hoffman, H. S., and Ratner, A. M. Reinforcement model of imprinting: Implications for socialization in monkeys and men. *Psychological Review,* 1973, 80, 527–544.

Hoffman, H. S., and Solomon, R. L. An opponent-process theory of motivation. III. Some affective dynamics in imprinting. *Learning and Motivation,* 1974, 5, 149–164.

Hoffman, M. L. Is altruism part of human nature? *Journal of Personality and Social Psychology,* 1981, 40, 121–137.

Hofstadter, D. R. *Metamagical themas: Questing for the essence of mind and pattern.* New York: Basic Books, 1985.

Hokanson, J. E. Psychophysiological evaluation of the catharsis hypothesis. In E. I. Megargee and J. E. Hokanson (Eds.), *The dynamics of aggression.* New York: Harper & Row, 1970.

Holland, D. C. How cultural systems become desire: A case study of American romance. In R. D'Andrade and C. Strauss (Eds.), *Human motives and cultural models.* Cambridge, England: Cambridge University Press, 1992, pp. 61–89.

Holman, G. L. Intragastric reinforcement effect. *Journal of Comparative and Physiological Psychology,* 1969, 69, 432–441.

Holt, E. B. *Animal drive and the learning process, an essay toward radical empiricism* (Vol. I). New York: Holt, 1931.

Hoon, P. W., Wincze, J. P., and Hoon, E. F. A test of "reciprocal inhibition": Are anxiety and sexual arousal in women mutually inhibitory? *Journal of Abnormal Psychology,* 1977, 86, 65–74.

Houston, A. I., and McFarland, D. J. Behavioral resilience and its relation to demand functions. In J. E. R. Staddon (Ed.), *Limits to action: The allocation of individual behavior.* New York: Academic Press, 1980.

Hovland, C. I., and Sears, R. R. Minor studies in aggression. VI. Correlation of lynchings with economic indices. *Journal of Personality,* 1940, 9, 301–310.

Hugdahl, K., and Öhman, A. Effects of instruction on acquisition and extinction of electrodermal response to fear-relevant stimuli. *Journal of Experimental Psychology: Human Learning and Memory,* 1977, 3, 608–618.

Hull, C. L. *Principles of behavior.* New York: Appleton-Century-Crofts, 1943.

———. *A behavior system: An introduction to behavior theory concerning the individual organism.* New Haven, CT: Yale University Press, 1952.

Humphrey, G. *Thinking: An introduction to its experimental psychology.* London: Methuen, 1951.

Hunt, E. On the nature of intelligence. *Science,* 1983, 219, 141–146.

Hunter, D. E., and Whitten, P. *The study of anthropology.* New York: Harper & Row, 1976.

Inoue, S., and Bray, G. A. Role of the autonomic nervous system in the development of ventromedial hypothalamic obesity. *Brain Research Bulletin,* 1980, 5 (Suppl. 4), 119–125.

Irwin, F. W. Stated expectations as functions of probability and desirability of outcomes. *Journal of Personality,* 1953, 21, 329–335.

Irwin, F. W. *Intentional behavior and motivation.* New York: Lippincott, 1971.

Isaacson, R. L. Relation between N achievement, test anxiety, and curricular choices. *Journal of Abnormal and Social Psychology,* 1964, 68, 447–452.

Isen, A. M., Means, B., Patrick, R., and Nowicki, G. Some factors influencing decision-making strategy and risk taking. In M. S. Clark and S. T. Fiske (Eds.), *Affect and cognition: The 17th annual Carnegie symposium on cognition.* Hillsdale, NJ: Lawrence Erlbaum, 1982.

Izard, C. E. Differential emotions theory and the facial feedback hypothesis of emotion activation: Comments on Tourangeau and Ellsworth's "The role of facial response in the experience of emotion." *Journal of Personality and Social Psychology,* 1981, 40, 350–354.

———. *The psychology of emotions.* New York: Plenum, 1991.

Jacobs, H. L., and Sharma, K. N. Taste versus calories: Sensory and metabolic signals in the control of food intake. *Annals of the New York Academy of Science,* 1969, 157, 1084–1125.

Jaffe, J. H. Drug addiction and drug abuse. In A. G. Gilman, T. W. Rall, A. S. Nies, and P. Taylor (Eds.), *Goodman and Gilman's The pharmacological basis of therapeutics.* New York: Pergamon, 1990, pp. 522–572.

James, W. *Principles of psychology.* New York: Holt, 1890.

Janis, I. L., and Mann, L. *Decision making: A psychological analysis of conflict, choice, and commitment.* New York: Free Press, 1977.

Johnson, D. B. Altruistic behavior and the development of the self in infants. *Merrill-Palmer Quarterly,* 1982, 28, 379–388.

Jolly, A. *The evolution of primate behavior.* New York: Macmillan Co., 1972.

Jones, E. E., and Davis, K. E. From acts to dispositions: The attribution process in person perception. In L. Berkowitz (Ed.), *Advances in experimental social psychology* (Vol. 2). New York: Academic Press, 1965.

Jordan, H. A. Voluntary intragastric feeding: Oral and gastric contributions to food intake. *Journal of Comparative and Physiological Psychology,* 1969, 68, 498–506.

———. Physiological control of food intake in man. In G. A. Bray et al. (Eds.), *Obesity in perspective.* Washington, D.C.: Fogarty International Center Series on Preventive Medicine, DHEW Publication No. (NIH) 75-708, 1975.

Jordan, H. A., Moses, H., MacFayden, B. V., and Dudrick, S. J. Hunger and satiety in humans during parenteral hyperalimentation. *Psychosomatic Medicine,* 1974, 36, 144–155.

Kagan, J. Differential reward value of incomplete and complete sexual behavior. *Journal of Comparative and Physiological Psychology,* 1955, 48, 59–64.

————. Attention and psychological change in the child. *Science,* 1970, 170, 826–832.

————. *Change and continuity in infancy.* New York: Wiley, 1971.

————. *The second year.* Cambridge, MA: Harvard University Press, 1981.

————. *The nature of the child.* New York: Basic Books, 1984.

Kagan, J., Kearseley, R. B., and Zelazo, P. R. *Infancy: Its place in human development.* Cambridge, MA: Harvard University Press, 1978.

Kahneman, D., Slovic, P., and Tversky, A. (Eds.). *Judgment under uncertainty: Heuristics and biases.* Cambridge, England: Cambridge University Press, 1982.

Kahneman, D., and Tversky, A. On the psychology of prediction. *Psychological Review,* 1973, 80, 237–251.

Kahneman, D., and Tversky, A. Choices, values and frames. *American Psychologist,* 1984, 39, 341–350.

Kakar, S. Stories from Indian psychoanalysis: Context and text. In J. W. Stigler, R. A. Shweder, and G. Herdt (Eds.), *Cultural psychology: Essays on comparative human development.* Cambridge, England: Cambridge University Press, 1990, pp. 427–445.

Kalat, J. W. *Biological psychology.* Belmont, CA: Wadsworth, 1981.

Kamil, A. C. Systematic foraging by a nectar-feeding bird *(Loxops virens). Journal of Comparative and Physiological Psychology,* 1978, 92, 388–396.

Kaye, K., and Marcus, J. Infant imitation: The sensory-motor agenda. *Developmental Psychology,* 1981, 17, 258–265.

Keesey, R. E. A set-point analysis of the regulation of body weight. In A. J. Stunkard (Ed.), *Obesity.* Philadelphia: Saunders, 1980.

Kelley, A., and Stinus, L. Neuroanatomical and neurochemical substrates of affective behavior. In N. A. Fox and R. J. Davidson (Eds.), *Affective development: A psychobiological perspective.* Hillsdale, NJ: Lawrence Erlbaum, 1984.

Kelley, H. H. Attribution theory in social psychology. In D. Levine (Ed.), *Nebraska Symposium on Motivation* (Vol. 15). Lincoln: University of Nebraska Press, 1967.

————. Attribution in social interaction. In E. E. Jones, D. E. Kanouse, H. H. Kelley, R. E. Nisbett, S. Valins, and B. Weiner (Eds.), *Attribution: Perceiving the causes of behavior.* Morristown, NJ: General Learning Press, 1972.

Kelley, H. H., and Thibaut, J. W. *Interpersonal relations: A theory of interdependence.* New York: Wiley, 1978.

Kennedy, G. C. The role of depot fat in the hypothalamic control of food intake in the rat. *Proceedings of the Royal Society (London),* Series B, 1953, 140, 578–592.

Kerr, S. On the folly of rewarding A, while hoping for B. *Academy of Management Journal,* 1975, 18, 769–783.

King, H. E. Psychological effects of excitation in the limbic system. In D. E. Sheer (Ed.), *Electrical stimulation of the brain.* Austin: University of Texas Press, 1961.

Kinsey, A. C., Pomeroy, W. D., and Martin, C. E. *Sexual behavior in the human male.* Philadelphia: Saunders, 1948.

Kisseleff, H. R. Food associated drinking in the rat. *Journal of Comparative and Physiological Psychology,* 1969, 67, 284–300.

Kisseleff, H. R., and Epstein, A. N. Exaggerated prandial drinking in the recovered lateral rat without saliva. *Journal of Comparative and Physiological Psychology,* 1969, 67, 301–308.

Klüver, H., and Bucy, P. C. Preliminary analysis of functions of the temporal lobes in monkeys. *Archives of Neurological Psychiatry,* 1939, 42, 979–1000.

Köhler, W. *The mentality of apes.* New York: Harcourt, Brace & World, 1925.

Kolb, B., and Whishaw, I. Q. *Fundamentals of human neuropsychology.* (2nd ed.) New York: Freeman, 1990.

Komaki, J. L., Coombs, T., and Schepman, S. Motivational implications of reinforcement theory. In R. Steers and L. Porter (Eds.), *Motivation and work behavior.* New York: McGraw-Hill, 1991, pp. 87–107.

Konner, M. J. Aspects of the developmental ethology of a foraging people. In N. Blurton Jones (Ed.), *Ethological studies of child behaviour.* New York: Cambridge University Press, 1972.

Kraemer, G. A psychobiological theory of attachment. *Behavioral and Brain Sciences,* 1992, 15, 493–541.

Kraly, F. S., and Smith, G. P. Combined pregastric and gastric stimulation by food is sufficient for normal meal size. *Physiology and Behavior,* 1978, 21, 405–408.

Krebs, J. R. Behavioral aspects of predation. In P. P. G. Bateson and P. H. Klopfer (Eds.), *Perspectives in ethology.* New York: Plenum, 1973.

Krebs, J. R., and Davies, N. B. *An introduction to behavioral ecology.* Oxford: Blackwell Scientific, 1981.

Kreuz, L. E., and Rose, R. M. Assessment of aggressive behavior and plasma testosterone in a young criminal population. *Psychosomatic Medicine,* 1972, 34, 321–332.

Krieckhaus, E. E., and Wolf, G. Acquisition of sodium by rats: Interaction of innate mechanisms and latent learning. *Journal of Comparative and Physiological Psychology,* 1968, 65, 197–201.

Kuo, Z. Y. The genesis of the cat's responses to the rat. *Journal of Comparative Psychology,* 1930, 11, 1–35.

Laird, J. D. Self-attribution of emotion: The effects of expressive behavior on the quality of emotional experience. *Journal of Personality and Social Psychology,* 1974, 29, 475–486.

Lamb, M. E., and Campos, J. J. *Development in infancy.* New York: Random House, 1982.

Landis, C., and Hunt, W. A. Adrenalin and emotion. *Psychological Review,* 1932, 39, 467–485.

Langer, E. J. The illusion of control. *Journal of Personality and Social Psychology,* 1975, 32, 311–328.

Langer, E. J., and Rodin, J. The effects of choice and enhanced personal responsibility for the aged: A field experiment. *Journal of Personality and Social Psychology,* 1976, 34, 191–198.

Lanzetta, J. T., Cartwright-Smith, J., and Kleck, R. E. Effects of nonverbal dissimilation on emotional experience and autonomic arousal. *Journal of Personality and Social Psychology,* 1976, 33, 354–370.

Lashley, K. The problem of serial order in behavior. In L. A. Jeffries (Ed.), *Cerebral mechanisms in behavior.* New York: Wiley, 1951.

Latané, B., and Darley, J. M. *The unresponsive bystander: Why doesn't he help?* New York: Appleton-Century-Crofts, 1970.

Latham, G. P., and Locke, E. Goal setting—a motivational technique that works. In R. Steers and L. Porter (Eds.), *Motivation and work behavior.* New York: McGraw-Hill, 1991.

Laudenslager, M. L., Ryan, S. M., Drugan, R. C., Hyson, R. L., and Maier, S. F. Coping and immunosuppression: Inescapable but not escapable shock suppresses lymphocyte proliferation. *Science,* 1983, 221, 568–570.

Lazarus, R. S. *Emotion and adaptation.* New York: Oxford University Press, 1991.

LeMagnen, J. Advances in studies of physiological control and regulation of food intake. In E. Stellar and J. M. Sprague (Eds.), *Progress in physiological psychology* (Vol. 4). New York: Academic Press, 1971.

———. Metabolic basis for the dual periodicity of feeding in rats. *Behavioral and Brain Sciences,* 1981, 4, 561–607.

Lepper, M. R., and Greene, D. (Eds.). *The hidden costs of reward.* Hillsdale, NJ: Lawrence Erlbaum, 1978.

Lepper, M. R., Greene, D., and Nisbett, R. E. Undermining children's intrinsic interest with extrinsic rewards: A test of the "overjustification" hypothesis. *Journal of Personality and Social Psychology,* 1973, 28, 129–137.

LeUnes, A. D., and Nation, J. R. *Sport psychology: An introduction.* Chicago: Nelson-Hall, 1989.

Levenson, R. W. Autonomic nervous system differences among emotions. *Psychological Science,* 1992, 3, 23–27.

Levy, R. I. *Tahitians.* Chicago: University of Chicago Press, 1973.

Lewin, K. A. *A dynamic theory of personality.* New York: McGraw-Hill, 1935.

Lewinsohn, P. M., Mischel, W., Chaplin, W., and Barton, R. Social competence and depression: The role of illusory self-perceptions. *Journal of Abnormal Psychology,* 1980, 89, 203–212.

Lewis, C. S. *The problem of pain.* New York: Macmillan Co., 1962.

Liberman, R. P., and Raskin, D. E. Depression: A behavioral formulation. *Archives of General Psychiatry,* 1971, 24, 515–523.

Liebert, R. M., Neale, J. M., and Davidson, E. S. *The early window: The effects of television on children and youth.* Elmsford, NY: Pergamon, 1973.

Liebling, D. S., Eisner, J. D., Gibbs, J., and Smith, G. P. Intestinal satiety in rats. *Journal of Comparative and Physiological Psychology,* 1975, 89, 955–965.

Linden, E. *Apes, men, and language.* New York: Pelican, 1976.

Lindsley, D. B. Attention, consciousness, sleep, and wakefulness. In *Handbook of physiology, Section 1, Neurophysiology,* Vol. III. Washington, DC: American Physiological Society, 1960.

Loftus, E. F. *Eyewitness testimony.* Cambridge, MA: Harvard University Press, 1979.

———. The reality of repressed memories. *American Psychologist,* 1993, 44, 518–537.

Loftus, E. F., and Klinger, M. R. Is the unconscious smart or dumb? *American Psychologist,* 1992, 47, 761–765.

Loftus, E. F., and Palmer, J. C. Reconstruction of automobile destruction: An example of the interaction between language and memory. *Journal of Verbal Learning and Verbal Behavior,* 1974, 13, 585–589.

Lorenz, K. Die angeborenen Formen moglicher Ernahrung. *Zeitschrift für Tierpsychologie,* 1943, 5, 235–409.

———. *Evolution and the modification of behavior.* Chicago: University of Chicago Press, 1965.

———. *On aggression.* London: Methuen, 1966.

Luborsky, L., Blinder, B., and Mackworth, N. Eye fixation and recall of pictures as a function of GSR responsivity. *Perceptual and Motor Skills,* 1963, 16, 169–183.

Ludwig, A. M., and Wikler, A. "Craving" and relapse to drink. *Quarterly Journal of Studies on Alcohol,* 1974, 35, 108–130.

Luria, A. R. *The working brain.* London: Penguin, 1973.

MacCorquodale, K., and Meehl, P. E. Edward C. Tolman.

In W. K. Estes et al., *Modern learning theory*. New York: Appleton-Century-Crofts, 1954.

MacDonnell, M. F., and Flynn, J. P. Control of sensory fields by stimulation of hypothalamus. *Science,* 1966, 152, 1406–1408.

Mahoney, E. R. *Human sexuality*. New York: McGraw-Hill, 1983.

Maier, F., Seligman, M. E. P., and Solomon, R. L. Pavlovian fear conditioning and learned helplessness: Effects on escape and avoidance behavior of (a) the CS-US contingency and (b) the independence of the US and voluntary responding. In B. A. Campbell and R. M. Church (Eds.), *Punishment and aversive behavior*. New York: Appleton-Century-Crofts, 1969.

Mandler, G. *Mind and Body*. New York: Norton, 1984.

Marcus, G. B. Stability and change in political attitudes: Observe, recall, and "explain". *Political Behavior,* 1986, 8, 21–44.

Mark, G. P., Blander, D. S., and Hoebel, B. G. A conditioned stimulus decreases extracellular dopamine in the nucleus accumbens after the development of learned taste aversion. *Brain Research,* 1991, 551, 308–310.

Mark, V. H., and Ervin, F. R. *Violence and the brain*. New York: Harper & Row, 1970.

Marks, R. W. The effect of probability, desirability and privilege on the stated expectations of children. *Journal of Personality,* 1951, 19, 332–351.

Markus, H. R., and Kitayama, S. Culture and the self: Implications for cognition, emotion, and motivation. *Psychological Review,* 1991, 98, 224–253.

Marlowe, W. B., Mancall, E. L., and Thomas, J. J. Complete Klüver-Bucy syndrome in man. *Cortex,* 1975, 11, 53–59.

Marshall, G. D., and Zimbardo, P. G. Affective consequences of inadequately explained physiological arousal. *Journal of Personality and Social Psychology,* 1979, 37, 970–988.

Marshall, J. F., Turner, B. H., and Teitelbaum, P. Sensory neglect produced by lateral hypothalamic damage. *Science,* 1971, 174, 523–525.

Martin, I., and Levey, A. B. Evaluative conditioning. *Advances in Behavior Research and Therapy,* 1978, 1, 57–102.

Maslach, C. Negative emotional biasing of unexplained arousal. *Journal of Personality and Social Psychology,* 1979, 37, 953–969.

Maslow, A. H. *Motivation and personality*. New York: Harper & Row, 1954.

———. Deficiency motivation and growth motivation. In M. R. Jones (Ed.), *Nebraska Symposium on Motivation*. Lincoln: University of Nebraska Press, 1955.

———. *Toward a psychology of being* (2nd ed.). New York: Van Nostrand, 1968.

———. *Motivation and personality* (2nd ed.). New York: Harper & Row, 1970.

Masserman, J. H., Wechkin, S., and Terris, W. "Altruistic" behavior in rhesus monkeys. *American Journal of Psychiatry,* 1964, 121, 584–585.

Matlin, M., and Stang, D. *The Pollyanna principle*. Cambridge, MA: Schenkman, 1978.

Matteo, S., and Rissman, E. F. Increased sexual activity during the midcycle portion of the human menstrual cycle. *Hormones and Behavior,* 1984, 18, 249–255.

May, E. R. *"Lessons" of the past*. New York: Oxford University Press, 1973.

Mayer, J. Regulation of energy intake and body weight: The glucostatic theory and the lipostatic hypothesis. *Annals of the New York Academy of Science,* 1955, 63, 15–43.

Mazur, J. E. Optimization theory fails to predict performance of pigeons in a two-response situation. *Science,* 1981, 214, 823–835.

———. Optimization: A result or a mechanism? *Science,* 1983, 221, 977.

———. *Learning and behavior* (3rd ed.). Englewood Cliffs, NJ: Prentice-Hall, 1994.

McClelland, D. C. Comments on Professor Maslow's paper. In M. R. Jones (Ed.), *Nebraska symposium on motivation*. Lincoln: University of Nebraska Press, 1955, pp. 31–37.

———. Some social consequences of achievement motivation. In M. R. Jones (Ed.), *Nebraska Symposium on Motivation*. Lincoln: University of Nebraska Press, 1955.

———. *The roots of consciousness*. Princeton, NJ: Van Nostrand, 1964.

———. Achievement and entrepreneurship: A longitudinal study. *Journal of Personality and Social Psychology,* 1965, 1, 389–392.

———. Managing motivation to expand human freedom. *American Psychologist,* 1978, 33, 201–210.

———. Epilogue. In D. R. Brown and J. Veroff (Eds.), *Frontiers of motivational psychology: Essays in honor of John W. Atkinson*. Berlin: Springer-Verlag, 1986, pp. 191–194.

McClelland, D. C., Atkinson, J. W., Clark, R. W., and Lowell, E. L. *The achievement motive* (2nd ed.). New York: Irvington, 1976.

McClelland, D. C., Clark, R. A., Roby, T. B., and Atkinson, J. W. The projective expression of needs. IV. The effect of need for achievement on thematic apperception. *Journal of Experimental Psychology,* 1949, 39, 242–255.

McClelland, D. C., Rindlisbacher, A., and de Charms, R. C. Religious and other sources of parental attitudes toward independence training. In D. C. McClelland (Ed.), *Studies in motivation.* New York: Appleton-Century-Crofts, 1955.

McClelland, L. A. Crowding and social stress. Unpublished doctoral dissertation, University of Michigan, 1974.

McClintock, M. Menstrual synchrony and suppression. *Nature,* 1971, 229, 244–245.

McDowell, J. J. The importance of Herrnstein's mathematical statement of the law of effect for behavior therapy. *American Psychologist,* 1982, 37, 771–779.

McHugh, P. R. Clinical issues in food ingestion and body weight maintenance. In E. M. Stricker, (Ed.), *Handbook of Behavioral Neurobiology* (Vol. 10: *Neurobiology of food and fluid intake*). New York: Plenum, 1990, pp. 531–547.

McHugh, P. Psychiatric misadventures. *American Scholar,* Fall 1992.

Mencimer, S. Love without the glove: The sad truth about why we don't use condoms. *Washington Post,* August 15, 1993, p. E1.

Menzel, E. W. Cognitive mapping in chimpanzees. In S. H. Hulse, H. F. Fowler, and W. K. Honig (Eds.), *Cognitive processes in animal behavior.* Hillsdale, NJ: Lawrence Erlbaum, 1978.

Meyerson, B. J., and Lindstrom, L. H. Sexual motivation in the female rat: A methodological study applied to the investigation of the effect of estradiol benzoate. *Acta Physiologica Scandinavica* (Suppl. 389), 1973, 1–80.

Michael, R. P., and Keverne, E. B. Pheromones in the communication of sexual status in primates. *Nature,* 1968, 218, 746–749.

Miller, G. A., Galanter, E., and Pribram, K. H. *Plans and the structure of behavior.* New York: Holt, Rinehart & Winston, 1960.

Miller, N. E. Liberalization of basic S-R concepts: Extensions to conflict behavior, motivation, and social learning. In S. Koch (Ed.), *Psychology: A study of a science* (Vol. 2). New York: McGraw-Hill, 1959, pp. 196–292.

Money, J., Wiedeking, C., Walker, P., Migeon, C., Meyer, W., and Borgaonkar, D. 47,XYY and 46,XY males with antisocial and/or sex-offending behavior: Antiandrogen therapy plus counseling. *Psychoneuroendocrinology,* 1975, 1, 165–178.

Mook, D. G. Oral and postingestional determinants of the intake of various solutions in rats with esophageal fistulas. *Journal of Comparative and Physiological Psychology,* 1963, 56, 645–659.

———. Some determinants of preference and aversion in the rat. *Annals of the New York Academy of Science,* 1969, 157, 1158–1175.

———. Satiety, specifications, and stop rules: Feeding as voluntary action. In A. N. Epstein and A. R. Morrison (Eds.), *Progress in Psychobiology and Physiological Psychology* (Vol. 14). New York: Academic Press, 1990, pp. 1–65.

———. Why can't altruism be selfish? *Psychological Inquiry,* 1991, 2, 139–141.

Mook, D. G., and Cseh, C. L. Release of feeding by the sweet taste in rats: The influence of body weight. *Appetite,* 1981, 2, 15–34.

Mook, D. G., and Kozub, F. J. Control of sodium chloride intake in the nondeprived rat. *Journal of Comparative and Physiological Psychology,* 1968, 66, 105–109.

Mook, D. G., Wagner, S. and Talley, C. E. P. Effect of body weight manipulations on sham feeding in the rat. *Appetite,* 1992, 18, 55–67.

Moreland, R. L., and Zajonc, R. B. Is stimulus recognition a necessary condition for the occurrence of exposure effects? *Journal of Personality and Social Psychology,* 1977, 35, 191–199.

———. Exposure effects may not depend on stimulus recognition. *Journal of Personality and Social Psychology,* 1979, 37, 1085–1089.

———. Exposure effects in person perception: Familiarity, similarity, and attraction. *Journal of Experimental Social Psychology,* 1982, 18, 395–415.

Morris, D. The reproductive behaviour of the ten-spined stickleback *(Pygosteus pungitius L.). Behaviour,* 1958, 61, 1–154.

Morruzi, G., and Magoun, H. W. Brainstem reticular formation and activation of the EEG. *Electroencephalography and Clinical Neurophysiology,* 1949, 1, 455–473.

Mowrer, O. H. *Learning theory and personality dynamics.* New York: Ronald Press, 1950.

Moyer, K. E. *The psychobiology of aggression.* New York: Harper & Row, 1976.

Murray, A. D. Infant crying as an elicitor of parent behavior: An examination of two models. *Psychological Bulletin,* 1979, 86, 191–215.

Mussen, P., and Eisenberg-Berg, N. *Roots of caring, sharing, and helping.* San Francisco: Freeman, 1977.

Neill, D., Gaar, L., Clark, A., and Britt, M. "Rate-free" measures of self-stimulation and microinjections: Evidence toward a new concept of dopamine and reward.

In B. G. Hoebel and D. Novin (Eds.), *The neural basis of feeding and reward*. Brunswick, ME: Haer Institute, 1982.

Nemeroff, C., and Rozin, P. Sympathetic magical beliefs and kosher dietary practices: The interaction of rules and feelings. *Ethos: The Journal of Psychological Anthropology*, 1992, 20, 96–115.

Netter, F. H. *The Ciba collection of medical illustrations*. Volume 1: *Nervous system*. New York: Ciba Pharmaceutical, 1958.

Nicholls, J. G. Achievement motivation: Conceptions of ability, subjective experience, task choice, and performance. *Psychological Review*, 1984, 91, 328–346.

Nisbett, R. E., and Ross, L. *Human inference: Strategies and shortcomings of social judgement*. Englewood Cliffs, NJ: Prentice-Hall, 1980.

Nisbett, R. E., and Wilson, T. D. Telling more than we can know: Verbal reports on mental processes. *Psychological Review*, 1977, 84, 231–259.

O'Brien, C. P. Experimental analysis of conditioning factors in human narcotic addiction. *Pharmacological Review*, 1976, 27, 533–543.

Ofshe, R. Inadvertent hypnosis during interrogation. *International Journal of Clinical and Experimental Hypnosis*, 1992, 11, 125–155.

Olds, J., and Milner, P. Positive reinforcement produced by electrical stimulation of septal area and other regions of rat brain. *Journal of Comparative and Physiological Psychology*, 1954, 47, 419–427.

Olson, J. M., and Zanna, M. P. A new look at selective exposure. *Journal of Experimental Social Psychology*, 1979, 15, 1–15.

Overmeir, J. B., and Seligman, M. E. P. Effects of inescapable shock upon subsequent escape and avoidance responding. *Journal of Comparative and Physiological Psychology*, 1967, 63, 28–33.

Patterson, C. J. Aggression, altruism, and self-regulation. In M. H. Bornstein and M. E. Lamb (Eds.), *Developmental psychology: An advanced textbook*. Hillsdale, NJ: Lawrence Erlbaum, 1984.

Paulus, P., McCain, G., and Cox, V. Death rates, psychiatric commitments, blood pressure and perceived crowding as a function of institutional crowding. *Environmental Psychology and Nonverbal Behavior*, 1978, 3, 107–116.

Peck, J. W., and Novin, D. Evidence that osmoreceptors mediating drinking in rabbits are in the lateral preoptic area. *Journal of Comparative and Physiological Psychology*, 1971, 74, 134–147.

Perin, C. T. Behavior potentiality as a joint function of the amount of training and the degree of hunger at the time

of extinction. *Journal of Experimental Psychology*, 1942, 30, 93–113.

Persky, H., Smith, K. D., and Basu, G. K. Relation of psychologic measures of aggression and hostility to testosterone production in man. *Psychosomatic Medicine*, 1971, 33, 265–277.

Peterson, C., and Seligman, M. E. Causal explanations as a risk factor for depression: Theory and evidence. *Psychological Review*, 1984, 91, 347–374.

Petit, C. Why they got pregnant. *San Francisco Chronicle*, January 14, 1975, 4.

Pettigrew, T. F. The ultimate attribution error: Extending Allport's cognitive analysis of prejudice. *Personality and Social Psychology Bulletin*, 1979, 5, 461–476.

Pfaff, D. W. Neurobiological mechanisms of sexual motivation. In D. W. Pfaff (Ed.), *The physiological mechanisms of motivation*. New York: Springer-Verlag, 1982.

Pfaff, D. W., and Pfaffmann, C. Behavioral and electrophysiological responses of male rats to female rat urine odors. In C. Pfaffmann (Ed.), *Olfaction and taste*. New York: Rockefeller University Press, 1969.

Pfaus, J. G., Damsma, G., Nomikos, G. G., Wenkstern, D. G., Blaha, C. D., Phillips, A. G., and Fibiger, H. C. Sexual behavior enhances central dopamine transmission in the male rat. *Brain Research*, 1990, 530, 345–348.

Pi-Sunyer, X., Kissileff, H. R., Thornton, J., and Smith, G. P. C-terminal octapeptide of cholecystokinin decreases food intake in obese men. *Physiology and Behavior*, 1982, 29, 627–630.

Platt, J. R. Interresponse-time shaping by variable-interval-like interresponse-time reinforcement contingencies. *Journal of the Experimental Analysis of Behavior*, 1979, 31, 3–14.

Pliner, P. The effects of mere exposure on liking for edible substances. *Appetite*, 1982, 3, 283–290.

Pliner, P., Herman, C. P., and Polivy, J. Palatability as a determinant of eating: Finickiness as a function of taste, hunger, and the prospect of good food. In E. D. Capaldi and T. L. Powley (Eds.), *Taste, experience, and feeding*. Washington, DC: American Psychological Association, 1990, pp. 210–226.

Plutchik, R. *Emotion: A psychoevolutionary synthesis*. New York: Harper & Row, 1980.

Polivy, J., and Herman, C. P. *Breaking the diet habit: The natural weight alternative*. New York: Basic Books, 1983.

———. Dieting and binging: A causal analysis. *American Psychologist*, 1985, 40, 193–201.

Porter, L. W. A study of perceived need satisfactions in bottom and middle management jobs. *Journal of Applied Psychology*, 1961, 45, 1–10.

Powell, G. E. *Brain and personality*. London: Saxon House, 1979.

Powley, T. L. The ventromedial hypothalamic syndrome, satiety and a cephalic phase hypothesis. *Psychological Review*, 1977, 84, 89–126.

Prelec, D. The empirical claims of maximization theory: A reply to Rachlin, and to Kagel, Battalio, and Green. *Psychological Review*, 1983, 90, 101–107.

Premack, D. Reversibility of the reinforcement relation. *Science*, 1962, 136, 235–237.

———. Minds with and without language. In L. Weiskrantz (Ed.), *Thought without language*. Oxford: Oxford University Press (Clarendon), 1988, pp. 46–65.

Price, R. A., Cadoret, R. J., Stunkard, A. J., and Troughton, E. Genetic contributions to human fatness: An adoption study. *American Journal of Psychiatry*, 1987, 144, 1003–1008.

Pylyshyn, Z. W. What the mind's eye tells the mind's brain: A critique of mental imagery. *Psychological Bulletin*, 1973, 80, 1–24.

Quinn, N. The motivational force of self-understanding: Evidence from wives' inner conflicts. In R. D'Andrade and C. Strauss (Eds.), *Human motives and cultural models*. Cambridge, England: Cambridge University Press, 1992, pp. 90–126.

Rachlin, H. *Behaviorism in everyday life*. Englewood Cliffs, NJ: Prentice-Hall, 1980.

Rachlin, H., Battalio, R., Kagel, J., and Green, L. Maximization theory in behavioral psychology. *Behavioral and Brain Sciences*, 1981, 4, 371–417.

Rachman, S. J., and Hodgson, R. J. *Obsessions and compulsions*. Englewood Cliffs, NJ: Prentice-Hall, 1980.

Rachman, S., Marks, I., and Hodgson, R. The treatment of chronic obsessive-compulsive neurosis by modeling and flooding in vivo. *Behavior Research and Therapy*, 1973, 11, 463–471.

Radke-Yarrow, M., Zahn-Waxler, C., and Chapman, M. Children's prosocial dispositions and behavior. In P. H. Mussen and E. M. Hetherington (Eds.), *Handbook of child psychology* (Vol. 4): *Socialization, personality, and social development* (4th ed.). New York: Wiley, 1983.

Rajecki, D. W., Lamb, M. E., and Obmascher, P. Toward a general theory of infantile attachment: A comparative review of aspects of the social bond. *Behavioral and Brain Sciences*, 1978, 1, 417–436.

Rathus, S. A. *Psychology*. Ft. Worth: Holt, Rinehart & Winston, 1990.

Redelmeier, D. A., Rozin, P., and Kahneman, D. Understanding patients' decisions: Cognitive and emotional perspectives. *Journal of the American Medical Association*, 1993, 270, 72–76.

Reid, E. C. Autopsychology of the manic-depressive. *Journal of Nervous and Mental Disease*, 1910, 37, 606–620.

Rheingold, H. L., Hay, D. F., and West, M. J. Sharing in the second year of life. *Child Development*, 1976, 47, 1148–1158.

Rescorla, R. A., and Solomon, R. L. Two-process learning theory: Relationships between Pavlovian conditioning and instrumental learning. *Psychological Review*, 1967, 74, 151–182.

Richter, C. P. A behavioristic study of the activity of the rat. *Comparative Psychology Monographs*, 1922, 1.

———. Symposium: Contributions of psychology to the problems of personality and behavior. IV. Biological foundations of personality differences. *American Journal of Orthopsychiatry*, 1932, 2, 345–354.

———. Total self-regulatory functions in animals and human beings. *Harvey Lectures*, 1942–43, 38, 63–103.

Rimm, D. C., and Masters, J. C. *Behavior therapy: Techniques and empirical findings* (1st ed.). New York: Academic Press, 1974.

———. *Behavior therapy: Techniques and empirical findings* (2nd ed.). New York: Academic Press, 1979.

Ristau, C. A. (Ed.). *Cognitive ethology: The minds of other animals*. Hillsdale, NJ: Lawrence Erlbaum Associates, 1991.

Ritter, S., and Taylor, J. S. Vagal sensory neurons are required for lipoprivic but not glucoprivic feeding in rats. *American Journal of Physiology*, 1990, 258, R1395–R1401.

Robbins, T. W., and Fray, P. J. Stress-induced eating: Fact, fiction, or misunderstanding? *Appetite*, 1980, 1, 103–133.

Robinson, R. G., Folstein, M. F., Simonson, M., and McHugh, P. R. Differential antianxiety response to caloric intake between normal and obese subjects. *Psychosomatic Medicine*, 1980, 42, 415–427.

Rodin, J. Current status of the internal-external hypothesis for obesity: What went wrong? *American Psychologist*, 1981, 36, 361–372.

Roiphe, K. *The morning after: Sex, fear, and feminism on campus*. Boston: Little, Brown, 1993.

Rolls, B. J. How variety and palatability can stimulate appetite. *Nutrition Bulletin*, 1979, 5, 78–86.

Rolls, B. J. The role of sensory-specific satiety in food intake and food selection. In E. J. Capaldi and T. L. Powley (Eds.), *Taste, experience, and feeding*. Washington, D. C.: American Psychological Association, 1990.

Rolls, B. J., Rowe, E. T., and Rolls, E. T. How sensory properties of food affect human feeding behavior. *Physiology and Behavior,* 1982, 29, 409–417.

Rosenhan, D. L., and Seligman, M. E. P. *Abnormal Psychology.* New York: W. W. Norton, 1984.

Ross, L. The intuitive psychologist and his shortcomings. In L. Berkowitz (Ed.), *Advances in experimental social psychology* (Vol. 10). New York: Academic Press, 1977.

Ross, L., and Anderson, C. Shortcomings in the attribution process: On the origins and maintenance of erroneous social assessments. In A. Tversky, D. Kahnman, and P. Slovic (Eds.), *Judgment under uncertainty: Heuristics and biases.* New York: Cambridge University Press, 1982.

Ross, L., Lepper, M. R., and Hubbard, M. Perseverance in self perception and social perception: Biased attributional processes in the debriefing paradigm. *Journal of Personality and Social Psychology,* 1975, 32, 880–892.

Ross, L., and Nisbett, R. E. *The person and the situation: Perspectives of social psychology.* New York: McGraw-Hill, 1991.

Rosvold, H. E., Mirsky, A. F., and Pribram, K. H. Influence of amygdalectomy on social behavior in monkeys. *Journal of Comparative and Physiological Psychology,* 1954, 47, 173–178.

Roth, S. R., Schwartz, M., and Teitelbaum, P. Failure of recovered lateral hypothalamic rats to learn specific food aversions. *Journal of Comparative and Physiolological Psychology,* 1973, 83, 184–197.

Rozin, P. Are carbohydrate and protein intakes separately regulated? *Journal of Comparative and Physiological Psychology,* 1968, 65, 23–29.

———. The evolution of intelligence and access to the cognitive unconscious. In E. Stellar and J. M. Sprague (Eds.), *Progress in psychobiology and physiological psychology* (Vol. 6). New York: Academic Press, 1976.

———. Disorders of food selection: The compromise of pleasure. *Annals of the New York Academy of Sciences,* 1989, 575, 376–386.

———. Social and moral aspects of food and eating. In I. Rock (Ed.), *The legacy of Solomon Asch: Essays in cognition and social psychology.* Hillsdale, NJ: Lawrence Earlbaum, 1990, pp. 97–110.

———. The importance of social factors in understanding the acquisition of food habits. In E. D. Capaldi and T. L. Powley (Eds.), *Taste, experience, and feeding.* Washington, DC: American Psychological Association, 1990, pp. 255–269.

———. Getting to like the burn of chili pepper: Biological,

psychological, and cultural perspectives. In B. G. Green, J. R. Mason, and M. R. Kare (Eds.), *Chemical senses* (Vol. 2: *Irritation*). New York: Marcel Dekker, 1990, pp. 231–269.

Rozin, P., Ebert, L., and Schull, J. Some like it hot: A temporal analysis of hedonic responses to chili pepper. *Appetite,* 1982, 3, 13–22.

Rozin, P., Gruss, L., and Berk, G. Reversal of innate aversions: Attempts to induce a preference for chili peppers in rats. *Journal of Comparative and Physiological Psychology,* 1979, 93, 1001–1014.

Rozin, P., Millman, L., and Nemeroff, C. Operation of the laws of sympathetic magic in disgust and other domains. *Journal of Personality and Social Psychology,* 1986, 50, 703–712.

Rozin, P., and Nemeroff, C. The laws of sympathetic magic: A psychological analysis of similarity and contagion. In J. W. Stigler, R. A. Shweder, and G. Herdt (Eds.), *Cultural psychology: Essays on comparative human development.* Cambridge, England: Cambridge University Press, 1990, pp. 205–232.

Rozin, P., Reff, D., Mack, M., and Schull, J. Conditioned opponent processes in human tolerance to caffeine. *Bulletin of the Psychonomic Society,* 1984, 22, 117–120.

Rozin, P., and Schull, J. The adaptive-evolutionary point of view in experimental psychology. In R. C. Atkinson, R. J. Herrnstein, G. Lindzey, and R. D. Luce (Eds.), *Stevens' handbook of experimental psychology* (Vol. 1: *Perception and motivation*). New York: Wiley, 1988, pp. 503–546.

Rozin, P., and Zellner, D. A. The role of Pavlovian conditioning in the acquisition of food likes and dislikes. In N. S. Braveman and P. Bronstein (Eds.), *Experimental assessments and clinical applications of conditioned food aversions. Annals of the New York Academy of Sciences* (Vol. 443). New York: New York Academy of Sciences, 1987, pp. 189–202.

Russek, M. Hepatic receptors and the neurophysiological mechanisms controlling feeding behavior. In S. Ehrenpreis (Ed.), *Neuroscience research.* New York: Academic Press, 1971.

Rymer, S. *Genie: An abused child's flight from silence.* New York: Harper Collins, 1993.

Sabini, J. *Social psychology.* New York: W. W. Norton, 1992.

Schachter, S. Some extraordinary facts about obese humans and rats. *American Psychologist,* 1971, 26, 129–144.

———. Recidivism and self-cure of smoking and obesity. *American Psychologist,* 1982, 37, 436–444.

Schachter, S., and Singer, J. E. Cognitive, social, and physiological determinants of emotional state. *Psychological Review,* 1962, 69, 379–399.

———. Comments on the Maslach and Marshall–Zimbardo experiments. *Journal of Personality and Social Psychology,* 1979, 37, 989–995.

Schafer, S. Sociosexual behavior in male and female homosexuals: A study in sex differences. *Archives of Sexual Behavior,* 1977, 6, 355–364.

Schallert, T., and Whishaw, I. Q. Two types of aphagia and two types of sensorimotor impairment after lateral hypothalamic lesions: Observations in normal weight, dieted, and fattened rats. *Journal of Comparative and Physiological Psychology,* 1978, 92, 720–741.

Schank, R., and Abelson, R. P. *Scripts, plans, goals and understanding: An inquiry into human knowledge structures.* Hillsdale, NJ: Lawrence Erlbaum, 1977.

Schmidt, R. A. *Motor control and learning.* Champaign, IL: Human Kinetics Publishers, 1982.

Schneirla, T. C. An evolutionary and developmental theory of biphasic processes underlying approach and withdrawal. In M. R. Jones (Ed.), *Nebraska Symposium on Motivation.* Lincoln: University of Nebraska Press, 1959.

Schwartz, B. Does helplessness cause depression, or do only depressed people become helpless? Comment on Alloy and Abramson. *Journal of Experimental Psychology: General,* 1981a, 110, 429–435.

———. Reinforcement-induced behavioral stereotypy: How not to teach people to discover rules. *Journal of Experimental Psychology: General,* 1982, 111, 23–59.

Schwartz, B. *Psychology of learning and behavior.* New York: W. W. Norton, 1984.

———. *The battle for human nature: Science, morality, and modern life.* New York: Norton, 1986.

———. On the creation and destruction of value. In M. Hechter, L. Nadel, and R. E. Michod (Eds.), *The origin of values.* New York: Aldine de Gruyter, 1993, pp. 153–186.

Schwartz, B., and Lacey, H. *Behaviorism, science, and human nature.* New York: Norton, 1982.

Schwartz, B., and Reisberg, D. *Psychology of learning and memory.* New York: Norton, 1991.

Schwartz, R. S., and Brunzell, J. D. Increase of adipose tissue lipoprotein lipase activity with weight loss. *Journal of Clinical Investigation,* 1981, 67, 425–430.

Scitovsky, T. *The joyless economy: An inquiry into human satisfaction and consumer dissatisfaction.* New York: Oxford University Press, 1976.

Sclafani, A. Nutritionally based learned flavor preferences in rats. In E. D. Capaldi and T. L. Powley (Eds.), *Taste, experience and feeding.* Washington, DC: American Psychological Association, 1990, pp. 139–156.

———. Conditioned food preferences. *Bulletin of the Psychonomic Society,* 1991, 29, 256–260.

Sclafani, A., and Springer, D. Dietary obesity in adult rats: Similarities to hypothalamic and human obesity syndromes. *Physiology and Behavior,* 1976, 17, 461–471.

Seligman, M. E. P. On the generality of the laws of learning. *Psychological Review,* 1970, 77, 406–418.

———. Phobias and preparedness. *Behavior Therapy,* 1971, 2, 307–320.

———. *Helplessness: On depression, development, and death.* San Francisco: Freeman, 1975.

———. *Learned optimism: How to change your mind and your life.* New York: Simon & Schuster, 1990.

Seligman, M. E. P., and Johnston, J. C. A cognitive theory of avoidance learning. In F. J. McGuigan and D. B. Lumsden (Eds.), *Contemporary approaches to conditioning and learning.* Washington, DC: Winston–Wiley, 1973.

Seligman, M. E. P., and Maier, S. F. Failure to escape traumatic shock. *Journal of Experimental Psychology,* 1967, 74, 1–9.

Selye, H. *The stress of life.* New York: McGraw-Hill, 1956.

Sevenster, P. Incompatibility of response and reward. In R. A. Hinde and J. Stevenson-Hinde (Eds.), *Constraints on learning.* New York: Academic Press, 1973.

Shafir, E., Simonson, I., and Tversky, A. Reason-based choice. *Cognition,* 1993, 49, 11–36.

Shattuck, R. *The forbidden experiment: The story of the wild boy of Aveyron.* New York: Farrar, Straus & Giroux, 1980.

Sheffield, F. D., and Roby, T. B. Reward value of a nonnutritive sweet taste. *Journal of Comparative and Physiological Psychology,* 1950, 43, 471–481.

Sheffield, F. D., Wulff, J. J., and Backer, R. Reward value of copulation without sex drive reduction. *Journal of Comparative and Physiological Psychology,* 1951, 44, 3–8.

Sherman, P. W. Nepotism and the evolution of alarm calls. *Science,* 1977, 197, 1246–1253.

Shettleworth, S. J. Foraging, memory, and constraints on learning. In N. S. Braveman and P. Bronstein (Eds.), *Experimental assessments and clinical applications of conditioned food aversions. Annals of the New York Academy of Sciences* (Vol. 443). New York: New York Academy of Sciences, 1987, pp. 216–226.

———. Function and mechanism in learning. In M. Zeiler and P. Harzem (Eds.), *Advances in analysis of behavior* (Vol. 3: *Biological factors in learning*). New York: Wiley, 1983.

Shimp, C. P. Perspectives on the behavioral unit: Choice behavior in animals. In W. K. Estes (Ed.), *Handbook of learning and cognitive processes*. Vol. 2. *Conditioning and behavior theory*. Hillsdale, NJ: Lawrence Erlbaum, 1975.

Shweder, R. A. *Thinking through cultures*. Cambridge, MA: Harvard University Press, 1991.

———. Ghost busters in anthropology. In R. D'Andrade and C. Straus (Eds.), *Human motives and cultural models*. Cambridge, England: Cambridge University Press, 1992, pp. 45–57.

Shweder, R. A., Mahapatra, M., and Miller, J. G. Culture and moral development. In J. W. Stigler, R. A. Shweder, and G. Herdt (Eds.), *Cultural psychology: Essays on comparative human development*. Cambridge, England: Cambridge University Press, 1990, pp. 130–204.

Sidman, M. Two temporal parameters of the maintenance of avoidance behavior by the white rat. *Journal of Comparative and Physiological Psychology*, 1953, 46, 253–261.

———. *Tactics of scientific research*. New York: Basic Books, 1960.

Siegel, S. Evidence from rats that morphine tolerance is a learned response. *Journal of Comparative and Physiological Psychology*, 1975, 89, 498–506.

Siegel, S., Hinson, R. E., Krank, M. D., and McCully, J. Heroin "overdose" death: Contribution of drug-associated environmental cues. *Science*, 1982, 216, 436–437.

Simon, H. A. *Models of thought*. New Haven, CT: Yale University Press, 1979.

Singer, W. Central-core control of visual-cortex functions. In F. O. Schmitt and F. G. Worden (Eds.), *The neurosciences: Fourth study program*. Cambridge, MA: MIT Press, 1979.

Skinner, B. F. *Behavior of organisms*. New York: Appleton-Century-Crofts, 1938.

———. An operant analysis of problem solving. In B. Kleinmutz (Ed.), *Problem solving*. New York: Wiley, 1966.

———. *Beyond freedom and dignity*. New York: Knopf, 1971.

Slochower, J., Kaplan, S. P., and Mann, L. The effects of life stress and weight on mood and eating. *Appetite*, 1981, 2, 115–125.

Slovic, P., Fischhoff, B., and Lichtenstein, S. Facts versus fears: Understanding perceived risk. In D. Kahneman, P. Slovic, and A. Tversky (Eds.), *Judgment under uncertainty: Heuristics and biases*. Cambridge, England: Cambridge University Press, 1982.

Smith, B., Fillion, T. J., and Blass, E. M. Orally mediated sources of calming in 1- to 3-day-old human infants. *Developmental Psychology*, 1990, 26, 731–737.

Smith, G. P. Satiety and the problem of motivation. In D. W. Pfaff (Ed.), *The physiological mechanisms of motivation*. New York: Springer-Verlag, 1982.

Smith, G. P., and Epstein, A. N. Increased feeding in response to decreased glucose utilization in the rat and monkey. *American Journal of Physiology*, 1969, 217, 1083–1087.

Smith, G. P., and Gibbs, J. Satiating effect of cholecystokinin. *Annals of the New York Academy of Sciences*, 1994, 713, 236–241.

Smith, J. N. M. The food searching behaviour of two European thrushes. I. Description and analysis of search paths. *Behaviour*, 1974a, 48, 276–302.

———. The food searching behaviour of two European thrushes. II. The adaptiveness of the search patterns. *Behaviour*, 1974b, 49, 1–61.

Snyder, C. R., Higgins, R. L., and Stucky, R. J. *Excuses: Masquerades in search of grace*. New York: Wiley, 1983.

Sokoloff, E. N. Neuronal models and the orienting reflex. In M. A. Brazier (Ed.), *The central nervous system and behavior*. New York: Macy, 1960.

Solomon, R. L. The opponent process theory of acquired motivation. *American Psychologist*, 1980, 35, 691–712.

Solomon, R. L., and Corbit, J. D. An opponent process theory of motivation. I. The temporal dynamics of affect. *Psychological Review*, 1974, 81, 119–145.

Solomon, R. L., Kamin, L. J., and Wynne, L. C. Traumatic avoidance learning: The outcomes of several extinction procedures with dogs. *Journal of Abnormal and Social Psychology*, 1953, 48, 291–302.

Southwick, C. H., Pal, B. C., and Siddiqi, M. F. Experimental studies on social intolerance in wild rhesus monkeys. *American Zoologist*, 1972, 12, 651–652.

Spence, K. W., Taylor, J. A., and Ketchel, R. Anxiety (drive) level and degree of competition in paired-associates learning. *Journal of Experimental Psychology*, 1956, 52, 306–310.

Spitzer, L., and Rodin, J. Human eating behavior: A critical review of studies in normal weight and overweight individuals. *Appetite*, 1981, 2, 293–329.

Staddon, J. E. R. *Adaptive behavior and learning*. Cambridge, England: Cambridge University Press, 1983.

———. Rationality, melioration, and law-of-effect models for choice. *Psychological Science*, 1992, 3, 136–141.

Staddon, J. E. R., and Hinson, J. M. Optimization: A result or a mechanism? *Science*, 1983, 221, 976–977.

Steers, R. M., and Porter, L. W. *Motivation and work behavior*. New York: McGraw-Hill, 1983.

Steers, R. M., and Spencer, D. G. The role of achievement

motivation in job design. *Journal of Applied Psychology,* 1977, 62, 472–479.

Steiner, J. E. Facial expressions of the neonate infant indicating the hedonics of food-related chemical stimuli. In J. M. Weiffenbach (Ed.), *Taste and development: The genesis of sweet preference.* Bethesda, MD: U. S. Department of Health, Education and Welfare, 1977.

Stellar, E. The physiology of motivation. *Psychological Review,* 1954, 61, 5–22.

———. Sweet preference and hedonic experience. In J. M. Weiffenbach (Ed.), *Taste and development: The genesis of sweet preference.* Bethesda, MD: U. S. Department of Health, Education and Welfare, 1977.

Stellar, J. R., Brooks, F. H., and Mills, L. E. Approach and withdrawal analysis of the effects of hypothalamic stimulation and lesions in rats. *Journal of Comparative and Physiological Psychology,* 1979, 93, 446–466.

Stephan, W. G., Berscheid, E., and Walster, E. Sexual arousal and heterosexual perception. *Journal of Personality and Social Psychology,* 1971, 20, 93–101.

Sternberg, R. J. A triangular theory of love. *Psychological Review,* 1986, 2, 119–135.

Strack, F., Martin, L. L., and Stepper, S. Inhibiting and facilitating conditions of the human smile: A nonobtrusive test of the facial feedback hypothesis. *Journal of Personality and Social Psychology,* 1988, 54, 768–777.

Strauss, C. Models and motives. In R. D'Andrade and C. Strauss (Eds.), *Human motives and cultural models.* Cambridge, England: Cambridge University Press, 1992, pp. 1–20.

———. What makes Tony run? Schemas as motives reconsidered. In R. D'Andrade and C. Strauss (Eds.), *Human motives and cultural models.* Cambridge, England: Cambridge University Press, 1992, pp. 191–224.

Stricker, E. M. Extracellular fluid volume and thirst. *American Journal of Physiology,* 1966, 211, 232–238.

———. Hyperphagia. *New England Journal of Medicine,* 1978, 298, 1010–1013.

———. Brain neurochemistry and the control of food intake. In E. Satinoff and P. Teitelbaum (Eds.), *Handbook of behavioral neurobiology: Vol. 6: Motivation.* New York: Plenum, 1990.

Stricker, E. M., Cooper, P. H., Marshall, J. F., and Zigmond, M. J. Acute homeostatic imbalances reinstate sensorimotor dysfunction in rats with lateral hypothalamic lesions. *Journal of Comparative and Physiological Psychology,* 1979, 93, 512–521.

Stricker, E. M., and Zigmond, M. J. Recovery of function after damage to central catecholamine-containing neu-

rons: A neurochemical model for the lateral hypothalamic syndrome. In J. M. Sprague and A. N. Epstein (Eds.), *Progress in psychobiology and physiological psychology* (Vol. 6). New York: Academic Press, 1976.

Stunkard, A. J., Sorenson, T. I. A., Harris, C., Teasdale, T. W., Chakraborty, R., Schull, W. J., and Schulsinger, F. An adoption study of human obesity. *New England Journal of Medicine,* 1986, 314, 193–198.

Suomi, S. J. Primate separation models of affective disorder. In J. Madden IV (Ed.), *Neurobiology of learning, emotion, and affect.* New York: Raven Press, 1991.

Svare, B. Psychobiological determinants of maternal aggressive behavior. In E. L. Simmel, M. E. Hahn, and J. K. Walters (Eds.), *Aggressive behavior: Genetic and neural approaches.* Hillsdale, NJ: Lawrence Erlbaum, 1983.

Symons, D. On the use and misuse of Darwinism in the study of human behavior. In J. H. Barkow, L. Cosmides, and J. Tooby (Eds.), *The adapted mind: Evolutionary psychology and the generation of culture.* New York: Oxford University Press, 1992, pp. 137–159.

Tavris, C. *Anger: The misunderstood emotion.* New York: Simon & Schuster, 1982.

Tavris, C., and Sadd, S. *The Redbook report on female sexuality.* New York: Delacorte, 1977.

Taylor, S. E. Adjustment to threatening events: A theory of cognitive adaptation. *American Psychologist,* 1983, 38, 1161–1173.

———. *Positive illusions: Creative self-deception and the healthy mind.* New York: Basic Books, 1989.

Taylor, S. E., and Brown, J. D. Illusion and well-being: A social psychological perspective on mental health. *Psychological Bulletin,* 1988, 103, 193–210.

Teitelbaum, P. Sensory control of hypothalamic hyperphagia. *Journal of Comparative and Physiological Psychology,* 1955, 48, 156–163.

———. Use of operant methods in the analysis and assessment of motivational states. In W. K. Honig (Ed.), *Operant behavior: Areas of research and application.* New York: Appleton-Century, 1966.

———. *Physiological psychology: Fundamental principles.* Englewood Cliffs, NJ: Prentice-Hall, 1967.

Teitelbaum, P., and Epstein, A. N. The lateral hypothalamic syndrome: Recovery of feeding and drinking after lateral hypothalamic lesions. *Psychological Review,* 1962, 69, 74–90.

Thibaut, J. W., and Kelley, H. H. *The social psychology of groups.* New York: Wiley, 1959.

Thibodeau, R., and Aronson, E. Taking a closer look: Reasserting the role of the self-concept in dissonance theory. *Personality and Social Psychology Bulletin,* 1992, 18, 591–602.

Thompson, D. A., and Campbell, R. G. Hunger in humans induced by 2-deoxy-D-glucose: Glucoprivic control of taste preference and food intake. *Science,* 1977, 198, 1065–1068.

Thorndike, E. L. *Animal intelligence.* New York: Macmillan Co., 1911.

Timberlake, W. The functional organization of appetitive behavior: Behavior systems and learning. In M. D. Zeiler and P. Harzem (Eds.), *Advances in analysis of behavior* (Vol. 3: *Biological factors in learning*). New York: Wiley, 1983.

Tinbergen, N. *The study of instinct.* New York and Oxford: Oxford University Press, 1951.

Tinkelpaugh, O. An experimental study of representative factors in monkeys. *Journal of Comparative Psychology,* 1928, 8, 197–236.

Tolman, E. C. *Purposive behavior in animals and men.* New York: Century, 1932.

———. Cognitive maps in rats and men. *Psychological Review,* 1948, 55, 189–208.

Tomkins, S. S. *Affect, imagery, consciousness.* Vol. 1, *The positive affects.* New York: Springer Pub., 1962.

———. *Affect, imagery, consciousness.* Vol. 2, *The negative affects.* New York: Springer Pub., 1963.

Tourangeau, R., and Ellsworth, P. C. The role of facial response in the experience of emotion. *Journal of Personality and Social Psychology,* 1979, 37, 1519–1531.

Trivers, R. L. The evolution of reciprocal altruism. *The Quarterly Review of Biology,* 1971, 46, 35–57.

Tuchman, B. W. *The march of folly.* New York: Knopf, 1984.

Turnbull, C. M. *The mountain people.* New York: Simon & Schuster, 1973.

Tversky, A., and Kahneman, D. The framing of decisions and the psychology of choice. *Science,* 1981, 221, 453–458.

Valenstein, E. S. *Brain control.* New York: Wiley, 1973.

Valins, S. Cognitive effects of false heart-rate feedback. *Journal of Personality and Social Psychology,* 1966, 4, 400–408.

Vallone, R. P., Griffin, D. W., Lin, S., and Ross, L. Overconfident prediction of future actions and outcomes by self and others. *Journal of Personality and Social Psychology,* 1990, 58, 582–592.

Van den Boom, D. Preventive intervention and the quality of mother-infant interaction and infant exploration in irritable infants. In W. Koops et al. (Eds.), *Developmental psychology behind the dikes.* Amsterdam: Eburon, 1990, pp. 249–270.

VanItallie, T. B., and Kissileff, H. R. Human obesity: A problem in body energy economics. In E. M. Stricker (Ed.), *Handbook of Behavioral Neurobiology* (Vol. 10: *Neurobiology of food and fluid intake*). New York: Plenum, 1990, pp. 207–240.

van Lawick-Goodall, J. *In the shadow of man.* Boston: Houghton Mifflin, 1971.

Veith, J. L., Buck, M., Getzlaf, S., Van Dalfsen, P., and Slade, S. Exposure to men influences the occurrence of ovulation in women. *Physiology and Behavior,* 1983, 31, 313–315.

von Neumann, J., and Morgenstern, O. *Theory of games and economic behavior.* Princeton, NJ: Princeton University Press, 1944.

Wahba, M. A., and Bridwell, L. G. Maslow reconsidered: A review of research on the need hierarchy theory. In R. M. Steers and L. W. Porter (Eds.), *Motivation and work behavior.* New York: McGraw-Hill, 1983.

Wallace, R. A. *Animal behavior: Its development, ecology, and evolution.* Santa Monica, CA: Goodyear Publishing, 1979.

Wallach, L., and Wallach, M. A. Why altruism, even though it exists, cannot be demonstrated by social psychological experiments. *Psychological Inquiry,* 1991, 2, 153–155.

Wallach, M. A., and Wallach, L. *Psychology's sanction for selfishness: The error of egoism in theory and therapy.* San Francisco: Freeman, 1983.

Walster, E., and Walster, G. W. *A new look at love.* Reading, MA: Addison-Wesley, 1978.

Warwick, Z. S., and Weingarten, H. P. Dissociation of palatability and calorie effects in learned flavor preferences. *Physiology and Behavior,* 1994, 55, 501–504.

Watson, J. B. Psychology as the behaviorist views it. *Psychological Review,* 1913, 20, 158–177.

———. *Behaviorism.* Chicago: University of Chicago Press, 1924.

Watson, J. S. Memory and "contingency analysis" in infant learning. *Merrill-Palmer Quarterly,* 1967, 13, 55–76.

Weber, M. *The Protestant ethic* (translated by Talcott Parsons). New York: Scribner's, 1930.

Wegner, D. M. *White bears and other unwanted thoughts.* New York: Viking, 1989.

———. You can't always think what you want: Problems in the suppression of unwanted thoughts. *Advances in Experimental Social Psychology,* 1992, 25, 193–224.

Wegner, D. M., and Erber, R. The hyperaccessability of suppressed thoughts. *Journal of Personality and Social Psychology,* 1992, 63, 903–912.

Wegner, D. M., Lane, J. D., and Dimitri, S. The allure of

secret relationships. *Journal of Personality and Social Psychology,* 1994, 66, 287–300.

Wegner, D. M., Schneider, D. J., Carter, S. R., III, and White, T. L. Paradoxical effects of thought suppression. *Journal of Personality and Social Psychology,* 1987, 53, 5–13.

Weiner, B. (Ed.). *Achievement motivation and attribution theory.* Morristown, NJ: General Learning Press, 1974.

Weiner, B. In the Atkinson tradition: The motivational function of emotion. In D. R. Brown and J. Veroff (Eds.), *Frontiers of motivational psychology: Essays in honor of John W. Atkinson.* Berlin: Springer-Verlag, 1986, pp. 26–39.

———. *Human motivation.* New York: Holt, Rinehart & Winston, 1989.

Weiner, B., and Sierad, J. Misattribution for failure and enhancement of achievement strivings. *Journal of Personality and Social Psychology,* 1975, 31, 415–421.

Weingarten, H. P. Diet palatability modulates sham feeding in VMH-lesion and normal rats: Implications for finickiness and evaluation of sham-feeding data. *Journal of Comparative and Physiological Psychology,* 1982, 96, 223–233.

———. Conditioned cues elicit feeding in sated rats: A role for learning in meal initiation. *Science,* 1983, 220, 431–433.

Weiss, J. M. Effects of coping response on stress. *Journal of Comparative and Physiological Psychology,* 1968, 65, 251–260.

Weisz, J. R. Development of control-related beliefs, goals, and styles in childhood and adolescence: A clinical perspective. In J. Rodin, C. Schooler, and K. Warner Schaie (Eds.), *Self-directedness: Cause and effects throughout the life course.* Hillsdale, NJ: Lawrence Erlbaum, 1990, pp. 103–145.

White, R. Selective inattention. *Psychology Today,* November 1971, pp. 47–50, 78–84.

Williams, D. R., and Williams, H. Automaintenance in the pigeon: Sustained pecking despite contingent non-reinforcement. *Journal of the Experimental Analysis of Behavior,* 1969, 12, 511–520.

Wilson, J. Q. *Thinking about crime.* New York: Basic Books, 1975.

———. *The moral sense.* New York: Free Press, 1993.

Wilson, T. D. Strangers to ourselves: The origins and accuracy of beliefs about one's own mental states. In J. H. Harvey and G. Weary (Eds.), *Attribution: Basic issues and applications.* Orlando, FL: Academic Press, 1985.

Wilson, T. D., and Kraft, D. Why do I love thee?: Effects of repeated introspections about a dating relationship on attitudes toward the relationship. *Personality and Social Psychology Bulletin,* 1993, 19, 409–418.

Wilson, T. D., Lisle, D. J., Schooler, J. W., Hodges, S. D., Klaaren, K. J., and LaFleur, S. J. Introspecting about reasons can reduce post-choice satisfaction. *Personality and Social Psychology Bulletin,* 1993, 19, 331–339.

Winch, R. F. *Mate selection: A study of complementary needs.* New York: Harper & Row, 1958.

Winterbottom, M. R. The relation of childhood training in independence to achievement motivation. Unpublished doctoral dissertation, University of Michigan, 1953.

Wise, R. A. Neuroleptic and operant behavior: The anhedonia hypothesis. *Behavior and Brain Sciences,* 1984, 5, 39–87.

———. The neurobiology of craving: Implications for the understanding and treatment of addiction. *Journal of Abnormal Psychology,* 1988, 97, 118–132.

Wise, R. A., Spindler, J., and Legault, L. Major attenuation of food reward with performance-sparing doses of pimozide in the rat. *Canadian Journal of Psychology,* 1978, 32, 77–85.

Wixon, D. R., and Laird, J. D. Awareness and attitude change in the forced-compliance paradigm: The importance of when. *Journal of Personality and Social Psychology,* 1976, 34, 376–384.

Wolchik, S. A., Beggs, V. E., Wincze, J. P., Sakheim, D. K., Barlow, D. H., and Mavissakian, M. The effect of emotional arousal on subsequent sexual arousal in men. *Journal of Abnormal Psychology,* 1980, 89, 595–598.

Wolf, A. V. *Thirst: Physiology of the urge to drink and problems of water lack.* Springfield, IL: Thomas, 1958.

Wolf, G. "Innate recognition" aids rats in sodium regulation. *Journal of Comparative and Physiological Psychology,* 1970, 73, 117–123.

Wolfe, J. B. Effectiveness of token-rewards for chimpanzees. *Comparative Psychology Monographs,* 1936, 12 (No. 60).

Wolgin, D. L., Cytawa, J., and Teitelbaum, P. The role of activation in the regulation of food intake. In D. Novin, W. Wyrwicka, and G. Bray (Eds.), *Hunger: Basic mechanisms and clinical implications.* New York: Raven Press, 1976.

Wolgin, D. L., and Teitelbaum, P. Role of activation and sensory stimuli in recovery from lateral hypothalamic damage in the cat. *Journal of Comparative and Physiological Psychology,* 1978, 92, 474–500.

Worschel, W., and Shebilske, W. *Psychology: Principles and applications.* Englewood Cliffs, NJ: Prentice-Hall, 1983.

Woytinski, W. S., and Woytinski, E. S. *World population and production*. New York: Twentieth Century Fund, 1953.

Wundt, W. *Principles of physiological psychology*. New York: Macmillan Co., 1910.

Yankura, J. *Doing RET: Albert Ellis in action*. New York: Springer, 1990.

Yerkes, R. M., and Dodson, J. D. The relation of strength of stimulus to rapidity of habit-formation. *Journal of Comparative Neurological Psychology*, 1908, 18, 459–482.

Young, P. T., and Shuford, E. H. Intensity, duration, and repetition of hedonic processes as related to acquisition of motives. *Journal of Comparative and Physiological Psychology*, 1954, 47, 298–305.

Young, R. C., Gibbs, J., Antin, J., Holt, J., and Smith, G. P. Absence of satiety during sham feeding in the rat. *Journal of Comparative and Physiological Psychology*, 1974, 87, 795–800.

Zahn-Waxler, C. The case for empathy: A developmental perspective. *Psychological Inquiry*, 1991, 2, 155–158.

Zajonc, R. B. Attitudinal effects of mere exposure. *Journal of Personality and Social Psychology, Monograph Supplement*, 1968, 9, 1–27.

Zajonc, R. B. Feeling and thinking: Preferences need no inferences. *American Psychololgist*, 1980, 35, 151–175.

Zanna, M. P., and Cooper, J. Dissonance and the attribution process. In J. H. Harvey, W. J. Ickes, and R. F. Kidd (Eds.), *New directions in attribution research* (Vol. 1). Hillsdale, NJ: Lawrence Erlbaum, 1976.

Zanna, M. P., and Olson, J. M. Individual differences in attitudinal relations. In M. P. Zanna, E. T. Higgins, and C. P. Herman (Eds.), *Consistency in social behavior: The Ontario symposium* (Vol. 2). Hillsdale, NJ: Lawrence Erlbaum, 1982.

Zellner, D. A., Rozin, P., Aron, M., and Kulish, C. Conditioned enhancement of humans' liking for flavor by pairing with sweetness. *Learning and Motivation*, 1983, 14, 338–350.

Zillman, D. Attribution and misattribution of excitatory reactions. In J. H. Harvey, W. J. Ickes, and R. F. Kidd (Eds.), *New directions in attribution research* (Vol. 2). Hillsdale, NJ: Lawrence Erlbaum, 1978.

Zimbardo, P. *The psychological power and pathology of imprisonment*. A statement prepared for the U. S. House of Representatives Committee on the Judiciary; Subcommittee No. 3: Hearings on Prison Reform, San Francisco, CA, October 25, 1971.

Zuckerman, E. *The day after World War III*. New York: Viking, 1984.

Credits and Permissions

Fig. 1-1A, Photo by Ralph Morse/Life Magazine © Time, Inc.

Fig. 1-1B, Photo courtesy of Bea Mook.

Fig. 2-1, Photo courtesy of the National Library of Medicine.

Fig. 2-2, Descartes, "De Hormine" in *Philosophical Works,* Cambridge University Press, 1911.

Fig. 2-3, Photo courtesy of Department of Library Services, American Museum of Natural History.

Fig. 2-4, Photo courtesy of The Warder Collection.

Fig. 2-5, Drawing by Whitney Darrow, Jr.; © 1976, *The New Yorker* Magazine, Inc.

Fig. 2-6, Photo courtesy of The Bettman Archive.

Fig. 3-1, Photo courtesy of Bea Mook.

Fig. 3-5, Adapted from Gilman, A., The relation between osmotic pressure, fluid distribution and voluntary water intake. *American Journal of Physiology,* 1937, *120,* 323–328. © 1937 by the American Psychological Association.

Fig. 3-14, Adapted from Craighead, L.W., Stunkard, A.J., and O'Brien, R., Behavior therapy and pharmacotherapy for obesity. *Archives of General Psychiatry,* 1981, 38. © 1981, The American Medical Association.

Fig. 3-17, Photos from Steiner, J.E., Facial expressions of the neonate infant indicating the hedonics of food-related chemical stimuli. In J.M. Weiffenbach (ed.), *Taste and development: The genesis of sweet preference.* Bethesda, Maryland: U.S. Department of Health, Education, and Welfare, 1977.

Fig. 3-19, Adapted from Fedorchak, P.M., and Bolles, R.C. Nutritive expectancies mediate cholecystokinin's suppression-of-intake effect. *Behavioral Neuroscience,* 1988, *102,* 451–455.

Fig. 3-20, Drawing by Maslin; © 1992 *The New Yorker* Magazine, Inc.

Fig. 3-21, Adapted from Herman, C.P., and Polivy, J. Restrained eating. In A.J. Stunkard (ed.), *Obesity.* Philadelphia: Saunders, 1980, 208–225.

Fig. 4-1, Adapted from Tinbergen, N., 1951.

Fig. 4-3, Photo used with permission from the Zoological Society of London.

Fig. 4-4, Photo courtesy of Roy and Sue Wagner.

Fig. 4-5, Photo by Charles Gatewood.

Fig. 4-6, Adapted from Bermant, G. Sexual behavior: hard times with the Coolidge Effect. In M.H. Siegel and H.P. Ziegler (eds.), *Psychological research: The inside story.* New York: Harper and Row, 1976. © 1976 by Michael H. Siegel and H. Philip Ziegler. Reprinted with permission from HarperCollins Publishers, Inc.

Fig. 4-7, Drawing by D. Reilly; © 1991 *The New Yorker* Magazine, Inc.

Fig. 4-9, Reproduced with special permission from *Playboy* Magazine: © 1975 by Playboy.

Fig. 4-11, Photo courtesy of Bea Mook.

Fig. 5-4, Adapted from Gallistel, 1980.

Fig. 5-9, Adapted with permission from Pfaus, J.G., Damsma, G., Nomikos, G.G., Wenkstern, D.G., Blaha, C.D., Philips, A.G., and Fibiger, H.C. *Brain Research,* 1990, *530,* 345–348.

Fig. 5-11, From Smith, B., Fillion, T.J., and Blass, E.M. Orally mediated sources of calming in 1- to 3-day-old human infants. *Developmental Psychology,* 1990, *26,* 731–737.

Fig. 5-14, Illustration from Damasio, H., Damasio, A.R., Grabowski, T., Frank, R., and Galaburda, A.M. The return of Phineas Gage. *Science,* 1994, *264,* 1102–1105.

Fig. 5-15, Photo courtesy of Bea Mook.

Fig. 6-1, From Perin, C.T. Behavior potentiality as a joint function of the amount of training and the degree of hunger at the time of extinction. *Journal of Experimental Psychology,* 1942, *30,* 93–113.

Fig. 6-2, From Spence et al. Anxiety (drive) level and degree of competition in paired-associates learning. *Journal of Experimental Psychology,* 1956, *52,* 306–10.

Fig. 6-3, After Harlow, 1950; photo courtesy of Wisconsin Primate Laboratory.

Fig. 6-6, From Erdelyi, M.H., *Psychoanalysis: Freud's Cognitive Psychology.* New York: W.H. Freeman & Co., 1985.

Fig. 6-7, Photo courtesy of DeBeers.

Fig. 6-10, After Cannon, W.B. *Bodily Changes in Pain, Hunger, Fear, and Rage.* New York: Appleton, 1929.

Fig. 6-11, After Netter, F.H., 1958.

Fig. 6-12, From Guyton, 1966.

Fig. 6-13, From Hebb, D.O. Drives and the CNS. *Psychological Review,* 1955, *62,* 243–254.

Fig. 7-4, From Bernstein, I.L. Learned taste aversions in children receiving chemotherapy. *Science,* 1978, *200,* 1302–1303.

Fig. 7-5, Photo courtesy of Susan Mineka.

Fig. 7-6, Photo courtesy of Yerkes Regional Primate Research Center, Emory University.

Fig. 7-7, Photo courtesy of Bob Daemmrich/Stock Boston.

Fig. 7-8, Photo courtesy of Nina Leen, *Life* Magazine, © 1964 Time, Inc.

Fig. 7-9, From Hoffmann et al. Reinforcement model of imprinting: Implications for socialization in monkeys and men. *Psychological Review,* 1973, *80,* 527–544.

Fig. 7-12, Ibid.

Fig. 8-1, Photo by W. Rapport, courtesy of B.F. Skinner.

Fig. 8-2, Adapted from Ayllon, T., and Michael, J. The psychiatric nurse as a behavioral engineer. *Journal of the Experimental Analysis of Behavior,* 1959, *2,* 323–334.

Fig. 8-3, From Liberman, R.P., and Raskin, D.E. Depression: a behavioral formulation. *Archives of General Psychiatry,* 1971, *24,* 515–523.

Fig. 8-4, Modified from Gray et al. Little brother is changing you. *Psychology Today*, 1974, 7, 42–46.

Fig. 8-5, From Allison, M.G., and Ayllon, T. Behavioral coaching in the development of skills in football, gymnastics, and tennis. *Journal of Applied Behavior Analysis*, 1980, *13*, 297–314.

Fig. 8-7, From Colwill, R.M., and Rescorla, R.A. Postconditioning devaluation of a reinforcer affects instrumental responding. *Journal of Experimental Psychology: Animal Behavior Processes*, 1990, *16*, 372–389.

Fig. 8-8, Photo courtesy of Animal Behavior Enterprises.

Fig. 9-3, From Shettleworth, S.J. Foraging, memory, and constraints on learning. In Braverman, N.S., and Bronstein, P. (eds.), Experimental assessments and clinical applications of conditioned food aversions. *Annals of the New York Academy of Sciences*, 1987, *443*, 216–226. © The New York Academy of Sciences, 1987.

Fig. 9-4, Modified from Krieckhaus, E.E., and Wolf, G. Acquisition of sodium by rats: interaction of innate mechanisms and latent learning. *Journal of Comparative and Physiological Psychology*, 1968, 95, 197–201.

Fig. 9-7, Modified from Wegner et al. Paradoxical effects of thought suppression. *Journal of Personality and Social Psychology*, 1987, *53*, 5–13.

Fig. 9-8, From Wegner, D.M., and Erber, R. The hyperaccessibility of suppressed thoughts. *Journal of Personality and Social Psychology*, 1992, *63*, 903–912.

Fig. 9-9, Data from Wegner et al., 1987.

Fig. 10-1, Drawing by Harris; © 1979 *The New Yorker* Magazine, Inc.

Fig. 10-5, Reprinted with permission from p. 150 of Kantowitz, Roediger, and Elmes, *Experimental Psychology*, 5th ed. © 1994 by West Publishing Co. All rights reserved.

Fig. 10-10, From Elner, R.W., and Hughes, R.N. Energy maximization in the diet of the shore crab, *Carcinus maenas*. *Journal of Animal Ecology*, 1978, *170*, 103–116. See also Rozin, P., and Schull, J., 1988.

Fig. 10-11, Adapted from Herrnstein, R.J. On the law of effect. *Journal of the Experimental Analysis of Behavior*, 1970, *13*, 243–266.

Fig. 11-2, Drawing courtesy of Sidney Harris.

Fig. 11-5, From Pettigrew, T.F. The ultimate attribution error: extending Allport's cognitive analysis of prejudice. *Personality and Social Psychology Bulletin*, 1979, *5*, 461–476.

Fig. 11-7, From Spence et al., 1956.

Fig. 12-2, From Darwin, C. *The Origin of Species*, 1859.

Fig. 12-3, (Left) photo by F.D. Schmidt, © 1985 The Zoological Society of San Diego; (Right) photo courtesy of B. Campbell.

Fig. 12-4, (Left) from M. Bertrand, The behavioral repertoire of the stumptail macaque, in *Bibliotecha Primatologia* #11, by permission from Karger Publishers; (right) photo courtesy of Gordon Menzig, © Photophile.

Fig. 12-5, From Ekman, P., *Darwin and Facial Expression*. Orlando, Florida: Academic Press, 1973.

Fig. 12-6, Photos courtesy of Paul Ekman.

Fig. 12-7, Photo courtesy of E. Eibl-Eibesfeldt.

Fig. 12-9, From Strack, F., et al. Inhibiting and facilitating conditions of the human smile: A nonobtrusive test of the facial feedback hypothesis. *Journal of Personality and Social Psychology*, 1988, *54*, 768–777.

Fig. 12-10, From Kagan, J. Attention and psychological change in the child. *Science*, 1970, *170*, 826–832.

Fig. 12-13, From Cohen, S., Tyrrell, D.A.J., and Smith, A.P. Psychological stress and susceptibility to the common cold. *New England Journal of Medicine*, 1991, *325*, 606–612.

Fig. 12-15, Drawing by Modell, © 1971 *The New Yorker* Magazine, Inc.

Fig. 12-16, Excerpted from *Washingtoon*, © 1993 by Mark Alan Stamaty.

Fig. 13-1, Photo courtesy of University of Wisconsin Primate Laboratory.

Fig. 13-2, From Kagan, J. et al., 1978.

Fig. 13-3, Data from Van Den Boom, 1990.

Fig. 13-5, Photo courtesy of The Bettman Archive.

Fig. 13-8, Photo courtesy of George D. Lepp/Bio-Tec Images.

Fig. 13-9, Adapted from Baumeister, R.F., and Cairns, K.J. Repression and self-presentation: when audiences interfere with self-defensive strategies. *Journal of Personality and Social Psychology*, 1992, *62*, 851–862.

Fig. 13-10, From Batson, D.C., and Shaw, L.L. Evidence for altruism: towards a pluralism of prosocial motives. *Psychological Inquiry*, 1991, *2*, 107–122.

Fig. 13-11, Photo courtesy of Benny Ortiz.

Fig. 13-12, Drawing by Modell; © 1953 by *The New Yorker* Magazine, Inc.

Fig. 14-1, Photo courtesy of David C. McLelland. From MacLelland et al., 1976.

Fig. 14-2, Ibid., from MacLelland et al., 1964.

Fig. 14-3, Ibid.

Fig. 14-5, Ibid.

Fig. 14-7, From Wiener, B., and Sierad, J. Misattribution for failure and enhancement of achievement strivings. *Journal of Personality and Social Psychology*, 1975, *31*, 415–421.

Fig. 14-9, Drawing by Ross; © 1993 *The New Yorker* Magazine, Inc.

Fig. 14-10, From Maier, S.F., et al., 1969.

Fig. 14-11, From Seligman, M.E.P., and Maier, S.F. Failure to escape traumatic shock. *Journal of Experimental Psychology*, 1967, *74*, 1–9.

Name Index

Subject Index